# Lecture Notes in Computer Science 9040

Commenced Publication in 1973
Founding and Former Series Editors:
Gerhard Goos, Juris Hartmanis, and Jan van Leeuwen

T0234087

More information about this series at http://www.springer.com/series/7407

Kentaro Sano · Dimitrios Soudris
Michael Hübner · Pedro C. Diniz (Eds.)

# Applied Reconfigurable Computing

11th International Symposium, ARC 2015
Bochum, Germany, April 13–17, 2015
Proceedings

 Springer

*Editors*
Kentaro Sano
Tohoku University
Sendai
Japan

Dimitrios Soudris
National Technical University of Athens
Athens
Greece

Michael Hübner
Ruhr-Universität Bochum
Bochum
Germany

Pedro C. Diniz
University of Southern California
Marina del Rey
California
USA

ISSN 0302-9743
Lecture Notes in Computer Science
ISBN 978-3-319-16213-3
DOI 10.1007/978-3-319-16214-0

ISSN 1611-3349 (electronic)

ISBN 978-3-319-16214-0 (eBook)

Library of Congress Control Number: 2015934029

LNCS Sublibrary: SL1 – Theoretical Computer Science and General Issues

Springer Cham Heidelberg New York Dordrecht London

Springer International Publishing AG Switzerland is part of Springer Science+Business Media
(www.springer.com)

# Preface

Reconfigurable computing provides a wide range of opportunities to increase performance and energy efficiency by exploiting spatial/temporal and fine/coarse-grained parallelism with custom hardware structures for processing, movement, and storage of data. For the last several decades, reconfigurable devices such as FPGAs have evolved from a simple and small programmable logic device to a large-scale and fully programmable system-on-chip integrated with not only a huge number of programmable logic elements, but also various hard macros such as multipliers, memory blocks, standard I/O blocks, and strong microprocessors. Such devices are now one of the prominent actors in the semiconductor industry fabricated by a state-of-the-art silicon technology, while they were no more than supporting actors as glue logic in the 1980s. The capability and flexibility of the present reconfigurable devices are attracting application developers from new fields, e.g., big-data processing at data centers. This means that custom computing based on the reconfigurable technology is recently being recognized as important and effective measures to achieve efficient and/or high-performance computing in wider application domains spanning from highly specialized custom controllers to general-purpose high-end programmable computing systems.

The new computing paradigm brought by reconfigurability increasingly requires researches and engineering challenges to connect capability of devices and technologies with real and profitable applications. The foremost challenges that we are still facing today include: appropriate architectures and structures to allow innovative hardware resources and their reconfigurability to be exploited for individual application, languages, and tools to enable highly productive design and implementation, and system-level platforms with standard abstractions to generalize reconfigurable computing. In particular, the productivity issue is considered a key for reconfigurable computing to be accepted by wider communities including software engineers.

The International Applied Reconfigurable Computing (ARC) symposium series provides a forum for dissemination and discussion of ongoing research efforts in this transformative research area. The series of editions was first held in 2005 in Algarve, Portugal. The second edition of the symposium (ARC 2006) took place in Delft, The Netherlands during March 1–3, 2006, and was the first edition of the symposium to have selected papers published as a Springer LNCS (Lecture Notes in Computer Science) volume. Subsequent editions of the symposium have been held in Rio de Janeiro, Brazil (ARC 2007), London, UK (ARC 2008), Karlsruhe, Germany (ARC 2009), Bangkok, Thailand (ARC 2010), Belfast, UK (ARC 2011), Hong Kong, China (ARC 2012), Los Angeles, USA (ARC 2013), and Algarve, Portugal (ARC 2014).

This LNCS volume includes the papers selected for the 11th edition of the symposium (ARC 2015), held in Bochum, Germany, during April 13–17, 2015. The symposium attracted a lot of very good papers, describing interesting work on reconfigurable computing-related subjects. A total of 85 papers were been submitted to the symposium from 22 countries: Germany (20), USA (10), Japan (10), Brazil (9), Greece (6),

Canada (3), Iran (3), Portugal (3), China (3), India (2), France (2), Italy (2), Singapore (2), Egypt (2), Austria (1), Finland (1), The Netherlands (1), Nigeria (1), Norway (1), Pakistan (1), Spain (1), and Switzerland (1). Submitted papers were evaluated by at least three members of the Technical Program Committee. After careful selection, 23 papers were accepted as full papers (acceptance rate of 27.1%) for oral presentation and 20 as short papers (global acceptance rate of 50.6%) for poster presentation. We could organize a very interesting symposium program with those accepted papers, which constitute a representative overview of ongoing research efforts in reconfigurable computing, a rapidly evolving and maturing field.

Several persons contributed to the success of the 2015 edition of the symposium. We would like to acknowledge the support of all the members of this year's symposium Steering and Program Committees in reviewing papers, in helping in the paper selection, and in giving valuable suggestions. Special thanks also to the additional researchers who contributed to the reviewing process, to all the authors who submitted papers to the symposium, and to all the symposium attendees. Last but not least, we are especially indebted to Mr. Alfred Hoffmann and Mrs. Anna Kramer from Springer for their support and work in publishing this book and to Jürgen Becker from the University of Karlsruhe for their strong support regarding the publication of the proceedings as part of the LNCS series.

January 2015                                                    Kentaro Sano
                                                            Dimitrios Soudris

# Organization

The 2015 Applied Reconfigurable Computing Symposium (ARC 2015) was organized by the Ruhr-University Bochum (RUB) in Bochum, Germany.

## Organization Committee

### General Chairs

Michael Hübner      Ruhr-Universität, Bochum, Germany
Pedro C. Diniz      University of Southern California/Information Sciences Institute, USA

### Program Chairs

Kentaro Sano      Graduate School of Information Sciences, Tohoku University, Sendai, Japan
Dimitrios Soudris      National Technical University of Athens, Greece

### Finance Chair

Maren Arndt      Ruhr-Universität, Bochum, Germany

### Publicity Chair

Ricardo Reis      Universidade Federal do Rio Grande do Sul, Porto Alegre, Brazil

### Web Chairs

Farina Fabricius      Ruhr-Universität, Bochum, Germany
Daniela Horn      Ruhr-Universität, Bochum, Germany

### Proceedings Chair

Pedro C. Diniz      University of Southern California/Information Sciences Institute, USA

### Special Journal Edition Chairs

Kentaro Sano      Graduate School of Information Sciences, Tohoku University, Sendai, Japan
Pedro C. Diniz      University of Southern California/Information Sciences Institute, USA
Michael Hübner      Ruhr-Universität, Bochum, Germany

**Local Arrangements Chairs**

Maren Arndt                          Ruhr-Universität, Bochum, Germany
Horst Gass                           Ruhr-Universität, Bochum, Germany

## Steering Committee

Hideharu Amano                       Keio University, Japan
Jürgen Becker                        Karlsruhe Institute of Technology, Germany
Mladen Berekovic                     Braunschweig University of Technology, Germany
Koen Bertels                         Delft University of Technology, The Netherlands
João M. P. Cardoso                   Faculdade de Engenharia da Universidade do Porto,
                                       Portugal
George Constantinides                Imperial College of Science, Technology and
                                       Medicine, UK
Pedro C. Diniz                       University of Southern California/Information
                                       Sciences Institute, USA
Philip H.W. Leong                    University of Sydney, Australia
Katherine (Compton) Morrow           University of Wisconsin-Madison, USA
Walid Najjar                         University of California Riverside, USA
Roger Woods                          The Queen's University of Belfast, UK
In memory of Stamatis Vassiliadis Delft University of Technology, The Netherlands

## Program Committee

Zack Backer                          Los Alamos National Laboratory, Los Alamos,
                                       USA
Jürgen Becker                        Karlsruhe Institute of Technology, Germany
Mladen Berekovic                     Braunschweig University of Technology, Germany
Koen Bertels                         Delft University of Technology, The Netherlands
Matthias Birk                        Karlsruhe Institute of Technology, Germany
João Bispo                           Instituto Superior Técnico/Universidade Técnica
                                       de Lisboa, Portugal
Stephen Brown                        Altera and University of Toronto, Canada
João Canas Ferreira                  Faculdade de Engenharia da Universidade do Porto,
                                       Portugal
João M. P. Cardoso                   Faculdade de Engenharia da Universidade do Porto,
                                       Portugal
Cyrille Chavet                       Université de Bretagne-Sud, France
Ray Cheung                           City University of Hong Kong, China
Daniel Chillet                       Inria Rennes, France
Kiyoung Choi                         Seoul National University, South Korea
Paul Chow                            University of Toronto, Canada
René Cumplido                        National Institute for Astrophysics, Optics, and
                                       Electronics, Mexico
Florent de Dinechin                  INSA Lyon, France

| | |
|---|---|
| Steven Derrien | Université de Rennes 1, France |
| Pedro C. Diniz | University of Southern California/Information Sciences Institute, USA |
| António Ferrari | Universidade de Aveiro, Portugal |
| Carlo Galuzzi | Delft University of Technology, The Netherlands |
| Diana Göhringer | Ruhr-Universität, Bochum, Germany |
| Frank Hannig | Friedrich-Alexander University Erlangen-Nürnberg, Germany |
| Jim Harkin | University of Ulster, Northern Ireland, UK |
| Reiner Hartenstein | Technische Universität Kaiserslautern, Germany |
| Dominic Hillenbrand | Karlsruhe Institute of Technology, Germany |
| Christian Hochberger | Technische Universität Dresden, Germany |
| Michael Hübner | Ruhr-Universität, Bochum, Germany |
| Waqar Hussain | Tampere University of Technology, Finland |
| Tomonori Izumi | Ritsumeikan University, Japan |
| Ricardo Jacobi | Universidade de Brasília, Brazil |
| Krzysztof Kepa | Virginia Bioinformatics Institute, USA |
| Andreas Koch | Technische Universität Darmstadt, Germany |
| Dimitrios Kritharidis | Intracom Telecom, Greece |
| Vianney Lapotre | LIRMM-CNRS, Montpellier, France |
| Philip H.W. Leong | University of Sydney, Australia |
| Gabriel M. Almeida | Leica Biosystems/Danaher, Germany |
| Eduardo Marques | University of São Paulo, Brazil |
| Konstantinos Masselos | Imperial College of Science, Technology and Medicine, UK |
| Antonio Miele | Politecnico di Milano, Italy |
| Takefumi Miyoshi | e-trees Inc., Japan |
| Horácio Neto | Instituto Superior Técnico, Portugal |
| Smail Niar | University of Valenciennes, France |
| Seda O. Memik | Northwestern University, Illinois, USA |
| Monica M. Pereira | University Federal do Rio Grande do Norte, Brazil |
| Christian Pilato | Columbia University, USA |
| Thilo Pionteck | University of Lübeck, Germany |
| Marco Platzner | Universität Paderborn, Germany |
| Dan Poznanovic | Cray Inc., USA |
| Kyle Rupnow | Nanyang Technological University, Singapore |
| Kentaro Sano | Tohoku University, Sendai, Japan |
| Marco D. Santambrogio | Politecnico di Milano, Italy |
| Yukinori Sato | Japan Advanced Institute of Science and Technology, Japan |
| Pete Sedcole | Celoxica, Paris, France |
| Yuichiro Shibata | Nagasaki University, Japan |
| Dimitrios Soudris | National Technical University of Athens, Greece |

| | |
|---|---|
| David Thomas | Imperial College of Science, Technology and Medicine, UK |
| Tim Todman | Imperial College of Science, Technology and Medicine, UK |
| Pedro Trancoso | University of Cyprus, Cyprus |
| Chao Wang | University of Science and Technology of China, China |
| Markus Weinhardt | Hochschule Osnabrück, Germany |
| Theerayod Wiangtong | Mahanakorn University of Technology, Thailand |
| Yoshiki Yamaguchi | University of Tsukuba, Japan |
| Peter Zipf | Universität Kassel, Germany |

## Additional Reviewers

| | |
|---|---|
| Andreas Agne | Universität Paderborn, Germany |
| Ihsen Alouani | University of Valenciennes, France |
| Jecel Assumpção Jr. | University of São Paulo, Brazil |
| Cristiano Bacelar de Oliveira | University of São Paulo, Brazil |
| Rico Backasch | Technische Universität Dresden, Germany |
| Mouna Baklouti | École Nationale d'Ingnieurs de Sfax, Tunisia |
| Davide B. Bartolini | Politecnico di Milano, Italy |
| Cristopher Blochwitz | Universität zu Lübeck, Germany |
| Anthony Brandon | Delft University of Technology, The Netherlands |
| Jae Min Cho | Seoul National University, South Korea |
| David de La Chevallerie | Technische Universität Darmstadt, Germany |
| Gianluca Durelli | Politecnico di Torino, Italy |
| Andreas Engel | University of Basel, Switzerland |
| Peter Figuli | Karlsruhe Institute of Technology, Germany |
| Philip Gottschling | Technische Universität Darmstadt, Germany |
| Adib Haron | Delft University of Technology, The Netherlands |
| Jan Heisswolf | Karlsruhe Institute of Technology, Germany |
| Gerald Hempel | Technische Universität Dresden, Germany |
| Rainer Hoeckmann | Osnabrück University of Applied Sciences, Germany |
| Matei Istoan | Inria, France |
| Moritz Joseph | Universität zu Lübeck, Germany |
| Lukas Jung | Technische Universität Darmstadt, Germany |
| Jehangir Khan | University of Valenciennes, France |
| Kyounghoon Kim | Seoul National University, South Korea |
| Jinho Lee | Seoul National University, South Korea |
| Jinx Liu | University of Ulster, Northern Ireland, UK |
| Charles Lo | University of Toronto, Canada |
| Thomas Marconi | Delft University of Technology, The Netherlands |

Fernando Martin del Campo     University of Toronto, Canada
Luiz Martins                   Federal University of Uberlandia, Brazil
Joachim Meyer                  Karlsruhe Institute of Technology, Germany
Alessandro A. Nacci            Politecnico di Milano, Italy
Sancta Pandit                  University of Toronto, Canada
Lazaros Papadopoulos           Democritus University of Thrace, Greece
Erinaldo Pereira               University of São Paulo, Brazil
Michael Raitza                 Technische Universität Dresden, Germany
Simon Reder                    Karlsruhe Institute of Technology, Germany
Guillaume Salagnac             INSA-Lyon, France
Shimpei Sato                   Japan Advanced Institute of Science and
                                 Technology, Japan
Ali Asgar Sohanghpurwala       Virginia Polytechnic Institute and State University,
                                 USA
Hyunjik Song                   Seoul National University, South Korea
Florian Stock                  Technische Universität Darmstadt, Germany
Berna Torun                    Delft University of Technology, The Netherlands
Erik Vermij                    IBM Research, The Netherlands
Alex Weiss                     Accemic gmbh, Germany
Tobias Wiersema                Universität Paderborn, Germany
Bartosz Wojciechowski          Wroclaw University of Technology, Poland
Jianfeng Zhang                 University of Toronto, Canada

# Contents

## Systems and Applications II

## Extended Abstracts (Posters)

Special Session 1: Funded R&D Running and Completed Projects
(Invited Papers)

Special Session 2: Horizon 2020 Funded Projects (Invited Papers)

# Architecture and Modeling

# Reducing Storage Costs of Reconfiguration Contexts by Sharing Instruction Memory Cache Blocks

Thiago Baldissera Biazus and Mateus Beck Rutzig[✉]

Federal University of Santa Maria, Santa Maria, RS, Brazil
thiago.biazus@ecomp.ufsm.br, mateus@inf.ufsm.br

**Abstract.** Reconfigurable architectures have emerged as energy efficient solution to increase the performance of the current embedded systems. However, the employment of such architectures causes area and power overhead mainly due to the mandatory attachment of a memory structure responsible for storing the reconfiguration contexts, named as context memory. However, most reconfigurable architectures, besides the context memory, employ a cache memory to store regular instructions which, somehow, cause a needless redundancy. In this work, we propose a Demand-based Cache Memory Block Manager (DCMBM) that allows the storing of regular instructions and reconfigurable contexts in a single memory structure. At runtime, depending on the application requirements, the proposed approach manages the ratio of memory blocks that is allocated for each type of information. Results show that the DCMBM-DIM spends, on average, 43.4% less energy maintaining the same performance of split memories structures with the same storage capacity.

## 1 Introduction

Nowadays, the increasing complexity of embedded systems, such as tablets and smartphones, is a consensus. One of the reasons of such complexity is the growing amount of applications, with different behaviors, running in a single device, being most of them not foreseen at design time. Thus, designers of such devices must handle severe power and energy constraints, since the capacity of battery does not scale with the performance requirements.

Companies conceive their embedded platforms with few general purpose processors surrounded by dozens of ASICs to deal with power and performance challenges of such embedded devices. General Purpose Processors (GPP) are responsible for interface controlling and operating system processing. Basically, ASICs are employed to execute applications that would overload the general purpose processor. Due to their specialization, ASICs achieve better performance and energy consumption than GPP when executing applications that belong to its domain. Thus, video, audio and telecommunication standards are employed as ASICs. However, as the technology evolves, the constant release of new standards becomes a drawback, since it should be incorporated in the platform as an ASIC. Besides making the design increasingly complex, this approach affects the time to market, since new tools and compilers should be available to support new ASICs.

K. Sano et al. (Eds.): ARC 2015, LNCS 9040, pp. 3–14, 2015.
DOI: 10.1007/978-3-319-16214-0_1

Reconfigurable architectures have emerged as energy efficient solution to increase the performance of the current embedded system scenario due to the adaptability offered by these architectures [1][2][3]. Due to its adaptive capability, reconfigurable architectures could emulate the behavior of ASICs employed in the current embedded platforms, being a candidate to replace them.

Typically, a reconfigurable architecture works by moving the execution of portions of code from the general purpose processor to reconfigurable logic, offering positive tradeoff between performance and energy, with area and power consumption penalties. Such area and power consumption overhead mainly relies on two structures: the reconfigurable logic and the context memory. The context memory is responsible for storing contexts. A context represents the execution behavior of a portion of code in the reconfigurable logic, where the execution happens indeed.

Several techniques have been proposed aiming to decrease the impact of reconfigurable logic [4][12] but few approaches have been concerned about the context memory overhead [5]. However, the efficiency of the reconfigurable systems relies in this storage component, since application speedup is directly proportional to the context memory hit rate.

Most dynamic reconfigurable architectures, besides the context memory, employ a cache memory to store regular instructions which, somehow, cause a needless redundancy [1][2][3]. Such redundancy is supported by the ordinary execution of these architectures. When the execution starts, most memory accesses are due to regular instruction, since, in this period of the execution, these instructions are being translated to contexts. After some execution time, due to the increasing use of reconfigurable architecture, the pattern on memory accesses changes, since accesses to fetch contexts increase while for regular instructions decrease.

In this work we propose a demand-based allocation cache memory that joins regular instructions and reconfigurable contexts in a single memory structure. Due to the aforementioned memory access pattern behavior, the proposed approach measures, at runtime, the best allocation ratio of cache memory blocks between contexts and regular instructions considering the demand for each data type. In order to achieve this goal, we propose the Demand-based Cache Memory Block Manager (DCMBM) to support the allocation of both data types and to decide which data type would be replaced in a single cache memory structure.

This paper is organized as follows. Section 2 shows a review of researches regarding context memory exploitation. Section 3 presents the proposed cache architecture. The methodology used to gather data about the proposed approach and the results are shown in Section 4. Section 5 presents the final remarks.

## 2    Related Work

Several researches have proposed different partitioning strategies aiming to increase the hit rate of cache memories. Most of them focus on sharing cache memory blocks among several threads that are running concurrently in a scenario of multiprocessor systems. In [6] is proposed a Gradient-based Cache Partitioning Algorithm to improve the cache hit rate by dynamic monitoring thread references and giving extra cache space for threads that require it. The cache memory is divided in regions and an algorithm calculates the affinity of threads to acquire certain cache region.

The proposal shown in [7] works over the premise that more cache resources should not be given for applications that have more demand and few resources but it should be provided for applications that benefit more from cache resources. A run-time monitor constantly tracks the misses of each running application, partitioning the number of ways of a set-associative cache among them. After each modification in the partitioning, the algorithm verifies the difference of miss rate of the threads in comparison with the previous partitioning and acts to minimize the global miss rate by varying the number of ways for each application. The approaches presented in [8][9] propose strategies to switch off ways depending on the cache miss rate aiming at saving energy.

Despite several researchers have proposed techniques to partition the cache memory among several threads/process, to the best of our knowledge, there is no work considering cache partitioning in the field of reconfigurable architectures. Aiming to support the importance of optimizing the storage components when reconfigurable architectures are considered, Table 1 shows the impact of the context memory showing the amount of bytes required to configure the reconfigurable fabric of three different architectures. As it can be seen in this Table, these architectures rely on a significant amount of bytes to store a single configuration. For instance, GARP [2], a traditional reconfigurable architecture, requires 786 KB to hold 128 configurations, such amount of memory would certainly provide a considerable impact in the power consumption of entire system.

**Table 1.** Bytes per Configuration Required by Different Reconfigurable Architectures

| Rec. Architecture | GARP[1] | DIM[3] | Piperench[2] |
|---|---|---|---|
| Bytes per Configuration | 6,144 | 4,261 | 21,504 |

In this work, we propose a cache partitioning technique for coarse-grained reconfigurable architecture where regular instructions and reconfigurable context share the same cache structure. Considering that the need for a large storage volume of each type of information occurs at different periods of the execution time, a Demand-based Cache Memory Block Manager (DCMBM) is proposed to handle such behavior by partitioning the cache memory blocks depending on the demand of each type of information.

# 3    Demand-Based Cache Memory Block Manager (DCMBM)

## 3.1    The Structure of the Cache Memory

Figure 1 shows the structure of the cache memory of the Demand-based Cache Memory Block Manager (DCMBM). As it can be seen in this Figure, DCMBM has almost the same structure of a traditional cache being composed of valid, tag and data fields. The valid bit is used to verify the truth of the stored data and tag is used to verify if the data of the address stored matches with requested address. Data field holds the information indeed. Additionally, every block of DCMBM has a field, named Type (t), to identify if the stored information is a regular instruction or a context. The DCMBM works as a traditional cache memory, if a cache miss happens in a certain line of the cache memory, the replacement algorithm chooses, in the case of a set associative cache, one of the blocks of the target set to be replaced.

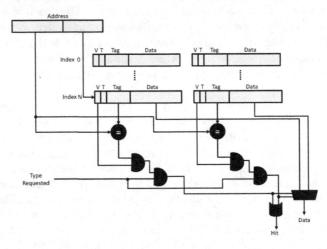

**Fig. 1.** Circuit of the DCMBM

## 3.2    Block Allocation Hardware

The Block Allocation Hardware (BAH) is responsible for managing the ratio of blocks that would be allocated to each type of information. The algorithm is based on a threshold and works over the cache associativity. Based on the demand for each type of information, the BAH uses the threshold to decide, when a write to the cache happens, which type of information should be replaced.

The BAH is implemented as a 4-bit circuit, thus the range of the values goes from 0 to 15. There is a 4-bit register for each cache set that holds a value in order to inform if a block that contains a context or a regular instruction would be replaced.

When a new context is created, it means that it should be stored in the cache memory (a write in the cache), and the value of the register of the target set is lower than a certain threshold (defined at design time), a block of regular instruction is selected as victim to be replaced. However, when the value is greater than a given threshold and a regular instruction causes a cache miss (a write in the cache), a context is chosen as victim to be replaced.

There are two scenarios where the value of the register of the set is updated:

•    When a context should be stored in the memory cache, the BAH algorithms decrements the value of the target set by one unit. This strategy focuses on increasing the number of blocks to store contexts instead of regular instructions, since the lower the value, the more blocks to store contexts will be opened in the set. Following the pattern of memory accesses of dynamic reconfigurable architectures, there are some periods of the application execution where the process to translate regular instructions to contexts boosts, thus the number of requests to store context would increase. Therefore, more cache blocks must be given to store contexts to maximize the context hit ratio and, consequently, to speed up the application.

- When neither a regular instruction nor a context has generated a hit of a certain address (a cache miss happens due to a regular instruction), the BAH algorithm increments the value of the target set by one unit. This strategy aims to increase the number of blocks to store regular instructions, since the higher the value, the more blocks to store regular instructions will be opened in the set. There is a high probability that a miss generated by both regular instruction and context is due to the first execution of a certain portion of code. It means that the dynamic reconfigurable architecture is starting to translate such portion of code and will not request a block to store the context related to such portion of code soon. However, as a new portion of code is being executed, more blocks for regular instructions would be necessary to increase the hit rate and to avoid penalties in the execution time of the application.

In the following topics, we summarize how the BAH handles each possibility of cache memory access:

1) When a miss happens from both regular instruction and context and the value of the register of the target set is:
   a. lower than a certain threshold, a block of regular instruction is selected as a victim and the value of the register is incremented by one unit.
   b. greater than a certain threshold, a block of context is selected as a victim and the value of the register is incremented by one unit.
2) When a new context is finished by the reconfigurable architecture (it means that it should be stored in the cache memory) and the value of the register of the target set is:
   a. lower than a certain threshold, a block of regular instruction is selected as a victim and the value of the register is decremented by one unit.
   b. greater than a certain threshold, a block of context is selected as a victim and the value of the register is decremented by one unit.
3) When a hit happens, both from regular instructions or context, the values of the registers are not updated.

## 3.3    Replacement Algorithm

As the DCMBM is based on the cache associativity, a replacement algorithm should be implemented to select the block, into target set, that would be victim to be replaced. We have selected the Least Recently Used (LRU) as the replacement algorithm since it is widely employed in the current processors in the market (e.g. ARM Cortex, Intel Core, etc). We have implemented a modified LRU to work together with the BAH. Unlike the original version of LRU, where any of the blocks into the target set would be victim to be replaced, the DCMBM algorithm works only over blocks, into the target set, that match with the type of information that was chosen to be victim by the BAH. It is implemented by just comparing the type of information that should be replaced (provided by BAH) and the type of information of every block into the target set (provided by the field t (type of date)).

# 4    Case Study

In this section we show how the Demand-based Cache Memory Block Manager (DCMBM) works together with a reconfigurable system. As a case study, we have selected the Dynamic Instruction Merging (DIM) [3]. Particularly, this architecture was selected since it has already shown to be energy efficient on accelerating a wide range of application behaviors [3]. In addition, such reconfigurable system has two memory structures (instruction memory and context memory) and would take advantage of the proposed approach since it is based on a hardware which builds contexts at runtime.

## 4.1    DIM Architecture

As shown in Figure 2, the entire reconfigurable system is divided into six blocks: the DIM hardware; the Reconfigurable Data Path; the MIPS R3000 processor; the context memory; the instruction and data memory. The next subsections give a brief overview of each block.

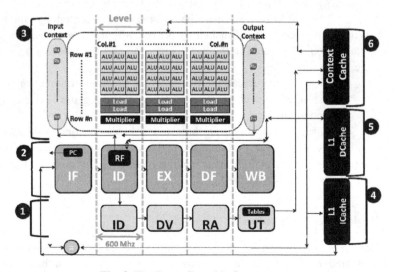

**Fig. 2.** The Reconfigurable System

*a.    DIM hardware*

A special hardware, named as DIM (Dynamic Instruction Merging), is responsible for detecting and extracting instruction level parallelism (ILP) from sequence of regular instructions that are executed by the general purpose processor and for translating them to data path contexts. A context is composed of bits that configure the functional units and make the route of the operands from the processor register file to the reconfigurable data path. The DIM hardware is based on a binary translation algorithm (BT) [3], thus no new instructions need to be implemented in the translation from regular instructions to contexts. As shown in Figure 2, the DIM is a 4-stage pipelined circuit and works in parallel with the processor, presenting no delay overhead in the pipeline structure. The detection, reconfiguration and execution processes follow these steps:

- At run time, the DIM unit detects sequences of instructions that can be executed in the reconfigurable architecture. In this step, the instructions, fetched from the instruction cache, are executed into processor pipeline stages.
- After that, this sequence is translated to a data path configuration, and saved in the context cache. These sequences are indexed by the instruction memory address of the first instruction of the context.
- The next time that such instruction memory address is found, this means that the beginning of a previously translated sequence of instructions was located, and the processor changes to a halt state. Then, the context for the respective sequence is loaded from the context cache, the data path is reconfigured and the input operands are fetched.
- This configuration is executed on combinational logic circuit of the reconfigurable data path.
- Finally, the write back in the registers and memory positions writes are done.

*b.    The Reconfigurable Data Path and MIPS R3000 processor*

The reconfigurable data path is tightly coupled to a MIPS R3000 processor, so no external accesses (relative to the core) are necessary. The R3000 processor is based on a 5-stage pipelined circuit and implements the MIPS I instruction set architecture.

The reconfigurable data path is composed of simple functional units (ALU, Multipliers and Memory Accesses) which generate a totally combinational circuit. The circuit is bounded by the input context registers and output context registers that hold the operands fetched from the processor register file and the results of the operations performed in the data path, respectively. The organization of the data path is divided in row and columns, instructions allocated by the DIM hardware at the same column are executed in parallel. In contrast, instructions allocated in different columns are executed in sequential way.

Connections between the functional units are made by multiplexers, which are responsible for routing the operands within the data path. Input multiplexers select the source operands from the input context to the functional units. Output multiplexers carry the execution results to the output context to make the write back into the processor register file.

*c.    Instruction and Data Cache Memories*

As the MIPS processor is based on Harvard Architecture, there are two cache memory structures to store data and regular instructions separately. Both caches are set associative caches and the way could be parameterized depending on the performance requirements and the power constraints of the design. In the experimental results section, we explain the methodology for the associativity degree used in this work.

*d.    Context Cache Memory*

Additionally to the data and instruction memories, there is another cache structure that holds the context built by the DIM hardware, named as Context Cache. The steps to fetch a context from the Context Cache are exactly the same as to fetch a regular instruction from the Instruction Cache since a context is indexed by the memory address of the first instruction of the translated sequence. In this way, the least significant bits of the memory address are reserved to provide the index information and the remaining bits are stored as tag. Like the other cache structures, the Context Cache is also set associative and the associativity degree depends on the design requirements and constrains.

## 4.2    Employment of DCMBM in the DIM Architecture

Aiming to employ the proposed approach in the DIM architecture the Context Cache (Block 6) and L1 ICache (Block 4) structures are replaced by a single cache memory that stores both contexts and regular MIPS instructions. Unlike the separated cache memory structures that rely on two concurrent memory accesses (one into the ICache to find out a regular instruction and other into the Context Memory to find out a context) for each change in the PC content, the DCMBM performs a single access to find out both a context and a regular instruction related to the PC address. If a hit happens in a context, the bits will be sent to the reconfigurable data path. On the other hand, if a hit happens in a regular instruction block, the bit will be sent to the 1st pipeline stage of the MIPS processor. Besides the area savings due to the elimination of an entire memory structure, the DCMBM provides energy savings (as it can be seen in the section 5) since the number of memory access would decrease significantly.

## 5      Experimental Results

To measure the efficiency of the proposed approach we have compared the original DIM architecture (Figure 2) (named as Or-DIM), that contains both Instruction Cache and Context memory structures, against the DIM architecture based on the DCMBM technique (named as DCMBM-DIM). For the sake of the comparison, we have created two scenarios aiming to show the efficiency of the DCMBM approach on handling the behavior of dynamic reconfigurable architectures. The first scenario compares Or-DIM and DCMBM-DIM conceived by memory structures with the same storage capacity, in terms of bytes. The second scenario compares DIM-DCMBM with half the storage capacity than Or-DIM. In all experiments we have used, for both DCMBM-DIM and Or-DIM, 8-way set associative cache memory structures. Both scenarios were evaluated varying the size of the L1 cache (where the DCMBM is implemented) from 16KB to 128KB. A 512-KB 16-way associative unified L2 cache was employed in all experiments.

To gather results about performance we have implemented the DCMBM hardware together with the cycle-accurate DIM architecture simulator [3]. We have conceived a reconfigurable data path with 45 columns, 4 ALU per row, 2 multipliers per row and 3 memory accesses per row. Such configuration of reconfigurable data path produces a context of 128 bytes, meaning that the block size of memory structure of both DCMBM-DIM and Or-DIM must have such amount of bytes. In addition, we have selected some benchmarks from MiBench (*susan edges, susan corners* and *blowfish*), Splash (*molecular dynamics (md), lu factorization (lu)* and *fast fourier transformation (fft)*) and PARSEC (*swaptions* and *blackscholes*) to measure the efficiency of the DCMBM with the behavior of real applications.

Finally, the energy consumption was evaluated by synthesizing the VHDL description of DCMBM hardware using CMOS 90nm technology. To gather data about cache memory structures we have used CACTI [10]. It is important to emphasize that the synthesis of the DCMBM reports that the circuit just increases 2% of access time of the original cache memory structure. Such overhead comes from the BAH algorithm that must decide, at runtime, which type of information should be replaced.

## 5.1  Same Storage Capacity

The results shown in this subsection reflects the comparison of DCMBM-DIM and Ori-DIM considering the same storage capacity in terms of L1 cache. For instance, in Table 2, the second column shows the comparison of a 8KB ICache plus 8KB Context Cache Or-DIM against a 16KB DCMBM-DIM, the results of such table is normalized to the execution of Ori-DIM. As it can be seen in this Table, most benchmarks are benefited from the dynamic behavior of DCMBM-DIM. As it would be expected, the smaller the cache memory is, the greater are the gains of DCMBM-DIM over Ori-DIM, since the BAH algorithm has the freedom to manage the cache blocks of DCMBM-DIM (twice than the capacity of each memory structure of Ori-DIM) to a certain type of information, depending on the demand of the application. *FFT, Susan Corners, Swaptions* and *Blackscholes* achieve performance improvements when DCMBM-DIM is employed due to higher hit rate in the reconfiguration contexts. It means that more portions of code are accelerated in the reconfigurable data path when the proposed approach is applied.

On the other hand, *LU* and *Susan Edges* show performance losses when DCMBM-DIM is employed. Despite the DCMBM-DIM achieving more hits in contexts, due to the significant size of their codes, both benchmarks show more misses in regular instructions than Ori-DIM when the storage capacity is small. When the size of the cache memory grows, both benchmarks show at least the same performance of Ori-DIM.

**Table 2.** Performance of DCMBM-DIM normalized to Ori-DIM Execution considering the same storage capacity

| | Performance Normalized to Ori-DIM Execution | | | | |
|---|---|---|---|---|---|
| | **16KB** | **32KB** | **64KB** | **128KB** | **256KB** |
| FFT | 0,92 | 0,98 | 1,03 | 1,00 | 0,99 |
| LU | 1,08 | 1,06 | 0,97 | 0,98 | 0,97 |
| MD | 0,99 | 1,00 | 1,02 | 1,00 | 0,99 |
| Susan E | 1,06 | 1,02 | 1,01 | 1,01 | 1,00 |
| Susan C | 0,97 | 0,97 | 1,00 | 1,00 | 1,00 |
| Swaptions | 0,97 | 0,96 | 0,97 | 1,00 | 0,99 |
| Blackscholes | 0,95 | 0,96 | 0,97 | 1,00 | 0,99 |
| Blowfish | 1,01 | 1,00 | 1,00 | 1,00 | 1,00 |
| *Average* | *0,99* | *0,99* | *1,00* | *1,00* | *0,99* |

Table 3 shows the energy consumption of DCMBM-DIM normalized to the Ori-DIM approach. As it can be seen in this Table, the proposed approach spends less energy in the execution of all benchmarks considering all cache sizes. The main source of the energy savings is the fewer memory accesses performed by DCMBM-DIM than Ori-DIM. While a single memory access is performed by DCMBM-DIM to find out a context and a regular instruction, the Ori-DIM must perform a instruction cache access and a context cache access. Despite the two memory accesses performed by Or-DIM are done into memory structures with half the storage capacity, the sum of the energy consumption is greater than a single access in a memory structure with twice storage capacity. Summarizing, the DCMBM-DIM spends, on average, 43.4% less energy maintaining the same performance of Ori-DIM when the same storage capacity is considered.

**Table 3.** Energy Consumption of DCMBM-DIM normalized to Ori-DIM Execution considering the same storage capacity

| | Energy Comsumption Normalized to Ori-DIM Execution | | | | |
|---|---|---|---|---|---|
| | **16KB** | **32KB** | **64KB** | **128KB** | **256KB** |
| FFT | 0,47 | 0,56 | 0,64 | 0,63 | 0,53 |
| LU | 0,61 | 0,64 | 0,61 | 0,64 | 0,54 |
| MD | 0,51 | 0,57 | 0,64 | 0,64 | 0,53 |
| Susan E | 0,59 | 0,59 | 0,61 | 0,62 | 0,52 |
| Susan C | 0,49 | 0,53 | 0,60 | 0,62 | 0,52 |
| Swaptions | 0,48 | 0,52 | 0,57 | 0,62 | 0,52 |
| Blackscholes | 0,47 | 0,52 | 0,57 | 0,62 | 0,52 |
| Blowfish | 0,52 | 0,55 | 0,60 | 0,61 | 0,51 |
| *Average* | *0,52* | *0,56* | *0,60* | *0,63* | *0,52* |

## 5.2    Halve the Storage Capacity

This subsection shows the results considering the DCMBM-DIM with half the storage capacity in comparison to Ori-DIM. For instance, the second column of Table 4 reflects the comparison of a 16KB ICache plus 16KB Context Cache Or-DIM against a 16KB DCMBM-DIM.

Table 4 shows the performance of DCMBM-DIM normalized to Ori-DIM execution. This table shows the efficiency of BAH algorithm on adapting to the demand required by the application. The performance losses by having a memory structure with half the storage capacity than Ori-DIM are almost insignificant in all benchmarks. In contrast, the energy saving remain almost the same of the comparison with the same storage capacity. When the proposed approach is employed, the execution of all applications spends, on average, 41 % less energy in comparison to Ori-DIM.

**Table 4.** Performance of DCMBM-DIM normalized to Ori-DIM Execution considering the half the storage capacity

| | Performance Normalized to Ori-DIM Execution | | | |
|---|---|---|---|---|
| | 32KB-16KB | 64KB-32KB | 128KB-64KB | 256KB-128KB |
| FFT | 1,03 | 0,99 | 0,99 | 0,99 |
| LU | 1,08 | 1,06 | 0,98 | 0,97 |
| MD | 1,00 | 1,01 | 1,03 | 0,99 |
| Susan E | 1,09 | 1,03 | 1,02 | 1,01 |
| Susan C | 1,04 | 1,01 | 1,00 | 1,00 |
| Swaptions | 0,99 | 0,99 | 1,01 | 0,99 |
| Blackscholes | 0,98 | 1,00 | 1,01 | 0,99 |
| Blowfish | 1,01 | 1,00 | 1,00 | 1,00 |
| *Average* | *1,03* | *1,01* | *1,00* | *0,99* |

**Table 5.** Energy Consumption of DCMBM-DIM normalized to Ori-DIM Execution considering the half the storage capacity

| | Energy Comsumption Normalized to Ori-DIM Execution | | | |
|---|---|---|---|---|
| | 32KB-16KB | 64KB-32KB | 128KB-64KB | 256KB-128KB |
| FFT | 0,57 | 0,54 | 0,53 | 0,78 |
| LU | 0,62 | 0,59 | 0,54 | 0,79 |
| MD | 0,53 | 0,55 | 0,56 | 0,78 |
| Susan E | 0,62 | 0,55 | 0,53 | 0,76 |
| Susan C | 0,54 | 0,53 | 0,52 | 0,77 |
| Swaptions | 0,51 | 0,51 | 0,53 | 0,76 |
| Blackscholes | 0,50 | 0,52 | 0,54 | 0,76 |
| Blowfish | 0,52 | 0,52 | 0,52 | 0,76 |
| *Average* | *0,55* | *0,54* | *0,53* | *0,77* |

# 6    Conclusions

In this work, we have proposed DCMBM-DIM, aiming to reduce the storage costs, in terms of energy and area, by sharing a single memory structure among regular instructions and reconfiguration contexts. A demand-based hardware, named as BAH, is proposed to manage the amount of blocks available for each type of information depending on the demand of the application. Considering memory designs with the same and half the storage capacity, DCMBM-DIM maintains the performance of dedicated structures and offers considerable energy savings.

# References

1. Goldstein, S.C., et al.: PipeRench: A Reconfigurable Architecture and Compiler. Computer **33**, 70–77 (2000)
2. Wawrzynek, J.R.H.: Garp: a MIPS processor with a reconfigurable coprocessor. In: Proceedings of IEEE Symposium on FPGA-Based Custom Computing Machines. ACM, Washington (1997)
3. Beck, A.C.S., et al.: Transparent reconfigurable acceleration for heterogeneous embedded applications. In: Proceedings of Design, Automation and Test in Europe, pp. 1208–1213. ACM, New York (2008)
4. Rutzig, M.B., et al.: Balancing reconfigurable data path resources according to application requirements. In: IEEE International Symposium on Parallel and Distributed Processing, IPDPS 2008, pp. 1–8, April 14–18, 2008
5. Lo, T.B., et al.: Decreasing the impact of the context memory on reconfigurable architectures. In: Proceedings of HiPEAC Workshop on Reconfigurable Computing, Pisa (2010)
6. Hasenplaugh, W., et al.: The gradient-based cache partitioning algorithm. ACM Trans. Archit. Code Optim. **8**(4), Article 44, January 2012
7. Qureshi, M.K., Patt, Y.N.: Utility-based cache partitioning: a low-overhead, high-performance, runtime mechanism to partition shared caches. In: 39th Annual IEEE/ACM International Symposium on Microarchitecture, MICRO-39, pp. 423–432, December 2006
8. Albonesi, D.H.: Selective cache ways: on-demand cache resource allocation. In: Proceedings of the 32nd Annual International Symposium on Microarchitecture, MICRO-32, pp. 248–259 (1999)
9. Suh, G.E., Rudolph, L., Devadas, S.: Dynamic Partitioning of Shared Cache Memory. J. Supercomput. **28**(1), 7–26 (2004)
10. Wilton, S.J.E., et al.: CACTI: an enhanced cache access and cycle time model. IEEE Journal of Solid-State Circuits, 677-688, May 1996
11. Clark, N., Tang, W., Mahlke, S.: Automatically generating Custom instruction set extensions. In: Workshop of Application-Specific Processors (2002)

# A Vector Caching Scheme for Streaming FPGA SpMV Accelerators

Yaman Umuroglu$^{(\boxtimes)}$ and Magnus Jahre

Department of Computer and Information Science,
Norwegian University of Science and Technology, Trondheim, Norway
{yamanu,jahre}@idi.ntnu.no

**Abstract.** The sparse matrix – vector multiplication (SpMV) kernel is important for many scientific computing applications. Implementing SpMV in a way that best utilizes hardware resources is challenging due to input-dependent memory access patterns. FPGA-based accelerators that buffer the entire irregular-access part in on-chip memory enable highly efficient SpMV implementations, but are limited to smaller matrices due to on-chip memory limits. Conversely, conventional caches can work with large matrices, but cache misses can cause many stalls that decrease efficiency. In this paper, we explore the intersection between these approaches and attempt to combine the strengths of each. We propose a hardware-software caching scheme that exploits preprocessing to enable performant and area-effective SpMV acceleration. Our experiments with a set of large sparse matrices indicate that our scheme can achieve nearly stall-free execution with average 1.1 % stall time, with 70 % less on-chip memory compared to buffering the entire vector. The preprocessing step enables our scheme to offer up to 40 % higher performance compared to a conventional cache of same size by eliminating cold miss penalties.

## 1 Introduction

Increased energy efficiency is a key goal for building next-generation computing systems that can scale the "utilization wall" of dark silicon [1]. A strategy for achieving this is accelerating commonly encountered kernels in applications. Sparse Matrix – Vector Multiplication (SpMV) is a computational kernel widely encountered in the scientific computation domain and frequently constitutes a bottleneck for such applications [2]. Analysis of web connectivity graphs [3] can require adjacency matrices that are very large and sparse, with a tendency to grow even bigger due to the important role they play in the Big Data trend.

A defining characteristic of the SpMV kernel is the *irregular memory access pattern* caused by the sparse storage formats. A critical part of the kernel depends on memory reads to addresses that correspond to non-zero element locations of the matrix, which are only known at runtime. The kernel is otherwise characterized by little data reuse and large per-iteration data requirements [2], which makes the performance memory-bound. Storing the kernel inputs and outputs in

© Springer International Publishing Switzerland 2015
K. Sano et al. (Eds.): ARC 2015, LNCS 9040, pp. 15–26, 2015.
DOI: 10.1007/978-3-319-16214-0_2

high-capacity high-bandwidth DRAM is considered a cost-effective solution [4]; however, the burst-optimized architecture of DRAM constitutes an ever-growing "irregularity wall" in the quest for enabling efficient SpMV implementations.

Recently, there has been increased interest in FPGA-based acceleration of computational kernels. The primary benefit from FPGA accelerators is the ability to create customized memory systems and datapaths that align well with the requirements of each kernel, enabling stall-free execution (termed *streaming acceleration* in this paper). From the perspective of the SpMV kernel, the ability to deliver high external memory bandwidth owing to high pin count and dynamic (run-time) specialization via partial reconfiguration are attractive properties. Several FPGA implementations for the SpMV kernel have been proposed, either directly for SpMV or as part of larger algorithms like iterative solvers [5,6], some of which present order-of-magnitude better energy efficiency and comparable performance to CPU and GPGPU solutions thanks to streaming acceleration. These accelerators tackle the irregular access problem by buffering the entire random-access data in *on-chip memory (OCM)*. Unfortunately, this *buffer-all strategy* is limited to SpMV operations where the random-access data can fit in OCM, and therefore not suitable for very large sparse matrices.

To address this problem, we propose a specialized vector caching scheme for area-efficient SpMV accelerators that can target large matrices while still preserving the streaming acceleration property. Using the canonical cold-capacity-conflict cache miss classification, we examine how the structure of a sparse matrix relates to each category and how misses can be avoided. By exploiting preprocessing (which is quite common in GPGPU and CPU SpMV optimizations) to specialize for the sparsity pattern of the matrix we show that streaming acceleration can be achieved with significantly smaller area for a set of test matrices. Our experiments with a set of large sparse matrices indicate that our scheme achieves the best of both worlds by increasing performance by 40% compared to a conventional cache while at the same time using 70% less OCM than the buffer-all strategy. The contributions of this work are four-fold. First, we describe how the structure of a sparse matrix relates to *cold*, *capacity* and *conflict* misses in a hardware cache. We show how cold misses to the result vector can be avoided by marking row start elements in column-major traversal. We propose two methods of differing accuracy and overhead for estimating the required cache depth to avoid all capacity misses. Finally, we present an enhanced cache with cold miss skip capability, and demonstrate that it can outperform a traditional cache in performance and a buffer-all strategy in area.

## 2   Background and Related Work

### 2.1   The SpMV Kernel and Sparse Matrix Storage

The SpMV kernel $y = A \cdot x$ consists of multiplying an $m \times n$ sparse matrix $A$ with $NZ$ nonzero elements by a dense vector $x$ of size $n$ to obtain a result vector $y$ of size $m$. The sparse matrix is commonly stored in a format which allows storing only the nonzero elements of the matrix. Many storage formats for

$$\begin{bmatrix} 1.1 & 0 & 0 \\ 0 & 2.2 & 3.3 \\ 4.4 & 0 & 5.5 \end{bmatrix}$$

```
colptr={0 2 3 5}                    for(j=0 to n-1)
values={1.1 4.4 2.2 3.3 5.5}    for(i=colptr[j] to colptr[j+1])
rowind={0 2 1 1 2}                    y[rowind[i]] += values[j] * x[j]
```

**Fig. 1.** A sparse matrix, its CSC representation and SpMV pseudocode. The random-access clause to y is highlighted.

sparse matrices have been proposed, some of which specialize on particular sparsity patterns, and others suitable for generic sparse matrices. In this paper, we will assume an FPGA SpMV accelerator that uses column-major sparse matrix traversal (in line with [4,6,7]) and an appropriate storage format such as Compressed Sparse Column (CSC). Column-major is preferred over row-major due to the advantages of maximum temporal locality on the dense vector access and the natural C-slow-like interleaving of rows in floating point multiplier pipelines, enabling simpler datapaths [6]. Additionally, as we will show in Section 3.2 it allows bypassing cold misses, which can contribute significantly to performance. Figure 1 illustrates a sparse matrix, its representation in the CSC format, and the pseudocode for performing column-major SpMV. We use the `variable` notation to refer to CSC SpMV data such as `values` and `colptr`. As highlighted in the figure, the result vector y is accessed depending on the `rowind` values, causing the random access patterns that are central to this work.

## 2.2   FPGA SpMV Accelerators and Result Vector Access

The datapath of a column-major SpMV accelerator is a multiply-accumulator with feedback from a random-access memory, as illustrated in Figure 2a. New partial products are summed into the corresponding element of the result vector, which can give rise to read-after-write (RAW) hazards due to the latency of the adder, as shown in Figure 2b. Addressing this requires a read operation to y[i] to be delayed until the writes to y[i] are completed, which is typically avoided by stalling the pipeline or reordering the elements.

   With growing sparse matrix sizes and typically double-precision floating point arithmetic, the inputs of the SpMV kernel can be very large. Combined with the memory-bound nature of the kernel, this requires high-capacity high-bandwidth external memory to enable competitive SpMV implementations. Existing FPGA SpMV accelerators [4–6] used DRAM as a cost-effective option for the storing the SpMV inputs and outputs, which is also our approach in this work. These designs typically address the random access problem by buffering the entire random-access vector in OCM [5,6]. Random accesses to the vector are thus guaranteed to be serviced with a small, constant latency. Unfortunately, this limits the maximum sparse matrix size that can be processed with the accelerator. To deal with y vectors larger than the OCM size while avoiding DRAM random access latencies, Gregg et al. [4] proposed to store the result vector in high-capacity DRAM and used a small direct-mapped cache. They also observed that cache misses present a significant penalty, and proposed reordering the matrix and processing in cache-sized chunks to reduce miss rate. However, this

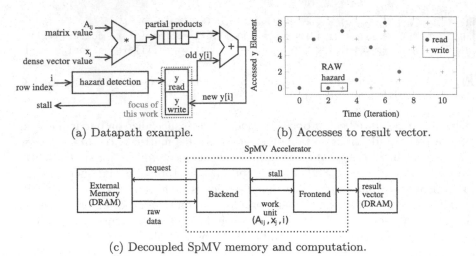

(a) Datapath example.                    (b) Accesses to result vector.

(c) Decoupled SpMV memory and computation.

**Fig. 2.** A column-major FPGA SpMV accelerator design

imposes significant overheads for large matrices. In contrast, our approach does not modify the matrix structure; rather, it extracts information from the sparse matrix to reduce cache misses, which can be combined with reordering for greater effect. Prior work such as [8] analyzed SpMV cache behavior on microprocessors, but includes non-reusable data such as matrix values and requires probabilistic models. FPGA accelerators can exhibit deterministic access patterns for each sparse matrix, which our scheme exploits for analysis and preprocessing.

To concentrate on the random access problem, we base our work on a decoupled SpMV accelerator architecture [7], which defines a *backend* interfacing the main memory and pushing *work units* to the *frontend*, which handles the computation. Our focus will be on the random-access part of the frontend. Since we would like the accelerator to support larger result vectors that do not fit in OCM, we add DRAM for storing the result vector, as illustrated in Figure 2c.

### 2.3   Sparse Matrix Preprocessing

The memory behavior and performance of the SpMV kernel is dependent on the particular sparse matrix used, necessitating a preprocessing step at runtime for optimization. Fortunately, algorithms that make heavy use of SpMV tend to multiply the same sparse matrix with many different vectors, which enables ameliorating the cost of preprocesing across speed-ups in each SpMV iteration. This preprocessing can take many forms [9], including permuting rows/columns to create dense structure, decomposing into predetermined patterns, mapping to parallel processing elements to minimize communication and so on. We also adopt a preprocessing step in our scheme to enable optimizing for a given sparse matrix, but unlike previous work, our preprocessing stage produces information to enable specialized cache operation instead of changing the matrix structure.

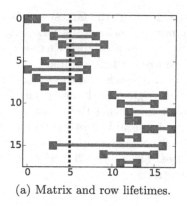

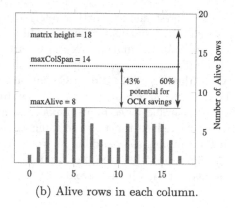

(a) Matrix and row lifetimes.      (b) Alive rows in each column.

**Fig. 3.** Example matrix Pajek/GD01_b and row lifetime analysis

# 3   Vector Caching Scheme

To tackle the memory latency problem while accessing the result vector from DRAM, we buffer a portion of the result vector in OCM and use a hardware-software cooperative *vector caching scheme* that enables per-matrix specialization. This scheme will consist of a runtime *preprocessing step*, which will extract the necessary information from the sparse matrix for efficient caching including the required cache size, and *vector cache* hardware which will use this information. Our goal is to shrink the OCM requirements for the vector cache while avoiding stalls for servicing requests from main memory.

## 3.1   Row Lifetime Analysis

To relate the vector cache usage to the matrix structure, we start by defining a number of structural properties for sparse matrices. First, we note that each row has a strong correspondence to a single result vector element, i.e $y[i]$ contains the dot product of row i with x. The period in which $y[i]$ is used is solely determined by the period in which row i accesses it. This is the key observation that we use to specialize our vector caching scheme for a given sparse matrix.

**Calculating maxAlive:** For a matrix with column-major traversal, we define the *aliveness interval* of a row as the column range between (and including) the columns of its first and last nonzero elements, and will refer to the interval length as the *span*. Figure 3a illustrates the aliveness intervals as red lines extending between the first and last non-zeroes of each row. For a given column j, we define a set of rows to be *simultaneously alive* in this column if all of their aliveness intervals contain j. The number of alive rows for a given column is the maximum size of such a set. Visually, this can be thought of as the number of aliveness interval lines that intersect the vertical line of a column. For instance, the dotted line corresponding to column 5 in Figure 3a intersects 8 intervals, and there are 8 rows alive in column 5. Finally, we define the *maximum simultaneously alive* *rows* of a sparse matrix, further referred to as `maxAlive`, as the largest number of rows simultaneously alive in any column of the matrix. Incidentally, `maxAlive` is equal to 8 for the matrix given in Figure 3a – though the alive rows themselves may be different, no column has more than 8 alive rows in this example.

**Calculating `maxColSpan`:** Calculating `maxAlive` requires preprocessing the matrix. If the accelerator design is not under very tight OCM constraints, it may be desirable to estimate `maxAlive` instead of computing the exact value in order to reduce the preprocessing time. If we define aliveness interval and span for columns as was done for rows, the largest column span of the matrix `maxColSpan` provides an upper bound on `maxAlive`. The column 3 in Figure 3a has a span of 14, which is `maxColSpan` for this matrix.

### 3.2   Avoiding Vector Cache Misses

We now use the canonical cold/capacity/conflict classification to break down cache misses into three categories and explain how accesses to the result vector relate to each category. For each category, we will describe how misses can be related to the matrix structure and avoided where possible.

**Cold Misses:** Cold (compulsory) misses occur when a vector element is referenced for the first time, at the start of the aliveness interval of each row. For matrices with very few elements per row, cold misses can contribute significantly to the total cache misses. Although this type of cache miss is considered unavoidable in general-purpose caching, a special case exists for SpMV. Consider the column-major SpMV operation $y = Ax$ where the $y$ vector is random-accessed using the vector cache. The initial value of each $y$ element is zero, and is updated by adding partial sums for each nonzero in the corresponding matrix row. If we can distinguish cold misses from the other miss types at runtime, we can avoid them completely: a cold miss to a $y$ element will return the initial value, which is zero[1]. Recognizing misses as cold misses is critical for this technique to work. We propose to accomplish this by introducing a *start-of-row bit* marked during preprocessing, as described in Section 3.3.

**Capacity Misses:** Capacity misses occur due to the cache capacity being insufficient to hold the SpMV result vector working set. Therefore, the only way of avoiding capacity misses is ensuring that the vector cache is large enough to hold the working set. Caching the entire vector (the buffer-all strategy) is straightforward, but is not an accurate working set size estimation due to the sparsity of the matrix. While methods exist to attempt to reduce the working set of the SpMV operation by permuting the matrix rows and columns, they are outside the scope of this paper. Instead, we will concentrate on how the working set size can be estimated. This estimation can be used to reconfigure the FPGA SpMV accelerator to use less OCM, which can be reallocated for other components. In this work, we make the assumption that a memory location is

---

[1] The more general SpMV form $y = Ax + b$ can be easily implemented by adding the dense vector $b$ after $y = Ax$ is computed.

in the working set if it will be reused at least once to reap all the caching benefits. Thus, the cache must have a capacity of at least `maxAlive` to avoid all capacity misses. This requires the computation of `maxAlive` during the preprocessing phase. If OCM constraints are more relaxed, the `maxColSpan` estimation described in Section 3.1 can be used instead. Figure 3b shows the row lifetime analysis for the matrix in Figure 3a and how different estimations of the required capacity yield different OCM savings compared to the buffer-all strategy.

**Conflict Misses:** For the case of an SpMV vector cache, conflict misses arise when two simultaneously alive vector elements map to the same cache line. This is determined by the nonzero pattern, number of cachelines and the chosen hash function. Assuming that the vector cache has enough capacity to hold the working set, avoiding conflict misses is an associativity problem. Since content-associative memories are expensive in FPGAs, direct-mapped caches are often preferred. As described in Section 4.2, our experiments indicate that conflicts are few for most matrices even with a direct-mapped cache, as long as the cache capacity is sufficient. Techniques such as victim caching [10] can be utilized to decrease conflict misses in direct-mapped caches, though we do not investigate their benefit in this work.

## 3.3 Preprocessing

Having established how the matrix structure relates to vector cache misses, we will now formulate the preprocessing step. We assume that the preprocessing step will be carried out by the general-purpose core prior to copying the SpMV data into the accelerator's memory space.

---

**Algorithm 1** Finding `maxAlive` and marking row starts.

---

**function** PREPROCESSMAXALIVE(CSCMatrix $A$)
  $Q \leftarrow priorityQueue(), currentAlive \leftarrow 0, maxAlive \leftarrow 0$
  $R \leftarrow toCSR(A)$
  **for** $i \leftarrow 0..m - 1$ **do**
    $start \leftarrow R.colind[R.rowptr[i]]; end \leftarrow R.colind[R.rowptr[i + 1] - 1]$
    $markRowStart(A, start, i)$
    $Q.insert(prio = start, elem = +1); Q.insert(prio = end, elem = -1)$
  **end for**
  **while** $!Q.empty()$ **do**
    $currentAlive \leftarrow currentAlive + Q.pop(); maxAlive \leftarrow max(currentAlive, maxAlive)$
  **end while**
  **return** $maxAlive$
**end function**

---

One task that the preprocessing needs to fulfill is to establish the required cache capacity for the sparse matrix via the methods described in Section 3.1. Another important function of the preprocessing is marking the start of each row to avoid cold misses. In this paper, we reserve the highest bit of the `rowind` field in the CSC representation to mark a nonzero element as the start of a row. Although this decreases the maximum possible matrix that can be represented, it avoids introducing even more data into the already memory-intensive kernel,

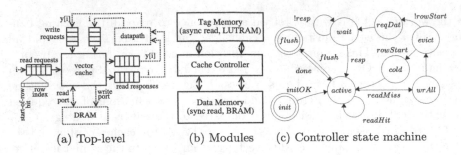

(a) Top-level        (b) Modules        (c) Controller state machine

**Fig. 4.** Design of the vector cache

and can still represent matrices with over 2 billion rows for a 32-bit `rowind`. At the time of writing, this is 18x larger than the largest matrix in the University of Florida collection [3].

For the case of computing `maxAlive`, we can formulate the problem as constructing an interval tree and finding the largest number of overlapping intervals. Algorithm 1The values inserted are +1 and -1, respectively for row starts and ends. `maxAlive` is obtained by finding the maximum sum the sorted values during the iteration. We do not present the algorithm for finding `maxColSpan`, as it is simply iterating over each column of the sparse matrix and finding the one with the greatest span.

### 3.4  Vector Cache Design

The final component of our vector caching scheme is the vector cache hardware itself. Our design is a simple increment over a traditional direct-mapped hardware cache to allow utilizing the start-of-row bits to avoid cold misses. A top-level overview of the vector cache and how it connects to the rest of the system is provided in Figure 4a. All interfaces use ready/valid handshaking and connect to the rest of the system via FIFOs, which simplifies placing the cache into a separate clock domain if desired. Row indices with marked start-of-row bits are pushed into the cache as 32-bit-wide read requests. The cache returns the 64-bit read data, as well as the requested index itself, through the read response FIFOs. The datapath drains the read response FIFOs, sums the `y[i]` value with the latest partial product, and writes the updated `y[i]` value into the write request FIFOs of the cache.

Internally, the cache is composed of data/tag memories and a controller, depicted in Figure 4b. Direct-mapped associativity is chosen for a more suitable FPGA implementation as it avoids content-associative memories required for multi-way caches. To increase performance and minimize the RAW hazard window, the design offers single-cycle read/write hit latency, but read misses are blocking to respect the FIFO ordering of requests. To make efficient use of the synchronous on-chip SRAM resources in the FPGA while still allowing single-cycle hits, we chose to implement the data memory in BRAM while the tag

**Table 1.** Suite with `maxColSpan` and `maxAlive` values for each sparse matrix

| # | Name | Dimension | Nonzeroes | NZ/col | Problem Type | maxColSpan | maxAlive |
|---|------|-----------|-----------|--------|--------------|------------|----------|
| 1 | webbase-1M | 1000005 | 3105536 | 3.10 | web connectivity matrix | 997552 | 283024 |
| 2 | mc2depi | 525825 | 2100225 | 3.99 | model of epidemic | 770 | 770 |
| 3 | scircuit | 170998 | 958936 | 5.61 | circuit simulation | 170975 | 80408 |
| 4 | mac_econ_fwd500 | 206500 | 1273389 | 6.17 | macroeconomic model | 2481 | 431 |
| 5 | cop20k_A | 121192 | 2624331 | 21.65 | accelerator cavity design | 121052 | 99843 |
| 6 | shipsec1 | 140874 | 3568176 | 25.33 | ship section detail | 10145 | 9797 |
| 7 | pwtk | 217918 | 11524432 | 52.88 | wind tunnel stiffness matrix | 189337 | 16070 |
| 8 | consph | 83334 | 6010480 | 72.13 | FEM concentric spheres | 46481 | 9074 |

memory is implemented as look-up tables. The controller finite state machine is illustrated in Figure 4c. Write misses are directly transferred to the DRAM to keep the cache controller simple. Prior to servicing a read miss, the controller waits until there are no more writes from the datapath to guarantee memory consistency. Regular read misses cause the cache to issue a DRAM read request, which prevents the missing read request from proceeding until a response is received. Avoiding cold misses is achieved by issuing a zero response on a read miss with the start-of-row bit set, without issuing any DRAM read requests.

# 4   Experimental Evaluation

We present a two-part evaluation of our scheme: an analysis of OCM savings using the minimum required capacity estimation techniques, followed by performance and FPGA synthesis results of our our vector caching scheme. For both parts of the evaluation we use a subset of the sparse matrix suite initially used by Williams et al. [2], excluding the smaller matrices amenable to the buffer-all strategy. The properties of each matrix is listed in Table 1.

## 4.1   OCM Savings Analysis

In Section 3.2 we described how the minimum cache size to avoid all capacity misses could be calculated for a given sparse matrix, either using `maxColSpan` or `maxAlive`. The rightmost columns of Table 1 list these values for each matrix. However, a vector cache also requires tag and valid bit storage in addition to the cache daha storage, which decreases the net OCM savings from our method. We compare the total OCM requirements of `maxColSpan`- and `maxAlive`-sized vector caches against the buffer-all strategy. The baseline is calculated as $64 \cdot m$ bits (one double-precision floating point value per y element), whereas the vector cache storage requires $(64 + \lceil log_2(W) \rceil + 1) \cdot W$ bits to also account for the tag/valid bits storage overhead, where W is the cache size. Figure 5a quantifies the amount of on-chip memory required for the two methods, compared to the baseline. For seven of the eight tested matrices, significant storage savings can be achieved by using our scheme. A vector cache of size `maxAlive` requires 0.3x of the baseline storage on average, whereas sizing according to `maxColSpan` averaged at 0.7x of the baseline. It should be noted that matrices 2, 4 and 6, which have a more

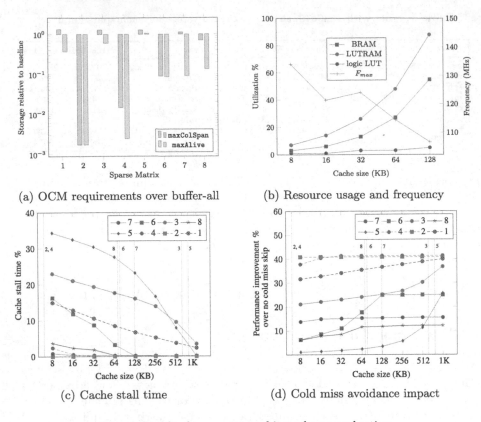

(a) OCM requirements over buffer-all   (b) Resource usage and frequency

(c) Cache stall time   (d) Cold miss avoidance impact

**Fig. 5.** Results from vector caching scheme evaluation

regular structure with elements clustered around the diagonal, already gain significant storage benefits from the low-overhead `maxColSpan` estimation. On the other hand, the irregular matrices 1 and 3 have no storage reduction benefits by using a `maxColSpan`-sized cache, so `maxAlive` must be used. For matrix #5, even `maxAlive` is only 17.6% smaller than the entire y, and therefore the savings from vector caching is not large enough to offset the tag overhead.

## 4.2  Vector Cache Evaluation

We use Chisel [11] to create a parametrizable hardware description for the vector cache, which is converted to Verilog via the Verilog backend. The generated Verilog code is fed into XST for FPGA synthesis in order to obtain frequency and area results for the cache, and passed through the Verilator tool to generate a cycle-accurate SystemC model. The model is used in a in-house SpMV frontend simulator, which is stimulated with inputs corresponding to the chosen sparse matrix and models the behavior of the accumulator datapath and DRAM for performance assessment. We assume a 100 MHz clock for the frontend, with delays of 7 cycles for the accumulator datapath and 10 cycles for DRAM reads.

**Area and Frequency:** We report area and frequency results from synthesis for a Xilinx Spartan-6 LX45 FPGA with -2 speed grade, chosen to demonstrate the potential of the technique with mediocre OCM. Our results indicate that the cold skip enhancement is with very little extra hardware cost (less than 1% in logic LUTs for the largest tested design), hence we do not report separate results for a baseline cache without this enhancement. Figure 5b shows the percent utilization of BRAM, LUTRAM and logic resources for a range of vector cache sizes, and the maximum frequency $F_{max}$ reported by the synthesis tool. A vector cache of 128 KB can fit on this relatively small FPGA, which is large enough to accommodate the maxAlive-sized working set of 5 of the 8 tested matrices. As can be expected, the utilization of BRAM and LUTRAM increases linearly with cache size, and the LUTRAM used for cache tags ultimately limits scaling to larger caches. Due to the simple design, the LUT utilization for implementing logic is rather small and occupies about 5% of the available resources for the largest design, which leaves plenty of room for implementing the more logic-intensive parts of the accelerator. The maximum attainable frequency is between 106 – 133 MHz for the tested designs, which is similar to the operating frequencies of previous SpMV accelerator designs. Further $F_{max}$ improvements can be achieved by using a more powerful FPGA or design optimizations.

**Cache Stall Time:** As our goal is to enable a stall-free cache, we evaluate the impact of cache stalls with our scheme. Figure 5c depicts the percentage of total execution time the accelerator with up to 1 MB of cache is stalled due to cache misses. The maxAlive of each matrix is indicated with numbered lines in the background. For 6 of the 8 matrices, allocating at least a maxAlive-sized cache with cold miss avoidance capability is enough to remove almost all cache misses, also indicating there are very few conflict misses. #3 is an exception, which suffers from conflict misses even with a large cache due to its nonzero pattern. The web connectivity matrix 1 has a working set larger than the maximum tested cache size, although its miss rate is already quite low. Low miss rates with cache sizes smaller than maxAlive is also observed for matrices 8 and 7, indicating that more relaxed working set definitions could be used for further reduction in required storage. Overall, by allocating at least maxAlive-sized caches, the cache stall time for our scheme is only 1.1% averaged across the test suite.

**Cold Miss Avoidance:** To show the gains from the cold miss avoidance technique, we plot the overall performance improvement due to removal of cold miss stalls in Figure 5d. The baseline for each data point is a vector cache of equal size without cold miss avoidance capabilities. The average performance improvement for at least maxAlive-sized caches is 28.6%. As the cache grows larger, fewer capacity misses are encountered and cold misses make up a larger percentage of the total. This increases the benefit from cold miss avoidance, until there are no cache misses left and the benefit levels off. Since larger sparse matrices exhibit more cold misses due to large y size, the greatest benefit is observed for the large matrices 1, 2 and 4, with up to 40% improvement. For matrix 5, the number of capacity misses with small caches is very large and very little benefit is observed until a cache size of 16K elements.

## 5   Conclusion and Future Work

We have studied how matrix structure relates to cache misses, and proposed a scheme that uses preprocessing to enhance the operation of a traditional hardware cache for FPGA SpMV accelerators. Specifically, we have proposed two methods to estimate required cache depth to avoid all capacity misses, and a way of enhancing the matrix representation to avoid all cold misses. Our experiments with a suite of large sparse matrices indicate that the scheme can service random accesses to the result vector with no or few stalls, while avoiding cold miss penalties that hamper traditional hardware caches. Future work will include evaluating the vector caching scheme in a complete FPGA SpMV accelerator context.

## References

1. Taylor, M.B.: Is dark silicon useful?: harnessing the four horsemen of the coming dark silicon apocalypse. In: Proc. of the Design Automation Conference (2012)
2. Williams, S., Oliker, L., Vuduc, R., Shalf, J., Yelick, K., Demmel, J.: Optimization of sparse matrix-vector multiplication on emerging multicore platforms. Parallel Computing **35**(3) (2009)
3. Davis, T.A., Hu, Y.: The University of Florida Sparse Matrix Collection. ACM Trans. Math. Softw. **38**(1) (2011)
4. Gregg, D., Mc Sweeney, C., McElroy, C., Connor, F., McGettrick, S., Moloney, D., Geraghty, D.: FPGA based sparse matrix vector multiplication using commodity DRAM memory. In: Int. Conf. on Field Prog. Logic and Applications (2007)
5. Fowers, J., Ovtcharov, K., Strauss, K., Chung, E.S., Stitt, G.: A high memory bandwidth fpga accelerator for sparse matrix-vector multiplication. In: IEEE Int. Symp. on Field-Programmable Custom Computing Machines (2014)
6. Dorrance, R., Ren, F., Marković, D.: A scalable sparse matrix-vector multiplication kernel for energy-efficient sparse-BLAS on FPGAs. In: Proc. of the ACM/SIGDA Int. Symp. on FPGAs (2014)
7. Umuroglu, Y., Jahre, M.: An energy efficient column-major backend for FPGA SpMV accelerators. In: IEEE Int. Conf. on Computer Design (2014)
8. Temam, O., Jalby, W.: Characterizing the behavior of sparse algorithms on caches. In: Proc. of the ACM/IEEE Conf. on Supercomputing (1992)
9. Toledo, S.: Improving the memory-system performance of sparse-matrix vector multiplication. IBM Journal of Res. and Dev. **41**(6) (1997)
10. Jouppi, N.P.: Improving direct-mapped cache performance by the addition of a small fully-associative cache and prefetch buffers. In: Proc. of the Int. Symp. on Computer Architecture (1990)
11. Bachrach, J., Vo, H., Richards, B., Lee, Y., Waterman, A., Avižienis, R., Wawrzynek, J., Asanović, K.: Chisel: constructing hardware in a scala embedded language. In: Proc. of the Design Automation Conference (2012)

# Hierarchical Dynamic Power-Gating in FPGAs

Rehan Ahmed[1,2]([⊠]), Steven J.E. Wilton[1,2],
Peter Hallschmid[1,2], and Richard Klukas[1,2]

[1] The University of British Columbia, Vancouver, Canada
[2] Blackcomb Design Automation, Vancouver, Canada
{rehan.ahmed,richard.klukas}@ubc.ca, stevew@ece.ubc.ca,
peter.hallschmid@blackcomb-da.com

**Abstract.** Dynamic power-gating has been shown to reduce FPGA
static leakage power significantly. In this paper, we propose a high-level
synthesis (HLS) compiler-assisted framework that automatically detects
the hierarchical power-gating opportunities, and turns off accelerators
when they are not required. Unlike previous work which considers turning off entire accelerators when they are not required, our technique is
more fine-grained, in that it allows turning off a portion of an accelerator when other parts of an accelerator are running. Results on CHStone
benchmarks show that hierarchical power-gating can save up to 31 %
of static energy when the parent and descendant accelerators are power-
gated independently. An additional savings of up to 25 % can be achieved
if the parent accelerator is power-gated while the sub-accelerator runs.

## 1 Introduction

As Field-Programmable Gate Arrays (FPGAs) are migrated to advanced processing nodes, power has become a first-class concern for many applications.
Compared to an Application-Specific Integrated Circuit (ASIC), an FPGA
implementation typically dissipates 14x more power [7]. One of the most effective
techniques to reduce the power dissipation in an FPGA is to turn off (power-
gate) part of the design when it is idle. Recent work has presented techniques
for dynamic power-gating (DPG) [3], in which parts of the FPGA can be turned
off at run time, under control of an on-state power controller.

Dynamic power-gating, however, presents a formidable challenge to a
designer. In ASIC design, in which power-gating is common, power-gating opportunities are identified manually and typically described in a standard format,
such as Unified Power Format (UPF). For FPGAs, many designers may not be
willing or able to invest the effort into this manual identification, reducing the
effectiveness of overall power-gating. Although techniques have been proposed
for identifying some power-gating opportunities from a netlist or dataflow graph,
these techniques typically focus on power-gating opportunities which are as short
as several cycles [2,6,8], limiting the effectiveness of power-gating. Automatically

© Springer International Publishing Switzerland 2015
K. Sano et al. (Eds.): ARC 2015, LNCS 9040, pp. 27–38, 2015.
DOI: 10.1007/978-3-319-16214-0_3

identifying significant power-gating opportunities from a netlist or RTL design remains a difficult challenge.

Identifying power-gating opportunities can be much easier, however, if the design is created using a higher-level design tool. In particular, high-level synthesis (HLS) methodologies are increasingly being used to raise the abstraction level of a design and improve designer productivity. In such a methodology, a designer specifies a design using a language such as C, and the tool generates a circuit. Importantly, the overall architecture of the resulting digital system is determined by the high-level synthesis compiler. The compiler not only knows about the structure of the circuit, but also its temporal behaviour which can be used to identify power-gating opportunities automatically.

In [1], a methodology is presented in which the schedule from a high-level synthesis tool is used to determine the idle periods of individual hardware accelerators in a synthesized system. The predicted length of these idle periods is used to determine whether the power saved by power-gating the accelerator is more than the overhead of turning the accelerator off and then on again at the end of the idle period. Based on this knowledge, individual accelerators can then be power-gated when it is deemed profitable. In this previous work, however, the granularity of power-gating is fixed at the accelerator level. An entire accelerator is turned off or on as a unit. For very large accelerators, it may be profitable to power gate at a finer granularity. If an accelerator has many phases, each of which is implemented by a separate logic circuit (which we call a sub-accelerator), then it may be desirable to turn off individual sub-accelerators when parent or other sub-accelerators are running.

In this paper, we present a HLS compiler-assisted framework that automatically detects the hierarchical power-gating opportunities from an application expressed in C language. We present a study in which we vary the granularity of power-gating and quantify the benefits of making power-gating decisions for each sub-accelerator separately, rather than simply at the accelerator level. We show that for some applications, this finer-granularity results in more effective power-gating, providing more power savings than the previous technique.

When determining whether an idle period is long enough to make power-gating worthwhile, [1] assumes a static schedule constructed using a single set of input vectors. If these input vectors change, the idle times experienced during the run of the application may deviate from the predicted idle times, potentially leading to sub-optimal power-gating decisions. For the accelerators considered in [1], the idle periods are long enough that this is not likely to be a concern. Finer-grained power-gating, however, implies shorter idle periods, meaning the optimal power-gating decisions may be more sensitive to changes in the inputs. In this paper, we investigate whether this is an issue as the granularity of power-gating decreases. Thus, this paper has three contributions:

1. We enhance the design framework in [1] to support hierarchical power-gating. Section 3 presents our compiler-assisted framework for automatically generating hierarchical power-gating decisions.

2. We study the impact of reducing the power-gating granularity to consider power-gating sub-accelerators as well as accelerators. Section 4 quantifies the impact of hierarchical power-gating.
3. We investigate whether the compiler-assisted power-gating approach used in [1] is sufficient as the granularity of power-gating decreases. Section 5 presents our findings across a large number of input patterns.

# 2 Context

Although our work will apply to any FPGA which provides dynamic power-gating control, and any high-level synthesis tool, we describe it in the context of the Dynamic Power-Gated FPGA architecture from [3] and the LegUp high-level synthesis tool from [4]. In this section, we present a brief background about each.

## 2.1 Dynamic Power-Gated Architecture

The DPG architecture from [3] is a typical island-style FPGA in which the logic and routing fabric have been augmented with header switches and associated control logic that allow regions of the chip to be selectively powered-down, under the control of signals from elsewhere on the chip (typically from a power-state controller). A Power-Gated Region (PGR) is the basic unit of power-gating which is turned on or off as a unit. Each of these regions consists of a small number of CLBs, as shown in Fig. 1. The flip-flops within each logic element are not turned off as this allows for a more rapid power-up sequence since state is retained. Table. 1 shows the simulated architecture parameters used in our experiments.

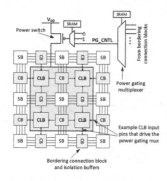

**Fig. 1.** Example power gating region supporting DPG [3]

**Table 1.** Simulated Architecture Parameters used in Experiments of Sect. 4

|  |  | PGR | SB |
|---|---|---|---|
| $P_{1 \to 0}$ | Power to Turn-Off | 1.22E-04 | 1.45E-05 |
| $P_{0 \to 1}$ | Power to Turn-On | 5.98E-04 | 5.53E-05 |
| $T_{1 \to 0}$ | Time to Turn-Off | 6.59E-09 | 4.12E-10 |
| $T_{0 \to 1}$ | Time to Turn-On | 7.14E-09 | 4.46E-10 |
| $P_{ON-leak}$ | On Leakage Power | 6.70E-05 | 5.36E-06 |
| $P_{OFF-leak}$ | Off Leakage Power | 2.03E-06 | 2.93E-07 |

## 2.2 LegUp High-Level Synthesis Framework

Our work is based on *LegUp*, a high-level open source synthesis framework [4]. LegUp automatically generates an SoC consisting of a MIPS processor and one or more accelerators from an application expressed in *C*. The application is first profiled on a hardware profiler to identify the functions that would benefit from hardware implementation. Based on this information, the tool then compiles each identified function into a *hardware accelerator*. The portions of the algorithm that are not selected for acceleration are mapped to the MIPS processor and will run as software. These accelerators and a MIPS processor are then combined using an Avalon fabric, creating an accelerated version of the original C code.

# 3    Hierarchical Power-Gating

As described above, LegUp automatically identifies functions in the input C code that are suitable for acceleration. The work in [1] considers each of these accelerators, along with a static schedule, and determines whether the benefit of turning off the accelerator is more than the overhead of doing so. In our work, we consider not only each function in the C code, but their sub-functions as well. In the hardware generated by LegUp, each sub-function is implemented as a separate hardware unit (which we refer to as a *sub-accelerator*) and our approach considers turning off each of these hardware units separately.

Our framework is shown in Fig. 2. We identify all the profitable idle phases across all the hierarchical accelerators and generate a static power-gating schedule. This is then passed on to HLS compiler which then generates Verilog descriptions of the datapath and controller circuit. The various phases of the framework are discussed below.

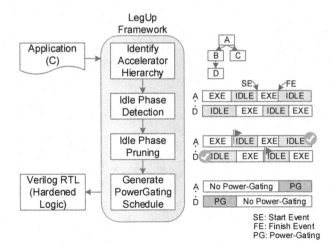

**Fig. 2.** HLS Compiler Assisted Hierarchical Power-Gating Framework

## 3.1   Identifying Accelerator Hierarchy

The (HLS) compiler operates on a C program and converts annotated (profitable) C-functions into hardware accelerators. In doing so, if the function has descendant functions, they are also converted into sub-accelerators. We keep track of the function calls in the program and build a hierarchical call tree for all the functions (annotated for acceleration) in the program. This enables us to identify all the hierarchical accelerators in the program, which later get synthesized into hardware modules. In this paper, we refer to the top accelerator in the hierarchy as a *parent accelerator* and the accelerators called by the top accelerator as *child accelerators*.

## 3.2   Idle Period Detection

Each accelerator (parent or child) typically has active and idle periods. The idle periods are potential power-gating opportunities. The goal of this phase is to identify all idle periods based on a static schedule, as determined by the scheduling algorithm in the HLS compiler, and to identify the start and end events associated with each idle period. Note that the actual duration of the idle period will typically vary from run to run as input patterns change. In Section 5, we evaluate the impact of changing inputs on the number of idle periods and their duration.

## 3.3   Pruning Idle Periods

The previous phase produces a list of all potential power-gating opportunities. However, many of these may not be profitable. Powering down (and later powering up) a power-gated region incurs both energy and delay overhead. Thus, for each power-gating opportunity, we must determine whether a power-gating event should be generated.

In general, an accelerator should be turned off when idle if the power saved by power-gating the accelerator is more than the overhead of turning the accelerator off and then on again at the end of the idle period. To make this determination, we first find the accelerator's energy break-even time – the minimum idle time at which the leakage-savings compensate the energy penalty for mode transition. If the predicted idle time duration, as determined in Section 3.2, is more than break-even time, we generate a power-gating event. Below, we briefly describe how we find an accelerator's break-even time.

**Determining Accelerator's Energy Break-Even Time:** Every time an accelerator transitions between the *sleep* and *execution* modes, there is an energy penalty. An accelerator should only be power gated if it will be idle long enough to compensate for this penalty. The energy break-even time is the minimum idle time for which an accelerator should be power gated, and can be calculated as:

$$T_{break-even} = \frac{(P_{1\to0} \times T_{1\to0}) + (P_{0\to1} \times T_{0\to1})}{P_{ON-leak} - P_{OFF-leak}} \tag{1}$$

where $P_{1\to0}$, $T_{1\to0}$, is the power and time required to enter power-saving mode. Similarly, $P_{0\to1}$ and $T_{0\to1}$ is the power and time required to exit the power-saving mode. $P_{ON-leak}$ and $P_{OFF-leak}$ is the leakage power in the turned-on and turned-off state respectively.

In context of our target DPG architecture, as discussed in Sec.2.1, the power-gated region (PGR) is the basic unit of granularity. Thus, an accelerator occupies an integral number of PGRs and switch-blocks (SBs). Therefore, the switching energy and power-saved can be expressed as,

$$E_{switch} = NumPGR \times (P_{switchPGR} \times T_{switchPGR}) \\ + NumSBs \times (P_{switchSB} \times T_{switchSB}) \tag{2}$$

$$P_{saved} = NumPGR \times (P_{PGR-on-leak} - P_{PGR-off-leak}) \\ + NumSBs \times (P_{SB-on-leak} - P_{SB-off-leak}) \tag{3}$$

where in (2) and (3), $NumPGR$ and $NumSBs$ is the number of PGRs and SBs, respectively, occupied by the accelerator. We find this by performing an initial mapping of the accelerator to the fabric, however, estimation techniques could also be used.

### 3.4  Power-gating Schedule Generation

Once all the profitable power-gating opportunities across all the hierarchical accelerators have been identified, a schedule with these decisions is generated. The power-gating schedule records the conditions (start and end events) that trigger a particular idle period in an accelerator. Each time these conditions are met at run-time, power-gating is triggered which would put the accelerator in sleep mode.

## 4  Experimental Results

### 4.1  Experimental Setup

We use the CHStone benchmarks suite developed for C-based high-level synthesis (HLS); these benchmarks represent diverse real-world application domains. The C-based source of each benchmark was provided as input to the Legup HLS framework, augmented with our tool flow, as shown in Fig.2. The RTL output from the framework, which contains datapath, controller and hierarchical power-gating schedule, is then mapped to the dynamic power-gating FPGA architecture from [3] to get the number of PGRs and SBs occupied by the accelerators. Since we have not fabricated an FPGA with our power-gating architecture, we do not generate a bitstream. However, the HSPICE simulated architecture parameter values, given in Table. 1, allows us to quantify the impact of hierarchical power-gating.

## 4.2   Hierarchical Power-Gating Evaluation

In order to quantify the impact of hierarchical power-gating, we apply the following power-gating policies to the parent and child accelerators in CHStone benchmarks suite [5] and compare their impact:

**Accelerator-Level Power-Gating; Policy-P1:** In this policy, the entire accelerator, including all the sub-accelerators of this accelerator, is considered as one power-gating unit. The sub-accelerators have no separate power-gating control. Whenever the parent accelerator is active at the end of it's idle period, all it's sub-accelerators in the hierarchy become active as well. This approach is similar to [1] and serves as the reference.

**Parent Runs while Child Runs; Policy-P2:** This approach represents intra-accelerator power-gating in which the parent and descendant accelerators are treated as independent units for power-gating i.e. each hierarchical accelerators can be switched independently. In this policy, the parent accelerator remains active and does not sleep after initiating the sub-accelerator. The sub-accelerator is power-gated, however, if only the parent is required to be active.

**Parent is Power-Gated while Child Runs; Policy-P3:** This approach also represents intra-accelerator power-gating. In this approach, we power-gate the parent accelerator after it is has started a sub-accelerator. Once the sub-accelerator has finished processing, the parent accelerator is woken up.

The proposed power-gating policies are evaluated based on the total leakage energy consumed by an accelerator in power-gating mode, denoted as $E\_PG$, in which the accelerator is turned-off during it's idle period if it is deemed profitable. The leakage energy in all execution and idle phases is added together to estimate $E\_PG$. By design, the DPG architecture in [3] suffers a 10% performance degradation due to the presence of power-gating circuitry; to account for this, we increase the idle and execution time periods by this degradation factor when calculating $E\_PG$. Of the circuits in the CHStone suite, we present results for two benchmarks below.

**JPEG:** The hierarchical call tree of JPEG benchmark is shown in Fig. 3. There are three parent-level and two child-level accelerators. We evaluate the above mentioned power-gating policies for *Decode_Block (DB)* accelerator as it has two descendants. The occupancy stats of various JPEG accelerators are reported in Table. 2. The columns labeled DTF show the number of power-gated regions (PGRs) and switch-blocks (SBs) for each accelerator that can be *dynamically*

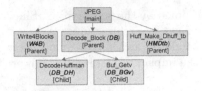

**Fig. 3.** JPEG Hierarchical Call Tree

**Table 2.** JPEG Occupancy Stats

| Accelerator | Total PGRs | PGRs (DTF) | SBs (DTF) | EBT | EBC | W.Cyc |
|---|---|---|---|---|---|---|
| W4B | 162 | 139 | 1576 | 4.43E-08 | 3 | 4 |
| DB | 222 | 155 | 659 | 6.01E-08 | 4 | 4 |
| HMDtb | 48 | 28 | 260 | 4.78E-08 | 4 | 1 |
| DB_DH | 31 | 21 | 96 | 5.91E-08 | 4 | 1 |
| DB_BGv | 25 | 19 | 54 | 6.50E-08 | 5 | 1 |

*turned off (DTF)* (typically not all PGRs and switch blocks can be turned off even when an accelerator is idle, since routing switches within a switch block or other parts of a PGR must remain active to implement parts of the circuit that have not been turned off). The fifth column shows the accelerator's energy-break even time (EBT) which is converted into energy-break even cycles (EBC) assuming a 66Mhz clock. The last column is the number of cycles to transfer from sleep to normal execution mode, denoted as *wake-up cycles* (W.Cyc), and are used to quantify the impact on execution length.

Fig. 4a shows the execution and idle time percentages across the three power-gating policies. The *Decode_Block (DB)* appears as a single accelerator in policy $P1$, as the parent and it's descendants are treated as one combined hardware module, while it's descendants are visible in the other two policies. As can be observed from Fig. 4a, the descendant accelerators executes briefly and remain idle most of the time during which they can be power-gated. The parent accelerator is power-gated in $P3$ while it's descendants are running which presents an additional power-savings opportunity. Fig. 4b shows the $E\_PG$ consumption comparison across power-gating policies. The $E\_PG$ for the parent and child accelerators are added together in $P2$ and $P3$. As can be observed in Fig. 4b, $E\_PG$ in $P2$ is 31.88% less than $E\_PG$ in $P1$ which indicates that in JPEG benchmark it would be worth considering the parent and child accelerators as stand-alone units for power-gating. Further, in this benchmark, the child accelerators have significant execution times, meaning that by turning off the parent when the children are executing (policy $P3$), further power reductions are possible. As shown in Fig. 4b, $E\_PG$ in $P3$ is 49.30% less than $E\_PG$ in $P1$.

**SHA:** The hierarchical call tree of SHA benchmark is shown in Fig. 5 and it's accelerators sizes are given in Table. 3. Note that the *Sha_Tansform* accelerator appears as both parent and child, and is instantiated twice when hardware is generated. We distinguish the child-level *Sha_Tansform (SU_ST)* accelerator by adding its parent name before it.

As can be observed in Fig. 6a, the child accelerator, *Sha_Tansform (SU_ST)*, is busy executing most of the time; during this time, it's parent, *Sha_Update (SU)*, can be turned off (Policy $P3$). The value of $E\_PG$ for each policy is shown in Fig. 6b. As can be seen, $E\_PG$ for policy $P3$ is 46.11% less than for policy $P1$, as the parent remains turned off 89% of the time. This comparison suggests that it is best to treat the parent and child as independent accelerators which, if

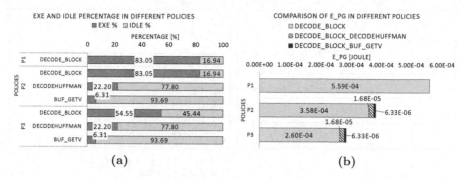

**Fig. 4.** JPEG Benchmark (a) Percentage of Execution and Idle Times (b) Comparison of Total Leakage Energy Consumed - in various Power-Gating Policies

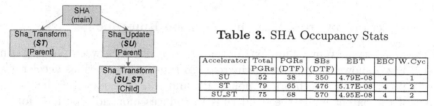

**Table 3.** SHA Occupancy Stats

| Accelerator | Total PGRs | PGRs (DTF) | SBs (DTF) | EBT | EBC | W.Cyc |
|---|---|---|---|---|---|---|
| SU | 52 | 38 | 350 | 4.79E-08 | 4 | 1 |
| ST | 79 | 65 | 476 | 5.17E-08 | 4 | 2 |
| SU_ST | 75 | 68 | 570 | 4.95E-08 | 4 | 2 |

**Fig. 5.** SHA Hierarchical Call Tree

are power-gated during their respective idle times can reduce, the leakage energy by 46%. Therefore, in case of SHA benchmark, policy $P3$ remains best overall.

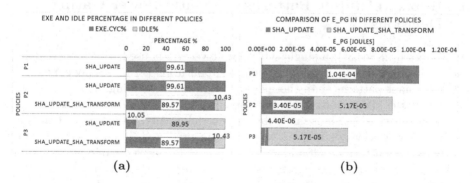

**Fig. 6.** SHA Benchmark (a) Percentage of Execution and Idle Times (b) Comparison of Total Leakage Energy Consumed - in various Power-Gating Policies

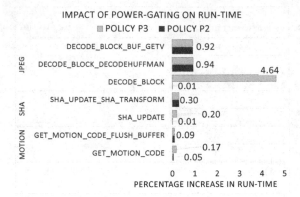

**Fig. 7.** Impact of Power-Gating on Run-Time

### 4.3 Impact of Power-Gating on Execution Run-time

Each power-gating event incurs extra cycles to transition between power-gating modes. Fig. 7 shows the percentage increase in run-time for various accelerators due to power-gating overhead in policy P2 and P3. In policy P3 the power-gating of the parent while the child runs introduces more idle periods for the parent which increase the overall overhead. As a result, the execution length of the parent accelerator increases more in P3 than in P2. As shown in Fig. 7, the run-time of the *decode-block* in policy P3, which is a parent accelerator in JPEG, is increased by 4.6% due to large number of calls to the two child accelerators during which the parent is power-gated.

## 5   Impact of Input Patterns on Static Power-Gating Decisions

As discussed in Sec.3.4, a single set of input vectors is used when constructing the static power-gating schedule. When the application is run, it may experience different input patterns than those assumed during scheduling. This may cause changes in the idle periods of accelerators and sub-accelerators. This may mean that power-gating decisions made during scheduling are sub-optimal. If the idle period of an accelerator is much smaller than predicted, it may be that more energy is wasted turning off and on the region than is saved while power-gated. If the idle period of an accelerator is longer than predicted, it may be that the scheduler decides that power-gating is not worthwhile, when in actuality, it would have been. To investigate this concern, we vary the input vectors ten thousand times and observe the impact on the number and duration of idle periods in an accelerator. In particular, we are interested in whether the change in input can reduce the idle period duration below energy break-even cycles leading to a sub-optimal decision.

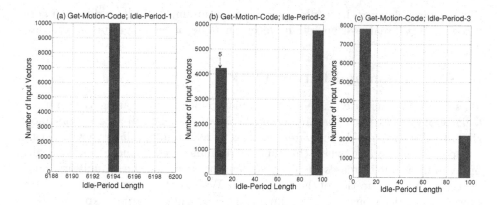

**Fig. 8.** Histograms showing the Variation in the Idle-Period Duration of Get-Motion-Code Accelerator (a) Idle-Period-1 (b) Idle-Period-2 (c) Idle-Period-3

We performed the experiment across nine accelerators in three of the CHStone benchmarks circuits. For each accelerator, we varied the input pattern by randomly selecting values for each input independently (the allowable range of values for each input was determined by examining the program). Ten thousand input sets are generated, and for each, the total number of and the duration of idle periods were recorded.

We found that in eight (out of nine) accelerators, there was no variation in the number of idle periods and the duration of each idle period remained the same. As a result, for these accelerators, the static power-gating scheduler makes the optimal decisions.

The ninth accelerator, *Get_Motion_Code (GMC)* in the Motion benchmark, exhibited variation in the duration of idle periods. This particular accelerator has three idle periods and the static power-gating schedule determines that power-gating is appropriate for all of them. Changing the input vector $10K$ times reveals the variation as illustrated in the histograms of Fig. 8. The X-axis of each histogram represents the number of idle cycles in an idle period and the Y-axis is the number of input vectors that led to that number of idle cycles. The first idle period does not show any variation, however, the second and third idle periods do show variation. In both cases, the periods were either 5 cycles long or 100 cycles long, depending on one of the input signals. For period 2, about 40% of input samples led to an idle period of 5 cycles. In this accelerator, the energy break-even point is exactly 5 cycles. As a result, the static scheduler always assumes that the accelerator should sleep for this idle period. If the period happens to be 5 cycles, the overall cost and benefit of power-gating are equal, but if the idle period is 100 cycles, significant power savings are obtained by power-gating. In either case, however, the decision to power gate during this idle period is optimal. This situation is the same for the third idle period, in which 20% of input vectors lead to long idle periods.

It is possible that this could occur if the minimum idle phase duration goes below energy break-even point, however, in none of our experiments did this occur.

# 6    Conclusion and Future Work

This paper demonstrates the potential of hierarchical power-gating to save static leakage power. We show that fine-grained control over the sub-accelerators allow them to sleep when only the parent context is required. Similarly, power-gating the parent accelerator when the child is running, creates more power saving opportunities but increases the program length. Reducing the granularity, however, reduces the duration of the idle periods. We show that the compiler-assisted power-gating decisions remain optimal as long as the idle period experienced at run-time is greater than the break-even point. The static power-gating predictions can be greatly improved if the application workload is known at compile-time. Adapting the power-gating decisions with varying workload at run-time, however, would require a dynamic power-gating predictor which is an interesting area for future investigation.

# References

1. Ahmed, R., Bsoul, A.A.M., Wilton, S.J.E., Hallschmid, P., Klukas, R.: High-level synthesis-based design methodology for dynamic power-gated fpgas. In: 24th International Conference on Field Programmable Logic and Applications, FPL 2014, Munich, Germany, September 2–4, 2014, pp. 1–4 (2014). http://dx.doi.org/10.1109/FPL.2014.6927433
2. Bharadwaj, R., Konar, R., Balsara, P., Bhatia, D.: Exploiting temporal idleness to reduce leakage power in programmable architectures. In: Proceedings of the 2005 Asia and South Pacific Design Automation Conference, ASP-DAC 2005, vol. 1, pp. 651–656, January 2005
3. Bsoul, A., Wilton, S.J.E.: An FPGA architecture supporting dynamically controlled power gating. In: Proc. of the 2010 Intl. Con. on Field-Programmable Technology (FPT), pp. 1–8 (2010)
4. Canis, A., Choi, J., Fort, B., Lian, R., Huang, Q., Calagar, N., Gort, M., Qin, J.J., Aldham, M., Czajkowski, T., Brown, S., Anderson, J.: From software to accelerators with legup high-level synthesis. In: Proc. of the 2013 Intl. Con. on Compilers, Architecture and Synthesis for Embedded Systems (CASES), pp. 1–9, September 2013
5. Hara, Y., Tomiyama, H., Honda, S., Takada, H., Ishii, K.: Chstone: a benchmark program suite for practical c-based high-level synthesis. In: ISCAS, pp. 1192–1195. IEEE (2008). http://dblp.uni-trier.de/db/conf/iscas/iscas2008.html#HaraTHTI08
6. Ishihara, S., Hariyama, M., Kameyama, M.: A low-power FPGA based on autonomous fine-grain power gating. IEEE Transactions on Very Large Scale Integration (VLSI) Systems 19(8), 1394–1406 (2011)
7. Kuon, I., Rose, J.: Measuring the gap between FPGAs and asics. IEEE Trans. on Computer-Aided Design of Integrated Circuits and Systems 26(2), 203–215 (2007)
8. Usami, K., Ohkubo, N.: A design approach for fine-grained run-time power gating using locally extracted sleep signals. In: International Conference on Computer Design, ICCD 2006, pp. 155–161, October 2006

# Tools and Compilers I

# Hardware Synthesis from Functional Embedded Domain-Specific Languages: A Case Study in Regular Expression Compilation

Ian Graves[1]([✉]), Adam Procter[1], William L. Harrison[1],
Michela Becchi[2], and Gerard Allwein[3]

[1] Department of CS, University of Missouri, Columbia, MO, USA
iangraves@mail.missouri.edu
[2] Department of ECE, University of Missouri, Columbia, MO, USA
[3] US Naval Research Laboratory, Code 5543, Washington, DC, USA

**Abstract.** Although FPGAs have the potential to bring software-like flexibility and agility to the hardware world, designing for FPGAs remains a difficult task divorced from standard software engineering norms. A better programming flow would go far towards realizing the potential of widely deployed, programmable hardware. We propose a general methodology based on domain specific languages embedded in the functional language Haskell to bridge the gap between high level abstractions that support programmer productivity and the need for high performance in FPGA circuit implementations. We illustrate this methodology with a framework for regular expression to hardware compilers, written in Haskell, that supports high programmer productivity while producing circuits whose performance matches and, indeed, exceeds that of a state of the art, hand-optimized VHDL-based tool. For example, after applying a novel optimization pass, throughput increased an average of 28.3 % over the state of the art tool for one set of benchmarks. All code discussed in the paper is available online [1].

## 1 Introduction

FPGAs are notably difficult to program and this has motivated research into high-level synthesis (HLS) from high level programming languages and, in particular, from domain-specific languages [2]. This language-based approach is attractive because of its potential to make hardware engineering more like software engineering with its support for modularity, reuse, and abstraction, and thereby create a wider group of developers for programmable hardware. This paper describes a methodology for deriving performant hardware implementations directly from high-level functional embedded domain-specific languages (EDSL).

This Research Was Supported by the Office of the Assistant Secretary of Defense for Research and Engineering, the U.S. Department of Education Under GAANN Grant Number P200A100053, NSF CAREER Award 00017806, and NSF Award CNS-1319748.

K. Sano et al. (Eds.): ARC 2015, LNCS 9040, pp. 41–52, 2015.
DOI: 10.1007/978-3-319-16214-0_4

**This work makes the following contributions.** We present ReWire [3], a subset of the Haskell functional language as a compiler target for compiling domain-specific languages to FPGAs. We show that ReWire can be effectively used as a compiler target because it supports the compilation of large input programs (over 100K LOC) and can generate competitively fast hardware implementations versus state of the art, domain-specific tools.

These contributions comprise a methodology supporting the "three P's" [4] for programming reconfigurable hardware: productivity, performance and portability. DSLs address the first two P's directly because domain specialization supports programmer productivity and, furthermore, allows aggressive optimization of domain-specific idioms. Portability is achieved by using ReWire, a retargetable language for specifying hardware devices.

New language constructs raise issues with respect to performance. Is there a performance price to be paid and, if so, is the increased expressiveness worth it? Does the increased expressiveness enable better performance and programmer productivity? In light of these questions, we evaluate our methodology via two case studies. The case studies presented here consider a purely functional framework for REHC construction, called RexHacc (for "Regular EXpression HArdware compiler-compiler"). RexHacc is an EDSL-structured compiler-compiler, implemented in Haskell, for Perl-compatible regular expressions (PCRE) similar to those seen in popular intrusion detection systems (e.g., Snort [5]).

**Overview of Methodology.** The methodology factors the problem of HLS into a series of translations between EDSLs. An EDSL is a domain-specific language that is defined as a collection of constructs within an existing high level language. The methodology is illustrated in the inset figure. A problem domain can be realized as a

**Fig. 1.** FP Methodology for HLS

DSL embedded in Haskell. DSL cross-compilers targeting ReWire enable synthesis onto an FPGA via the ReWire compiler. Sec. 2 presents a more in-depth discussion of our methodology.

The case studies involve regular expression to hardware compilation (see Fig. 2) in which we generate artifacts that perform as well as and often better than state of the art approaches. The case studies reported here consider the problem domain of regular expression to hardware compilers (REHC) [6]. Following Fig. 1, we developed a reusable and modular framework for REHC called *RexHacc* and demonstrated that circuits produced with it meet or exceed the performance of state-of-the-art REHC.

**The RexHacc Framework.** We performed an experiment in which we compared RexHacc to the performance of the state-of-the-art REHC of Becchi and Crowley [7] (henceforth `reg2vhdl`) against its own benchmarks. The goal is to

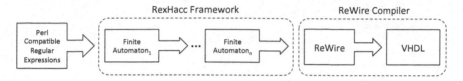

**Fig. 2.** Combining the ease of use of traditional EDSLs with the power and run-time performance of a virtualized language

demonstrate both the productivity gain and high performance achievable via our methodology in the construction and testing of compilers generated by RexHacc. The presentation here is deliberately high-level. We suppress the definitions of functions and data types; the code is online [1].

The entry point for RexHacc is the function rexhacc with Haskell type:

$$\texttt{rexhacc :: (NFA a -> NFA a) -> RegEx a -> ReWire}$$

The declaration form "::" is pronounced "has type". The function rexhacc takes two inputs, an optimization function (of type NFA a -> NFA a) as well as a regular expression (of type RegEx a). The type NFA a (resp., RegEx a) represents non-deterministic finite automata (resp., regular expressions) over an alphabet of type a. A regular expression compiler is generated with RexHacc by applying the top-level rexhacc function to an optimization pass, opt:

(‡)
```
compiler :: RegEx a -> ReWire
compiler = rexhacc opt
  where opt = (o₁ . ⋯ . oₙ)
```

Each $o_i$ is an optimization pass of functional type NFA a -> NFA a, all of which are composed using Haskell's function composition operator (i.e., the infix ".") into a single pass. This composition corresponds to the middle box in Fig. 2 and each $o_i$ is a phase inside that box. The generated compiler takes a regular expression over an alphabet of type a and converts it into an NFA a, which is then fed to the optimization pass opt. The optimization pass produces an NFA a from which ReWire code is generated. The ReWire output from this compiler can either be translated into VHDL by the ReWire compiler or executed as software in any standard Haskell environment.

**Summary of Case Study Results.** Secs. 4 and 5 each describe the definition of an REHC in the RexHacc framework. Each case study was tested against reg2vhdl using existing test suites [7] with respect to standard metrics for circuit size, clock speed and throughput (see Fig. 3). The first case study (Sec. 4) implements the same optimization passes as reg2vhdl, and it was clear that this compiler generally matched or exceeded the performance of the hand-optimized compiler reg2vhdl with a tiny increase in circuit size. It was observed that one of the benchmarks (tcp25) seemed to be particularly challenging for both the first case study compiler and reg2vhdl with respect to throughput. This observation motivated the second case study (Sec. 5), which

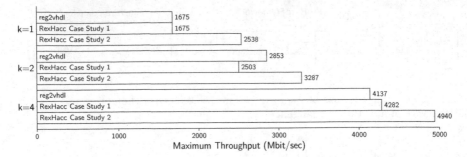

**Fig. 3.** Maximum throughput for the `tcp25` benchmark, comparing `reg2vhdl` and the RexHacc case study compilers (Secs. 4 and 5). Parameter k indicates stride length (Sec. 4). Case study 2 shows an average of 28.3% throughput increase over `reg2vhdl`.

improves on the first with an (apparently novel) optimization pass that results in better performance than `reg2vhdl` on the `tcp25` benchmark.

## 2    A Methodology for Synthesis from Functional EDSLs

Synthesis from pure functional languages (e.g., Haskell, www.haskell.org) is appealing because combinational hardware is functional in nature, functional languages have powerful features supporting programmer productivity (e.g., modularity, expressive data types, static type inference, etc.), and the absence of side effects (e.g., destructive update) simplifies synthesis. But general purpose functional languages also contain a number of features that cannot be represented in hardware (e.g., general recursion and garbage collection) and this makes HLS directly from existing functional languages more challenging.

ReWire [3] is a proper *sublanguage* of Haskell—i.e., any ReWire program is a Haskell program, but not all Haskell programs are ReWire programs. ReWire programs, in contrast with general purpose functional languages like Haskell, are always synthesizable to hardware. ReWire restricts Haskell by disallowing the use of higher-order functions and general recursion at runtime (though techniques like partial evaluation may enable their use at compile time). RexHacc uses the ReWire hardware compiler as a back-end for producing VHDL implementations.

*Front End.* The RexHacc compilation process begins with a collection of regular expressions written in Perl-compatible regular expression (PCRE) syntax. We use the parser combinator library Parsec in Haskell to parse the regular expressions in the source file. The regular expression is converted to the NFA type via a textbook translation of regular expressions to NFAs [8]. The resulting NFA is passed to the optimization portion of the compilation chain.

*Simulating Circuits in Haskell.* Because ReWire is a sublanguage of Haskell, we can execute ReWire code as software in any Haskell environment with a test

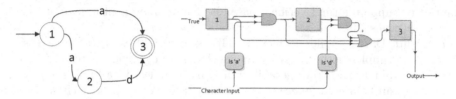

**Fig. 4.** An NFA and its corresponding Sidhu and Prasanna-style implementation

harness for executing reactive resumptions. The implementation of rexhacc was tested and debugged using a test harness in Haskell which is included in the code base [1].

## 3   Related Work

The conversion of sets of regular expressions into NFAs is a well-known procedure [8]. Sidhu and Prasanna [6] have proposed an efficient FPGA implementation of NFAs. Their solution is based on the one-hot encoding scheme; the use of an NFA representation avoids the $O(2^n)$ space complexity that is characteristic of DFA (deterministic finite automata) representations, typically adopted in memory-based regular expression matching implementations [9–12]. Subsequent efforts on FPGA [7,13–15] have refined Sidhu and Prasanna's implementation and achieved gigabit/sec processing throughputs on real-world pattern sets.

There are a number of efforts to apply ideas and techniques from functional programming to hardware design and synthesis. Arvind [16] describes the Bluespec synthesis language as "a relatively simple DSL (GAAs *[Guarded Atomic Actions]* and modules) with a fully functioning Haskell-like meta programming layer on top." The methodology advocated here employs metaprogramming as well, in that ReWire programs (which are also Haskell programs) are ultimately produced by the rexhacc function. Within the Haskell community, perhaps the most well known system for hardware synthesis is Lava [17]. Lava is a domain-specific language for hardware specification embedded in Haskell. Primitives in Lava are essentially structural and specify circuits at the level of signals. ReWire, by contrast, compiles a subset of Haskell itself to hardware circuits, and relies on an abstract set of behavioral primitives. The primary motivation for developing ReWire is as a vehicle for the design, implementation, and formal verification of high assurance hardware.

CλasH [18], is a compiler for a subset of Haskell to VHDL. Like ReWire, CλasH uses Haskell itself as a source language. CλasH requires some limits be placed on the kinds of algebraic data types used as well as the basic operating types. ForSyDe is a platform to compile models of hardware written in Haskell to circuitry [19]. This paper demonstrates that the ReWire compiler works at scale as the generated ReWire programs are on the order of 100K LOC. Great care was taken in the design of ReWire so that it possesses a rigorous denotational semantics to support formal verification while maintaining synthesizability for all of its programs [20].

The Delite DSL compiler framework [4] seeks to address the "three P's" with respect to implementing software on parallel, heterogeneous systems. Delite addresses portability (i.e., retargetability of DSL compilers to a broad range of parallel hardware) through *language virtualization*. ReWire is also a virtualized DSL in that it has a separate compiler backend for producing FPGA-based implementations while reusing large parts of its host language's infrastructure— including Haskell's type system, front end, etc. In George, et al., [2], the Delite framework is adapted to the generation of hardware from DSLs, specifically the hardware acceleration of kernels in a heterogeneous setting.

## 4   Case Study 1: Matching State of the Art

We undertake the construction of a tool equivalent in functionality to the state of the art [7] (reg2vhdl) and to examine the feasibility of duplicating this functionality with our approach. The purpose of this case study is to demonstrate the *ease* with which such a tool can be constructed. The optimizations were chosen to match those of Becchi and Crowley [7] and include *head zipping*, *striding*, *alphabet compression*, and *epsilon elimination*. These results indicate that the rexhacc-based compiler compares favorably to and often surpasses reg2vhdl where throughput is concerned, and area utilization is similarly competitive. Each optimization phase was implemented in a few dozen lines of Haskell code; this is a rough indication that the amount of programmer effort required is small.

- *Head zipping.* Head zipping is a transformation that merges outbound transitions from a state that have the same transition labels. Nodes with more than one inbound transition are not head zipped because this would result in a non-equivalent NFA. Head zipping is performed by merging the destination nodes of the matching transitions into one node that includes all of the outbound transitions from the merged nodes.
- *Striding.* Striding is an optimization pass that doubles the number of characters an NFA matches at each transition. Striding traverses the graph's edges and looking two transitions ahead from each state, converts two-transition sequences to a single transition consuming two characters.
- *Alphabet compression.* Alphabet compression is a technique that increases sharing of logic by exploiting the identical treatment of different characters by an NFA. If two characters always result in the same transitions between all states, then these characters are compressed into one character class.
- *Epsilon elimination.* Eliminating $\epsilon$-transitions reduces the complexity and size of NFAs and simplifies code generation. NFAs with $\epsilon$-transitions allow state transitions without consuming input. States connected to an NFA solely by $\epsilon$-transitions can be eliminated. Eliminating unnecessary states reduces the number of flip flops required to implement the NFA on an FPGA. A textbook $\epsilon$-elimination algorithm is used [8].

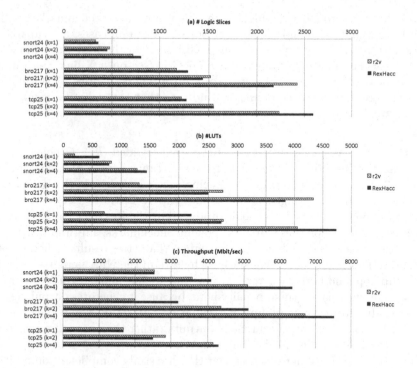

**Fig. 5.** Performance comparisons of RexHacc to reg2vhdl tool (here, "r2v")

**Experiments and Evaluation.** To test the performance of RexHacc, we selected three benchmark sets of regular expressions from the literature [7,9]. Snort24 is a set of 24 regular expressions drawn from the Snort network intrusion detection system [5]. Tcp25 is a set of 79 regular expressions designed to match malicious SMTP traffic, also drawn from the Snort NIDS. Bro217 is a set of 217 regular expressions drawn from the Bro NIDS [21]. Matchers for each of these benchmarks were generated using reg2vhdl, as well as RexHacc. Each benchmark was tested at stride lengths $k = 1$, $k = 2$, and $k = 4$, producing circuits that consume input streams at one, two, and four bytes per clock cycle. The resulting VHDL was then synthesized using Xilinx's XST synthesis tool for the Xilinx Spartan-3E X3CS500E FPGA, speed grade -4. The synthesis tools are optimized for speed. The frequencies that we list are synthesis estimates.

Fig. 5 compares the resulting circuits in terms of three performance metrics: (a) logic slice utilization, (b) LUT utilization, and (c) maximum throughput as measured in megabits per second. (Flip flop utilization was extremely close between the two tools and thus is not shown.) RexHacc compares favorably with reg2vhdl on virtually all fronts.

*Throughput.* RexHacc matches or exceeds reg2vhdl's total throughput for all but one of the nine benchmarks. In the best case (benchmark bro217, $k =$

1) throughput is around 60% higher. In the worst case (benchmark `tcp25`, $k = 2$) throughput is around 13% lower. Both tools, in all cases, are capable of processing input at a rate of more than 1 Gbit/sec. In the best case, RexHacc is capable of handling input rates up to 7.5 Gbit/sec on a Xilinx Spartan-3E FPGA at a relatively low clock rate. Tests on a Xilinx 7-series platform (not presented here, but available online [1]) indicate that throughputs of up to 25 Gbit/sec are achievable with a more modern FPGA.

*Logic utilization.* With the exception of the single-strided ($k = 1$) benchmarks, LUT utilization for RexHacc-generated circuits ranged from 88% to 116% of their `reg2vhdl` counterparts. In the specific case where $k = 1$, RexHacc tends to produce circuits with higher LUT counts (up to 219% higher), suggesting that the combinational next-state logic produced by the RexHacc code generator is more complicated for these circuits. For all benchmarks, flip flop utilization for RexHacc was close to, but slightly higher than, the results generated by `reg2vhdl`. This is not surprising since each state in the NFA is represented by a single flip flop, and both tools tend to generate similar numbers of NFA states. RexHacc, however, pays a small penalty here, because it generates output signals synchronously, storing them in flip flops, while `reg2vhdl` does not. Please note, however, that the choice of synchronous outputs rather than asynchronous ones is optional in the most recent version of ReWire.

The results exhibited here suggest that the case study compiler is competitive with the state of the art. The extra flexibility of the modular, purely functional design does not come at a prohibitive cost in terms of circuit size, and indeed brings substantial benefits with respect to throughput.

## 5   Case Study 2: Surpassing State of the Art

In this case study, we demonstrate the *agility* of the RexHacc approach by identifying an opportunity for an optimization, and rapidly implementing that optimization as a compiler phase in RexHacc. The modular nature of RexHacc made it easy both to identify a key performance bottleneck, and to implement a new optimization pass to address it.

*Identifying the bottleneck.* While conducting the experiments of Sec. 5, we noticed that one of the benchmarks, `tcp25`, stood out for its relatively low maximum throughput when processed by RexHacc as well as by `reg2vhdl`. While striding enabled our compiler to produce circuits with maximum throughput in excess of 6 Gbit/sec for `snort24` and `bro217`, maximum throughput for `tcp25` just barely exceeded 4 Gbit/sec. The throughput advantage over `reg2vhdl` observed for `snort24` and `bro217` was essentially nonexistent for `tcp25`.

To explore the reasons for this, we instrumented our compiler pipeline by using the Haskell Functional Graph Library's built-in support for generating

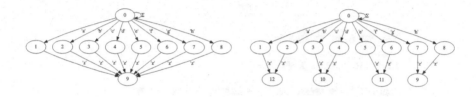

**Fig. 6.** NFA for $(a|b|c|d|e|f|g|h)z$, before state splitting (left) and after (right)

graph visualizations via GraphViz (www.graphviz.org). We observed that the `tcp25` NFA exhibited a structural feature that was not present in the `snort24` and `bro217` NFAs. Specifically, the `tcp25` NFA contained one state that had a large number of inbound transitions. A simplified example of this problem is exhibited in Fig. 6 (left), where state 9 has eight inbound transitions. A large number of inbound transitions emerges when the source regular expression contains a long chain of choice operators. This pattern is not uncommon in packet inspection rulesets (e.g., consider a long chain of alternative filenames followed by the common suffix ".exe").

In the circuit implementation the inbound transitions translate to a large fan-in of signals that must be ORed together to determine whether to activate that state. As the size of this fan-in grows large, the combinational logic involved begins to dominate the critical path of the circuit. The result is a sharp reduction in maximum operating clock frequency, and therefore throughput. This suggested an opportunity for optimization: namely, to transform the NFA in such a way as to reduce the number of inbound transitions to heavily-loaded states.

*State Splitting Optimization.* To address the performance bottleneck, we extended the compiler of Sec. 4 with an optimization called *state splitting*. Suppose we have in our NFA a state $s$ with inbound transitions $e_1, \cdots, e_n$, and assume without loss of generality that $s$ has no self-loops. Observe that we can produce an *equivalent* NFA by "splitting" $s$ in two: that is, introducing a new state (call it $s'$), and reassigning half of the inbound transitions (say, $e_1, \cdots, e_{\lceil n/2 \rceil}$) to $s'$ instead of $s$. State splitting works by applying this transformation to each node whose indegree exceeds a certain fixed threshold $t$. Fig. 6 (right) illustrates the results of applying state splitting to the NFA for $t = 2$. N.b., the maximum indegree has been reduced from 8 to 2 in this example.

The reader may note that this optimization may have the effect of *increasing* the number of inbound transitions for successor states of split nodes. This is generally not a problem for two reasons: first, as long as state splitting succeeds in reducing the *maximum* indegree, it is likely to pay off even if some states see their number of inbound transitions increased. Second, state splitting may be iterated; if the splitting of state $s_1$ results in state $s_2$ exceeding the split threshold, $s_2$ itself may be split.

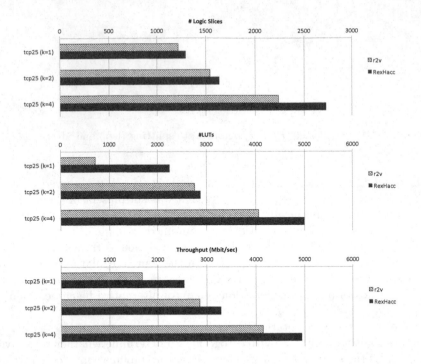

**Fig. 7.** Comparisons of RexHacc with state splitting enabled to reg2vhdl (here, "r2v") tool

The full code for the state-splitting optimization, consisting of 17 lines of code, is given as the splitStates function in the code base [1]. We can insert the state-splitting into the optimization pipeline simply by adding an extra phase to the rexhacc call; this is an instance of (‡) from Sec. 1:

## 6  Conclusions and Future Work

This research is a substantial case study utilizing the ReWire compiler at scale. ReWire is a subset of Haskell limited in expressive power to ensure the synthesizability of every ReWire program. There is a potential drawback to such restrictions: it excludes many powerful functional programming idioms. In spite of this potential drawback, we demonstrate that ReWire maintains sufficient expressiveness to support the design and implementation of high level DSLs for specifying fast hardware accelerators. Future work aims to improve the resource usage of ReWire-generated devices by optimizing ReWire's code generation stages.

The methodology leverages the intrinsic power of Haskell and functional programming. RexHacc is modular and customizable in the sense that optimization passes can be easily added and removed. Because the ordering of passes is exposed as function composition in Haskell, experimentation with optimization ordering is enabled. A RexHacc-generated compiler can be instrumented in a straightforward manner as we did with GraphViz and take advantage of existing external Haskell tools.

The flexibility of the RexHacc framework derives from the cross-compilation to ReWire and the ability of ReWire to generate VHDL synthesizable to efficient circuits. The methodology we have introduced lowers the barrier to entry for reconfigurable computing for functional programmers. At the same time, it provides an opportunity for hardware designers to leverage the power of the functional paradigm to improve productivity. The choice of a purely functional language does not come at a performance cost: our benchmarking demonstrates that we match or exceed the performance of a state-of-the-art hand-tuned compiler for a number of real-world tests.

The two research directions we are pursuing have to do with increasing the expressiveness of the type system to support metaprogramming and hardware security. The current methodology is based on metaprogramming (i.e., ReWire/Haskell programs are generated by Haskell programs) and there are type systems for staged programming (e.g., MetaML [22]) that we believe will improve programmer productivity further while automatically enforcing type safety. We developed a type system for enforcing fault isolation on ReWire [23] and we are currently extending to information flow security.

**Acknowledgments.** The authors would like to thank Jason Agron of Intel Corporation and David Andrews of the University of Arkansas for their helpful feedback.

# References

1. Graves, I., Procter, A., Harrison, W.L., Becchi, M., Allwein, G.: ARC 15 Code Base. http://goo.gl/efJ6SO
2. George, N., Lee, H., Novo, D., Rompf, T., Brown, K., Sujeeth, A., Odersky, M., Olukotun, K., Ienne, P.: Hardware system synthesis from domain-specific languages. In: Proc. of 24th Int. Conf. on Field Prog. Logic and App. (FPL 2014) (2014)
3. Procter, A., Harrison, W., Graves, I., Becchi, M., Allwein, G.: Semantics-directed machine architecture in ReWire. In: 2013 Int. Conf. on Field Programmable Technology (FPT 2013), pp. 446–449 (2013)
4. Lee, H., Brown, K., Sujeeth, A., Chafi, H., Rompf, T., Odersky, M., Olukotun, K.: Implementing domain-specific languages for heterogeneous parallel computing. IEEE Micro **31**(5), 42–53 (2011)
5. Roesch, M.: Snort - lightweight intrusion detection for networks. In: Proc. of the 13th USENIX Conf. on System Administration. LISA 1999, pp. 229–238 (1999)
6. Sidhu, R., Prasanna, V.K.: Fast regular expression matching using FPGAs. In: Proc. of the 9th Annual IEEE Symp. on Field-Programmable Custom Computing Machines, pp. 227–238 (2001)
7. Becchi, M., Crowley, P.: Efficient regular expression evaluation: theory to practice. In: Proc. of the 4th ACM/IEEE Symp. on Architectures for Networking and Communications Systems, pp. 50–59. ACM (2008)

8. Hopcroft, J.E., Motwani, R., Ullman, J.D.: Introduction to Automata Theory, Languages, and Computation, 3rd edn. Addison-Wesley (2006)
9. Becchi, M., Crowley, P.: An improved algorithm to accelerate regular expression evaluation. In: Proc. of the 2007 ACM/IEEE Symp. on Architecture for Networking and Communications Sys., pp. 145–154 (2007)
10. Kumar, S., Dharmapurikar, S., Yu, F., Crowley, P., Turner, J.: Algorithms to accelerate multiple regular expressions matching for deep packet inspection. In: Proc. of the 2006 Conf. on Applications, Technologies, Architectures, and Protocols for Computer Communications, SIGCOMM 2006, pp. 339–350 (2006)
11. Brodie, B.C., Taylor, D.E., Cytron, R.K.: A scalable architecture for high-throughput regular-expression pattern matching. In: 2006 ISCA, pp. 191–202 (2006)
12. Becchi, M., Crowley, P.: A hybrid finite automaton for practical deep packet inspection. In: Proc. of the 2007 ACM CoNEXT Conf., pp. 1–12 (2007)
13. Mitra, A., Najjar, W., Bhuyan, L.: Compiling PCRE to FPGA for accelerating SNORT IDS. In: Proc. of the 2007 ACM/IEEE Symp. on Architecture for Networking and Communications Sys., pp. 127–136 (2007)
14. Sourdis, I., Bispo, J.a., Cardoso, J.a.M., Vassiliadis, S.: Regular expression matching in reconfigurable hardware. J. Signal Process. Syst. 51(1), 99–121 (2008)
15. Yang, Y.H.E., Jiang, W., Prasanna, V.K.: Compact architecture for high-throughput regular expression matching on fpga. In: Proc. of the 2008 ACM/IEEE Symp. on Architectures for Networking and Communications Sys., pp. 30–39 (2008)
16. Arvind: Bluespec and haskell. In: Proc. 1st Ann. Workshop on Fun. Prog. Concepts in Domain-specific Languages, pp. 1–2 (2013)
17. Bjesse, P., Claessen, K., Sheeran, M., Singh, S.: Lava: hardware design in haskell. In: 3rd ICFP, pp. 174–184 (1998)
18. Baaij, C., Kuper, J.: Using rewriting to synthesize functional languages to digital circuits. In: McCarthy, J. (ed.) TFP 2013. LNCS, vol. 8322, pp. 17–33. Springer, Heidelberg (2014)
19. Sander, I., Jantsch, A.: System modeling and transformational design refinement in ForSyDe. IEEE Transactions on Computer-Aided Design of Integrated Circuits and Systems 23(1), 17–32 (2004)
20. Procter, A.: Semantics-Driven Design and Implementation of High-Assurance Hardware. PhD thesis, Univeristy of Missouri, Department of Computer Science (2014)
21. Paxson, V.: Bro: a system for detecting network intruders in real-time. In: Proc. of the 1998 Conf. on USENIX Security Symp., p. 3 (1988)
22. Taha, W., Sheard, T.: Metaml and multi-stage programming with explicit annotations. Theoretical Computer Science 248(1), 211–242 (2000)
23. Harrison, W.L., Procter, A., Allwein, G.: The confinement problem in the presence of faults. In: Aoki, T., Taguchi, K. (eds.) ICFEM 2012. LNCS, vol. 7635, pp. 182–197. Springer, Heidelberg (2012)

# ArchHDL: A Novel Hardware RTL Design Environment in C++

Shimpei Sato[1]([✉]) and Kenji Kise[2]

[1] Japan Advanced Institute of Science and Technology, Nomi, Ishikawa, Japan
[2] Tokyo Institute of Technology, Tokyo, Japan
shimpei.sato@jaist.ac.jp, kise@cs.titech.ac.jp

**Abstract.** LSIs are designed in four stages including architectural design, logic design, circuit design, and physical design. In the architectural design and the logic design, designers describe a hardware in RTL. However, they generally use different languages. Typically a general purpose programming language such as C or C++ and a hardware description language such as Verilog HDL or VHDL are used in the architectural design and the logic design, respectively. In this paper, we propose a new hardware description environment for the architectural design and logic design which aims to describe and verify a hardware in one language. The environment consists of (1) a new hardware description language called ArchHDL which enables to simulate a hardware faster than Verilog HDL simulation and (2) a source code translation tool from ArchHDL to Verilog HDL. ArchHDL is a new language for hardware RTL modeling based on C++. The key features of this language are that (1) designers describe a combinational circuit as a function and (2) the ArchHDL library implements non-blocking assignment in C++. Using these features, designers are able to write a hardware in a Verilog HDL-like style. The source code of ArchHDL is able to convert to Verilog HDL by the translation tool and is able to synthesize for an FPGA or an ASIC. We implemented a many-core processor in ArchHDL. The simulation speed for the processor by ArchHDL achieves about 4.5 times faster than the simulation speed by Synopsys VCS. We also convert the code to Verilog HDL and estimated the hardware resources on an FPGA. To implement the 48-node many-core processor, it needs 71 % of entire resources of Virtex-7.

## 1 Introduction

VLSI chips such as high performance processors and SoCs with many hardware elements are designed in the flow of (1) architectural design, (2) logic design, (3) circuit design, and (4) physical design. In architectural design and logic design, simulations in register transfer level (RTL) are indispensable for efficient debugging and logical verification. For these RTL modeling and simulation, some hardware description languages such as Verilog HDL and VHDL are often used.

Architectural design and logic design are also important for hardware FPGA implementation. Available hardware resources in FPGAs are increasing, and requirements to implement a large scale hardware are also increasing. So, the

© Springer International Publishing Switzerland 2015
K. Sano et al. (Eds.): ARC 2015, LNCS 9040, pp. 53–64, 2015.
DOI: 10.1007/978-3-319-16214-0_5

elapsed time of an RTL simulation for such large scale design is becoming very long even if using a fast RTL simulator. Therefore, CAD systems which realize high-speed RTL simulation are strongly required.

We have proposed *ArchHDL*[11] as a new hardware description language for RTL modeling and high-speed architectural simulation. In this paper, we propose a new hardware description environment for architectural design and logic design which aims to write and verify a hardware in one language. This environment comprises of (1) a hardware description language called ArchHDL which enables to simulate a hardware faster than Verilog HDL simulation and (2) a source code translation tool from ArchHDL to Verilog HDL.

ArchHDL is a hardware description language for hardware RTL modeling based on C++. The key features of this language are that (1) a combinational circuit description is handled as a function call and (2) non-blocking assignment support in C++ by the ArchHDL library. The goal of the proposed environment is to attain following three points.

– Easy hardware modeling in RTL
– High-speed simulation compared to Verilog HDL simulation

In the previous work, we found that RTL simulation speed using ArchHDL is much faster than a Verilog HDL simulation using Icarus Verilog[6] which is a well known free software. However, the simulation was performed with a simple hardware like 8-bit counter circuit, and it was not a practical evaluation to confirm the usefulness of ArchHDL. In this paper, we implement a many-core processor as a practical hardware in ArchHDL and evaluated the simulation speed. The source code of ArchHDL is transformed into Verilog HDL by the translation tool and the Verilog HDL code is synthesized for an FPGA. We convert the many-core processor code to Verilog HDL using the translation tool and measure the hardware resources on an FPGA.

## 2    A New Hardware Description Environment

We propose a new hardware design environment which consists of a new hardware description language called ArchHDL[11] and source code translation tool from ArchHDL to Verilog HDL. In this section, the hardware description in ArchHDL and development of the translation tool are delivered.

### 2.1    Concept of ArchHDL

ArchHDL is a hardware description language based on C++. It provides a C++ library to describe hardware in RTL. The library includes definitions of *Module* class, *reg* class, *wire* class, and functions for simulation.

The key features of this language are: (1) implementing combinational circuits as functions and (2) supporting non-blocking assignment to registers. To describe a combinational circuit as a function, the lambda expression which is newly added to the C++ standard library called C++11 is used. Non-blocking

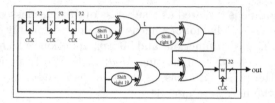

**Fig. 1.** A block diagram of sample circuit used for explanation of hardware description in ArchHDL. (Xorshift random value generator)

```
1  class Xorshift : public Module {
2  public:
3    wire<uint_1> i_rst_x;
4    wire<uint_1> i_enable;
5    wire<uint_32> i_seed;
6    wire<uint_32> o_out;
7
8    reg<uint_32> x;
9    reg<uint_32> y;
10   reg<uint_32> z;
11   reg<uint_32> w;
12   wire<uint_32> t;
13
14   void Assign() {
15     t = [=]() { return x() ^ (x() << 11); };
16     o_out = w;
17   }
18   void Always() {
19     if (!i_rst_x()) {
20       x <<= 123456789;
21       y <<= 362436069;
22       z <<= 521288629;
23       w <<= 88675123 ^ i_seed();
24     } else {
25       if (i_enable()) {
26         x <<= y();
27         y <<= z();
28         z <<= w();
29         w <<= (w() ^ (w() >> 19)) ^ (t() ^ (t() >> 8));
30       }
31     }
32   }
33 };
```

**Fig. 2.** A sample description of Xorshift random value generator in ArchHDL

assignment, which is generally supported in hardware description languages such as Verilog HDL or VHDL, is not supported in general purpose programming languages. ArchHDL implements non-blocking assignment by the library in C++.

ArchHDL realizes an RTL hardware description with Verilog HDL-like style by these features and defined classes in the library. A source code described in ArchHDL is able to compile with general C++ compilers, then the simulation of the hardware is delivered by the execution of the binary file. The simulation speed is faster than the simulation using Verilog HDL simulator.

## 2.2 Hardware RTL Modeling in ArchHDL

Fig. 1 is a block diagram of the sample circuit used for explanation of Arch-HDL hardware description in this section. The circuit is a 32-bit pseudo random value generator using Xorshift algorithm. It employs four registers and generates random value by XOR and shift operations. Initialization mechanisms of register values and input of seed, which are contained in the sample description we present later, are omitted in this figure.

Fig. 2 is a sample description of Xorshift random value generator in Arch-HDL. Descriptions about inclusion of standard libraries are omitted.

A hardware module is declared as a subclass of *Module* class which is defined in the ArchHDL library. Behavior of a hardware module is mainly described using *reg* class, *wire* class, *Assign* function, and *Always* function, which are defined in the library. A class defined by inheriting *Module* class corresponds to a *module* in Verilog HDL. Here, *Xorshift* class is declared as a subclass of *Module* class and it represents the hardware module.

An instance of *wire* class and *reg* class can be regarded as a *wire* and *reg* in Verilog HDL respectively. These classes are implemented as a template class in the ArchHDL library. Therefore, users must specify the data type into the angled bracket when they declare an instance of *wire* or *reg*. In Fig. 2, *uint_1* and *uint_32* are used as data types for *wire* and *reg*. The number at the end of these data types represents the bit width of the data, and is intended to simplify the analysis by the source code translation tool. These data types are defined in the library. However, these are actually implemented as an alias of *unsigned int*. Therefore, a value declared with these data type is not masked by the represented bit width. Also, user defined structure is able to use as a data type for a *wire* class and *reg* class instance. The *wire* class and the *reg* class are implemented as functional objects in the library, so a value of these instance can be referred by a function call of the class instance.

A module description in ArchHDL does not employ ports. Therefore, the description about connections between modules is implemented by referring directly to *wire* or *reg* class instances declared in a module. To simplify the analysis by the translation tool, some naming rules are applied. As indicated from the 3rd line to the 6th line in the Fig. 2, an instance name starting from "i_" is an input port and an instance name starting from "o_" is an output port. These rules are also applied to an instance which declared using array.

Combinational circuits are defined by assigning a functional object to a *wire* class instance. All of assignment statements to instances are written in *Assign* function as denoted from the 14th line to the 17th line in the Fig. 2. In the case of this example, combinational circuits which are able to describe in the Verilog HDL assign statement are only used. However, using the lambda expression of C++11 denoted in the 15th line, designers are able to define various combinational circuits in ArchHDL.

The ArchHDL library supports non-blocking assignment of a *reg* class instance. Statements of non-blocking assignment are described using "<<=" operator, and they are written in *Always* function as indicated from the 18th line to the 32nd line in the Fig. 2. The *Always* function is equivalent to "always @(posedge CLK)" in Verilog HDL.

## 2.3   Testbench in ArchHDL

Fig. 3 shows a sample testbench in ArchHDL for the random value generator shown in Fig. 2. Descriptions of inclusion of standard libraries are omitted. This code is to display generated random values for 30 cycles. The seed value for the random value generator is set at 1.

```
 1  #include "common/xorshift.h"
 2
 3  class TestTop : public Module {
 4  public:
 5    static const int HALT_CYCLE = 30;
 6
 7    reg<uint_1> HALT;
 8    reg<int> cycle;
 9
10    wire<uint_1> rst_x;
11    reg<unsigned int> seed;
12    wire<unsigned int> rand;
13    Xorshift xorshift;
14
15    void PortConnect() {
16      xorshift.i_rst_x = rst_x;
17      xorshift.i_enable = rst_x;
18      xorshift.i_seed = seed;
19      rand = xorshift.o_out;
20    }
21    void Assign() {
22      rst_x = [=]() { return (cycle() < 1) ? 0 : 1; };
23    }
24    void Initial() {
25      HALT = 0;
26      cycle = 0;
27    }
28    void Always() {
29      cycle <<= cycle() + 1;
30      HALT  <<= (cycle() >= HALT_CYCLE);
31
32      if (!rst_x()) {
33        seed <<= 1;
34      } else {
35        printf("%08x\n", rand());
36      }
37    }
38  };
39
40  int main() {
41    TestTop testtop;
42    do {
43      ArchHDL::Step();
44    } while (!testtop.HALT());
45    return 0;
46  }
```

**Fig. 3.** A sample testbench for Xorshift in ArchHDL

In the main function from the 40th line, the *TestTop* module is generated and then the *Step* function provided by the library is called in the do-while loop. At the time of the *TestTop* instance is generated, all of *reg*, *wire*, and *Module* class instances are stored in a data area prepared in the ArchHDL library. The *Step* function calls the *Always* function of all *Module* class instances stored in the library data area, Therefore, the call of the function simulates the hardware behavior in one cycle.

*PortConnect* function is used to connect ports of Xorshift module as denoted from the 15th line to the 20th line. The role of this function is same to *Assign* function mentioned above. However, it is necessary to describe *PortConnect function* and *Assign* function separately to simplify the analysis of the translation tool. From the 24th line to the 28th line, register initializations are described in *Initial* function. This function is equivalent to the initial block in Verilog HDL.

## 2.4   Advantages and Disadvantages of ArchHDL over Verilog HDL

The advantages of ArchHDL are (1) the intuitive module description by object-oriented programming and (2) the flexible testbench description using C++ standard environment.

Hardware resources on LSIs or FPGAs are increasing, and opportunities to describe a hardware which implements a lot of the same module like many-core processors are also increasing. Designers are able to declare modules, registers, or wires using an array in ArchHDL. Therefore, they also able to use for statements to describe the behavior of such hardware intuitively.

Architectural verification needs plenty of simulations using various parameters, and requires a flexible description to the testbench. The testbench description in ArchHDL is able to use the random value generators, variable-length array and so on which are included in C++ standard library. Therefore, the flexibility of the testbench description is equal to typical software simulators. Furthermore, the simulation speed is faster than Verilog HDL simulation which described in same abstraction level.

To simplify the implementation of ArchHDL library and the source code translation tool, the current ArchHDL has some restrictions compared with the description capability of Verilog HDL. The main restrictions are (1) the described hardware may use only one clock signal, (2) the assignment of value to a register is done only in a positive edge of the clock and (3) the designers describe registers and wires using C++ integer type like 32-bit int or 64-bit int.

ArchHDL supports a hardware which allows assigning a value to a register in a positive edge of a single clock. Therefore it does not support to use multiple clocks and to assign a value in a negative edge of a clock. Although SFL[9] has similar constraint, it was used for variety of hardware descriptions[5, 7].

ArchHDL uses C++ integer type like 32-bit int or 64-bit int for the data type of registers and wires. The declaration of registers and wires of any bit width are not supported. ArchHDL supports C++ common operators, and does not support the bit selection operation and the bit concatenation operation which are supported in Verilog HDL.

The ArchHDL library is implemented with about 200 lines of source code and it is simple. Users are able to expand the library to introduce other clock signals or data types. We think that these restrictions are caused by an initial stage implementation of the library. Therefore, they will be eliminated with the progress of this work.

## 2.5   Translation Tool from ArchHDL to Verilog HDL

We are developing a code translator from ArchHDL to Verilog HDL. It is able to automatically generate a Verilog HDL code from ArchHDL.

As shown in some examples of hardware description in ArchHDL, its description style becomes Verilog HDL-like description style by using classes such as reg class or wire class provided by the library. Especially, designers are expected to describe the same statement about an assignment and an arithmetic expression in ArchHDL and Verilog HDL. Thus, the code translation from ArchHDL to Verilog HDL can be delivered without any optimization.

Fig. 4 shows the translation flow from ArchHDL code to Verilog HDL code. The tool receives ArchHDL code as an input and outputs the Verilog HDL. The translation is delivered as follows: (1) code scanning, (2) information generation for Verilog HDL code by string replacement and parsing.

In the parsing process, statements which are not able to describe in Verilog HDL syntax are analyzed. Basically it is not necessary to parse statements written in ArchHDL in detail, because they must be the same statements in Verilog HDL.

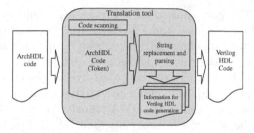

**Fig. 4.** Translation flow from ArchHDL code to Verilog HDL code

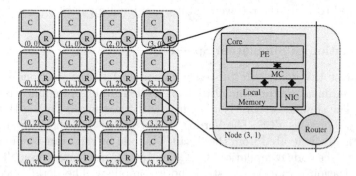

**Fig. 5.** M-Core Architecture used as a practical hardware for evaluation

The main restrictions of description in ArchHDL which can be converted to Verilog HDL are as follows: (1) using only reg class or wire class as a data type and (2) using up to 2-dimensional array for instance declaration.

In particular, the reason of the limitation for the array depends on that the Verilog HDL syntax limitation and the multidimensional array is not supported in some Verilog HDL simulator. We think that we can describe a practical hardware sufficiently in ArchHDL under such restrictions.

## 3   Experimental Results

We evaluate our proposed hardware description environment which consists of ArchHDL and the source code translation tool in two aspects: (1) The simulation speed of a hardware described in ArchHDL, and (2) The FPGA resource utilization of a hardware synthesized from Verilog HDL code generated by the the source code translation tool.

### 3.1   A Sample Hardware for Practical Evaluation

We implemented M-Core Architecture[12], a many-core processor employs scratchpad memories, as a sample hardware for evaluation. Fig. 5 shows the M-Core Architecture. Each node of the M-Core Architecture is composed of a core and a router. The core consists of a Processing Element (PE), a memory controller (MC), a local memory, and a Network Interface Controller (NIC). The PE is a 32-bit five-stage pipelined MIPS processor[10]. Each node is connected to the mesh network via the router. The router architecture is the conventional Input-buffered Virtual Channel router[3] with five-stages pipeline, four virtual channels per input port, and 4-flit buffer per virtual channel.

For a data transfer between cores, DMA transfer is used. DMA command is send from a PE to its NIC via memory-mapped IO. NIC reads data from the local memory using these information. After that, packets are generated and injected into the network. When a packet arrives a node, the information of the packet is used to write the received data to the local memory.

## 3.2  Evaluation of Simulation Speed

We implement the many-core processor introduced in the previous section in ArchHDL and measure the simulation time while running an application on the processor. The simulation time is compared with the time of Verilog HDL simulation using Synopsys VCS. The Verilog HDL code used in the VCS simulation is automatically generated from the ArchHDL code by our translation tool. For ArchHDL source code compilation, GCC and Intel Compiler are used. The compiler optimization option is -Ofast for both compilers. The detailed computer environment for simulation is as follows

- CPU: Intel Xeon E5-2687W
- Memory: 32 GB
- OS: Ubuntu 13.04 x86_64
- GCC (g++): version 4.7.3, optimization -Ofast
- Intel Compiler (ICPC): version 14.0.1 optimization -Ofast
- Synopsys VCS: version H-2013.06

In the simulation, various number of cores (from $2\times2$ to $10\times10$) of the many-cores processor are used. The many-core processor executes an application that every cores communicate with each other in every 100 cycles. The total execution cycles of the simulation is 100,000 cycles. The simulation is performed 10 times for each configuration, and the average simulation time of them is used as the final result.

ArchHDL simulation can be parallelized using OpenMP. This parallelization is supported by the ArchHDL library and users do not need to change their source code. The parallelized simulation accuracy is same as that of before parallelization. For the parallelized simulation, we use a computer which has the 8 physical cores (16 logical cores using SMT) CPU.

Fig. 6 illustrates the simulation results in case of using 1 thread. The X-axis indicates the node counts of the sample many-core processor and the Y-axis represents the simulation time in second.

We can see that the simulation time increases when the number of nodes increases. The simulation by VCS is fastest (maximum 2.9 times faster than GCC and maximum 2.7 times faster than Intel Compiler). However, the speedup of

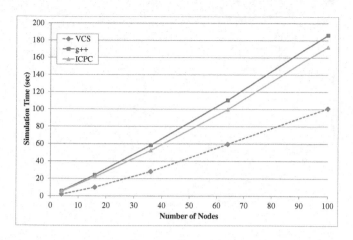

**Fig. 6.** The simulation time comparison using just single-threaded

the VCS simulation compared to other simulations (GCC and Intel Compiler) decreases when the number of nodes increases, In particular, the speedup is maximum when the number of nodes is 4 (2×2 network) and minimum when the number of nodes is 100 (10×10 network).

Fig. 7 shows the simulation results in case of parallelized simulation (with 8-thread and 16-thread). "VCS" and "ICPC 1 thread" in Fig. 7 are same as ones illustrated in Fig. 6.

We can see that every parallelized simulation is faster than the VCS simulation. The parallelized simulation is 4.5 times faster in maximum than the VCS simulation when using 16-thread. The simulation results also show that the speedup of the parallelized simulation compared to the VCS simulation increases when the number of nodes increases.

### 3.3 FPGA Resource Utilization of the Many-core Processor Synthesized from Converted Verilog HDL Code

Here, we estimate the FPGA resource utilization of M-Core architecture. The target device is Xilinx Virtex-7 XC7VX485 on the evaluation kit VC707.

The number of nodes to implement is 48 (8×6). The register files on the Processing Element of each node is implemented using LUT-RAM. The local memory in each core and the input buffers in each router are implemented using Block-RAM. Parameters of the local memory on each core are 32-bit data width, 32 KB total size, and 3 port (2 read, 1 write). Parameters of the input buffer are 38 bit data width, 16 entry (4 entry for each 4 virtual channels in a port), and 2 port (1 read, 1 write). The number of router port except the edge node of the processor is 5. Therefore, five Block-RAMs are used for input buffers in a router.

Table 1 shows the hardware resources of the processor which are delivered during place and route. The processor occupied 54,509 slices which is 71% of

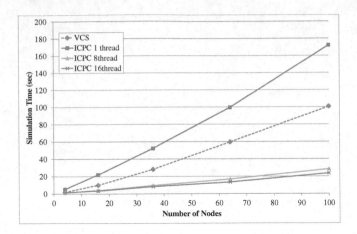

**Fig. 7.** The parallelized simulation time in ArchHDL. Note that the simulation time of VCS is single-thread.

**Table 1.** Hardware Resource of a 64-node many-core processor on Virtex-7

|  | Slice | Reg | LUT | BRAM (RAMB36E1)) |
|---|---|---|---|---|
| Used | 54,509 | 79,641 | 158,103 | 1,007 |
| Utilization | 71% | 13% | 52% | 97% |

entire resources, and runs at 114.9 MHz according to the synthesis report. The number of slices for each element in a node are about 460 slices for Processing Element, about 25 slices for Memory Controller, about 280 slices for Network Interface Controller, and about 400 slices for router.

From the result of hardware resources, we found that the scale of the hardware generated by the converted Verilog HDL code by the translation tool is appropriate.

## 4    Related Works

Chisel[2], SystemC[1], and MyHDL[4] are hardware description languages that are able to compile as a program of general-purpose programming language. Although hardware designers are able to describe hardware in RTL in these languages, the hardware description style in those languages is very different from the style of Verilog HDL.

SystemC is designed based on C++ and it is implemented as a C++ class library. The hardware described in SystemC is able to compile and execute as a C++ program. Hardware designers describe hardware using classes and macros which are provided in the SystemC library. While most of the HDLs like Verilog HDL, VHDL and proposed ArchHDL support the RTL of design, SystemC originally supports the design at a higher abstraction level to model large hardware systems.

MyHDL is designed based on Python. The hardware described in MyHDL is compiled and is executed as a Python program. The project provides a tool to convert a source code in MyHDL to Verilog HDL and VHDL for hardware synthesis. It is reported that the architectural simulation speed of MyHDL is about 3 times faster[8] than the speed of Verilog HDL compiled by Icarus Verilog. Although this project is unique using Python, MyHDL has not been used extensively.

Chisel is designed based on Scala. The hardware description in Chisel is converted to C++ code for high-speed simulation, and also is converted to Verilog HDL code for ASIC synthesis. It is reported that the simulation speed of Chisel C++ simulation is 7.8 times faster against Synopsys VCS.

SFL[9] is a unique language and PARTHENON is a high-level CAD tool for SFL developed by NTT(Nippon Telegraph and Telephone Corporation). In SFL, the designer does not describe a clock signal explicitly and the system assumes the existence of the global clock implicitly. This strategy is the same as ArchHDL. Although SFL is an attractive language, the development and maintenance of PARTHENON system had stopped.

## 5  Conclusion

In this paper, we propose a new hardware description environment for architectural design and logic design which aim to write and verify a hardware in one language. The environment comprises of (1) A hardware description language called ArchHDL and (2) A source code translation tool from ArchHDL to Verilog HDL. The goals of the proposed environment are to attain following: (1) Easy hardware modeling in RTL, (2) Realizing the environment which is able to verify both architectural design and logic design in one description, and (2) High-speed simulation compared to Verilog HDL simulation.

We evaluate our proposed hardware description environment in two aspects: (1) The simulation speed of hardware described by ArchHDL and (2) The amount of resources usage of hardware when synthesizing Verilog HDL code generated from ArchHDL code by the translation tool. For practical evaluation, we implemented a many-core processor in ArchHDL and also converted the source code to Verilog HDL by the translator. The simulation speed of ArchHDL was about 4.5 times faster than the simulation speed using Synopsys VCS which is one of the fastest Verilog HDL simulator. The resource utilization of the 48-node many-core processor on Virtex-7 was 54,509 in occupied slices. From the result, we found that the scale of the hardware generated by the converted Verilog HDL code by the translation tool is appropriate.

As future works, we consider about that: (1) The detailed verification of the converted code from ArchHDL to Verilog HDL, (2) To develop a source code translation tool from Verilog HDL to ArchHDL to obtain the first RTL simulation, and (3) Implement the hardware described in ArchHDL into FPGAs and confirm its behavior.

# References

1. IEEE standard for Standard SystemC Language Reference Manual. IEEE std. 1666–2011 (2011)
2. Bachrach, J., Vo, H., Richards, B., Lee, Y., Waterman, A., Avižienis, R., Wawrzynek, J., Asanović, K.: Chisel: constructing hardware in a scala embedded language. In: Proceedings of the 49th Annual Design Automation Conference, DAC 2012, pp. 1216–1225. ACM, New York (2012). http://doi.acm.org/10.1145/2228360.2228584
3. Dally, W., Towles, B.: Principles and Practices of Interconnection Networks. The Morgan Kaufmann Series in Computer Architecture and Design. Elsevier Science (2004)
4. Decaluwe, J.: Myhdl: a python-based hardware description language. Linux J. **2004**(127), 5 (2004). http://dl.acm.org/citation.cfm?id=1029015.1029020
5. Hayasaka, H., Haramiishi, H., Shimizu, N.: The design of pci bus interface. In: Proceedings of the 2003 Asia and South Pacific Design Automation Conference, ASP-DAC 2003, pp. 579–580 (2003)
6. Icarus Verilog Web page: http://iverilog.icarus.com
7. Kon, C., Shimizu, N.: The design of an i8080a instruction compatible processor with extended memory address. In: Proceedings of the 2003 Asia and South Pacific Design Automation Conference, ASP-DAC 2003, pp. 571–572 (2003)
8. MyHDL Web page: http://www.myhdl.org/doku.php/performance
9. Parthenon Web page: http://www.kecl.ntt.co.jp/parthenon/
10. Patterson, D., Hennessy, J.: Computer Organization and Design: The Hardware/software Interface. Morgan Kaufmann Series in Computer Graphics. Morgan Kaufmann (2012)
11. Sato, S., Kise, K.: ArchHDL: a new hardware description language for high-speed architectural evaluation. In: Proceedings of IEEE 7th International Symposium on Embedded Multicore SoCs (MCSoC 2013), pp. 107–112, September 2013
12. Uehara, K., Sato, S., Miyoshi, T., Kise, K.: A study of an infrastructure for research and development of many-core processors. In: Proceedings of International Conference on Parallel and Distributed Computing, Applications and Technologies (PDCAT), pp. 414–419, December 2009

# Operand-Value-Based Modeling of Dynamic Energy Consumption of Soft Processors in FPGA

Zaid Al-Khatib$^{(\boxtimes)}$ and Samar Abdi

Electrical and Computer Engineering, Concordia University, Montreal, Canada
z_alk@live.concordia.ca, samar@ece.concordia.ca

**Abstract.** This paper presents a novel method for estimating the dynamic energy consumption of soft processors in FPGA, using an operand-value-based model at the instruction level. Our energy model contains three components: the instruction base energy, the maximum variation in the instruction energy due to input data, and the impact of one's density of the operand values during software execution. Using multiple benchmarks, we demonstrate that our model has only 4.7% average error and 12% worst case error compared to the reference post-place-and-route simulations, and is more than twice as accurate as existing instruction-level models.

**Keywords:** Energy modeling · Soft processors · Power estimation

## 1 Introduction

Processor core energy consumption is a first order metric for FPGA-based embedded system design, due to its direct impact on battery life. Early and accurate modeling of soft-processor performance and energy consumption, for a given application, is needed to perform early design space exploration with reasonable confidence. A fine-grained and rapid estimation tool is also important for reconfiguration and customization of system architecture as well as optimization of software implementation for energy consumption.

Modeling the dynamic energy consumption of a soft processor remains a major challenge. Power measurement techniques typically used with ASIC processors, as in the work presented by Bazzaz *et al.* [1] cannot be adopted to measure the power dissipated in the FPGA resources implementing the soft processor core, independent of the other FPGA components. Hence, low level post-place-and-route models and simulations are preferred as they enable capturing the switching activity of the final FPGA logic resources [2]. However these are incredibly slow, thereby making the design space exploration and SW optimization process impractical. Alternatively, energy models based on processor power states are used for quick estimates but they can be very inaccurate. Instruction-level models promise higher accuracy than mode-based models, however, it is very difficult to accurately characterize the energy consumption of individual instructions in soft processors implementations. In fact, conventional methods used in previous work to isolate the energy consumed by an instruction examine its execution under very unique states that do not accurately

© Springer International Publishing Switzerland 2015
K. Sano et al. (Eds.): ARC 2015, LNCS 9040, pp. 65–76, 2015.
DOI: 10.1007/978-3-319-16214-0_6

reflect the energy it would consume when it is executed as part of a normal application run. Our goal is to build a concise instruction-level model that can provide fast and accurate estimates of dynamic energy consumption for soft processors in FPGA. Using a heuristic approach, our model accounts for both the inter-instruction effects and the operand values of the instructions for estimating the energy consumption.

Previous work suggest insignificant impact of operand values on processor power dissipation in ASIC [3]. However, we observed that the operand values greatly impact the energy consumed by soft processor cores in FPGA. This is due to the fact that Soft-processor data-path units are implemented on several Configurable Logic Blocks (CLBs) and DSPs. This requires the operand values propagate through much longer routes between these block than in ASIC, giving them higher charge capacitance. These signals are also frequently reset to Zero by instructions like the NOP and small operand operations [4]. As such, there's an increased probability of signals switching after the execution of instructions operating with values containing many ones. The higher density of ones in an instructions operands, the larger the probability of switching, hence higher power dissipation and energy consumption by the processor core. A profiling and estimation tool is required to calculate this operand value metric and to apply the energy models to large applications.

The novel contributions of this paper are as follows:

1. We designed a novel energy data model for a soft-processor FPGA implementation that can be generated heuristically without analysing the processor architecture and pipeline, using sets of applications described in Section 3.
2. We designed an estimation tool that analyses C code at the machine instruction level, applies the energy data model and annotation techniques to estimate the energy of each instruction executed in a given run, as described in Section 4.

## 2   Related Work

There are several modeling techniques to estimate energy consumption of soft processors. They can be categorized based on the model's abstraction level. The most accurate models simulate the processor at the gate level using post-place and route simulations, tracking the switching rate all internal signals. Examples of tools, based on such models, include Xilinx's XPower Analyzer XPA [1], [5] and Synopsys's Power Compiler [6]. Accurate, low level simulation models suffer from very slow simulation speeds. In fact, in order to estimate the energy consumed executing the Dhrystone benchmark [7] on a Microblaze processor core [8] using XPA took over 2 days of simulation time. This simulation was done on a quad-core i7 PC with 16 GB RAM.

Higher level modeling of processor energy and power is typically done by characterizing the workload of the processor. These can be divided in three broad groups based on the number of contributing factors in each model. We will refer to these groups as first, second and third order models. They are identified as follows:

- First order models are state-based, in which the energy consumption is derived from the state of the processor. An average dynamic power value is assigned to each power state. The dynamic energy is then estimated by multiplying the weighted average power by the total execution time. Jouletrack implements a very simple first order model [3]. System level estimation tools like Softwatt [9], Wattch [10], and other state-based estimation techniques [11] use first order processor models because of their simplicity. Energy aware scheduling techniques using first order models have also been proposed utilizing such models [12]. However, first order models do not reflect the processor energy savings from software optimizations independently of performance. For example, re-ordering assembly instructions to increase the number of repeating instructions reduces energy consumption. This effect cannot be observed by first order models.

- Second order models assign an estimated average energy value for each instruction in the processor's instruction set. The energy required to execute a program is then estimated as the sum of the energy values assigned to all the executed instructions. Many completed works use this technique such as [3], [13], [14]. More work however is required to prove the accuracy of these models to estimate large applications running on soft processors. In fact, we observed very negligible accuracy improvement over the first order models.

- Third order processor models incorporate inter-instruction energy effects. When analyzing the energy required for completing an instruction, the neighboring instructions are also accounted for. The reasoning is that neighboring instructions indicate the state of the processor before and after executing an instruction. Several processors, including an Intel 486DX2 processor [1] and a Fujitsu DSP [15], have been modeled using this approach. VLIW processors have also been modeled using third order models [16]. Third order models have been applied to estimate system-level energy consumption [17]. However, third order models do not take the effects of input data for the application into account, which can lead to significant errors.

The techniques proposed in these works were adopted to generate three models of an implementation of the Microblaze processor implemented on a Xilinx Virtex5 FPGA. The Microblaze instruction set architecture is similar to the RISC-based DLX architecture [18]. We used these models to evaluate the applicability of these techniques on a modern soft processor. The results presented in this paper demonstrate significant errors in excess of 100%. In the quest of identifying the causes of these inaccurate results, we derived results showing significant impact of operand value on energy consumption. The following section describes the proposed model, generated using a novel instruction characterization technique.

## 3    Operand-Value-Based Processor Energy Model

This section describes the proposed methodology for creating an Operand-Value-Based Model (OVBM) for a processor implementation consisting of:

- The base energy cost for each instruction, with zero operands,
- The maximum energy variance, due to operand values, for each instruction, and
- Linear parameters, slope and intercept (m and b) modeling the correlation between the one's density and the energy consumed in the processor data-path signals.

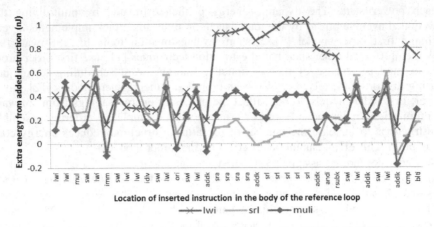

**Fig. 1.** Location Based Energy Profile of three instructions (Load Word, Shift Right Logic, and Multiply)

A single OVBM is sufficient to estimate the processor energy cost of any application running on a given implementation of the processor. A separate model is required for alternative design configurations and optimizations of the processor.

## 3.1 Base Energy Cost of Instructions

The minimum dynamic energy required by the processor to complete an instruction is defined as the base energy cost of the instruction. It is determined by the type and operation of the instruction as well as the state of the processor's internal signals prior to executing the instruction. This state dependency is referred to as the inter-instruction energy effect. Normally, we expect two consecutive instructions of the same type to consume less energy than two of different types.

Most instruction energy estimation techniques suggested in the literature rely on measuring or estimating the average power consumed by the processor while

**Table 1.** Base energies and maximum energy variations for Microblaze in Nanojoules (nJ)

| Inst. | Base energy after instruction from class: | | | Max. instr. Energy Variance |
|---|---|---|---|---|
| | *Arithmetic & Logic* | *Memory* | *Shift* | |
| add | 0.1147 | 0.4882 | 0.1608 | 1.0034 |
| rsubk | 0.3461 | 1.0352 | 0.7762 | 0.7872 |
| mul | 0.1233 | 0.4819 | 0.4019 | 0.9795 |
| idiv | 0.1850 | 0.5401 | 0.4419 | 0.7602 |
| and | 0.0892 | 0.5306 | 0.4213 | 0.6977 |
| xori | 0.3257 | 0.6345 | 0.5921 | 0.6977 |
| cmp | 0.1821 | 0.7108 | 0.5727 | 1.0456 |
| nop | 0.1343 | 0.4808 | 0.1959 | 0 |
| lwi | 0.7680 | 0.3536 | 0.9858 | 0.5310 |
| swi | 0.8159 | 0.4108 | 0.9761 | 0.2208 |
| srl | 0.1628 | 0.5550 | 0.1124 | 1.0782 |
| sra | 0.1571 | 0.5836 | 0.1899 | 1.0373 |

repeatedly executing an instruction or a pair of instructions in either an infinite loop or in very long programs of the repeating instructions [1], [3], [13, 14, 15, 16]. This, however, accounts for a very special and limited execution case of the instruction, not representative of its expected executions in real applications. The inaccuracy of such models is clearly demonstrated in the Section 5.

In order to accurately characterize the base energy required by an instruction while also accounting for inter-instruction effect, we designed a reference application that executes a single basic block of approximately 100 diverse instructions operating on changing values in an infinite loop. This is done to represent a general and diverse environment in which we examine the energy characteristics of the instruction. A set of benchmarking applications is created for each instruction. In each application, an instruction is inserted between a different pair of instructions in the reference application. To ensure a minimum energy consumption, we set the operands values of this instruction to zero. Hence, we create as many applications per instruction as there are instructions in the reference application. The low level model of the processor is then used to evaluate the increase of the energy consumed as a result of the inserted instruction. Presented graphically, we plot the energy of the instruction when it was inserted after the instruction of reference application as shown on the horizontal axis as in Figure 1. We refer to each plot as the *Location-Based Energy Profiles* (LBEP) of the instruction.

We derived LBEPs for all Microblaze instructions, three of which are shown in Figure 1. We observed a strong similarity in the patterns of instructions that utilize the same processor data-path units. The energy consumed by each instruction is minimum when it is inserted after an instruction of the same type, and varies when inserted after other types of instructions. This implies that the Microblaze instruction set can be grouped based on the data-path units they utilize. These groups are: memory access, shift operation, and arithmetic and logic operations. Figure 1 illustrates the LBEP of three instructions: memory load (lwi), logical right shift (srl) and integer multiplication (muli). The X-axis represents the sequence of instructions of the reference application. The Y-axis is the increase in energy consumption due to the insertion of the instruction before the reference application instruction on the X-axis. The LBEPs for the arithmetic and logic instructions are similar to that exhibited by (muli). Similarly, the LBEPs of the shift and memory instructions are similar to those for (srl) and (lwi).

To derive the base energy cost of instructions from its LBEP, we consider only the sample points in which the instruction is inserted between instructions of the same type. Thus, we obtain three base energy costs for each instruction, one for each case where it executes following instructions of one of three groups identified. For instance, from the energy profile of the load word instruction (lwi) given in Figure 1, we first consider the energy values corresponding to the lwi instruction inserted between pairs of logic or arithmetic instructions. The average of these energy estimates is recorded as the base energy cost of the load instruction following a logic or arithmetic operation. Similarly, estimates for the base energy cost of the lwi instruction following memory and shift instructions, are also evaluated. The second group of columns in Table 1 presents the three base energy costs of Microblaze instructions when they follow an instruction from one of the three groups. This constitutes the first parameter of the OVBM.

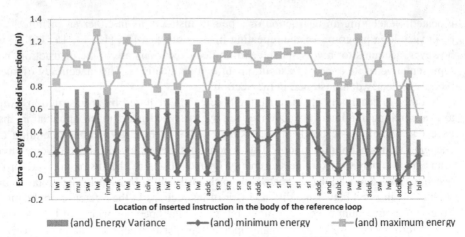

**Fig. 2.** Maximum energy variance, maximum, and minimum LBEP of an *and* instruction

## 3.2 Maximum Instruction Energy Variance

The dynamic power consumed by the soft processor cores implemented on an FPGA is dependent on the operand values of the instruction as discussed in Section 1. To incorporate the influence of operand values, we introduce a new parameter to the OVBM, called maximum instruction energy variance. It is defined as the maximum difference between the energy cost of an instruction with large operands and the instruction's base energy cost. To observe this variance, a copy of the energy benchmarks used to generate the LBEPs, described in the previous subsection, is created. The operand values of the inserted instructions are then changed to the maximum positive values of 0x7fffffff instead of zero, generating a maximum energy profile for the instruction. The two plots in Figure 2 illustrate the location-based maximum and base energy profiles of the (and) instruction. The difference between the profiles is presented as a bar graph in Figure 2.

As seen in Figure 2, the difference between the maximum energy and the base energy does not vary significantly with the location of the inserted instruction. The small variance is due to the different average one's densities of the instructions of the reference loop. The differences are averaged to obtain a single value of maximum energy variance for each instruction. The total energy consumed by an instruction $i$ is modeled using equation (1).

$$E_i = E_{base}(i,j) + k(operand\ value\ property) \cdot EV(i) \qquad (1)$$

$E_{base}(i,j)$ is the base energy of instruction $i$ following instruction $j$. $EV(i)$ is the maximum energy variance of instruction $i$, and $k$ is a factor that determines the what fraction of the maxim energy variance of instruction i given the operand values.

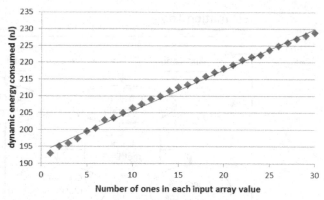

**Fig. 3.** Relation between the energy consumed running an application and the one's count of its input values

### 3.3    Energy Impact of Operand Values

As described in Section 1, the density of ones in the operand value impacts the energy consumed by soft-processors. To examine this correlation, we generated a different set of benchmarks where a fixed set of varying instructions operate on values with increasing densities. An application containing a source array of 10 elements and a loop with instructions is to load a value from the source array and perform several operations using it is first implemented. A total of 30 applications were then derived from it, in each the array values were initialized to different positive integers containing the same number of ones. The energy required to execute these application is estimated using reference estimation tools, plotted in Figure 3.

Figure 3 demonstrates a linear correlation of the energy consumption and operand densities. The lowest value, at 194.7 nJ, corresponds to the least dense operands. This value is in fact only 0.4% less than the sum of the base energies of the instructions in the benchmark (which evaluates to 195.4 nJ using values from Table 1). The additional energy consumed, beyond the base energy cost of 195 nJ, is the accumulation of energy consumed in the data-path signal result of the of instructions in the benchmark (the $k \cdot EV(i)$ term in equation (1)).The $k$ factor in equation (1) is expressed as a linear function of the one's density as given in equation (2). The one's density of the operands of instruction $i$, is denoted by $OD(i)$ with slope $m$ and y-intercept $b$.

$$k = m \cdot \big(OD(i)\big) + b \qquad (2)$$

By substituting k using equation (2) into equation (1) we can express the estimated energy of a basic block of $N$ instruction using equation (3) as the sum of the estimated energy consumed for each instruction making the basic block.

$$E_{est} = \sum_{i=1}^{N} E(i) = \sum_{i=1}^{N} E_{base}(i, i-1) + \sum_{i=1}^{N}(m \cdot OD(i) + b) \cdot \Delta E(i) \qquad (3)$$

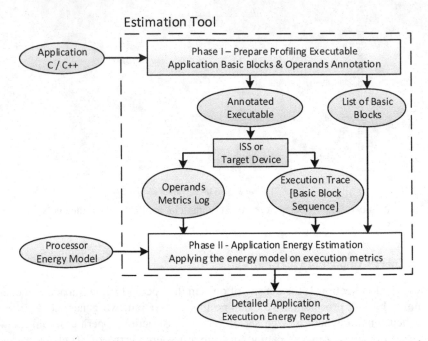

**Fig. 4.** Proposed automated application analysis, annotation, and energy estimation tool

In order to derive the values for $m$ and $b$ for a given processor, we equated the linear approximation equation in (3) to the reference energy estimation for each of the 30 applications, generating a system of 30 linear equations. Substituting in the known values from the OVBM in Table 1, we are able to calculate the sum of base energies and energy variance for the fixed instructions in all 30 applications. The average one's densities of each instruction are found using the profiling stage of the estimation tool described Section 4 instead of the one's density of the input array. This results with an over-determined system of 30 equations and two unknowns, m and b. An approximate solution at m = 0.016 and b = -0.061 for the Microblaze processor is determined once and added to the model parameters.

## 4      Energy Estimation and Annotation

We have developed a tool to automatically apply the proposed model to an embedded application. The tool works in two phases as shown in Figure 4.

In the first phase, the tool annotates the source code with instructions aimed to identify the instructions that will execute, and run-time operand value metrics (one's density). It also identifies the basic-blocks of the application. After executing the annotated application, the logged profiling data is sent to the host PC for processing in the second phase. These annotations:

1. Record the execution sequence of the basic blocks,
2. Record the opcode of each instruction executed, as well as the values of their destination registers,
3. Calculate the average of the one's densities of all values used by each non-repeating shift instruction, and
4. The tool also generates a list of the basic blocks and the instructions in each basic block. Using an object-dump utility [17] the exact machine instructions of each basic block are identified

The second phase of the estimation tool uses the processor energy model, parameters obtained from the execution of the annotated application, and list of basic blocks, to estimate the energy consumed by each executed instruction using equation (3) described in Section 3. The estimated energy consumed by each basic block is then be evaluated as the sum of the estimated energy of all its instructions. The total energy consumption is then found using the estimated energy of the basic blocks and the execution trace.

**Table 2.** Baseline energy estimates using XPA [5]

| Application | Time  (µs) | Power (mW) | Energy (mJ) |
|---|---|---|---|
| Dhrystone | 39.35 | 33.35 | 1.31 |
| Quicksort | 164.20 | 33.78 | 5.55 |
| ReadBMPBlock | 251.61 | 39.96 | 10.05 |
| DCT | 166.68 | 30.84 | 5.14 |
| Quantize | 58.20 | 25.52 | 1.49 |
| Zigzag | 25.33 | 30.98 | 0.78 |
| Huffman Encode | 471.95 | 40.70 | 19.21 |
| JPEG | 973.77 | 37.66 | 36.67 |

## 5    Experimental Results

To evaluate the proposed estimation method, we developed an OVBM of the Microblaze soft processor implementation on a Virtex5 FPGA as described in Section 3. The processor was implemented without cache, connected via a Local Memory Bus (LMB) to 64 kB block RAM, which stores the program and data of the application. The system clock is operating as a frequency of 125 MHz. To compare OVBM to the state of the art, we also developed three different energy models using the techniques surveyed in Section 2. We implemented the estimation tool described in Section 4 to automatically annotate and analyze applications targeted for a Microblaze processor. The automatic annotation tool was expanded to accept all generated energy models.

### 5.1    Estimation Accuracy

We examine the accuracy of the models using a set of 8 application benchmarks listed in Table 2 re used. The execution time and average dynamic power consumed by the processor for each benchmark were obtained using Xilinx XPA [5] and used to calculate the energy consumed by each benchmark. These estimations are highly accurate and can be used as baseline to compare the accuracy of all models. The benchmarks are Dhrystone, an implementation of the Quicksort algorithm, and five functions of a JPEG [19] encoder: Read BMP Block, *Discrete Cosine Transfer* (DCT), Quantize, Zigzag, and Huffman encode.

**Table 3.** Estimated energy in Millijoule (mJ) and estimation error, relative to references in Table 2, comparing the accuracy of proposed model to $1^{st}$, $2^{nd}$, and $3^{rd}$ order energy models generated using previous work methods.

| Application | $1^{st}$ Order | | $2^{nd}$ Order | | | | $3^{rd}$ Order | | | | OVBM | |
|---|---|---|---|---|---|---|---|---|---|---|---|---|
| | E | Err | E | Err | E* | Err | E | Err | E* | Err | E | Err |
| Dhrystone | 1.31 | 0.0% | 3.6 | 171% | 1.31 | 0.0% | 3.3 | 155% | 1.31 | 0.0% | 1.30 | -0.7% |
| Quicksort | 5.48 | -1.3% | 16 | 185% | 5.07 | -8.7% | 13 | 128% | 4.95 | -10.7% | 5.37 | -3.2% |
| ReadBMPBloc | 8.39 | -16% | 25 | 145% | 7.90 | -21% | 22 | 116% | 8.50 | -15% | 8.82 | -12.3% |
| DCT | 5.56 | 8.2% | 18 | 253% | 5.82 | 13.2% | 18 | 253% | 7.12 | 38.5% | 4.96 | -3.5% |
| Quantize | 1.94 | 30% | 6.4 | 329% | 2.04 | 38% | 4.0 | 169% | 1.57 | 5.4% | 1.47 | -0.9% |
| Zigzag | 0.84 | 7.7% | 2.3 | 195% | 0.74 | -5.3% | 2.3 | 194% | 0.90 | 15.3% | 0.78 | -0.6% |
| Huffman Enc. | 15.74 | -18% | 51 | 164% | 16.26 | -15% | 48 | 148% | 18.68 | -2.7% | 17.64 | -8.2% |
| JPEG | 32.48 | -11.4% | 102 | 179% | 32.76 | -11% | 94 | 156% | 36.77 | 0.3% | 33.67 | -8.2% |
| Average error | | 13.4% | | 203% | | 16% | | 165% | | 12.6% | | 4.7% |
| Std. Deviation of error | | 9.5% | | 60% | | 11% | | 43% | | 12.8% | | 4.3% |

Table 3 presents the dynamic energy estimations obtained using the four models for the examined benchmarks. The first order model uses the average dynamic power consumed by Microblaze executing the Dhrystone benchmark as the average power parameter. The estimated energy consumed by the remaining benchmarks are the products of the execution times by the average power. Naturally, the error in estimating the Dhrystone benchmark using this method is zero. The error in estimating the other benchmarks ranges between -18% and 30.7%, when compared to the reference values in Table 2. It is important to note that the accuracy of the first order model depends on the choice of the average power paramter used. In this instance, using the average power of Dhrystone resulted in reasonable estimates for benchmarks like quicksort and ReadBMPBlock, however, as it's tested with more applications, the unpredictablitiy of this method becomes apparent.

The second and third order models, initially, produced large errors. The energy for an instruction in the second order model is obtained using low level simulations of the given instruction in a loop as done in [3], [13, 14, 15, 16]. Similarly, the energy for a pair of instructions in the third order model is obtained using low level simulation of the instruction pair in a loop. Clearly, this technique does not produce accurate estimates of the energy cost of an instruction. As suggested in [3], the models are calibrated using the Dhrystone estimation error. However, despite calibration, the second and third order models generated worst case errors of up to 37.6%, and 38.5% respectively. The average errors were also high at 16% and 12.6%. Furthermore, the high deviation of estimate errors further demonstrates that these models cannot be used with confidence.

The energy estimates generated using our approach are given in the final column, titled OVBM. It outperforms other models, both in terms of average accuracy and estimation confidence. The worst case error obtained is -12.3%, with an average error of only 4.7%. Therefore, dynamic energy estimates obtained using the proposed approach can be used with confidence for early design space exploration as well as system and software reconfiguration and optimization efforts.

**Table 4.** Execution time of PVBM-based estimation tool compared to Post-place-and-route simulation (XPA)

| Application | OVBM Tool (Seconds) | | | XPA (Minutes) |
|---|---|---|---|---|
| | Phase 1 + 2 (Host) | Execution (Target) | Total | |
| Dhrystone | 0.03 | 7.49 | 7.53 | 72 |
| Quicksort | 0.01 | 23.08 | 23.09 | 147 |
| ReadBMPBlock | 0.21 | 5.88 | 6.08 | 202 |
| DCT | 0.03 | 10.85 | 10.88 | 148 |
| Quantize | 0.01 | 8.40 | 8.41 | 85 |
| Zigzag | 0.01 | 4.41 | 4.42 | 65 |
| Huffman Encode | 0.07 | 65.04 | 65.11 | 340 |
| JPEG | 0.28 | 104.24 | 104.52 | 638 |

### 5.2    Estimation Speed

In addition to having a higher average accuracy and confidence over other instruction-level models, the proposed estimation technique generates energy estimates within seconds. Table 4 compares the time required by our tool to XPA [5] to derive the presented estimations. The simulation host was utilized a Nehalem based Intel i7 quad-core processor and 16 GB of DDR3 RAM. The time presented includes the time required to execute both estimation phases presented in Section 4 and the execution time of the annotated application. In our experiments, we used a Microblaze implementation on a Xilinx Virtex5 FPGA development board to run the annotated executable. The total time required to complete the two phases running on the host for the JPEG benchmark was under one second. The time needed to run the annotated executable and transfer the logs to the host was under two minutes. As such, the total estimation time this benchmark was under two minutes. In contrast, it took over 10 hours to obtain the baseline estimate using XPA. As such, our model demonstrates 3 orders of magnitude speedup over post-place-and-route models.

## 6    Conclusion

We presented a novel dynamic energy modeling technique for soft processors in FPGA based on the operand values of instructions. We showed that energy estimates obtained from our model are significantly more accurate than the state of the art energy models. The energy model can be used for early software optimization, system architecture reconfiguration and customization as well as design space exploration. In the future, we expect to validate our model with more applications and other embedded processors.

# References

1. Bazzaz, M., Salehi, M., Ejlali, A.: An accurate instruction-level energy estimation model and tool for embedded systems. IEEE Trans. On Instrumentation and Measurement **62**(7) (2013)
2. Xilinx Inc, Power Methodology Guide UG786 (2011). http://www.xilinx.com/support/documentation/sw_manuals/xilinx13_1/ug786_PowerMethodology.pdf
3. Sinha, A., Chandrakasan, A.P.: JouleTrack-a web based tool for software energy profiling. In: Proceedings, Design Automation Conference pp. 220–225 (2001)
4. Krishnaswamy, A., Gupta, R.: Dynamic coalescing for 16-bit instructions. ACM TECS **2005**, 3–37 (2005)
5. Xilinx Inc, XPower Analyzer (2011). http://www.xilinx.com/products/design_tools/logic_design/verification/xpower.htm
6. Synopsys Inc. Power Compiler (2012). http://www.synopsys.com/Tools/Implementation/RTLSynthesis/Pages/PowerCompiler.aspx
7. Weicker, R.P.: Dhrystone: a synthetic systems programming benchmark. Comm. of the ACM **27**, 1013–1030 (1984)
8. Xilinx Inc.: LogiCORE IP, MicroBlaze micro controller system. http://www.xilinx.com/tools/microblaze.htm
9. Gurumurthi, S., Sivasubramaniam, A., Irwin, M.J., Vijaykrishnan, N., Kandemir, M.: Using complete machine simulation for software power estimation: The SoftWatt approach. HPCA, pp. 141–150 (2002)
10. Brooks, D., Tiwari, V., Martonosi, M.: Wattch: A framework for architectural-level power analysis and optimizations. ISCA, pp. 83–94 (2000)
11. Ahmadinia, A., Ahmad, B., Arslan, T.: A state based framework for efficient system-level power estimation of costum reconfigurable cores. In: Proceedings, SOC Conf., pp. 1–4 (2008)
12. Chen, J., Thiele, L.: Task partitioning and platform synthesis for energy efficiency. In: Proceedings. RTCSA, pp. 393–402 (2009)
13. Brandolese, C., et al.: Software energy estimation based on statistical characterization of intermediate compilation code. Symposium. Low Power Electronics and Design (ISLPED), pp. 333–338 (2011)
14. Tiwari, V., Tien-Chien Lee, M.: Power analysis of a 32-bit embedded microcontroller. ASPDAC, pp. 141–148 (1995)
15. Tien-Chien Lee, M., Tiwari, V., Malik, S., Fujita, M.: Power analysis and minimization techniques for embedded DSP software. IEEE VLSI, (5), pp. 123–135 (1997)
16. Roy, S., Bhatia, R., Mathur, A.: An accurate energy estimation framework for VLIW processor cores. In: Proceedings. ICCD, pp. 464–469 (2006)
17. Kim, J., Kang, K., Shim, H., et al.: Fast estimation of software energy consumption using IPI(inter-prefetch interval) energy model. In: VLSI-SoC, pp. 224–229 (2007)
18. Sailer, P.M., Philip, M., Kaeli, R.: The DLX Instruction Set Architecture Handbook (1st ed.). Morgan Kaufmann Publishers Inc., CA, USA (1996)
19. Wallace, G.K.: The JPEG still picture compression standard. IEEE Trans. On Consumer Electronics **38**, xviii–xxxiv (1992)

# Systems and Applications I

# Preemptive Hardware Multitasking in ReconOS

Markus Happe$^{(\boxtimes)}$, Andreas Traber, and Ariane Keller

Communication Systems Group, ETH Zurich, Zürich, Switzerland
{markus.happe,ariane.keller}@tik.ee.ethz.ch, atraber@student.ethz.ch

**Abstract.** Preemptive hardware multitasking is not supported in most reconfigurable systems-on-chip (rSoCs), which severely limits the scope of hardware scheduling techniques on these platforms. While modern field-programmable gate arrays (FPGAs) support dynamic partial reconfiguration of any region at any time, most hardware tasks cannot be preempted at arbitrary points in time, because context saving and restoring is not supported out of the box by the vendors. Although hardware task preemption techniques have been proposed in the past, they cannot be found in today's rSoCs. In this paper we therefore propose a novel methodology for preemptive hardware multitasking that does not require any changes at the task level and show that our approach can be seamlessly integrated to an established execution environment for rSoCs, called ReconOS. Our experimental results show that we can successfully capture and restore the states of all flip-flops and block RAMs in a reconfigurable region on a Xilinx Virtex-6 FPGA at arbitrary points in time. Context capturing/restoring can be performed at a bandwidth of 22-28 MB/s, which allows for context switches in the order of milliseconds.

**Keywords:** Preemptive hardware multitasking · Context save and restore · Partial reconfiguration · Reconfigurable system-on-chip · ICAP

## 1 Introduction

Dynamic partial reconfiguration (DPR) is one of the most exciting features of modern field-programmable gate arrays (FPGAs). DPR allows to reconfigure partial regions of the FPGA fabric without affecting the rest of the system. Reconfigurable systems-on-chip (rSoCs) combine processor(s) with multiple reconfigurable hardware regions (slots) on a single chip and use DPR to dynamically switch between multiple hardware tasks in a slot. For instance, rSoCs can dynamically map the most used tasks to hardware according to the current workload to increase the system performance. However, hardware tasks can not be preempted in most rSoCs and either have to run to completion or need to be terminated during execution, before they can be replaced by other hardware tasks. This severely limits the scope for hardware multitasking, where multiple hardware tasks share the same reconfigurable slots over time.

In contrast to this, software systems support preemptive multitasking where multiple software tasks share a single processing unit. A scheduler selects the next

© Springer International Publishing Switzerland 2015
K. Sano et al. (Eds.): ARC 2015, LNCS 9040, pp. 79–90, 2015.
DOI: 10.1007/978-3-319-16214-0_7

software tasks which should be executed on the processor by following a given scheduling algorithm. Using preemptive multitasking, a scheduler can preempt and resume all tasks at arbitrary points in time and therefore ensure fairness amongst competing software tasks, minimize starvation and improve the responsiveness of the tasks by applying smart scheduling algorithms. Unfortunately, we do not see similar benefits for most reconfigurable hardware systems to fully exploit the DPR feature on today's FPGAs, preemptive hardware multitasking should be supported in rSoCs. One major challenge of preemptive hardware multitasking is the saving/restoring of the task's context. Unlike software tasks that have a well-defined context, the context of a hardware task is stored in a large number of state-holding elements, such as flip-flops, DSP blocks, LUT-RAMs and block RAMs, which complicates context switching.

Several research projects have developed preemptive hardware multitasking techniques, which either follow a (i) `task-specific` or a (ii) `bitstream read-back` preemption technique. The task-specific techniques add dedicated hardware structures to the hardware tasks, e.g. scan-chains [2,5], such that the context of a task can be extracted/inserted. However, task-specific methods generate a considerable overhead in hardware resources and require modifications of the tasks at source code or netlist level. It would be highly preferable, if the hardware tasks do not need to be modified at all (similar to software tasks).

The second class of preemptive hardware multitasking techniques reads-back the current configuration of the slot area over the internal configuration access port (ICAP). Related work has shown that preemptive hardware multitasking is possible using bitstream read-back for Virtex-e [4], Virtex-4 [3] and Virtex-5 [8] FPGAs. Unfortunately, the bitstream read-back methods have to be tailored to the FPGA families, since the FPGA architectures and bitstream format change from one FPGA family to the next. Most proposed methods require modifications at the task-level, which complicates their integration to existing rSoCs.

Although preemptive hardware multitasking seems to be highly beneficial, no advanced execution environment for rSoCs seems to support any of these techniques. Therefore, we show in this paper that our novel preemptive hardware multitasking technique can be integrated into a multithreaded execution environment called ReconOS. To the best of our knowledge, this is the first paper that investigates hardware task preemption on Virtex-6 FPGAs using bitstream read-back over the ICAP interface.

This paper provides the following contributions:

1. We give detailed instructions how to capture and restore flip-flops and block RAMs on Virtex-6 FPGAs, revealing many information that cannot be found in the official Xilinx documentation. Our novel preemptive hardware multitasking technique does not require any changes at task level.
2. We extended the ReconOS execution environment for rSoC architectures to support our preemptive hardware multitasking technique. For this purpose, we implemented a new hardware ICAP controller that supports all required functionality for capturing/restoring a task's context.

3. Finally, we show in our experimental evaluation on a ReconOS system that we can efficiently restore the contexts of four different hardware threads on a Virtex-6 FPGA at arbitrary points in time.

The paper is structured as follows: Section 2 discusses related work and Section 3 presents our preemptive hardware multitasking methodology. In Section 4 we show how the presented multitasking methodology can be embedded to the ReconOS execution environment. Finally, Section 5 presents our experimental results and Section 6 concludes the paper.

## 2    Related Work

Several context save and restore approaches have been studied in the past 15 years. Simmler et. al. [9] first proposed a technique for transparent context saving and restoring by bitstream read-back and manipulation. By refining these concepts, Kalte and Porrmann [4] implemented an architecture for relocatable hardware tasks which allows the extraction of state values from an FPGA's storage elements and their injection into partial bitstreams for reconfiguration in a different location on the device. Their approach is transparent to the hardware module's designer, but was tailored to outdated Xilinx Virtex-e FPGAs.

More recent related work has demonstrated that context saving and restoring can also be performed on newer Xilinx FPGAs, such as Virtex-4/5 FPGAs, by reading back the configuration data over the ICAP interface. For instance, Jozwik et al. [3] have used a Virtex-4 FPGA to capture and restore the context of hardware tasks. However, in contrast to our approach they needed additional combinational logic inside the reconfigurable regions to be able to restore the task's context. Morales-Villanueva and Gordon-Ross [8] have presented a technique to capture and restore the context of hardware tasks over the ICAP interface on Virtex-5 FPGAs. They have also demonstrated that it is possible to relocate hardware tasks between reconfigurable regions. Our work fits well to the approaches that read-back all registers of a reconfigurable region over the ICAP interface [3,8]. Unlike related work, we focus on newer Virtex-6 FPGAs and additionally capture and restore the state of block RAMs.

As an alternative approach, Jovanovic et. al. [2] as well as Koch et al. [5] proposed linking registers together in a serial scan-chain that can be used to read or write a hardware module's context in a transparent manner. Compared to the previous preemption techniques, the time overhead for a task preemption is reduced at the cost of additional hardware. Although the scan-chain approach can be applied to all FPGA families, it requires modifications of the hardware modules. In contrast to this approach, we can preempt hardware tasks without any modification at the source code or netlist level.

Lübbers and Platzner [7] extended the multithreaded programming model provided by ReconOS to support cooperative scheduling techniques. In cooperative multitasking a hardware thread informs the operating system whether it can be preempted. At thread preemption the thread saves its context to a shared memory that can be accessed by the operating system. This approach can significantly reduce the thread context and allows for thread migrations to other reconfigurable regions. However, in contrast to our approach cooperative multitasking requires deep modifications of the hardware threads at source code level and does not allow for thread preemptions at arbitrary points in time.

## 3   Methodology: How To Preempt Hardware Tasks

This section introduces our novel methodology for hardware task preemption on Xilinx FPGAs at arbitrary points in time. We assume that the vendor design tools are used to generate an rSoC, which contains at least one reconfigurable region. The Xilinx design tools for partial reconfiguration [10] generate (i) a full bitstream that contains the configuration of the entire FPGA fabric and (ii) multiple partial bitstreams that contain task-specific configurations of the reconfigurable regions (slots). At system start, the full bitstream has to be downloaded to the FPGA configuration memory, which contains the entire rSoC configuration. At run-time, the rSoC can dynamically replace a hardware task in a reconfigurable slot by downloading the partial bitstream of the next hardware task over the ICAP interface. We assume that the partial bitstreams are stored in external memory, e.g. a compact flash card. It is important to note that the RESET_AFTER_RECONFIG attribute has to be set for all reconfigurable regions in the user constraint file (UCF), when the vendor tools are executed. Otherwise the state of the FPGA resources can not be restored for these regions.

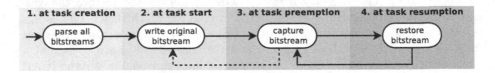

**Fig. 1.** Preemptive hardware multitasking approach for a reconfigurable region

The Xilinx approach for partial reconfiguration does not support saving and restoring a task's context out of the box. Therefore, we propose a novel methodology for Xilinx FPGAs which captures/restores the context of a partial region to allow for preemptive hardware multitasking. Our methodology does not require any modification of the hardware tasks, but we assume that each task has a clock and a reset signal. Our preemption methodology relies on the capabilities of the ICAP interface and the bitstream format of the FPGA family. Currently, we only support the Xilinx Virtex-6 family. Figure 1 shows the main stages of our multitasking approach for one reconfigurable region. The four stages of our methodology are described in the following subsections.

### 3.1   At Task Creation: Parse All Partial Bitstreams

In an initial stage, we parse all partial bitstream of a reconfigurable region to identify certain configuration metadata. The partial bitstreams of a Xilinx

Virtex-6 contains three different kinds of configuration frame blocks: (i) configurable logic blocks (CLBs), input/output blocks, clocks, (ii) BRAM contents and (iii) a CFG_CLB block. The CFG_CLB block defines which part of the FPGA needs to be reset or reconfigured. It only appears in a partial bitstream, if the RESET_AFTER_RECONFIG attribute has been set for this region [10,11]. Figure 2 shows an abstract overview of a partial bitstream with three frame blocks.

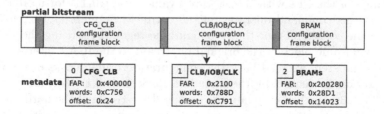

**Fig. 2.** Parsing metadata of a partial bitstream

We store the frame address register (FAR), the number of 32-bit words and the offset inside the partial bitstream of each frame block as metadata. This metadata is required when we want to capture the context of a hardware task. Furthermore, the rSoC creates a working copy of each original bitstream at run-time, called 'captured bitstream'. This working copy is stored in main memory. It gets updated, whenever the corresponding task is preempted, to store the captured context. It can be deleted, when the task terminates. Similar to Liu et al. [6], we replace the cyclic redundancy check (CRC) at the end of the captured bitstream with a 'no operation' command, thus we do not need to update the CRC value at task preemption. Note that this might cause reliability issues.

### 3.2 At Task Start: Write Original Bitstream

In the second stage, we configure a hardware task for a first time. Hence, no context needs to be restored. Therefore, we only need to write the original partial bitstream that has been generated by the Xilinx bitgen tool to the ICAP interface. Details on how to write (partial) bitstreams to the ICAP interface can be found in the corresponding user guide [11].

We set the reset signal of the hardware task during the reconfiguration process. This reset signal should also be connected to the static interfaces that connect the hardware task to the rest of the system. If the static interfaces to the reconfigurable region are active during reconfiguration, it might happen that data is sent accidentally from the partial region to the interfaces.

### 3.3 At Task Preemption: Capture Bitstream

In the third stage, a hardware thread is preempted and we need to store the contents of its state-holding elements, such as flip-flops (FFs) and block RAMs

(BRAMs). We deactivate the clock of the hardware task during the capturing process to freeze the task execution.

In a first step, we capture the current state of all flip-flops in hidden registers in the configuration memory (INIT0/INIT1) by calling the GCAPTURE command over the ICAP interface. The hidden registers INIT0/INIT1 contain the initial states of all FFs and are used during the initial configuration of the FPGA. The GCAPTURE command must be sent over ICAP to the device, which replaces the initial values of the FFs with the captured values, see [10, 11] for more details. Per default this command operates on the entire FPGA fabric. Therefore, we need to define constraints for the reconfigurable region by writing the CFG_CLB configuration frame block of the original bitstream to the ICAP interface.

In a second step, we read back the configuration frame blocks of the reconfigurable region as defined by the metadata in Section 3.1 (with an exception for the CFG_CLB block). We update the captured bitstream of the hardware task by overwriting the configuration frames with the captured configuration frames. Instructions for reading back configuration frame blocks can be found in [11].

In a final step, we need to modify certain configuration bits in order to restore the BRAM contents at a later point. We believe that these bits define for each BRAM whether its memory contents should be restored. We have found out that these bits follow a certain pattern by investigating the bitstreams for different reconfigurable regions. Hence, this step can be automated. According to our observations, we have to modify a single bit of specific 32-bit words in the configuration frame blocks for BRAMs by following this equation:

$$w'_i(j) = \begin{cases} 0, & \text{if } \exists k \in \mathbb{N}_0 : i = \frac{81k+36}{8} \wedge j = 17 \\ w_i(j), & \text{otherwise} \end{cases}$$

where $w_i(j)$ is the $j$-th bit of the $i$-th configuration word (31 downto 0).

### 3.4   At Task Resumption: Restore Bitstream

In the final stage, we write a captured bitstream back to the reconfigurable region to restore the previously preempted hardware task. After this reconfiguration we need to trigger the global set/reset port of the STARTUP_VIRTEX6 primitive. Otherwise, the states of the FFs and BRAMs will not be restored. The partial bitstreams contain a GRESTORE command, which is probably supposed to call this startup primitive. However, similar to [8] we have observed in our experiments that the GRESTORE command did not restore the states of the FFs and BRAMs. Therefore, we manually trigger the startup method over the global set/reset (GSR) port over the STARTUP_VIRTEX6 interface after writing back the captured bitstream. Furthermore, we set the reset signal of the hardware task in order to prevent unexpected behavior of the hardware task during reconfiguration of the reconfigurable region. We unset the reset signal before we trigger the GSR event. Similar to the capturing stage, we disable the clock in this stage.

# 4   ReconOS Architecture For Hardware Multitasking

We have integrated our multitasking methodology to the operating system ReconOS. Although ReconOS supports the dynamic reconfiguration of hardware modules (hardware threads) out of the box, there was no support for preemptive hardware multitasking. In this section we describe the ReconOS architecture and introduce our new ReconOS ICAP hardware controller and software scheduler, which can preempt and resume hardware tasks in reconfigurable regions at arbitrary points in time.

## 4.1   ReconOS Multithreading Approach and Architecture

The operating system ReconOS [1] extends the multithreaded programming model to the domain of reconfigurable hardware. Instead of regarding hardware modules as passive coprocessors to the system CPU, they are treated as independent hardware threads on an equal footing with software threads running on the system. ReconOS allows hardware threads to use the same operating system (OS) services for communication and synchronization as software threads, providing a transparent programming model across the hardware/software boundary. The hardware threads are represented by delegate threads in software, which call the operating system services on behalf of the hardware threads.

ReconOS has been implemented as an extension to (embedded) operating system kernels, such as Linux or Xilkernel. ReconOS is targeted at platform FPGAs integrating microprocessors and reconfigurable logic. It takes advantage of the dynamic partial reconfiguration capabilities of Xilinx FPGAs to reconfigure hardware threads during run-time. This allows multiple hardware threads to transparently share the reconfigurable resources.

Figure 3 shows the hardware architecture of a ReconOS system that supports preemptive hardware multitasking. The architecture contains a single reconfigurable hardware region (reconfigurable slot), which can hold one hardware thread at a time. A dedicated hardware OS interface (OSIF) handles the hardware threads OS requests and forwards them to the operating system kernel running on the CPU. It also manages the low-level synchronization. Each hardware thread is connected to the memory subsystem over a memory interface (MEMIF), such that each thread can autonomously access the main memory.

In Figure 3 the hardware thread A is configured to the reconfigurable slot. However, a software scheduler can replace the currently running hardware thread with another thread (B, C, or D). The original and captured partial bitstreams of all available hardware threads (A–D) are stored in the main memory. The captured bitstreams include the captured states of the FFs and the BRAMs.

In ReconOS a hardware thread is connected to its delegate thread and to the memory subsystem over FIFO-based interfaces. The threads should not be preempted while the thread sends/receives data to/from the FIFO interfaces, since this data is currently not captured (and restored). Hence, the scheduler should wait until all FIFO interfaces of a thread are empty, before it preempts the thread. We assume that our hardware threads are computing for the majority

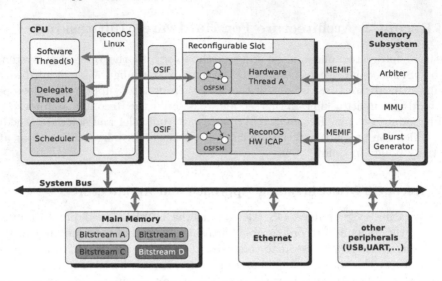

**Fig. 3.** ReconOS architecture with one hardware slot and four hardware threads (A–D)

of the time and only access the OSIF/MEMIF interface once in while. Hence, we believe that this restriction of the interruptibility can be neglected in practice.

## 4.2   ReconOS ICAP Controller

We have implemented a new hardware ICAP controller and a software scheduler, which support preemptive hardware multitasking in ReconOS. The scheduler is a Linux user-space task that controls all stages of our multitasking methodology and performs the required modifications of the captured bitstreams. The ReconOS HW ICAP controller was implemented as a ReconOS hardware thread, such that the controller has a separate interface to the main memory. Therefore, the software scheduler only needs to send read/write commands and main memory addresses to the ReconOS HW ICAP thread to read-back or write partial bitstreams. The scheduler can also set the reset signals and enable/disable the clock signals for all reconfigurable hardware slots. Furthermore, the scheduler can trigger the global set/reset port of the STARTUP_VIRTEX6 interface, which is instantiated in the ReconOS HW ICAP thread.

Figure 4 shows the block diagram of the ReconOS HW ICAP controller. The ICAP interface is connected to a local dual-port memory which is controlled by a separate finite state machine (ICAP_FSM) that manages the transfer of the bitstream between the local memory and the ICAP interface. This local memory can be accessed by a second finite state machine (Reconos_FSM) that manages the communication with the operating system and the main memory. The local memory is not large enough to hold a complete bitstream. Thus, the ICAP controller splits the bitstreams into chunks. We use double-buffering for writing original/captured bitstreams and single-buffering for reading back the configuration frame blocks of a slot.

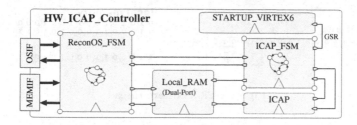

**Fig. 4.** ReconOS HW ICAP controller

## 5   Experimental Results

In this chapter we present experimental results for our preemptive hardware multitasking approach on Virtex-6 FPGAs. We have performed all measurements on a Xilinx Virtex-6 ML605 evaluation board (XC6VLX240T FPGA).

In our experiments, we have used a ReconOS design with a single reconfigurable slot as depicted in Figure 3. The processor, all hardware modules and hardware threads were clocked at 100 MHz. We have tested four reconfigurable hardware threads: ADD, SUB, MUL, and LFSR, which are described below:

1. The ADD thread contains three 32-bit registers $R_{1-3}$. The thread continuously computes $R_3 = R_1 + R_2$. The registers can be accessed by a software application over the OSIF interface.
2. The SUB thread is similar to the ADD thread, but computes $R_3 = R_1 - R_2$.
3. The MUL thread computes the product of $R_1$ and $R_2$ in $R_1$ steps. The (intermediate) result is stored in $R_3$. The result $R_3$ is computed as the addition of $R_2$ with itself $R_1$ times, i.e. $R_3 = \sum_{i=1}^{R_1} R_2$. In each step, $R_1$ is decremented by one and $R_3$ is updated to the current intermediate result. Hence, we can preempt the thread during computation and validate if the register values have been correctly captured/restored. This thread is used to validate the cycle-true state restoration of flip-flops.
4. The LFSR thread stores the values of several linear feedback shift registers (LFSRs) in a local memory of 8KB and continuously shifts their register values. The thread only implements a single 16-bit linear feedback shift register, which processes all LFSRs sequentially. For this purpose, the hardware thread loads the value of one LFSR at a time from the local memory, shifts its 16-bit register for one bit and stores the register value back to the local memory; and then continues with the next LFSR. Figure 5 shows the overview of the LFSR thread.
   The initial values for the LFSRs are copied from the main memory to the local BRAMs over the MEMIF interface. The LFSR thread is used to validate the cycle-true state restoration of flip-flops and BRAMs. In our experiments, we have stored four LFSRs in the local memory.

The ADD, SUB, and MUL threads also contain an 8KB local memory each, which can be accessed from software over the MEMIF interface in order to test, if the

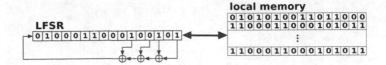

**Fig. 5.** LFSR hardware thread

BRAM entries have been captured and restored correctly. However, these threads do not alter their local memories internally during computation. Hence, we can not validate a cycle-true state restoration of the BRAMs for these threads.

In extensive experiments, we validated that all hardware threads could be successfully preempted and restored at arbitrary points in time. For the MUL and LFSR thread, we could validate that the state restoration was cycle-true for both FFs and BRAMs. Table 1 shows the results of our performance measurements for two bitstream sizes. We have randomly selected two regions on the FPGA fabric, where the first region covers about 2% of the FPGA area (bitstream size: 361 KB) and the second region covers about 4% of the FPGA area (bitstream size: 741 KB). It can be seen that context capturing takes longer than context restoring and that the execution times depend linearly on the bitstream size.

**Table 1.** Context capture/restore performance

| bitstream size | $t_{capture}$ | $t_{restore}$ | $t_{total}$ | bandwidth | max swaps/s |
|---|---|---|---|---|---|
| 741 KB | 16.0 ms | 9.7 ms | 25.7 ms | 28 MB/s | 38 |
| 361 KB | 10.3 ms | 5.5 ms | 15.8 ms | 22 MB/s | 63 |

The capture time $t_{capture}$ of a partial bitstream depends on the number and size of reconfiguration frames and the overhead to trigger the readback requests over the ICAP interface. For performance reasons, successive reconfiguration frames can be combined to a single readback request, which lowers the overhead caused by the ICAP interface. For both cases, the partial bitstreams can be read back with two readback requests only, one for the CLB configurations and one for the BRAM configurations. Since the performance overhead for the two readback operations is the same for both bitstream sizes, the relative bandwidth is higher for the larger bitstream size in Table 1. However, the maximum number of task swaps per second is lower for the larger bitstream.

Scheduling algorithms for reconfigurable hardware threads are not in the scope of this paper. However, we have performed an example measurement over time for a manually-defined schedule that uses all four hardware threads, which is shown in Figure 6. In this example, all four threads are scheduled periodically in the following sequence: ADD→SUB→LFSR→SUB→ADD→MUL). The individual time slices have been predefined manually (not by a scheduling algorithm) and we assume that the threads are independent from each other. We can see that it is possible to swap several times between the hardware threads in the interval of

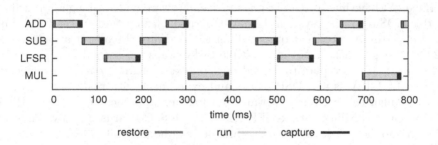

**Fig. 6.** Preemptive multitasking with four hardware threads

**Table 2.** Resource consumption

| component | #FFs | #LUTs | #BRAMs |
|---|---|---|---|
| HW slot | 5616 | 2808 | 7 |
| ADD/SUB | 375 | 603 | 2 |
| MUL | 474 | 751 | 2 |
| LFSR | 474 | 810 | 2 |
| ReconOS HW ICAP | 323 | 741 | 2 |
| XPS_HWICAP | 750 | 804 | 1 |

a single second. The partial bitstream size was 361 KB in this example, which corresponds to about 2% of the FPGA area.

Table 2 lists the resource consumption for the partial reconfigurable slot, for our reconfigurable hardware threads and for the ReconOS HW ICAP controller. It can be seen that our hardware threads only use a fraction of the actual slot area. However, we always capture and restore all flip-flops and BRAMs of the partial region. Hence, the capture and restore times for this slot are always the same. This means that we could implement more complex threads than the ADD,SUB,MUL,LFSR thread for this slot without increasing the capture/restore times. The ReconOS HW ICAP controller represents the entire hardware overhead of our multitasking approach, since we do not introduce any extra logic to the hardware threads in contrast to most related work. However the resource consumption of our HW ICAP controller is comparable to the resource consumption of the Xilinx XPS_HWICAP controller. Hence, we conclude that the area overhead of our approach is negligible.

## 6   Conclusion and Future Work

In this paper, we have shown a novel methodology that allows for preemptive hardware multitasking on Xilinx Virtex-6 FPGAs without requiring modifications at the task level. Our approach reads back the contents of all FFs and block RAMs of a predefined reconfigurable region on an FPGA fabric over the ICAP interface. We have integrated our preemptive hardware multitasking approach to the ReconOS operating system. In our experiments, we could successfully capture and restore the context of four different hardware threads at a bandwidth of 22-28 MB/s, which allows for multiple tasks swaps per second.

In future work we plan to extend our context capturing / restoring mechanisms to LUT-RAMs and DSP blocks and experiment with real-world applications. We plan to port our hardware multitasking approach to further FPGA families, such as Xilinx Virtex-7 FPGAs or Zynq SoC boards. Finally, we want to investigate how task relocation techniques can be integrated to ReconOS.

# References

1. Agne, A., Happe, M., Keller, A., Lübbers, E., Plattner, B., Platzner, M., Plessl, C.: ReconOS - An Operating System Approach for Reconfigurable Computing. IEEE Micro **34**(1), 60–71 (2014)
2. Jovanovic, S., Tanougast, C., Weber, S.: A hardware preemptive multitasking mechanism based on scan-path register structure for FPGA-based reconfigurable systems. In: NASA/ESA Conf. on Adaptive Hardware and Systems (2007)
3. Jozwik, K., Tomiyama, H., Honda, S., Takada, H.: A novel mechanism for effective hardware task preemption in dynamically reconfigurable systems. In: Int. Conference on Field Programmable Logic and Applications (2010)
4. Kalte, H., Porrmann, M.: Context saving and restoring for multitasking in reconfigurable systems. In: FPL Conference. IEEE (2005)
5. Koch, D., Haubelt, C., Teich, J.: Efficient hardware checkpointing: Concepts, overhead analysis, and implementation. In: FPGA Symp. ACM (2007)
6. Liu, S., Pittman, R.N., Forin, A.: Minimizing partial reconfiguration overhead with fully streaming DMA engines and intelligent ICAP controller. In: ACM/SIGDA Int. Symposium on Field Programmable Gate Arrays (2010)
7. Lübbers, E., Platzner, M.: Cooperative multithreading in dynamically reconfigurable systems. In: FPL Conference. IEEE (2009)
8. Morales-Villanueva, A., Gordon-Ross, A.: HTR: On-Chip Hardware Task Relocation for Partially Reconfigurable FPGAs. ARC 2013. LNCS, vol. 7806, pp. 185–196. Springer, Heidelberg (2013)
9. Simmler, H., Levinson, L., Männer, R.: Multitasking on FPGA coprocessors. In: Int. Workshop on Field Programmable Logic and Applications. Springer (2000)
10. Xilinx: Partial Reconfiguration - User Guide UG702 v14.5 (2013). http://www.xilinx.com/support/documentation/sw_manuals/xilinx14_7/ug702.pdf
11. Xilinx: Virtex-6 FPGA Configuration - User Guide UG360 v3.7 (2013). http://www.xilinx.com/support/documentation/user_guides/ug360.pdf

# A Fully Parallel Particle Filter Architecture for FPGAs

Fynn Schwiegelshohn$^{(\boxtimes)}$, Eugen Ossovski, and Michael Hübner

Embedded Systems for Information Technology, Ruhr-Universität-Bochum,
Bochum, Nord-Rhein-Westfalen, Germany
{fynn.schwiegelshohn,eugen.ossovski,michael.huebner}@rub.de

**Abstract.** The particle filter is a nonparametric filter which approximates the posterior system state through a finite number of state samples i.e. particles drawn from a probability distribution. It consists of three steps which are motion update, sensor update and resampling. The first two steps are easily parallelized since the calculations do not depend on other particles. The resampling step however requires all particles to determine the particle set for the next iteration of the particle filter. In this paper, we introduce a novel FPGA optimized resampling (FO-resampling) approach to solve the parallelization problem of the resampling step by introducing virtual particles. Compared to multinomial resampling, FO-resampling achieves similar results with the added benefit of being able to completely parallelize all the steps of the particle filter. Additional to evaluating our approach with simulations, we implement a particle filter with FO-resampling on an FPGA.

**Keywords:** Particle filter · FPGA · Resampling · Parallelization · Robotics · Localization · Sensor update · Motion update · FPGA optimized resampling

## 1 Introduction

The particle filter is an alternative to the common and well known Kalman filters which use Gaussian techniques for state estimation. They have been successfully employed in a wide variety of robotic application scenarios [9]. Since they do not make strong parametric assumptions on the posterior density, they are able to represent complex multi-modal beliefs. Due to this fact, particle filters are often used in robotics when a robot might face data association problems which result into several different system hypothesis. The accuracy of the state estimation depends on the amount of samples that are drawn from the probability distribution by the particle filter. An infinite amount of samples lets the particle filter converge to the correct posterior state. Therefore, the particle filter usually operates with a large number of particles. In [8], the authors state that autonomous robots can benefit from FPGAs as processing platforms due to their ability to execute tasks in parallel and to fully utilize elastic algorithms. In order

© Springer International Publishing Switzerland 2015
K. Sano et al. (Eds.): ARC 2015, LNCS 9040, pp. 91–102, 2015.
DOI: 10.1007/978-3-319-16214-0_8

to achieve the best performance from a given processing platform, the algorithm has to be adapted accordingly. If the robot is able to execute the particle filter algorithm in parallel, the localization accuracy would only influence the particle filters processing time slightly compared to a sequential implementation.

A lot of research has been conducted on the parallelization of particle filters [3,4,6,7]. Gong et al. introduce a parallel resampling method for shared memory architectures based on systematic resampling [4]. With the shared memory approach, they are able to eliminate the dependency between the left and right boundary when choosing a particle from the particle set and thus are able to parallelize the resampling step. Through the use of shared memory, this solution is not easily implemented on FPGAs but is useful for graphical processing units (GPU). Choppala et al. propose to use a random network as fixed resampling unit for the particle filter [3]. Here, each particle will interact with a fixed set of other particles provided by the network. The resampler then samples one particle form the respective set either deterministically or stochastically. Miao et al. developed a parallel particle filter architecture for FPGAs which uses independent Metropolis-Hastings sampling to increase performance on the root mean square error value [6]. They successfully achieved high speed and accurate performance with their implementation. However, only several processing elements responsible for 250 particles each are used thus no full parallelization is implemented. Mountney et al. present another parallel particle filter architecture for neural signal processing [7]. Here, the time needed to execute the particle filter is independent of the number of particles. This is not the case in the other particle filter architectures since they use processing elements to calculate several particles. We aim to let the processing time be independent from the number of particles.

Therefore, this paper proposes a novel, fully parallel particle filter architecture. It's main contribution is a new resampling scheme to fully parallelize each step of the particle filter for each particle. This new resampling scheme is based on the idea of Gibbs sampling and does not require the complete particle set to execute the resampling step. In order to adapt each state hypothesis to the current sensor data, virtual particles are generated that randomly move through the state space. If one virtual particle achieves a higher importance factor than the actual particle, the real particle assumes the state hypothesis of the virtual particle. The performance of this new resampling approach has been evaluated against the multinomial resampling scheme through MATLAB simulations. The implementation of the particle filter is done on a Zynq7000 System on Chip where further performance measurements and evaluations are conducted. There, we analyze the frequency at which the particle filter can be driven, the amount of real particles that can be utilized when using the complete chip area, and the performance of the particle filter on hardware compared to the MATLAB implementation.

In the following section, we will introduce each component and in our architecture before explaining our implementation in Section 3. Section 4 presents our results with several test cases for the particle filter with FO-resampling. Finally, we will conclude our work in Section 5.

## 2    Architecture Design

In order to be able to parallelize the particle filter, it is necessary to examine the algorithm and detect the parallelizable parts. Code 1 shows the basic particle filter algorithm and its functionality.

**Code 1.** Algorithm of the Particle Filter

```
1:    particle_filter(χ_{t-1}, u_t, z_t)
2:    {
3:            χ̄_t = χ_t = ∅
4:            for m = 1 to M do
5:                    sample x_t^{[m]} ~ p(x_t | u_t, x_{t-1}^{[m]})
6:                    w_t^{[m]} = p(z_t | x_t^{[m]})
7:                    χ̄_t = χ̄_t + ⟨x_t^{[m]}, w_t^{[m]}⟩
8:            endfor
9:            for i = 1 to M do
10:                   draw i with probability
11:                   add x_t^{[i]} to χ_t
12:           endfor
13:           return χ_t
14:   }
```

$\chi_{t-1}$ resembles the set of particles from the particle filter iteration, $u_t$ describes the most recent control input, and $z_t$ stands for the current sensor measurement. In Line 5, the algorithm generates a first state hypothesis for the current particle based on the particle $x_{t-1}^{[m]}$ and the control input $u_t$. In robotic localization, this step is also known as the motion update step. In Line 6, a weight is then calculated for the sampled particle from Line 5 with the help of the sensor measurement $z_t$. The function with which the weight is calculated can be an environment model or a simple Gaussian distribution function. Calculation of the importance factor is generally called sensor update step in robotics. Line 8 simply saves all sampled particles with their respective weights in a temporary set $\bar{\chi}_t$. The last step, which involves the Lines 9 to 12 of Code 1, is called the resampling step and is the most important one of the particle filter. Here, the algorithm draws $M$ particles from the temporary set $\bar{\chi}_t$. The probability for each particle to be selected is defined by the respective weight $w_t^m$ which has been calculated in Line 6. Therefore, each particle can be selected multiple times, thus changing the composition of the final set $\chi_t$ compared to the temporary set $\bar{\chi}_t$. After the resampling step, all particles have uniform weights until the sensor update step is executed again.

### 2.1    FPGA Optimized Resampling

Instead of replacing particles with a small importance factor through particles with a high one, FPGA optimized resampling (FO-resampling) requires the particles to increase their weight by themselves. This approach eliminates the possible interrelationship between each particle from the former particle set $\chi_{t-1}$ to the current particle set $\chi_t$. Code 2 shows the FO-resampling algorithm in pseudo code with $N$ being the number of particles.

**Code 2.** Algorithm of FPGA optimized resampling

```
1: foreach particle i ∈ {1,...,N}
2:     fo_resampling(xᵢ,wᵢ)
3:     {
4:         for n = 1 to B do
5:             sample r ~ U(−1,1)
6:             x̂ᵢ,ₙ = xᵢ + σₓᵢ · r
7:             ŵᵢ,ₙ = p(zₜ | x̂ᵢ,ₙ)
8:             if ŵᵢ,ₙ > wᵢ then
9:                 xᵢ = x̂ᵢ,ₙ
10:                wᵢ = ŵᵢ,ₙ
11:            endif
12:        endfor
13:    return xᵢ
14: }
```

In FO-resampling, every particle has a constant number of $B$ opportunities to increase its weight $w_i$, see Line 4. In every opportunity, a virtual particle $\hat{x}_{i,n}$ will be randomly generated around the actual particle $x_i$. This is shown in Line 5 and 6. First we draw a random number $r$ from a uniform distribution with the boundaries $[-1, 1]$. This random number is multiplied with the standard deviation $\sigma_{x_i}$ and then added to the current particle state $x_i$. The standard deviation $\sigma_{x_i}$ is used to define the spread of $\hat{x}_{i,n}$ around $x_i$. If the initial importance factor is very low, a higher standard deviation can be chosen in order to potentially reach regions where higher weights can be achieved. If the initial weight is already very high, a smaller value for $\sigma_{x_i}$ should be chosen since the position with the highest probability is close by and only minor corrections are required in order to reach the highest possible weight. Consequently, if the importance factor $\hat{w}_{i,n}$ of the virtual particle achieves a higher value than the corresponding factor $w_i$ of the real particle, $x_i$ will be replaced with $\hat{x}_{i,n}$. If $\hat{w}_{i,n} < w_i$ is true, the real particle is not replaced and the virtual particle from the next iteration will be compared to the real particle again. In Code 2, Line 8 to 11 show the replacement of the real with the virtual particle parameters. After $B$ iterations, all particles $x_i$ are incorporated into the posterior estimation.

In this resampling method, no operations are used which require a relation between all particles $x_i$. This enables the design of a complete parallel particle filter architecture and is thus optimized for parallel architectures such as FPGAs. One of the main benefits from this architecture is that each component is reused for creating and evaluating the virtual particles for each particle. Generally, the motion and sensor models of particle filters are computationally the most complex components. This leads to a high processing time when these components are reused on a general purpose processor. When implemented on an FPGA, these components consume a lot of chip area when implemented as hardwired logic circuits but do not have a high processing time. Therefore, we do not add additional components to the particle filter for resampling but use the components which are already implemented. This leads to an efficient chip area usage on FPGAs and is the reason why we call this resampling technique FO-resampling.

An argument against our novel resampling technique is that FO-resampling is biased since it does not eliminate particles with low weights through replacement and the iteration value $B$ is finite. We will empirically show in Section 4 that an estimation of the iteration value $B$ can be made in order to achieve satisfactory weight quality for each particle.

## 3     Implementation

As mentioned in the previous section, the particle filter consists of the three components motion model, sensor model, and FO-resampler. We will discuss the implementation of each component in this section. The particle filter receives as input control data $u_t$, sensor data $z_t$, and random numbers from a random number generator (RNG). The particle's state hypothesis is represented by the parameter triple $x_i = (x, y, \theta)$, with x and y being the coordinates in a 2D space and $\theta$ being the orientation of the object which is to be localized, in this use case the robot.

All particle filter components have to be connected to each other in order to create the parallel particle filter architecture. Figure 1 shows the particle filter's architecture. Here, the parallel calculation of each particle can be clearly seen as well as the reuse of the motion and sensor model components. The RNG, which is required by the motion model, is implemented as a linear feedback shift register. The RNG generates normally distributed random numbers. Since several random number have to be available at once, we decided to let the RNG run continuously and fill a shift register with it's random numbers. When the motion model components require the random numbers, three of them for each system state parameter will be sent to each component. This approach enables us to use only one RNG for the complete particle filter and not one RNG for each particle. After the resampling step is completed, the particle set has to be interpreted in order to gain a position estimation. This is done through calculation of the mean for each parameter of all particles. This approach is only feasible when no multi-modality is present in the system but is easily adaptable to support multi-modality when required. After calculating the mean, the position estimation is ready to be sent to an output for further processing.

The control logic, for enabling each component is not present in Figure 1. It's state machine is designed as a Moore machine and is presented in Figure 2. Here, the value "calc_en" stands for the enable signal for the motion and sensor model and the value "res_en" stands for the enable signal for the resampling component. The state machine is in the state "undefined" directly after initialization,

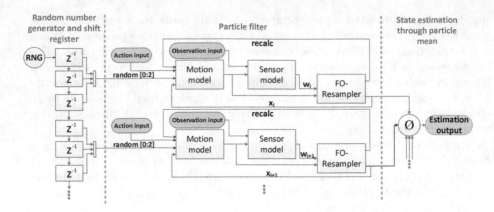

**Fig. 1.** Complete particle filter architecture

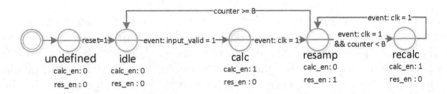

**Fig. 2.** The control logic to enable the respective component for each particle filter state

as undefined signals may be present on the control logic inputs. The particle filter is brought to a defined state through the "reset" signal. This signal also lets the state machine transition from the "undefined" state to the "idle" state. In this state, all components of the particle filter are locked and wait for valid input signals. The "input_valid" signal indicates that valid inputs are available for the particle filter and that the motion and sensor model can start processing the inputs. This is shown in the state machine by the transition from the "idle" state to the "calc" state through the "input_valid" signal. The results of both components are available after one clock cycle and the state machine can transition at the clocks rising edge "clk=1" to the state "resamp", where evaluation of the particle state hypothesis through FO-resampling takes place. The state machine will alternate between the "recalc" and "resamp" state for the creation and evaluation of the $B$ virtual particles. After $B$ iterations of both states, the final particle state hypothesis has been calculated and will be sent to the output of the FO-resampling component. The state machine will then transition from the "resamp" state into the "idle" state, where it will wait until the next valid input is available for processing.

# 4     Evaluation and Results

Since FO-resampling is a novel resampling approach, it's accuracy performance should be compared to other established resampling methods. Traditional resampling methods only have the number of particles to increase accuracy. In FO-resampling however, both the number of real and virtual particles can be adjusted in order to reach the desired accuracy. For this purpose, we investigate the accuracy performance of FO-resampling at first in simulation, see Section 4.1, before evaluating the implementation, see Section 4.2.

## 4.1     Simulation of FO-resampling

We employ a well established model for evaluating resampling methods [1,2,6] with the following functions

$$x_{k+1} = \frac{x_k}{2} + \frac{25 \times x_k}{1 + x_k^2} + 8cos(1.2k) + v_k \tag{1}$$

$$z_k = \frac{x_k^2}{20} + n_k. \tag{2}$$

$x_k$ describes the current actual state the device under test (i.e the robot) is in. $z_k$ are the sensor readings which the particle filter receives. $v_k$ and $n_k$ are zero mean Gaussian random variables with the variances $\sigma_{v_k}^2 = 10$ and $\sigma_{n_k}^2 = 1$. This system model's equation (1) has a high nonlinearity which makes localization very challenging. We compare FO-resampling with multinomial resampling on this system model. The number of particles in both particle filters is $N = 100$ and additionally, the particle filter with FO-resampling is executed with $B = 10$ virtual particle iterations. The variance of the motion update is $\sigma_{mot}^2 = 1$ and of the sensor model $\sigma_z^2 = 0.05$ The results are depicted in Figure 3.

When comparing both estimations with the true system states, it is apparent that both resampling method perform satisfactory in accuracy and robustness. Even when estimations prove to be very wrong, both resampling methods manage to recover and regain a correct estimation for the system state. Since the model for the sensor data induces a dual-modality to the system through $x_k^2$, the performance of both particle filters can be increased when a more sophisticated clustering scheme is used to determine the posterior system state. In order to quantify the performance of the particle filter, we use the Root Mean Square Error (RMSE) value $RMSE = \sqrt{\frac{1}{k}\sum_{t=0}^{k}(x_t - \hat{x}_t)^2}$. The RMSE is traditional measure of performance for Bayes filters. The RMSE value was determined with different numbers of particles $N$ for multinomial resampling and with different numbers of particles $N$ and iterations $B$ for FO-resampling. The system model described in the equations (1) and (2) was used for each simulation. The parameters $\sigma_{mot}^2$, $\sigma_z^2$, $\sigma_{v_k}^2$, and $\sigma_{n_k}^2$ have not been changed. Table 1 shows the RMSE results for 1 to 10000 particles.

A poor performance with a small number of particles is expected. Even with a small number of 10 particles, a significant improvement in the RMSE value can

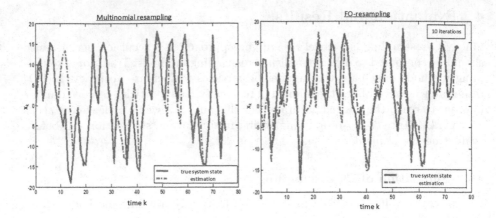

**Fig. 3.** Comparison between multinomial resampling and FO-resampling

**Table 1.** RMSE values for multinomial resampling dependent on the number of particles

| Number of particles $N$ | 1 | 5 | 10 | 50 | 100 | 1000 | 10000 |
|---|---|---|---|---|---|---|---|
| RMSE | 0.220 | 0.159 | 0.062 | 0.065 | **0.044** | **0.049** | **0.045** |

be seen. With a particle number above 100, we see the RMSE value converging towards $\sigma_z$ without any indication for further improvement. Table 2 shows the RMSE values of FO-resampling dependent on the particle number $N$ and the number of virtual particles $B$.

**Table 2.** RMSE values for FO-resampling dependent on the number of particles and the number of iterations

| RMSE | | Number of particles $N$ | | | | | |
|---|---|---|---|---|---|---|---|
| | / | 1 | 5 | 10 | 50 | 100 | 1000 |
| | 1 | 0.381 | 0.216 | 0.206 | 0.292 | 0.244 | 0.267 |
| **Number** | 5 | 0.069 | 0.148 | 0.140 | 0.163 | 0.151 | 0.152 |
| **of** | 10 | 0.097 | 0.077 | 0.071 | 0.114 | 0.104 | 0.092 |
| **iterations** $B$ | 50 | **0.031** | **0.037** | **0.043** | **0.046** | **0.036** | **0.039** |
| | 100 | 0.042 | 0.033 | 0.041 | 0.044 | 0.048 | 0.030 |

If FO-resampling is compared to multinomial resampling solely based on the particle number $N$ ($B=1$), multinomial resampling is far superior. This is due to the fact that multinomial builds the final particle set out of the particles with the highest weights and therefore is able to converge faster to the true system state. However, as the number of virtual particles increases, we can see that even with a small number of particles a similar RMSE performance is achieved. With

$B = 50$ and $N = 10$, the RMSE value is in the same region as with multinomial resampling. Furthermore, we can see that at certain values for $N$ and $B$ no significant improvement regarding the RMSE value is made. This shows that FO-resampling converges towards a final estimation even with small values for $N$ and $B$. This is especially attractive for parallel hardware implementations, as the $N$ defines the chip area usage of the particle filter.

## 4.2  Performance of FO-resampling on Real Hardware

We implemented the particle filter with FO-resampling on the programmable logic of a Zynq7020 [5]. In order to send data to the particle filter, the ARM Cortex-A9 dual core processor has to communicate with the programmable logic. This is done with an AXI-Lite bus. The ARM processor executes a program which sends simulated sensor and motion data to the particle filter. When the position estimation is complete, the particle filter will send its result to the processor. In order to determine how many particles we are able to use for our test case, we synthesize our implementation with different number of particles. Table 3 shows the resource requirements for $N = 1$, $N = 10$, and $N = 14$.

**Table 3.** Resource usage of the particle filter with $N = 1$, $N = 10$, and $N = 14$ particles

|  | $N = 1$ **particle** | | $N = 10$ **particles** | | $N = 14$ **particles** | | |
| --- | --- | --- | --- | --- | --- | --- | --- |
| **Resources** | Used | in % | Used | in % | Used | in % | **Available** |
| Slice LUTs | 4079 | 7.66 | 28860 | 54.24 | 52412 | 98.51 | **53200** |
| Slice Registers | 1549 | 1.45 | 4636 | 4.35 | 5934 | 5.57 | **106400** |
| DSPs | 22 | 10 | 220 | 100 | 214 | 97.27 | **220** |

It can be seen that a maximum of $N = 14$ particles is possible on a FPGA from the Artix-7 family. With 14 particles, the slice lookup tables (LUT) have almost been fully utilized with 98.51%. The particle filter does not require that much slice registers, but fully utilizes the available DSPs. The DSPs are used for calculating the estimations in the motion and sensor model as well as in the RNG. What is interesting to point out is, that all of the DSPs are already used at $N = 10$, but at $N = 14$ only 97.27% are utilized. This is due to the synthesizing process, which remaps some components to LUTs when the preferred component is not available.

Another important attribute of the hardware implementation of the particle filter, is the operating frequency that can be achieved. We therefore simulated the complete particle filter after synthesis to analyze the number of clock cycles needed to perform one position estimation. Figure 4 shows a snippet of the cycle accurate simulation. Here, the signals "clk" for the clock, "action[0:2]" for the control data input, "observ[0:2]" for the measurement, "x_estimate[0:2]" for the particle state estimation, "random" for the random number generation, and

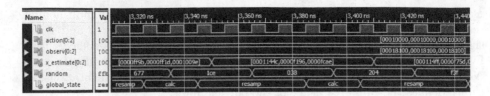

**Fig. 4.** Excerpt of the implemented particle filter simulation

"global_state" for the control logic state machine are depicted. The calculation of a new random variable takes three clock cycles. This random variable is then written to the shift register which updates all of the other shift register's contents. The process of calculating a new particle state estimation "x_estimate[0:2]" calc state requires both control logic states *resamp* and *calc*. *calc* can only be executed after the random variable shift register is updated, as it requires unbiased random variables. Therefore, one iteration of *resamp* and *calc* determines the time for calculating one iteration of "x_estimate[0:2]". As can be seen in Figure 4, this takes six clock cycles. We can determine the processing time with the equation $t_{pf} = 6 \times B \times \frac{1}{f_{max}}$, with $B$ being the number of iterations for FO-resampling and $f_{max}$ being the maximum operating frequency of the synthesized design on the Zynq7020 for $N = 10$ particles. Based on the information from the Synthesis tool, we are able to operate the particle filter at a clock frequency of $f_{max} = 150MHz$. With $B = 100$, this leads to a processing time of $t_{pf} = 6 \times 100 \times \frac{1}{150MHz} = 3.996\mu s$ for one final position estimation by the particle filter.

While the maximum number of particles seems rather small, we can still achieve a comparable performance to multinomial sampling with $N = 1000$ particles when we execute our particle filter with $N = 10$ particles and $B = 100$ virtual particles. These are our architecture parameters for the use case validation. First we evaluate our implementation with five very simple test cases. The initial position for all particles is $x_{init} = (0, 0, 0)$, with the parameters being the x-, the y-coordinate, and the rotation $\theta$ respectively. In every test case, the particle filter receives the motion control input $u = (1, 1, 1)$. The sensor measurement $z$ is different with each test case in order to analyze the performance of the implemented particle filter, when the initial position estimation is increasingly inaccurate. Here, we assume that the measurement $z$ does not suffer from severe interferences and closely resembles the actual system state. The results of these test cases are presented in Table 4.

The results from $x_{est}$ shows that particle filter can reach an accurate state estimation even when the measurement $z$ is far off compared to the control input $u$. In our final use case, we assume the particle filter is performing the localization step of a robot. The robot follows a trajectory which resembles a hexagon. After each time step $\Delta t$, the robot performs localization based on it's odometric model with the control data $u_t$ for respective time step. The particle filter receives the actual system state overlayed with white Gaussian noise with

**Table 4.** Test cases to determine the performance of the particle filter with increasing inaccurate initial state estimations

| Initial state | Control input $u$ | Measurement $z$ | Estimated state $x_{est}$ |
|---|---|---|---|
| $(0,0,0)$ | $(1,1,1)$ | $(1,1,1)$ | $(1.0190, 1.0281, 0.9896)$ |
| $(0,0,0)$ | $(1,1,1)$ | $(1.35, 1.35, 1.35)$ | $(1.3784, 1.3926, 1.3329)$ |
| $(0,0,0)$ | $(1,1,1)$ | $(1.5, 1.5, 1.5)$ | $(1.4502, 1.4829, 1.5159)$ |
| $(0,0,0)$ | $(1,1,1)$ | $(1.75, 1.75, 1.75)$ | $(1.7451, 1.7633, 1.7548)$ |
| $(0,0,0)$ | $(1,1,1)$ | $(2,2,2)$ | $(1.8904, 1.8987, 1.8320)$ |

a variance of $\sigma^2 = 1$. The following Figure 5 shows the localization results of the particle filter. The starting point of the robot is the position $(0,0)$. It then follows

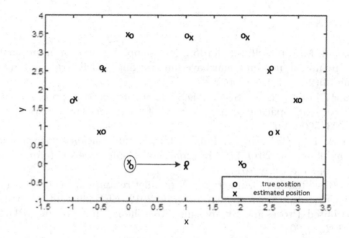

**Fig. 5.** State estimation in the robot use case

a hexagon form counterclockwise until it is at the starting point again. It can be clearly seen that the particle filter is able to follow the robot's trajectory very closely and that the estimated positions do not have a large deviation from the true position. This can also be seen by the RMSE value of 0.0469 of this use case. The particle filter with FO-resampling managed to generate accurate estimate in several different scenarios. Of course more tests have to be conducted with different parameters, but for an initial evaluation, the particle filter performed satisfactory.

## 5    Conclusion

In this paper, we introduced a novel resampling scheme, FO-resampling, for particle filters. Normally, the resampling step cannot be fully parallelized, since the next particle set is created out of the current particle set based on each particles importance factor. FO-resampling eliminates this bottleneck by treating each particle individually. In order to gain a better importance factor without considering every other particle in the set, we FO-resampling introduced the concept of virtual particles which are spread around the initial particle estimation. The importance factor of these virtual particles is compared to the importance factor of the real particle and replaced if the virtual particle's weight is higher. FO-resampling shows promising results in terms of accuracy and stability for the test cases we conducted. However, more use cases have to be implemented and different motion and sensor models have to be implemented in order to fully evaluate this new resampling scheme. This will be done in our ongoing research. Furhtermore, we aim to implement this architecture on larger FPGAs such as Virtex-7 or a rapid prototyping machine like Chipit, in order to better evaluate the implemented particle filter's performance with a larger number of particles.

# References

1. Arulampalam, M., Maskell, S., Gordon, N., Clapp, T.: A tutorial on particle filters for online nonlinear/non-gaussian bayesian tracking. IEEE Transactions on Signal Processing **50**(2), 174–188 (2002)
2. Carlin, B.P., Polson, N.G., Stoffer, D.S.: A monte carlo approach to nonnormal and nonlinear state-space modeling. Journal of the American Statistical Association **87**(418), 493–500 (1992)
3. Choppala, P., Teal, P., Frean, M.: Particle filter parallelisation using random network based resampling. In: 2014 17th International Conference on Information Fusion (FUSION), pp. 1–8 (July 2014)
4. Gong, P., Basciftci, Y., Ozguner, F.: A parallel resampling algorithm for particle filtering on shared-memory architectures. In: 2012 IEEE 26th International Parallel and Distributed Processing Symposium Workshops PhD Forum (IPDPSW), pp. 1477–1483 (May 2012)
5. Inc., X.: Zynq 7000 all programmable soc. Tech. rep.. (http://www.xilinx.com/products/silicon-devices/soc/zynq-7000.html)
6. Miao, L., Zhang, J., Chakrabarti, C., Papandreou-Suppappola, A.: A new parallel implementation for particle filters and its application to adaptive waveform design. In: 2010 IEEE Workshop on Signal Processing Systems (SIPS), pp. 19–24 (October 2010)
7. Mountney, J., Silage, D., Obeid, I.: Parallel field programmable gate array particle filtering architecture for real-time neural signal processing. In: 2010 Annual International Conference of the IEEE Engineering in Medicine and Biology Society (EMBC), pp. 2674–2677 (August 2010)
8. Schwiegelshohn, F., Huebner, M.: An application scenario for dynamically reconfigurable fpgas. In: 2014 9th International Symposium on Reconfigurable and Communication-Centric Systems-on-Chip (ReCoSoC), pp. 1–8 (May 2014)
9. Thrun, S., Burgard, W., Fox, D.: Probabilistic Robotics, chap. Chapter 4.3 The Particle Filter, pp. 96–112. Intelligent Robotics and Autonomous Agents series, The MIT Press (2006)

# TEAChER: TEach AdvanCEd Reconfigurable Architectures and Tools

Kostas Siozios[1]([✉]), Peter Figuli[2], Harry Sidiropoulos[1], Carsten Tradowsky[2],
Dionysios Diamantopoulos[1], Konstantinos Maragos[1], Shalina Percy Delicia[2],
Dimitrios Soudris[1], and Jürgen Becker[2]

[1] School of Electrical and Computer Engineering,
National Technical University of Athens, Athina, Greece
{ksiop,harry,diamantd,komaragos,dsoudris}@microlab.ntua.gr,
http://proteas.microlab.ntua.gr/teacher
[2] Institute for Information Processing Technologies,
Karlsruhe Institute of Technology, Karlsruhe, Germany
{peter.figuli,carsten.tradowsky,shalina.ford,juergen.becker}@kit.edu

**Abstract.** This paper presents an on-going collaboration project, named TEAChER for providing breakthrough knowledge to students and young researchers on reconfigurable computing and advanced digital systems. The project is intended to cover topics like architectures and capabilities of field-programmable gate arrays, languages for the specification, modeling, and synthesis of digital systems. Furthermore design methods, computer-aided design tools, reconfiguration techniques and practical applications are taught. The virtual laboratory enables the remote students to easily interact with a set of reconfigurable platforms in order to control experiments through the internet. By using the user-friendly interface, the remote user can change predefined system parameters and observe system response either in textual, or graphical format. In addition such a virtual laboratory includes a booking system, which enables remote users to conduct experiments in advance.

**Keywords:** Engineering education · Reconfigurable computing · Virtual prototyping · 3-D Architecture · CAD Algorithms · FPGA Prototyping

## 1 Introduction

The reconfigurable architectures and more specifically the Field-Programmable Gate Arrays (FPGAs) carry out a true revolution in the world of digital circuits. After being initially reserved almost exclusively for prototyping tasks, they are now very quickly evolving as an implementation medium for a great number of different demanding application domains. The key to their popularity is their feature to support application implementation by appropriately (re-)configuring the functionality of hardware resources. This allows FPGAs to provide higher flexibility, rapid product prototyping and significantly reduced non-recurring engineering (NRE) costs, as compared to Application-Specific Integrated Circuit (ASIC) devices.

© Springer International Publishing Switzerland 2015
K. Sano et al. (Eds.): ARC 2015, LNCS 9040, pp. 103–114, 2015.
DOI: 10.1007/978-3-319-16214-0_9

The characteristics and capabilities of these architectures have changed and improved significantly the last two decades from arrays of Look-Up Tables (LUTs), to heterogeneous devices that integrate a number of hardware components (e. g., LUTs with different sizes, microprocessors, DSP modules, RAM blocks, etc.). In other words, the logic fabric of an FPGA changed gradually from a homogeneous and regular architecture to a heterogeneous (or piece-wise homogeneous) device.

Such architectureal enhancements have been already taken into consideration from educational perspective, since the impact of FPGAs on different development directions is growing continuously. When FPGAs were first introduced, they were predominantly used for implementing simple random and glue logic, whereas nowadays even undergraduate students are capable of constructing quite complex digital devices on a single FPGA chip.

Usually, in the classical university curriculum there is a hard distinction between hardware and software: the former is under the responsibility of the electrical engineering (EE) or computer engineering (CE) department, whereas the latter is taught at the computer science (CS) department. However, nowadays with hardware/software co-design this clear-cut frontier is dissolving, requiring a fundamental change in the engineering curriculum. Towards this direction, a number of universities introduce lessons related to design of embedded systems, which has inherent the concept of hardware/software co-design.

In addition to this, there is a deep chasm between reconfigurable computing and the way, how classical computer science people look at parallelism. This situation is similar to the well-known hardware/software chasm. In education until recently reconfigurable computing has been subject of embedded systems, or System-on-Chip (SoC) design within EE departments, whereas most classical CS departments have ignored the enormous speed-up opportunities which can be obtained from this field. Only a few departments provide special courses mostly attended by a small percentage of graduate students.

Teaching reconfigurable architectures and CAD tools as part of embedded systems domain, are key driving innovation factor in leading European industry sectors, whereas the increased awareness of designing efficient embedded systems is also stated into a number of reports and road maps (e. g., ARTEMIS, HIPEAC, EUROPE2020, ITRS, etc). These documents highlight also the strategic decision about enhancing both the excellence, as well as the design of embedded systems in Europe, in order to improve the competitiveness of companies.

This paper describes a collaborative project between German (Karlsruhe Institute of Technology) and Greek (National Technical University of Athens) universities for developing educational material related to advanced reconfigurable architectures and CAD algorithms lessons. The emphasis (short and long term) for the outcomes of TEAChER project are summarized as follows:

- Increase the availability of educational material for topics related to the embedded systems community. This is further improved with the e-learning services introduced with the virtual laboratory.
- Provide training to young engineers, as well as to researchers through the transfer of breakthrough knowledge in embedded system technology. For this

purpose, lessons will be based on state-of-the-art reconfigurable architectures and CAD tools.
- Enable research and development of future and emerging technologies, such as 3-D integration, optical on-chip interconnects and system virtualization.
- Bring novel ideas in the embedded systems domain, which is one of the flagships of European industry. This is also expected to support the enhancement of Europe's position in the embedded system market.

Towards these directions, two complementary flavors of educational material will be developed during the TEAChER project. The first of them affects the programming of reconfigurable architectures. The second one deals with the design of reconfigurable architecture and the development of CAD algorithms used for architecture-level exploration and application mapping onto FPGA devices. Both of these flavors exhibit a lot of challenges that have to be sufficiently addressed in order to produce high-quality educational material. Among others, it is crucial to manage the distribution and the interactions between the technical and conceptual parts. For instance, in case the focus was mainly directed at technical skill development, then students would not have the ability to adapt their experience to other programming languages and environments, as well as to reuse programming strategies.

The educational material for programming reconfigurable architectures covers all the necessary programming models that enable students to ease the design of an ad-hoc component structure for a specific digital application. Furthermore, all the necessary mechanisms for improving performance (e. g., through parallelization, pipeline, etc), or reducing the development time (e. g., with the usage of a high-level synthesis tool) will also be covered. In contrast, the material for the second flavor puts emphasis on academic toolflows that enable the simulation of reconfigurable architectures. The requirement for academic tools relies mostly on the availability of source code for the employed CAD algorithms, which in turn enables students to model either more advanced reconfigurable platforms, or to introduce novel algorithms for application implementation onto them.

The paper is organized as follows: Section 2 highlights the motivation for this initiative, as well as the objectives that we aim to address during this 3-years project. The framework for designing 2-D/3-D reconfigurable architectures and the supported (both for exploration phase and for application mapping) CAD algorithms/tools are discussed in Section 3. Section 4 summarizes the topics of educational material. Sections 5 describes the underline platforms for supporting the customization of existing reconfigurable devices. The employed educational and pedagogical methods are described in Section 6. In Section 7 we show how emerging research fields can benefit from the TEAChER framework. Finally, Section 8 concludes the paper.

## 2   Motivation and Objectives of the TEAChER Project

The TEAChER project focuses clearly on modern learning and teaching methods to optimally provide state-of-the-art knowledge to young engineers and researchers in order to enhance later their career prospects. For this purpose, within TEAChER project we aim to develop educational material, as well as to organize university lessons, for the domain of reconfigurable architectures and the supporting CAD algorithms/tools. Instead of focusing exclusively on conventional techniques found in existing lessons, we plan to incorporate in-house technology developed from other E.U. funded research projects that the consortium of TEAChER participated, in order to teach young researchers about how it is possible to employ state-of-the-art technologies to their designs.

This section highlights the open issues found in teaching reconfigurable architectures and CAD tools and proposes how these are addressed within this project.

*Transfer knowledge to young researchers, students, etc., based on the markets needs:* Since the participant laboratories from the German and Greek universities have already established a tight co-operation (through research activities and projects) with research institutes and R&D departments of companies in the domain of reconfigurable architectures across the whole Europe, it is expected that the students that attend these lessons will earn industry-oriented skills, which potentially would be crucial for new jobs. Moreover, by strengthening the state-of-the-art knowledge in the domain of reconfigurable architectures and the supporting CAD tools, we expect to improve the competitiveness of young researchers not only inside Germany and Greece, but worldwide.

*Disseminate the knowledge and tools developed during this project to the community of reconfigurable architectures:* This objective is one of the most important goals of the TEAChER project. By disseminating the educational material (e. g., books, software tools, etc) to the research community, it is possible to achieve the maximum possible visibility for the outcomes of this project. Such a selection was already applied by the two partners regarding the former version of toolflows developed during the AMDREL project, which are publicly available to the internet for online execution [16].

*Help universities with similar studies to improve their educational procedure:* Towards this goal, either the educational material developed from TEAChER project could be shared to other universities, or the partners of this project may participate to specialized lessons/workshops at these universities.

## 3   The TEAChER Framework

The consortium of the TEAChER project comprises partners with an impressive academic track record and proven expertise on a variety of fields related to reconfigurable architectures and CAD tools. Through joining of the above partners' fields of expertise, the TEAChER project will focus on the development of an educational material for teaching advanced topics in the design of reconfigurable architectures, as well as the software tools that automate the procedures

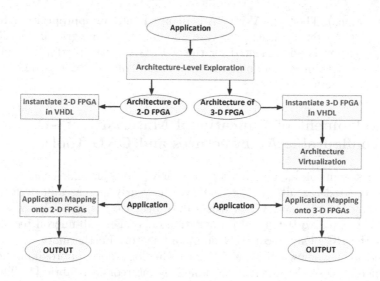

**Fig. 1.** Flow diagram for the topics addressed during the TEAChER project

of architecture-level exploration of these platforms and perform application mapping onto them, with the usage of state-of-the-art technologies.

Starting from an application, initially we perform architecture-level exploration in order to determine the most suitable reconfigurable architecture for application implementation. During this analysis, a number of application properties are identified. Among others, the memory requirements, the demands for supporting high-speed connectivity among distinct kernels, as well as the existence, or not, of complex arithmetic operations (e. g., floating-point operations) are identified.

The conclusions of this step provide an overview for the architectural organization of the target reconfigurable device. These parameters are appropriately handled in order to instantiate the FPGA implementation using the Hardware Description Language VHDL. An initial form of this description regarding the 2-D FPGA instantiation was already available to the consortium, due to previous collaboration between participating universities. However, for the scopes of the TEAChER project, this description should be appropriately modified in order to be used also for academic purposes.

In case we are studying the 2-D flow (see Figure 1 left), then the VHDL description of the Virtual FPGA (V-FPGA) is mapped onto an existing reconfigurable platform (e. g., provided by Altera or Xilinx), whereas the application mapping onto the V-FPGA is performed with the extended version of 2-D MEANDER flow [5]. Otherwise, when looking at the 3-D branch (see Figure 1 right), the VHDL description of the V-FPGA has to be appropriately modified in order to take into consideration inherent constraints posed by the third dimension (i. e., the existence of vertical connections that minimize the wire length of long connections). Then, the V-FPGA is mapped onto an appropriate hardware platform (i. e., Virtex-7), which is aware about the 3-D integration Finally the actual application is implemented for the V-FPGA target platform (similar to the 2-D flavor of our methodology). The concept of V-FPGA is described in more detail in section 5.

## 4    Development of Educational Material for 3-D Reconfigurable Architectures and CAD Tools

For decades, semiconductor manufacturers have been shrinking the transistor size in Integrated Circuits (ICs) to achieve the yearly increases in performance described by Moores Law, which exists only because the RC delay was negligible, as compared to the signal propagation delay. For sub-micron technology, however, the RC delay becomes a dominant factor. Furthermore, a study by Magen et. al. has shown that at 130nm technology node approximately 51 % of the microprocessor's power is consumed by interconnect fabric [4]. This has generated many discussions concerning the end of device scaling as we know it today and has hastened the search for solutions beyond the perceived limits of current 2-D devices.

Three dimensional (3-D) chip stacking is considered by many as the silver bullet technology that will accommodate for all the aforementioned requirements [6]. Stacking multiple dies in the vertical axis and interconnecting them by using very fine-pitch Through Silicon Vias (TSVs) enable the creation of chips with very diverse functionalities implemented in different process technologies in a very small form factor. Introducing locality along the $z$-axis enables on average shorter interconnections between system components, which in turn leads to reduced signal propagation delay compared to conventional, i. e., 2-D, architectures [6]. Additionally, by stacking smaller dies rather than manufacturing a large planar die also leads to yield, hence cost, improvement because the probability that a die is defective is positively correlated with its size. Consequently, the shift from horizontal to vertical stacking of circuits has the potential to rewrite the conventions of electronics design. Although 3-D integration promises considerable benefits, several challenges need to be satisfied. Among others, new methodologies and software tools that support efficient design space exploration are required.

The educational material that will be developed towards this direction will cover the following topics:

- Improve interconnection networks for 3-D reconfigurable architectures [10].
- Design customized interconnection networks for 3-D reconfigurable architectures [11].
- Quantify the impacts of 3-D architectures with commercially available physical prototyping CAD tools (e. g., Cadence SoC Encounter) [1].
- Perform architecture-level exploration of 3-D reconfigurable architectures [8].
- Support fault-tolerance for 3-D reconfigurable architectures [13].

- Model thermal and reliability degradation in 3-D reconfigurable architectures [12].
- Design heterogeneous 3-D reconfigurable architectures [9].
- Develop CAD algorithms for application mapping onto 3-D reconfigurable architectures [7].
- Customize 3-D reconfigurable architectures through virtualization [14].
- Enhance 3-D reconfigurable architectures with Network-on-Chip topology [17].

## 5   Virtual Laboratories

The reconfigurable architecture and CAD algorithms courses in university departments face a significant challenge: the migration from theory to practice. This is especially crucial for lessons, which deal with boards that are usually difficult and too expensive to be bought by students. Any engineering curricula should present a significant level of practical component. The developed practical skills should inspire the students to, among other issues, test learned theoretical concepts, interact with equipment, and analyze experimental data. Within engineering disciplines, laboratory experiments are essential to apply the studied theory and observe the differences between studied models and real equipment.

Working in real laboratories, where the user interacts directly with the equipment by performing physical actions (e. g., manipulating with the hands, turning knobs, pressing buttons, etc) and receiving sensory feedback (e. g., visual, audio and tactile), similar to the case depicted in Figure 2(a) has become more and more expensive. Even though interacting with real equipment offers a higher level of training, more advanced educational techniques are absolutely necessary to be employed. In order to overcome the limited resources (human and material), the large number of students allocated to each experiment, as well as the time and space restrictions, alternative approaches for laboratory exercises have to be considered.

Towards this direction, it is feasible to provide the same interaction at a distance with the assistance of the remote infrastructure. This is a new layer that sits in between the student and the laboratory equipment. Such a layer is responsible for conveying user actions and receiving sensory information from the equipment, similar to the case depicted in Figure 2(b). The derived virtual laboratories incorporate also simulation environment in order to become an alternative to overcome the real laboratory disadvantages. Hence, they can be a good interactive medium, providing a good explanation of learned theoretical concepts.

A number of features are provided with the usage of such a virtual laboratory. Among others, the equipment is available worldwide 24 hour per day, there are no time or place restrictions, the laboratory infrastructure is maintained at a considerable low cost. Furthermore it provides flexibility and friendly user interface, while the students can, at any time, repeat the experiment and reevaluate their results.

We have to mention that the concept of virtual laboratory does not rely only on simulation environment. More specifically, even though such an approach can accurately simulate real equipment (depending on the considered and/or developed models), the use of real laboratory experiments has an extra educational and pedagogical value, ensuring the reliability of the experiment.

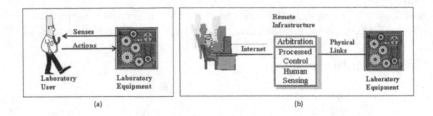

**Fig. 2.** Differences between traditional and virtual laboratories

## 5.1   Virtual 2D/3D FPGAs

Key role in this procedure plays the virtualization, which as we already mentioned recently becomes mainstream in the product development tool-chain. Thus, virtual platforms can sufficiently support concurrent hardware/software system design. In more details, the usage of virtualization enables to model a hardware platform, which might include different processing cores, memories, interconnection schemes, as well as various peripherals, in a form of a simulator. Figure 3 (left) depicts a schematic view of the employed architecture. Fundamental role in this architecture is given to the virtual FPGA (V-FPGA) architecture, which is an island-style FPGA. The architectural properties (e. g., the LUT size and the number of LUTs per slice) of each V-FPGA are customizable depending on the applications requirements.

The architecture of these V-FPGAs was developed at generic HDL-level and then mapped onto a Virtex-7 FPGA board. This, allows our system to incorporate features, such as partial reconfiguration at slice level, or the interconnection with 3-D process technology, which otherwise would not be available. Hence, the V-FPGA interacts as an intermediate layer for our solution, between the actual (fabricated) Virtex-7 platform and the applications. Additional details about the architecture of V-FPGA can be found in [3,15].

The educational material planned to be developed during the TEAChER project pays effort to teach students and new researchers about how to use such a virtual hardware (V-FPGA) in order to introduce additional features to existing (fabricated) devices, which would otherwise not be supported. Students will gain deep knowledge on FPGA architectures and will be able to build highly efficient systems with custom embedded FPGA fabrics. They will get deep insight in the special 2D/3D toolflow for future design methodologies, comprising computer aided design space exploration and dealing with trade-offs in area, performance, power, costs. Furthermore the students will learn and experience the design of heterogeneous system-on-chip solutions with hardware/software

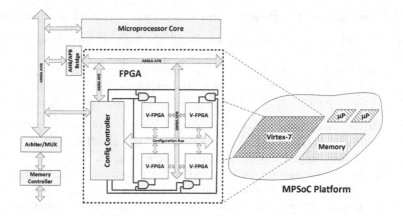

**Fig. 3.** The concept of V-FPGA

co-design methodologies, where one or more processor cores are interconnected on-chip with the reconfigurable hardware fabric, interacting with each other. Due to the virtualization layer, students will be able to quickly prototype the application specific system on off-the-shelf physical FPGAs.

### 5.2    Development of Academic Tools

During this project, a number of new tools will be released in order to support the educational procedure. The new tools will be developed under the GPL license in order to be easily redistributed to other universities with similar lessons, as well as to the interested researchers. This selection will contribute to the broad acceptance of the new tools, whereas the researchers (e. g., master/PhD students, engineers, etc) are expected to contribute also with content refinements and updates based on the actual demands posed by the research community.

Such an approach was already applied to the MEANDER framework [5], in which a number of CAD algorithms were actually developed from PhD students from different other than the original contributors' universities.

## 6    Employed Educational and Pedagogical Methods

Apart from conventional educational methodologies applied in the electrical engineering domain, during the TEAChER project we will develop also an e-learning solution. Thus the students will be able to remotely use the educational material, as well as the laboratory infrastructure (e. g., FPGA boards, CAD tools, etc). Towards this goal, a 'hybrid learning' approach is proposed, which refers to a solution, in which the traditional classroom time is reduced but not eliminated, and it is complemented with some online learning.

Next we summarize the main features of our online educational platform:

– Support synchronous e-learning, where all the participants (i. e., students) interact simultaneously in real-time.
– Support asynchronous e-learning, where the students are self-paced, allowing among other participants to engage in the exchange of ideas or information without the dependency of other participants' involvement at the same time.

Apart from the conventional technologies, which are used to facilitate e-learning, such as books, CD/DVD, etc, throughout the TEAChER project, we propose to use the virtual classroom. More specifically, the virtual classroom is formed by mixing a number of different communication technologies, such as web-conference software that enables students and instructors to communicate with each other via web cam, microphone, and real-time chatting in a group setting. Participants to this classroom are able to write on the board and even share their desktop, when given rights by the teacher. Similar communication technologies that are available in a virtual classroom include text notes, microphone rights, and breakout sessions, which enable the participants to work collaboratively in a small group setting to accomplish a task as well as allow the teacher to have private conversations with his or her students. The virtual classroom also will provide the opportunity for students to receive direct instruction from a qualified teacher in an interactive environment. Consequently, the students will be able to have direct and immediate access to their instructor for instant feedback and direction. In addition to this, the virtual classroom will provide a structured schedule of classes, which can be helpful for students who may find the freedom of asynchronous learning to be overwhelming. Another feature provided by the virtual classroom affects the opportunity to record a lesson. In such a case, each class is recorded and stored on a server, which allows for instant playback of any class over the course of the school year. This can be extremely useful for students to review material and concepts for an upcoming exam. This also provides students with the opportunity to watch any class that they may have missed, so that they do not fall behind.

# 7    Towards Future FPGA Technologies

The proposed TEAChER framework is able to address groups of various expertise level. Undergraduate students, new to the field of reconfigurable hardware, start with application development for a given hardware architecture. More advanced students dive into design space exploration with varying architectural parameters, tuning the target platform for specific objectives (e.g., performance, power, area, thermal distribution, etc.). Furthermore, the TEAChER framework encourages experts and researchers to cross the boundaries of state-of-the-art by developing and exploring future FPGA technologies. This is supported by deep parameterizable technology process models, as well as APIs for customizing the CAD toolflow. An emerging field of research that can early benefit from the TEAChER framework is Teratronics, which is briefly introduced in the following subsection.

## 7.1   Teratronics

Terahertz technology has become a highly emerging research field, surfacing the known knowledge of the advancing world and making it to step into the unexploited gap called Terahertz gap, that lies in full potential, sandwiching itself between the microwave and infrared frequency ranges. This unharnessed gap has led to the birth of a new field called Teratronics which convolves within the key aspects of electronics and photonics. The continuously growing FPGA domain with the blooming parallelization, pipelining and reconfiguration facilities is aimed to make its mark in the future scientific world by bringing terahertz frequency application into reality. However, for now, advances in the context of Teratronics are mainly on fundamental physical layer, dealing with low complexity. There is a big gap to the application domain and the system level, because today's and near future FPGAs are not meeting the Terahertz demands.

The TEAChER framework can support the researchers to close this gap by developing and exploring future FPGA technologies that incorporate latest promising breakthrough physical technologies, such as optical on-chip interconnects and 3D integration, combined with tailored reconfigurable architectures.

Furthermore, the Helmholtz International Research School of Teratronics [2] can use the TEAChER framework to train the young researchers on future FPGA technologies and toolflows, that are not yet manufactured and marketed, thus leveraging the advance in research. The first step of learning about reconfiguring the functionality of the hardware resources will motivate the students to peep into the frequency hopped region which lay as a stepping stone for the future innovations. The intelligence of system virtualization will not only aid the students in designing 3D architectures but also will facilitate them to implement their designed model with the required interconnects in virtual FPGAs (V-FPGAs). These highly efficient systems built on V-FPGAs will thereby assist the students to get connected to a higher bandwidth in a cost effective way, thereby triggering the terahertz frequencies into life.

## 8   Conclusions

In this paper we have presented a project, we call TEAChER, for developing educational material for teaching reconfigurable computing to undergraduate and postgraduate students. Since reconfigurable computing is a fast evolving discipline, such an approach is expected to be a key issue in order to offer companies well-educated, innovation aware, and highly concerned engineers. Moreover, newly developed tools will be released under the GPL license in order to be easily redistributed to other universities with similar lessons, as well as to the interested researchers or companies.

**Acknowledgments.** The authors would like to thank the German and Greek sections of the German Academic Exchange Service (DAAD) for their substantial financial support. This work is also partially supported by the Helmholtz International Research School for Teratronics (HIRST) and by the German Research Foundation (DFG) within Invasive Computing (SFB/TR 89).

# References

1. Diamantopoulos, D., Siozios, K., Soudris, D.: Framework for performing rapid evaluation of 3d socs. Electronics Letters **48** (June 2012)
2. HIRST: Helmholtz International Research School for Teratronics. http://www.teratronics.kit.edu
3. Huebner, M., Figuli, P., Girardey, R., Soudris, D., Siozios, K., Becker, J.: A heterogeneous multicore system on chip with run-time reconfigurable virtual fpga architecture. In: Parallel and Distributed Processing Workshops (IPDPSW) (2011)
4. Magen, N., Kolodny, A., Weiser, U., Shamir, N.: Interconnect-power dissipation in a microprocessor. In: SLIP 2004 Proceedings of the 2004 International Workshop on System Level Interconnect Prediction, ACM, New York, NY, USA (2004)
5. MEANDER. 2D and 3D MEANDER Framework. http://proteas.microlab.ntua.gr
6. Pavlidis, V.F., Friedman, E.G.: Three-dimensional Integrated Circuit Design. Morgan Kaufmann Publishers Inc., San Francisco, CA, USA (2009)
7. Sidiropoulos, H., Siozios, K., Figuli, P., Soudris, D., Huebner, M., Becker, J.: Jitpr: A framework for supporting fast application's implementation onto fpgas. ACM Trans. Reconfigurable Technol. Syst. **6**(2) (August 2013)
8. Sidiropoulos, H., Siozios, K., Soudris, D.: A framework for architecture-level exploration of communication intensive applications onto 3-d fpgas. In: 2011 International Conference on Field Programmable Logic and Applications (FPL) (2011)
9. Sidiropoulos, H., Siozios, K., Soudris, D.: On supporting rapid exploration of memory hierarchies onto fpgas. J. Syst. Archit. **59**(2) (February 2013)
10. Sidiropoulos, H., Siozios, K., Soudris, D.: A novel 3-d fpga architecture targeting communication intensive applications. J. Syst. Archit. **60**(1) (January 2014)
11. Siozios, K., Pavlidis, V.F., Soudris, D.: A novel framework for exploring 3-d fpgas with heterogeneous interconnect fabric. ACM Trans. Reconfigurable Technol. Syst. **5**(1) (March 2012)
12. Siozios, K., Rodopoulos, D., Soudris, D.: On supporting rapid thermal analysis. Computer Architecture Letters **10**(2) (July 2011)
13. Siozios, K., Soudris, D.: A low-cost fault tolerant solution targeting commercial fpga devices. J. Syst. Archit. **59**(10) (November 2013)
14. Siozios, K., Soudris, D., Huebner, M.: A framework for customizing virtual 3-d reconfigurable platforms at run-time. In: IPDPSW 2014 Proceedings of the 2014 IEEE International Parallel & Distributed Processing Symposium Workshops, IEEE Computer Society (2014)
15. Siozios, K., Soudris, D., Huebner, M.: A framework for customizing virtual 3-d reconfigurable platforms at run-time. In: IPDPSW 2014 Proceedings of the 2014 IEEE International Parallel & Distributed Processing Symposium Workshops, pp. 183–188. IEEE Computer Society, Washington, DC, USA (2014)
16. Soudris, D., Nikolaidis, S., Siskos, S., Tatas, K., Siozios, K., Koutroumpezis, G., Vasiliadis, N., Kalenteridis, V., Pournara, H., Pappas, I., Thanailakis, A.: Amdrel: a novel low-energy fpga architecture and supporting cad tool design flow. In: Proceedings of the Asia an South Pacific Design Automation Conference (2005)
17. Tatas, K., Siozios, K., Soudris, D., Jantsch, A.: Designing 2D and 3D Network-on-Chip Architectures. Springer (2014)

# Tools and Compilers II

# Dynamic Memory Management in Vivado-HLS for Scalable Many-Accelerator Architectures

Dionysios Diamantopoulos$^{(\boxtimes)}$, S. Xydis, K. Siozios, and D. Soudris

School of Computer Engineering, National Technical University of Athens,
Athina, Greece
diamantd@microlab.ntua.gr

**Abstract.** This paper discusses the incorporation of dynamic memory management during High-Level-Synthesis (HLS) for effective resource utilization in many-accelerator architectures targeting to FPGA devices. We show that in today's FPGA devices, the main limiting factor of scaling the number of accelerators is the starvation of the available on-chip memory. For many-accelerator architectures, this leads in severe inefficiencies, i.e. memory-induced resource under-utilization of the rest of the FPGA's resources. Recognizing that static memory allocation – the defacto mechanism supported by modern design techniques and synthesis tools – forms the main source of "resource under-utilization" problems, we introduce the DMM-HLS framework that extends conventional HLS with dynamic memory allocation/deallocation mechanisms to be incorporated during many-accelerator synthesis. We integrated the proposed framework with the industrial strength Vivado-HLS tool, and we evaluate its effectiveness with a set of key accelerators from emerging application domains. DMM-HLS delivers significant increase in FPGA's accelerators density (3.8× more accelerators) in exchange for affordable overheads in terms of delay and resource count.

## 1 Introduction

Breaking the exascale barrier [1] has been recently identified as the next big challenge in computing systems. Several studies [2], showed that reaching this goal requires a design paradigm shift towards more aggressive hardware/software co-design architecture solutions. Recently, many-accelerator heterogeneous architectures have been proposed to overcome the utilization/power wall [3–5].

From an electronic design automation (EDA) perspective, high-level synthesis (HLS) tools are expected to play a central role [6] in enabling effective design of many-accelerator computing platforms. Raising the design abstraction layer, designers can now quickly evaluate the performance, power, area and

This work was partially supported by "TEAChER: TEach AdvanCEd Reconfigurable architectures and tools" project funded by DAAD (2014) and CIDCIP and MENELAOS projects funded by the Greek Ministry of Development under the National Strategic Reference Framework NSRF 2007-2013, action "Creation of innovation clusters" "A GREEK PRODUCT, A SINGLE MARKET: THE PLANET"

© Springer International Publishing Switzerland 2015
K. Sano et al. (Eds.): ARC 2015, LNCS 9040, pp. 117–128, 2015.
DOI: 10.1007/978-3-319-16214-0_10

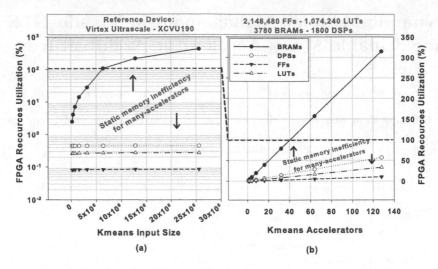

**Fig. 1.** Memory bottleneck of $K_{means}$ clustering algorithm, with $A_i$-Accelerators, $N_p$-Points, $P_k$-Clusters=3, $V_j$-Point Values=Rand(0,1000) on:
(a)Workload scalability ($A_i$=1, $N_p = [2 \times 10^4 : 2\times : 256 \times 10^4]$),
(b)Accelerators scalability ($A_i = [1 : 2\times : 128]$, $N_p = 2 \times 10^4$)

cost requirements of a differing accelerator configurations, thus providing controllable system specifications with reduced effort over traditional HDL-based development flow.

From a hardware perspective, heterogeneous FPGAs are proven to form an interesting platform solution for many-accelerator architectures. However, in such diverse and large pool of accelerators the memory organization forms a significant performance bottleneck, thus a carefully designed memory subsystem is required in order to keep accelerator datapaths busy [7], [8]. In [7], the authors propose a many-accelerator memory organization that statically shares the address space between active accelerators. Similarly in [8], a many-accelerator architectural template is proposed that enables the reuse of accelerator memory resources adopting a non-uniform cache architecture (NUCA) scheme. Both [7] and [8] are targeting ASIC-like many-accelerator systems and they mainly focusing on the performance implications of the memory subsystem.

In this paper, we extend the scope of the aforementioned research activities by showing that the memory subsystem is not only a performance bottleneck but it rather forms the main limiting factor regarding the scalability of such many-accelerator architectures for FPGA devices. Specifically, we show that in modern high-end FPGA devices, the main limiting factor of scaling the number of accelerators is the starvation of the available on-chip memory. This leads in severe resource under-utilization of the FPGA. In fact modern FPGA design tools (both at the RTL or HLS-level) allow only static memory allocation, which dictates the reservation of the maximum memory that an application needs, for the entire execution window. While static allocation works fine for a limited number of accelerators, it does not scale to a many-accelerator design paradigm. Figure 1 shows a study on the resource demands when scaling (i) the dataset workload and (ii) the number of parallel accelerators implementing the $K_{means}$ clustering algorithm on the Virtex Ultrascale XVCU190 FPGA device, i.e. the FPGA with the highest storage of on-chip block RAM (BRAM), total size: 132.9Mb. It is clearly shown that in both cases the BRAM memory is the resource that saturates faster than to the rest FPGA resources types (FFs, LUTs, DSPs), thus forming the main limiting factor of higher accelerator densities as well as generating large fractions of under-utilized resources.

In this paper, we propose to alleviate the "resource under-utilization" problem by eliminating the pessimistic memory allocation forced by static approaches. Specifically, we propose the adoption of dynamic memory management (DMM) during HLS for the design of many-accelerator FPGA-based systems, to enable each accelerator to dynamically adapt its allocated memory according to the runtime memory requirements.

To the best of our knowledge, only [9] and [10] studied the dynamic memory allocation for high-level synthesis. However they do not target many-acclerator systems, supporting only fixed size intra-accelerator allocations. We introduce the DMM-HLS framework that (i) extends typical HLS with DMM mechanisms and (ii) provides API function calls which enable source-to-source modifications that transform the statically allocated code to dynamic one, similar to malloc/free API of glibc. We extensively evaluated the effectiveness of the proposed DMM-HLS framework over several many-accelerator architectures for representative applications of emerging computing domains. We show that DMM-HLS delivers in average 3.8× increase on the accelerator count in comparison to typical HLS with static memory allocation, leading in all cases to more uniform resources allocation and better scalability.

## 2  On the Memory-Induced Resource Under-Utilization in Many-Accelerator FPGAs

In this section, we further analyze the memory-induced resource under-utilization problem found in many-accelerator FPGAs. We show that the on-chip BRAM memory size forms the resource that exhibits the most severe limitation regarding to accelerator count scaling. We further strengthen the previous argument by showing that memory-induced resource under-utilization is consistent across several commercial FPGA devices with different platform characteristics. To drive analysis, we consider a many-accelerator FPGA architecture targeting the $K_{means}$ clustering kernel. Each accelerator implements an instance of $K_{means}$ kernel with statically allocated memory and it is scheduled independently from the rest of accelerators.

We study the FPGA resource utilization when scaling the number of the allocated $K_{means}$ hardware kernels. We consider four type of resources, i.e. BRAMs, look-up tables (LUTs), flip-flops (FFs) and digital signal processing blocks (DSPs). We are interest to identify which esource types form the most severe scaling bottleneck. Thus, for each of these resources, we scale the number

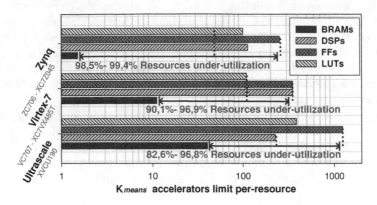

**Fig. 2.** Resource under-utilization impact on $K_{means}$ algorithm

of accelerators up to the point that the specific resource becomes starved, under the ideal assumption that there is an infinite number of rest of the resources. In order to characterize accelerator scaling under differing platform configurations, we perform the analysis on three Xilinx FPGA devices [11], i.e. (i) Virtex Ultrascale XVCU190 (highest on-chip memory on the market), (ii) Virtex-7 VC707, XC7VX485T (high-end development board) and (iii) Zynq-7000, ZC706 XC7Z045 (embedded development board).

Figure 2 depicts the maximum number of accelerators that can be allocated, up to the point of resource starvation. As shown, the on-chip memory (BRAM type) is the resource type that starves faster, exhibiting this consistent behavior across all the examined FPGA devices. As expected the size of the on-chip memory has a significant impact on the maximum number of allocated accelerators, ranging form 41 for the Ultrascale down to 1 for the Zynq device. In more detail, the memory-induced resource under-utilization ranges between 98.5% - 99.4%, 90.1% - 96.9% and 82.6% - 96.8% for the Zynq, Virtex-7 and Ultrascale FPGA devices, respectively. Previous analysis indicates that the memory-induced resource under-utilization is an existing and critical limiting factor regarding to effective scaling of many-accelerator FPGA designs. We identify static memory allocation, i.e. managing accelerator's memory based on worst-case memory footprint estimates, as the main source of this "resources under- utilization" problem, which strongly motivated our DMM-HLS proposal to enable dynamic adaptation of allocated memory according to the accelerator's runtime memory requirements.

## 3   Dynamic Memory Management for Many-Accelerators

### 3.1   Dynamic Memory Management in Vivado-HLS

Figure  3 shows an overview of the proposed DMM-HLS design and verification flow. The flow is based on Xilinx Vivado-HLS, a state-of-art and industrial strength HLS tool. The DMM-HLS extension works explicitly to the high-level source code of the application, thus it keeps minimum implementation overhead to the designers. A source-to-source code modification stage is the step where the original code is transformed from statically allocated to dynamically allocated using specific function calls from the proposed DMM-HLS API. For the targeted many-accelerator systems, the static-to dynamic-allocation code transformation is performed on data structures found within the global scope of the application. The transformed code is augmented by the DMM-HLS function calls and it is synthesized into RTL implementation through the back-end of Vivado HLS tool.

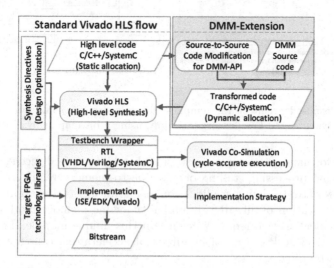

**Fig. 3.** Proposed extension on Vivado HLS flow to support dynamic memory management for many-accelerators FPGA-based systems

DMM-HLS framework extends the architectural template originally supported in Vivado-HLS by (i) supporting emerging many-accelerator systems and (ii) allowing the on-chip BRAM to by dynamically allocated among accelerators at runtime. The proposed architecture, Fig. 4, is divided in two subsystems: the processor subsystem and the accelerators subsystem. The processor subsystem typically consists of soft or hard IPs, such as the processor (e.g. ARM A9 in Zynq), executing three main code segments: the application control flow; the computationally non-intensive code kernels; and the code which shall be executed on CPU due to the need of high accuracy or high FPGA implementation cost (e.g. floating point division). The accelerators subsystem holds the computationally intensive kernels of the application. The accelerators are modeled in high-level language and synthesized using Vivado-HLS. The on-chip BRAMs are considered as a shared-memory communication link between processor and accelerators datapaths. Although we propose the dynamic allocation of on-chip memory, DMM-HLS framework supports the description of accelerators with both statically and dynamically allocated data stored in BRAMs.

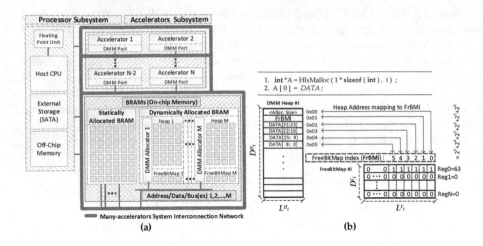

**Fig. 4.** (a) Proposed architectural template for memory efficient many-accelerator FPGA-based systems. (b) Free-list organization, using a bit-map array.

A key performance factor of the system is the ability to feed accelerators with data so that no processing stalling occurs due to memory read/write latency. Moving from static to dynamic allocation using an aggressive approach could lead to the allocation of all BRAMs under the same memory module so that all allocation/deallocation requests occurs on this unique module. This implies serialization bottleneck in case of hundreds of accelerators, thus memory level parallelism is required.

Similar to multi-threaded dynamic memory management [12], [13], DMM-HLS supports fully-parallel memory access paths, by grouping BRAM modules into unique memory banks, named heaps (Fig. 4). Every heap instantiation has its own DM allocator. Each heap-$i$ is highly parameterizable on a number of design options, most important of which are (i) the heap depth $D_i^H$ (the total number of unique addresses), (ii) the heap word length $L_i^H$, (iii) the allocation alignment $A_i$ (the minimum number of bytes per allocation so that every new allocation starts from a unique address) and (iv) the meta-data header size $H_i$ (the number of bytes reserved on first address(es) of every allocation to store meta-data related to the allocation, e.g. allocation length). In a similar manner we define the free depth $D_i^F$ and free word length $L_i^F$ for the FreeBitMap memory.

The proposed DM allocator for HLS supports arbitrary size allocation/deallocation, i.e. enables allocation on the same heap of any simple data type (integers, floats, doubles etc.), as well as more complex data types (structs of same or combined simple data types and 1-D arrays). A FreeBitMap structure, i.e. bit-map free-list holding information about the free space inside this heap, tracks the occupied memory space. FreeBitMap, is an array of registers, every bit of which maps to a single byte of Heap. The term "maps" refers to the allocation status (allocated or free) of this byte. Given that $_i^F \times L_i^F = (D_i^H \times L_i^H)/8$, in every case the FreeBitMap's size is 8× smaller of the heap size. Figure 4(b) depicts the organization of FreeBitMap, using an example of the allocation of 1 integer (4 bytes on x86).

## 3.2  DMM-HLS Allocation Mechanisms

The DM allocator can be employed through the DMM API, which is composed of two main function calls for memory allocation and deallocation. We adopt a similar to *glibc* malloc/free function call API:

- `void* HlsMalloc(size_t size, uint heap_id)`
- `void HlsFree(void *ptr, uint heap_id)`

, where **size** is the requested allocation size in bytes, **heap_id** is the identification number of the heap on which allocation shall occur and **\*ptr** is the pointer which shall be freed up.

The allocator currently implements a first fit algorithm to find a free continuous memory space according to requested bytes. Since we reserve two extra bins to hold meta-data related to allocation, the first fit function returns the index of $FreeBitMap$, so that there are continuous $(size + 2)$ free positions (equal to 0) at $FreeBitMap[index]$-$FreeBitMap[index + size + 2]$. Next the allocator calculates the address of heap based on this $index$. However the heap word length $L_i^H$ defines the smallest unit of memory access, i.e. each memory address specifies different number of bytes. Thus in order to allow any arbitrary allocation size we implemented a $L_i^H$-byte aligned memory address access. For that scope the mapped address $CandidateAddr$ is padded with extra bytes in order to be aligned. Next the corresponding bits in $FreeBitMap$ for the aligned address space reserved are marked (set to 1), and finally the meta-data are written to the first two bins while the aligned address is returned. The $HlsFree$ function has minimum execution overhead since the meta-data for every allocation store all necessary information for deallocation. The function exits with the deallocation of corresponding bits in $FreeBitMap$ for the requested pointer.

Finally, the shared hardware interface of $HlsMalloc$ and $HlsFree$ limits execution parallelism when multiple accelerators request to allocate/free memory simultaneously, even if the accesses affect data across different heaps. To overcome this issue, we apply function inlining of the $HlsMalloc$ and $HlsFree$[1] which increases resource occupation, but also allows the unconstrained parallel access on heaps from many-accelerators.

## 3.3  DMM-HLS Allocation Runtime Issues

There are three major runtime issues related to the DMM in many accelerator systems, i.e. memory fragmentation, memory coherency and memory access conflicts. Fragmentation is defined as the amount of memory used by the allocator

---

[1] Using the "*#pragma AP inline*" preprocessor pragma of Vivado-HLS.

relative to the amount of memory requested by the program. In many accelerator systems, we recognize two fragmentation types, alignment and request fragmentation. Alignment fragmentation accounts for the extra bytes reserved for keeping every allocation padded to the heap word length $L_i^H$, including allocation size and header metadata information. As long as the size of DMM requests (malloc/free) is multiple of $L_i^H$, the alignment fragmentation is zero. Request fragmentation refers to the situation that a memory request skips freed memory blocks to find a continuous memory space equivalent to the size of the request. In the worst case scenario the request cannot be served even if there are available memory blocks in the heap if they are merged. Request fragmentation is strongly dependent on the memory allocation patterns of each accelerator. In case of an homogeneous many-accelerator system, i.e. each accelerator allocates the same memory size, request fragmentation is zero. Due to the first-fit policy, the worst request fragmentation appears on many-accelerator systems with heterogeneous memory size allocation requests, and only in the case of subsequent memory requests, where the second allocation requests a larger memory block than the last freed one.

In the proposed architectural template of many-accelerator systems, memory coherency problems are eliminated inherently, since every accelerator has its own memory space, thus no other accelerator may access it. However memory access conflicts may become a performance bottleneck in case that a large set of accelerators share the same heap. We alleviate this issue by enabling multi-heaps configurations that relax the pressure on the dynamic memory management infrastructure.

## 4   Experimental Results

We evaluated the efficiency of the proposed DMM-HLS framework considering many-accelerator architectures targeting to emerging application domains. Recently, Microsoft showed that such many-accelerator systems on reconfigurable fabrics form promising solution to accelerate portions of large-scale software [14]. A medium-scale deployment on a bed of 1,632 servers, measuring its efficacy in accelerating the Bing web search engine, reported improvements on the ranking throughput of each server by a factor of 95%. In this paper, we considered six applications (Table 1) from the Phoenix MapReduce framework [15].

While the DMM-1 setup (one heap for all accelerators) allows the highest number of accelerators (3.8×), it express low throughput since all accelerators are executed sequentially, thus the low system's latency outperforms the massive performance budget of the increased number of accelerators. As long as more heaps are added, the overall system exhibits higher throughput up to the point that the extra overhead of multi-heaps causes the decrease of accelerators, i.e. although there are available idle heaps, the accelerators are not so many to fully utilize them, leading to throughput decrease. However, the proposed DMM-HLS framework aided the instantiation of many-accelerator systems that exhibit an

**Table 1.** Applications Characterization

| Kernel | Description | Parameters |
|---|---|---|
| Histogram | Determine frequency of image's RGB channels. | $M_{size} = 640{\times}480$ |
| Matrix Mul/tion | Dense integer matrix multiplication. | $M_{size} = 100{\times}100$ |
| String Match | Search file with keys for 4 encrypted words | $N_{file-keys} = 307{,}200$ |
| Linear Regression | Compute the best fit line for a set of points. | $N_{points} = 100{,}000$ |
| PCA | Principal components analysis on a matrix. | $M_{size} = 250{\times}250$ |
| $K_{means}$ | Iterative clustering algorithm to classify 3-D | $N_{points} = 20{,}000$ |
|  | data points into groups. | $P_{clusters} = 10$ |

average throughput increase of 21.4× over the static allocation obtained by the conventional Vivado-HLS flow. On average, considering both the DMM infrastructure and accelerators, the on-chip memory utilization is around 60% while the rest FPGA resources are increased by a factor of 6.3×, 17.6× and 29.7× for DSPs, FFs and LUTs respectively.

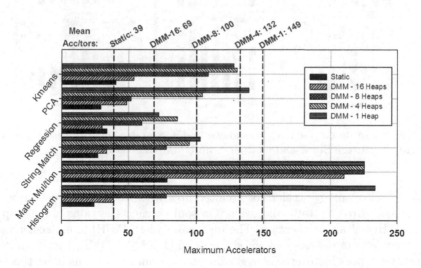

**Fig. 5.** DMM-HLS efficiency on the maximum number of deployed accelerators: 3.8× more accelerators in average, compared to static allocation

We evaluate the practical performance improvements delivered by the proposed DMM-HLS framework in a twofold manner. First, we evaluate the maximum number of accelerators that can be programmed onto the FPGA[2] in order to find the realistic saturation point for many-accelerator systems due to the starvation of the resources. Figure 5 shows that the proposed DMM-HLS framework

---

[2] For all measurements reported in section 4 we selected the Virtex Ultrascale XVCU190 as target device.

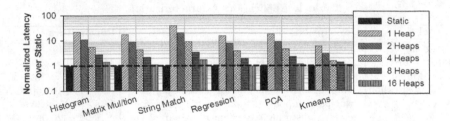

**Fig. 6.** Per-accelerator latency overhead for different number of heaps

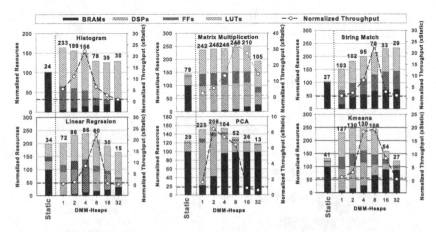

**Fig. 7.** Comparison on resources breakdown and accelerators density versus system's throughput, between Static and multiple-heap DMM-HLS setups

is able to deliver many-accelerator architectures with 3.8× more accelerators in average, compared to static allocation. On some kernels the gains may be up to 9.7×, i.e. Histogram application. The high gains of DMM-HLS on accelerator's density come from the usage of one single heap (DMM-1). DMM-1 configuration has the least possible overhead regarding the resources consumed by the DM manager. As long as configurations with more heaps are adopted (e.g. DMM-4 etc), the extra resources needed to implement the corresponding allocators decrease the maximum number of accelerators, i.e. the instantiation of 16 heaps delivers an average gain of 1.7×.

In order to evaluate the per-accelerator latency overhead due to DMM mechanisms, Figure 6 depicts the normalized latency of the employed kernels for the case of 16 accelerators using 1,2,4,8 and 16 heaps. As shown, the average overhead for all accelerators is 19.9× when only one heap is employed, while it drops to 10×, 4.7×, 2.3× and 1.2× as long as the heaps are doubled. The increase of heaps allows higher memory level parallelism to be achieved, since less accelerators are sharing the same heap. Yet, even in the case that every accelerator has its own unique heap, i.e. 16-accelerators - 16-heaps configuration, the latency overhead still persists (1.2×), due DMM internal operation (freelist check, first-fit operation, etc.). However the DMM-HLS framework enables effective system configurations, which trade-off accelerator density and heap sharing.

To express the aforementioned effectiveness, of multiple-heap DMM setups, we measure the throughput achieved when allocating the maximum number of accelerators considering differing multiple-heap DMM configurations. The throughput metric is obtained as the workload size (in Mbytes) over the latency of a kernel to process it (in us). Figure 7 depicts the aggregated results. Each diagram corresponds to the many-accelerator architectures for each specific application. The x-axis refers to the system's setup, ranging from static allocation and DMM allocation with number of heaps equal to 1, 2, 4, 8, 16 and 32, respectively. The left y-axis refers to the normalized resources[3]. All the stacked vertical bars refer to this axis. The right y-axis refers to the normalized throughput, with reference to throughput obtained from static allocation, which is highlighted as a dashed horizontal line of value 1. Accelerators' density (i.e. maximum number of deployed accelerators) for every system setup is depicted on top of every stacked bar.

## 5  Conclusions

This paper targeted the scalability issues of modern many-accelerator FPGA systems. We showed that the on-chip memory resource impose severe bottlenecks on the maximum number of deployed accelerators, leading to large resource under-utilization in modern FPGA devices. By developing the DMM-HLS, we manage the incorporation of dynamic memory management during HLS to alleviate the resource under-utilization inefficiencies mainly induced by the static memory allocation strategies used in modern HLS tools. The proposed approach has been extensively evaluated over real-life many-accelerator architectures targeting to emerging applications, showing that its adoption delivers significant gains regarding to accelerators density and throughput improvements.

## References

1. Flynn, M.J., Mencer, O., Milutinovic, V., Rakocevic, G., Stenstrom, P., Trobec, R., Valero, M.: Moving from petaflops to petadata. Commun. ACM **56**(5), 39–42 (2013)
2. Shalf, J., Quinlan, D., Janssen, C.: Rethinking hardware-software codesign for exascale systems. Computer **44**(11), 22–30 (2011)
3. Venkatesh, G., Sampson, J., Goulding, N., Garcia, S., Bryksin, V., Lugo-Martinez, J., Swanson, S., Taylor, M.B.: Conservation cores: Reducing the energy of mature computations. SIGARCH Comput. Archit. News **38**(1), 205–218 (2010)

---

[3] Every stacked vertical bar contains the cumulative percentage of the four studied resources (BRAMs, DSPs, FFs and LUTs), thus the theoretical maximum value of left y-axis, on the diagrams of Fig. 7, is 400%.

4. Chen, Y.-T., Cong, J., Ghodrat, M., Huang, M., Liu, C., Xiao, B., Zou, Y.: Accelerator-rich cmps: From concept to real hardware. In: 2013 IEEE 31st International Conference on Computer Design (ICCD), pp. 169–176. October 2013

5. Cong, J., Ghodrat, M.A., Gill, M., Grigorian, B., Reinman, G.: Architecture support for domain-specific accelerator-rich cmps. ACM Trans. Embed. Comput. Syst. 13(4s), 131:1–131:26 (2014)

6. Cong, J., Liu, B., Neuendorffer, S., Noguera, J., Vissers, K., Zhang, Z.: High-level synthesis for fpgas: From prototyping to deployment. IEEE Trans. on Computer-Aided Design of Integrated Circuits and Systems 30(4), 473–491 (2011)

7. Lyons, M.J., Hempstead, M., Wei, G.-Y., Brooks, D.: The accelerator store: A shared memory framework for accelerator-based systems. ACM Trans. Archit. Code Optim. 8(4), 48:1–48:22 (2012)

8. Cota, E., Mantovani, P., Petracca, M., Casu, M., Carloni, L.: Accelerator memory reuse in the dark silicon era. IEEE Computer Architecture Letters 99, no. RapidPosts, p. 1 (2012)

9. Semeria, L., De Micheli, G.: Spc: synthesis of pointers in c application of pointer analysis to the behavioral synthesis from c. In: ICCAD 98. Digest of Technical Papers. 1998 IEEE/ACM International Conference on Computer-Aided Design, pp. 340–346 November 1998

10. Shalan, M., Mooney, V.J.: A dynamic memory management unit for embedded real-time system-on-a-chip. In: Proceedings of the 2000 International Conference on Compilers, Architecture, and Synthesis for Embedded Systems, ser. CASES 2000. ACM, New York, NY, USA, pp. 180–186 (2000)

11. Xilinx, Inc. [Online]. (http://www.xilinx.com)

12. Xydis, S., Bartzas, A., Anagnostopoulos, I., Soudris, D., Pekmestzi, K.Z.: Custom multi-threaded dynamic memory management for multiprocessor system-on-chip platforms. In: ICSAMOS, pp. 102–109 (2010)

13. Sade, Y., Sagiv, M., Shaham, R.: Optimizing c multithreaded memory management using thread-local storage. In: Bodik, R. (ed.) CC 2005. LNCS, vol. 3443, pp. 137–155. Springer, Heidelberg (2005)

14. Putnam, A., Caulfield, A., Chung, E., Chiou, D., Constantinides, K., Demme, J., Esmaeilzadeh, H., Fowers, J., Gopal, G.P., Gray, J., Haselman, M., Hauck, S., Heil, S., Hormati, A., Kim, J.-Y., Lanka, S., Larus, J., Peterson, E., Pope, S., Smith, A., Thong, J., Xiao, P.Y., Burger, D.: A reconfigurable fabric for accelerating large-scale datacenter services. In: 41st Annual International Symposium on Computer Architecture (ISCA) June 2014

15. Ranger, C., Raghuraman, R., Penmetsa, A., Bradski, G., Kozyrakis, C.: Evaluating mapreduce for multi-core and multiprocessor systems. In: IEEE 13th International Symposium on, High Performance Computer Architecture, HPCA 2007, pp. 13–24 February 2007

# SET-PAR: Place and Route Tools for the Mitigation of Single Event Transients on Flash-Based FPGAs

Luca Sterpone[✉] and Boyang Du

Dipartimento di Automatica e Informatica, CAD Group, Politecnico di Torino,
Torino, Italy
luca.sterpone@polito.it

**Abstract.** Flash-based Field Programmable Gate Arrays (Flash-based FPGAs) are becoming more and more interesting for safety critical applications due to their re-programmability features while being non-volatile. However, Single Event Transients (SETs) in combinational logic represent their primary source of critical errors since they can propagate and change their shape traversing combinational paths and being broadened and amplified before sampled by sequential Flip-Flops. In this paper the SET sensitivity of circuits implemented in Flash-based FPGAs is mitigated with respect to the working frequency and different FPGA routing architecture. We outline a parametric routing scheme and placement and routing tools based on an iterative partitioning algorithm able to generate high performance circuits by reducing the wires delay and reducing the SET sensitivity. The efficiency of the proposed tools has been evaluated on a Microsemi Flash-based FPGA implementing different benchmark circuits including a RISC microprocessor. Experimental results demonstrated the reduction of SET sensitivity of more than 30% on the average versus state-of-the-art mitigation solutions and a performance improvement of about 10% of the nominal working frequency.

**Keywords:** Flash-based FPGAs · Single Event Transients · Mitigation · Electric filtering

## 1 Introduction

As technology nodes continuously scale, VLSI devices are becoming increasingly vulnerable to Single Event Effects (SEEs) induced by highly charged particles such as heavy ions, affecting in particular electronic devices working in harsh environments such as aerospace or avionics ones. Among various reconfigurable devices, Flash-based Field Programmable Gate Arrays (FPGAs) are becoming increasingly adopted in safety-critical applications [1] [2]. The main reason of their success is due to their non-volatile configuration memory. However, although Flash-based configuration memory cells are immune to permanent loss of the configuration data due to the strike of a high charged particle; the floating gate switches composing the FPGA configurable logic and routing nodes may suffer transient effects also called Single Event Transients (SETs) [3]. Two cases distinguish a SET phenomenon: the former consists of the modification of the content of a storage cell such as a latch or a Flip-Flop (FFs);

© Springer International Publishing Switzerland 2015
K. Sano et al. (Eds.): ARC 2015, LNCS 9040, pp. 129–140, 2015.
DOI: 10.1007/978-3-319-16214-0_11

the latter involves a particle hit of a routing or logic cell gate provoking an electrical pulse that may propagate through the logic [4]. While in the first case, traditional redundancy-based mitigation solutions consisting in the modular triplication and voting of the sequential element can efficiently avoid error propagations; in the second case the electrical pulse traversing logic data path and routing wires may become indistinguishable from effective electrical signal, since during the propagation the pulse width can be broadened and the amplitude amplified [5]. Considering this scenario, the width of the SET pulse at the input of the storage element is crucial and should be minimized in order to reduce the impact of SETs on a circuit implemented on Flash-based FPGAs.

Recently, several researchers analyzed the nature of SET phenomena on Flash-based FPGAs [6] [7]. Several works analyzed the source of these events, studying the propagation of the transient pulses traversing combinational logic paths and routing segments [8]. SET propagation has also been investigated through radiation test experiments [9] and fault injection approaches [10]. In particular recent experiments demonstrated a peculiar SET pulse-width broadening modulation when SET electrical pulses traverse different type of logic gates and routing switch. On the other hand, many hardening solutions based on redundancy and logic filtering has been proposed. Even though these approaches can efficiently mitigate errors within sequential elements, they are not able to cope with transient pulses originated within sensitive nodes of logic gates or routing switches. The main reason behind this gap is due to an invalid or incomplete logic and routing model that leads to incorrect filtering balance, unable to properly mitigate pulse propagation. Besides these approaches introduce very large overhead in terms of logic and routing resources degrading the overall circuit performances.

Recently, Computer Aided Design (CAD) tools able to perform SET aware implementation of circuits on Flash-based FPGAs have been proposed as a viable solution to mitigate SETs [11]. Although experimental results are encouraging, this solution is only able to mitigate a limited set of transient pulses requiring an expensive characterization of the device sensitivity depending on high charged particle hit rate and experimental radiation test. Other approaches presented in [12] are effective but cannot be directly applied to various Flash-based FPGAs since the applicability on a general purpose circuit is neither automatic nor parametric and the FPGA model is not available.

In the present paper we propose a new framework of algorithms specifically oriented to the mitigation of SET phenomena on Flash-based FPGAs. The framework includes three main modules: a novel parametric scheme of a generic Flash-based FPGA logic and routing architecture which can be suitably adapted to the desired user device, a placement algorithm able to implement routable circuits and performing a SET filtering-oriented positioning of logic elements and a routing algorithm based on a resistive and capacitive-driven approach able to wisely choose fast long lines minimizing the number of short wires thus providing an optimal working frequency of the mapped circuit with effective SET mitigation.

The main contributions of this paper are focused on two key aspects. First, the proposed approach is the first solution integrating an accurate routing and logic model of generic Flash-based FPGA architectures, which can be flexibly adapted to various topology organizations, programmable and hardwire segments and logic elements definition oriented to the SET mitigation. Secondly, the developed placement algorithm performs unbalanced logical path positioning increasing the intrinsic filtering capabilities of routing and logic paths while guaranteeing full routability. Besides, the developed routing algorithm is the first one based on a two dimensional mesh topological organization of the resources which allows reduced computational time and effective optimal working frequency.

The whole framework has been evaluated on several benchmark circuits belonging to the ITC'99 benchmarks including a RISC microprocessor. The SET sensitivity has been measured through electrical fault injection on an effective set of transient pulses. Experimental results demonstrated that our approach is able to decrease the SET sensitivity of more than 30% on the average. Besides, the performance of the circuits in terms of working frequency has been improved of 10% on the average.

The paper is organized as follows. Section 2 reports an overview of the related works concerning SET mitigation approaches; Section 3 describes the developed parametric model of the FPGA architecture, while Section 4 depicts the proposed framework describing the developed placement and routing algorithm and the interface tools to commercial Flash-based FPGAs workflow. Experimental results and analysis are provided in Section 5. Finally, conclusions and future works are drawn in Section 6.

## 2    Related Works

In previous works, radiation beam experiments and benchmarking test had characterized SETs on two main Flash-based FPGA architectures: commercial and low-power. They both have almost the same internal architecture, except for the manufacturing process, leading the second one to be a very low-power FPGA with a power consumption in the order of microwatts. They both undergo internal architecture analysis and radiation test in order to evaluate SET sensitivity. On the other side these experiments have proven the immunity of Flash-based FPGAs to Single Event Upsets (SEUs) in their configuration memory [1].

Different approaches proposed algorithms and physical layout model for the mitigation of SETs. Two main SET mitigation categories are considered: transistor resizing and logic redundancy. If transistor resizing is not feasible on Flash-based FPGAs since physical logic cells and Flip-Flops (FFs) modifications are not applicable on FPGA regular fabric; logic redundancy methods based on traditional fault-tolerant techniques such as Triple Modular Redundancy (TMR) [13] have been applied. Another set of previously developed techniques includes time and spatial redundancy. In [14] authors proposed a synthesis algorithm which is able to divide a Flip-Flop implementation into two latches block obtaining a dual-sampling latch able to filter transient phenomena. However, these techniques have been demonstrated to be ineffective for a large set of transient pulses. The reasons of that have been demonstrated by more advanced studies showing that SET propagation may be altered through the transient pulse traversing of the circuit logical path [4] in relation to the kind of logic elements and routing segments traversed [5]. On the idea foreseen by [10], it has been proven that by modifying the placement positions of logic gates and therefore changing the interconnection characteristics in terms of delay and capacitive load, it is possible to attenuate the propagation and eventually nullify it before a pulse is sampled by a sequential element. A preliminary place and route algorithm developed for this specific purpose has been proposed in [15], while a placement retiming algorithm has been proposed in [12]. However, an accurate radiation experiment evaluation of this approach [11] showed that it is only capable to partially reduce the overall SET sensitivity of a circuit, while most of the transient errors are bypassing the filtering optimizations. The main limitation of these previous approaches is due to the application of the mitigation strategies on an already available place and route solution. Indeed, such kind of techniques firstly analyzes the sensitive nodes of an already mapped circuit basing on the probability of having a sensitive node on specific critical logic gates, secondly the mapper and the place and route algorithms are applied on the previously estimated sensitive nodes in order to minimize the SET sensitivity. A second relevant limitation of the previously developed methods is characterized by the absence of detailed routing data, since both routing infrastructure and routing algorithm are not available. The missing availability of routing information and algorithm provokes an evident limit on the applicability of transient filtering, since routing segment capacitive and resistive loads are only estimated by placement. However, the approach proposed in this paper is based on a place and route flow, which does not require a previous map of the circuit. Instead, it works directly from the synthesized netlist, besides it includes a detailed FPGA logic and routing model which allows the execution of both placement and routing algorithms on the basis of the used Flash-based FPGA architecture.

## 3    The FPGA Logic and Routing Model

Contemporary FPGA architectures are generally characterized by the well-known island-style FPGA model [16] including a two-dimensional array of logic elements that are interconnected via a programmable routing network. On the basis of these resources organization, FPGA families may have different architecture depending on the number of logic elements, local and global routing wires as well as pin locations and short wires granularity. In the present section, we describe the FPGA logic and routing model developed for supporting the placement and routing algorithm oriented to the SET mitigation. The model has been developed following a parametric format we named *Generic Array Format* (GAF) is supported by a two dimensions matrix mesh format where all the FPGA resources refer too. Basically, all the resources are defined by nodes and lines organized on the two dimensions mesh space.

The parametric format, whose graphical organization is illustrated in Figure 1.a, allows the definition of the following FPGA characteristics:

1. *2-D mesh matrix space*: it defines the maximal space area and the number of logic elements and *switch matrix column* and *rows*. This parameter allows also the identification of FPGA regions that are not used for reconfigurable switches (e.g., in particular when these areas are used for embedded hardwired microprocessors, memory blocks or DSP modules).
2. *Switch matrix and logic element block*: it defines the number, dimension and organizations of the routing and logic element areas. A traditional island style FPGA has generally one or more logic elements for each switch matrix block, our model allows different organizations where routing segments are divided

into more switch blocks and logic elements are organized in different position. Please note that since both the switch matrix block and the logic elements are defined by rectangular shape with proper dimensions on the 2D-mesh, our model supports any kind of FPGA architecture and it can be eventually adapted to novel FPGA logic and routing topology.

3. *Internal routing resources*: it defines the programmable interconnection points of a switch matrix block. Each resource is defined by a segment with a source and destination point that can be placed according to the user definition in any position of the two dimensions mesh matrix (e.g., reasonably source and destination points are placed on the same switch matrix frame).

4. *Hardwired routing resources*: it defines the starting and ending points of all the hardwired lines on the FPGA architecture. It includes the *horizontal* and *vertical hardwires lines*, *horizontal* and *vertical long lines* as well as the *logic element input/outputs*. Each single routing line is defined by a set of points identifying the source point and the destination points. Please note that the position of the source and destination points must correspond to the one of the internal routing resource.

5. *Input / Output pins*: it defines the position of the I/O pins. They can be located on all the available two dimensions mesh matrix space allowing the modeling of all the kinds of FPGA pin-out organizations.

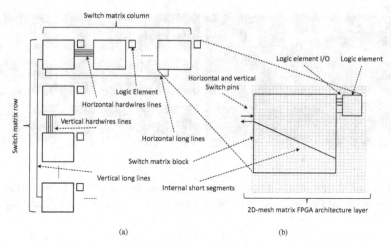

**Fig. 1.** Parametric architectural FPGA model for mesh-matrix oriented place and route algorithms (a) and the mesh matrix format in two dimensions (b)

The GAF parametric architectural FPGA model has been defined within a textual file where it is possible to specify regular or not regular resources, by this way it is not necessary to define internal short segments for all the switch matrix elements, since they are replicated on all of them, and, using the same model, it is possible to define singular routing and logic resources. The main advantage of this format is the extremely high flexibility to be adapted to various kinds of FPGA architectures covering almost all the state-of-the-art FPGA devices.

## 3.1    Flash-Based FPGA Modeling

For the purpose of this work, the developed GAF model has been created for mimic the model of a Microsemi Flash-based FPGA device of the ProASIC family and model A3P250 using a package PQ208 [17]. This FPGA device is characterized by an array of 6,144 cells organized in 48 rows by 128 columns of VersaTiles, 157 input/output pins. The FPGA logic and routing resources are organized in a single switch matrix block associated with a logic element, characterized by three inputs and one output. The three inputs can be used as functional inputs for a combinational logic gate implementation or as data, clock and reset/clear inputs for a sequential element implementation (both Flip-Flop and Latch). The routing architecture has been identified as routing infrastructure with 328 vertical long lines and 1,070 horizontal long lines connecting VersaTiles with a distance ranging from 5 to 13 switch matrix blocks. Finally, the internal routing short segment architecture has been devised using 2,755 programmable interconnection segments covering all the possible input and output combinations.

The developed model, a sub-set of which is illustrated in Figure 2 as an empty array space (a) and a placed and routed one (b), counts up to 17,168,752 routing interconnection segments.

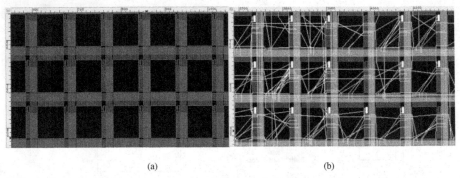

(a)                                                      (b)

**Fig. 2.** A graphical view obtained from the developed environment of the Microsemi ProASIC3 A3P250 Flash-based FPGAs logic and routing model as empty (a) and placed and routed (b) array

## 4     SET-PAR: Placement and Routing Tools for SET Mitigation

The developed place and route algorithm (SET-PAR) for implementing SET-aware circuits on Flash-based FPGAs starts by reading the netlist description of a synthesized netlist. For the purpose of this work, the tool has been interfaced with the Synopsys Synplify synthesizer and loads the net-list in the Actel Flattened Netlist (AFL) format. The algorithm, compatible with the standard Microsemi Libero SoC design flow, is illustrated in Figure 3.

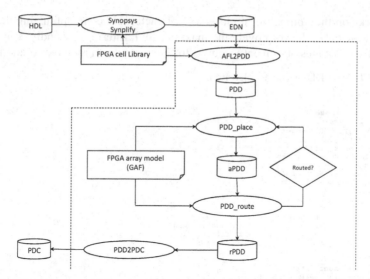

**Fig. 3.** The integrated Microsemi Libero SoC and SET-PAR place and route flow

In detail, the AFL netlist format is a traditional flattened netlist including detailed FPGA gate level description and nets between cells that can be generated through the Synopsys synthesizer embedded within the Microsemi Libero SoC tool.

The SET-PAR flow consists in a preliminary phase where the AFL is elaborated by the developed *AFL2PDD* tool. This tool consists in a parser algorithm that generate a Physical Design Description file (PDD) containing the graph based representation of the synthesized circuit where logic elements (both combinational gates and Flip-Flops) are modeled as graph vertices while nets are modeled by graph edges. Besides, the tool includes into the PDD file the functional maps related to each combinational gate generated from the FPGA cell library database provided by the manufacturer. Once this preliminary phase is completed the SET-PAR flow executes the placement and the routing algorithms in two distinct phases. The details of the two algorithms are depicted in the following subsections.

## 4.1    The PDD Placement Algorithm

The goal of the PDD placement algorithm is to find an effective placement for each logic node while optimizing the filtering capabilities of each logical path and mini-mizing the overhead delay of the circuit. The algorithm reads from the PDD circuit description the logic nodes, their interconnections and the I/O pins; while it loads the FPGA architectural characteristics, in terms of switch matrices rows and columns from the FPGA array model. The core of the placement algorithm is based on an av-erage Manhattan distance optimization technique including a detailed logical path analysis. The placement strategies consist in two phases, as it is illustrated in Algo-rithm 1. After the initialization of the placement environment, the PDD placement firstly works on the optimal local placement of each logic cone optimizing the filtering capabilities in order to provide the maximal SET filtering; secondly it optimizes the overall logic cones placement locations for guaranteeing a routable solution.

**Algorithm 1.** The PDD placement algorithm

```
PDD_place (PDD description)
   {
   /*Preliminary Phase*/
   L_Elements (type, locations) = reading_logic(PDD)
   For each Logic ∈ L_Element
        io_net(Logic) = read_inout_logic (Logic);
   P_Area = create_placement_area (PDD, GAF);
   /*Local Logic Cone Placement, Phase 1*/
   Cone_Macro(i) = extract_cone(P_area);
    K = optimal_SET(Macro_set);
   For each Cone_Macro(i){
        Local_k = 0;
            do until (SET_k <= ( K+D))
               {
                For each Logic ∈ Cone_Macro(i)
                    Place_Macro = Place_Manhattan_Min (Logic, local_K);
                (SET_k,D) = compute_SET_filters(Place_Macro);
                If (SET_k < K) then local_K++;
               }
       }
   /*Global Placement, Phase 2*/
   do until (to_place_element == 0)
     {
      For each Place_Macro(i)
          Shared_logic = Global_place(Place_Macro(i));
          Place_Area(Shared_Logic, Place_Macro(i));
   }
   create_PDD(P_area);
      }
```

In details, during the initialization phase, the circuit description is loaded into a directed graph called *L_element*, where each node is characterized by a type and an initial unplaced location and the set of input output nets (*io_nets*) is identified. Based on the PDD and Generic Array Format information, the placement area (*P_Area*) is generated. At the beginning of the first phase, it is computed the optimal filtering capabilities of each logic cone without considering the routing characteristics. This coefficient, named $\Delta K$, provides the best SET filtering coefficient that a specific logic cones can achieve. The placement is then performed analyzing the type of logic elements involved and each gate is characterized by a specific inverting coefficient which is calculated on the basis of the probability that the logic function provides in output the logical opposite value of input. The *Place_Manhattan_Min* function generates a temporal placement following: if a couple of connected gates have an inverting coefficient greater than 0.5, the placement is performed locating the two gates with a minimal distance; in the other cases, the placement is performed in a longer distance limited by the *local_k* coefficient. This process is repeated until the temporary placement has a SET coefficient (*SET_k*) which is equivalent to the optimal one with a degree of freedom provided by a flexibility coefficient D.

The second phase consists in the global placement; all the temporary placement macros are placed on *P_area*. During this phase, the major issue is due to the logic gates sharing multiple logic cones. These gates are identified and the placement modified accordingly minimizing the distance between their original positions with respect to the temporary placement. Finally, a new placement annotated PDD file (*aPDD*) including the placement location of each logic element within the FPGA array is generated.

## 4.2    PDD Routing Algorithm

The PDD routing algorithm consists of the most complex part of the proposed Flash-based FPGA design tools. At the beginning of the routing phase, the circuit description is already with a placement solution that may guarantee the optimal SET filtering capabilities of the considered circuit. However, depending on the kind of routing segment used to physically generate all the interconnections the SET filtering characteristics may be deteriorated nullifying the placement optimization. This penalization phenomenon has been observed in previously developed approaches that were not able to control the routing process [11][12][15], while our approach is able to avoid this degradation.

The PDD routing algorithm, illustrated in Algorithm 2, firstly loads the entire Generic Array Format (GAF) model of the FPGA generating an internal memory storage area composed of all the routing interconnection and logic details included into the GAF model. Secondly, it reads all the placement solution from the *aPDD* file and updates the internal memory storage area.

The routing phase consists of two phases: the sorting of the nets and the detailed routing phase. First, the algorithm performs the selection of longer interconnections first; the function *Greater_first_sort* properly generates this order on the basis of the maximal Manhattan distance between the logic cells involved in the on-going routing process of the net. Secondly, the PDD router performs the detailed routing where each net is routed selecting the routing segments by optimizing the resistive capacitive load with respect to the SET filtering introduced by each routing segment. Please note that the selection of the physical interconnection is therefore not performed for minimizing the routing delay, thus maximizing the usage of long lines, but properly selecting programmable interconnection segments, short wires and long lines in order to achieve the RC capacitive load estimated for each routed net, characterized by the *RC_load_min* parameter.

**Algorithm 2**. The PDD routing algorithm.

```
PDD_router (aPDD, GAF)
  {
    /*Preliminary Phase*/
    Routing_Area (GAD,PDD locations) = reading_place (aPDD)
    /*Distance order, Phase 1*/
    Net_order = Greater_first_sort (Nets, PDD type);
    Max_distance = Max_First_Sort (Net_List);
    /*Detailed Routing phase 2*/
    do until (Max_distance == 0)
    {
        For each Nete Net_order {
            Route = FALSE;
            Flex = 0;
            While (Route != TRUE)
            {
            RC_load_min = estimate_RC_coefficient (Net_Path(Net));
            Route = Find_Routing_Path (Source(Net),Drain(Net),RC_load, Flex);
            If (Route == FALSE) then Flex++;
            }
            Update_Route_Area();
        }
    }
    create_rPDD(Routing_Area);
  }
```

## 5    Experimental Results

The developed SET-PAR tools have been experimentally evaluated in order to probe the efficiency and the improvements of the SET filtering techniques with respect to previously developed SET optimization approaches on Flash-based FPGAs. Two experimental analyses have been performed. The former aimed at evaluating the improvements of the SET mitigation on transient error pulses set ranging from 10 ps to 10 ns. The latter consists of a detailed timing analysis measuring the maximum delay of the critical path between the different solutions of the implemented circuits. Both the evaluations have been performed using some benchmark circuits included in the ITC'99 benchmarks and including a RISC processor core [18]. Besides, all the circuits have been implemented using a Microsemi A3P250 Flash-based FPGA based on 130nm CMOS manufacturing process and counting up to 6,144 logic cells [17].

The characteristics of the implemented circuits are illustrated in Table I, where for each circuit is reported the number of logic cells, the number of nets and the number of routing segments including short and long wires, obtained with commercial tools and with the proposed SET-PAR approach.

As it is possible to observe the physical routing used by the SET-PAR algorithm provides a number of routing segments ranging from 10% to 20% lower than the one obtained using commercial solutions based on the previously developed method [11].

**Table 1.** Characteristics of the implemented benchmark circuits

| Circuit | Logic Cells [#] | Routing Nets [#] | Commercial tools and [11] Short Wires [#] | Long Lines [#] | SET-PAR approach Short Wires [#] | Long Lines [#] |
|---|---|---|---|---|---|---|
| B03 | 131 | 466 | 1,365 | 555 | 1,112 | 432 |
| B05 | 544 | 2,070 | 6,407 | 2,573 | 6,301 | 2,509 |
| B07 | 244 | 1,038 | 2,821 | 1,066 | 2,373 | 893 |
| B08 | 149 | 464 | 1,326 | 545 | 1,199 | 486 |
| B09 | 115 | 480 | 1,705 | 663 | 1,348 | 535 |
| B10 | 168 | 474 | 1,375 | 543 | 1,251 | 486 |
| B11 | 311 | 1,290 | 3,798 | 1,423 | 3,094 | 1,197 |
| B12 | 619 | 2,856 | 7,731 | 2,905 | 6,916 | 2,404 |
| B13 | 222 | 584 | 1,429 | 516 | 1,203 | 450 |
| B14 | 3,872 | 16,722 | 71,621 | 27,025 | 70,517 | 26,636 |
| RISC | 3,425 | 11,814 | 36,368 | 13,112 | 33,642 | 11,951 |

The analysis of the Single Event Transient sensitivity has been performed with the Single Event Transient Analyzer platform [10] using a large set of transient pulses ranging from 10ps to 10ns thus covering the entire realistic transient events induced in a harsh radiation environment. The validation has been obtained by randomly choose the location where to electrically inject the pulses and by applying random input stimuli to the tested circuits. Then, we classify a result as wrong answer, if during the test application produces at least one output pattern that differs from the expected one. Finally, we count the number of SETs provoking errors on the circuit outputs. The results we gathered are illustrated in Figure 4, where we indicated the reduction, in percentage, of the SET number provoking errors within the output of the implemented circuits. The reduction is extremely high since around 30% of SETs are correctly mitigated with respect to the previously developed approach. Besides, it is possible to notice that the SET-PAR tool works properly independently from the complexity of the implemented circuit (e.g., the overall SET-induced errors reduction is always greater than 27% whatever is the circuit under analysis).

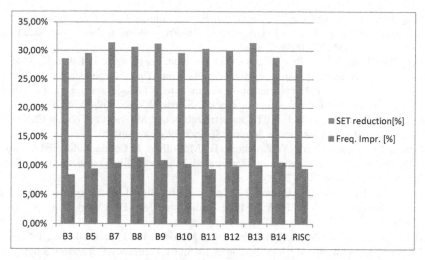

**Fig. 4.** Single Event Transient reduction and Frequency improvements of the SET-PAR implemented circuits with respect to the previously developed solution based on Microsemi Commercial tools.

Finally, the benchmark circuits have been timing analyzed using Microsemi vendor's software in order to estimate the maximum working frequency. The results obtained with the timing analysis are reported on Figure 4 as percentage of frequency improvement provided by the SET-PAR tools with respect to the previous solution. The results demonstrate that the SET-PAR algorithm is efficiently implementing circuits on Flash-based FPGA.

## 6 Conclusions and Future Works

In this paper a new place and route algorithm oriented to the mitigation of Single Event Transients (SETs) phenomena on Flash-based FPGAs has been presented. The presented method is the first solution integrating an accurate routing and logic model of generic Flash-based FPGA architectures able to be flexibly adapted to various type of architectures. Furthermore, the proposed approach is able to perform unbalanced logical path placement and routing increasing the SET filtering capabilities and thus reducing the overall SET sensitivity of the circuits implemented on Flash-based FPGAs. Experimental results demonstrated a SET sensitivity reduction of more than 30% with respect to previously developed approach and a performance improvement of about 10% of the nominal working frequency.

## References

1. Speers, T., Wang, J.J., Cronquist, B., McCollum, J., Tseng, H., Katz, R., Kleyner, I.: "0.25 μm FLASH memory based FPGA for space applications. presented at the Military Aerospace Programmable Logic Devices Conference (MAPLD), Greenbelt, MD (1999)

2. Rezgui, S., Wang, J.J., Sun, Y., Cronquist, B., McCollum, J.: New reprogrammable and non-volatile radiation tolerant FPGA: RTA3P. In: Proceedings of IEEE Aerospace Conference, pp. 1–11 (March 2008)
3. Berg, M., Wang, J.J., Ladbury, R., Buchner, S., Kim, H., Howard, J., Label, K., Phan, A., Irwin, T., Friendlich, M.: An analysis of Single Event Upsets dependencies on high frequency and architectural implementation within Actel RTAX-S family Field Programmable Gate Arrays. IEEE Transactions on Nuclear Science 53(6), 3569–3574 (2006)
4. Rezgui, S., Won, R., Tien, J.: SET Characterization and Mitigation in 65-nm CMOS Test Structures. IEEE Transactions on Nuclear Science 59(4), August 2012
5. Rezgui, S., Wang, J.J., Sun, Y., Cronquist, B., McCollum, J.: Configuration and routing effects on the SET propagation in Flash-based FPGAs. IEEE Transactions on Nuclear Science 55(6), 3328–3335 (2008)
6. Wang, J.J., Kuganesan, G., Charest, N., Cronquist, B.: Biased-Irradiation characteristics of the floating gate switch in FPGA. In: IEEE Radiation Effects Data Workshop, pp. 101–104 (2006)
7. Battezzati, N., Gerardin, S., Manuzzato, A., Merodio, D., Paccagnella, A., Poivey, C., Sterpone, L., Violante, M.: Methodologies to Study Frequency-Dependent Single Event Effects Sensitivity in Flash-based FPGAs. IEEE Transactions on Nuclear Science 56(6, pt. 1), 3534–3541 (2009)
8. Sterpone, L., Battezzati, N., Kastensmidt, F.L., Chipana, R.: An Analytical Model of the Propagation Induced Pulse Broadening (PIPB) Effects on Single Event Transient in Flash-based FPGAs. IEEE Transactions on Nuclear Science 58, 2333–2340 (2011)
9. Wang, J.J., Samiee, S., Chen, H.-S., Huang, C-K., Cheug, M., Borillo, J., Sun, S.N., Cronquist, B., McCollum, J.: Total ionizing dose effects on Flash-based Field Programmable Gate Array. IEEE Transactions on Nuclear Science 51(pt. 2), 3759–3766 (2004)
10. Sterpone, L., Battezzati, N., Ferlet-Cavrois, V.: Analysis of SET Propagation in Flash-based FPGAs by means of Electrical Pulse Injection. IEEE Transactions on Nuclear Science 57(pt. 1), 1820–1826 (2010)
11. Sterpone, L., Du, B.: Analysis and mitigation of single event effects on flash-based FPGAs. In: IEEE European Test Symposium, pp. 1–6 (2014)
12. Xu, W., Wang, J., Hu, Y., Lee, J.-Y., Gong, F., He, L., Sarrafzadeh, M.: In-Place FPGA Retiming for Mitigation of Variational Single-Event Transient Faults. IEEE Transactions on Circuits and Systems 58(6), 1372–1381 (2011)
13. Baze, M.P., Buchner, S.P., McMorrow, D.: A Digital CMOS Design Techniques for SEU hardening. IEEE Transactions on Nuclear Science 6, 2603–2608 (2000)
14. Microsemi aa.vv., "Using Synplify to Design in Microsemi Radiation-hardened FPGAs". Application Note, AC139, p. 9 (2012)
15. Sterpone, L., Battezzati, N.: On the mitigation of SET broadening effects in integrated circuits. In: IEEE 13th International Symposium on Design and Diagnostic of Electronic Circuits and Systems (DDECS), pp. 36–39 (2010)
16. Betz, V., Rose, J., Marquardt, A.: Architecture and CAD for Deep-submicron FPGAs. Springer, Boston (1999)
17. ProASIC3 Flash-based FPGAs, datasheet
18. ITC 1999, ITC 1999 Benchmark home page, http://www.cerc.utecas.edulitc99-benchmark slbench.html

# Advanced SystemC Tracing and Analysis Framework for Extra-Functional Properties

Philipp A. Hartmann[1], Kim Grüttner[1(✉)], and Wolfgang Nebel[2]

[1] OFFIS – Institute for Information Technology, Oldenburg, Germany
pah@computer.org, gruettner@offis.de
[2] Department for Computer Science, University of Oldenburg, Oldenburg, Germany
nebel@informatik.uni-oldenburg.de

**Abstract.** System-level simulations are an important part in the design flow for today's complex systems-on-a-chip. Trade-off analysis during architectural exploration as well as run-time reconfiguration of applications and their mapping require detailed introspection of the dynamic effects on the target platform. Additionally, extra-functional properties like power consumption and performance characteristics are important metrics to assess the quality of a design. In this paper, we present an advanced framework for instrumentation, pre-processing and recording of functional and extra-functional properties in SystemC-based virtual prototyping simulations. The framework is based on a hierarchy of so-called *timed value streams*, allowing to address the requirements for highly configurable, dynamic architectures while allowing tailored introspection of the required system characteristics under analysis.

## 1 Introduction

One of the main challenges for extra-functional property monitoring in today's complex embedded systems is the correct attribution of platform activity (computation, communication and e.g. the resulting power dissipation) to the currently active (software) applications running on the platform. Especially in dynamic reconfigurable scenarios, where multiple applications share the same processing elements, interconnects, memories, peripherals and even energy sources over time, the implicit, parasitic interference along extra-functional dimensions can be hard to quantify and consequently to control.

In order to integrate such a monitoring infrastructure in a virtual platform simulation enhanced with extra-functional properties, several requirements have to be fulfilled, both for the functional models used in the simulation, as well as for the recording and pre-processing capabilities provided by the simulation environment. Last but not least, as some use cases require an online feedback (e.g. power management, power-aware scheduling, etc.), the modelling of extra-functional sensors and probes needs to be integrated in the same simulation environment as well.

Fig. 1 shows a typical virtual platform simulation model. Here, the extra-functional activity is ultimately consumed at the architecture level within processing elements, interconnects, memories and peripherals. For multi-application

© Springer International Publishing Switzerland 2015
K. Sano et al. (Eds.): ARC 2015, LNCS 9040, pp. 141–152, 2015.
DOI: 10.1007/978-3-319-16214-0_12

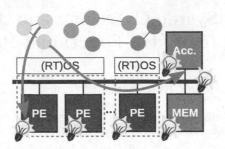

**Fig. 1.** Application-aware platform activity monitoring

scenarios, the correct attribution to the triggering application tasks needs to be ensured. Moreover, the hardware and software architecture consists of multiple service layers, including operating and run-time layers and potentially further platform support for dynamic reconfiguration. Starting from the activity recording at the SoC component level, the requirements for an application-aware simulation infrastructure are summarized in the following.

- **Simplicity:** Only use those (dynamic) parameters needed for the current use case (e.g. ignore area, when not looking for thermal behaviour).
- **Composability:** Derive combined values from physical relations between individual contributors (e.g. total power, temperature-dependent power, capacitance-based power).
- **Hierarchy:** Put parameters on "correct" geometric level, inheriting parameters from the context and/or the environment.
- **Adaptivity:** Allow changing parameters during run-time to support the modelling of dynamic (e.g. power management) subsystems.
- **Abstraction:** Allow flexible selection and structural/temporal abstraction according to the current analysis and monitoring requirements.

From the simulation infrastructure perspective, this requires a flexible and composable framework to describe customized, use case specific, extra-functional models. As the extra-functional simulation infrastructure has to deal with physical quantities (like capacitance, temperatures, etc.), a shortcoming of many C/C++-based environments is the lack of a proper checking for correctly combined quantities. To avoid such modelling errors, strongly-typed **physical units support** is needed, where composition errors can be caught by the compiler.

Today's system-level simulations oftentimes use sophisticated mechanisms to improve the simulation speed. In virtual platform simulations, *temporal decoupling* is a widespread technique to achieve the required simulation performance to run complex software stacks on the simulated platform. Another approach includes *co-simulation* with models described in other simulators (e.g. RTL, custom instruction-set simulators, Matlab/Simulink) or the integration of emulators or hardware/prototypes in the loop. Even third-party extra-functional models might need to be integrated into a single system simulation. Both of these aspects require the separation of the **functional and the extra-functional simulation time progression**. This means that functional blocks need to be able to inject their property updates independently from a global simulation time, preferably in a distributed manner. Hence, a separate update and synchronisation mechanism is required for the extra-functional model.

In this paper, we present a highly flexible instrumentation, tracing, and analysis infrastructure for SystemC-based virtual platform simulations. This framework can be used to record arbitrary (physical) values and quantities over time, based on so-called *timed value streams*. These streams can be combined to a run-time (pre-)processing hierarchy before recording the required data for offline analysis. The paper is organised as follows: In Section 2, we give an overview of the state-of-the-art and refine the goals behind this work. The details of the *timed value streams* semantics are given in Section 3 and the recording and instrumentation of the functional models is described in Section 4. The stream processing and analysis capabilities are then presented in Section 5, and Section 6 concludes the paper with an outline of future work based on the presented infrastructure.

## 2   Goals of this Framework beyond the State-of-the-Art

The main motivation for a dedicated tracing and analysis framework explicitly targeting extra-functional modelling in SystemC is the lack of physical quantity support in the existing, standardized SystemC tracing facilities. Additionally, based on the requirements given in Section 1, more flexibility for the instrumentation, tracing and analysis is needed.

- `sc_core::sc_trace` [5] is not flexible enough, e.g. by being tied to the global simulation time and lacking pre-processing and filtering capabilities.
- `sca_core::sca_trace` [9] is SystemC AMS-specific, not widely supported in commercial environments, and not compatible with temporal decoupling.
- SCV transaction recording [10] not appropriate for physical quantities.
- Some advanced instrumentation APIs are partly available in commercial tools [11], but usually not flexible enough for online preprocessing.

Explicit support for dimensional analysis based on the Boost.Units library [1] has been added to SystemC-AMS in [7]. This approach addresses the lack of proper composition of physical quantities in (SystemC AMS) models. It does not address their tracing, recording, and preprocessing explicitly, though.

Extended tracing frameworks for SystemC have been proposed in the research literature already [3,6]. These approaches focus on transaction-level modelling and do not address the need for the separation of the functional model and the run-time preprocessing of platform activity information. The DUST framework [6] is designed for transaction-level introspection and analysis with advanced storage and online debugging capabilities. The (transaction) recording itself is based on the SCV API [10] and not suitable for extra-functional properties. In [3], "CULT: A Unified Framework for Tracing and Logging C-based Designs" has been proposed. The main features include support for custom back-

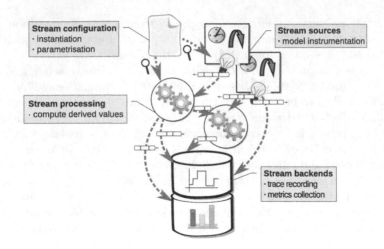

**Fig. 2.** Composable stream processing framework for activity extraction, pre-processing, monitoring and recording

ends and an minimal-invasive instrumentation of the functional models. Explicit support for physical quantities and their online processing is not addressed.

To cover all of the requirements and to provide the required flexibility and composability, we present an instrumentation framework based on *timed value streams*. The basic idea is shown in Fig. 2. The source streams contents are produced by (functional) components, recording the relevant activity information according to their distributed time model (to support temporal decoupling). These primary traces are then processed by a set of stream processors to derive the physical quantities based on the extra-functional property model.

## 3   Timed Value Streams

The underlying core technique of the extra-functional monitoring framework presented to the user is based on so-called *timed value streams*, consisting of a sequence of (`value`,`duration`) tuples.

The basic timed value stream infrastructure is shown in Fig. 3: The leaf annotations in the functional model (1) are `pushed` as tuples according to the current local simulation time of the producing process. These incoming tuples are buffered within the stream (2) without advancing the local time of the stream itself. Once the stream writer explicitly `commits` its updates, the local simulation time of the stream is advanced and the pending tuples are sent to the listening readers (3). Each reader receives its own copy of the tuples, in order to allow independent consumption of the tuples in the following *stream processors* (Section 5).

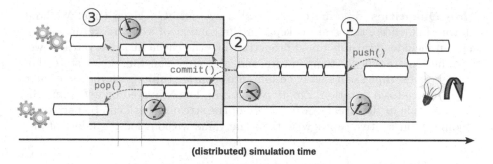

**Fig. 3.** Basic *timed value stream* infrastructure

**Definition 1 (timed value stream).**
A *timed value stream* $\mathcal{S} = \langle (v_0, \tau_0), \ldots, \rangle$ is a sequence of tuples $(v_i, \tau_i)$ with $v_i \in V(\mathcal{S})$ and $\tau_i \in \mathcal{T} \subseteq \mathbb{R}_{>0}$, where

- $V(\mathcal{S})$ is the value domain of the stream, optionally with a *physical dimension*,
- $\tau_i$ denote the *durations* of each tuple, taken from the *time domain* $\mathcal{T}$.

A *stream window* $\mathcal{S}_t^n$ is a finite subsequence of a stream $\mathcal{S}$ of length $n$, where

- $t$ denotes the starting time, with $\exists j : t = \sum_{i=0}^{j} \tau_i$,
- and $n$ tuples in the stream $\langle (v_j, \tau_j), \ldots, (v_{j+n}, \tau_{j+n}) \rangle$.[1]     ♣

During simulation, the (infinite) stream stays a theoretical concept and the following discussion uses finite stream windows instead. Together with the distributed time model, this leads to the phased approach shown in Fig. 3, where individual streams can advance separately and independently from the SystemC simulation time.

It is important to note, that according to above's definition each stream has a strictly monotonic time advance and consists of gapless windows. On the other hand, the activity recording can lead to empty intervals. Furthermore, during the stream processing, streams with unaligned tuples need to be normalized (i.e. split into aligned tuples) to define the time resolution (tuple durations) of the output streams. Both aspects need to be addressed properly in the context of physical quantities.

### 3.1 Support for Extra-Functional/Physical Quantities

Especially in light of extra-functional properties, the values held by a *timed value stream* need to be classified according to their semantics. While functional tracing usually observes the *state* of a system over time, extra-functional properties emerge both as *state quantities* and *process quantities*.[2]

---

[1] We sometimes omit $j$ for improved readability.
[2] This classification is loosely adopted from the theory of thermodynamics. Sometimes, these classes are called state and process *functions*.

**State Quantities** describe the state of a system at a given time. Without external influences, this state is kept. In the context of system-level modeling, this can include extra-functional properties like the cache hit/miss rates, power consumption, (ambient) temperature and of course the functional state. For timed streams, tuples can simply be split into separate tuples with the same value and the same total duration. Empty periods can be completed by extending the previous tuple in the stream. A reduction of the stream length can be performed by joining consecutive tuples with the same value without loosing information.

**Process Quantities** describe a *state change* with an associated duration. Examples include the amount of cache hits/misses,the energy needed for a dynamic frequency/voltage switch, or number of transferred bytes in a transaction. Timed stream tuples of such quantities cannot be split, joined or completed in the same way as state quantities. Instead, splitting requires the distribution of the state change into two (or more) intermediate steps with a combined value equivalent to the original value. Empty periods can be filled with a dedicated "silence value" (usually 0) and a lossless reduction of the stream length is not possible without reducing accuracy of the temporal resolution.

**Timed Stream Traits** are used in the implementation to address the need for the above distinction. A special template parameter defining the different stream tuple policies can be given. The different policies provide an implementation for the different stream (tuple) operations, like splitting, joining and merging tuples.

An example for the default traits of the more interesting *process quantity traits* is given in Listing 1.1. For state quantities corresponding traits classes are available as well. The `merge_policy` is needed for conflicting `push`es to a stream (see Section 4). If the default traits are not sufficient, users can define their own traits (and policies) by inheriting from the default classes and overriding the nested `typedef`s.

```
template<typename ValueType> struct timed_process_traits {
  typedef ValueType value_type;
  // provide default value for empty periods
  typedef timed_silence_policy<value_type>    empty_policy;
  // distribute values proportionally to duration
  typedef timed_divide_policy<value_type>     split_policy;
  // keep tuples separate
  typedef timed_separate_policy<value_type>   join_policy;
  // resolve conflicts by accumulating values
  typedef timed_accumulate_policy<value_type> merge_policy;
}; // timed_process_traits<ValueType>

timed_stream<energy_quantity, timed_process_traits> energy_stream;
timed_stream<power_quantity> power_stream; // state traits by
default
```

**Listing 1.1.** Timed stream traits for process quantities

## 3.2   Distributed Time Model and Synchronisation

In order to support the integration of the stream-processing with a temporally decoupled simulation, the different components integrate into a distributed time model, enabling hierarchical synchronisation between different components.

To finalise the values written to a particular temporarily decoupled timed stream, the pushes need to be explicitly committed. This finalizes the current stream window with all tuples written to the stream until the current local time offset. Subsequent pushes with explicit timestamps earlier than the committed time lead to a run-time error. In addition, attached tracing observers (processors or backends, see Section 5) are notified that new data is available for processing.

In case of multiple independent streams in a single component, the local time offsets need to be consistent as well. Furthermore, the driving SystemC process may need to consume the SystemC simulation time at some point. Both operations are tightly coupled, therefore a second overload of sync functions is provided by the timed streams. Having the same semantics for their arguments, these explicit sync functions return the offset to the current absolute SystemC simulation and perform a commit on *all streams in the current component*. With this, a common idiom to finalise a local computation is the wait(sync) call using one of the streams explicitly as shown in Listing 1.2. Alternatively, a convenience macro to mark such a synchronisation point explicitly is available as well.[3]

```
void commit();                               // commit all pending pushes
void commit( duration_type const & offset ); // ... explicit window
void commit( time_type const & offset );     // ... until offset

time_type sync();                            // commit & synchronise
time_type sync( duration_type const & offset ); // ... explicit window
time_type sync( time_type const & offset );  // ... until offset

#define SYSX_SYNCHRONISATION_POINT() \
  sc_core::wait( [stream_scope].sync() )
```

**Listing 1.2.** Stream synchronisation API

# 4   Activity Recording – Stream Sources

Writing to a *timed stream* can be done explicitly by using a timed_writer object attached to a stream (push interface), or based on implicit extraction of stream updates from variables within the functional model (annotation interface).

## 4.1   Explicit Writing to a Timed Stream

Explicitly pushing to a *timed value stream* can be performed via a *stream writer*, attached to the stream. Writers can be attached and removed from a stream dynamically during runtime, either based on the streams name or in terms of a direct C++ reference.

---

[3] The current "scope" is determined by the tracing framework automatically.

```
void push( value_type const & value, duration_type const & duration ); // (1)
void push( time_type  const & offset
         , value_type const & value, duration_type const & duration ); // (2)
void push( value_type const & value );                                 // (3)
```

Listing 1.3. Stream push interface

Overload (1) adds a given value for a given duration to the current end of the stream. Since each stream maintains a local time offset, this time offset is automatically advanced by the given duration, when this interface call is used. This interface is particularly well suited for annotating local computations without requiring external synchronisation in-between.

The push (2) function can be used to write (future) values to a stream, delayed relatively to the stream's local time as given by the offset parameter. When using this overload, the local time of the stream is not advanced. This variant can be used to support out-of-order temporal decoupling and potentially leads to overlapping tuples that need to be merged according to the stream's merge_policy (creating an error by default).

The final overload (3) can be used in case of an unknown duration (only suited for *state quantities*). In this case, the value is assumed to be held indefinitely until overwritten again. Again, the stream's local time is not advanced until the next commit.

## 4.2    Block-Based Annotations

A frequent use case of the annotation framework is the augmentation of application source code with extra-functional properties. If only a single stream is driven from within a process, no inter-stream synchronisation is needed and the local time of the component is equal to the local time of the (only) stream. If multiple streams are maintained, each of which has different update characteristics, keeping the local time offsets consistent quickly becomes inconvenient. Therefore, a higher level abstraction for block-based annotations of execution time durations is provided, separating the time annotation from the actual value updates again and handling the synchronisation transparently for the user.

```
timed_stream<process_state>                  state_str;    // IDLE
timed_stream<unsigned, timed_process_traits> mem_load_str; // 0

void faculty(int in0, int& out0) {
    timed_var<process_state> state( state_str );      //traceable var
    timed_var<unsigned>      mem_load( mem_load_str ); //traceable var
    timed_ref<int>           in      ( in0 );         // alias parameter

    SYSX_TIMED_BLOCK( sc_time(500, SC_NS) ) {  // functionality
        state    = BUSY;
        mem_load = 10;
        // ...
    } // automatic push to all streams in scope

    while(tmp0) SYSX_TIMED_BLOCK( sc_time(200, SC_NS) ) {
        state    = BUSY;
```

```
     mem_load = 2;
   } // automatic push to all streams in scope
   SYSX_SYNCHRONISATION_POINT}(); // commit and sync with SystemC
   return;
}
```

**Listing 1.4.** Simple example of tracing multiple local values

The different basic blocks for annotations are wrapped within `SYSX_TIMED_BLOCK` C++ scopes providing the duration of the block. Instead of explicit pushes to different streams, `timed_var` objects can be used and updated via plain assignments. These timed variables (or their `timed_ref` counterpart, aliasing an existing variable) are used to implicitly push the corresponding tuples upon exit of the annotated block.

## 5   Run-Time Extra-Functional Property Monitoring – Stream Processing

As sketched in Fig. 2, the actual processing of the leaf instrumentation towards derived extra-functional properties is performed by a hierarchical set of so-called *stream processors*. These processors are triggered based on the object-oriented *Observer pattern*, without relying on the SystemC simulation itself (no SystemC processes, events, channels) to facilitate a separation of the models and to allow dynamic reconfiguration of the analysis environment during runtime. Stream processors can attach to a (set of) `timed_readers` and subscribe to `commits`, either for each extension of a pending window or just for the start of new windows.

```
   void notify( timed_reader_base & src );
```

**Listing 1.5.** Stream observer interface

Subsequently reading pending values via a `timed_reader` can be done in several ways. For most pre-processing operations, the `(const_)tuple_iterator` based interface is sufficient. The streams provide the output interface for consuming the committed data sketched in the following listing:

```
value_type const & get() const;                          // read a
value value_type const & get( duration_type const & o ) const;
// ... at given offset

tuple_type const & front() const;                        // read
first tuple tuple_type const & front( duration_type const & d );
// ... for a duration

void pop_front();                                        // drop
first tuple void pop_until( time_type const & until );
// ... for a duration void pop_all();
// ... all tuples

const_tuple_iterator begin() const;        // get iterators to the
pending tuples const_tuple_iterator end()    const;
```

**Listing 1.6.** Stream reader interface

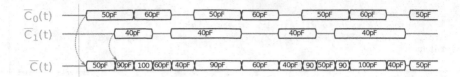

**Fig. 4.** Structural abstraction: Accumulating switching activity by stream processing

Additionally, various querying functions about the different time offsets and other utility functions are available in the stream base class.

### 5.1 Time Normalisation of Streams

When combining streams with different time resolutions, a *time normalisation* needs to be performed. This means that tuple boundaries need to be aligned before combining their values according to the stream processor's output function.

For a stream processor listening to multiple streams $\mathcal{S}_0, \ldots, \mathcal{S}_k$, the pending windows[4] $\mathcal{S}_{i,t_0}^{n_i}$ are transformed to *normalised windows* $\mathcal{S}_{i,t_0}^{n'}$ by applying the stream's `split_policy` according to the following rules:

$$\mathcal{S}_{i,t_0}^{n'} = \left\langle \left(v'_{i,0}, \tau'_0\right), \ldots, \left(v'_{i,n'-1}, \tau_{n'-1}\right)\right\rangle$$
$$= \left\langle \left(v'_{i,0}, (t'_1 - t_0)\right), \ldots, \left(v'_{i,n'-1}, (t'_{n'-1} - t'_{n'-2})\right)\right\rangle, \text{with}$$
$$t_{i,j} = t_0 + \sum_{l<j} \tau_{i,l}$$
$$t'_j = \inf_{0 \le i \le k} \left\{ t_{i,l} : t_{i,l} > t'_{j-1}\right\}, t'_0 = t_0$$
$$v'_i = \text{SplitPolicy}(\mathcal{S}_{i,t_0}^{n_i}, \tau'_i)$$

This normalisation can be performed by the stream processor base class to simplify the stream processor implementation itself. An example for this operation is shown in Fig. 4, which depicts a *structural abstraction* by combining two (average) switching activity streams from two functional components into a joint switching activity stream.

Another dimension for stream abstraction is the reduction of the time resolution, called *temporal abstraction*. A stream processor can for instance reduce the number of tuples in a stream by averaging the values over a fixed time window. This is useful to reduce the amount of tuples that need to be processed and helps improving the simulation performance.

### 5.2 Offline Analysis – Stream Backends

Especially for offline or post-mortem analysis, a special set of stream processors can be used, so called *stream backends*. Compared to a generic stream processor,

---

[4] The starting time is assumed to be aligned already.

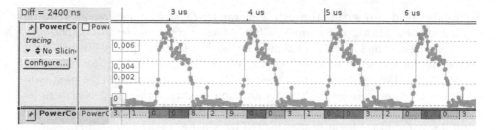

**Fig. 5.** Example trace integration into Synopsys Virtualizer

a stream backend has no outgoing timed streams on its own and merely processes (a set of) incoming streams for specific purposes. Different use cases for stream backends are to be considered, as described in the following. The detailed external interface of these backends are specific to these use cases and therefore out of the scope of this paper.

**Trace File Generation.** One of the most obvious backends for a tracing and analysis infrastructure is the generation of value-over-time trace files, e.g. based on the Value Change Dump (VCD) format [4]. This widespread text-based format is supported by most graphical analysis tools and can be generated by the standard SystemC `sc_trace` API as well. Consequently, a VCD backend has been implemented for timed streams.

Secondly, some commercial simulation environments provide additional analysis capabilities beyond a mere visualisation of traces. One example for such an environment is the Synopsys Virtualizer tool suite [11], which includes an generic data analysis API suitable for the integration with the timed value streams extension. An example excerpt of a dynamic power trace stream visualized by the Virtualizer user interface is shown in Fig. 5.

**Metrics/Statistics Collection.** Another frequent requirement of system-level simulations is the gathering of compact performance or quality metrics for example to drive an automatic design space exploration. To enable the collection of such metrics or statistical information, user-defined stream backends can be used as well. These specific metric backends then report their value(s) at the end of the simulation (or explicitly upon request). As there is no feedback to the simulation model itself, the computation of the design metrics can run independently of the SystemC simulation time.

## 6   Conclusion

In this paper, we have presented a novel approach for instrumentation, preprocessing and analysis of extra-functional properties in system-level simulations. The SystemC-based implementation uses *timed value stream* to transport such extra-functional properties through a hierarchy of stream processors towards dedicated backends for offline analysis (trace files or report generators). The approach is currently included in our simulation environment for power-aware virtual prototypes [2].

As a special extension, we will now start to define a dedicated set of stream backends to allow simulation-based validation of extra-functional contracts [8] (assumption/guarantee pairs covering extra-functional properties). The underlying linear-temporal logic properties (LTL) will be used to run-time monitors based on stream processors. With the capability to store a continuous window of tracing history (see Section 5), the stream-based infrastructure is perfectly suited for this kind of temporal monitoring.

**Acknowledgments.** This work has been partially supported by the EU integrated projects COMPLEX (FP7-247999) and CONTREX (FP7-611146).

# References

1. Boost. Units library 1.1.0. http://www.boost.org/doc/html/boost_units.html
2. Grüttner, K., Hartmann, P.A., Hylla, K., Rosinger, S., Nebel, W., Herrera, F., Villar, E., Brandolese, C., Fornaciari, W., Palermo, G., Ykman-Couvreur, C., Quaglia, D., Ferrero, F., Valencia, R.: The COMPLEX reference framework for HW/SW co-design and power management supporting platform-based design-space exploration. Microprocessors and Microsystems 37(8,C), 966–980 (2013), Special Issue on European Projects in Embedded System Design (EPESD 2012)
3. Hong, W., Joshi, J., Vieh, A., Bannow, N., Kramer, A., Post, H., Bringmann, O., Rosenstiel, W.: Advanced features for industry-level logging and tracing of C-based designs. In: Forum on Specification and Design Languages (FDL 2013). IEEE (September 2013)
4. IEEE Standard Verilog Hardware Description Language. IEEE Std. 1364–2005, IEEE Computer Society (April 2006) ISBN 0-7381-4851-2
5. IEEE Standard SystemC Language Reference Manual. IEEE Std. 1666–2011. IEEE Computer Society (January 2012). http://standards.ieee.org/getieee/1666/ ISBN 978-0-7381-6801-2
6. Klingauf, W., Geffken, M.: Design structure analysis and transaction recording in SystemC designs: A minimal-intrusive approach. In: Forum on Specification and Design Languages (FDL 2006). IEEE (September 2006)
7. Maehne, T., Vachoux, A.: Supporting dimensional analysis in SystemC-AMS. In: IEEE Behavioral Modeling and Simulation Workshop (BMAS 2009), pp. 108–113 (September 2009)
8. Nitsche, G., Grüttner, K., Nebel, W.: Power contracts: A formal way towards power-closure?! In: Proc. of the 23rd Intl. Workshop on Power and Timing Modeling, Optimization and Simulation (PATMOS), pp. 59–66 (September 2013)
9. Standard SystemC AMS extensions 2.0 Language Reference Manual. Accellera Systems Initiative (March 2013). http://accellera.org/downloads/standards/systemc
10. SystemC Verification Library 2.0. Accellera Systems Initiative (July 2014). http://accellera.org/downloads/standards/systemc
11. Synopsys: Virtualizer. http://www.synopsys.com/systems/virtualprototyping

# Run-Time Partial Reconfiguration Simulation Framework Based on Dynamically Loadable Components

Xerach Peña[✉], Fernando Rincon, Julio Dondo, Julian Caba,
and Juan Carlos Lopez

Universidad de Castilla-La Mancha, CP:13071 Ciudad Real, Spain
xerach.pena@uclm.es

**Abstract.** In this paper a SystemC-based framework for run-time partial reconfiguration modeling and simulation is introduced which allows to perform early design space exploration for dynamically reconfigurable systems. Besides, a middleware to extend the capability of TLM introducing a semantic to interconnect components described at different abstraction levels or languages is added. This middleware allows to automate the creation of the corresponding communication adapters to these new components. Finally, the services provided by the middleware are described and experimental results are presented to validate the proposal.

**Keywords:** SystemC · Dynamic reconfiguration · Middleware

## 1 Introduction

Nowadays, embedded systems composed by one or several microprocessors plus reconfigurable hardware are gaining importance in the implementation of a large range of applications. Their success is largely due to its flexibility, the capability to exploit hw reconfiguration and the high ratio of performance versus power consumption. In this context, partial reconfiguration capability is one of the most important features concerning many of these reconfigurable devices. However, although run-time reconfiguration enables new possibilities in the reconfigurable computation field, it also introduces new challenges such as how to get an efficient use of the reconfigurable resources, including how to obtain an optimum management of the reconfiguration process. These reconfigurable resources are used to host different components during design life-cycle. However, the characteristics of these resources such as occupied area size, shape, location, communication interface, etc., must be defined in the first stages of the design process, forcing developers to deal not only with traditional co-design techniques and high-level design problems, but with efficient reconfiguration process scheduling as well. Moreover, there is a lack of tools to handle the modeling of partially reconfigurable FPGAs at high level of abstraction making almost impossible to explore the impact of reconfigurable sub-systems on the performance and behaviour of the system as a whole in early design phases.

© Springer International Publishing Switzerland 2015
K. Sano et al. (Eds.): ARC 2015, LNCS 9040, pp. 153–164, 2015.
DOI: 10.1007/978-3-319-16214-0_13

To solve this problem, there have been some proposals, based on sw/hw systems for dynamic resource management in FPGAs, that combine both scheduling and instantiation tasks, and providing a complete flow management to support the design of dynamically reconfigurable hw [12]. However, this kind of solution lead designers to the need of a platform where designs could be tested and simulated, in order to avoid the implementation in hw until the design has been correctly checked out. Thus, the capability to model partial reconfiguration devices in this sort of platform is revealed as a fundamental requirement in the design flow. Furthermore, due to the ever increasing complexity of hw and hw/sw co-designs, developers strive for higher levels of abstraction in the early stages of the design flow.

In this context, SystemC [1] language has been revealed as an important tool to deal with not only modelling in high level of abstraction, but also to work at all stages of the design flow in hw/sw co-designs. SystemC allows the design and verification of sw, hw or mixed systems. It allows also describing a system at different levels of abstraction, from RTL up to functional models that may be timed or untimed. SystemC mainly consists of a class library of C++, composed of classes, macros and templates; and a simulation kernel, forming together a framework. This framework has the capability to model a concurrent system using modules, communications mechanisms and hw-oriented data types. A module is formed by one or several processes modeling its behaviour; ports to communicate with other modules; and internal variables to save its states. The communication ports can be interconnected by using channels. In a SystemC model hierarchy is allowed so a module can contain other modules. This hierarchy is dynamically constructed during the execution of the model elaboration phase and it cannot be changed once the simulation phase has started. This implies a major difficulty to model the partial dynamic reconfiguration using SystemC.

The simulation kernel executes a SystemC model scheduling and calling C++ functions registered by using SC_THREAD, SC_CTHREAD or SC_METHOD processes. This execution is divided into two phases: the elaboration phase and the simulation phase[2]. During the elaboration phase the modules are instantiated and initialized by executing their constructor. It is in this phase where the processes are also registered. Following, the connections between modules are established as a part of the initialization phase.

## 1.1 Dynamic Reconfiguration in SystemC

A reconfigurable system is one that can change part of its configuration at runtime. Dynamically reconfigurable FPGAs can modify part of its structure to implement different components with different functionalities in the same area whereas the rest of the system is running.

Modelling a reconfigurable system requires modelling its behavior as a whole, in where all possible configurations are taken into account. However, the main problem that a developer faces when trying to model dynamic reconfiguration in SystemC is that new instances can't be generated once the simulation phase has already started. This limitation can be solved by stopping the simulation phase, opening the elaboration phase in order to make all necessary changes, and running again the simulation phase. However in this way the dynamic reconfiguration process is still not modeled.

Therefore, in a system formed by a set of microprocessor and dynamically reconfigurable FPGAs, a platform that allows the simulation, testing and verification of the system including dynamic reconfiguration at the first stage of the design, arises as a need.

To address these problems, in this paper a simulation framework is proposed, where reconfiguration takes place at two diffent levels. On one side, it allows the reconiguration of the interconnection infrastructure at run-time, where components can be described at different abstraction levels and languages, such as C/C++, SystemC RTL, or VHDL. On the other side partial run-time reconfiguration of components is modeled after the use of dynamically loadable libraries, which do not imply the modification of the simulation kernel, and provides a simple and homogeneous mecanism for the replacement of the different behaviors associated to a reconfigurable area. This framework is based on a lightweight middleware, using TLM-2.0 as the common transport layer.

The remainder of the paper is structured as follows: in Sect. 2, we discuss works related to SystemC and partial reconfiguration modeling. Section 3 introduces our simulation framework and the way to model dynamically reconfigurable systems, and Sect. 4 presents the application used to validate it. Finally, we discuss conclusions of our work in Sect. 5.

## 2    Related Works

Although there are some authors who have proposed a solution based on a modified SystemC kernel as presented in [3] and [4], most of the researchers have chosen to stay into the standard and not modify the simulation kernel.

Regarding an unmodified simulation kernel, works shown in [5] associated to ADRIATIC (Advanced Methodology for Designing Reconfigurable SoC and Application Targeted IP-entities in wireless Communications) Project, carries out the concept of Dynamic Reconfigurable Fabric. The fabric is a special component that contains several contexts and the capability to dynamically switch from one context to another. This paper propose a methodology for modeling dynamically re-configurable blocks, that takes as an input a SystemC model of a static system and transforms it into a code implementing a reconfigurable module. Candidate modules to a dynamic implementation are chosen by their common interface. The main drawback of this work is that it is necessary to have all the functionalities implemented in each reconfigurable module and it is not allowed to change it once the simulation has began.

Sharing the same point of view, authors in [6] present their approach to model partial reconfiguration as a SystemC library, called ReChannel. Although the concept of reconfigurable zone is added, a reconfigurable module consists in instantiating all possible modules for each reconfigurable zone, as the previous case, where only one module is activated at a time by a dynamic circuit switching.

To connect the set of reconfigurable modules and the remaining system, a portal is used by handling the basic channel defined on SystemC. The control to manage reconfiguration is carried out by dedicated portals. However, not only the tasks are assigned once at the beginning of the simulation, which means that it is not possible to move the task from one reconfigurable zone to another, but also, it is not allowed to add new modules in run-time either.

One approach closely related to the architecture of Xilinxs FPGAs, especially Virtex-II, Virtex-4 and Virtex-5 is shown in [7] and [8]. In this case, the authors put forward a simulation model where reconfiguration capabilities are included as well. The starting point is in the smallest unit that can be reconfigured at the hw level, generating a 1D sequence of columns or 2D grid of tiles, using a tile as a container encapsulating all needed functionalities. The inner process of a SystemC module is implemented using SC_CTHREAD, SC_THREAD and SC_METHOD to represent a synchronous sequential, asynchronous sequential, and combinational circuits, respectively. The method bodies only consists of a function pointer that indicates the currently configured functionality. Communication between tiles has been implemented by manifold ports, modelling the bus macros used as connectors in the FPGA. When components use more than one tile, there will be a master tile that execute the task while the others are functionally switched off, or simply route signals to neighbour tiles. This is an excellent solution to simulate dynamic systems in this type of FPGAs, however there are several aspects to take into account. Firstly, the set of ports per edge is given by the superset of ports required by all implemented functionalities. Thus every tiles must implement all possible communication protocols. Besides, every systemC module must include an empty function as well as those implementing simple signal transfers from incoming to outgoing ports, increasing simulation time. Finally, this simulation platform does not allow inclusion of new functionalities once the simulation has started, nor reuse it in architectures other than 1D or 2D meshes.

In [9], authors presented OSSS+R by adding reconfigurable support to the extension OSSS (Oldenburg System Synthesis Subset), and where they proposes the automatic synthesis of a reconfigurable system. This synthesisable subset of SystemC is extended by additional elements for high-level modelling, like shared variables, polymorphism or transaction level modelling. The C++ polymorphism concept is used to assign different modules to one reconfigurable zone, as long as they share the same static interface. This reconfigurable zone are modeled as a special container called osss_recon, which is the basis to take into account the reconfiguration and the context switch times to provide a RTL model. However, tasks are assigned to a reconfigurable zone within this container in a static way, and it is not allowed to change or add one in run-time.

The capability to enable, disable, resume and kill process on systemC were concepts introduced in SystemC-2.1 as dynamic threads, and it had been used by authors in [10]. In contrast of static threads, dynamic threads may be spawned during runtime and not only during the elaboration phase. In this work a reconfigurable module is composed of two dynamic threads: one for the actual user process, modeling the functionality; and the other one for the creation and destruction processes (control). This work also define the concept of dynamic port, making possible the construction of a port after the elaboration phase. However the dynamic port comprises a set of static channels that generate instance of channel pool before the simulation, and manages the connection and disconnection of channels in the channel pool. Concerning the two dynamic threads that compose a reconfigurable module, the control thread is not part of the reconfiguration process, since it is not the module which is in charge of the reconfiguration process.

In [11] authors present a simulator, based on the separation of concerns between the application and the architecture, and it can be used either in early development stages, or during the implementation phase. As already mentioned in previous works, they use the concept of reconfigurable zone characterized by a set of resources. Through their methodology they have taken into account functionality changing and resources sharing. During simulation, a manager is used to map the reconfigurable modules into the appropriate zone according to available resources. In order to model the dynamic behaviour of the tasks, a module is set up with two dynamic threads. The first one is the User Algorithm and represents the functionality of a dynamically reconfigurable module, spawning at runtime. The second one is the Reconfiguration Control, that communicates with the configuration interface and it is responsible for the creation and the destruction of the User Algorithm. All the communications in this work (between modules and from the reconfiguration manager to a module) were described using OSCI TLM-2.0 standard.

Encapsulating a reconfigurable task, modeling its dynamic behaviour by SystemCs dynamic threads, and carrying out the communication by using TLM is by far the most flexible and complete method to work with partial dynamic reconfiguration on SystemC.

Extending some issues shown in related works, we presented in [12] a framework to manage partially dynamic reconfiguration in a completed transparent way for both the user and the application. In this work a Reconfiguration Engine has been designed to efficiently handle the reconfiguration process without processor intervention, and reducing considerably the reconfiguration time. Furthermore, we extended the use of TLM [13] not only to communicate between modules, or between a module and the remaining system, but also to show a method to widen flexibility concerning to the topology of the reconfigurable modules. Although the capability to change or add tasks in run-time on SystemC has not been successfully treated yet, in [14] is shown a method to work with plugins in C++ that opens a way for reconfigurable modules in run-time on SystemC.

Our approach relies on a combination between dynamic threads of SystemC and plugins of C++ to change the functionality of modules during run-time, and on transaction level modeling for all the communications. One of the most important features of our proposal is that it is not necessary to change the simulation kernel of SystemC, and therefore, it is in the line followed by the standard.

# 3  Simulation Framework

## 3.1  Heterogeneous Component Integration

One of the contributions of the paper is the definition of a common integration environment, where different kinds of heretogeneous (hw and sw) comoponents can be integrated at different abstraction levels. This is achived thanks to the use of a TLM communication infrastructure, and therefore to the separation of concerns between communcation and functionality. However, TLM is only used as the communication physical layer because, as novel contribution in this work, a middleware is added, incorporating a new logical layer, and appending a set of semantic rules to TLM (See Fig: 1).

The TLM layer works as a communication network that routes messages from one physical TLM destination to another. On the other side, each component has a logical identifier, and follows some simple and predefined rules for the construction and parsing of the communication messages, which define the fields to include in the message as well as the way data must be serialized to be consistent in both ends of the communication process. The purpose of the logical layer is to stablish a biunivocal correspondence between the behavior representation of the component as a set of functions and parameters, and how their invocations and return values are translated into messages. However, components may be modelled at any abstraction layer, as far as their final interface is compatible with the logical messages defined.

The separation of both the physical and logical planes of the communication is the key to provide transparency between components, and avoid unnecessary coupling between functionality and low-level integration details. However it relies on the use of a specific adapter, called CA (Communication Adapter), provided as part of the framework, and which will act as a bridge between both worlds.

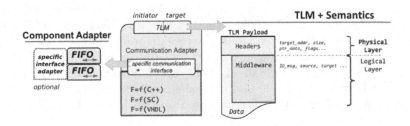

**Fig. 1.** Communication adapter

## 3.2  Communication Adapter Architecture

As a result, the simulation framework allows the interconnection of not only a set of components described in different abstraction levels, but also any other entity (such a external subsystem), as long as it is done through a specific CA. For instance, it is possible to connect our system to an emulator, where an specific sw is running, and which makes use of a component simulated in our tool as a hw accelerator.

As its name describes, the purpose of the Communication Adapter (figure 1) is the adaptation of the component interface to the TLM communication infrastructure that links the rest of components in the system. On the TLM side, operation requests and data are encapsulated following the payload format described in the TLM-2.0 standard. On the component side, communication is performed by a double set of input/ouput FIFOs. The use of a FIFO interface may seem restrictive with respect to the use of a richer component interface at a first glance. However, the payload format used by TLM perfectly fits this approach with almost no overhead, and additionally, it is possible to add an specific adapter to map it into a more appropriate one.

The CA is a library component provided by the simulation framework. From the physical communication point of view, it can be configured to act as a TLM initiator and/or target. Each kind of interface has its counterpart input and output FIFOs in the component side. But from a logical point of view, the CA is the responsible for the implementation of the basic middleware services, which in the simplest case implies that communication transparency between components is guaranteed. This is achieved by the:

- **separation between physical and logical addressing spaces**. The physical one relates to the references used by TLM, which are used to route messages from initiators to targets and vice-versa. Logical references are used by the components, regardless of their physical location. Logical addresses are mapped into physical ones depending on the topology defined in the model. The mapping can be hardcoded in the CA, or may be delegated into a location service, such as the one described in section 3.6.
- **message format**. Messages are routed by the TLM infrastructure based on the information in their headers, which corresponds to the physical addressing space. The TLM data field of the payload can be divided into two parts. The first one can be considered the logical header of the message, and includes the logical address from the source and target, as well as a message identifier, that the CA can use to link return values with the requests. Finally the last part of the message includes the real data of the message, serialized following a set of fixed rules. That data can be directly forwarded to the component interface FIFOs.
- **message protocol**. In this case a simple request/replay protocol is used.

### 3.3    Partial Dynamic Run-Time Reconfiguration

As already mentioned in the introduction, SystemC suffers from some limitations when considering partial dynamic reconfiguration modelling.The main conclusion to be drawn from these limitations is that there is no direct way to add functionality to a component at runtime without modifying the simulation kernel.

Alternatively, this paper proposes of a novel technique for modelling partial dynamic reconfiguration using SystemC, which is based in the combination of dynamic libraries, plus the use of a special component adaptor: the Reconfigurable Unit (RU). Such units can be configured to embed completely different behaviors, that may be replaced during the life cycle of the application. RUs and regular components are integrated into the simulation model using the CA described in section 3.2, since once configured, RUs act as any other component in the system.

RU reconfiguration is performed by the Reconfiguration Controller (RC). The task of the controller is to dynamically (at run-time) load the behaviors associated to each RU, and configure the CA to be accessible from other components in the system. The RU doesn't take any reconfiguration decisions by itself, but it provides a very simple abstraction layer for reconfiguration management. Currently the framework doesn't include any facility such as a reconfiguration scheduler, so it must be modelled as part of the application. However, nothing prevents from building it as a service on top of the RC.

Finally a directory service is required, in order to map logical references of the components into their physical TLM identity. As part of the reconfiguration process both the logical and physical identities of the component in the CA of the RU are updated.

### 3.4  Reconfigurable Unit Architecture

RUs are not real components but an almost empty frame that provides the FIFO interfaces described in section 3.2 (figure 2), as well as a reference variable that can instantiate different component behaviors, not statically determined (figure 2). The reconfiguration process then consists in the instantiation of a certain behavior included in a dynamic library, which can be loaded at runtime, just like a sw plugin. Once the library is downloaded, the reference is updated, and the RU behaves as specified in the library.

As it happens with plugins, something to take into account is that the interface of the component is fixed at design time, and therefore every component that maps into a RU must comply with it. However, that's not really a problem because in the proposed model, the entry point to the component are FIFO channels. If a more specific interface is required (for third party IP integration, for example), it can be easily adapted. The reconfigurable behavior thus will include the adaptor as part of the model. Furthermore, the existance of a fixed interface resembles the real physical behavior of reconfigurable logic in FPGAs.

### 3.5  Reconfiguration Controller

The Reconfiguration Controller includes a list of the available RUs in the system. This list is defined at compile, when the concrete number of available RUs is fixed. Therefore there is no limitation in the number of different behaviors used in the RUs, but the number of different RUs remains constant.

After elaboration, at run-time, the RC waits for the reception of reconfiguration requests. The RC works at a different plane than the RUs in the system, and does not share the same TLM communication infrastructure. The requests

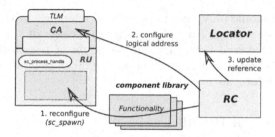

**Fig. 2.** Communication adapter

are received though the input FIFO as a serialized message, that can include one of the following type of operations:

- **start**: for the activation of the component, either because it has been previously stopped or it has just been configured
- **stop**: that disables both the execution and reception of messages
- **reconfigure**: the request includes the name of the behavior to download, as well as the physical and logical identities of the new resulting component.

From the simulator point of view, the reconfiguration process involves three operations, all of them managed from the RC:

1. First the binary code of the new behavior must be downloaded from a dynamic library. Previously the source code of the model must be compiled, and the compatibility of the interface has to be ensured. Once downloaded, the RU reference to the real code is updated (through a $sc\_process\_handle$ reference).
2. The next step consists in the configuration of the logical addressing in the CA of the RU, so the new component becomes available to the rest of components in the system. At the same time such reference must be updated in the directory service (locator), so it can be queried by other CAs during logical to physical address translation.
3. Finally, a call to the $sc\_spawn$ function will initiate the execution of the process that acts as the entry point to the component behavior, which is equivalent to the *start* operation.

The procedure described above can also include time modelling, and a reconfigurable latency can be asociated in the form of a parametrizable function.

## 3.6   Location Service

This service is used to map physical and logical addresses, and can be easily implemented using a table. The use of a table even allows for the dynamic replacement of the references, a necessary feature to implement partial dynamic reconfiguration.

Components should only refer to the logical references of their targets so the models are not dependant from the concrete topology of the implementation. The translation between both of them should be a responsibility of the CA which will request for it to the location service. Such requests can be cached in the adapter to reduce the execution overhead.

## 4  Experimental Results

In order to check the validity of the approach two simple experiments have been carried out. The first one consists in the reconfiguration of a simple signal generator component with two versions, one producing a sinusoidal output, and the other generating a saw shaped signal. The top of the system simply instantiates one RU plus the corresponding CA, and the RC, and data communication reduces to a single message for starting/stopping the generation procedure. The result of the execution is shown in figure 3.

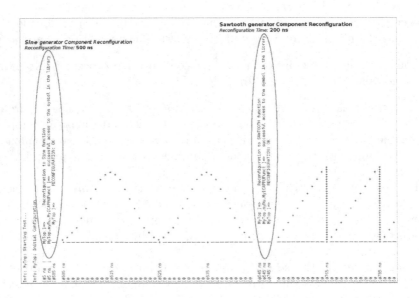

**Fig. 3.** Simulation of a reconfiguration

The second experiment consists in the simulation of a set of several versions of the Features from Accelerated Segment Test (FAST) Corner Detection algorithm [15] [16], used to detect corners in an image. In this experiment different versions of the algorithm are implemented in the same RU, and taking 9, 10, 11 or 12 pixels in the working out for each version. This experiment is used to model a dynamically reconfigurable part of a system in which the execution of this algorthm is accelerated in reconfigurable areas of a FPGA in which the hw implementation of the algorithm can be reconfigured in run-time according to

the version required [17]. In this experiment for each version, a golden reference model exists to check the correct performance of the algorithm. The top
application uses the dynamically reconfigurable environment to keep the same
system simulation environment to systematically evaluate all different versions.
The model includes a test module that consecutively loads a different configuration into a single RU, injects the corresponding data through the TLM infrastructure, receives the results of the computation, and finally checks the correct
performance of the model.

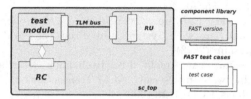

**Fig. 4.** FAST test simulation

However, the framework described is not limited to the use of a single dynamically reconfigurable component. Any number of them can be combined, including
the static part of the design, or even linked with a third party models, as far as
the communication takes place through the appropriate CA. This framework is
specially well suited for the simulation of highly adaptable systems, such as the
ones used in mixed mode genetic architectures, for example.

## 5 Conclusions

The main contribution presented in this paper has been a straightforward way to
model partial dynamic reconfiguration in SystemC without the need to modify
the simulation kernel of the language. Although the work mostly refers to reconfigurable components, it can be extensible to the whole model of the system,
since the use of a communication middleware ensures communication flexibly
and transparency between heterogeneous components. Such middleware is based
in the use of TLM as the physical transport layer for messages, and therefore
inherits the benefits in the modelling capabilities as well as the flexibility already
provided by the standard.

Moreover, the proposed technique for reconfiguration implies almost no simulation overhead, since the number of components instantiated are kept to the
minimum, there is only one active processes in execution per RU, and there is
not any other in the background, disabled or waiting to be resumed. Finally,
the extension of the system through the inclusion of new behaviors that can be
instantiated into the RUs, implies no modification in the simulation model.

# References

1. www.accelera.org
2. Black, D.C., Donovan, J., Bunton, B., Keist, A.: SystemC: From the Ground Up. Springer (2005)
3. Bhattacharyya, B., Rose, J., Swan, S.: Language Extensions to SystemC: Process Control Constructs. In: Procs. of the 44th Annual Conference on Design Automation (DAC), NY, USA, pp. 35–38 (2007)
4. Brito, A.V., Kuhnle, M., Hubner, M., Becker, J., Melcher, E.U.K.: Modelling and Simulation of Dynamic and Partially Reconfigurable Systems using SystemC. In: Procs. of ISVLSI, pp. 35–40 (2007)
5. Pelkonen, A., Masselos, K., Cupak, M.: System-Level Modeling of Dynamically Reconfigurable Hardware with SystemC. In: Procs. of Parallel and Distributed Processing Symposium (2003)
6. Raabe, A., Hartmann, P.A., Anlauf, J.K.: Rechannel: Describing and Simulating Reconfigurable Hardware in SystemC. ACM Transactions on Design Automation of Electronic Systems 13(1), 1–18 (2008)
7. Albrecht, C. Pionteck, T., Koch, R., Maehle, E.: Modelling Tile-Based Run-Time Reconfigurable Systems Using SystemC. In: Proc. of the European Conference on Modelling and Simulation (ECMS), Prague (2007)
8. Pionteck, T., Albrecht, C., Koch, R., Brix, T., Maehle, E.: Design and Simulation of Runtime Reconfigurable Systems. In: Procs. of IEEE Workshop on Design and Diagnostics of Electronic Circuits and Systems (2008)
9. Schallenberg, A., Nebel, W., Herrholz, A., Hartmann, P.A., Oppenheimer, F.: OSSS+R: a framework for application level modelling and synthesis of reconfigurable systems. In: Procs. of the Conference on Design, Automation and Test in Europe (DATE), Belgium, pp. 970–975 (2009)
10. Asano, K., Kitamichi, J., Kenichi, K.: Dynamic Module Library for System Level Modeling and Simulation of Dynamically Reconfigurable Systems. Journal of Computers 3, 55–62 (2008)
11. Duhem, F., Muller, F., Lorenzini, P.: Methodology for designing partially reconfigurable systems using transaction-level modeling. In: Procs. of Design and Architectures for Signal and Image Processing (DASIP), pp. 1–7 (2011)
12. Cervero, T., Dondo, J., Gomez, A., Rincon, F., Lopez, S., Peña, X., Sarmiento, R., Lopez, J.C.: A resource manager for dynamically reconfigurable FPGA-based embedded systems. In: Procs. of Conference on Digital Systems Design (EUROMICRO), Santander (2013)
13. Open SystemC Initiative (OSCI), OSCI TLM-2.0 Language Ref. Manual (2009)
14. Dynamic Class Loading for C++ on Linux. http://www.linuxjournal.com/article/3687
15. Rosten, E., Drummond, T.: Fusing Points and Lines for High Performance Tracking. In: Procs. of the IEEE Intl. Conference on Computer Vision (ICCV) (2005)
16. Rosten, E., Drummond, T.W.: Machine Learning for High-Speed Corner Detection. In: Leonardis, A., Bischof, H., Pinz, A. (eds.) ECCV 2006, Part I. LNCS, vol. 3951, pp. 430–443. Springer, Heidelberg (2006)
17. Dondo, J.D., Villanueva, F., Garcia, D., Gonzalez, C., Vallejo, D., Lopez, J.C.: Distributed FPGA-based Architecture to Support Indoor Localisation and Orientation Services. Journal of Network and Computer Application 45, 181–190 (2014)

# Network-on-a-Chip

# Architecture Virtualization for Run-Time Hardware Multithreading on Field Programmable Gate Arrays

Michael Metzner[1]([✉]), Jesus A. Lizarraga[2], and Christophe Bobda[3]

[1] Department of Computer Science, University of Potsdam, Potsdam, Germany
metzner@cs.uni-potsdam.de
[2] Instituto Politecnico Nacional, Mexico City, Mexico
[3] CSCE Department, University of Arkansas Fayetteville, Fayetteville, AR, USA
cbobda@uark.edu

**Abstract.** In this paper a novel coarse-grained architecture virtualization for Field Programmable Gate Arrays (FPGA) is presented which can be used as basis for run-time dynamic hardware multithreading. The architecture uses on-chip networking to interconnect routers and computational elements providing a flexible and highly configurable structure. Quadratic routers are reducing total router count while ensuring short communication paths and minimal resource overhead.

**Keywords:** Architecture Virtualization · On-Chip-Networking · Hardware Multi-Threading

## 1 Introduction

Decreasing size of transistors and increasing packing density have led the transition from high-clocked single processors to multicore. However, pure multicore solutions without customized computing components will not be able to provide the required performance in many computational fields such as image processing, oil and gas exploration, and programmatic financial trading, which requires complex 3D convolutions on large data arrays and tight requirements on memory and IO [10]. Studies are predicting that increase in power as result of chip density will drastically reduce the usage of manycores to a maximum of 75% [7]. Heterogeneous architectures made upon general purpose processors and specialized computing components, intelligent methods to dynamically adapt chip resources to run-time computational and power consumption requirements can improve the performance of future multicores [10]. Reconfigurable logic such as FPGAs can be used for this purpose, as part of heterogeneous multiprocessors, either on the same die or as separate co-processor. However, for such platforms to be successful, the FPGA must be able to dynamically accommodate multiple threads running as hardware tasks. Dynamically placing and replacing those threads on the FPGA to allow critical parts of applications to be accelerated at

© Springer International Publishing Switzerland 2015
K. Sano et al. (Eds.): ARC 2015, LNCS 9040, pp. 167–178, 2015.
DOI: 10.1007/978-3-319-16214-0_14

run-time is done today using partial reconfiguration, a process technically and conceptually limited in currently FPGAs. Firstly, there is currently no support for communication among tasks arbitrarily placed on FPGA at run-time. The modular design flow used for partial reconfiguration in today's FPGAs places high restrictions on designs, requesting computational bins and direct communication tracks to be specified at compile-time. Once fixed, this structure cannot be modified at run-time, which drastically reduces the flexibility. The process is done manually for every design and is very sensitive to small changes. Secondly, FPGA configuration is very fine-grained, which increases reconfiguration overhead, particularly when tasks consuming large amount of resources must be frequently placed on the device. Finally, the programmability of FPGAs is essentially reduced to hardware design, a difficult process that prevents its adoption in the software community where the bulk of programmers are to be found. Hardware virtualization can help overcome the aforementioned hurdles by placing a coarse-grained reconfigurable hardware overlay between hardware tasks and raw FPGA. This reduces the configuration overhead, allows design decision to be made on-line and reduce the programmability burdens through compilers that can map instructions to coarse-grained processing elements. Overlay architectures recently proposed for FPGAs are based on existing concepts of coarse-grained reconfigurable architectures. They consist of microarchitectural components like ALU, multiplexers and direct interconnection among neighboring or distant cores. Existing overlays are accessible as a single large monolithic block that can accommodate only one hardware function at a time. Their communication is based on direct interconnection paradigm, which must be fixed at design time and never changed at run-time. As result, their communication infrastructure does not promote hardware multithreading. Tasks cannot to be randomly placed on the reconfigurable device at run-time and be accessible by other tasks, either on the same device or on external devices.

In this work, we propose a novel virtualization architecture for FPGAs which allows for unrestricted communication among hardware tasks running on the device. The architecture combines direct interconnection for high-performance at local level within a task's boundary, while using reduced overhead network-on-chip for global communication beyond component boundary. The architecture is based on a quadratic router access mechanism that drastically reduce the number of routers, thus leading to short communication paths and reduced resource overhead. We address the inefficient resource usage with a novel class of routers that can be dynamically recycled as computing resource in modules in the boundary of which they are placed at run-time. The viability of our approach is demonstrated with benchmarks in signal and image processing, which shows a performance difference between applications running on raw FPGAs and the same applications running on the virtualization layer.

The paper is organized as follow: Section 2 provides a motivation of the problem solved in this paper with help of a case study. In section 3 we discuss coarse-grained reconfigurable architectures and recent work in FPGA virtualization. In section 4, we present our architecture and explain design choices we made to address problems of existing overlays. Section 5 shows our evaluation approach and the meaning of the results, while section 6 concludes the paper and provide some indication of our future work.

## 2   Motivation Example

The problem addressed in this work, namely hardware multitasking on coarse-grained reconfigurable devices is illustrated in Figure 1. Consider a device with a 2-D mesh and a global and flexible form of communication, in this case a network on chip. The first set of threads on the device represent the execution of a video communication application consisting of a video capture module, a video compressor after the H.264 protocol and a communication using WLAN. This implementation is constrained by the two already placed components CR1 and CR2, which cause the communication between the compressor and the WLAN modules to go through 5 hops. Upon completion of CR1 and CR2, a relocation can be done, which reduces the distance between the compressor and the WLAN to just 3 hops. The WLAN modules can further be replaced by a Bluetooth module with a much smaller footprint, lower power and performance, which reduces the distance between the two modules to just 2 hops, without altering the distance between the compressor and the video capture module.

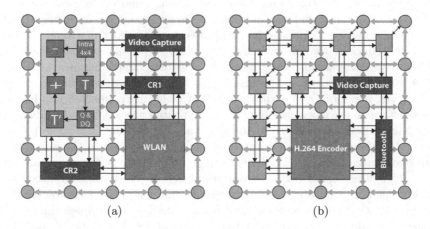

(a)                                           (b)

**Fig. 1.** Video capture, compression and transmission (left) and performance improvement through reconfiguration and relocation.

Resource organization for efficient temporal execution of those tasks at run-time is very challenging. *High performance* and *accessibility* are the two main objectives to be reached. High performance is defined by architectural considerations and efficient run-time organization and management, while accessibility allows hardware tasks running of the device to be reachable regardless of their placement location and later relocation. While virtualization on FPGA provides an answer to the first challenge, existing implementation do not address accessibility since they are tailored only for fixed usage. As consequence, no existing coarse-grained architecture and overlay can handle the scenario previously described.

Our main contribution in this work is the design of a novel virtualization infrastructure allowing a flexible and unrestricted communication among hardware tasks arbitrarily placed on the virtual hardware at run-time.

## 3   Related Work

Published work in coarse-grained reconfigurable architectures and FPGA overlays such as [3,11,15] are essentially *dataflow machines*, ususally consisting of small arithmetic and logic units, register files, all of which are immersed in an switch-based interconnect structure. Data-flow machines are mostly used in systems as co-processors for acceleration of a single tasks, which can be replaced by configuring the entire device. Communication is based on direct interconnect among neighbor or distant processing elements. While data-flow machines fulfill high-performance requirements, they do not address accessibility, which is mostly enforced by the communication mechanism. Bus systems currently in use in system-on-chips represent a potential communication alternative in coarse-grained architectures. However, current bus-based architectures will not be able to sustain the communication load among hundreds of processing elements a coarse-grained overlay would be able to accommodate in future FPGAs. The overhead needed to manage hundred of connected cores on a single bus will drastically reduce system performance and offset all parallelism gains. Network-on-Chip (NoC) was designed as a means to overcome the communication bottleneck in high density chips in the future [1,6]. In NoC, messages are exchanged among cores, memories and peripherals, all of which are connected in a network infrastructure on the chip, instead of using dedicated wires. While the advantage of NoCs have been quantitatively and qualitatively elucidated in some publications [2,13], they also present some drawbacks, mostly due to the adoption of regular computer network paradigms in the chip domain. NoCs are usually provided as a 2-dimensional grid with routers placed at intersections between lines and columns and connected to homogeneous PEs. This approach creates three main problems: 1) communication within the boundary of complex components split across several PEs is message-based instead of directed and dedicated, thus leading to performance degradation; 2) Routers in the 2D Mesh are tailored for the general case. As consequence, dedicated topologies must be mapped to the 2D mesh, which increases resource redundancy; 3) the number of routers on many routes in the 2D are usually more than needed to route a packet to destination, which increases the routing time. Routing techniques such as virtual-cut-through are able to bypass some idle routers to improve the speed, but they don't address the redundancy issue. As solution to the three mentioned problems, Application Specific NoCs (ASNoC) have been proposed in several publications [5,8,12]. In a ASNoC large components spanning beyond a single PEs are implemented in dedicated area, where direct interconnections within the module boundary are used to increase their speed. The topology of the network is usually determined by the communication pattern of the system, which eliminates redundancies and improves performance. However, the main drawback of ASNoCs is their lack of flexibility. For each application an ASNoC-Chip must be built, which incurs high design and production costs that most companies cannot afford. The resulting chip is optimal for the targeted application, but cannot be used for others applications. The Zippy architecture [4] attempts to provide an answer to accessibility and high-performance though a mixture of direct connection for neighbor PE and bus for global interconnect. Beside low performance, the use of a bus restricts the placement of components to certain location on the chip, thus limiting device's flexibility. In [14] preliminary results of a dynamic network-on-chip paradigms was presented. However, high-router count and large resource overhead of routers prevented the usage of this technology, particularly on FPGA devices.

In this work, we propose a novel architecture that combines coarse-grained elements, a mixture of network-on-chip and direct interconnection. With router reuse in components, our approach overcomes the problems of current coarse-grained reconfigurable devices and FPGA overlays.

## 4   The Novel Architecture

We present our architecture in this section and discuss our design choices. The overall architecture organization is first explained at high level, with emphasis on local and global connectivity. Thereafter, processing elements and interconnect are explained in more details.

### 4.1   General Device Organization

We propose the general organization of figure 2d, which goes far beyond the capabilities of the most advance architectures proposed so far. For instance the Zippy architecture [4](Figure 2a) uses direct interconnect locally and a bus for global interconnection. The bus is used to access every single PE from an external processor attached to the device. Interconnection between modules executing on chip must go through an external memory or external processor, which drastically slows down computations. Using a regular NoC (figure 2b) to provide communication among modules on the chip would be very efficient and flexible. However, the performance of large modules split across many processing element will suffer because of the message-based data exchange within a component boundary. Our proposed architecture reduces the number of router by 4 by providing one router for a group of four PEs, similar to the Arteris FlexNoC architecture (figure 2c). However, as oppose the FlexNoC, our proposed architecture also provides direct interconnection to neighbor PE, thus increasing the streaming bandwidth among PEs used in the same module. This fulfills the high-performance requirement. Each component consisting of several PEs will access the network and be reachable through one of the routers in the set of routers it covers, which fulfills the accessibility requirement. The last innovation of our architecture is that remaining routers will be used to provide additional computational power to that component. To our best knowledge, no existing device has make use of this paradigm. We call our architecture *Quattuor* because it connects 4 PE on a single router.

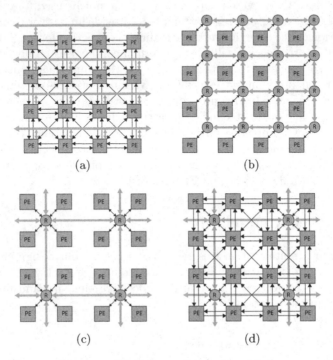

(a)                                                    (b)

(c)                                                    (d)

**Fig. 2.** The Zippy architecture [4] (2a) uses buses for global communication, while regular NoC (2b) exhibits high routers redundancy. Arterix FlexNoC [9] (2c) has less routers, but does not provide direct connection between neighbor modules. Our proposed architecture (2d) extends the best of existing architectures with direct interconnect, network-on-chip and router reuse.

## 4.2  Processing Elements

Like other coarse-grained reconfigurable architectures, the Quattuor processing elements consist of several arithmetic and logic units for data processing, register files for data storage, multiplexers and demultiplexers for controlling the flow of data among the units. The processing elements (PE) proposed in this section are kept relatively simple due to the early stage of development. More complex functional units are planned for the future. The organization of a Quattuor-PE is presented in Figure 3. The computation is done using ALUs, each of which provides 8 arithmetic and logic operations: addition, subtraction, multiplication, division, nop, and, or and xor.

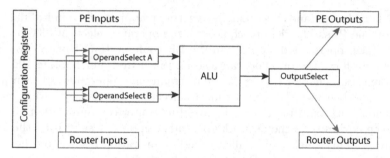

**Fig. 3.** Structure of a Quattuor-PE

The register files as well as the ALUs within a 4-block are connected to the router and neighbor PEs, so they can receive exchange operands and results of computation. The configuration of a PE is done by the configuration register which is connected to all units in the PE. Configuring a unit consists of defining its behavior at certain point until the next configuration or a repeating operation. Each processing element has a unique address and receives its configuration through the network using its closest router. Sending configuration data through the network removes the need for dedicated configuration lines present in existing coarse-grained architecture and overlays. Because we use one router for 4 PEs, the configuration path is reduced by 4. Furthermore depending on the geographic location on the chip, configuration data can be sent from the closest router to the PE, which further reduce configuration time.

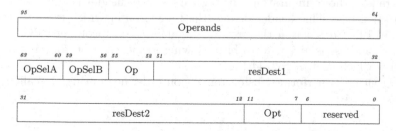

**Fig. 4.** Configuration Bits of a Quattuor-PE.

The format of configuration data is shown in Figure 4. It consists of a 96-bit packet. The bits 95-64 define operands for the ALU if they are needed. The following eight bits 63-56 control the operand multiplexers and define the source of each operand. The bits 55-52 select the operation for the ALU. The following bits 51-12 define the destinations for the result of the ALU operation. The possibility to define more than one destination offers a great flexibility to implement data-flow graphs in the network. The bits 11-8 define what should be done with the result. Bit 7 can be set to allow a continuous operation of the current PE configuration. The last bits are reserved for future use.

The flexible operand selection allows the mapping of complex data-flow graphs on the PEs. The default choice for the operand selection (0000) is that the ALU takes operands directly from the PE configuration. But to allow more complex data-flows the operand can also be taken from neighboring PEs. This direct connection enables fast exchange of results and operands between multiple ALUs and because of the Quattuor architecture complex operations can be implemented with multiple PEs while avoiding router communication.

To keep flexibility in the network operands can be also sent using the router interconnect. This functionality allows sending operation results to other partitions in the network while no PE has to be blocked for the transfer.

The result output of a PE can be configured in various ways. The default action is to define the ALU result as final result which will be reported back to the processor. The type of result will be sent to the Quattuor network output by using the router interconnect. Another possibility is to deliver the result to a neighboring PE using the direct interconnect. This is the fastest transfer possible in the network. For transferring results to a more distant location in the network the router interconnect can be used.

### 4.3   Router Architecture

Besides the processing elements, routers are one of the most important components on our dynamic network on chip concept. Our router is created with a set of FIFOs and a controller. There is one input FIFO that collects the four inputs of the router using a round-robin mechanism. All messages get collected and delivered to the designated outputs.

To transfer the configurations for the PEs a small header is added to the 96 configuration bits. This header defines the target router which is connected to the target PE. Considering the growing capabilities of upcoming FPGA series the router address is given by 16 bits allowing to identify 256 routers in every dimension which lead to 262144 PEs.

The routing is performed using dimension ordering routing, so called Y-X routing.

### 4.4   Quattuor-PE Direct Interconnect

As stated earlier, then main differentiation of the Quattuor-Architecture is the capability of using direct interconnect locally, within a task for fast data exchange among the sub-modules, and global communication using messages beyond components boundary. The first approach is useful when building computational data-flow graphs that leverages parallelism within a task. Direct communication between two neighbor PE takes just 1 clock cycle. In the second case, global communication goes through the router and depends on the distance between the two hardware tasks. We do not address this part in this work and simply assume that a function in change of run-time resource management will keep components which heavily communicate close to each other.

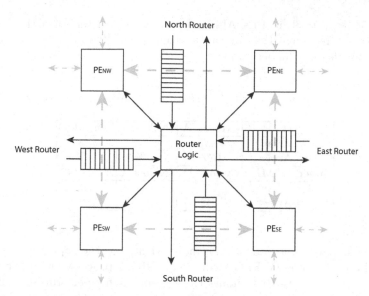

**Fig. 5.** Internal structure of routers with PEs

The delay of ALU operation depends on the implementation of the single operations. While bit manipulations like shift, and, or, xor etc. can be handled in a single clock cycle, more complex operations like division may take longer. As mentioned before the router implements a round-robin scheduling on the router inputs. That leads to a variable input delay of one to four clock cycles plus a delay depending on the FIFO implementation of the input buffers. All communication between routers implements a hand-shake-algorithm to ensure data integrity even if a router buffer is completely filled. Communication between router and the connected PEs is done in a single clock cycle.

## 5   Evaluation

For evaluation, we implemented the Quattuor-Architecture on various FPGA in diverse configurations. Our first objective was assess the resource consumption on diverse FPGAs, which will then give an estimate of the size of the overlay that can be accommodated on contemporary devices. Beside resource consumption, we also wanted to measure the performance decrease resulting from the implementation of applications on the overlay compare to their implementation on the raw FPGA.

Table 1 summarizes the resource consumption for single Quattuor-Elements as well as Quattuor-Arrays of size (in number of routers) of 3x3 (6x6 PEs) and 4x4 (8x8 PEs) in 3 different FPGA-Types: Cyclone IV (Altera EP4CE115F29C7), Cyclone V (Altera 5CSXFC6D6F31C6), Zynq-7000 (Xilinx XC7Z020-3-CLG484). The chosen FPGAs are considered the low-cost series from Altera and Xilinx. Our tests show that even these device are capable of hosting 3x3 and 4x4 router arrays providing 36 respectively 64 PEs. Also an important characteristic of the design is the operational frequency. Here we can see that on the Zynq platform the design achieves a significantly higher frequency.

**Table 1.** Evaluation of the Quattuor-Architecture in term of area and speed on various FPGAs

| Area | Cyclone-IV | Cyclone-V | Zynq-7000 |
|---|---|---|---|
| 3x3 Array | 37% | 37% | 34% |
| 4x4 Array | 67% | 67% | 61% |
| **Speed in MHz** | Cyclone-IV | Cyclone-V | Zynq-7000 |
| 3x3 Array | 147 | 173 | 223 |
| 4x4 Array | 142 | 165 | 223 |

Our second part of the evaluation is more oriented on the application side and performed on a Cyclone IV FPGA running a NIOS2 processor together with a Quattuor network. For the benchmark the system-on-chip performs several operations which will be compared to raw software and raw FPGA implementations. The following section shows how a Quattuor configuration is derived from an application on the example of 3x3 matrix multiplication.

$$a = \begin{pmatrix} a_{00} & a_{01} & a_{02} \\ a_{10} & a_{11} & a_{12} \\ a_{20} & a_{21} & a_{22} \end{pmatrix} \qquad b = \begin{pmatrix} b_{00} & b_{01} & b_{02} \\ b_{10} & b_{11} & b_{12} \\ b_{20} & b_{21} & b_{22} \end{pmatrix} \qquad (1)$$

$$c = \begin{pmatrix} a_{00}b_{00} + a_{01}b_{10} + a_{02}b_{20} & \ldots & a_{00}b_{02} + a_{01}b_{12} + a_{02}b_{22} \\ a_{10}b_{00} + a_{11}b_{10} + a_{12}b_{20} & \ldots & a_{10}b_{02} + a_{11}b_{12} + a_{12}b_{22} \\ a_{20}b_{00} + a_{11}b_{10} + a_{22}b_{20} & \ldots & a_{20}b_{02} + a_{21}b_{12} + a_{22}b_{22} \end{pmatrix} \qquad (2)$$

Each component of the final result matrix can be implemented using three multiplications and two additions and be represented using the following data-flow graph (for the first element of the result matrix):

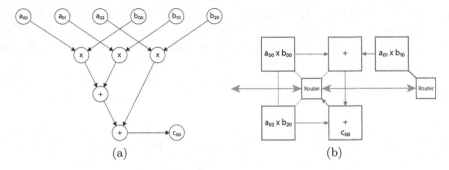

(a)                                        (b)

**Fig. 6.** Data-flow for matrix component $c_{00}$ and mapping on PEs

Now there are some possibilities for the implementation. The first intention is that every component of the result matrix can be build by the same operations only changing the operands. That means one implementation would be to map this particular set of operations shown in the data-flow graph to the Quattuor array like in Figure 6b.

To evaluate the performance of this implementation we created a small system-on-chip on the Cyclone-IV FPGA consisting a NIOS2 soft-core CPU. The complete system (CPU, Quattuor, memory) is running at 50 MHz and the results are compared to others systems.

**Table 2.** Evaluation of the Quattuor-Performance for a 3x3 Matrix Multiplication

| Application | Quattuor/NIOS2 | NIOS2 | Intel 2.1GHz | FPGA |
|---|---|---|---|---|
| 3x3 Matrix | 4.8ms (6us) | 504us | 2us | 405us (720ns) |
| 3x1 Matrix | 1.8ms (2us) | 120us | 1us | 149us (240ns) |

In Table 2 the results for the performance evaluation are listed. We can state that in this example using the Quattuor network creates a large overhead. The measured execution time is about five milliseconds for the complete 3x3 matrix multiplication but calculating the results takes only 6 $\mu$s. The rest of the execution time is taken by the configuration of the PEs which has to be done for every component of the result matrix and the communication between the Quattuor network, CPU and memory. This can also be seen in comparison with a raw FPGA implementation. This was done by creating a small IP core with bus interface implementing the data-flow as seen in Figure 6a. Even in this implementation we can see that for operand writing to and result reading from the IP core there is a large overhead.

# 6    Conclusion and Future Work

In this paper, we presented a concept and implementation of a novel coarse-grained architecture virtualization for Field Programmable Gate Arrays. The Quattuor architecture allows for run-time dynamic hardware multithreading by using a combination of direct interconnection to allow for high-performance communication within task boundaries, low-overhead network-on-chip for communication beyond component boundaries. Our evaluation shows a performance lost toward raw software and FPGA implementations which is generated by the communication overhead which is needed to configure the PEs via the bus connection of the Quattuor IP core and the interconnect latency in the network. The future work on the topic will focus on effective PE configuration and configuration reusing to minimize the impact for real world applications. Also in our future work we are going to investigate how to automatically map applications on the network without requiring users to recode their programs. For instance binary synthesis will be made possible with our approach, with the goal of extracting parallel kernel at run-time and synthesizing them for FPGA acceleration.

# References

1. Benini, L., Micheli, G.D.: Networks on chips: A new soc paradigm. IEEE Computer **35**(1), 70–78 (2002)
2. Bjerregaard, T., Mahadevan, S.: A survey of research and practices of network-on-chip. ACM Comput. Surv. 38(1), June 2006
3. Brant, A., Lemieux, G.G.: Zuma: An open fpga overlay architecture. In: Annual IEEE Symposium on Field-Programmable Custom Computing Machines, 93–96 (2012)
4. Christian Plessl, G., Platzner, M.: Hardware virtualization on dynamically reconfigurable processors. In: Khalgui, M., Hanisch, H.-M. (eds:) Reconfigurable Embedded Control Systems: Applications for Flexibility and Agility. IGI Global (2011)
5. Dall'Osso, M., Biccari, G., Giovannini, L., Bertozzi, D., Benini, L.: xpipes: a latency insensitive parameterized network-on-chip architecture for multi-processor socs. In: Proceedings of the 21st International Conference on Computer Design, ICCD 2003, p. 536. IEEE Computer Society, Washington, DC (2003)
6. Dally, W.J., Towles, B.: Route packets, not wires: on-chip interconnection networks. In: Proceedings of the Design Automation Conference, Las Vegas, NV, pp. 684–689, June 2001
7. Esmaeilzadeh, H., Blem, E., St. Amant, R., Sankaralingam, K., Burger, D.: Dark silicon and the end of multicore scaling. SIGARCH Comput. Archit. News, 39(3), 365–376 (2011)
8. Goossens, K., Dielissen, J., Radulescu, A.: Aethereal network on chip: Concepts, architectures, and implementations. IEEE Des. Test **22**(5), 414–421 (2005)
9. A. Inc., Arteris FlexNoC Interconnect IP. Arteris, Inc. Sunnyvale, CA, USA
10. Michael, M.C.: Challenges in high speed reconfigurable computing (June 2009)
11. Mirsky, E., DeHon, A.: MATRIX: A reconfigurable computing architecture with configurable instruction distribution and deployable resources. In: Pocek, K.L., Arnold, J. (eds.) IEEE Symposium on FPGAs for Custom Computing Machines, pp. 157–166. IEEE Computer Society Press, Los Alamitos (1996)
12. Penolazzi, S., Jantsch, A.: A high level power model for the nostrum noc. In: Proceedings of the 9th EUROMICRO Conference on Digital System Design. DSD 2006, pp. 673–676. IEEE Computer Society, Washington, DC (2006)
13. Probell, J.: Routing Congestion: The Growing Cost of Wires in Systems-on-Chip. Arteris, Inc., Sunnyvale, CA, USA
14. O. F. B. Review. In
15. Toi, T., Awashima, T., Motomura, M., Amano, H.: Time and space-multiplexed compilation challenges for dynamically reconfigurable processors. In: Midwest Symposium on Circuits and Systems, pp. 1–4 (2011)

# Centralized and Software-Based Run-Time Traffic Management Inside Configurable Regions of Interest in Mesh-Based Networks-on-Chip

Philipp Gorski, Tim Wegner$^{(\boxtimes)}$, and Dirk Timmermann

Institute of Applied Microelectronics and Computer Engineering, University of Rostock, Richard-Wagner Str. 31, 18119 Rostock-Warnemnde, Germany
{philipp.gorski2,tim.wegner,dirk.timmermann}@uni-rostock.de

**Abstract.** This work proposes the introduction of multiple spatially independent network interfaces in order to connect computational resources to mesh-based Networks-on-Chip (NoCs). Furthermore, a flexible system for traffic monitoring is introduced supporting runtime reconfigurability as well as software-based centralized data aggregation and evaluation. These approaches are combined to form a sophisticated framework for runtime traffic management of NoC-based many-core systems exploiting the dual-path options of the underlying network.

Simulations show that this framework is capable of significantly decelerating thermal wear-out, while improving performance characteristics (e. g. packet delay) at moderate additional costs (i. e. power dissipation).

**Keywords:** Networks-on-Chip · Adaptive routing · Many-core systems · Run-time traffic management

## 1 Introduction

Networks-on-Chip (NoCs) emerged as the next generation of communication infrastructures for modern many-core systems applying packet-based communication inside a networked topology of routers. The most commonly used NoC topology is the 2-dimensional $N_X \times N_Y$ mesh (2D-mesh) reverting to XY-routing and wormhole-switching. This supports a regular physical layout as well as scalability and provides the required degree of parallelism [1]. Typically, each computational resource is served by one dedicated router. In many cases routers are enhanced by techniques like dual-path routing (e. g. XY/YX-routing), the utilization of virtual-channels (VCs) or deepening of the logical router pipeline by additional stages [2]. This paper introduces different modifications and enhancements for the introduced 2D-meshes. Contributions are as follows:

- Application of a quadrant-based mesh (QMesh) connecting each computational resource to the routers of all surrounding quadrants. Average hop distances are reduced and the integration of dual-path routing without using VCs is enabled. The basic structure of the 2D-mesh is maintained.

© Springer International Publishing Switzerland 2015
K. Sano et al. (Eds.): ARC 2015, LNCS 9040, pp. 179–190, 2015.
DOI: 10.1007/978-3-319-16214-0_15

- The QMesh is equipped with Flexible Traffic Monitoring (FTM). The observation of reconfigurable rectangular clusters is supported utilizing adaptable algorithms and policies for monitoring and data evaluation. For each cluster traffic recording is provided including run-time end-to-end traffic analysis.
- Combination of the dual-path capabilities of the QMesh with FTM to enable intra-cluster path updates at run-time.

The resulting NoC infrastructure represents a flexible, configurable solution for adaptive routing at run-time. The overall framework is outlined in Figure 1. As it can be seen, FTM and potential path reconfigurations are performed on a cluster-basis, while monitoring is done individually for each NoC tile within a cluster. Aggregation of monitoring data collected for all tiles of a cluster is performed by a designated master-tile. Traffic evaluation and adaptations are executed by SW solutions, while basic monitoring functions as well as the aggregation of monitoring data are realized in HW. Furthermore, regular network traffic is separated from monitoring and control packets by utilizing two fully independent networks (i. e. DNoC and SNoC). This approach is expected to yield improvements regarding incidence of network saturation, average packet delay, fault-tolerance and thermally induced wear-out of NoC components. At the same time, additional power dissipation and area overhead shall be kept moderate.

The remainder of this paper is organized as follows. Section 2 contains the related work on multi-ported topologies, run-time traffic monitoring and path adaptation mechanisms. Section 3 introduces the QMesh infrastructure, while in Section 4 the concept of FTM is addressed. Subsequently, in Section 5 the approach for run-time adaptation of routing paths is introduced. Section 6 provides experimental results regarding impact on performance and reliability. The paper is concluded in Section 7.

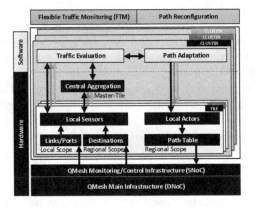

**Fig. 1.** Partition of the NoC-based infrastructure into clusters and tiles for traffic monitoring, evaluation and adaptation of routing paths

## 2   Related Work

In the following state-of-the-art approaches, the implementation of multi-ported resources in NoCs is mainly driven by the separation of traffic classes in order to improve communication performance. Furthermore, the introduction of additional resource connectivity differs between specialized and generalized policies.

In [3] a hybrid NoC (HNoC) combining a 2D-mesh with point-to-point (P2P) buses is proposed. These P2P connections exclusively serve to cover nearest-neighbor communication to adjacent resources. The approach in [4] deploys two independent network interfaces (NIs) in order to connect resources to two 2D-meshes handling dedicated traffic classes. Both approaches apply multi-ported resources to integrate additional NoC infrastructure elements.

In [5–7] the focus is on enhancements of single-network meshes. In [5] a dual NI is explored to increase the fault-tolerance of 2D-meshes. Each resource is connected to two spatially independent routers of the same row of the mesh to provide higher path independence. However, this approach cannot provide full path independence for all source-destination pairings, since the connection to routers of the same row leads to shared XY-path segments for a significant amount of destinations.

In [6,7] the NR-Mesh is introduced connecting each resource to up to four adjacent routers. Traffic injection follows a random policy for the selection of a dedicated NI for each packet, while at the destination dynamic selection of the ejection NI is applied. For the routing policy, deterministic XY-routing as well as adaptive XY/YX-routing are proposed. However, the concept of injection port selection as well as the routing policy seem to be only proof-of-concept studies.

Regarding the combination of run-time traffic monitoring and routing, distributed adaptive strategies represent the most commonly applied approaches. Typically, distributed minimal routing algorithms with full or partial adaptivity are applied adapting the path for each packet at the hop-to-hop level. Continuous regional traffic monitoring of buffer or crossbar utilization is proposed in [8]. Gathered information concerning the local traffic situation is considered by minimal, partially adaptive solutions like odd-even or west-first/negative-first/north-last adaptations deviated from the work in [9].

Local traffic monitoring with adaptive non-minimal routing is combined in [11]. Probabilistic and source-based selection between minimal XY- and YX-routing is implemented in [12] offering nearly optimal throughput without additional costs for path selection.

## 3   Quadran T-Based Mesh Topology

The basic structure of the QMesh topology is illustrated in Figures 2a and 2b. Furthermore, different packet transfer scenarios and resulting dual-path options with applied XY-routing are depicted. Inside a regular 2D-mesh packets are generated at an arbitrary source (SRC) and are then injected into the NoC at the router located at $Q_0$. Subsequently, packets are forwarded along the X-direction

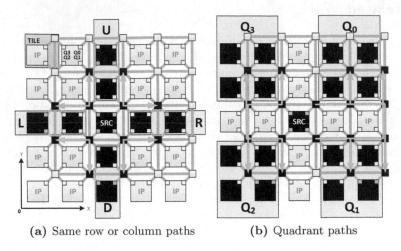

(a) Same row or column paths          (b) Quadrant paths

**Fig. 2.** 5×5 QMesh: dual-path options for the available SRC/DST constellations

and then along the Y-direction until the router at $Q_0$ at the destination (DST) is reached. Therefore, simple XY-coordinates of the 2D-mesh are sufficient for unique addressing. For the scenario in Figure 2a DSTs are designated U, R, D, L, while in Figure 2b DSTs are labeled $Q_0$ to $Q_3$ relative to the SRC.

**Table 1.** Dual-path options in the QMesh including constraints and hop distances compared to a regular 2D-mesh (from the perspective of a SRC)

| DST | Path A | | | Path B | | | |
|---|---|---|---|---|---|---|---|
| | $Q_{in,src}$ | $Q_{out,router}$ | Hop dist. | $Q_{in,src}$ | $Q_{out,router}$ | Hop dist. | Constraint |
| Up (U) | $Q_0$ | $Q_3$ | $n_{hop,2D}-1$ | $Q_3$ | $Q_0$ | $n_{hop,2D}-1$ | $x_{src}>0$ |
| Right (R) | $Q_0$ | $Q_1$ | $n_{hop,2D}-1$ | $Q_1$ | $Q_0$ | $n_{hop,2D}-1$ | $y_{src}>0$ |
| Down (D) | $Q_1$ | $Q_2$ | $n_{hop,2D}-1$ | $Q_2$ | $Q_1$ | $n_{hop,2D}-1$ | $x_{src}>0$ |
| Left (L) | $Q_3$ | $Q_2$ | $n_{hop,2D}-1$ | $Q_2$ | $Q_3$ | $n_{hop,2D}-1$ | $y_{src}>0$ |
| $Q_0$ | $Q_0$ | $Q_0$ | $n_{hop,2D}-2$ | $Q_1$ | $Q_3$ | $n_{hop,2D}$ | $y_{src}>0$ |
| $Q_1$ | $Q_1$ | $Q_1$ | $n_{hop,2D}-2$ | $Q_0$ | $Q_2$ | $n_{hop,2D}$ | none |
| $Q_2$ | $Q_2$ | $Q_2$ | $n_{hop,2D}-2$ | $Q_3$ | $Q_1$ | $n_{hop,2D}$ | $x_{base,dst}>0$ |
| $Q_3$ | $Q_3$ | $Q_3$ | $n_{hop,2D}-2$ | $Q_2$ | $Q_0$ | $n_{hop,2D}$ | $y_{src}\&x_{base,dst}>0$ |

In contrast, the QMesh allows for the injection/ejection of packets via different routers placed around the SRC/DST. For this reason, the routing information comprises not only the XY-coordinates of the DST router, but also the input interface $Q_{in,src}$ at the SRC and the correct output port $Q_{out,router}$ at the DST router to address the correct DST tile. Thus, addressing must be extended by 4 bits for $Q_{in,src}$ and $Q_{out,router}$ (2 bits each). The required information is derived from a programmable path table (PT), which is integrated at each tile representing the basis for dynamic path updates. The resulting overhead of $(N_X \times N_Y - 1) \times 4$ bits per tile is acceptable (i.e. around 32 byte for an 8×8 QMesh) and small compared to the kbyte-sized buffer (BUF) at the resources.

For SRC/DST pairs with identical X- or Y-coordinates (see Figure 2a) two different path options with the same hop distance exist. If the DST is located inside one of the quadrants (see Figure 2b) with different X- and Y-coordinates (SRC's perspective), the path options vary in their distances by two hops. The PT lookup of $Q_{in,src}$ and $Q_{out,router}$ is performed when a message is written into the SRC's transmission buffer prior to packetization and is based on the DST's base address ($x_{base,dst}$, $y_{base,dst}$). The XY-coordinates of the base address are identical to the coordinates of the destination router in a standard 2D-mesh (i.e. router connected to NI at $Q_0$). In order to address the correct $Q_{out,router}$ the destination address is modified to match the correct endpoint router address.

In comparison to a regular 2D-mesh the resulting path lengths are reduced by up to two hops. Additionally, nearest-neighbor traffic is removed from the links and the average router traffic load is reduced. Furthermore, nearly all destinations can be served via a second path. The combinations for all possible SRC/DST constellations as well as constraints for alternative paths and resulting reductions in hop distance are provided in Table 1. The QMesh provides deterministic dual-path capabilities at increased communication locality representing an optimal candidate for the realization of region-based adaptation strategies at run-time.

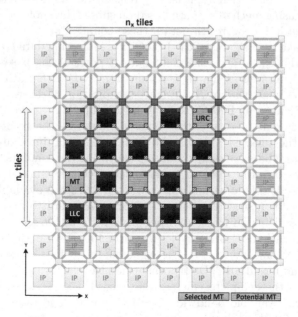

**Fig. 3.** A 4×5 cluster inside an 8×8 QMesh

## 4    Regional Traffic Monitoring

The applied periodic run-time traffic monitoring operates on reconfigurable clusters formed by NoC tiles within regions-of-interest. Furthermore, a centralized data aggregation is provided in each cluster being performed by so called master-tiles (MTs). The proposed approach for Flexible Traffic Monitoring (FTM) is designed for cluster sizes of up to 64 tiles. Multiple rectangular-shaped FTM clusters are permitted but overlapping is prohibited. Each cluster can be configured with an individual timing period selected from a discrete set fitting the requirements of its assigned workload fractions. The centralized processing and evaluation of monitoring data is performed by a software module managing cluster setup and reconfiguration as well. The initial decision for cluster formation and subsequent sizing adaptations derive from higher system-level services (e. g. application mapping), since they possess a more global view. Figure 3 illustrates a 4×5 FTM cluster inside an 8×8 QMesh NoC. Due to the focus of this paper on traffic management, the description of FTM is kept short focusing on the main capabilities. Detailed discussions on FTM are provided in [13,14].

The FTM communication regarding monitoring and control packets is realized via a fully independent network called SNoC, while data transfers of the applications are realized via the DNoC (see Figure 1). Both networks provide full QMesh connectivity for each tile. Parameters like buffer sizing, link width or operating frequency can be customized independently to meet the requirements of particular traffic classes. Thus, the SNoC can be designed with reduced buffering and link width. Furthermore, it is fully reusable for additional scenarios [14].

The FTM sensing mechanisms are based on simple threshold counters at each tile implemented in hardware. In detail, these counters are sourced by existing specific handshake logic signals of the DNoC tiles indicating data traversals along the quadrant NIs ($Q_0$ to $Q_3$), the eight output ports of the base router at $Q_0$ (i. e. U, R, D, L as well as $Q_0$ to $Q_3$), and for (N-1) E2E paths terminating inside the cluster consisting of N tiles. After expiration of discretely adjustable sensor periods defined as DNoC clock cycles ($2^5$ up to $2^{12}$ cycles) all counters of a tile are checked. In case a threshold is exceeded, the resulting overflow is reported to the selected MT via the SNoC. The MT integrates additional groups of hardware-based overflow counters capturing the contents of monitoring packets of each slave-tile (ST) of its associated cluster. In order to improve flexibility and fault-tolerance multiple potential MTs are available within the QMesh allowing for migration of the monitoring software to another MT (see Figure 3). The anticipated fraction of potential MTs within the QMesh is 25 %.

At the end of each monitoring cycle (i. e. after 100 sensor periods), DNoC load values for the tile outputs ($T_{load}$), the eight outgoing links of the base routers at $Q_0$ ($L_{load}$) and for all SRC/DST paths inside the cluster ($P_{load}$) are provided by the FTM for the complete cluster. The recorded load values represent the utilization of the available bandwidth with maximum and average monitoring errors of 2 % and 0.5 % [13].

To conclude, the introduced FTM represents a run-time configurable solution enabling a globalized view on the current traffic situation of a specific spatial

NoC region. For 4×4 and 8×8 clusters within an 8×8 QMesh the allowed monitoring cycles are $25.6 \cdot 10^3$ and $102.4 \cdot 10^3$ DNoC clock cycles (see Section 6). As it is shown [15], such timing is sufficient to keep pace with the dynamic behavior of typical workload. The combination of software-based integration of the evaluation logic and flexibility regarding spatial sizing and placement offers similar traffic management capabilities as the hardware-only implementation in [2].

## 5  Software-Based Run-Time Adaption of Routing Paths

The QMesh provides path adaptations through reprogramming of PTs (see Section 3), while FTM data serves to explore existing E2E path options for each SRC/DST pair inside a cluster. In this section an approach for run-time path adaptions is introduced combining the concepts of the QMesh and FTM. The evaluation of potential path updates is performed periodically after expiration of monitoring cycles (see Section 4) and is executed by the currently selected MT of the cluster. The processing order of the cluster tiles for path update evaluation is considered static, beginning at the lower left corner (LLC) and proceeding to the upper right corner (URC) row-by-row (see Figure 4). For each SRC tile along this route the monitoring software evaluates each path to cluster-internal DSTs. The static fashion is applied in order to achieve a convergence in the traffic optimization over several monitoring cycles. The path evaluation operates on copies of the tile output and link utilization maps ($T^*_{load}$ and $L^*_{load}$). The update evaluation is only performed for valid paths, which requires the availability of at least one more path option and a monitored path utilization that is greater than a defined threshold $P_{load} > 0$. Note that in the QMesh some paths from/to tiles at the left and lower edge do not meet this condition (see Table 1).

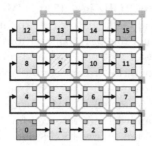

**Fig. 4.** Processing order for path update evaluation

The flow for path evaluation and potential adaptations is divided into five steps. First, the given $T^*_{load}$ and $L^*_{load}$ maps along the currently selected path $SP_{old} = $ (A or B) are prepared by removing the monitored utilization (given by $P_{load}$) for this path. This is required for a fair comparison of both path options.

Second, the metric for comparison of the path options ($SUM_A$ and $SUM_B$) is calculated from the prepared values of $T^*_{load}$ and $L^*_{load}$. The metric values are calculated by parsing through the corresponding maps along the path coordinates and summing up the utilization data.

Third, the values for $SUM_A$ and $SUM_B$ are compared and the new path $SP_{new} = $ (A or B) is selected depending on which path offers the minimal utilization sum. If the chosen path differs from the old one, this is registered by incrementing the number of occurred updates for path evaluations of the current SRC.

Fourth, $T^*_{load}$ and $L^*_{load}$ maps are updated along the selected XY-path $SP_{new}$ by adding the utilization (given by $P_{load}$) for the currently evaluated SRC/DST pair. This ensures that successive path evaluations operate on the adapted traffic situation. Furthermore, the PT entry of the corresponding SRC/DST pair is updated to the new path.

Finally, if all path options of the examined SRC are evaluated for all DSTs inside the cluster, the path setup of the SRC is checked for changes. In case paths were adapted, the updated PT is transmitted to the SRC via the SNoC. Afterward, the next SRC is evaluated.

# 6    Experimental Results

For experimental evaluation, the QMesh as well as a regular 2D-mesh are integrated into a cycle-accurate SystemC-based simulator [16]. This simulator considers traffic-load-driven thermal impacts for NoC routers and links and therefore allows for estimation of temperature-based wear-out effects. Furthermore, FTM is integrated to facilitate path update computations. For this purpose, a C++-based implementation of the FTM software module was profiled at the instruction level using the Sniper simulator [18] at version 5.1. For the MT core the built-in Intel Nehalem setup was deployed as processing architecture operating with a clock frequency of 2 GHz in a 45 nm CMOS technology.

Network configurations and traffic pattern setup for the SystemC-based simulations can be obtained from Table 2. All simulations are executed deploying a 8×8 QMesh with cluster sizes of 4×4 and 8×8 and reverting to synthetic traffic patterns. Applied patterns comprise transpose, bit reverse, bit complement and shuffle traffic. Additionally, nearest-neighbor (NN), hotspot (HOT) and Rentian (RENT) traffic patterns are examined. For the former, fractions of 20 %, 40 %, 60 % and 80 % of the total bandwith are reserved for NN communication, while for the second these fractions are reserved for 8 hot modules along the edges of the QMesh. The RENT traffic pattern applies a power law distribution along hop distances [17].

Generally, the PTs of the QMesh tiles are configured to select the shortest path A by default (see Table 1). The QMesh (unmanaged and managed) is compared to a regular 2D-mesh regarding relative improvements of the network saturation $\Delta_{sat}$, the power overhead $\Delta_{power}$ and packet delay reduction $\Delta_{delay}$. Furthermore, thermal related wear-out effects at minimum and maximum packet injection rates ($a_{MTTF}$ at $PIR_{low}$ and $PIR_{high}$) are analyzed.

**Table 2.** Basic simulation setup for the evaluation of the traffic management

| Parameter | DNoC | SNoC |
|---|---|---|
| Link width/flit size | 64 bits | 16 bits |
| Router buffer size | 9 flits | 1 flit |
| Clock cycle | 1 ns | 1 ns |
| Packet size | 20 % with 2 flits, 80 % with 9 flits (7.6 flits on average) | |

## 6.1  Reliability Analysis

The mean-time-to-failure (MTTF) describes the average period of time after that a CMOS device fails under constant operating conditions. The acceleration factor $a_{MTTF}$ in turn indicates if the variation of a parameter induces a decrease or an increase of the MTTF. In this context, Equation 6.1 represents the relationship between the MTTF for a QMesh ($t_{QMesh}$) and the MTTF for a regular 2D-mesh ($t_{2DMesh}$) focusing on the temperature-related increase ($a_{MTTF}<1$) or decrease ($a_{MTTF}>1$) of wear-out progress. $E_a$ is the activation energy specific to a certain wear-out effect in electron volts (0.7 eV at 45 nm), k is the Boltzmann's constant ($8.6 \cdot 10^{-5}\,eV/K$), and $T_{QMesh}$ and $T_{2DMesh}$ describe the absolute mesh temperatures in Kelvin. In the following $a_{MTTF}$ is utilized to compare the QMesh with the 2D-mesh regarding thermal wear-out improvements for router and link components.

$$a_{MTTF} = \frac{t_{QMesh}}{t_{2DMesh}} = e^{\frac{E_a}{k} \cdot (\frac{1}{T_{QMesh}} - \frac{1}{T_{2DMesh}})} \tag{1}$$

The results for $a_{MTTF}$ are depicted in Figure 5. As it can be seen, the QMesh (in conjunction with FTM and runtime path adaptation) yields significant improvements for various traffic patterns tested for cluster sizes of 4×4 and 8×8 inside a 8×8 NoC. This applies for both low and high packet injection rates (PIR) and results in an increase of the MTTF by almost 0.6 (for 4×4 clusters) and 0.4 (for 8×8 clusters) on average. This can be mainly attributed to improvements in communication locality and the reduction of router and link activities.

## 6.2  Traffic Analysis

The following charts summarize the impact of the managed QMesh on run-time costs as well as performance. Regarding the evaluation of power dissipation, for the QMesh the corresponding results of the FTM units as well as the SNoC are integrated to provide a comprehensive and realistic analysis.

The results in Figures 6a and 6b illustrate the improvement of network saturation $\Delta_{sat}$ of the QMesh relative to the 2D-mesh. Figure 6a indicates that BP patterns at both cluster sizes profit most with average improvements of 380 % and 394 %

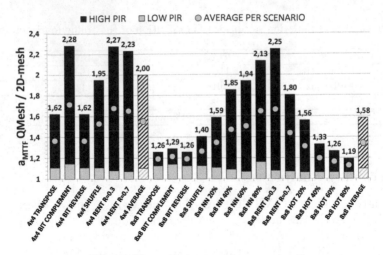

**Fig. 5.** Thermal wear-out improvement

for 4×4 and 8×8 cluster sizes. In contrast, PD patterns in Figure 6b reveal a more moderate growth of the NoC saturation limits. Only in case the communication locality is high enough (i. e. NN), the QMesh provides significant gains resulting in an average increase of 53 % compared to the 2D-mesh.

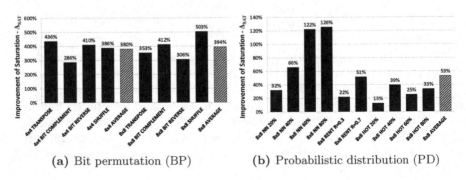

(a) Bit permutation (BP)        (b) Probabilistic distribution (PD)

**Fig. 6.** Saturation improvements for the analyzed traffic patterns

In Figures 7a and 7b the deviation of average total power dissipation $\Delta_{power}$ and average packet header delay $\Delta_{delay}$ of the QMesh in relation to the 2D-mesh is depicted. Similar to improvements regarding network saturation, Figure 7a shows that the QMesh provides better results for BP patterns. Generally, packet delay can be reduced due to application of runtime path adaptation, while power consumption is increased by additional hardware. For 4×4 clusters, NoC power increases by 48 % averaged over all simulated BP patterns, while packet delay can be reduced by around 63 %. Deployment of 8×8 clusters yields an average increase of power by 60 % and an average reduction of packet delay by 47 %.

Figure 7b illustrates that the power overhead is constantly higher for PD patterns resulting in an average increase of 74 %. In parallel, packet delay is reduced by 55 % on average. Only for PD patterns with high communication locality (NN at 60 % and 80 % and RENT) reductions of packet delay outweigh the related power increase. However, values are restricted to traffic ranges where the 2D-Mesh is able to operate at, while the QMesh provides capacities beyond. Therefore, more beneficial results regarding the ratio of power increase to packet delay reduction are anticipated, if the PIR per tile is increased.

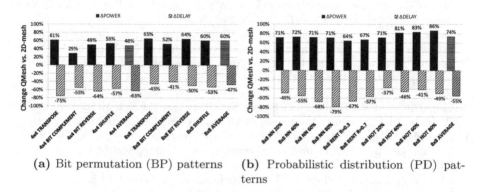

(a) Bit permutation (BP) patterns    (b) Probabilistic distribution (PD) patterns

**Fig. 7.** Relative changes of power dissipation and packet delay

## 7 Conclusion

This paper introduces two independent approaches to many-core systems based on Networks-on-Chip (NoCs). Firstly, this concerns the concept of multiple spatially independent network interfaces deployed for connecting the computational resources of such systems to mesh-based NoCs. This yields the option of selecting different end-to-end paths for data transfers depending on the current load profile of the mesh. Additionally, reliability is benefited, since computational resources remain accessible in case of faulty routers or network interfaces.

Secondly, this concerns a flexible system for traffic monitoring offering the possibility of run-time reconfiguration of local monitoring clusters. Within these clusters a software-based monitoring module is responsible for aggregation and evaluation of recorded communication activities and traffic loads.

Moreover, these two approaches are combined to enable run-time traffic management by software-based adaptation of routing paths. Basically, this management utilizes the traffic information gathered from the monitoring system to decide which of the available paths is preferable regarding impact on load distribution.

Results indicate that major run-time characteristics of many-core systems can be improved by the proposed run-time traffic management. This especially applies to network saturation and packet transfer delay. Furthermore, temperature-related wear-out effects are decelerated significantly, while additional costs (i. e. power dissipation due to additional hardware) are acceptable.

# References

1. Agarwal, A., Iskander, C., Shankar, R.: Survey of Network on Chip (NoC) Architectures and Contributions. J. Eng. Comp. Arch. **3**(1), 1–15 (2009)
2. Manevich, R. et al.: A Cost Effective Centralized Adaptive Routing for Networks-on-Chip. In: 14th Euromicro Conf. Digit. Syst. Des. 9(2), pp. 39–46, August 2011
3. Zarkesh-Ha, P. et al.: Hybrid Network on Chip (HNoC): Local Buses with a Global Mesh Architecture. In: 12th SLIP, pp. 9–14 (2010)
4. Volos, S. et al.: CCNoC: Specializing On-Chip Interconnects for Energy Efficiency in Cache-Coherent Servers. In: 6th Internat. Symposium on NoCs, pp. 67–74 (2012)
5. Zonouz, A. E. et al.: A Fault Tolerant NoC Architecture for Reliability Improvement and Latency Reduction. In: 12th DSD, Methods and Tools, pp. 473–480 (2009)
6. Camacho, J. et al.: Towards an Efficient NoC Topology through Multiple Injection Ports. In: 14th Euromicro Conference on Digital System Design, pp. 165–172 (2011)
7. Camacho, J. et al.: A power-efficient network on-chip topology. in: 5th Internat. Workshop on Interconnection Network Arch. on-Chip, Multi-Chip, pp. 23–26 (2011)
8. Chen, L., Hwang, K., Pinkston, T.: RAIR: Interference Reduction in Regionalized Networks on Chip. In: 27th IPDPS, pp. 1–12 (2013)
9. Chiu, G.: The odd-even turn model for adaptive routing. IEEE Trans. Parallel Distrib. Syst. **11**(7), 729–738 (2000)
10. Glass, C.J., Ni, L.M.: The turn model for adaptive routing. ACM SIGARCH Comput. Archit. News **20**(2), 278–287 (1992)
11. Ebrahimi, M. et al.: LEAR - A Low-Weight and Highly Adaptive Routing Method for Distributing Congestions in On-chip Networks. In: 20th Euromicro Intl. Conference on Parallel, Distributed and Network-Based Processing, pp. 520–524 (2012)
12. Ali, A., Rafique, N., Thottethodi, M.: Near-Optimal Worst-Case Throughput Routing for Two-Dimensional Mesh Networks. In: 32nd ISCA, pp. 432–443 (2005)
13. Gorski, P., Timmermann, D.: Centralized traffic monitoring for online-resizable clusters in Networks-on-Chip. In: 8th ReCoSoC, pp. 1–8 (2013)
14. Gorski, P. et. al.: RedNoCs: A Runtime Configurable Solution for Cluster-based and Multi-objective System Management in Networks-on-Chip. In: 8th internat. Conference on Systems, pp. 192–201 (2013)
15. Mishra, A. K., Mutlu, O., Das, C. R.: A heterogeneous multiple network-on-chip design: an application-aware approach. In: 50th DAC, pp. 1–10 (2013)
16. Gag, M., Wegner, T., Gorski, P.: System level modeling of Networks-on-Chip for power estimation and design space exploration. MBMV **2013**, 25–34 (2013)
17. Manevich, R., Cidon, I., Kolodny, A.: Handling global traffic in future CMP NoCs", Internat. Workshop on System Level Interconnect Prediction, pp. 40–48 (2012)
18. Carlson, T.E., Heirman, W., Eeckhout, L.: Sniper: Exploring the Level of Abstraction for Scalable and Accurate Parallel Multi-Core Simulation, pp. 1–12. Internat. Conf. for High Performance Computing, Networking, Storage and Analysis (2011)

# Survey on Real-Time Network-on-Chip Architectures

Salma Hesham[1(✉)], Jens Rettkowski[2],
Diana Göhringer[2], and Mohamed A. Abd El Ghany[1,3]

[1] German University in Cairo, Cairo, Egypt
{salma.hesham,mohamed.abdel-ghany}@guc.edu.eg
[2] Ruhr-University Bochum, Bochum, Germany
{jens.rettkowski,diana.goehringer}@rub.de
[3] TU Darmstadt, Darmstadt, Germany
mohameds@ies.tu-darmstadt.de

**Abstract.** Networks-on-Chip (NoCs) are the backbone of communications in a Multi-Processor System-on-Chip (MPSoC) platform. MPSoCs are becoming an unavoidable trend especially with the growing complexity of embedded applications requiring massive parallel computation. Real-time applications make out a significant portion of the embedded field, which cannot be overlooked. However, the use of NoCs in real-time systems imposes complex constraints on the overall design. In this paper, challenges faced, when designing NoCs for real-time applications are discussed. Contributions in this area are surveyed on the level of QoS support, fault tolerance and adaptivity. The surveyed work provides a comprehensive overview of existing real-time NoC architectures and gives an insight towards future promising research points in this field.

## 1   Introduction

The past four decades have witnessed an impressive spring for modern electronic technologies and products overrunning our daily life, starting by consumer electronics reaching to automotive electronics, industrial machinery and robotics. This advance in micro-electronic products was driven by the recent developments in nanotechnology which allowed the integration of multiple processing elements (PEs) onto a single chip creating the multiprocessor systems-on-chip (MPSoCs). Today's MPSoCs hold tens of sophisticated processing cores or possibly up to hundreds of simple cores such as the recent Knights Core with 50 cores from Intel [1]. Future MPSoCs are expected to embrace thousands of processing cores within the next few years [2]. Networks-on-Chips (NoCs) [3] have been proposed as the emerging solution for the increasingly complicated communication requirements of MPSoCs and future Many-Cores. NoCs offer a scalable and flexible communication infrastructure with highly supported modularity and powerful performance [5].

MPSoCs have proved their merit as the typical platform for embedded and cyber physical systems for their massive computational power and unique energy efficiency provided in a compact design. Real-time applications make out a significant portion of the embedded field, which cannot be overlooked. However, the use of NoCs in

© Springer International Publishing Switzerland 2015
K. Sano et al. (Eds.): ARC 2015, LNCS 9040, pp. 191–202, 2015.
DOI: 10.1007/978-3-319-16214-0_16

real-time systems imposes complex constraints on the overall design. These constraints are implied by the fact that real-time communication performance relies on both the logical result as well as the completion time bound. A data packet received by a destination too late could be useless (soft real-time applications) or even cause a severe consequence (hard real-time applications). Accordingly, both the computation and the communication between the components must complete within certain deadlines for the system to behave correctly.

In this paper, the implications of real-time applications on NoC design are discussed. Existing contributions covering Quality-of-Service (QoS) support, fault tolerance and adaptivity aspects within real-time NoCs are reviewed. The presented survey work provides a comprehensive overview of existing real-time NoC architectures and gives an insight about open research points in this field. Several NoC surveys were previously conducted providing a comprehensive introduction to the NoC field [6]; an advanced introduction to the area of NoC-based MPSoC design [7]; or focusing on specific challenges in the NoCs design [8]. However, to the best of the authors' knowledge, this is the first survey specifically targeting real-time NoCs. The paper is organized as follows. In Section 2, challenges faced, when designing NoCs for real-time applications are discussed. Section 3 surveys the state-of-the art techniques for QoS support in NoC architectures. Existing reliability approaches for real-time NoCs are presented in Section 4. Adaptivity within real-time NoCs is further reviewed in Section 5. Finally, Section 6 concludes the work and discusses future insights.

## 2     Real-Time Challenges in NoC Design

NoC-based MPSoCs constitute a scalable, reusable energy efficient platform for embedded systems with supported high degree of parallelism and powerful performance. Extensive research is found in the literature for efficient NoC designs allowing applications requirements to be achieved by proper customization of NoC features. However, the use of NoC in real-time systems imposes complex constraints on the overall design. This comes from the fact that all performance metrics in a real-time NoC become interlocked with an extra paramount constraint, namely predictability. Messages belonging to a real-time flow have a strict deadline denoting the maximum time by which they must reach their destination. Missed deadlines are as faulty as a lost packet. In hard real-time systems, no deadline is allowed to be missed even under worst case communication scenarios, as it would cause a catastrophic consequence. On the other hand, soft real-time systems can tolerate a small number of missed deadlines at the expense of temporary weakened performance. Accordingly, transmission delays between the NoC routers must be predictable in order to be able to guarantee an end-to-end latency which in the worst case does not exceed the imposed deadline. However, predictability is a very challenging constraint in a NoC as a shared medium between several concurrent applications and basically in congestion situations. In that context, a NoC supporting real-time applications must provide guaranteed services in terms of bandwidth and end-to-end latency [10]. Section 3 surveys the different existing NoC architectures providing quality of service (QoS) support for real-time NoCs.

Though predictability is the most important constraint for real-time applications, it is not exclusive. As a branch of embedded systems, real-time applications are also restricted by other requirements such as reliability and energy efficiency. The continuous shrinking in the silicon technology process puts reliability and fault tolerance among the most noticeable research problems in NoC designs [11]. However, tackling this outstanding problem in real-time NoCs has its unique challenges such as maintaining the same timing behavior before and after failure isolation [12]. On the level of energy efficiency, several approaches were presented in the literature to minimize NoC power consumption. However, such conventional techniques affect the timing behavior of the NoC. Therefore, their application is not suitable for real-time NoCs, highlighting the need for new techniques to minimize energy consumption while committing to timing constraints [14]. Furthermore, efficient execution of real-time applications on NoC-based MPSoCs is governed by a powerful task scheduling and mapping technique on the available cores [15]. Additionally, real-time MPSoCs are subject to varying workloads and application-specific demands during runtime making adaptive techniques highly justified in this area. System characteristics are dynamically changed to fulfill the requirements at runtime. In this survey, only reliability and adaptivity of real-time NoCs are covered.

## 3    NoC Architectures for QoS Support

Quality of service denotes the ability of the network to provide the communication requirements and abide to the constraints imposed by the executed application. Several parameters define these requirements and constraints such as packet loss, latency, jitter and throughput. From a QoS perspective, NoC designs can be classified into two main categories: best effort services (BE) and guaranteed services (GS) [16]. The correctness and completion of transmission is the only ensured service in a BE NoC. On the other hand, a GS NoC offers guaranteed commitment to performance bounds allowing for predictability. Accordingly, GS NoCs are the main concern in real-time domain, where predictability is the basic endeavor implying throughput and/or latency QoS guarantees. According to Mello et al. [17], existing techniques for QoS support in NoC designs fall under one of the following approaches: (1) tailoring the network dimensions to fit the bandwidth requirements of all executed tasks in the system; (2) supporting connection –oriented communication; (3) implementing connection-less communication with priority scheduling; and (4) hybrid combinations of previous techniques. The first approach is adopted by Xpipes NoC [19]. Xpipes is sized at the design phase with adjustment of channels bandwidths according to the applications requirements. This approach is based on a pre-design phase and postulates a prior knowledge of the executed load on the system which does not comply with today's complex applications. Furthermore, it does not guarantee a congestion-free design even with largely increased bandwidth [17]. The other three approaches have been extensively evolving in the literature. The different contributions in each approach are detailed in the following.

## 3.1   Connection-Oriented Approach

The connection-oriented approach is based on the idea of resources reservation. The communication links from the source to the final destination of the data are reserved establishing a complete connection path for the packets before being injected into the network. This approach is implemented either by using the pure circuit switching technique or by applying the concept of virtual circuits. In a pure circuit switching NoC, communication is achieved over three basic steps: (1) path setup phase to check for free route and reserve the corresponding links; (2) actual data transmission; (3) cancellation phase to release the resources. For hard real-time applications, this approach has indisputable advantage in terms of reliable QoS support providing hard throughput guarantees and tight latency bounds. Since an established route is an ownership for the traffic source, routers complexity is reduced and data is transferred at full rate of the links with no contention. Latency becomes only a factor of the route length and the dependency between traffics is confined to the route setup phase which fails or succeeds based on the traffic situation. These advantages are challenged by three main drawbacks namely non-scalability, path setup delay and inefficient resource utilization due to wasted resources to cover worst case behavior. Therefore, contributions in connection-oriented NoCs are mainly concerned with efficient path setup schemes and improved resource utilization.

SoCBUS, the first pure circuit switched NoC is presented in [20]. It uses mesochronous clocking and proposes a new packet-based setup scheme termed packet connected circuit (PCC). Special request packets are sent for path establishment following a distributed dynamic minimum path routing. A request reaching its destination locks all the temporary reserved links traveled throughout the path. A blocked request route at any node initiates a retry phase by retracing the partially established path and waiting for the occupied channels to become available. Such channel blocking situation is addressed by Wolkotte et al. [21] as well as by Pham et al. [22] to avoid high setup latencies. In [21], the spatial division multiplexing (SDM) concept is introduced in a synchronous circuit switching NoC. A lane division multiplexing technique is proposed allowing for physical separation between data streams. Links are divided into lanes and each lane can be used for separate physical connection. A connection may use one or more lanes based on the bandwidth requirements. The proposed router provides flexibility, however, the use of an external central coordination node (CCN) to configure the path setup and NoC routing limits the scalability of the design. In contrast, Pham et al. in [22] propose a new distributed dynamic path setup scheme based on backtracking probing to avoid blocked channels. Instead of waiting for busy channels to become available, the setup headers are allowed to flexibly backtrack and seek minimum paths alternatives.

Nostrum [23] and AEthereal [24] are two pioneering NoC examples based on time division multiplexing (TDM) for better resource utilization while maintaining the hard performance guarantees. TDM is an alternative to pure circuit switching which allows links to be shared in a contention-free scheme by reserving resources for specific points in time. Data are injected into the network at dedicated time slots following a periodic schedule. TDM schedules are either static or dynamically computed and they may be placed locally at each router for distributed routing or globally in the network interfaces (NIs) only for source routing [25], [26], [27]. Nostrum [23] supports guaranteed service by implementation of virtual circuits based on TDM. Virtual

circuits are set up semi-statically with fixed routes at design time however with variable bandwidth in runtime using the concept of looping containers. A special type of
packets called container are loaded with information and are looped between the
source and destination. As much bandwidth reservation is required for any virtual
circuit that is set up, as much containers are looped. AEthereal TDM NoC has been
evolving through [24], [28] and [27]. AEthereal [24] supports both BE and GS traffic
with static distributed TDM slot tables. In AEthereal, the TDM approach is implemented based on global synchronicity where all routers must always be in the same
time slot. The next version AElite [28] is the light version of AEthereal which supports source routing for GS [25].Its main contribution is the introduction of the distributed global notion of time through mesochronous and asynchronous routers. AElite
is further developed to the dAElite [27], namely distributed-aelite, in order to provide
multicast. dAElite supports only GS with a new configuration technique based on a
dedicated broadcast network which increases the speed of setting up and release of
connections and distributed routing. Finally, Argo [26] TDM NoC is presented using
mesochronous NIs to keep common notion of time however with asynchronous routers. Explicit need for synchronization between routers is revoked by exploiting the
fact that pipelined asynchronous circuits behave as FIFOs. The proposed self-timed
router allows masking of the skew between the NIs. Table 1 summarizes the presented contributions in this subsection with respect to the adopted approach, the
routing methodology, clocking scheme and supported traffic. On the other hand, Table 2 presents the reported hardware results. The tabulated results promote the dAelite
for the minimum hardware cost. However, the Argo asynchronous TDM NoC provides the highest bandwidth/link and highest operating frequency resulting in 30% of
Gb/s/ link more than dAelite.

**Table 1.** Summary of Contributions for Connection-Oriented Approach

| NoC | Approach | Routing | Clocking | Traffic |
|---|---|---|---|---|
| [20] | Circuit switching using PCC | Distributed | Mesochronous | GS |
| [21] | SDM | Distributed | Synchronous | GS |
| [22] | Circuit switching with backtracking | Distributed | Wave-pipelining source-synchronous | GS |
| [23] | TDM, loop containers | Unspecified | Unspecified | GS/BE |
| [24] | TDM | Source/Distributed | Synchronous | GS/BE |
| [28] | TDM | Source | Mesochronous | GS |
| [27] | TDM | Distributed | Synchronous | GS |
| [26] | TDM | Distributed | Asynchronous | GS |

**Table 2.** Circuit Switching Routers Hardware Implementation Results

| Router | Ports | Data width | Tech. | Area | Max freq. | BW/link |
|---|---|---|---|---|---|---|
| [21] | 5 | 16-bit | 0.13 µm | 0.0506 mm$^2$ | 1075 MHz | 17.2 Gb/s |
| [22] | 5 | 16-bit | 0.18 µm | 0.0315 mm$^2$ | 923 MHz | 14.76 Gb/s |
| [24] | 6 | 32-bit | 0.13 µm | 0.175 mm$^2$ | 500 MHz | 16 Gb/s |
| [28][1] | 5 | 32-bit | 65 nm | 3416 µm$^2$ | 885 MHz | 28.32 Gb/s |
| [27] | 5 | 32-bit | 65 nm | 3475 µm$^2$ | 926 MHz | 29.63 Gb/s |
| [26] | 5 | 34-bit | 65 nm | 7715 µm$^2$ | 1.13 GHz | 38.4 Gb/s |

---

[1] The results obtained from comparison with dAelite router in [22].

## 3.2    Connection-Less Approach

The connection-less approach is another alternative to provide QoS in NoCs based on packet switching with priorities. This approach is promoted by the typical use of NoC-based MPSoCs in multifunctional systems where diverse applications run in parallel bidding for different service requirements real-time or non-real-time. Traffic flows are clustered according to their QoS requirements into different groups each assigned a priority value. In contention situations, higher priority flows are serviced first and have the right to interrupt the lower priority ones. In connection-less NoCs, routers work in an independent manner. Wormhole switching with virtual channels is typically used for its high throughput and low buffering requirements. Additionally, the prioritized traffic flows are highly applicable for a virtual channel flow control router, where each VC has a particular priority that corresponds to one of the traffic clusters.

The connection-less approach has several benefits in terms of bandwidth and network resources utilization as well as adaptation to the varying network traffic. However, these advantages run against several challenges in terms of complexity and latency problems in addition to weak QoS support due to sharing of resources which is always critical regarding predictability. Nonetheless, a quantitative comparison presented in [29] demonstrated that for variable bit-rate applications, connection-less approach proves better performance over connection-oriented approach in terms of guaranteed end-to-end delay for individual flows with better prediction of transmission latency. However, these guarantees are only attainable for higher priority traffics. Progression of lower priority traffics through the network highly depends on the load of the higher priority flows possibly leading to long time stalls. State-of-the art techniques tackle the above mentioned problems by presenting efficient priority assignment techniques, priority arbitration techniques, and architectural solutions.

QNoC [30] is a packet switching NoC supporting four different classes of communication services. Each class has a fixed priority and additional service levels can be further defined by adhering priority ranking. Packets with higher priority are serviced first and round robin arbitration is applied for contending packets within same service level.

The QoS aware BiNoC is proposed in [31] supporting GS traffic with a reduced end-to-end latency. BiNoC is based on Wormhole switching with prioritized virtual channels. However, it offers dynamically self-reconfigurable bidirectional communication channels based on the real-time traffic need providing better bandwidth utilization. Idle channels can temporarily change their direction of operation to resolve congestions on the opposite direction. Furthermore, a new prioritized routing scheme is proposed supporting dynamic odd-even routing algorithm for GS real-time traffic.

The work in [32], [33], [34] and [35] address the problem of blocked lower priority data. In [32], two new mechanisms are proposed. First is an aging mechanism which tackles the starvation problem of blocked data; the priority of the blocked data is incremented after certain number of cycles. The second is a discarding mechanism which improves the bandwidth utilization by dropping packets of lower priority data if their deadlines are missed and if the number of dropped packets can be tolerated within the soft real-time application. On the other hand, a predictable reconfigurable

NoC (PRNoC) is proposed in [33] with a new round-based priority arbitration scheme. The term round refers to the set of packets arriving simultaneously when a new arbitration is initiated. The proposed arbitration guarantees QoS for higher priority packets while avoiding starvation for lower priority ones. In PRNoC, the network interface component supports PE reconfiguration. Furthermore, switches support both deterministic XY routing as well as the odd-even turn adaptive routing model. In contrast to conventional approaches, the NoC architecture proposed in [34] handles the situation in a reverse manner. Low QoS traffic is prioritized over guaranteed throughput traffic as long as enough resources are available for the guarantees. Cheshmi et al. [35] present a similar approach however for GALS NoCs. They propose a new priority scheduling algorithm for QoS guarantees in asynchronous routers. The algorithm is based on a quota setting methodology providing guaranteed end-to-end delay in a non-preemptive method. Lower priority flows are allowed to use the channel even with the existence of high priority ones. However, their access is limited to a certain small portion of the channel based on an assigned quota table. The required performance guarantees can be achieved by adjusting the values in the quota table.

## 3.3   Hybrid Techniques

The previous two subsections highlighted the advantages as well as the drawbacks of both NoC approaches: connection-oriented and connectionless. Specifically, connection-oriented approach can provide hard performance guarantees for GS traffics while connection-less approach offers soft guarantees with better adaptation to the varying network traffic as well as better bandwidth and resource utilization. In fact, real-time applications, mainly targeting MPSoCs, invoke a mixture of traffic types with different predictability and QoS requirements. In that context, hybrid NoC designs are promoted to provide the right mix of soft and hard real-time guarantees and to efficiently handle both streaming and best effort traffics generated by real-time applications. The MANGO NoC [36] is one typical asynchronous hybrid architecture where the routers internally consist of a BE router and a GS router implemented separately. The BE router supports simple source-routing for connection-less data packets. On the other hand, the GS router utilizes virtual channels (VCs) routing to establish hard GS connections. Virtual circuits are implemented by reserving a sequence of independently buffered VCs. Since the GS router provides non-blocking switching, link arbitration becomes the basis for guaranteed service. In [37], Lusala et al. propose a hybrid NoC architecture for real-time applications. The proposed NoC consists of two sub-networks: circuit- and packet switching. The circuit switching sub-network is based on a combination between the SDM and TDM techniques in an attempt to provide a guaranteed service with increased path diversity and improved resource utilization. The performance results proved that implementing SDM with TDM technique boosts the positive response to source requests for time slots reservation as the impact of scheduling constraint is significantly alleviated. Table 3 presents the reported hardware results of the hybrid routers. The results highlight the ultimately high operating frequency provided by the hybrid SDM-TDM router [37] when compared with the dAelite [27] and Argo [26] routers presented in Table 2, however at the expense of a more complex router.

**Table 3.** Hybrid Routers Hardware Implementation Results

| Router | Ports | Data width | Tech. | Area | Max freq. |
|--------|-------|-----------|-------|------|-----------|
| [36] | 5 | 32-bit | 0.12 µm | 0.188 mm$^2$ | 515 MHz |
| [37] | 6 | 18-bit$^2$ | 65 nm | 86499.9 µm$^2$ | 2 GHz |

## 4    Fault Tolerance

The continuous shrinking in the silicon technology process puts reliability and fault tolerance among the most noticeable research problems in NoC designs [11]. Two possible types of faults are considered: transient and permanent faults which may be data or control faults due to component or connection failure. A detailed classification of the different possible faults scenarios is presented in [38]. Transient faults are handled using flow control based methods where error correction/detection codes are implemented with possible retransmission mechanisms. On the other hand, in order to tolerate permanent errors, a reliable NoC should be able to detect the error, precisely locate the fault to finally isolate the failure and recover the lost data. Each of the previously mentioned phases is a stand-alone reliability research issue. In this section, existing efforts targeting fault tolerance within real-time NoCs are surveyed. Yue et al. [39] developed a metric to measure timing similarities between two different NoC topologies for real-time applications. Their work is based on the core-level redundancy approach to improve the reliability of NoC-based many-core chips. A fine-tuned polynomial time algorithm based on Hungarian method is proposed to reconfigure a defect tolerant core. The algorithm makes use of the developed timing similarity metric to select the optimum virtual core replacing the defected one while keeping the timing variations minimized between the original and the reconfigured virtual topologies. The work of Yue et al. is elaborated in [12] by Li et al. Two new algorithmic solutions were proposed to achieve the utmost similarities in the timing behavior using a GSNoC model. On the other hand, the work presented in [40] focus on fault detection coverage. A comprehensive system-level analysis is presented for the behavior of a typical real-time2D mesh NoC in mixed-critical systems under the effect of faults. A failure mode and effect analysis (FMEA) is performed in addition to a classification of error effects regarding duration and ability to compromise task isolation with full coverage of potential single faults. On the same focus of fault detection, NoCAlert [41] presents a comprehensive on-line real-time hardware-assertions-based fault detection mechanism for NoCs. The proposed methodology is based on invariance checking and covers only illegal faults. System is continuously checked for illegal outputs through several distributed checker micro-modules. An illegal output is an operational decision that violates the functional correctness rule(s) of a particular

---

$^2$ Total width of the physical link with four 18-bit wide sub-channels design

NoC component. The micro-modules provide real-time on-line fault detection without interfering or interrupting NoC operation. Finally, Amin et al. [42] propose a system level flexible design method to tolerate faults on heterogeneous MPSoC platforms with mesh based NoC interconnects under real-time constrains. The proposed system addresses the fault tolerance and performance tradeoffs by including two types of processing nodes one is a high fault tolerance and the other is a high performance one. Table 4 provides a summary for the surveyed reliability approaches presented in this section. The surveyed efforts regarding reliability of real-time NoCs indicate that this research area is still wide for new contributions and open for improvement. Specifically considering heterogeneous many-core systems and adaptive routing would make worthwhile contributions in this area.

**Table 4.** Summary of Contributions for Reliability in Real-Time NoCs

| Ref. | Reliability Coverage | Approach | Platform | Routing |
|------|---------------------|----------|----------|---------|
| [39] | Fault isolation | Virtual cores | Homogeneous many-core with 2D mesh NoC | XY |
| [40] | Fault detection | FMEA | 2D mesh NoC | Deterministic source routing |
| [41] | Fault detection | Invariance checking | CMP with 2D mesh NoC | Custom[3] |
| [42] | Fault tolerance vs. performance tradeoffs | Flexible system level method | Heterogeneous MPSoC with 2D mesh NoC | XY |

# 5    Adaptive Techniques in Real-Time NoCs

Since application-specific demands vary for a wide range of real-time applications during runtime, adaptive techniques are justified in this area. They change dynamically system characteristics to fulfill the requirements at runtime. In this section, the focus is on adaptive techniques improving dynamically demands such as the utilization of resources in real-time NoCs. An adaptive on-chip communication, called AdNoC (Adaptive Network-on-Chip), is presented in [43]. The contribution of this paper is an adaptive path allocation algorithm which meets a level of QoS concerning to bandwidth. A connection is established by (re-)allocating dynamically buffer blocks on demand. This is enabled by decisions made locally at each router depending on the bandwidth in each direction to the adjacent routers. The advantage of such an adaptive algorithm is an efficient utilization of buffers. Pionteck et al. [44] describe a NoC with prioritizing semi-static data streams. Semi-static data streams consist of a number of consecutive packets which have the same path for a period of time. The NoC presented in this paper detects locally semi-static data streams in each router to establish a point-to-point connection. Since routing is done only for the first packet, the point-to-point connection sets a fixed latency for packets forwarding through this data stream. The adaptivity of the NoC is the detection and determination of the data stream. A scalable NoC, called Rerouting, with a self-optimization is presented in [45]. Rerouting provides

---

[3]   The NoCAlert is applicable to any router microarchitecture by deriving its corresponding invariances.

real-time by establishment of GS connections. In order to ensure this, a message is sent to allocate a path from source to destination. This allocation is static for most NoCs. Nevertheless, further requests of GS connections can lead to inefficient usage of paths allocated in NoCs. Therefore, Rerouting changes automatically the path of established GS connections to improve the exploitation of the NoC. Göhringer et al. introduce the Star-Wheels NoC [46] designed as a hybrid topology between star and spidergon. This provides the advantages of both topologies. In addition to packet-switched transmissions, Star-Wheels NoC provides circuit-switched connections. Hence, a connection guaranteeing a determined transmission time is enabled. Furthermore, Star-Wheels NoC adapts the size of the topology at runtime. More precisely, switches can be added or removed dynamically based on partial dynamic reconfiguration. Thus, the power consumption of the system is adjustable. In [14], a further approach for real-time NoCs with energy constraints is described. In order to fulfill this demand, a methodology to minimize the energy consumption without violating the predefined time constraints is presented. An adaptive algorithm determines the allowed slack of a packet. Based on this information, the algorithm decreases the energy consumption by applying voltage and frequency scaling. To sum up, Table 5 gives an overview of these NoCs. The adaptive technique based on the respective approach, the platform and the routing algorithm are listed.

**Table 5.** Summary of Contributions for Adaptive Techniques in Real-Time NoCs

| Ref. | Adaptive Technique | Approach | Platform | Routing |
|------|--------------------|----------|----------|---------|
| [43] | Adaptive path allocation | Buffer allocation algorithm | 2D mesh NoC | Weighted XY |
| [44] | Assigning of semi-static data streams | Monitoring router | 2D mesh NoC | XY |
| [45] | Rerouting | Selection strategy | 2D mesh NoC | Adaptive |
| [46] | Size of topology | Dynamic partial reconfiguration | Star-Wheels NoC | Deterministic |
| [14] | Energy efficiency | Slack exploitation | 2D Mesh NoC | Dimension order |

# 6   Conclusion

This paper discussed the challenges faced on the different design level of NoCs for real-time applications. A comprehensive survey was presented for existing real-time NoC architectures covering QoS support, fault tolerance and adaptivity. On the level of QoS support, TDM is widely used for connection-oriented techniques mainly with global synchronicity for hard real-time guarantees. Asynchronous TDM NoCs is a recent proposal that attracts interest for further exploration with an ultimate bandwidth per link approaching the 40 Gb/s. Connection-less techniques were also presented on the level of architectures, schedulability and priority arbitration schemes. Furthermore, hybrid techniques are highlighted as a significant solution to provide the critical mix between hard and soft real-time applications. The surveyed efforts regarding reliability of real-time NoCs indicate that this research area is still wide for new contributions and open for improvement. For future research, integrating run-time adaptivity and system reconfiguration with fault tolerance techniques for real-time NoCs would make significant contributions in this area. Furthermore, techniques to provide high link bandwidth in the range of hundreds of Gb/s in real-time NoCs may be investigated to cope with the increasing performance of real-time applications.

# References

1. Intel® Many Integrated Core Architecture - Advanced. http://www.intel.com
2. Borkar, S.: Thousand core chips: A technology perspective. In: (DAC) (2007)
3. Dally, W., Towles, B.: Route packets not wires: On-chip interconnection networks. In: 38th Design Automation Conference (DAC), pp. 684–689 (2001)
4. Abd, E.I., Ghany, M., El-Moursy, M., Ismail, M.: High throughput architecture for high performance NoC. In: Data Storage. Florin Balasa (2010)
5. Bjerregaard, T., Mahadevan, S.: A survey of research and practices of Network-on-chip. ACM Comput. Surv. 38(1) (2006)
6. Ogras, U., Marculescu, R.: Literature survey. In: Modeling, Analysis and Optimization of Network-on-Chip Communication Architectures 184. Springer Netherlands, pp. 9–32 (2013)
7. Abbas, A., et al.: A survey on energy-efficient methodologies and architectures of network-on-chip. Computers & Electrical Engineering 40(8), 333–347 (2014)
8. Sparsoe, J.: Design of networks-on-chip for real-time multi-processor systems-on-chip. In: 12th (ACSD), pp. 1–5 (2012)
9. Marculescu, R., Ogras, U.Y., Peh, L.-S., Jerger, N.E., Hoskote, Y.: Outstanding Research Problems in NoC Design: System, Microarchitecture, and Circuit Perspectives. IEEE Transactions on CAD 28(1), 3–21 (2009)
10. Li, Z., Li, S., Hua, X., Wu, H., Ren, S.: Maintaining real-time application timing similarity for defect-tolerant NoC-based many-core systems. In: ACM Transactions (2013)
11. Zhan, J., Stoimenov, N., Ouyang, J., Thiele, L., Narayanan, V., Xie, Y.: Designing energy-efficient NoC for real-time embedded systems through slack optimization. In: DAC (2013)
12. Davis, R., Burns, A.: A survey of hard real-time scheduling for multiprocessor systems. ACM Computing Surveys 43(4), 35.1–35.44 (2011)
13. Goossens, K., Dielissen, J., Meerbergen, J., Poplavko, P., Rădulescu, A., Rijpkema, E., Waterlander, E., Wielage, P.: Guaranteeing the Quality of Services in Networks on Chip. In: Jantsch, A., Tenhunen, H. (eds.) Networks on Chip, pp. 61–82. Springer, US (2003)
14. Mello, A., Tedesco, L., Calazans, N., Moraes, F.: Evaluation of current QoS mechanisms in networks on chip. In: IEEE Int. Symp. on System-on-Chip, pp. 1–4 (2006)
15. Bertozzi, D., Benini, L.: Xpipes: a network-on-chip architecture for gigascale systems-on-chip. IEEE Circuits and Systems Magazine 4(2), 18–31 (2004)
16. Wiklund, D., Liu, D.: SoCBUS: Switched network on chip for hard real time embedded systems. In: Proceedings of IPDPS, pp. 22–26 (2003)
17. Wolkotte, P., Smit, G., Rauwerda, G., Smit, L.: An energy-efficient reconfigurable circuit-switched network-on-chip. In: 19th IEEE IPDPS, p. 155a (2005)
18. Pham, P.-H., Park, J., Mau, P., Kim, C.: Design and implementation of backtracking wave-pipeline switch to support guaranteed throughput in network-on-chip. IEEE Trans. on VLSI Systems 20(2), 270–283 (2012)
19. Millberg, M., Nilsson, E., Thid, R., Jantsch, A.: Guaranteed bandwidth using looped containers in temporally disjoint networks within the nostrum network on chip. In: DATE 2, pp. 890–895 (2004)

20. Goossens, K., Dielissen, J., Radulescu, A.: The Æthereal network on chip: Concepts, architectures, and implementations. IEEE D&T of Computers **22**(5), 414–421 (2005)
21. Goossens, K., Hansson, A.: The aethereal network on chip after ten years: Goals, evolution, lessons, and future. In: 47th DAC, pp. 306–311 (2010)
22. Kasapaki, E., Spars, J.: Argo: A time-elastic time-division-multiplexed noc using asynchronous routers. In: 20th IEEE Int. ASYNC, pp. 45–52 (2014)
23. Stefan, R., Molnos, A., Goossens, K.: dAElite: A TDM NoC Supporting QoS, Multicast, and Fast Connection Set-Up. IEEE Transactions on Computers **63**(3), 583–594 (2014)
24. Hansson, A., Subbaraman, M., Goossens, K.: Aelite: A flit-synchronous network on chip with composable and predictable services. In: DATE 2009, pp. 250–255 (2009)
25. Harmanci, M., Escudero, N., Leblebici, Y., Ienne, P.: Quantitative modelling and comparison of communication schemes to guarantee quality-of-service in networks-on-chip. In: ISCAS, pp. 1782–1785 (2005)
26. Bolotin, E., Cidon, I., Ginosar, R., Kolodny, A.: QNoC: QoS architecture and design process for network on chip. JSA **50**(2–3), 105–128 (2004)
27. Lo, S.-H., Lan, Y.-C., Yeh, H.-H., Tsai, W.-C., Hu, Y.-H., Chen, S.-J.: QoS aware BiNoC architecture. In: 24th IEEE IPDPS, pp. 1–10 (2010)
28. Corrêa, E., Silva, L., Wagner, F., Carro, L.: Fitting the router characteristics in NoCs to meet QoS requirements. In: 20th SBCCI, pp. 105–110 (2007)
29. Lu, C.-H., Chiang, K.-C., Hsiun, P.-A.: Round-based priority arbitration for predictable and reconfigurable network-on-chip. In: 8th IEEE Int. Conf. on FPT, pp. 403–406 (2009)
30. Diemer, J., Ernst, R., Kauschke, M.: Efficient throughput-guarantees for latency-sensitive networks-on-chip. In: 15th ASP-DAC, pp. 529–534 (2010)
31. Cheshmi, K., Trajkovic, J., Soltaniyeh, M., Mohammadi, S.: Quota setting router architecture for quality of service in GALS NoC. In: 23rd Int. Symp. on RSP, pp. 44–50 (2013)
32. Bjerregaard, T., Sparso, J.: A router architecture for connection-oriented service guarantees in the MANGO clockless network-on-chip. In: DATE **2**, pp. 1226–1231 (2005)
33. Lusala, A.K., Legat, J.: A hybrid NoC combining SDM-TDM based circuit-switching with packet-switching for real-time applications. In: IEEE 10th NEWCAS, pp. 17–20 (2012)
34. Goehringer, D., Lukas, M., Oey, O., Becker, J.: Reliable and adaptive network-on-chip architectures for cyber physical systems. ACM TECS **12**(1), 51:1–51:21 (2013)
35. Yue, K., Lockom, F., Li, Z., Ghalim, S., Ren, S., Zhang, L., Li, X.: Hungarian algorithm based virtualization to maintain application timing similarity for defect-tolerant NoC. In: ASP-DAC (2012)
36. Rambo, E.A., Tschiene, A., Diemer, J., Ahrendts, L., Ernst, R.: Failure analysis of a network-on-chip for real-time mixed-critical systems. In: DATE (2014)
37. Prodromou, A., Panteli, A., Nicopoulos, C., Sazeides, Y.: NoCAlert: An on-line and real-time fault detection mechanism for network-on-chip architectures. In: MICRO (2012)
38. Amin, M., Tagel, M., Jervan, G., Hollstein, T.: Design methodology for fault-tolerant heterogeneous MPSoC under real-time constraints. In: ReCoSoC (2012)
39. Al Faruque, M.A., Ebi, T., Henkel, J.: Run-time adaptive on-chip communication scheme. In: IEEE/ACM International Conference on Computer-Aided Design (ICCAD) (2007)
40. Pionteck, T., Osterloh, C.: Prioritizing semi-static data streams in network-on-chips for runtime reconfigurable systems. In: HPCS (2013)
41. Heisswolf, J., Singh, M., Kupper, M.; Konig, R., Becker, J.:Rerouting: Scalable NoC self-optimization by distributed hardware-based connection reallocation. In: ReConFig(2013)
42. Goehringer, D., Oey, O., Huebner, M., Becker, J.: Heterogeneous and runtime parameterizable star-wheels network-on-chip. In: SAMOS (2011)

# Cryptography Applications

# Efficient SR-Latch PUF

Bilal Habib$^{(\boxtimes)}$, Jens-Peter Kaps, and Kris Gaj

Electrical and Computer Engineering Department, George Mason University,
Fairfax, VA, USA
{bhabib,jkaps,kgaj}@gmu.edu

**Abstract.** In this paper we present an efficient SR-Latch based PUF design, with two times improvement in area over the state of the art, thus making it very attractive for low-area designs. This PUF is able to reliably generate a 128-bit cryptographic key. The proposed design is compact and the effect of inter-CLB routing is eliminated. The PUF response is generated by quantifying the number of oscillations during the metastability state for preselected latches. The derived design has been verified on 25 Xilinx Spartan-6 FPGAs (XC6SLX16). The uniqueness measure is 49.24%. In addition the design has been tested at ± 5% of core voltage and also over the rated temperature range [0-85°C]. The reliability at +5% of nominal voltage is 99.18%, while at -5% of nominal voltage it is 97.54%. We also propose a novel area-efficient error correcting scheme that assures that a key generated in the field, at the extreme values of voltage and temperature supported by the commercial-grade Spartan-6 FPGAs, is the same as the key generated during enrollment at nominal operating conditions.

**Keywords:** Physical Unclonable Functions · SR-Latch · Metastability · FPGAs

## 1 Introduction

Recent research has led to an increased interest in security measures, especially in solutions that are physically unique and unclonable. In this regard, different structures of Physical Unclonable Functions (PUFs) have been developed and investigated to efficiently meet the requirements of these solutions. PUFs are physical primitives that produce unclonable and device-specific measurements of silicon Integrated Circuits (ICs). These measurements are then processed to generate either responses in challenge-response schemes or secure keys for cryptographic functions. Manufacturing process variations give physical uniqueness, but many physical unclonable functions (PUFs) are noisy and exhibit low circuit efficiency. Therefore, while designing new PUF structures, we need to focus on the efficiency and reliability besides the unclonability and uniqueness measures.

PUF structure is incorporated in the silicon devices for targeting two major applications. First one is the identification of silicon devices and another one is secure key generation for cryptographic functions. In this paper we are targeting the secure key generation application using SR-latch PUF.

© Springer International Publishing Switzerland 2015
K. Sano et al. (Eds.): ARC 2015, LNCS 9040, pp. 205–216, 2015.
DOI: 10.1007/978-3-319-16214-0_17

In Section 2, we describe the previous work for a better understanding of our study on PUF. Section 3 explains the design methodology. In Section 4, we explain the bit-string generation. Results and analysis are covered in Section 5. The conclusion and future study are described in Section 6.

## 2     Related Work

Since 2002, silicon based PUFs have been extensively investigated. There are two categories of silicon based PUF circuits: Delay based PUFs and Memory based PUFs. Delay based PUFs include Arbiter PUF [1, 2, 3], Ring-Oscillator (RO) PUF [4, 9], and S-ArbRO PUF [15]. In [14], a PUF based on programmable delay lines is presented.

Another category of silicon PUF is based on memory. It includes SRAM PUF [5], Butterfly PUF [7], and Latch PUF [6]. In [10], the concept of transient effect ring oscillator (TERO) is presented. A true random number generator (TRNG) is developed by counting the oscillations of elements during metastability. The least significant bit of that count is selected as a random bit. It is important to mention that the design proposed in [10] is implemented on Spartan-3 devices which are a 90nm technology while our design is tested on Spartan-6 which is a 45nm technology. The source of entropy is dependent on many factors, like the technology used, design implemented and testing methodology. The TERO approach is further developed in [13], where an element with PUF capability is presented. In [17], PUF design is developed which is based on (TERO) cells. The randomness is harvested by measuring the metastable oscillator counts. Final bits are generated by averaging the oscillation counts and then reading the most significant two (or four) bits of an eight bit counter for each latch. In order to assure the reproducibility of these bits, each latch count is measured $2^{18}$ times.

In [16], SR-latch based PUF is developed; it has been implemented on Spartan-3 and Spartan-6 devices. In Spartan-6 based design, 128 SR-latches have been implemented. Each latch is configured by using two neighboring CLBs in each column. Inside each CLB a Look up Table (LUT) and a Flip Flop (FF) are used. PUF response is determined by the final state of the latch. All the latches are excited by a 2.5MHz clock signal. For each latch two bits are contributed towards the PUF response. If the final state of the latch is logic '0' in 1000 repetitions of the experiment, the corresponding response bits are '00'. If the final state is logic '1' in 1000 repetitions of the experiment, the corresponding response bits are '11'. If the final state changes at least once during 1000 repetitions of the experiment, this state is declared random, and encoded as '10'. A detection circuit determines all three cases and generates the response bits in each case. In our proposed design, we tried to improve the circuit efficiency of this design. In addition, our source of entropy is based on the exact number of oscillations at the output of an SR-latch during the metastable state, rather than a final state of each latch, as in [16]. Because of the encoding method, in [16] the goal is to increase the number of random latches, while in our work, we decrease the number of random latches. We include only the most stable latches, i.e., latches generating consistently the same number of oscillations in the metastable state, in the bit generation step during enrollment. On top of that, the method of [16] does not differentiate between the behavior of latches that generate no oscillations at the output from the behavior of latches that generate an even number of oscillations. This distinction is clearly made in our scheme. Furthermore, the method of [16] is prone to the influence of neighboring logic. We diminished this influence by prohibiting the tool from assigning any resources of the latch CLB to any external logic.

## 3    Design Methodology

In our design, an SR-latch is made from two LUTs configured as a NAND gate each. Additionally, two flip-flops are used in this latch to reduce the clock skew. Initially, a latch is forced into a metastable state by applying a rising-edge at a 'ctrl' signal, as shown in Fig. 1. Transitory oscillations in the loop start if the following two conditions are fulfilled [10]: A) the circuit must have a positive feedback and B) The RC time constant (defined by the parasitic resistance and capacitance) must be shorter than the total delay of all logic elements involved in the loop. In our design the delay of a loop is equal to the propagation delay of a single LUT. In Spartan 6 FPGAs, this delay is equal to 0.21ns [20]. Adding more elements to the loop increases the propagation delay. The longer loops will be more strongly affected by the routing delays of FPGA fabric; therefore we kept the loop as small as possible.

During the metastable state, the SR-latch oscillates. An eight-bit counter is used to count these oscillations. Once the metastable state is over, the latch stops oscillating, and the counter value is stored into the block RAM (BRAM). Before applying the 'ctrl' signal, the two flip-flops (FF) are reset. It is done to ensure that latches always start oscillations with the same initial state. This reset functionality is not incorporated in either [13] or [17]. Additionally, both [13] and [17] are based on a loop made of AND gates and inverters. Our loop is based only on NAND gates. Since in an FPGA implementation, an additional gate requires an extra LUT, therefore we chose NAND gate to keep the loop as short as possible. This small modification results in the reduction of the propagation delay. It needs to be mentioned that by keeping the loop small has two major advantages. First, we can place four SR-latches inside a single CLB; secondly, propagation delays are minimally affected by routing delays. This way, the randomness due to process variations is the dominant factor, while in a longer loop the routing delays become the dominant factor in the propagation delay [8].

Once the process of the characterization is over for all the latches, the data from the BRAM is read-out to the PC via Enhanced Parallel Port (EPP) protocol as shown in Fig. 2. In our design, a 9-bit multiplexer address line selects a particular latch. This latch is then excited by applying a low to high transition at the 'ctrl' signal, as shown in Fig. 2. The eight-bit counter, available at the output of the multiplexer, counts the number of oscillations during the metastable state. These values are then stored in the neighboring BRAM. The bit generation and analysis are done during post-processing. It must be mentioned that only one latch is characterized at any given time. This is done to prevent any correlation between the neighboring latches and also to save the FPGA logic resources.

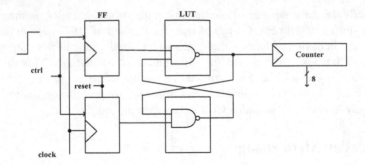

**Fig. 1.** A single SR-Latch design

Therefore, only one counter is used to measure the latch-counts during the metastable state. In addition, all the control signals are provided by the FSM. 512 latches are implemented, which requires 128 CLBs. The prototype design requires BRAM and EPP, because we want to analyze all the latch counts. However, in the final product, EPP can be replaced by a different interface and the size of the required BRAM will be reduced. The placement of latches is constrained by the slice location attribute. All the latches are placed in a rectangular matrix of CLBs. The dimensions of this matrix are 16x8 as shown in Fig. 3.

We implemented our design on Spartan-6 (XC6SLX16) device. Four latches are implemented inside a single CLB in our design. These four latches (L1, L2, L3 and L4) are shown in Fig. 4, each with a different color scheme. This design is developed to eliminate the inter-CLB routing. We believe that due to the capacitance of long wires, the variation due to routing delays become significant, as explained in [8].

As evident from the above figure, each latch consists of two LUTs and two FF. All the LUTs inside the CLB are utilized in the implementation of latches, thus, achieving a hardware efficiency of 100% in terms of LUTs. By comparison, the design proposed in Fig. 12 in [16], has 12.5% LUT utilization because, only two LUTs are utilized from the two adjacent CLBs. In addition, the circuit efficiency for FF is 50%, while it is only 6.25% in [16].

## 4    Bit Generation

Each latch is sampled 100 times and the corresponding latch count values are stored in the BRAM. Once all the latches are characterized, we select highly stable latches and ignore the remaining ones. In our method, a latch is defined to be stable if the latch count value remains the same for all 100 samples. The value 100 is chosen due to the fact that it is easier to interpret it as a percentage of the total. This number is in fact a trade-off between reliability, execution time and the storage resources in BRAM. During enrollment, we store for each latch, a latch number, a corresponding bit showing whether this latch is stable, and the latch count value (i.e., we store: {Latch #, stable, count}).

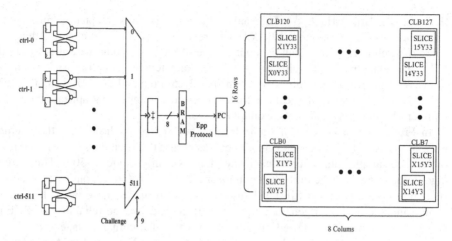

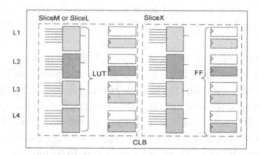

**Fig. 2.** SR-latch PUF design.          **Fig. 3.** Layout on FPGA

**Fig. 4.** Our proposed design: Implementation of 4 SR-latches per CLB

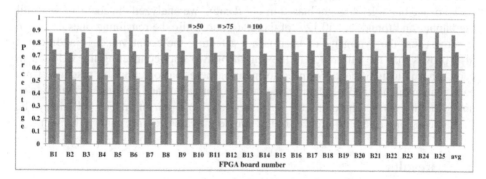

**Fig. 5.** Proposed design: Percentage of stable latches per board at 1.2V and 25°C. This result corresponds to the design from Figure 4.

For bit generation during enrollment, only the stable latch count values are considered. In this method the count values for L+1 latches are used. These values are used to generate the L bit PUF response. We number stable latches in a snake-like fashion: $L_1, L_2, L_3, \dots L_{L+1}$, and then we do the comparisons of neighboring latches $[L_1, L_2]$,

$[L_2, L_3], [L_3, L_4], ...., [L_L, L_{L+1}]$. The snake-like comparison is adopted to mitigate the effect of systematic variations [9]. A binary response bit '1' is generated if the count value of latch $L_i$ is greater than the count value of latch $L_{i+1}$; otherwise it is '0'. In the field, the count value of stable latches is recalculated by sampling each latch 100 times. We get 100 count values between 0 and 255, e.g., {127, 127, 128, 127, 127, 127... 128, 127}. For further calculations, we use the number that appears the largest number of times, e.g., 127 in the example above.

In Fig. 5, the percentage of stable latches per device is shown. On the average, 87% of latches (0.87*512 = 445) in all devices repeat the latch count at least 50 times out of 100 samples during enrollment (i.e., have stability mode "> 50"). This percentage drops to 51.4% when the latch counts are identical 100 times out of 100 samples (i.e., have stability mode "100"). Now the question arises, how many latches we should include in the bit generation process. It depends on the reliability of PUF response. In this work, we tested our boards at +5% of nominal voltage and -5 % of nominal voltage. It needs to be mentioned that on our Nexys-3 FPGA boards, the nominal voltage is equal to 1.2V. We believe that the high number of stable latches is achieved due to the fact that external logic has minimal affect on the latch operation. This is accomplished by using all the LUTs of Latch-CLBs for implementing SR latches.

It should be mentioned, that our method for a PUF ID generation is completely different than the method used in [17]. In [17], the most significant bits of a count value for a single TERO loop are used. In our design, all bits of two count values, obtained using two neighboring stable SR latches, are compared with each other to generate a single bit of a PUF ID. As a result, our design allows obtaining the same (or higher) reliability using much fewer repetitions of the count measurement ($2^{18}$ in [17] vs. $100 \times 100 < 2^{14}$ in our design). Because of that, our PUF has a shorter response time than the PUF described in [17].

To prove that a latch is not biased in our design, we analyzed the count value of all the latches and found that 50.12% of them are odd while the remaining ones are even. It proves that the symmetry of latch is not affecting the count value. In addition, it also proves that the difference in the length of two nets connecting the LUTs with each other is insignificant. We need to mention here that our final bit response from each pair of latches is dependent on the latch count values and not on the final state of any particular latch. Therefore, the bit response from a pair of latches will always be the same as long as the differences of the two count values do not change the sign.

## 5     Results

We compare our results with [16]. This comparison is summarized in Tables 1 and 2. The uniqueness is calculated using the following equation:

$$\text{Uniqueness} = \frac{2}{N(N-1)} \sum_{i=1}^{N-1} \sum_{j=i+1}^{N} \frac{HD(R_i, R_j)}{L} \times 100\% \qquad (1)$$

**Table 1.** Details of dataset

|  | This work | Yamamoto et al. [16] |
|---|---|---|
| No. of Chips (N) | 25 | 20 |
| PUF per Chip | 1 | 2 |
| Samples (T) | 100 | 100 |
| ID size (L) bits | 256 | 256 |
| SR-Latches (M) | 512 | 128 |
| FPGA (Device used) | XC6SLX16-3CSG324 | XC6SLX16-2CSG324 |

Similarly, reliability is calculated according to the following equations:

$$HD_{INTRA_i} = \frac{1}{T} \sum_{t=1}^{T} \frac{HD(R_i, R'_{i,t})}{L} \times 100\%$$    (2)

$$Reliability_i = 100\% - HD_{INTRA_i}$$    (3)

$$Average\ Reliability = \frac{1}{P} \sum_{j=1}^{P} Reliability_j$$    (4)

**Table 2.** Comparison with Yamamoto et al [16]

|  | This work | [16] | Ideal |  |
|---|---|---|---|---|
| Uniqueness | 49.24% | 49% | 50% | Ri = Response of chip i |
| Reliability @ 1.14v | **97.54%** | 94.70% | 100% | Rj = Response of chip j |
| Reliability @ 1.20v | **99.5%** | 99.14% | 100% | HD= Hamming distance |
| Reliability @ 1.26v | **99.18%** | 95.20% | 100% | T = Total number of samples /ID |
|  |  |  |  | t = Index of a sample ($1 \leq t \leq T$) |

Reliability shown in Table 2 is the average reliability of five random boards from a set of 25 boards. Average Reliability of P chips can be calculated using equation (4). Equations 1, 2 and 3 are based on the definitions of PUF quantitative metrics proposed in [18]. It needs to mention that Uniqueness shown in Table 2 is calculated for 25 FPGA devices.

## 5.1    Uniqueness

In Fig. 6, the normalized inter-chip Hamming distance, (HD (Ri, Rj)/L)*100% is shown. The mean is 49.24%, while the standard deviation is 3.36%. This data is generated from 25 FPGA boards at 25°C and 1.2V supplied as the core voltage.

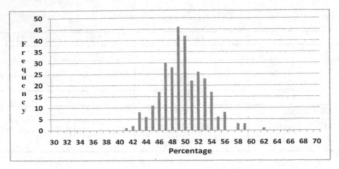

**Fig. 6.** Normalized inter-chip Hamming distance (Mean=49.24%)

The total number of combinations (i.e., the total number of board pairs $\{i,j\}$) is $\binom{25}{2}$= 300. The y-axis (denoted frequency) shows the total number of times a given normalized inter-chip Hamming distance was obtained.

## 5.2   Reliability

In Table 3, the information on bit flips for five boards is shown. It is clear from this table that the worst case is 13 bit flips. The Maximum intra-chip Hamming distance is defined as (HD ($R_i$, $R'_{i,t}$)), when tested under all conditions.

**Table 3.** Voltage vs. Intra-chip Hamming Distance

| Board No. | No. of stable latches at 1.2V | Bit flips at 1.26V | Bit flips at 1.14V | Maximum HD($R_i$,$R'_{i,t}$) | Worse case HD |
|---|---|---|---|---|---|
| B2 | 260 | 1 | 4 | 4 | |
| B4 | 280 | 1 | 13 | 13 | |
| B6 | 264 | 1 | 6 | 6 | 13 |
| B1 | 275 | 5 | 1 | 5 | |
| B2 | 262 | 3 | 9 | 9 | |

**Table 4.** Temperature vs. Intra-chip Hamming Distance

| Board No. | Bit length | Bit flips at 0°C | Bit flips at 85°C | Maximum HD($R_i$, $R'_{i,t}$) | Worse case HD |
|---|---|---|---|---|---|
| B1 | 256 | 4 | 11 | 11 | |
| B2 | 256 | 7 | 12 | 12 | |
| B3 | 256 | 2 | 12 | 12 | |
| B4 | 256 | 0 | 7 | 7 | |
| B5 | 256 | 3 | 13 | 13 | 16 |
| B6 | 256 | 2 | 7 | 7 | |
| B7 | 256 | 3 | 10 | 10 | |
| B8 | 256 | 7 | 16 | 16 | |
| B9 | 256 | 8 | 8 | 8 | |
| B1 | 256 | 5 | 8 | 8 | |

We tested the boards at 0°C and 85°C. Table 4 shows the results for 10 boards. From Table 4, it is evident that for reliability the effect of 85°C is always worse than the effect of 0°C. Overall the worse case Hamming distance is 16. We also tested the five FPGA boards at 1.14V and four different temperatures, as shown in Fig. 7.

## 5.3    Reliability vs. Error Correction

For error correction, we propose a novel method, inspired by the designs described in [19]. This method is based on the use of BCH code. It consists of two procedures: Generation and Reproduction. Generation is carried out at the room temperature and nominal voltage, while Reproduction is carried out in the field.

During the generation process, Secure Sketch (SS) is applied to PUF output w, as shown in Fig. 8. The second input to SS is the key K, generated using a True Random Number Generator, RNG1. The output of SS, denoted by s, is stored as helper data in the database. During the reproduction process, the helper data is used to regenerate the key K from a noisy PUF response w'. BCH decoder is used to regenerate the 131 bit key as shown in the figure. We propose to use BCH with the following parameters: (n=255, k=131, t=18) code. The meaning of these parameters is as follows: n=255 is the output block size, k=131 is the input block size (in our case, the size of the key to be encoded), and t=18 is the number of errors that can be corrected by this code. We chose these parameters because the code with these parameters can easily correct the worse case errors shown in Tables 3 and 4, and Fig. 7. Please note that in our scheme, the key K is not a function of the PUF response during the Generation process, but becomes a function of the PUF response during the Reproduction process in the field. This feature differentiates our scheme from two methods presented in [19].

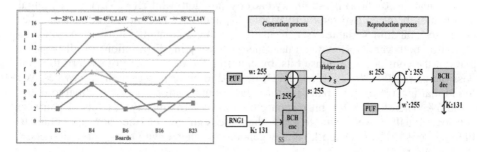

**Fig. 7.** Bit flips at 1.14V [25°C-85°C].          **Fig. 8.** Error correction scheme

## 5.4    Entropy Analysis

Actual entropy of a PUF is a function of complex physical processes. Therefore, it is close to impossible to calculate the actual entropy of a PUF response. Normally, only the estimated upper bounds on the underlying entropy can be calculated. These bounds can be calculated using at least the following two methods.

1. Based on the analysis of single bits
2. Based on the analysis of pairs of bits

Both these methods have been explained in [12]. The first method assumes that an adversary knows a bias for each position of a PUF response. In this method every bit position in a PUF response vector will have its own bias. This upper bound, called the bit-dependent bias entropy bound, can be calculated by using,

$$H(Y^n) = \sum_{i=1}^{n} h(p_i) \qquad (5)$$

In equation (5), h(pi) is the binary entropy function, it has been calculated for n = 256 bit positions. We calculated bit-dependent bias entropy bound based on PUF responses of 25 FPGAs. This entropy bound appeared to be equal to 0.959 or 95.9%. This result implies that the 256-bit response contains a maximum of 245 bits of entropy.

The second method is based on the analysis of a pair of PUF response bits. This method assumes that an adversary knows pairwise joint distributions for pairs of consecutive bits i and i+1.This bound is tighter than the bound given by (5). It is called pairwise joint distribution entropy bound. It can be calculated using equations (6) and (7).

$$H(Y^n) = \sum_{i=1}^{n} h(p_i) - \sum_{i=1}^{n-1} I(Y_i, Y_{i+1}) \qquad (6)$$

Where,

$$I((Y_1, Y_2) = \sum_{y1 \in y1} \sum_{y2 \in y2} p(y1, y2). log_2 \frac{p(y1,y2)}{p(y1)p(y2)} \qquad (7)$$

In equation (6), h(pi) is the binary entropy function, while $I(Y_i, Y_{i+1})$ is the mutual information between two random variables $Y_i$ and $Y_{i+1}$. The mutual information between two random variables is a measure for the amount of information which is shared by both variables. We estimate the pairwise joint distributions of all possible pairs of the considered response bits, by counting the occurrences of each of the four possible pairs ('00', '01', '10', and '11') in the 256 bit response of all 25 devices. We found that for n = 256; the pairwise joint distribution entropy bound is equal to 0.866 or 86.6%. Therefore, a 256-bit response contains approximately 221 bits of pairwise entropy. Finally, we want to add that the entropy of the key is equal to PUF_entropy*131 in our top-level key generation scheme with error-correction code, shown in Fig. 8.

## 5.5    Cost

It has been stated in [16] that the unused LUTs in each CLB can be used by the tool for other purposes. Therefore it is claimed that the circuit efficiency is still higher. However, we believe that neighboring logic, routed through the CLB, adversely affects the PUF response bits. To prove this claim we implemented ring-oscillators inside the latch-CLB for the design proposed in Fig. 12 in [16]. The result is listed in Table 5. We believe this change can become significant at different voltage.

**Table 5.** Effect of external signals on SR-latch

|  | Without Ring oscillators [16] | With Ring oscillators |
|---|---|---|
| Reliability @ 1.2v | 99% | 92% |

Therefore it is highly recommended to prohibit the external signals from being routed through the latch-CLBs. In our design, the external signals cannot be routed through any CLBs designated to be used for SR-latches. We also prohibit the tool from using any resources inside the latch-CLBs for external logic. Therefore, the effect of external signal on the latch performance is eliminated.

As shown in Fig. 1, the latch requires only two LUT input pins. Thus we connect the remaining four input pins of each LUT to logic '0', and lock them. It must be mentioned that we implement our PUF only on even rows of CLBs. This is done to leave one set of rows for additional logic to be implemented by the tool. This logic includes multiplexer, decoder, registers, and counters. We would like to emphasize that the latch in our design is compact and does not share a switch-box with any other external signal (each CLB is associated with a single switch-box). Based on this discussion, the design proposed in [16] for Spartan-6 FPGAs is two times more expensive than the one we are proposing in this work. Table 6 lists the FPGA resources used by both designs.

**Table 6.** Comparison with [16]

|  | This work | [16] |
|---|---|---|
| Total latches configured | 512 | 128 |
| Total CLBs used for PUF (latches only) | 128 | 256 |
| Response bit length | 256 | 256 |
| Latch/#CLB | 4 | 0.5 |
| Response bits/#CLB | 2 | 1 |
| Response bits entropy | 221 | 167.9 |
| Response bits entro- | 1.72 | 0.65 |
| Multiplexer size (CLBs) | 16 | 4 |
| Extra logic (CLBs)* | 18 | N/A |

† Latches only. Registers, counters, control logic.

## 5.6    Characterization Time

We record 100 samples of data from each latch. The delay between any two samples is 10,000 clock cycles. The on-board clock frequency is 100MHz. As a result, the frequency of the ctrl signal is set to 10 kHz. The total characterization time for each FPGA is equal to (512 x 100 x 10,000)/ (100 MHz) = 5.12 sec.

## 6    Conclusion and Future Work

We presented a highly reliable SR-latch PUF in this work. The latch is designed to keep the effect of routing at minimum and extract the randomness at the same time. The design is two times more efficient from the circuit efficiency point of view. The

PUF responses exhibit high resistance to temperature and voltage variations. The uniqueness is close to the ideal value. We tested the design on a set of 25 FPGA devices and the results were very promising. We plan to incorporate the bit-generation step into the circuit, thus eliminating the requirement for post-processing. In addition, we plan to implement the on-chip error correction scheme.

# References

1. Gassend, B., Clarke, D., van Dijk, M., Devadas, S.: Controlled Physical Random Functions. In: Proc. ACSAC 2002, pp. 149–160 (2002)
2. Lee, J.W., Lim, D., Gassend, B., Suh, G.E., van Dijk, M., Devadas, S.: A Technique to Build a Secret Key in Integrated Circuits for Identification and Authentication Application. In: Proc. Symposium on VLSI Circuits 2004, pp. 176–159 (2004)
3. Lim, D.: Extracting Secret Keys from Integrated Circuits. Master's thesis, MIT, MA, USA (2004)
4. Suh, G.E., Devadas, S.: Physical unclonable functions for device authentication and secret key generation. In: Proc. DAC 2007, pp. 9–14 (2007)
5. Guajardo, J., Kumar, S.S., Schrijen, G., Tuyls, P.: FPGA intrinsic PUFs and their use for IP protection. In: Proc. CHES 2007, pp. 63–80 (2007)
6. Su, Y., Holleman, J., Otis, B.: A 1.6pJ/bit 96% stable chip-ID generating circuit using process variations. In: Proc. ISSCC 2007, pp. 406–611 (2007)
7. Kumar, S.S., Guajardo, J., Maes, R., Schrijen, G.-J., Tuyls, P.: Extended abstract: The butterfly PUF protecting IP on every FPGA. In: Proc. HOST 2008, pp. 67–70 (2008)
8. Morozov, S., Maiti, A., Schaumont, P.: An analysis of delay based PUF implementations on FPGA. In: Proc. ARC 2010, pp. 382–387 (2010)
9. Maiti, A., Schaumont, P.: Improved Ring oscillator PUF: An FPGA Friendly Secure Primitive. Journal of Cryptology **24**, 375–397 (2010)
10. Varchola, M., Drutarovsky, M.: New High Entropy Element for FPGA Based True Random Number Generators. In: Proc. CHES 2010, pp. 351–365 (2010)
11. Hospodar, G., Maes, R., Verbauwhede, I.: Machine learning attacks on 65nm Arbiter PUFs: Accurate modeling poses strict bounds on usability. In: Proc. WIFS 2012, pp. 37–42 (2010)
12. Maes, R.: Physically Unclonable Functions: Constructions, Properties and Applications. PhD Thesis, KatholiekeUniversiteit Leuven (2012)
13. Varchola, M., Drutarovsky, M., Fischer, V.: New Universal Element with Integrated PUF and TRNG Capability. In: Proc ReConFig 2013, pp. 1–6 (2013)
14. Habib, B., Gaj, K., Kaps, J.: FPGA PUF Based on Programmable LUT Delays. In: Proc. DSD 2013, pp. 696–704 (2013)
15. Ganta, D., Nazhandali, L.: Easy-to-build Arbiter Physical Unclonable Function with enhanced challenge/response set. In: Proc ISQED 2013, pp. 733–738 (2013)
16. Yamamoto, D., Sakiyama, K., Iwamoto, M., Ohta, K., Takenaka, M., Itoh, K.: Variety enhancement of PUF responses using the locations of random outputting RS latches. Journal of Cryptographic Engineering **3**, 197–211 (2013)
17. Bossuet, L., Ngo, X., Cherif, Z., Fischer, V.: A PUF Based on a Transient Effect Ring Oscillator and Insensitive to Locking Phenomenon. In: Proc. TETC 2013, pp. 30–36 (2013)
18. Maiti, A., Gunreddy, V., Schaumont, P.: A Systematic Method to Evaluate and Compare the Performance of Physical Unclonable Functions In: Embedded Systems Design with FPGAs, pp. 245–267. Springer (2013)
19. Kang, H., Hori, Y., Katashita, T., Hagiwara, M., Iwamura, K.: Cryptographic Key Generation from PUF Data Using Efficient Fuzzy Extractors. In: Proc. ICACT 2014, pp. 23–26 (2014)
20. http://www.xilinx.com/support/documentation/data_sheets/ds162.pdf

# Hardware Benchmarking of Cryptographic Algorithms Using High-Level Synthesis Tools: The SHA-3 Contest Case Study

Ekawat Homsirikamol [✉] and Kris Gaj

Volgenau School of Engineering, George Mason University,
Fairfax 22030, Virginia
{ehomsir,kgaj}@gmu.edu

**Abstract.** The growing number of candidates competing in the cryptographic contests, such as SHA-3, makes the hardware performance evaluation extremely time consuming, tedious, and imprecise, especially in the early stages of the competitions. The main difficulties include the long time necessary to develop and verify HDL (hardware description language) codes of all candidates, and the need of developing (or at least tweaking) codes for multiple variants and architectures of each algorithm. High-level synthesis (HLS), based on the newly developed Xilinx Vivado HLS tool, offers a potential solution to the aforementioned problems. In order to verify a potential validity of this approach, we have applied our proposed methodology to the comparison of five Round 3 SHA-3 candidates. Our study has demonstrated that despite a noticeable performance penalty, caused by the use of high-level synthesis tools vs. manual design, the ranking of the evaluated candidates, in terms of four major performance metrics, frequency, throughput, area, and throughput to area ratio, has remained unchanged for Altera Stratix IV FPGAs.

**Keywords:** FPGA · High-level synthesis · Secure hash algorithm · SHA-3 · Cryptography · Benchmarking · Evaluation · Hardware · Case study

## 1  Introduction & Motivation

The first open competition for a new cryptographic standard was announced by the National Institute of Standards and Technology (NIST) in 1997 [1]. The Advanced Encryption Standard (AES) [2], currently one of the most well-known and widely-used symmetric-key block ciphers, is the result of this competition. Since then, there has been a proliferation of open competitions with different cryptographic transformations targeted in each of them. One of the most important of them was the contest for the new cryptographic hash function standard, SHA-3. This contest attracted over 50 candidates, and required about four years for their evaluation.

The cryptographic competitions have become the norm for the development of new cryptographic standards for several reasons. First, the open nature of a competition and its submitted algorithms provides assurance for future users

© Springer International Publishing Switzerland 2015
K. Sano et al. (Eds.): ARC 2015, LNCS 9040, pp. 217–228, 2015.
DOI: 10.1007/978-3-319-16214-0_18

that any potential backdoor (i.e., an ability to decrypt a message without the knowledge of the key used for its encryption) is unlikely to exist. Secondly, the winner of such competition is guaranteed to have a strong security with good performance in software and hardware. Additionally, as cryptography is a broad field, studied by a limited number of scientists, a public competition enables focusing the attention of the entire cryptographic community on a specific area of cryptography, such as design of hash functions. As a result of an active involvement of the entire community, including leading experts in the specific area, the winning algorithm is likely to get endorsed and accepted as a new standard much faster than any algorithm developed by national intelligence organizations, such as the U.S. National Security Agency (NSA).

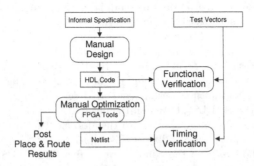

**Fig. 1.** Traditional Hardware Development and Benchmarking Flow

While security has been commonly recognized as the most important evaluation criterion, it is also a measure that is most difficult to evaluate and quantify, especially during a relatively short period of time reserved for the majority of contests. The typical outcome is that, after eliminating a fraction of candidates based on security flaws, a significant number of remaining candidates must be ranked based on their performance in hardware and software. In the past competitions, the differences among the competing algorithms in terms of their performance in hardware seemed to be particularly large, and often served as a tiebreaker when other criteria failed to identify a clear winner.

A traditional hardware benchmarking flow, shown in Fig. 1, typically starts with the translation of an informal specification to a hardware description language (HDL) code, e.g., the code written in VHDL or Verilog. Then, functional verification is performed based on test vectors generated using a reference software implementation. The post-place & route results are generated either using default options of FPGA tools, or tool options are optimized manually. Finally, the obtained netlist undergoes a timing verification for the last check up. This process has been further improved with the development of the Automated Tool for Hardware EvaluatioN (ATHENa) [3], allowing an automated optimization of FPGA tool options. This tool is application agnostic and works across supported FPGA vendors of Xilinx and Altera.

Nevertheless, hardware development for the purpose of benchmarking remains difficult due to various factors. These factors include a large number of candidates, large amount of time required to develop and verify HDL sources, multiple variants of algorithms, multiple hardware architectures targeting different needs, and dependence on skills of the designers.

A potential solution to the majority of aforementioned problems is High-Level Synthesis (HLS). HLS allows designers to use a high-level programming language, such as C, C++, or Java, to generate synthesizable HDL. Until recently, this approach has been impractical due to the inadequate quality and high cost of HLS tools [4]. This situation has changed when Xilinx acquired AutoESL Design Technologies Inc. in 2011, and incorporated its HLS tool, AutoPilot, into its latest toolchain, Vivado, in 2012 [5]. The availability of the industrial-quality, low-cost tool has allowed the HLS-based design approach to become more realistic.

Previous studies have demonstrated that HLS can reduce the development time, while maintaining good performance as compared to software [6–8]. It has also been shown that a design using HLS-based approach can compete against a hand-written Register Transfer Level (RTL) code [9–13], at least in selected domains.

Apart from the use of HLS to benchmark candidate algorithms during cryptographic contests, the use of HLS could also provide an earlier feedback for designers of cryptographic algorithms. Traditionally, a design of a cryptographic algorithm involves only security analysis and software benchmarking. This situation has created several unpleasant surprises when the resulting algorithms performed poorly in hardware, which was the case for Mars in the AES contest, as well as BMW, ECHO and SIMD in the SHA-3 Contest.

As a result, this study aims to analyze and test the following hypothesis:

*Ranking of candidate algorithms in cryptographic contests in terms of their performance in modern FPGAs will remain the same independently whether the HDL implementations are developed manually or generated automatically using High-Level Synthesis tools.*

## 2    Methodology

The development and benchmarking process used for the HLS-based design approach is shown in Figure 2. In this process, a designer modifies a reference software implementation, which is typically provided by the algorithm's designers in C. These modifications typically involve the addition of HLS tool directives, provided as pragmas, and small tweaks in the reference implementations that make them more suitable for HLS. Once these modifications are completed, the code is verified in software for the correct functionality. Afterward, the HLS-ready C code is processed by the HLS tool to generate an RTL HDL code. This code is further processed using the design methodology described in Section 1. In case, the obtained results are worse than expected, e.g., in terms of the number of clock cycles required to process a single input block, the HLS-ready C code must be further tweaked, and possibly extended with additional pragmas.

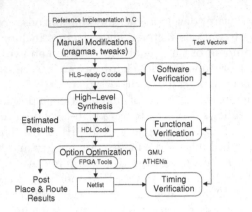

**Fig. 2.** HLS-Based Development and Benchmarking Flow

In order to verify our hypotheses, the five finalists of the SHA-3 competition were selected as our test case. The most efficient (in terms of the throughput to area ratio) high-speed architectures were selected for each algorithm [14–16]. These architectures included: two times horizontally folded architecture of BLAKE (\2h), four times unrolled architecture of Skein (x4), and the basic iterative architectures for Groestl, JH and Keccak (x1).

To provide a fair and reliable reference for comparison, the designs developed manually, using the RTL-based approach, based on the studies published in [14,17], have been benchmarked using the same FPGA families. These designs were selected for the following reasons:

- **Source codes** of the reference designs in RTL VHDL are easily accessible to the public [18]. This availability allows everybody to easily replicate the obtained results.
- **Detailed diagrams** of each design are available in public domain [18].
- **Uniform and realistic interface**. The aforementioned studies utilized a standard FIFO-based interface, which can be easily adapted to support any bus-based interface for a system-on-chip, e.g., the AXI-4 Stream interface.
- **Standalone**. The reference designs are completely self-sufficient. They require the minimum number of external control signals.

The reference C codes for the HLS-based approach are based on the submission packages available from the SHA-3 contest website [19]. Each reference C implementation is then manually modified to create an optimum HLS-ready C code, and verified in software. This C code is then passed as an input to Vivado HLS, and the corresponding VHDL code is automatically generated. This VHDL code is then simulated for functional correctness, and the number of clock cycles required to process a block of data is determined. If the results are incorrect, or the number of clock cycles too high, the HLS-ready code needs to be modified, and the entire process repeated. If the HDL code performs as expected, this code is benchmarked using ATHENa, and the final netlist verified using timing simulation.

In order to minimize any discrepancies between the rankings obtained using HLS and RTL-based approaches, we apply the same tools and optimization techniques to both manually written and automatically generated HDL codes. The synthesis of HDL codes is accomplished using Vivado HLS v2014.1, with VHDL as a target language. Logic synthesis and implementation (mapping, placing, and routing) are performed by ISE Design Suite v14.7 and Quartus II v13.0sp1, for Xilinx and Altera FPGAs, respectively. The gathering and uniform optimization of results were facilitated by ATHENa [3]. For the ease of comparison between the rankings, no dedicated FPGA resources, such as Block RAMs or DSP units are used. Our results are generated using two modern FPGA families: Stratix IV from Altera and Virtex 6 from Xilinx. Finally, it must be noted that HDL code generated from Vivado HLS is generally vendor independent. So far, we have found that as long as we do avoid the use of dual-port memory, the tool is able to generate a design that is compatible with Altera tools as well.

## 3   Design

### 3.1   Top-Level Interconnect

The interface and the communication protocol used in this study are based on the designs proposed in [17]. As we are operating at full speed, the input and output units must operate at the same time when a cryptographic core is hashing. The current HLS tool is not yet capable of generating a design that can perform these tasks automatically. As a result, these modules need to be connected manually at the top-level. The top-level diagram of all crypto cores is shown in Fig. 3. Each crypto core is comprised of three primary modules, *input processor*, *hash core* and *output processor*. Each module is generated using HLS tools independently, using a separate HLS-ready C code, in order to allow them to operate concurrently. Communications between modules in critical area are registered to improve timing. Endianness of incoming and outgoing data for the hash core are

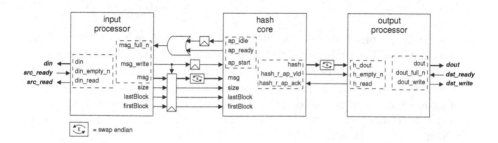

**Fig. 3.** Top-level diagram

swapped for correct operation. This is because the ARRAY_RESHAPE pragma organizes each word in little-endian format while big-endian is used from the hardware perspective.

## 3.2  Design Techniques

Design techniques play an important role in inferring our desired hardware architecture. These techniques are summarized below:

– **Match the code to the architecture.** In order to ensure that the synthesis tool can infer the desired hardware architecture from the reference C code, it is important to organize and modify the reference C code to match the target architecture as much as possible. An example is shown in Listing 1.1 and 1.2. In these example, the diagonal step is replaced by a second run through the column step, after the necessary permutation of the internal state words, as our target architecture (folded horizontally by a factor of two) contains only a half-round of BLAKE.

**Listing 1.1.** Original code before modification.

```
// (a) Before modification
/* do 14 rounds */
for(round=0; round<NB_ROUNDS32;
    ++round)
{
    /* column step */
    G32( 0,  4,  8,12,  0);
    G32( 1,  5,  9,13,  1);
    G32( 2,  6,10,14,  2);
    G32( 3,  7,11,15,  3);

    /* diagonal step */
    G32( 0,  5,10,15,  4);
    G32( 1,  6,11,12,  5);
    G32( 2,  7,  8,13,  6);
    G32( 3,  4,  9,14,  7);
}
```

**Listing 1.2.** HLS-compatible code after modification.

```
// (b) After modification
/* do 14 rounds */
for(round=0; round<NB_ROUNDS32*2;
    ++round)
{
    /* column step */
    G32( 0,  4,  8,12,  0);
    G32( 1,  5,  9,13,  1);
    G32( 2,  6,10,14,  2);
    G32( 3,  7,11,15,  3);

    // Permutation
    if (round % 2 == 0)
        for(i=0; i<4; i++)
            for(j=0; j<4; j++)
                tmp[i*4+j] = v[((j+i)%4)+
                    i*4];
    else
        for(i=0; i<4; i++)
            for(j=0; j<4; j++)
                tmp[i*4+j] = v[((j+4-i)
                    %4)+i*4];
```

– **No timing constraints.** The HLS tool can optimize the HDL code to meet any specific timing constraints. Unfortunately, the desired hardware architecture is not guaranteed. In fact, if a design is overly constrained, it is more likely to generate a sub-optimal hardware architecture. For the purpose of benchmarking, this can be very counterproductive. As a result, it is often better to remove any timing constraints, in order to avoid an automatic optimization of the architecture by the HLS tool.

**Listing 1.3.** Original code before modification.

```
// (a) Before modification
for(round=0; round<NB_ROUNDS; ++
    round)
{
  if (round == NB_ROUNDS-1)
    single_round(state, 1);
  else
    single_round(state, 0);
}
```

**Listing 1.4.** Code after modification for reduction of resource usage.

```
// (b) After modification
for(round=0; round<NB_ROUNDS; ++
    round)
{
  if (round == NB_ROUNDS-1)
    x = 1;
  else
    x = 0;
  single_round(state, x);
}
```

- **Keep design small by reusing functions.** Each function call in the HLS-ready code generally translates to a new block of hardware. This feature can increase the design size significantly. While this effect is straightforward to understand, it can be counterintuitive to utilize in software. An example of such situation is shown in Listing 1.3 and 1.4. In this example, a *single_round()* function accepts either *1* or *0* as its second input. In software, the two approaches would have an almost identical performance and memory usage. However, in the hardware generated by HLS, the design inferred by (a) requires twice as many resources as the design inferred by (b). This is because the *single_round()* function is called twice in (a), while it is being called only once in (b).

PRAGMAs used by the aforementioned techniques are described in [13]. All our HLS-ready source codes are available at [18].

## 4    Results and Discussion

### 4.1    Ranking of Results

The results of all our implementations for the RTL and HLS-based design flows are summarized in Fig. 4 and Fig. 5. Each algorithm is represented using a different shape marker, with lines across the markers helping to compare the throughput to area ratios. The higher the gradient of the line, the more efficient the corresponding algorithm is. All diagrams demonstrate a very good correlation between the HLS and RTL results in case of Altera Stratix IV FPGAs, and a moderate correlation in case of Xilinx Virtex 6 FPGAs. The details of all results and the corresponding ratios are listed in Table 1.

In Table 2, all Round 3 SHA-3 candidates are ranked according to four major performance measures: frequency, throughput, area, and throughput to area ratio. A reference ranking based on the RTL approach is followed by the new ranking based on the HLS approach. Underneath each of the first four candidates is the distance in percents to the next candidate, denoted as $\Delta(i+1)$, i.e., a relative difference between the candidate at position i in ranking and the algorithm at position i+1. The algorithms that have their positions changed in the HLS-based approach are marked in bold, with upward and downward arrows signifying the direction of change.

**Table 1.** Results for the HLS and RTL-based approaches. Notation: Freq.: clock frequency, A: area in ALUTs for Altera Stratix IV and CLB slices for Xilinx Virtex 6, TP: Throughput in Mbits/s, TP/A: throughput over area ratio, RTL/HLS: ratio of the RTL result to the corresponding HLS result.

| | Altera Stratix IV | | | | | | | | | | | |
|---|---|---|---|---|---|---|---|---|---|---|---|---|
| | HLS | | | | RTL | | | | RTL/HLS | | | |
| | Freq. | TP | A | TP/A | Freq. | TP | A | TP/A | Freq. | TP | A | TP/A |
| BLAKE | 119.6 | 2040 | 4557 | 0.45 | 132.3 | 2337 | 3543 | 0.66 | 1.11 | 1.15 | 0.78 | 1.47 |
| Groestl | 218.8 | 4871 | 7290 | 0.67 | 236.9 | 5776 | 7404 | 0.78 | 1.08 | 1.19 | 1.02 | 1.17 |
| JH | 336.8 | 3919 | 3256 | 1.20 | 399.7 | 4759 | 3210 | 1.48 | 1.19 | 1.21 | 0.99 | 1.23 |
| Keccak | 271.4 | 11356 | 4156 | 2.73 | 317.7 | 14401 | 3541 | 4.07 | 1.17 | 1.27 | 0.85 | 1.49 |
| Skein | 97.9 | 2387 | 5752 | 0.41 | 96.2 | 2592 | 3936 | 0.66 | 0.98 | 1.09 | 0.68 | 1.59 |
| | Xilinx Virtex 6 | | | | | | | | | | | |
| | HLS | | | | RTL | | | | RTL/HLS | | | |
| | Freq. | TP | A | TP/A | Freq. | TP | A | TP/A | Freq. | TP | A | TP/A |
| BLAKE | 150.6 | 2570 | 1289 | 1.99 | 126.1 | 2226 | 1257 | 1.77 | 0.84 | 0.87 | 0.98 | 0.89 |
| Groestl | 242.7 | 5403 | 2016 | 2.68 | 296.1 | 7220 | 1870 | 3.86 | 1.22 | 1.34 | 0.93 | 1.44 |
| JH | 291.8 | 3395 | 1141 | 2.98 | 454.6 | 5412 | 849 | 6.37 | 1.56 | 1.59 | 0.74 | 2.14 |
| Keccak | 211.2 | 8838 | 1494 | 5.92 | 261.2 | 11839 | 1086 | 10.90 | 1.24 | 1.34 | 0.73 | 1.84 |
| Skein | 107.3 | 2616 | 1426 | 1.83 | 125.2 | 3373 | 1005 | 3.36 | 1.17 | 1.29 | 0.70 | 1.83 |

**Table 2.** Algorithm rankings based on four major performance metrics. $\Delta(i+1)$ represents the relative difference in the measured metric between the algorithm at the current ranking position $i$ and the algorithm at the subsequent position $i+1$.

| Approach | Frequency rankings | | | | | Area rankings | | | | |
|---|---|---|---|---|---|---|---|---|---|---|
| | 1 | 2 | 3 | 4 | 5 | 1 | 2 | 3 | 4 | 5 |
| | Altera Stratix IV | | | | | | | | | |
| RTL | JH | Keccak | Groestl | BLAKE | Skein | JH | Keccak | BLAKE | Skein | Groestl |
| $\Delta(i+1)$ | 26% | 34% | 79% | 38% | | -9% | -0% | -10% | -47% | |
| HLS | JH | Keccak | Groestl | BLAKE | Skein | JH | Keccak | BLAKE | Skein | Groestl |
| $\Delta(i+1)$ | 24% | 24% | 83% | 22% | | -22% | -9% | -21% | -21% | |
| | Xilinx Virtex 6 | | | | | | | | | |
| RTL | JH | Groestl | Keccak | BLAKE | Skein | JH | Skein | Keccak | BLAKE | Groestl |
| $\Delta(i+1)$ | 54% | 13% | 107% | 1% | | -16% | **-7%** | **-14%** | -33% | |
| HLS | JH | Groestl | Keccak | BLAKE | Skein | JH | BLAKE↑ | Skein↓ | Keccak↓ | Groestl |
| $\Delta(i+1)$ | 20% | 15% | 40% | 40% | | -11% | -10% | -5% | -26% | |
| Approach | Throughput rankings | | | | | Throughput/Area rankings | | | | |
| | Altera Stratix IV | | | | | | | | | |
| RTL | Keccak | Groestl | JH | Skein | BLAKE | Keccak | JH | Groestl | BLAKE | Skein |
| $\Delta(i+1)$ | 149% | 21% | 84% | 11% | | 175% | 90% | 18% | 0% | |
| HLS | Keccak | Groestl | JH | Skein | BLAKE | Keccak | JH | Groestl | BLAKE | Skein |
| $\Delta(i+1)$ | 133% | 24% | 64% | 17% | | 127% | 80% | 49% | 8% | |
| | Xilinx Virtex 6 | | | | | | | | | |
| RTL | Keccak | Groestl | JH | Skein | BLAKE | Keccak | JH | Groestl | Skein | BLAKE |
| $\Delta(i+1)$ | 64% | 33% | 60% | 52% | | 71% | 65% | 15% | **90%** | |
| HLS | Keccak | Groestl | JH | Skein | BLAKE | Keccak | JH | Groestl | BLAKE↑ | Skein↓ |
| $\Delta(i+1)$ | 64% | 59% | 30% | 2% | | 99% | 11% | 34% | 9% | |

This table clearly demonstrates that for Stratix IV, all rankings remain perfectly the same. For Virtex 6, the rankings remain the same in case of frequency and throughput. In case of area, BLAKE moves from the position number 4 to the position number 2. In case of the throughput to area ratio, Skein and BLAKE swap places at positions 4 and 5.

The first of these changes can be explained by looking at the RTL/HLS ratios for area in Table 1. For Keccak and Skein, the HLS implementation trails the RTL implementation by about 30%. At the same time, for BLAKE, the area is almost identical in case of both design flows. Interestingly, in case of Altera, the ratios of RTL to HLS results are much better balanced for the aforementioned three candidates (Skein: 0.68, BLAKE: 0.78, Keccak: 0.85).

In case of ranking in terms of throughput to area ratio, the swap of places between Skein and BLAKE can be explained by the fact that unexpectedly, the HLS implementation of BLAKE outperforms the RTL implementation in terms of throughput, and is almost identical in terms of area. At the same time, the HLS implementation of Skein trails the corresponding RTL implementation by about 30% for both throughput and area. Interestingly, nothing similar happens for the same VHDL source codes in case of Altera Stratix IV. Thus, the only reasonable explanation seems to be a different operation of Xilinx and Altera tools for logic synthesis, mapping, placing, and routing, which favors some combinations of algorithms and VHDL coding styles (RTL vs. HLS-generated), and is disadvantageous for the others.

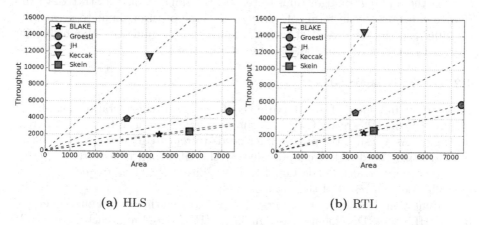

(a) HLS                    (b) RTL

**Fig. 4.** Manual RTL vs. HLS-based Results for Altera Stratix IV

**Table 3.** RTL/HLS performance ratios across investigated algorithms

| FPGA Family | Freq. | Throughput | Area | TP/A |
|---|---|---|---|---|
| Altera Stratix IV | 0.98-1.19 | 1.09-1.27 | 0.68-1.02 | 1.17-1.59 |
| Xilinx Virtex 6 | 0.84-1.56 | 0.87-1.59 | 0.70-0.98 | 0.89-2.14 |

In Table 3 we summarize the spread of ratios, RTL/HLS, across investigated algorithms, for all performance metrics and the two investigated FPGA families. In case of frequency, for Altera FPGAs, the ratio varies between 0.98 to 1.19, the spread of only about 20%, which is not likely to affect the ranking of the candidates. The same spread of ratios for Xilinx Virtex 6 exceeds 70%, which is

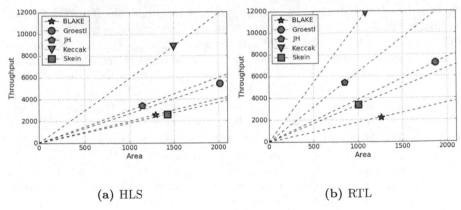

(a) HLS                                          (b) RTL

**Fig. 5.** Manual RTL vs. HLS-based Results for Xilinx Virtex 6

much more significant. For area, both spreads are similar, in the range of 30% for both Stratix IV and Virtex 6. Still, a particular combination of algorithms is causing the rankings of algorithms to remain the same in case of Stratix IV, and change substantially in terms of Virtex 6. In case of throughput to area ratio, the difference in the spread of ratios is much more significant (about 40% for Startix IV and more than 100% in case of Virtex 6).

## 4.2   Lessons Learned

The correct inference of architecture requires careful consideration for almost each line of the HLS-ready C code. A simple mistake can lead to vastly different outcomes. As a result, the programmer needs to repeatedly check the estimated results, using the design cycle provided by the HLS tool, to ascertain whether the output circuit has no additional logic. Additionally, clock frequency can be also affected as a result of this issue as well.

Latency, on the other hand, is largely dependent on the control unit generated by the HLS tool. Developing this unit in the HLS-based approach is relatively straightforward compared to the manual RTL approach, as the control unit is generated automatically, based on the code in C. In the manual hardware design, the creation of the control logic is often the primary bottleneck in terms of the design time. The ability of HLS tools to automatically generate and verify the schedule of the circuits can save a huge amount of time.

Nonetheless, the generated control unit tends to be sub-optimal. This is because the generated unit is not capable of supporting an overlap between the completion of the last round of encryption/decryption and reading the next input block. Moreover, one additional clock cycle is required to initiate processing of the subsequent data block. As a result, the throughput of the HLS-based design tends to be lower than the throughput of the manual one, even if they both operate at the same frequency. The throughput formulas for the RTL and HLS-based approach are given by equations 1 and 2, respectively.

$$Throughput_{RTL} = Block\_size/(\#Rounds * T_{clk}) \tag{1}$$

$$Throughput_{HLS} = Block\_size/((\#Rounds + 2) * T_{clk}) \tag{2}$$

## 5  Conclusions

High-level synthesis offers a potential to allow hardware benchmarking in early stages of cryptographic contests. It can also be an effective method for gauging the hardware performance of early variants of a cryptographic algorithm during the design process by groups of cryptographers with limited experience in hardware design.

Our case study based on the five final SHA-3 candidates has demonstrated the correct ranking for Altera Stratix IV FPGAs in terms of all major performance measures: frequency, throughput, area, and the throughput to area ratio. For Xilinx Virtex 6 FPGAs, the rankings matched perfectly only in case of two out of four performance measures.

Thus, at this point, we recommend only the use of Altera FPGAs for HLS-based candidate benchmarking. Interestingly, the recommended development flow combines the use of HLS tools from Xilinx (Vivado HLS), lower-level FPGA tools from Altera (Quartus II), and open-source script-based tools for option optimization (ATHENa).

In order for the HLS-based design approach to be an effective replacement for the manual design approach, there are a few obstacles that need to be still overcome. These obstacles include for example the limited correlation between the manual RTL designs and the HLS-based designs for Xilinx FPGAs, and the generation of sub-optimal control units by Vivado HLS tools. Additionally, the preparation of the HLS-ready C code needs to be simplified, for example by an automatic preprocessing of the generic C codes developed without high-level synthesis in mind.

**Acknowledgments.** This work is supported by the US National Science Foundation (NSF) under grant number #1314540.

## References

1. National Institute of Standards and Technology. Report on the Development of the Advanced Encryption Standard (AES), October 2000. http://csrc.nist.gov/archive/aes/round2/r2report.pdf
2. National Institute of Standards and Technology, FIPS PUB 197: Advanced Encryption Standard (AES), November 2001. http://csrc.nist.gov/publications/fips/fips197/fips-197.pdf
3. Gaj, K., Kaps, J., Amirineni, V., Rogawski, M., Homsirikamol, E., Brewster, B.: ATHENa - automated tool for hardware evaluatioN: toward fair and comprehensive benchmarking of cryptographic hardware using FPGAs. In: 2010 International Conference on Field Programmable Logic and Applications (FPL), pp. 414–421, August 2010

4. Martin, G., Smith, G.: High-Level Synthesis: Past, Present, and Future. IEEE Design & Test of Computers **26**(4), 18–25 (2009)
5. Maxfield, C.: First public access release to Xilinx Vivado design suite, July 2012. http://www.eetimes.com/document.asp?docid=1317376
6. Rupnow, K., Liang, Y., Li, Y., Chen, D.: A study of high-level synthesis: Promises and challenges. In: 2011 IEEE 9th International Conference on ASIC (ASICON), pp. 1102–1105, October 2011
7. Liang, Y., Rupnow, K., Li, Y., Min, D., Do, M.N., Chen, D.: High-level Synthesis: Productivity, Performance, and Software Constraints. Journal of Electrical and Computer Engineering 2012, Article ID 649057, 14 (2012)
8. Davis, J., Buell, D., Devarkal, S., Quan, G.: High-level synthesis for large bit-width multipliers on FPGAs: a case study. In: Third IEEE/ACM/IFIP International Conference on Hardware, Software Codesign and System Synthesis: CODES+ISSS 2005, pp. 213–218, September 2005
9. El-Araby, E., Taher, M., Abouellail, M., El-Ghazawi, T., Newby, G.: Comparative analysis of high level programming for reconfigurable computers: methodology and empirical study. In: 2007 3rd Southern Conference on Programmable Logic, SPL 2007, pp. 99–106, February 2007
10. Gruian, F., Westmijze, M.: VHDL vs. Bluespec System Verilog: A case study on a java embedded architecture. In: Proceedings of the 2008 ACM Symposium on Applied Computing, SAC 2008, pp. 1492–1497 (2008)
11. Berkeley Design Technology, Inc., High-Level Synthesis Tools for Xilinx FPGAs (2010), http://www.bdti.com/MyBDTI/pubs/Xilinxhlstcp.pdf
12. Cong, J., Liu, B., Neuendorffer, S., Noguera, J., Vissers, K., Zhang, Z.: High-Level Synthesis for FPGAs: From Prototyping to Deployment. IEEE Transactions on Computer-Aided Design of Integrated Circuits and Systems **30**(4), 473–491 (2011)
13. Homsirikamol, E., Gaj, K.: Can high-level synthesis compete against a hand-written code in the cryptographic domain? A case study. In: 2014 International Conference on Reconfigurable Computing and FPGAs (ReConFig), December 2014
14. Gaj, K., Homsirikamol, E., Rogawski, M., Shahid, R., Sharif, M.U.: Comprehensive Evaluation of High-Speed and Medium-Speed Implementations of Five SHA-3 Finalists Using Xilinx and Altera FPGAs, Cryptology ePrint Archive, Report 2012/368 (2012)
15. Guo, X., Huang, S., Nazhandali, L., Schaumont, P.: Fair and comprehensive performance evaluation of 14 second round SHA-3 ASIC implementations. In: The Second SHA-3 Candidate Conference, August 2010
16. Gürkaynak, F., Gaj, K., Muheim, B., Homsirikamol, E., Keller, C., Rogawski, M., Kaeslin, H., Kap, J.-P.: Lessons learned from designing a 65nm ASIC for evaluating third round SHA-3 candidates. In: The Third SHA-3 Candidate Conference, March 22-23 (2012)
17. Gaj, K., Homsirikamol, E., Rogawski, M.: Fair and comprehensive methodology for comparing hardware performance of fourteen round two SHA-3 candidates using FPGAs. In: Mangard, S., Standaert, F.-X. (eds.) CHES 2010. LNCS, vol. 6225, pp. 264–278. Springer, Heidelberg (2010). http://dx.doi.org/10.1007/978-3-642-15031-9_18
18. CCERG. GMU Source Codes. https://cryptography.gmu.edu/athena/index.php?id=sourcecodes
19. National Institute of Standards and Technology. Third (Final) Round Candidates, March 2014. http://csrc.nist.gov/groups/ST/hash/sha-3/Round3/submissionsrnd3.html

# Dual CLEFIA/AES Cipher Core on FPGA

João Carlos Resende and Ricardo Chaves$^{(\boxtimes)}$

Instituto Superior Técnico, Universidade de Lisboa / INESC-ID,
Rua Alves Redol 9, Lisbon 1000-029, Portugal
joaocresende@tecnico.ulisboa.pt, ricardo.chaves@inesc-id.pt

**Abstract.** In this paper a compact high throughput dual-cipher hardware structure is proposed, supporting the novel CLEFIA algorithm and the encryption standard AES. Currently, the more efficient and dedicated structures only allow to process the CLEFIA or the AES encryption algorithms. On the other hand, the existing multi-algorithm processors impose significantly higher area costs and are not able to achieve the throughputs of dedicated solutions. The presented work shows that by adequately scheduling and merging the processing structures, and with the proper use of the existing components in current FPGA technologies, it is possible to achieve a compact and efficient structure capable of computing the novel CLEFIA cipher while also supporting the well implanted AES cipher. Overall, the proposed structure allows for a throughput up to 1Gbps in feedback modes with low area cost, achieving identical efficiency metrics as the existing single cipher state of the art.

## 1 Introduction

With the rapid evolution of digital communications, and its expansion into everyday electronics, ensuring the safety and privacy of systems and their data has become a mandatory requirement. To achieve this, efficient implementations of existing and novel cryptographic algorithms are needed.

One such algorithm is the CLEFIA encryption algorithm, a novel symmetrical block cipher proposed and developed by SONY Corporation [15]. In 2012, CLEFIA was declared a International Standard in ISO/IEC 29192-2, and more recently a Candidate Recommended Cipher by the Japanese Cryptographic Research and Evaluation Committees (CRYPTREC) in the 2013 revision. However, given the implantation and robustness of the Advanced Encryption Standard (AES) [12], it is unlikely that this novel cipher can overthrown it. Nevertheless, CLEFIA particular focus on Digital Rights Management (DRM), increased use in Japan and by Sony, and the algorithm added robustness against differential and linear attacks [18], makes it a relevant alternative for future systems.

Both CLEFIA and AES are symmetrical block ciphers and share similar ciphering techniques, such as diffusion matrices and byte substitution (SBoxes). The major differences reside on the fact that CLEFIA is based on a Feistel Network, while the AES algorithm is based on a Substitution-Permutation Structure.

© Springer International Publishing Switzerland 2015
K. Sano et al. (Eds.): ARC 2015, LNCS 9040, pp. 229–240, 2015.
DOI: 10.1007/978-3-319-16214-0_19

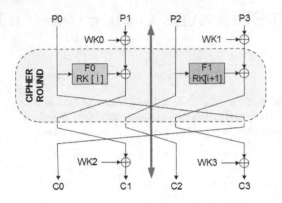

**Fig. 1.** CLEFIA Datapath

The main goal of this work is to show that, with efficient resource re-utilization, a dedicated CLEFIA/AES cryptographic engine can be achieved, capable of high throughputs with relatively low area footprints. To achieve this, state of the art compact structures for dedicated AES [2,3,5,14] and CLEFIA [10,13] algorithms are considered.

In order to provide a proof of concept, Field Programmable Gate Arrays (FPGA) is herein used as targeted technology, given their increasing deployment in embedded systems, adaptability, and ease of prototyping. Due to the added cost and complexity of partial reconfiguration techniques [9], and its low usage in current embedded system, this feature is herein not considered.

This paper is organized as follows: an introduction to the CLEFIA and AES algorithms is presented in Section 2. Section ?? discusses the most relevant state of the art. The proposed solution and its particular implementation details are presented in Section 4, while the obtained results and the analysis with the existing related work are presented in Section 5. Section 6 concludes this paper with some final remarks.

## 2    Considered Ciphers

### 2.1    CLEFIA Algorithm

The CLEFIA algorithm is a 128-bit block cipher, based on a 4-branched Feistel network, accepting key lengths of 128, 192 and 256 bits, processed over 18, 22, or 26 rounds. The 128 bits (16 bytes) of plain text are arranged into an array of four 32-bit words, processed over $N$ round sets of instructions, as depicted in Figure 1.

The first step of the encryption process is to XOR the second and fourth words of the plain text with the first and second 32 bits of the original key, performing a key whitening procedure. After this operation the rounds are executed.

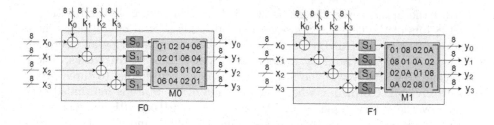

**Fig. 2.** CLEFIA F-function

In each round, the four input words are processed, where copies of the first and third input words go through a 32-bit output non-linear function, F0 and F1 respectively. After each one, the result is XORed with the second and fourth words. The resulting four words are then swapped by left-round shifting them.

After all rounds are computed, the final output values are obtained by XOR-ing, one last time, the second and fourth final words with the last two Whitening Keys, instead of a last word swap.

Each function, F0 and F1, receives a different 32-bit Round Key in a total of $(N \times 2)$ 32-bit keys (where $N$ is the number of rounds). Both functions use two 8x8 bits SBoxes for byte replacement, S0 and S1, and one matrix multiplication, M0 or M1, as depicted in Figure 2.

In order to perform the decryption process, one simply needs to invert the processing direction: the input becomes the ciphered text and the different keys are supplied in the inverted order (including the Whitening Keys).

## 2.2   AES Algorithm

The AES algorithm is also a 128-bit block cipher based on the Rijndael algorithm, accepting key lengths of 128, 192, and 256 bits, processed over 10, 12 or 14 rounds, repetitively. Each 128-bit (16 bytes) block of plain text is organized column wise, in a 4x4 byte matrix (named State), processed over $N$ rounds, as depicted in Figure 3.

| |
|---|
| AddRoundKey(State, ekey)<br>**for** round= 1, round<Nr, round++ **do**<br>  SubBytes(State)<br>  ShiftRows(State)<br>  MixColumns(State)<br>  AddRoundKey(State, ekey[round])<br>**end for**<br>SubBytes(State)<br>ShiftRows(State)<br>AddRoundKey(State, ekey[Nr]) |

| |
|---|
| AddRoundKey(State, dkey)<br>**for** round= 1, round<Nr, round++ **do**<br>  InvSubBytes(State)<br>  InvShiftRows(State)<br>  InvMixColumns(State)<br>  AddRoundKey(State, dkey[round])<br>**end for**<br>InvSubBytes(State)<br>InvShiftRows(State)<br>AddRoundKey(State, dkey[Nr]) |

**Fig. 3.** AES Encryption/Decryption operations

After the initial key addition, in which the plain text is XORed with the first 128 bits of the key, the State goes through the several operations. These round operations are: **SubBytes**, where each byte is replaced by another one, which can be implemented by a Look Up Table (SBox); **ShiftRows**, where the second to fourth row of the State are left-round shifted one to three bytes, respectively; **MixColumns**, where each column of the State is multiplied over $GF(2^8)$ by the values depicted in Figure 4; and **AddRoundKey**, where the entire State is XORed with the corresponding 128-bit Round Key. The decryption process of the AES cipher is performed identically to the encryption, but with the inverse operations. Note that the last round is slightly different since no (Inv)MixColumns operation is performed.

$$
\begin{bmatrix} r_{0i} \\ r_{1i} \\ r_{2i} \\ r_{3i} \end{bmatrix} = \begin{bmatrix} 02 & 03 & 01 & 01 \\ 01 & 02 & 03 & 01 \\ 01 & 01 & 02 & 03 \\ 03 & 01 & 01 & 02 \end{bmatrix} \begin{bmatrix} a_{0i} \\ a_{1i} \\ a_{2i} \\ a_{3i} \end{bmatrix} \qquad \begin{bmatrix} r_{0i} \\ r_{1i} \\ r_{2i} \\ r_{3i} \end{bmatrix} = \begin{bmatrix} 0E & 0B & 0D & 09 \\ 09 & 0E & 0B & 0D \\ 0D & 09 & 0E & 0B \\ 0B & 0D & 09 & 0E \end{bmatrix} \begin{bmatrix} a_{0i} \\ a_{1i} \\ a_{2i} \\ a_{3i} \end{bmatrix}
$$

**Fig. 4.** AES MixColumns and InvMixColumns matrixes

## 3    Related State of the Art

When considering block ciphers implementations on dedicated architectures, the improvements in the state of the art are mainly based on round folding, with unrolled or rolled structures; on the type of components used for the typical substitution operation, with dedicated logic or lookup tables; and with operation rescheduling [13,14].

One of the most direct ways to obtain a trade off between area and throughput is with round folding/expansion. In unrolled structures the round computation is expanded and pipelined. With this, multiple rounds of the algorithm can be executed independently and in parallel. These approaches are known for imposing higher area demands but, on the other hand, allowing for higher thoughputs and working frequencies in particular cases (such as in ECB mode). When ciphering in feedback modes (such as CBC) with dependencies between blocks, the throughput improvements cannot be achieved. When folding the round computation, each round is performed in one or more clock cycles, resulting in more compact structures. Consequently, lower throughputs are typically achieved [7].

Another major implementation differentiation in the state of the art is in the substitution operation. These vary from a fine grained implementation of the byte substitution (Logic based), to more coarse grained ones using equivalent lookup tables (Memory based). Logic based structures implement the byte substitution operations and matrix multiplications by hard-wiring their actual mathematical definition through logic components. They are cipher-specific and can be the most area efficient but usually the slowest to complete. Typically in FPGAs, the most efficient implementations to perform the byte substitution are lookup table based [14]. These use multiple FPGA LUTs, or even BRAMs, to implement an equivalent lookup table for byte substitution, and in some cases part of additional operations such as the matrix multiplication of AES, creating a so called TBox. Memory based approaches can lead to faster circuits at the cost of memory blocks.

### 3.1 AES Previous Work

*Chodowiec et al.* [3] propose a FPGA based AES compact implementation performing 1/4 of a round computation (32 bits) per cycle. The authors also choose to use two embedded dual-port 512x8b BRAMs, of a Xilinx Spartan II, for a memory based SBox (and InvSBox). The authors also improve their design by implementing the AES Shift Rows operation through the use of the dedicated, multi-addressable, 16-bit deep shift registers, implemented using the SRL16 LUT mode of the Xilinx devices. With this, the intermediate results are stored in shift registers that can always address any 4 bytes of the State, avoiding unnecessary logic for shifting operations. The remaining computation is implemented using a logic based approach.

The use of shift registers for the Shift Rows operation is also considered by *Rouvroy et al.* [14]. These authors further reduce the area resources by using the dual-port BRAMs to implement the AES algorithm based on TBoxes.

*Chaves et al.*[2] propose an AES implementation performing one round computation per clock cycle, also based on TBoxes. They choose to implement the Shift Rows operation by hard-wired and multiplexed path and perform the key expansion in software, resulting in a simpler structure. Additionally, the authors also improve the last round computation by noticing that, by XORing all the TBox matrix coefficients, one can obtain the original substitution value. This is valid for both encryption and decryption (Fig 4), as demonstrated by:

$$01 \cdot a_i = 03 \cdot a_i \oplus 01 \cdot a_i \oplus 01 \cdot a_i \oplus 02 \cdot a_i; \tag{1}$$

$$01 \cdot a_i = 0B \cdot a_i \oplus 0D \cdot a_i \oplus 09 \cdot a_i \oplus 0E \cdot a_i; \tag{2}$$

### 3.2 CLEFIA Previous Work

CLEFIA is based on a Feistel network, requiring identical byte substitution and matrix multiplication. *Kryjak et al.* [10] proposes four methods for the CLEFIA's SBoxes computation, all using FPGA LUTs. The structure allows for key scheduling and uses a pipelined unrolled round architecture.

*Proença et al.* [13] strive for a more compact implementation, with a folded full-round and folded half-round implementations, both based on TBoxes within BRAMs. Similarly to [2], it uses an extra BRAM to store the expanded keys.

## 3.3  Multi-Cryptographic Co-Processors

Aside from the single algorithm dedicated cipher structures, multi-cryptographic co-processors have also been proposed. However, these resembled general processors, making them more suitable for general encryption systems, with lower encryption throughputs. COBRA [6], MorphoSys [16] and CryptoManiac [19] are examples. Herein, we focus on a compact high performance dedicated structure.

# 4  Proposed Architecture and Implementation

As stated above, the main goal of this work it to achieve a compact high throughput CLEFIA FPGA implementation also capable of efficiently computing the AES algorithm. To achieve this, we start by combining the best compact structures in the state, for AES and CLEFIA, into a single structure.

The proposed structure considers the use of a folded structure, computing each round in multiple iterations with a datapath of 32 bits using a TBox approach, as depicted in Figure 5. The 32-bit folded structure is suggested by the state of the art to be the best compromise towards a compact structure still capable of achieving near Gbps throughputs.

Since the initial step for both algorithms is to XOR the plain text with the first input keys, a 32-bit XOR operation is considered before the Shift Register, as depicted by ① at the top left of Figure 5.

For the AES Shift Rows operation, a byte addressable 32-bit wide 16-bit deep shift register is considered ②, given the resulting compactness of this solution on Xilinx FPGAs when using the SRL16 LUT mode, as demonstrated in the state of the art. This Shift Register is used to temporarily store and address the State.

To allow for a more efficient datapath, a forwarding multiplexer is used to select the data fed to the TBoxes. This block is also used to add Round Keys, as in the case of the CLEFIA computation.

The main computation is performed in the TBox ④, used to store the lookup tables that process the byte substitution and the coefficient multiplications. The remaining part of the matrices multiplication, the necessary $GF(2^8)$ additions, are performed by a XOR tree stage ⑤.

The last computation of an AES round is the XORing of the Round Key, which is performed either in block ①, or partially in ③. Finally, a XOR tree stage ⑥ is used to add all coefficient multiplications of the AES MixColumns, as described in (1) and (2) and add the last Round Key. The CLEFIA computation also uses this stage to add the last Whitening Keys.

### TBoxes into BRAMs

AES and CLEFIA require SBox operations followed by a matrix multiplication, which can be partially compressed into a TBox if a memory based implementation is adopted.

In the AES algorithm the same SBox substitution is performed for all input Bytes. Following this, each Byte output is multiplied in $GF(2^8)$ by the coefficients $\{3,1,1,2\}$ for encryption and $\{B,D,9,E\}$ for decryption. The result, four sets of 32 bits, are then shifted and added by a 32-bit XOR tree resulting in a 32-bit result.

The CLEFIA algorithm does not require a different computation for encryption and decryption, since it is based on a Feistel network. However, as described in Section 2, four different TBoxes are required in each round. This is due to the two different SBoxes (S0 and S1) and two different MDS matrices (M0 and M1).

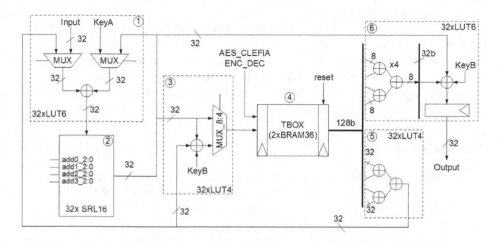

**Fig. 5.** Proposed CLEFIA/AES Datapath

## Implementation Details

In order to obtain adequate results, the proposed structure has been design and implemented considering the available resources in the target technology.

As illustrated in Figure 5, the needed computation has been divided into blocks of 6 and 4 inputs, in order to match the existing LUT6 logic blocks in the device. Block ① is responsible for adding the AES Round Keys *or* the CLEFIA swapped words, while ③ is mainly responsible for adding CLEFIA Round Keys *and* swapped words. The two stages could be sequential but the amount of resources would be the same, while the critical path would be longer. Note that in the foreseen critical path (block ⑤ to block ③) 4 input LUTs are considered. This is due to the fact that experimental results suggest better delay results when the existing LUTs are used in a 4 input LUT4 configuration.

For the Shift Register (block ②), the SRL16 LUT configuration is used. This configuration allows LUTs to operate as a 1-bit wide, 16-bit deep, addressable shift register with synchronous writing and asynchronous reading. The Shift Register is implemented by combining 4 groups of 8 LUTs (using only 8 deep positions). With proper scheduling the Shift Register is able to perform the CLEFIA Feistel word swap.

Having the more recent Virtex families from Xilinx as the target technology, 36Kb BRAMs are considered for the TBox implementation and key storage. Considering a structure with a 32-bit data path, two dual-port BRAMs are required. In each input port of each BRAM, the first 8 bits of address are used by the respective byte input. The 9th address bit of the BRAM is use to differentiate between encryption/decryption mode when computing AES or between a F0/F1 TBox when computing the CLEFIA algorithm. A final 10th bit is used to select which algorithm is being considered, addressing different memory locations with different TBox mappings. Given the 32-bit output word of each BRAM a total of 32Kb per BRAM is required.

A particular care needs to be taken regarding the mapping of the BRAMs outputs. As described in Figure 2 and Figure 4, each algorithm shifts the column coefficients in a particular way. Nevertheless, this shifting can coincide if the columns are properly paired. By using this characteristic when defining the connection and content of the BRAMs, the shifting path can still be hard-wired without the use of selection logic.

### Data Scheduling

With a 32-bit datapath a new State column, or word, is processed in each cycle. In the AES case, a round can only be started after all words of the previous round are computed. This is due to the fact that each new 32-bit word is derived from one byte from all the four 32-bit words produced in the previous round. Given the two cycle latency of the BRAM implemented TBox, one empty cycle is imposed between the processing of the last word of round $i$ and the first word of round $i + 1$. This imposes a 5 cycle processing for each AES round. Given the Feistel structure in the CLEFIA processing, the above data dependency is not imposed, allowing for a new round to be processed every 2 cycles. In the CLEFIA computation 6 additional cycles are required to perform the final key addition and final block output.

## 5   Result Analysis

In this section, experimental results for the proposed structure and the related state of the art are presented and compared on several Xilinx FPGA technologies. The obtained results were obtained using the Xilinx ISE Design Suite (v14.5) with the design described using VHDL. The values presented for the proposed design were obtained after Place&Route processing with software default parameters, namely Synthesis Normal Speed Optimization Effort, and High Optimization Effort in Mapping and Place&Route, with no extra effort. The obtained results for the proposed structure and those presented in the state of the art are depicted in Table 1. A few particularities have to be considered when analysing these results.

Regarding the achieved throughput, the presented values define the average rhythm at which the circuit processes the input blocks. In unrolled structures higher throughputs can be achieved, but only if multiple blocks are processed simultaneously. When considering a single data stream in a feedback mode, such as CBC, these structures cannot be efficiently used due to the data dependency between blocks. In Table 1 the throughput values are depicted as presented by their authors, while between brackets are the throughput values considering a single data stream in feedback mode.

Efficiency wise, we consider the use of the Throughput per Slice metric. This metric can be contested as a biased measurement, since it does not take into account other FPGA modules such as BRAMs or DSPs. However, given the difficulty in extracting equivalency values, this is herein used as the efficiency comparison metric. Between brackets are the efficiency metrics considering the throughput in feedback mode.

Regarding the key expansion, two main approaches are used, either computing them locally with dedicated logic, or computing them off chip and then storing them in local memory. Although being possible to share some resources with the datapath to perform the key expansion computation, dedicated logic is still required [17]. The off chip computation of the key expansion and loading to an auxiliary BRAM typically yields in more compact and efficient designs [17].

As depicted in Table 1, the proposed structure allows for a ciphering throughput of 1Gbps for the CLEFIA algorithm and near 850Mbps for the AES algorithm. These results are achieved at a cost of 123 Slices and 3 BRAMs on a Virtex 5 device, including the control unit and the extra BRAM for the expanded keys storage. On a Virtex 6 device, similar results are achieved.

The AES encryption mode results in a lower throughput, in regard to the CLEFIA computation, given the empty $5^{th}$ cycle per round, as discussed in the previous section. The throughput values are presented regarding the use of a single data stream in a feedback mode, considered as the most used and secure encryption mode. This implies that computation of data block $i$ can only be started after the computation of the data block $i - 1$ is concluded.

If independent data blocks were considered, the proposed structure could be used to cipher two data blocks simultaneously, by changing the control unit, and fully using the 16 positions available in the SRL16 Shift Register. This would eliminate the $5^{th}$ empty cycle in the AES computation, which would result in a throughput of about 1Gbps.

Considering the CLEFIA state of the art, the dedicated unrolled structure [10] allows for a throughput of 21Gbps in non-feedback modes. In feedback modes a maximum throughput of 1.2Gbps can be achieved. With a area cost of 2479 Slices, an efficiency of 0.48 is achieved for feedback modes. The structure proposed in [13] allows for a throughput of 1.7Gbps at a cost of 170 Slices. The same authors also proposed a more compact structure, allowing for a throughput of 1.3Gbps at a cost of 86 Slices, resulting in efficiency of 15.13. With a maximum CLEFIA throughput of 1Gbps, the structure herein proposed has an efficiency of 8.72, higher than most of the CLEFIA state of the art, but still 42% lower

**Table 1.** Performance comparison between CLEFIA designs [10,13] and AES designs [1,2,4,5,8,11]

| Operation[a] | KeySch. | Device | Resources Slices | Resources BRAM | Freq. [MHz] | Throughput[b] [Gbps] | Efficiency[b] [Mbps/Slice] |
|---|---|---|---|---|---|---|---|
| Kryjak[10] E+D | Y | xc5vlx30 | 2479 | 0 | 167 | 21.376 (1.188) | 8.62 (0.48) |
| Proença[13] E+D | N | xc5vlx30 | 170 / 86 | 4+1 / 2+1 | 240 / 366 | 1.707 (=) / 1.301 (=) | 10.04 (=) / 15.13 (=) |
| Ours CLEFIA AES E+D | N | xc5vlx30-3 | 123 | 2+1 | 352 | 1.073 (=) / 0.850 (=) | 8.72 (=) / 6.91 (=) |
| Ours CLEFIA AES | | xc6vlx240t-3 | 115 | | 332 | 1.012 (=) / 0.802 (=) | 8.80 (=) / 6.97 (=) |
| Chaves[2] E+D | N | xc5vlx30-3 | 407 | 8+2 | 189,5 | 2.427 (=) | 5.96 (=) |
| Drimer[4] E | N | xc5vsx50t-3 | 107 | 2+1 | 550 | 1.76 (0.88) | 16.45 (8.22) |
| Drimer[4] | | | 212 | 2+1 | 550 | 1.76 (0.88) | 8.30 (4.15) |
| El Maraghy[5] E | Y | xc5vlx50 | 303 | 8+2 | 425 | 1.327 (=) | 4.38 (=) |
| Liu[11] E | Y | xc5vlx85 | 3579 | 0 | 360 | 46.093 (2.305) | 12.88 (0.64) |
| Liu[11] | | xc6vlx240t | 3121 | 0 | 347,5 | 64.128 (3.206) | 20.55 (1.03) |
| Bulens[1] E | Y | xc5v | 400 | 0 | 350 | 4.07 (1.07) | 10.18 (2.67) |
| Bulens[1] D | | | 550 | 0 | | 4.07 (1.07) | 7.40 (1.94) |
| HELION[8] Tiny E+D | Y | xc5v.-3 | 94 | 0 | n.a. | >0.077 (n.a.) | >0.82 (n.a.) |
| HELION[8] Standard E | Y | xc5v.-3 | 155 | 0 | n.a. | >0.84 (n.a.) | >5.42 (n.a.) |

[a] Encryption and/or Decryption. [b] Values within (brackets) are for feedback modes.

that the highly optimized structure proposed in [13]. These lower results are due to the additional logic used to support the AES cipher. This additional logic also has a negative impact in the maximum achievable frequency.

In regard to the related AES state of the art, the unrolled architecture proposed in [11] allows for a throughput above 60Gbps in ECB mode. However, when considering feedback modes the maximum throughput is of 3.2Gbps with a area cost of 3121 Slices resulting in a Throughput per Slice efficiency of 1.03. The 128-bit folded datapath structure, single cycle per round, presented in [2] achieves a throughput of 2.4Gbps with an efficiency of 5.96 at a cost of a higher BRAM usage. A more compact structure is proposed in [4] allowing for a throughput up to 1.76Gbps requiring 107 Slices. However, if feedback modes are used, the maximum throughput lowers to 880Mbps. An important characteristic of this proposal is the use of 4 DSP blocks to implement the XOR operations, instead of regular Slices. With this option an efficiency of 8.22 Throughput per Slice is achieved. Note that DSPs are Xilinx FPGA dedicated components and are also not considered in the efficiency metric herein applied. Without the use of DSPs, 212 Slices are needed instead, resulting in a efficiency of 4.15 when considering feedback modes. Given this, it can be concluded that, when not considering DSPs blocks, the structure herein proposed allows for the highest AES efficiency while still allowing for the CLEFIA computation.

Overall, the proposed structure allows for a throughput between 1Gbps and 850Mbps in feedback modes for CLEFIA and AES algorithms, respectively, at a cost of 123 Slices and 3 BRAMs. The resulting efficiency metric is better than most of the state of the art, supporting only the CLEFIA or the AES algorithms.

## 6 Conclusion

In this paper, a dual-cipher compact architecture is proposed for the novel CLEFIA cipher, also supporting the AES cipher. While using identical computation mechanisms, these algorithms have relatively different computational approaches. AES is based on a Substitution-Permutation Network while CLEFIA uses the traditional Feistel Network structure. This work shows that by adequately scheduling and merging the processing structure, and with the use of a LUT based addressable Shift Register, a compact and efficient design can be devised on Xilinx FPGAs allowing both ciphers to coexist simultaneously. The result analysis suggests that, by properly exploring and reusing the existing FPGA logic, the proposed structure allows for a CLEFIA/AES dual-cipher design at a low area cost of 123 Slices on a Virtex 5 device, achieving high throughputs of about 1Gbps with a Throughput per Slice efficiency up to 8.72.

**Acknowledgments.** This work was supported by the ARTEMIS Joint Undertaking under grant agreement n° 621429 and by national funds through Fundação para a Ciência e a Tecnologia (FCT) with reference UID/CEC/50021/2013.

## References

1. Bulens, P., Standaert, F.-X., Quisquater, J.-J., Pellegrin, P., Rouvroy, G.: Implementation of the AES-128 on virtex-5 FPGAs. In: Vaudenay, S. (ed.) AFRICACRYPT 2008. LNCS, vol. 5023, pp. 16–26. Springer, Heidelberg (2008)
2. Chaves, R., Kuzmanov, G., Vassiliadis, S., Sousa, L.: Reconfigurable memory based AES co-processor. In: 20th International on Parallel and Distributed Processing Symposium, IPDPS 2006, p. 8. IEEE (2006)
3. Chodowiec, P., Gaj, K.: Very compact FPGA implementation of the AES algorithm. In: Walter, C.D., Koç, Ç.K., Paar, C. (eds.) CHES 2003. LNCS, vol. 2779, pp. 319–333. Springer, Heidelberg (2003)
4. Drimer, S., Güneysu, T., Paar, C.: DSPs, BRAMs, and a pinch of logic: Extended recipes for AES on FPGAs. ACM Transactions on Reconfigurable Technology and Systems (TRETS) **3**(1), 3 (2010)

5. El Maraghy, M., Hesham, S., Abd El Ghany, M.A.: Real-time efficient FPGA implementation of aes algorithm. In: 2013 IEEE 26th International on SOC Conference (SOCC), pp. 203–208. IEEE (2013)
6. Elbirt, A.J., Paar, C.: An instruction-level distributed processor for symmetric-key cryptography. IEEE Transactions on Parallel and Distributed Systems 16(5), 468–480 (2005)
7. Good, T., Benaissa, M.: AES on FPGA from the fastest to the smallest. In: Rao, J.R., Sunar, B. (eds.) CHES 2005. LNCS, vol. 3659, pp. 427–440. Springer, Heidelberg (2005)
8. HELION. http://www.heliontech.com
9. Kashyap, H., Chaves, R.: Secure partial dynamic reconfiguration with unsecured external memory. In: 2014 24th International Conference on Field Programmable Logic and Applications (FPL), pp. 1–7. IEEE (2014)
10. Kryjak, T., Gorgon, M.: Pipeline implementation of the 128-bit block cipher CLEFIA in FPGA. In: International Conference on Field Programmable Logic and Applications, FPL 2009, pp. 373–378. IEEE (2009)
11. Liu, Q., Xu, Z., Yuan, Y.: A 66.1Gbps single-pipeline AES on FPGA. In: 2013 International Conference on Field-Programmable Technology (FPT), pp. 378–381. IEEE (2013)
12. NIST: FIPS 197: Advanced encryption standard (AES). Federal Information Processing Standards Publication 197, 441–0311 (2001)
13. Proenca, P., Chaves, R.: Compact CLEFIA implementation on FPGAs. In: 2011 International Conference on Field Programmable Logic and Applications (FPL), pp. 512–517. IEEE (2011)
14. Rouvroy, G., Standaert, F.X., Quisquater, J.J., Legat, J.: Compact and efficient encryption/decryption module for FPGA implementation of the AES Rijndael very well suited for small embedded applications. In: Proceedings of the International Conference on Information Technology: Coding and Computing, ITCC 2004, vol. 2, pp. 583–587. IEEE (2004)
15. Shirai, T., Shibutani, K., Akishita, T., Moriai, S., Iwata, T.: The 128-Bit blockcipher CLEFIA (Extended Abstract). In: Biryukov, A. (ed.) FSE 2007. LNCS, vol. 4593, pp. 181–195. Springer, Heidelberg (2007)
16. Singh, H., Lee, M.H., Lu, G., Kurdahi, F.J., Bagherzadeh, N., Chaves Filho, E.M.: MorphoSys: An integrated reconfigurable system for data-parallel and computation-intensive applications. IEEE Transactions on Computers 49(5), 465–481 (2000)
17. Sklavos, N., Koufopavlou, O.: Architectures and VLSI implementations of the AES-proposal Rijndael. IEEE Transactions on Computers 51(12), 1454–1459 (2002)
18. Tsunoo, Y., Tsujihara, E., Shigeri, M., Suzaki, T., Kawabata, T.: Cryptanalysis of CLEFIA using multiple impossible differentials. In: International Symposium on Information Theory and its Applications, ISITA 2008, pp. 1–6. IEEE (2008)
19. Wu, L., Weaver, C., Austin, T.: CryptoManiac: A fast flexible architecture for secure communication. In: Proceedings of the 28th Annual International Symposium on Computer Architecture, pp. 110–119. IEEE (2001)

# Systems and Applications II

# An Efficient and Flexible FPGA Implementation of a Face Detection System

Hichem Ben Fekih, Ahmed Elhossini$^{(\boxtimes)}$, and Ben Juurlink

Embedded Systems Architectures (AE), Technical University of Berlin, Einsteinufer 17, 10587 Berlin, Germany
hichem.f@live.de,
{ahmed.elhossini,b.juurlink}@tu-berlin.de

**Abstract.** This paper proposes a hardware architecture based on the object detection system of Viola and Jones using Haar-like features. The proposed design is able to discover faces in real-time with high accuracy. Speed-up is achieved by exploiting the parallelism in the design, where multiple classifier cores can be added. To maintain a flexible design, classifier cores can be assigned to different images. Moreover using different training data, every core is able to detect a different object type. As development platform, the Zynq-7000 SoC from Xilinx is used, which features an ARM Cortex-A9 dual-core CPU and a programmable logic (FPGA). The current implementation focuses on the face detection and achieves a real-time detection at the rate of 16.53 FPS on image resolution of $640 \times 480$ pixels, which represents a speed-up of 6.46 times compared to the equivalent OpenCV software solution.

**Keywords:** Face detection · Computer vision · Zynq · FPGA

## 1 Introduction

Several applications in different domains require a reliable fast detection system, where the location and scale of faces in the image are extracted. Face detection is widely used as a first stage for applications, such as face recognition, video surveillance, eyes detection to measure the driver drowsiness in modern cars or in advertisement industry to collect information like gender and age range for targeted advertisements. Face detection is a fundamental technique that enables a natural human-computer interaction (HCI). There were several approaches based on different feature sets and methods that have dealt with face detection. Many of them were too complex and time consuming, since the difficulty associated with the face detection can be attributed to various factors, such as variation in scale, location, pose, lighting condition, etc.

On 2001 Viola and Jones [13] have proposed a new face detection framework based on Haar features that is able to process images rapidly. Since its publication, it has received considerable attention, because it can achieve very high detection rate. An open-source implementation of the detector made by Rainer

© Springer International Publishing Switzerland 2015
K. Sano et al. (Eds.): ARC 2015, LNCS 9040, pp. 243–254, 2015.
DOI: 10.1007/978-3-319-16214-0_20

Lienhart [9] exists already in the OpenCV library [1], which includes ready training data. Viola and Jones approach is primarily developed for face detection, but the algorithm is able to detect any object by using different training data.

This paper focuses on the face detection task based on Viola and Jones algorithm. A new software-hardware co-design approach is investigated, which enhances the performance of the original approach and achieves real time face detection performance. A hardware accelerator is developed to perform most of the computationally intensive tasks and implements all necessary components participating in the face detection. To maintain a flexible design, this paper presents the architecture of an Evaluator core, which can be duplicated to improve the performance. Adding more cores will increase the frame-rate on the cost of more resources and possibly power consumption. The Evaluator core contains a Read Only Memory (ROM), which can be adapted to detect any object by using the respective training data. Moreover, the design can be accessed as a network service throuth the network so multiple sources and multiple face detection systems can be integrated togather to increase the overall throughput of the system and flexibility of the design.

The remainder of this paper is organized as follows. Section 2 covers the relevant background information needed in order to perform the work presented in this paper. Section 3 lists the related work that focuses on software as well as hardware solutions for the face detection task. The actual high-level design and implementation are presented in Section 4, which includes a discussion about crucial design decisions and some used techniques in order to accelerate the process. Section 5 presents the evaluation results of the system and performs a comparison with equivalent software and hardware implementations. Finally, Section 6 includes the conclusions of the paper.

## 2    Background

On 2010, Nikolay Degtyarev et al. [4] have presented some research comparing many different face detection algorithms based on the false face rejection rate, false acceptance rate and speed. It turned out that the extended realization of the Viola and Jones object detection algorithm [9] is the best open source available algorithm based on the performance and the detection rates. It is considered the first real-time object detection framework providing very good detection rates. A complete software realization of the algorithm already exists in the OpenCV library [1]. Basically the face detection algorithm tries to locate specific Haar features of human faces and consists of two phases, training and detection. This paper will only cover the implementation of the detection phase on the FPGA, since the training data can be generated off-line on a typical PC. The training data used for the detection are created by Rainer Lienhart and are located in the OpenCV library [1].

### 2.1    Cascade Architecture

Viola and Jones algorithm consists of many cascaded stages, which are constructed during the training phase. A stage represents a strong classifier, which gets a sub-window as input and gives an output value indicating if the current window is a face candidate. Viola and Jones have proved in their work that only one stage containing 200 Haar features is able to detect faces successfully, but it will consumes a lot of time to process the complete image. Thus, stages are arranged in a cascaded form, where the first stages are less complex than the ones at the end of the cascade. In the case that any stage returns a negative result, the current sub-window will be immediately rejected otherwise next stage will be activated. If the sub-window passes all stages then it will be considered as a face candidate. This process is illustrated in Figure 1. Because the number of non-face candidates in an image is much more than face candidates, the first few stages are constructed to reject most of negative examples before more complex stages are activated. The performance is increased by rejecting negative sub-windows as early as possible. For this reason the first few stages are designed to contain only a few number of features.

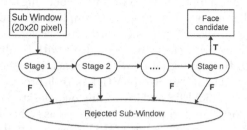

**Fig. 1.** Schematic depiction of the detection cascade

A single stage (also called a strong classifier), is responsible for classifying a sub-window as a face or a non face candidate. In this paper, the stage consists of many decision trees. Each tree evaluates the image and return an output value (h). These "h" values are summed up and compared to the stage threshold ($\theta$) as shown in Equation 1.

$$H(\theta) = \begin{cases} 1 & if \sum h \geq \theta \\ 0 & otherwise \end{cases}$$

(1)

In Equation 1, H is the strong classifier function, an output value 1 means that the current sub-window may contain a face and should be further analysed. The output value 0 means that the current sub-window is a negative image and has to be immediately rejected.

## 3    Related Work

There exist several techniques to detect faces in still images. Some attempts are based on detecting faces by skin color [10,12]. Such methods have the disadvantage, that they do not work with all types of skin color and are very vulnerable to different lighting conditions.

On 2007, S. Liao et al. have presented a face detection system based on Viola and Jones algorithm [8]. Instead of using Haar features, they have used

Local Binary Patterns values (LBP), which are showing less accuracy compared to Haar features. Since LBP features are integer, the detection and training phase are much faster than with Haar features. Another attempt made by X. Zhi et al. [17] presents a unified model for face detection and pose estimation. An experimental result over faces larger than 150 px shows a good detection rate but no information are mentioned about the performance, as well as, the detection rate for faces smaller than 150 px.

The work presented in this paper is based on the work made by R. Lienhart et al. [9], which presents an extended Haar feature set for the face detection system of Viola and Jones. The work of R. Lienhart et al. shows better detection rates than the algorithms presented in [8,10,12]. The trained classifiers are able to detect faces larger than 24 px. The software solution detects frontal faces in images (320x240) at 5 FPS on a Pentium-4 2 Ghz using a rescaling factor of 1.2. Since Viola and Jones approach is the most used and extended algorithm. A lot of work has been done in attempts to accelerate it. Depending on the host platform, software solutions that use optimized OpenCV implementations can reach 3 FPS on images consisting of 640x480 pixels. In order to accelerate the calculation of the Haar features, many researches have been dealt with hardware approaches.

In the work of D. Hefenbrock [5] a GPU approach is proposed, which is programmed using CUDA [11] and tested on NVIDIAs Tesla processors. The final GPU implementation reached 15.2 FPS and is running on a desktop server containing 4 Tesla GPUs. The reported performance is considered as sufficient and can be used in real-time applications. However using 4 GPU processors will consume certainly much power and typical quad-Tesla desktop supercomputers are expensive.

Another work by Hung-Chih Lai et al. [7] describes a face detection implementation on FPGA, where the classification process is done in only one clock cycle and the integral image is stored in registers. Such approaches can reach an enormous high speed detection but the system is only using 52 Haar features for the classification. Each one has a direct connection to the integral image. Using such a small number of features may affect the accuracy of the detection. Unfortunately, no information are mentioned about the accuracy of the system. Their hardware design may become infeasible when the number of features increases, because the number of classifiers will increase, which have a direct connection to the size of the integral image registers.

Cho et al. [2,3] have proposed an FPGA design, where images are stored in BRAMs and the integral image is stored in registers. Their design supports multiple classifiers, which enables processing many Haar features in parallel. The reported performance reached 16.08 FPS using 8 classifiers, which is the best reported frame rate with good accuracy. Nevertheless, the work presented in [3] is showing a decreased frame rate when the number of faces in the image is growing. Their design consumes relatively much FPGA resources and can not be adopted for lower end FPGAs.

A lot of promising work has been presented in the literature for face detection. The majority of them meets the real-time constraints. However, this paper will presents a complete new hardware solution, where the processing time is reduced and a flexible design is provided, which minimizes the reserved hardware resources and enables low end FPGAs to be used to extend their functionality.

## 4    Design and Implementation

This section discusses some design decisions and presents the FPGA implementation of the described face detection system. The first sub-section introduces the complete detection system. The remaining sub-sections will deal in details with the design of all required modules.

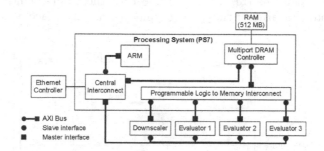

**Fig. 2.** Complete System Overview

### 4.1    System Overview

In the proposed system, images are captured on the PC and transferred via Ethernet to the system using the UDP protocol. An application running on the PC developed using C++ is responsible for sending images and presenting the results. The ARM-CPU on the Zynq Chip handles receiving the pixel data and ensures storing them in an external memory (DDRAM). The RAM acts as shared memory between all components. The Processing System (PS7) [14] includes four high performance AXI slave ports, which allow accessing the shared memory from four different modules. The Evaluator classifies a 20x20 pixel image as a face or non face candidate. It implements the task of the cascade architecture presented in Section 2. In Figure 2, three instances of the "Evaluator" are included to improve the performance of the face detection system. Each one will be assigned to a part of the image and thus the processing time will be reduced. On the other hand, a module is required to accelerate the image down-scaling, which is called Downscaler and it includes an AXI master port to read/write image pixels directly from/to the memory. The current version of the module resizes the image using the nearest neighbor interpolation algorithm with a scale factor of 1.2. The Downscaler and the 3 instances of the Evaluator are connected to the ARM CPU via AXI Bus. The CPU takes the mission to command and synchronize the modules. It also assigns image regions to the Evaluator instances for classification. More Evaluator cores can be connected to increase the performance.

## 4.2  The Evaluator Core

The Evaluator is the main module of the proposed architecture. It is responsible for classifying a 20x20 sub-window and it implements the cascaded strong classifiers described in Section 2. Figure 3 shows an overview of the Evaluator structure. The Preprocessing Engine module reads the pixels from memory and computes the integral image. Then, the Evaluator core starts reading the training data from the ROM module and it selects the required pixels for the classification from the integral image buffer. The tree receives the node threshold values, three node inputs and the rectangle data required for the computation of the Haar features. Then, the tree selects a value from the inputs, which represents the output vote indicating if the current window contains a face or not.

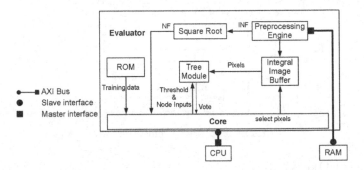

**Fig. 3.** Evaluator Overview

The ROM module consists of Block RAMs and contains the training data needed for the face detection. Overall, the training data includes 20 stages, 1047 trees, 2094 nodes (Haar features) and 4535 rectangles. These data are converted to a compressed binary format and are accessed by the evaluator core at each stage of the processing.

**Preprocessing Engine.** To perform the classification, 4535 rectangles have to be read from the ROM. Each rectangle needs four memory accesses to be computed. Hence, it is essential to copy a part of the original image to an internal cache to reduce the memory accesses and increase the performance. The Preprocessing Engine module uses the AXI Master Burst component from Xilinx to communicate with the memory and to copy 24x22 window to the internal cache. To minimize the effect of different lighting conditions when detecting faces, the implemented Evaluator uses training data, that have been generated using variance normalized images. It is therefore necessary during the detection to normalize images before processing them. The normalization is simply performed by multiplying the node thresholds with a normalization factor (NF), which is computed for each sub-window.

**Integral Image Buffer.** The integral image facilitates the Haar feature calculation. The face detection system processes one tree every cycle (four rectangles

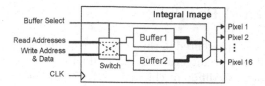

**Fig. 4.** Block Diagram of the Integral Image Buffer

in total) to ensure real-time performance. This component consists mainly of dual-port block RAMs, each one permits maximal two simultaneous accesses. As shown in Figure 4, it contains two buffers, each one consists of 8 BRAMs. Using the Buffer Select signal one buffer can be chosen for read accesses and the other one for write operations, which enables data to be read and written in the same time doubling the final frame rate.

**Decision Tree.** The tree contains two nodes, as shown in Figure 5, which predict an output value starting from two Haar features. Each node receives the Haar feature data from the integral image buffer and then it computes the feature value and compares it to the threshold received from the ROM module. Depending on the result a vote is selected.

Figure 5 shows the internal architecture of the proposed node design. It receives as inputs 3 rectangle definitions (a, b, c and d), weight of the second rectangle, a threshold value and a polarity (p).

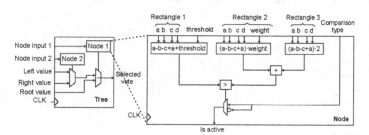

**Fig. 5.** Tree Architecture

### 4.3 Summary

The system presented in the previous sections receives the image data from the video source using the network interface. The software running on the ARM core is responsible for receiving the image through the network interface, storing it in the memory, and transmitting sub-windows to the evaluator core(s) for evaluation. It also controls the scaling module to scale sub-windows before processing them by the evaluator. Finally, the software transferes the evaluation results (locations of faces) back to the image source. This configuration allows the system to receive images from different sources and also multiple versions of the system can be used in parallel to process images from the same source. Higher resolutions as well as higher frame rates can be achieved using this approach.

# 5    Evaluation and Results

Several experiments are presented in this section to evaluate the performance and accuracy of the proposed architecture. In our evaluations we use two development boards equipped with two different chips of Xilinx Zynq-7000 All Programmable SoCs. The two boards are the ZedBoard [16] and Xilinx ZC706 Evaluation Kit [14]. Individual components were modelled in VHDL and validated using RTL simulation and by integration with the ARM Based SoC using Xilinx EDK 14.7 [15].

## 5.1    Resource Utilization

Xilinx EDK [15] platform is used to synthesis the proposed architecture. Based on the synthesis result, the FPGA can operate at a maximum clock speed of 144.32 MHz for the Z706 board and 100MHz for the ZedBoard. Table 1 shows the resources utilized by the face detection system on the ZC706 and ZedBoard when it includes 1, 2 or 3 Evaluator cores (running in parallel). The most consumed resources by the design are the BRAMs, which contain the training data and the integral image. The required resources increase linearly with the number of the used Evaluator cores. Depending on the available FPGA resources, the number of cores can be chosen. From these results, it is clear that the proposed design is portable and can be implemented on different FGPA architecture.

**Table 1.** Device Utilization Characteristics for the Face Detection System

| Board Name | ZedBoard | | | | | | ZC706 | |
|---|---|---|---|---|---|---|---|---|
| Target Device | xc7z020-1-clg484 | | | | | | xc7z045-ffg900 | |
| Number of Evaluator Cores | 1 | | 2 | | 3 | | 3 | |
| Number of Slice Registers | 4113 | 3% | 7011 | 6% | 9908 | 9% | 9908 | 9% |
| Number of Slice LUTs | 4596 | 8% | 7852 | 14% | 11004 | 20% | 11047 | 5% |
| Number of used BRAMs | 28 | 20% | 56 | 40% | 84 | 60% | 84 | 15% |
| Number of DSP48E1s | 11 | 4% | 22 | 8% | 33 | 15% | 33 | 3% |

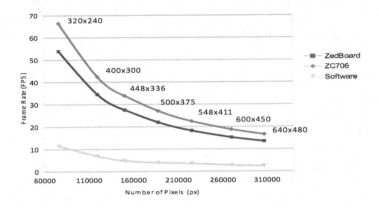

**Fig. 6.** Performance Measurement of the Face Detector Dystems using Different Image Sizes

**Table 2.** Performance Comparison of the Proposed Detector and the Original Implementation

(a) The ZedBoard

| Number of Faces | | 1 | 8 | 21 |
|---|---|---|---|---|
| Software Detector | | 3.03 FPS (1.00x) | 2.75 FPS (1.00x) | 2.56 FPS (1.00x) |
| Hardware | 1 core | 6.19 FPS (2.04x) | 6.17 FPS (2.24x) | 6.14 FPS (2.40x) |
| | 2 core | 10.54 FPS (3.47x) | 10.51 FPS (3.82x) | 10.46 FPS (4.09x) |
| | 3 core | 13.48 FPS (4.45x) | 13.47 FPS (4.90x) | 13.43 FPS (5.25x) |

(b) The ZC706 Evaluation Board

| Number of Faces | | 1 | 8 | 21 |
|---|---|---|---|---|
| Software Detector | | 3.03 FPS (1.00x) | 2.75 FPS (1.00x) | 2.56 FPS (1.00x) |
| Hardware | 1 core | 7.69 FPS (2.54x) | 7.68 FPS (2.79x) | 7.64 FPS (2.98x) |
| | 2 core | 13.08 FPS (4.32x) | 13.05 FPS (4.75x) | 13.00 FPS (5.08x) |
| | 3 core | 16.58 FPS (5.47x) | 16.57 FPS (6.03x) | 16.53 FPS (6.46x) |

## 5.2   Performance Comparison

The proposed face detector is based on the OpenCV implementation of the algorithm[9] and uses the same training file. In this section we introduce a comparison between the proposed implementation and the software implementation using OpenCV. The performance of the OpenCV implementation is determined by measuring the computation time required for analysing images on a PC having an Intel Core i5-4200U CPU (2.30 GHz), 8 GB DDR3L RAM (1600 MHz), Microsoft Windows 8.1. To make the comparison possible both implementations of the hardware and software use exactly the same parameters. To study the influence of the image size over the performance, an experiment was conducted, which consists of measuring the frame rate of the face detector using different image sizes. The result is depicted in Figure 6. It shows a decreasing frame rate when the size of the image is increased. Higher resoultions are supported as well, with the cost of more processing time.

Since the classifier spends more time on face sub-windows, images containing a lot of faces will require more time to process and hence will reduce the frame rate. Thus, the second measurement covers a performance comparison by processing 640x480 images containing different number of faces and using variant number of Evaluator cores. The results are shown in Tables 2a and 2b for the ZedBoard and ZC706 evaluation board respectivly.

On the ZedBoard the 1 core face detection system is capable of processing images at an average speed of 6.19 FPS. The 2 cores face detection system is capable of processing images at an average speed of 10.54 FPS, which represents a performance improvement of 1.70 times over the 1 core version. The 3 core face detection system has the best speed results and it is able to process the image at an average speed of 13.48 FPS. The ZC706 evaluation board shows better performance, since it has a better speed grade and the programmable logic is operating at higher frequency. The highest frame rate of an average of 16.5 FPS is achieved using 3 Evaluator cores. This represents an improvement of 6.46 times compared to the software version and 1.23 times relative to the 3 core detector on the ZedBoard. Using 2 cores on the ZC706 board provides almost the same performance of the ZedBoard when using 3 Evaluator cores. The higher number of faces in the image has an insignificant effect on the performance of the hardware solution compared to the software because of the double buffers used in the evaluator core to hide the latency.

## 5.3   Accuracy Comparison

In this section, the detection rate and the false positive rate of the hardware and software solutions are measured. A set of images (484 images containing 641 faces) from the database presented in [6] are used to perform the required measurements.

**Table 3.** Accuracy comparison

|          | Detected Faces | Detection Rate | False Alarms | False Positive Rate |
|----------|----------------|----------------|--------------|---------------------|
| Hardware | 590            | 92%            | 1055         | 0.034%              |
| OpenCv   | 619            | 97%            | 1551         | 0.050%              |

The result shown in Table 3 indicates that the software implementation has a better detection rate compared to the hardware version. There exists two possible reasons for the accuracy degradation. The first is that the hardware detector uses only 7 bits from the 8 bit pixel of the original image to compute the integral image. Using less bits reduces the amount of memory needed to store the integral image, but it reduces the accuracy of the system as well. The second reason encompasses the different downscaling algorithms applied in both implementations. While the linear interpolation is applied for downscaling images in the software, the hardware uses the nearest neighbour interpolation, which may result in a substantial information loss when resizing.

## 5.4   Comparison with Similar Works

The proposed face detection system is compared to two similar face detection systems presented in [2,5] and are discussed in Section 3. The comparison is made based on the results presented in both publications. Table 4 illustrates the reached frame rate of the proposed face detector compared to the work presented in [2,5]. All algorithms use the same scale factor 1.2. On image resolution 640x480, the GPU implementation [5] operates at 15.2 FPS utilizing 4 GPUs. The FPGA implementation [2] reached 16.08 FPS using 8 classifiers (where a classifier is equivalent to a node in this paper). The detection rate and the false positive rate of the referenced works are not mentioned, but in the best case, they are comparable to the rates of the OpenCV implementation.

**Table 4.** A Comparison of Different Accelerated Versions of Viola and Jone's Algorithm

| Approach | Number of Features | Resolution | Frame Rate |
|----------|--------------------|------------|------------|
| Proposed |                    | 320x240    | 66.45      |
| System   | 2094               | 640x480    | 16.53      |
| FPGA [2] |                    | 320x240    | 61.02      |
|          | 2135               | 640x480    | 16.08      |
| GPU [5]  | x                  | 640x480    | 15.2       |

## 5.5 Image Results

A sample output of the proposed hardware face detection system is shown in Figure 7a. The white squares present the detected face on the image. The result shows that in most cases, faces are successfully detected. Some of the undetected faces has a small rotation angle. This can be explained by the actual training data, which are generated using frontal faces. Some white rectangles point to non-face subwindows. A simple filter can be implemented to remove such wrong rectangles. An existing face in an image is usually classified in many overlapped rectangles. This property can be exploited to search for overlapped rectangles and rejects single rectangles, which does not overlap with others as illustrated in Figure 7.

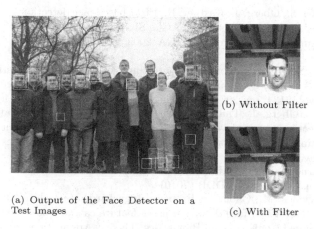

(b) Without Filter

(a) Output of the Face Detector on a Test Images

(c) With Filter

**Fig. 7.** Sample System Output

## 6 Conclusions

In this paper a software-hardware co-design approach is presented, that enables the detection of frontal faces in real time. This work is based on the object detection framework of Viola and Jones, which makes use of a cascade of classifiers to reduce the computation time and identifies particular Haar features to detect faces. The proposed architecture is flexible, as it allows the use of multiple instances of the face detector. This makes developers free to choose the speed range and reserved resources for this task. For small applications, that requires a face detection speed of 6 FPS or less, only one core will be sufficient, so that the design can fit into low capacity FPGAs. The current implementation runs on the Zynq SoC and receives images over IP network which allows exposing the face detection task as a remote service, that can be consumed from any device connected to the network. Using three Evaluator cores, the ZedBoard system achieves a maximal average frame rate of 13.4 FPS when analysing an image containing 640x480 pixels. This stands for an improvement of 5.25 times compared to the software solution and represents an acceptable results for most real-time systems. On the ZC706 evaluation board, a higher frame rate of 16.58

FPS is achieved. The proposed hardware solution achieved %92 accuracy which
is low compared to the software solution (%97) due to the low precision used in
the arithmetic operations and different scaling algorithm. The proposed solution
achieved higher frame rate compared to other solutions found in the literature.

# References

1. Bradski, G.: Opencv library. Dr. Dobb's Journal of Software Tools (2000)
2. Cho, J., Benson, B., Mirzaei, S., Kastner, R.: Parallelized architecture of multiple classifiers for face detection. In: 20th IEEE International Conference on Application-specific Systems, Architectures and Processors, ASAP 2009, pp. 75–82, July 2009
3. Cho, J., Mirzaei, S., Oberg, J., Kastner, R.: Fpga-based face detection system using haar classifiers. In: Proceedings of the ACM/SIGDA International Symposium on Field Programmable Gate Arrays, FPGA 2009, pp. 103–112. ACM, New York (2009)
4. Degtyarev, N., Seredin, O.: Comparative testing of face detection algorithms. In: Elmoataz, A., Lezoray, O., Nouboud, F., Mammass, D., Meunier, J. (eds.) ICISP 2010. LNCS, vol. 6134, pp. 200–209. Springer, Heidelberg (2010)
5. Hefenbrock, D., Oberg, J., Thanh, N., Kastner, R., Baden, S.: Accelerating viola-jones face detection to fpga-level using gpus. In: 2010 18th IEEE Annual International Symposium on Field-Programmable Custom Computing Machines (FCCM), pp. 11–18, May 2010
6. Jain, V., Learned-miller, E.: Fddb: A benchmark for face detection in unconstrained settings. Tech. rep, FDDB (2010)
7. Lai, H.C., Savvides, M., Chen, T.: Proposed fpga hardware architecture for high frame rate (<<100 FPS) face detection using feature cascade classifiers. In: First IEEE International Conference on Biometrics: Theory, Applications, and Systems, BTAS 2007, pp. 1–6, September 2007
8. Liao, S.C., Zhu, X.X., Lei, Z., Zhang, L., Li, S.Z.: Learning multi-scale block local binary patterns for face recognition. In: Lee, S.-W., Li, S.Z. (eds.) ICB 2007. LNCS, vol. 4642, pp. 828–837. Springer, Heidelberg (2007)
9. Lienhart, R., Maydt, J.: An extended set of haar-like features for rapid object detectio. In: Proceedings of the 2002 International Conference on Image Processing, vol. 1, pp. I-900–I-903 (2002)
10. Liu, Q., zheng Peng, G.: A robust skin color based face detection algorithm. In: 2010 2nd International Asia Conference on Informatics in Control, Automation and Robotics (CAR), vol. 2, pp. 525–528, March 2010
11. NVIDIA: Cuda developer zone (2014). https://developer.nvidia.com/about-cuda
12. Störring, M.: Computer Vision and Human Skin Colour: A Ph.D. Dissertation. Computer Vision & Media Technology Laboratory, Aalborg University (2004)
13. Viola, P., Jones, M.: Robust real-time face detection. International Journal of Computer Vision **57**(2), 137–154 (2004)
14. Xilinx: Zynq-7000 soc zc706 evaluation kit (2013). http://www.xilinx.com/publications/prod_mktg/Zynq_ZC706_Prod_Brief.pdf
15. Xilinx: Embedded devlopment kit 14.7 (2014). http://www.xilinx.com/tools/platform.htm
16. ZedBoard.org: Zedboard hardware users guide (2013). http://www.zedboard.org
17. Zhu, X., Ramanan, D.: Face detection, pose estimation, and landmark localization in the wild. In: 2012 IEEE Conference on Computer Vision and Pattern Recognition (CVPR), pp. 2879–2886, June 2012

# A Flexible Software Framework for Dynamic Task Allocation on MPSoCs Evaluated in an Automotive Context

Jens Rettkowski(✉), Philipp Wehner, Marc Schülper, and Diana Göhringer

Ruhr-University Bochum, Bochum, Germany
{jens.rettkowski,philipp.wehner,marc.schuelper,
diana.goehringer}@rub.de

**Abstract.** For a wide variety of applications such as multimedia applications, the number of tasks running simultaneously on Multiprocessor Systems-on-Chip (MPSoCs) changes dynamically at runtime. An intelligent resource management is required to efficiently map these tasks onto the processing elements. In this paper, a new flexible software framework for allocating tasks dynamically onto a heterogeneous MPSoC is presented. This MPSoC contains an ARM processor and multiple MicroBlazes. The framework maps the tasks on the MicroBlazes based on various strategies which are selectable to meet the application-specific demands. The performance of the framework is evaluated by an automotive application. In this context, an electronic control unit uses the proposed framework to avoid collisions with other vehicles. Thereby, realistic data given by a car simulator is distributed to the processing elements of the MPSoC. Here, the distance of vehicles influences the scheduling. The evaluation shows that this approach exploits the MPSoC scalability and simplifies the programming and efficient use of such systems.

**Keywords:** Dynamic task allocation · MPSoC · Automotive application · Car2Car communication · FPGA

## 1 Introduction

Due to the rising demands for a large number of various applications, the trend towards integration of Multiprocessor Systems-on-Chip (MPSoCs) in embedded systems increases [1]. To achieve high energy efficiency for the target application, these MPSoCs typically consist of a set of heterogeneous processing elements (PEs). In recent times, Networks-on-Chip (NoCs) arise as the most promising communication infrastructure for MPSoCs with a high number of PEs [2]. Several applications, each consisting of several different tasks, can be executed simultaneously on the MPSoC. However, the programmability becomes more complex and task mapping on the PEs influences significantly the system characteristics, in terms of performance and power. In order to exploit the benefits of such systems, an intelligent resource manager allocating tasks to system resources is needed. Algorithms for task allocation can be

© Springer International Publishing Switzerland 2015
K. Sano et al. (Eds.): ARC 2015, LNCS 9040, pp. 255–266, 2015.
DOI: 10.1007/978-3-319-16214-0_21

divided into dynamic and static mappings. The latter implies a fixed assignment to all tasks at design time. Since the number of tasks vary at runtime for a lot of applications, a static mapping can be inefficient. Using dynamic task mapping allows adding, moving and removing of application tasks at runtime. Thus, a better exploitation of ressources is guaranteed. However, this allocation of tasks is application specific. As a result, different strategies are necessary for a flexible software framework.

The main contribution of this paper is a new software framework for dynamic task allocation. This flexible software framework is applicable for several applications to simplify the programmability of such systems. The framework is evaluated by an automotive application in which tasks occur dynamically and in a non–deterministic manner.

The automotive context is given by a control unit to avoid collisions between vehicles. Considering that a vehicle receives information about surrounding vehicles in terms of position, velocity and direction, a safety-critical system can stop its car in case of an impending accident. Therefore, this safety-critical system must decide which vehicle has the greatest potential to cause an accident. As a result a priority scheme is necessary. The respective task of one vehicle can be processed independently from other vehicles. Hence, a multicore system is predestined for this application. In this case, the processing of data must be allocated onto PEs. In this paper, three different priority schemes ("first come first serve", distance-based and a specific sector-based heuristic) and two mapping algorithms (load-depended and uniform distribution) are presented. The framework manages the allocation of tasks and therefore simplifies the programming. While the framework is not limited to the number of PEs, it exploits the MPSoC scalability and   the efficient use of such systems.

For this purpose, a heterogeneous MPSoC consisting of an ARM processor and several MicroBlazes (µBs) is utilized as a platform for the software framework. The PEs communicate via a Network-on-Chip (NoC). A car simulator generating realistic data for the evaluation is employed. The performance of several strategies given by the framework is verified by the automotive application.

The rest of the paper is organized as follows: Section II presents related work in this area. The system architecture used in this paper is described in Section III. Section IV explains the software framework for dynamic task allocation. The evaluation and results of the framework is given by Section V. Finally, Section VI summarizes the paper and gives an outlook for future research.

## 2    Related Work

In [3] an overview of mapping algorithms and heuristics on multi- and many-core systems is given. The work categorizes the mapping phase in design-time and runtime methodologies and summarizes related work regarding centralized and distributed management techniques. In this paper, the framework has a central manager to allocate tasks at runtime. A comparison between static and dynamic allocation is given in [4]. A static allocation has a better quality of mapping regarding to a global view of the application. But, it implies deterministic behavior of the tasks. A dynamic allocation is capable to allocate new tasks. In case of the automotive context, the tasks arrive in a non-deterministic manner. Therefore, a dynamic task allocation is used in this work.

Especially the work of Moreira et al. [5] needs to be pointed out, as the authors use a runtime-based mapping methodology for a homogeneous architecture with a centralized control manager and virtual cores. They optimize against resource utilization which is an important aspect. Nevertheless, virtual cores are neither implemented nor necessary for the content of this paper. The estimated execution time of an application is an additional optimization goal in MPSoC.

Hong et al. [6] present a homogeneous architecture using an allocation methodology to reduce the execution time, where the workload of the network influences the mapping decisions. As a result, the allocation algorithm is optimized for a specific application. In comparison, several strategies for dynamic allocation are presented in this paper. Feasible criteria for the dynamic allocation of tasks are also introduced in [7], [8] and [9]. To reduce communication costs, dependent tasks are placed on the PEs as closely as possible in terms of the topology. That does not automatically mean the spatial distance, but a positioning regarding optimal data throughput and latency. On the opposite, loosely coupled tasks that do not produce significant communication overhead are located widely separated. As a side effect, unused resources are available closely to related PEs that run at capacity [10].

In this paper it is assumed that execution time is negatively influenced by network segments running at full capacity. The presented dynamic allocation mechanism is capable of distributing tasks to unused cores with the goal to achieve a load balancing in the MPSoC.


# 3    System Architecture

Realistic datasets are necessary for reasonable evaluation. Hence, the driving simulator from the company FOERST [11] is used to provide respective data and to react on the commands generated by the presented system. The simulator consists of three monitors mounted in front of a cockpit. All necessary and required peripherals, like the driver's seat, steering wheel and foot pedals are available, as shown in Fig. 1b. The driving simulator is fully remote controllable via an Ethernet interface. In addition, an MPSoC is used for the implementation of the dynamic task allocation. This MPSoC is realized on a Xilinx Zynq device [12] which provides an ARM processor besides an FPGA. In this approach, the FPGA contains 10 μBs, as shown in Fig. 1a. The processing elements (PEs) are connected by RAR-NoC [13] to provide a flexible on-chip communication. The routers of RAR-NoC are constructed in a 3x4 mesh topology. Moreover, the ARM processor communicates via two general purpose ports (GP) to the network. This result in a higher throughput between the FPGA and the ARM processor compared to one Port. To minimize the buffer size of the routers, wormhole routing is used. Additionally, the MPSoC supports reconfigurable PEs as well as reconfigurable routers supplied by RAR-NoC.

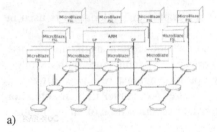

a)                                                                b)

**Fig. 1.** MPSoC using RAR-NoC (a) and the car simulator from the company FOERST (b)

# 4    Structure of the Software Framework

In example of an automotive application, this section presents an algorithm for a dynamic task allocation. The signal flow between the involved components is considered. The structure of the program is shown in Fig. 2. In the following, the reference vehicle is the vehicle controlled by the MPSoC. Surrounding vehicles are vehicles, which are detected by the MPSoC.

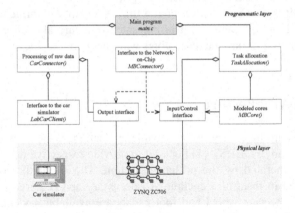

**Fig. 2.** Program structure

## 4.1    Data Acquisition

For the dynamic task allocation, input of raw data is required. It is encapsulated in so called task containers to separate the raw data from payload. Each task container object consists of a unique id, the respective priority and a data container. The latter is realized by a C++ structure with variable payload. Referring to [14], amongst a timestamp, the data container includes the position, the speed and the direction of the vehicle. The task allocation uses these data only for potential heuristics regarding the assignment of priorities. An important aspect is that the container class provides methods for (de-)serialization of the data container, as it is only possible to transmit data in form of 32 bit-words over the NoC.

After initialization of all modules, the main program continuously requests the positions of all surrounding cars in the virtual driving environment. This is done in the CarConnector class by acquiring, processing and committing the appropriate data. Request commands in form of strings are sent to the driving simulator via an Ethernet socket. To determine the position, speed and direction, two strings per vehicle are necessary. As the driving simulator does not provide an interface to identify active vehicles, it is required to request all 256 possible cars in the virtual environment. Hence, 512 requests are sent to the driving simulator per iteration. The data of the driver's car can be determined using two different methods: On the one hand, so called driver-functions can be used to directly request appropriate data, on the other side, the set of the 256 vehicles also includes the own car. It is of high importance to know the identification number of the vehicle to exclude it from the collision detection. Otherwise, a mismatch of a few milliseconds would result in two different positions for the driver's car. A widespread documentation regarding the Ethernet-Interface can be found in [11]. The received answer is buffered at first and then parsed for each vehicle to extract the relevant information. To achieve a higher performance of the µB processors, the return values are converted from floating point to integer.

## 4.2    Task Allocation

Distribution of allocated tasks can either be done evenly to all or load-dependent to a subset of the network attendees. For the latter, new tasks are distributed to already engaged cores. Other cores are activated when a defined threshold $load_{max}$ is reached. Conversely a cyclic delay function checks, if cores undercut a minimal load $load_{min}$. If that happens, remaining tasks are distributed to the other cores, providing that enough resources are available. Hence it is possible to switch off individual cores. It is obvious that a shorter calculation time is expected by using all cores. Processing the requests in a "first come – first serve" manner is a trivial solution for allocating capacities of a restricted resource. On the one hand, the process requests minimal resources, but on the other hand critical data is potentially processed after secondary information, as no priorities are considered. The second algorithm for the dynamic task allocation implements a priority allocation, based on the arbitrary distance between two objects. The underlying assumption of this heuristic implies, that the relevance of surrounding objects is reciprocal to the respective distance. Especially for collision prediction, it is obvious that closer cars are of higher relevance than vehicles in the far. In Fig. 3a, $dist_i$ is the Euclidean distance between the driver's car $f_R$ and surrounding vehicles $f_i$. It can be calculated from the return values of the driving simulator. Due to the time delay of data acquisition, a linear method with constant proportion is used for the priority allocation. Therefore, all vehicles within the defined radius $dist_{min}$ have the highest priority. The highest priority has the value 0 while the lowest priority is marked with 10. To enable a subsequent correction of the priority, the maximum value $prio_{max}$ can be lower than the highest system priority. The highest range $dist_{max}$ is required for normalization. It has to be determined considering the radius of reception of the surrounding cars:

$$dist_i = \sqrt{(x_R - x_i) + (y_R - y_i) + (z_R - z_i)} \quad (1)$$

$$prio(f_i) = prio_{max} + \left\lfloor \frac{prio_{min} - prio_{max}}{dist_{max} - dist_{min}} (dist_i - dist_{min}) \right\rfloor \quad (2)$$

The third method, the sector heuristic as shown in Fig. 3b, was developed for the specific use case presented in this paper. Compared to the task allocation, it is capable to deal with several factors for the priority allocation but with a greater effort. In contrast to the distance-based method, the positions of surrounding vehicles influence the assigned priority significantly. Priorities are assigned as follows:

- The highest priority is assigned to the vehicles $f_i$ within the critical radius $dist_{min}$ (orange inner circle), similar to the distance-based heuristic.
- The next lower priority is assigned to cars that are inside the blue trapezoid which is partially overlapped by $dist_{min}$.

The grey sectors represent the remaining area of the emulated car to car communication. The lowest priority is also assigned to vehicles in the left light grey sector, as they are slightly relevant for the prediction of collisions. Information of vehicles in the right dark grey sector is neither time critical and only relevant to caution against fog and traffic jam. A low priority is therefore assigned to them.

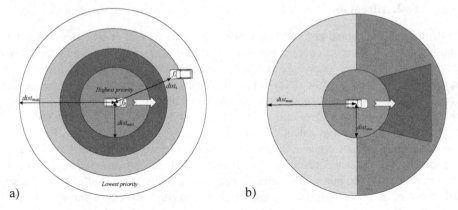

a)                                    b)

**Fig. 3.** Scheme of distance-based (a) and sector-based (b) priority heuristic

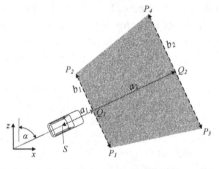

**Fig. 4.** Sketch for the calculation of the trapezoid edges

The Euclidean distance is used to determine, if the observed car is located within the critical area. The data is forwarded to a µB processor with highest priority, if this is the case. Otherwise, if the car is located in the blue trapezoid, as shown in Fig. 4, the vertices $P_1$ to $P_4$ are calculated based on $Q_1$ and $Q_2$ and the angle $\alpha$:

$$Q_1 = S + a_i \begin{pmatrix} \sin \alpha \\ \cos \alpha \end{pmatrix} \tag{3}$$

$$P_i = Q_i + a_i \begin{pmatrix} \sin (\alpha \pm 90°) \\ \cos (\alpha \pm 90°) \end{pmatrix} \tag{4}$$

Determination of the vehicles location is done by an adaptive PNPOLY algorithm [15]. The vertices of the polygon are sequentially listed in an array. A high priority is always assigned if the vehicle is located within the polygon. A low priority is assigned if the car is neither located within the critical radius nor within the trapezoid. In this case, the vehicles are located behind the driver's car.

### 4.3    Transmission via Network-on-Chip

Directly after the dynamic task allocation, data of the individual task container or control information is transmitted over the network. For this reason, a software interface, given by the class *MBConnector()*, provides a messaging protocol for ARM and µB processors. However, transmission errors cannot be ruled out. Failures of the processing elements or the routers induced by rough environment conditions (e.g. high temperature) can occur. Therefore, a reliability layer is included in the interface. To ease general usage, this layer is transparent. A single error is detected by means of parity bits and corrected. If more than one error occurs, the errors are identified by the µBs and the ARM processor gets informed. Data is transferred in the form of packets, which are classified into two types: data-packets and control-packets. Data-packets transmit the content of the task container. For the automotive application, the interface supports 7 different data-packets. These packets listed below can also be used or extended for other applications.

- Standard Packet: Packet contains the task container of surrounding vehicles. It is sent from ARM processor to µB.
- Extended Packet[1]: Besides the data of a standard packet, the extended packet contains additional information.
- Complete Packet: Packet is used to reallocate a task.
- Reference Standard Packet: Packet contains the task container of the reference vehicle. It distributes data within the Network.
- Reference Extended Packet[1]: Besides the data of a reference standard packet, the reference extended packet contains additional information.
- Reference Standard Broadcast Packet: Packet containing a note to broadcast and the task container of the reference vehicle is sent from the ARM processor to a µB.
- Reference Extended Broadcast Packet[1]: Besides the data of a reference standard broadcast packet, the reference extended broadcast packet contains additional information.

---

[1] Not used in the context of this paper.

Data-packets are divided into packets containing either task containers of reference vehicles or surrounding vehicles. Besides the content of the task container, further data can be sent by an extended packet. When a task is moved to another processor, the complete information about the task is transmitted by a complete packet. Moreover, the ARM processor supports broadcasting of a packet, which includes the task container of the reference vehicle and, if necessary, further data. As mentioned, the second type of packet is called control-packet. This packet subdivides data for transmission of status information, requests and control information. The size of this packet amounts the minimum number of flits for a message. It consists of a header flit which includes an identifier and a tail flit. The identifier specifies the packet type. The packet can be extended for further applications.

## 4.4   Data Processing by Microblazes

The processing of the task is performed by µBs. To facilitate this, each µB contains the same software framework. Due to the limited memory resources of the µBs, the lightweight operating system Xilkernel [16] is utilized. It provides functions such as the use of threads. Two separate threads are launched within the program. The computation of the tasks is executed by *calc_thread()*. Furthermore, *receive_thread()* takes care about the receiving of messages. In order to enable a rapid computation of the tasks, all calculations are executed with fixed-point numbers, as is this faster and provides a sufficient accuracy for the target application. *Receive_thread()* receives incoming packets and determines the type of the packet. In case of control-packets, the thread analyzes the packet to determine the action requested. An action may (re-) initialize the µB, reallocate or delete a task. In case of data-packets, it is stored with a new index in the data memory. Thus, a unique assignment is facilitated by the index. The maximum number of tasks running on a single µB is configurable. The presented implementation manages 30 tasks. This number is determined based on several program runs and sufficient to process the realistic data of the car simulator. Incoming data of an index already existing is postponed to the history of this data. The current implementation can store one additional data packet. However, this is also configurable. This means that in case of the automotive application two data sets of the same vehicle can be stored. Furthermore, data of the reference vehicle is broadcasted over the NoC. For this purpose, a predefined µB receives the data and subsequently, broadcast them to remaining µBs. A function is implemented which examines if unprocessed data is available and returns the data with the highest priority in every iteration. If priorities are equal, the data is returned depending on the order of incoming data. In order to distinguish between processed and unprocessed data, a label is available inside the task container. The processing of data is application-specific. Taking the proposed automotive application, collisions of vehicles are prevented. Hence, the risk of an accident must be determined by a strategy. To detect an impending accident, two cases are distinguished. On the one hand, vehicles are driving quasi-parallel independent from the direction of travel. On the other hand, the trajectories of vehicles approximated by a line intersect at an angle which is greater than 5 degrees. Based on these considerations, a µB which predicts an impending collision sends a warning to the ARM processor. This message leads the ARM processor to slow down the vehicle. Fig. 5a depicts the reference vehicle $f_R$ and a surrounding vehicle $f_i$ with quasi-parallel trajectories. The distance between these lines is calculated by Eq. 5. The approximation of the lines results from the difference $(dist_{i,x}, dist_{i,z})$ of the current coordinates $(x_i(k), z_i(k))$ and the coordinates $(x_i(k-1), z_i(k-1))$ given by the previous iteration.

$$(dist_{axial,2})^2 = \frac{(dist_{i,x}[z_i(k-1)-z_R(k)]-dist_{i,z}[x_i(k-1)-x_R(k)])^2}{dist_{i,x}^2+dist_{i,z}^2} \tag{5}$$

A distance between these trajectories, which is smaller than a threshold value, initiates to check whether the vehicles are approaching each other. If both cars drive in the same direction, the following condition must be fulfilled to start the slowing-down process of the vehicle.

$$v_{rel} = v_R - v_i > 0 \tag{6}$$

$$v^2_{rel} > dist_{i,R}^2 - dist_{sec}^2 - \frac{v_i^2}{2} \tag{7}$$

The velocity $v_{rel}$ describes the relative velocity between the cars. $dist_{sec}$ is a predefined security distance. The condition (8) is used for cars, which drive in opposite directions, to send a brake command.

$$dist_{i,R}^2 < v_i^2 + v_R^2 + dist_{sec}^2 \tag{8}$$

An example for two trajectories of cars intersecting at an angle which is greater than 5 degree is shown in Fig. 5b. In this case, the intersection point is calculated by means of Eq. 9 at first.

$$s^2 = 100 \, \frac{[-dist_{R,z}(x_R(k-1)-x_i(k-1))+dist_{R,x}(z_R(k-1)-z_i(k-1))]^2}{dist_{R,x} \cdot dist_{i,x}-dist_{i,z} \cdot dist_{R,z}} \tag{9}$$

$$t^2 = 100 \, \frac{[-dist_{i,z}(x_R(k-1)-x_i(k-1))+dist_{i,x}(z_R(k-1)-z_i(k-1))]^2}{dist_{R,x} \cdot dist_{i,x}-dist_{i,z} \cdot dist_{R,z}} \tag{10}$$

The stretch factor s represents the number of iterations until the reference vehicle reaches the intersection point. By analogy, the stretch factor t depicts the number of iterations of the surrounding car. $t_R$ and $t_i$ describe the respective time interval. In order to predict an initiating collision, the equation (11) gives a sufficient condition.

$$\frac{t_R \, t^2}{t_i \, s^2} \approx 1 \tag{11}$$

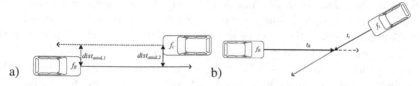

a)                                                                              b)

**Fig. 5.** Distance calculation (quasi-parallel vehicles (a) and non-parallel vehicles (b))

### 4.5    Data Processing by the ARM Processor

Messages sent by the µBs to the ARM processor are divided in information for the task allocation and the car simulator interface. Each type of message is transmitted via a separate port to the ARM processor. Possible messages for the task allocation are information, warnings, errors and requests, such as adapting the priority or reallocation of a task. An information message can be used to realize a UART output of the µBs. In this automotive application, the car simulator processes only requests regarding a slowing-down process of the vehicle. However, the interface can also be extended or adapted for other applications.

## 5    Evaluation and Results

The performance of the algorithms for dynamic task allocation is estimated through empiric time measurements. As the performance measurement is always a snapshot of the surroundings, it is impossible to reproduce exactly the same conditions. The significance of data is therefore given by the central limit theorem of stochastic processes.The response time of the system is a feasible definition in the context of automotive applications. It is obvious that approximately 90% of execution time is needed for the data acquisition in Fig. 6. Considering the time delay between transmission of the brake command and response of the car simulator, a ratio of 20:1 is the result. For meaningful results of the task allocation algorithms, the time needed for data acquisition is excluded in the following. Thus, the performance is defined as the difference between the beginning of the task allocation and the receipt of the brake command (step 2 to 4).

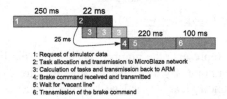

1: Request of simulator data
2: Task allocation and transmission to MicroBlaze network
3: Calculation of tasks and transmission back to ARM
4: Brake command received and transmitted
5: Wait for "vacant line"
6: Transmission of the brake command

**Fig. 6.** Performance of the dynamic task allocation

Initial measurements result in nearly the same response times for all algorithms. Neither the execution time of the heuristics, nor the calculation on the µB processors influences the overall response time significantly. On average, the response time and therefore the independent time constant of the network amounts to 20 milliseconds. Clearly recognizable is the accurate task management, as shown in Table 1. Tasks are specified by a Task ID, the respective time and priority are listed in the tables. Each task represents the data of one vehicle. By using all cores, a similar result for the distance heuristic is given for a high number of tasks. Prioritization has almost no effect for less than ten tasks, as each core handles only one task. Table 2 presents the results. First come first serve results in a congruent behavior for both distribution algorithms. To get significant results anyhow, additional measurement series are recorded. By using a *sleep()* command, the execution time of the μB processors is artificially increased. It can therefore be compared to the processing of complex calculations. It is important that the time constant of the network, which is independent from the data volume, is not changed anyhow. As shown in Table 3, the prioritized processing results in significantly faster reactions compared to the trivial "first come first served" approach. Due to the *sleep()* command, a simulated processing time of 3 milliseconds is added. While brake commands are mostly handled with the highest priority by the sector heuristic, using the distance heuristic results in some cases in occurrences as shown in Table 4. The grey row indicates a task that triggers a brake action. Although the heuristic is active, the task is handled with a relatively low priority. It is nevertheless obvious, that the supposed inaccurate heuristic decreases the response time by 6 milliseconds compared to the sector heuristic in this specific case. Due to the strict constraints of the car simulator regarding the number of cars, it is not possible to utilize the μB network to capacity with the used mathematic functions.

**Table 1.** Execution time for the sector heuristic and minimal number of cores (1 iteration)

| Task ID | 48 | 25 | 117 | 152 | 47 | 119 | 26 |
|---|---|---|---|---|---|---|---|
| Priority | 1 | 1 | 2 | 3 | 9 | 10 | 10 |
| Time [ms] | 20 | 20 | 20 | 21 | 21 | 21 | 21 |

**Table 2.** Execution time for the distance heuristic and maximum number of cores (1 iteration)

| Task ID | 1 | 3 | 10 | 20 | 26 | 35 |
|---|---|---|---|---|---|---|
| Priority | 10 | 2 | 1 | 9 | 4 | 9 |
| Time [ms] | 20 | 20 | 20 | 20 | 20 | 21 |

**Table 3.** Time measurement for the sector heuristic, minimal number of cores and *sleep()* command (1 iteration)

| Task ID | 10 | 35 | 119 | 26 | 19 | 48 | 3 | 117 | 29 |
|---|---|---|---|---|---|---|---|---|---|
| Priority | 1 | 3 | 3 | 4 | 9 | 10 | 10 | 10 | 10 |
| Time [ms] | 20 | 24 | 27 | 30 | 33 | 37 | 40 | 44 | 48 |

**Table 4.** Time measurement for the distance heuristic, minimal number of cores and *sleep()* command (1 iteration)

| Task ID | 25 | 32 | 26 | 48 | 38 | 19 | 1 | 27 |
|---|---|---|---|---|---|---|---|---|
| Priority | 1 | 1 | 3 | 3 | 5 | 7 | 7 | 9 |
| Time [ms] | 21 | 24 | 28 | 31 | 34 | 38 | 41 | 47 |

## 6 Conclusion and Future Prospects

A software framework for dynamic task allocation on MPSoCs has been presented and evaluated in an automotive context. Tasks, mapped by an ARM processor, were distributed onto a μB network by several strategies. The presented application targets a collision avoidance algorithm that uses the Euclidean distance of vehicles to esti-mate a priority of appropriate reactions. Amongst the Euclidean distance, a sector based heuristic that is specialized for the automotive application, has also been pre-sented. Additionally a "first come first serve" methodology has been implemented that processes task independently from any heuristic. The approach exploits the scala-bility and simplifies the programming and efficient use of MPSoCs. In the near future, dynamic partial reconfiguration will be implemented to add or remove PEs at runtime.

# References

1. Baloukas, C., Papadopoulos, L., Soudris, D., et al.: Mapping embedded applications on MPSoCs: the MNEMEE approach. In: IEEE Computer Society Annual Symposium on VLSI, pp. 512–517 (July 2010)
2. Pasricha, S., Dutt, N.: On-Chip Communication Architectures. Morgan Kaufmann Pub-lishers (2008)
3. Singh, A.K., Shafique, M., Kumar, A., Henkel, J.: Mapping on multi/many-core systems: survey of current and emerging trends. In: DAC, pp. 1–10 (May-June 2013)
4. Carvalho, E., Marcon, C., Calazans, N., Moraes, F.: Evaluation of static and dynamic task mapping algorithms in NoC-based MPSoCs. In: SoC 2009 (2009)
5. Moreriam, O., Mol, J.J.-D., Bekooij, M.: Online resource management in a multiprocessor with a network-on-chip. In: SAC, pp. 1557–1564 (2007)
6. Hong, S., Narayanan, S.H.K., Kandemir, M., Özturk, O.: Process variation aware thread mapping for chip multiprocessors. In DATE, pp. 821–826 (2009)
7. Ngouangal, A., Sassatelli, G., Torres, L., Gil, T., Soares, A., Susin, A.: A contextual re-sources use: a proof of concept through the APACHES' platform. In: DDECS, pp. 42–47 (April 2006)
8. Chou, C.-L., Marculescu, R.: User-Aware dynamic task allocation in networks-on-chip. In: DATE, pp. 1232–1237 (March 2008)
9. Liu, Y., Zhang, X., Li, H., Qian, D.: Allocating tasks in multi-core processor based parallel system. In: Network and Parallel Computing Workshops, NPC Workshops, pp. 748–753 (September. 2007)
10. Wildermann, S., Ziermann, T., Teich, J.: Run time mapping of adaptive applications onto homogeneous NoC-based reconfigurable architectures. In: FPT, pp. 514–517 (December 2009)
11. Foerst GmbH, Programming Tool Reference (2012). www.driving-simulators.eu
12. Xilinx Inc., ZC706 Evaluation Board for the Zynq-7000 XC7Z045 All Programmable SoC, UG954 (2013). www.xilinx.com
13. Rettkowski, J., Goehringer, D.: RAR-NoC: A reconfigurable and adaptive routable net-work-on-chip for FPGA-based multiprocessor systems. In: International Conference on ReConFigurable Computing and FPGAs (ReConFig) (December 2014)
14. Car 2 Car Communication Consortium, C2C-CC Manifesto (August 2007). www.car-2-car.org
15. Franklin, W.R.: PNPOLY - Point Inclusion in Polygon Test. www.ecse.rpi.edu
16. Xilinx Inc., Xilkernel, EDK 9.1i (December 2006). www.xilinx.com

# A Dynamically Reconfigurable Mixed Analog-Digital Filter Bank

Hiroki Nakahara[1]($\boxtimes$), Hideki Yoshida[2], Shin-ich Shioya[2],
Renji Mikami[3], and Tsutomu Sasao[4]

[1] Ehime University, Matsuyama, Japan
nakahara@cs.ehime-u.ac.jp
[2] Kagoshima University, Kagoshima, Japan
[3] Cypress Corp., Chiba, Japan
[4] Meiji University, Tokyo, Japan

**Abstract.** A cochlea filter bank for an audible frequency range is used for an acoustic diagnosis, which detects defects of the outer wall. However, a straightforward implementation of a cochlea filter bank by conventional FIR filters uses a large number of taps. Thus, it requires a large amount of hardware. This paper proposes two methods to reduce the amount of hardware. The first one is to use a mixed analog-digital filter, which reduces the number of taps of the FIR filter. The second one is to apply a dynamic reconfiguration which reduces the number of filter banks. We implemented the filter bank by the PSoC1 and the Spartan 6 FPGA. Experimental results shows that the number of taps for the proposed one is reduced by 99.1% from a straightforward realization. Implementation of the acoustic diagnostic system shows the usefulness of the proposed one.

## 1 Introduction

### 1.1 Acoustic Diagnosis of Outer Walls

An acoustic diagnosis detects defects[1] of outer walls. Troubleshooters knock at the outer wall by hammers to observe reverberating sound. And, they check if they have defects or not. In Japan, since diagnosis of outer walls of public structures is requested by the government, social demands for diagnosis are growing. An acoustic diagnosis has an advantage to ensure the safety of structures without destruction. However, its disadvantage is that the proficiency of the expert troubleshooters is required and their decisions are based on past experience. Recently, with the advance of the computer technology, expert systems have been practically used. Fig. 1 shows an acoustic diagnostic system. A reverberating sound is collected by a microphone. Since the diagnostic part requires a large amount of signal processing (complicated filtering), the diagnosis is often performed by an off-line PC. However, real time (on-line) computation is desired.

---

[1] For example, cracking of the outer wall, peeling of interior finish, or a water leakage due to rain.

© Springer International Publishing Switzerland 2015
K. Sano et al. (Eds.): ARC 2015, LNCS 9040, pp. 267–279, 2015.
DOI: 10.1007/978-3-319-16214-0_22

**Fig. 1.** Acoustic diagnostic system

Furthermore, a diagnostic system should be implemented by inexpensive devices. Since a diagnosis is performed at outer walls or tunnels all days, a lightweight and battery-powered system is desired.

## 1.2 Cochlea Filter Bank for Audible Frequency Range

The auditory portion of the inner ear is called the *cochlea*. It can distinguish band-limited waves [2]. From psychological experiments, the cochlea feature was modeled as a filter bank [12]. Various applications using cochlea filter banks have been reported: They recognize footsteps [6], hand claps [14], percussive sound [8], and engine noise of a car [3]. In general, a cochlea filter bank requires many taps. When a cochlea filter bank is realized by conventional digital filters, the amount of hardware tends to be large [17].

## 1.3 Related Works

The first implementation of a cochlea filter bank consists of 24 filters [20]. To the best of our knowledge, the most accurate cochlea implementation uses 1400 banks [5]. We proposed a cochlea filter bank for an audible frequency range consisting of 10 filters [17].

Various compact digital filters have been proposed: An infinite impulse response (IIR) filter with a dual fixed-points representation [16]; a finite impulse response (FIR) filter consisting of only on-chip memories [15]; an FIR filter with a dynamically changing sampling clock frequency [11]; and a dynamically reconfigurable FIR filter [10].

Programmable analog circuits have been proposed as follows: A mixed analog-digital programmable circuit [4]; and a filter on a field programmable analog array (FPAA) [1].

## 1.4 Contributions of the Paper

In general, a cochlea filter bank tends to require a large number of taps. Since the conventional realization used only digital filters (FIR or IIR filters), a large amount of hardware is required. This paper proposes a dynamically reconfigurable mixed analog-digital filter, which requires fewer taps. The combination of the proposed technique and conventional filters will reduce the amount of hardware. Our contributions are:

**Proposed a mixed analog-digital filter and implemented it:** An analog filter is a compact, while its roll-off characteristic is bad. On the other hand,

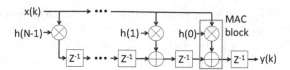

**Fig. 2.** FIR filter (straightforward realization)

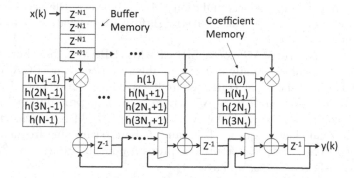

**Fig. 3.** FIR filter (transpose multi-MAC realization)

a digital filter tends to require a large amount of hardware, while its roll-off characteristic is good. The mixed analog-digital filter is compact and has good roll-off characteristic. We realized a mixed filter by the PSoC1 and the FPGA.

**Proposed a dynamically reconfigurable mixed filter:** It dynamically changes the filter characteristic to make the circuit compact.

**Applied to an acoustic diagnostic system:** We observe a syndrome of a reverberating sound to diagnose. Since the proposed system consists of a PSoC1 and a small FPGA (Spartan 6), it can be embedded into a pole of a hammer. Also, since the proposed system consumes a small amount of power, it can be operated by a battery to be used at outdoors.

### 1.5  Organization of the Paper

The rest of the paper is organized as follows: Chapter 2 introduces a cochlea filter bank; Chapter 3 shows a mixed analog-digital filter bank; Chapter 4 shows a dynamically reconfigurable filter bank; Chapter 5 shows experimental results; and Chapter 6 concludes the paper.

## 2  Cochlea Filter Bank by FIR Filters

### 2.1  FIR Filter

**A finite impulse response (FIR) filter** computes

$$y(k) = \sum_{i=0}^{N-1} h(i)x(k - i), \tag{1}$$

where $N$ denotes the number of **taps**, $h(i)$ denotes a **filter coefficient**, $x(k)$ denotes an input value $X$ at the time $k$, $y(k)$ denotes an output value $Y$ at the time $k$, and $k = 0, 1, \ldots$ We also assume that all the values are represented by $q$-bit fixed point binary numbers. Fig. 2 shows a straightforward realization of an FIR filter, where $z^{-1}$ denotes a delay element realized by a $q$-bit register. This realization requires $N$ registers of $q$-bit, $N$ adders, and $N$ multipliers. Since a modern FPGA has multiply-accumulation (MAC) blocks [2], the necessary number of MAC blocks is $N$. Note that, the straightforward realization is impractical for a large number of $N$.

An FPGA consists of MAC blocks, block RAMs (BRAMs), distributed RAMs, and flip-flops. We will maximally utilize available resource of an FPGA to realize the FIR filter. Fig. 3 shows the transpose multi-MAC realization of an FIR filter. Consider a decomposition $N = N_1 N_2$, where $N_1$ is **the parallelization**. This architecture computes Expr. (1) by $N_2$ steps using $N_1$ MAC blocks. Let $f_{sys}$ be the operational clock frequency [Hz], and $f_s$ be the sampling frequency [Hz]. For every $\frac{1}{f_s}$ second, this architecture computes $N_2$ output values until $N_1$ input values are transferred. Thus, we have

$$\frac{N_2}{f_{sys}} \leq \frac{1}{f_s}.$$

From this, we have

$$N_1 = \left\lceil \sqrt{\frac{f_s}{f_{sys}} N} \right\rceil. \tag{2}$$

This architecture uses $N_1$ MAC blocks and $N_1 q \times N_2 = Nq$ bit memory. Therefore, the reduction of the number of taps $N$ will reduce the amount of hardware. This paper considers the reduction of $N$.

## 2.2  Cochlea Filter Bank Using FIR Filters

Fig. 4 shows a cochlea filter bank consisting of 10 filters for audible frequency range (20-20,480 [Hz]) [17]. Each filter supports an octave. Previous research showed that, pitch, loudness and timbre of complex sounds can be reconstructed by both the maximal and the minimal of filtered waveforms [19]. Since the filter bank requires more computation than the detection part of the maximal and the minimal [18], we focus on the filter bank. Fig. 4 shows the frequency characteristic of the FIR filter bank realizing the cochlea filter bank for an audible frequency range. In the lower frequency bands, since a sharp cut-off characteristic is required, the number of taps is [17]:

$$N' \simeq \frac{f_s}{f_B} \times 2, \tag{3}$$

---

[2] The Xilinx Spartan 6 FPGA has DSP48A blocks.

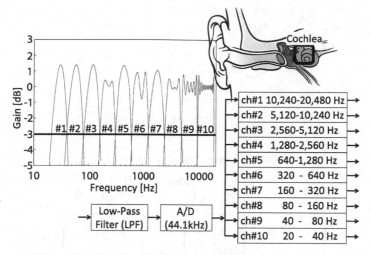

**Fig. 4.** Cochlea filter bank for audible frequency range [17]

where $f_s$ denotes the sampling frequency, and $f_B$ denotes the pass bandwidth for each filter bank. Table 1 shows lower center, and upper cut-off frequencies and the numbers of taps of the FIR filter. Table 1 shows that the direct realization of cochlea filter banks requires a large amount of hardware.

**Table 1.** Pass bandwidth and the number of taps of an FIR filter bank [17]

| ch# | lower cut-off freq.[Hz] | center freq.[Hz] | upper cut-off freq.[Hz] | # of taps |
|---|---|---|---|---|
| 1 | 10,240 | 14,482 | 20,480 | 89 |
| 2 | 5,120 | 7,241 | 10,240 | 89 |
| 3 | 2,560 | 3,620 | 5,120 | 89 |
| 4 | 1,280 | 1,810 | 2,560 | 89 |
| 5 | 640 | 905 | 1,280 | 295 |
| 6 | 320 | 453 | 640 | 295 |
| 7 | 160 | 226 | 320 | 883 |
| 8 | 80 | 113 | 160 | 1,103 |
| 9 | 40 | 57 | 80 | 2,205 |
| 10 | 20 | 28 | 40 | 4,409 |

# 3 Mixed Analog-Digital Filter Bank

## 3.1 PSoC1 Architecture

Fig. 5 shows an architecture of Cypress Inc. PSoC1 (Programmable System-on-Chip) [13]. The PSoC1 consists of programmable digital blocks and analog blocks. A digital block can be configured to be a timer, a counter, a PWM, or an UART, while an analog block can be configured to be a filter, an AD converter, a DA converter, or an amplifier. An analog block of the PSoC1 has an opamp circuit. It is roughly divided into three blocks: an analog switched capacitor

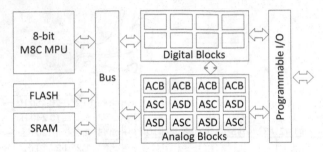

**Fig. 5.** Architecture for a PSoC1

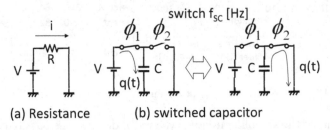

(a) Resistance          (b) switched capacitor

**Fig. 6.** Principle of an equivalent resistance using a switched capacitor

type C (ASC) block, an analog switched capacitor type D (ASD) block, and an analog continuous time type B (ACB) block. Both ASC and ASD blocks have **a switched capacitor block** which can be configured to be a programmable equivalent resistance. Fig. 6 shows a principle of an equivalent resistance using a switched capacitor. The current $i$ flows from the power source $V$ to the ground through the resistance $R$ (Fig. 6 (a)). Then, we have

$$R = \frac{V}{i}. \tag{4}$$

Suppose that the switched capacitor has two switches $\phi_1$ and $\phi_2$ (Fig. 6 (b)). When $\phi_1$ is closed and $\phi_2$ is opened, the capacitor $C$ stores charge $q$ as follows:

$$q = CV. \tag{5}$$

When $\phi_1$ is opened and $\phi_2$ is closed, the stored charge $q$ is discharged to the ground node. By switching back and forth of $\phi_1$ and $\phi_2$, the charge $q$ is moved from the power source to the ground. Thus, it can be considered as the equivalent current. Let $t_{SC}$ be switching period of the switched capacitor. Then, **the switching frequency** $f_{SC}$ is $\frac{1}{t_{SC}}$. The equivalent current of the continuous switching is $i = \frac{q}{t_{SC}} = q f_{SC}$. Expr. (5) shows that we have $i = CV \cdot f_{SC}$. Expr. (4) shows that the equivalent resistance $R_{SC}$ for the switched capacitor is

$$R_{SC} = \frac{1}{C \cdot f_{SC}}. \tag{6}$$

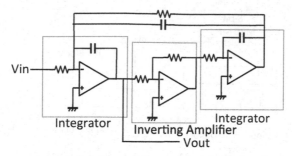

**Fig. 7.** Bi-quad band-pass filter

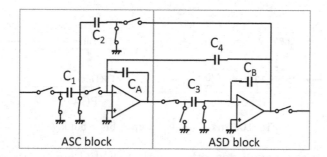

**Fig. 8.** Two-pole band-pass filter

From Expr. (6), the equivalent resistance is inversely proportional to $C$ and $f_{SC}$. In the PSoC1, the capacitor $C$ can be changed by a program. Since switches $\phi_1$ and $\phi_2$ cannot be opened or closed simultaneously, we cannot use high frequency $f_{SC}$ [3].

### 3.2 Realization of a Band-Pass Filter on a PSoC1 [13]

Fig. 7 shows a bi-quad band-pass filter. It consists of two integrators and one inverting amplifier. We can replace the resistance with the switched capacitor. If we reverse the switching timing, the output polarity is reversed. Thus, the center inverting amplifier can be replaced by the reversed switching capacitor. Fig. 8 shows **a two-pole band-pass filter (2pBPF)** consisting of two analog blocks. Let $f_c$ be the center frequency, and $Q$ be the quality factor. Then, we have

$$f_c = \frac{1}{2\pi} \frac{f_{SC}}{\sqrt{\frac{C_A C_B}{C_2 C_3} - \frac{1}{4} - \frac{C_4}{2C_2}}}, \tag{7}$$

$$Q = \frac{f_c}{f_B} = \frac{C_2}{C_4} \sqrt{\frac{C_A C_B}{C_2 C_3} - \frac{1}{4} - \frac{C_4}{2C_2}}, \tag{8}$$

---

[3] In the PSoC1, the capacitance can be configured with multiple of 0.05 [pF]. The maximum $f_{SC}$ is 2 [MHz].

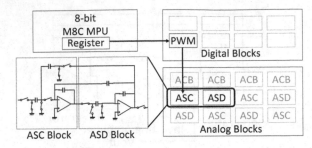

**Fig. 9.** Realization of a two-pole band-pass filter (2p-BPF) on a PSoC1

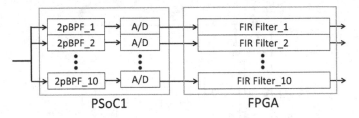

**Fig. 10.** Mixed analog-digital filter bank

where $f_B$ denotes a pass bandwidth [4]. Both $f_c$ and $Q$ are determined by $f_{SC}$ and the capacitances. Fig. 9 shows a realization of the 2pBPF on the PSoC1. As shown in Fig. 9, the 2pBPF requires two analog blocks and one digital block generating a switching clock with a period of $\frac{1}{f_{SC}}$.

### 3.3  Mixed Analog-Digital Filter Bank

Fig. 10 shows a mixed analog-digital filter bank. In the PSoC1, since the roll-off characteristic of the 2pBPF (analog filter) is poor, it is used as a noise elimination filter. On the other hand, since the roll-off characteristic of the FIR filter (digital filter) is good, it is used as a cochlea filter. Expr. (3) shows that the number of taps is proportional to the sampling frequency $f_s$. The 2pBPF which removes the unnecessary frequency component also reduces $f_s$. Thus, the mixed filter can reduce the number of taps in the FIR filter.

## 4    Dynamically Reconfigurable Filter Bank for an Acoustic Diagnostic System

### 4.1  Dynamically Reconfigurable Filter

Expr. (7) shows that, when the capacitances are fixed, $f_c$ is proportional to $f_{SC}$. Expr. (8) shows that, $\frac{f_c}{f_B}$ is constant. Thus, $f_B$ is also proportional to $f_{SC}$. As shown in Fig. 9, $f_{SC}$ can be changed by rewriting the register of the

---

[4] We assume that the pass band width is the difference of frequencies at 3 [dB] attenuation.

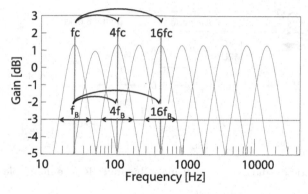

**Fig. 11.** Frequency characteristic of a dynamically reconfigurable analog band-pass filter on a PSoC1

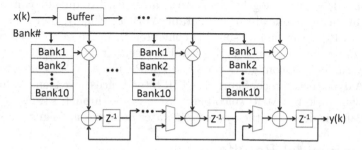

**Fig. 12.** Dynamically reconfigurable FIR filter

M8C MPU. Therefore, we can dynamically change the frequency characteristic at a high speed. Fig. 11 shows the frequency characteristic for the dynamically reconfigurable p2BPF on the PSoC1. As for the filter for a channel #1, its lower cut-off frequency $f_l$ is 20 [Hz] and its upper one $f_u$ is 40 [Hz]. In this case, the center frequency $f_c$ is $\sqrt{f_l f_u} = 28.8$ [Hz]. We configured each capacitance and $f_{SC}$ to cover $f_B$ (20 [Hz] to 40 [Hz]). The increase of $f_{SC}$ to $p \times f_{SC}$ also increases $f_c$ and $f_B$ to $p \times f_c$ and $p \times f_B$, respectively. Thus, the dynamically reconfigurable p2BPF efficiently realizes the octave divided filter bank shown in Fig. 4

Fig. 12 shows a dynamically reconfigurable FIR filter based on the transpose multi-MAC shown in Fig. 3. It changes the frequency characteristic by changing the coefficients corresponding to the bank number ($Bank\#$).

## 4.2   Application to an Acoustic Diagnostic System

Fig. 13 shows an acoustic diagnostic system using a dynamically reconfigurable mixed analog-digital filter bank. It emulates the filter bank shown in Fig. 4 by executing each channel sequentially. First, the microphone collects a reverberating sound. Second, it is transferred to the PSoC1 through the DC cut capacitor. The OpAmp for the PSoC1 is driven by a single power supply, and cannot handle the negative voltage. We use an analog block to generate a bias voltage (AGND:

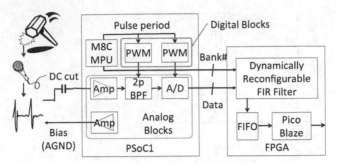

**Fig. 13.** Acoustic diagnostic system using a dynamically reconfigurable mixed filter

analog GND). Thus, the PSoC1 handles the positively biased voltage. Third, it is amplified by an analog block. Fourth, an unused frequency component is removed by the dynamically reconfigurable 2pBPF. Finally, digitized signal is sent to the FPGA through a 8-bit AD converter [5]. At the same time, the bank number (*Bank #*) and the enable signal are sent from the M8C MPU. The PSoC1 dynamically reconfigures both the 2pBPF and the AD converter, while the FPGA dynamically reconfigures the FIR filter. Since the extreme value detection is a light task, the MPU (pico blaze) executes it through FIFOs. When the extreme value is detected, the system generates an abnormal signal.

## 5    Experimental Results

### 5.1    Implementation Environment

We implemented the dynamically reconfigurable mixed analog-digital filter on Cypress Inc. PSoC1 (CY8C27443-24PXI: 8 digital blocks, 12 analog blocks, and 24 MHz internal clock frequency) and e-Trees Inc. exStick board (FPGA: Xilinx Inc. Spartan 6 (XC6SLX16-2CSG225C)) [7]. As for the design of the 2pBPF, we used Cypress Inc. PSoC filter design wizard. To generate coefficients for the FIR filter, we used MathWorks Inc. MATLAB and Xilinx Inc. FIR compiler. We realized the FIR filter with a rectangle window function and 18-bit fixed binary point numbers.

### 5.2    Implementation Results

Table 2 shows the lower and upper cut-off frequencies and the number of taps for the mixed analog-digital filter bank which emulates a cochlea for acoustic frequency ranges. Since we cannot decrease the sampling frequency for the high frequency band, the maximum number of taps is 89 for the filter bank #10. To make the design simple, rather than to reduce hardware, the numbers of taps for the filters are set to 89. Table 1 shows that the direct FIR filter realization requires 9,546 taps, while Table 2 shows that the mixed analog-digital filter

---

[5] Since the PSoC1 supports up to a 8-bit AD converter with an interrupt, we adopt it.

**Table 2.** Lower and upper cut-off frequencies and the number of taps for the mixed analog-digital filter

| ch# | Analog | | | A/D $f_s$ | Digital | | | # of taps |
|---|---|---|---|---|---|---|---|---|
| | lower [Hz] | center [Hz] | upper [Hz] | [kHz] | lower [Hz] | center [Hz] | upper [Hz] | |
| 1 | 17 | 27 | 42 | 0.89 | 20 | 28 | 40 | 89 |
| 2 | 34 | 54 | 85 | 1.78 | 40 | 57 | 80 | 89 |
| 3 | 68 | 108 | 171 | 3.56 | 80 | 113 | 160 | 89 |
| 4 | 136 | 216 | 342 | 7.12 | 160 | 226 | 320 | 89 |
| 5 | 282 | 439 | 682 | 14.24 | 320 | 453 | 640 | 89 |
| 6 | 543 | 861 | 1,364 | 28.48 | 640 | 905 | 1,280 | 89 |
| 7 | 1,086 | 1,721 | 2,726 | 44.10 | 1,280 | 1,810 | 2,560 | 89 |
| 8 | 2,173 | 3,442 | 5,452 | 44.10 | 2,560 | 3,620 | 5,120 | 89 |
| 9 | 4,514 | 7,150 | 11,324 | 44.10 | 5,120 | 7,241 | 10,240 | 89 |
| 10 | 8,695 | 13,771 | 21,810 | 44.10 | 10,240 | 14,482 | 20,480 | 89 |

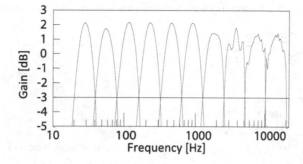

**Fig. 14.** Frequency characteristic for the mixed analog-digital filter bank

realization requires only 890 taps. Since the single dynamically reconfigurable filter bank emulates 10 banks, the total number of taps is only 89. Thus, the proposed one reduces the number of taps by 99.1%. Fig. 14 shows the frequency characteristic for the mixed analog-digital dynamically reconfigurable filter bank. The proposed one realizes the pass band characteristic which is similar to the original filter bank shown in Fig. 4.

### 5.3 Comparison of Used Resource

Table 3 compares used resource. Since the exStick board has 25 [MHz] clock source, we set to $f_{sys} = 25 \times 10^6$ [Hz]. We set the system sampling clock frequency $f_s$ to $44.1 \times 10^3$ [Hz]. We obtain $N_1$ from Expr. (2). Compared with the direct FIR filter realization (*FIR only*), although the proposed dynamically reconfigurable filter realization (*Dyn. Recf.*) uses more analog blocks, it drastically reduces the FPGA resource. Compared with the non-dynamically reconfigurable mixed filter realization (*Mixed*), it reduces both the PSoC1 and FPGA resources. Thus, the proposed one is suitable for a low-cost FPGA realization.

### 5.4 Implementation of an Acoustic Diagnostic System

We embedded the proposed mixed analog-digital filter bank on the acoustic diagnostic system shown in Fig. 15. We used the "Kororin" diagnostic stick [9]

**Table 3.** Comparison of used resource

| Filter bank realization | # taps N | N₁ | FPGA Resource DSP48A #Blks | Memory [bits] | PSoC1 Resource Analog #Blks | Digital #Blks |
|---|---|---|---|---|---|---|
| FIR only | 9,546 | 5 | 5 | 343,656 | 3 | 1 |
| Mixed | 890 | 2 | 2 | 32,040 | 50 | 20 |
| Dyn. Recf. | 89 | 1 | 1 | 3,204 | 5 | 2 |

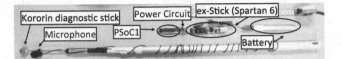

**Fig. 15.** Implemented acoustic diagnostic system on a stick

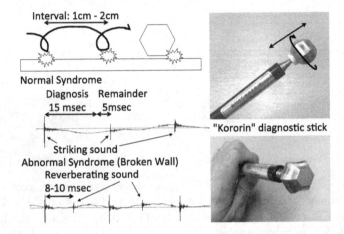

**Fig. 16.** Syndrome of a reverberating sound using the "Kororin" diagnostic stick

whose top has a hexagonal shape shown in Fig. 16. By rolling of the top, we collect reverberating sound every tens millisecond in a stable period. When the wall has an anomaly, a spike noise is observed after 10 millisecond by rolling the top. Since we take 15 millisecond for a margin, the remaining time is about 5 millisecond for the dynamic reconfiguration. The reconfiguration time for the PSoC1 is less than one millisecond, and its period is a short enough to receive the next reverberating sound. To emulate the filter bank, at least ten reconfigurations are necessary. The Kororin diagnostic stick can knock more than 10 times for tens centimeter interval. Thus, it is enough for the outer wall diagnosis.

# 6   Conclusion

In this paper, we proposed a mixed analog-digital dynamically reconfigurable filter bank to emulate a cochlea for an audible frequency range. To reduce the number of taps, we used a mixed analog-digital filter using both the PSoC1 and the FPGA. To reduce the number of filters, we used a dynamically reconfiguration technique. Compared with the direct FIR filter realization, the proposed one reduced the number of taps by 99.1%. We embedded the proposed acoustic diagnosis system to the PSoC1 and Spartan 6 FPGA.

# References

1. Becker, J., Manoli, Y.: Synthesis of analog filters on a continuous-time FPAA using a genetic algorithm. In: FPL 2006, pp. 1–4 (2006)
2. Bekesy, G.: Experiments in hearing. McGraw-Hill (1960)
3. Choe, H.C., Karlsen, R.E., Gerhert, G.R., Meitzler, T. : Wavelet-based ground vehicle recognition using acoustic signal. In: Wavelet Applications III, vol. 2762, pp. 434–445 (1996)
4. Chow, P., Chow, P., Gulak, P.G.: A field-programmable mixed-analog-digital array. In: FPGA 1995, pp. 104–109 (1995)
5. Deng, L., Geisler, C.D.: A composite auditory model for processing speech sounds. J. Acoust. Soc. Am. 82(2), 2001–2012 (1987)
6. Ekimov, A., Sabatier, J.M.: Vibration and sound signatures of human footsteps in buildings. J. Acoust. Soc. Am. 120, 762–768 (2006)
7. e-Trees.Japan Inc., exStick. http://e-trees.jp/
8. Freed, D.J.: Auditory correlates of perceived mallet hardness for a set of recorded percussive sound events. J. Acoust. Soc. Am. 87, 311–322 (1990)
9. Kuwaki Civil co. Ltd. http://www.k-civil.co.jp/
10. Llamocca, D., Pattichis, M.S., Vera, G.A.: Partial reconfigurable FIR filtering system using distributed arithmetic. Int. J. Reconfig. Comp., 1–14 (2010)
11. Martnez, J.J., Toledo, F.J., Garrigs, F.J., Vicente, J.M.F.: FPGA implementation of an area-time efficient FIR filter core using a self-clocked approach. In: FPL 2006, pp. 547–550 (2006)
12. Patterson, R.D.: Auditory filter shape. J. Acoust. Soc. Am. 55, 802–809 (1974)
13. Cypress Corp., PSoC Programmable System-on-Chip. http://www.cypress.com/?docID=45148
14. Repp, B.H.: The sound of two hands clapping: An exploratory study. J. Acoust. Soc. Am. 81(4), 1100–1109 (1987)
15. Sasao, T., Iguchi, Y., Suzuki, T.: On LUT cascade realizations of FIR filters. In: DSD 2005, pp. 467–474 (2005)
16. Wong, C.K., Leong, P.H.W.: An FPGA-based electronic cochlea with dual fixed-point arithmetic. In: FPL 2006, pp. 1–6 (2006)
17. Yoshida, H., Nakano, M., Yukimasa, T., Matsumura, S., Yokono, K., Hayama, Y.: Phase error reflects subjective sound quality. International Journal of BSCHS 16(1), 69–80 (2010)
18. Yoshida, H., Kakui, K., Maeda, Y., Fujiwara, Y.: Least-squares estimation of the extrema in the narrow-band music data. IJ-BSCHS 15(2), 85–91 (2010)
19. Yoshida, H., Kakui, K., Maeda, Y., Fujiwara, Y.: The adaptive extremal sampling based on a simple acoustic model, Bio-signals: Data acquisition, processing and control. IJ-BSCHS 14(2), 27–34 (2009)
20. Zwicker, E.: Uber psychologische und Methodische grundlagen der lautheit. Acustica 8, 237–258 (1958)

# The Effects of System Hyper Pipelining on Three Computational Benchmarks Using FPGAs

Tobias Strauch[(⊠)]

R&D EDAptix, Munich, Germany
tobias@edaptix.com

**Abstract.** C-Slow Retiming (CSR) generates concentric design clusters and improves the performance per area factor of a design by reusing the combinatorial logic in a time sliced fashion. The limitation of CSR is, that all C copies of the design have to be continuously executed. The paper proposes System Hyper Pipelining (SHP), which overcomes the limitations of CSR by adding thread stalling, bypassing and fork-join queueing techniques. The impact of SHP on multithreading and multiprocessing system is manifold. This paper concentrates on techniques to improve the performance of individual threads of SHP based CPUs. SHP is ideal for FPGAs with their high number of registers and their flexible memory usage. The paper compares standard implementations of CPUs with their CSR and SHP versions. Results based on three state-of-the-art 32-bit processors are shown.

**Keywords:** C-Slow Retiming · Symmetrical Multiprocessing · Multiprocessor Systems · Simultaneous Multithreading · NoCs

## 1   Introduction

Running complex software on a single processor can be very limited. Today's technologies to execute software on multiple processors or multithreading systems are very much advanced. Running software on networks-on-chip (NoCs), multiple processors or multithreading systems implemented on an FPGA gets more and more popular. The upcoming references [1..10] use FPGAs as their target technology. The discussed system architectures are already standard on ASICs.

NoCs technology applies networking theory and methods to on-chip communication. Abdelfattah et al. show in a recent publication [1], that FPGAs nowadays support high speed interfaces and on-chip data processing capabilities.

Symmetric Multiprocessing (SMP) systems are tightly coupled multiprocessor systems with a pool of homogeneous processors running independently. They have the capability to share common resources (memories, bus-systems, ...). With a proper operating system support, SMP systems can move tasks between processors to balance the workload efficiently. Matthews et al. show in [2] a multicore system with Linux SMP support. Vallina et al. discuss a similar environment with the emphasis on signal processing in [3]. In [4] Klimm et al. discuss the memory access of a multiprocessor system and its scalability, which is also an important element of the work of Wallentowitz et al. in [5]. How a multiprocessor system supports a bio-inspired robot is shown in [6] by Henrey et al..

© Springer International Publishing Switzerland 2015
K. Sano et al. (Eds.): ARC 2015, LNCS 9040, pp. 280–290, 2015.
DOI: 10.1007/978-3-319-16214-0_23

Simultaneous Multithreading (SMT) is a technique to improve the overall efficiency of superscalar CPUs with hardware multithreading. SMT permits the execution of multiple independent threads to better utilize the resources provided by modern processor architectures. A thread synchronization unit (or thread controller) is the essential element of such a technology, which is discussed by Lu et al. in [7], Tatas et al. in [8] and Labrecque et al. in [9] and [10].

C-Slow Retiming (CSR) provides C copies of a given design by inserting registers and reusing the combinatorial logic in a time sliced fashion. CSR therefore improves the performance per area factor. Leiserson et. al. introduced the concept of C-Slow Retiming (CSR) in [11]. CSR on netlists has been shown by Waver et al. in [12] and timing driven CSR on RTL by Strauch in [13]. In recent publications, CSR is used to maximize the throughput-area efficiency in [14] by Su et al., CSR is used on SMT-processors in [15] by Akram et al., and to improve performance in consumer image devices by Cadenas et al. in [16].

All C design copies have to be continuously executed, which is good for stream processing. Processors based on CSR are also called barrel processors. Nevertheless, parallel processing methods require a flexible number and a flexible execution order of threads to be run on a given multiprocessor or multithreading system. SMP and SMT solutions can be realized on CSR-ed designs [16]. In both cases, individual threads need to be stalled to be continued later (in case of a cache miss, for instance). It is of great benefit, when alternative threads can easily be executed during unused time slots to better utilize the design resources. This cannot be accomplished by designs using the standard CSR method.

This paper shows, how the limitations of CSR can be overcome by System Hyper Pipeline (SHP), which is a combination of C-Slow Retiming (CSR) and Parallel Processing (PP). SHP adds a higher flexibility to the pure CSR based multithreading. The number of active threads can range from zero active threads to a number of threads greater than C. Individual threads can be stalled, bypassed and reordered and therefore be executed at different speeds.

The goal of this paper is to explain SHP and to discuss the impact of SHP on various applications (mainly CPUs and MPSoC) as well as other aspects. It shows a case study of two processors implemented on an FPGA.

Section 2 explains the SHP technology. A thread controller to support SHP is proposed in section 3. Section 4 discusses various hardware related aspects and how the performance of individual threads in an SHP based processor environment is discussed in section 5. The paper finishes with result and conclusion sections.

## 2      CSR and SHP Technology

System Hyper Pipelining (SHP) is based on C-Slow Retiming (CSR). It enhances CSR with thread stalling, bypassing and reordering techniques by replacing the original registers of the design with memories and by adding a thread controller (TC). In the remainder of this paper, processors are used to demonstrate the SHP technology, but the method is not limited to processors. Nevertheless, the word "thread" is used synonym for the execution of a program or algorithm.

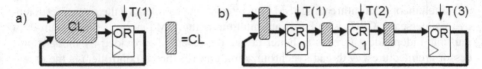

**Fig. 1.** a) Simplified single clock design. b) Applying CSR technique.

Figure 1a shows the basic structure of a sequential circuit with its inputs, outputs, combinatorial logic (CL) and original registers (OR). The sequential circuit handles one thread T(1). Figure 1b shows the CSR technique. The original logic is sliced into C (here C=3) sections, and each original path has now C-1 additional registers. This results in C functionally independent design copies T(C=1..3) which use the logic in a time sliced fashion. Each thread has its own thread index. For each design copy it now takes C micro-cycles to achieve the same result as in one cycle of the original design. The implemented register sets are called "CSR Registers", CRs. They are placed at different C-levels (CR0, CR1, ...).

$$\{CR0, CR1, OR\} = [\{T(1), T(2), T(3)\}, \{T(3), T(1), T(2)\}, \{T(2), T(3), T(1)\}] \qquad (1)$$

The sequence (1) shows how the complete design states (threads) traverse through the logic each cycle. There is no interaction between threads and each thread uses the complete design in a time sliced fashion. The modifications shown so far are very much understood and discussed in the literature [11-16]. Their fundamental understanding is required to follow the modifications towards the usage of SHP.

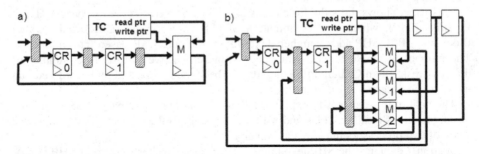

**Fig. 2.** a) SHP-ed design with thread controller, memories and less CRs. b) Advanced SHP.

Figure 2a shows the modifications of a CSR-ed design towards SHP. Assuming the ORs are now replaced by a memory (M). The incoming threads are stored at the relevant address (write pointer) based on the thread index. D is the number of threads which the memory can hold (memory depth). The outgoing thread can now be freely selected within D available threads (read pointer), except the threads already passing through the design logic.

$$\{CR0, CR1, M\} = [\{T(a), T(b), \{T(a), ..., T(p)\}\}, \{T(i), T(a), \{T(a), ..., T(p)\}\},$$
$$\{T(f), T(i), \{T(a), ..., T(p)\}\}] \qquad (2)$$

Equation (2) shows that an SHP-ed design can run any thread (T <= D) in any possible order. Same threads must not be executed at the same time.

A CSR-ed design has usually many shift registers. OR are followed by a series of CR registers. In the SHP-ed version, many memory data outputs are connected to CRs directly. In this case, the shift register chain at the outputs can be replaced by a register chain at the read address inputs of the memories. Figure 2b shows this advanced SHP version. The memory is sliced into individual sections (M0, M1, M2) and each section has a delayed read of the thread. The outputs can now be directly connected to the relevant combinatorial logic and the shift registers can be removed.

CSR has been formal proven in many publications [11]. Replacing a register with a memory or retiming a register from a memory output to the read address input has been proven in practice on many designs. The formal proof of SHP is therefore neglected.

$$Fcsr = Forig * C \tag{3}$$

$$0 <= T <= D \tag{4}$$

$$0 <= Ft <= Forig \tag{5}$$

$$Fshp = \Sigma\, Ft \tag{6}$$

The maximum frequency of the original design (Figure 1a) is defined as Forig and the maximum frequency of a CSR-ed design (Figure 1b) as Fcsr. Fscr depends on how many registers are inserted on the critical path. By generating C independent copies of the design, all running – theoretically – at Forig, Fcsr can be calculated as in (3). The maximal number of design copies is now defined by the memory depth D (and not by C). The design can now execute T individual threads (4), whereas the design states can now be stalled and the thread execution order can be freely selected. Threads can also run at much slower speeds (over a period of time) than Forig and can even be stalled (5). The maximal system frequency of an SHP-ed design Fshp is the sum of all individual active threads (6).

Pipelining techniques have been discussed throughout the last decades. Most numerous the pipelining of CPUs. In this sense, CSR and SHP are not necessarily pipelining methods with (register) inter-dependencies of different pipeline stages. Instead, they multiply the functionality of a design, whereas all threads are independent of each other. An already pipelined CPU can be simplified with Figure 1a, and CSR/SHP can still be applied on it (Figure 2b), without changing the behavior or pipeline stages of the original CPU. The only difference is, that it takes now C times as many cycles for a design state to pass through the combinatorial logic compared as to what can be achieved in a single cycle in the original design.

There are two key observations when SHP is used on a design. First, just like CSR, SHP can be applied automatically, which can be seen as a formal design transformation process. Weaver et al. show the usage of CSR on a post-placement netlist in [12]. Strauch shows in [13], how CSR can be applied on RTL. Compared to CSR, SHP additionally replaces the original registers with memories and adds a thread controller. This can also be done automatically.

Secondly, threads don't interact with each other. There is no register dependency between the individual threads. The runtime of each thread is therefore deterministic.

The variable latency that the execution per thread may experience due to different behavior in if-branches for instance is not an issue, because all threads work independent of each other.

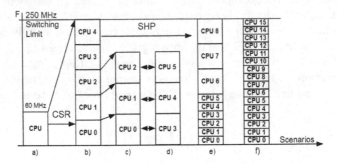

**Fig. 3.** Histogram of different scenarios (a-f) of running CSR and SHP

Figure 3 shows the advantages of CSR and SHP over the original design. The x-axis shows different scenarios. Assuming a single CPU runs at 60MHz on an FPGA (Figure 3a). It can be seen, how CSR improves the system performance of the original system implementation, (Figure 3b). When using CSR, the system performance is not necessarily limited by the critical path of the original design, but - for instance - by the switching limit of the FPGA (e.g. 250MHz) or the external memory access instead.

For executing multiple programs on multiple CPUs (symmetrical multi-processing), SHP allows a more efficient usage of the system resources (Figure 3b to 3f). It adds the possibility to distribute the system performance over a minimum (C, Figure 3b), and a maximum set of processors (D, Figure 3f), whereas any solution in between can be realized, Figure 3e. This load balancing is handled by a thread controller (TC).

Running a higher and flexible number of programs and threads (C = 5 <= T <= 16 = D) cannot be realized with CSR and improving the system performance up to the switching limit cannot be done with parallel processing (PP) alone. This is why SHP as a combination of CSR and PP is so beneficial.

## 3    Thread Controller

A TC is proposed, which is steered by a special function register set TR (Thread Register) which is accessible by all design copies. Figure 4 shows how the Thread ID (TID) is provided for the SHP memories. Figure 4 also gives an overview of the special function register sets of the TC which are mentioned in this section. When a thread is executed, its TID passes through the ID-Queue (IDQ). It is reinserted into the IDQ or in the ID-FIFO, if the relevant bit in the TR shows that the thread is still valid and not on hold or killed. When less than C threads are valid, active threads need to be re-executed, but the valid bit V of the IDQ indicates, that its state copies should not be stored. When more than C threads are executed or an additional thread is inserted, then the TID is parked in the ID-FIFO. Threads can be added by the CPU or by an interrupt source.

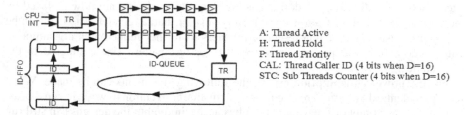

**Fig. 4.** Thread Controller Mechanism and Special Functional Register Sets

Threads can be added to the active thread list by setting the thread-specific active A bit in the TR. Threads can be hold by setting the hold H bit or killed by clearing the active A bit in the TR. When the thread priority bit P is set in the TR, then a thread execution has a higher priority than the threads stored in the ID-FIDO or threads resulting from an interrupt or the CPU. It is therefore directly inserted into the IDQ again and not stored into the ID-FIFO. The following actions are executed when the TR is accessed:

- Start a new thread at a given program address,
- handle the current thread:
    - kill the current thread now (clear A bit) or
    - continue the current thread in parallel or
    - continue the current thread (set H bit) once
        - the new thread is done or
        - all threads started from the current one are done.

To cope with fork-join queueing, the calling thread increments its sub threads counter (STC) register. It can stall itself by setting its H bit when needed. Each called thread saves the TID of its calling threads in the CAL register. Once a called thread is done, it decrements the STC of its caller and gets killed. Once the STC value gets zero, the calling thread continues by clearing its H bit.

This mechanism generates a TC with low complexity. It can stall and bypass individual threads and it is capable of handling fork-join queues. The software flow is entirely controlled through access to special function registers and is therefore compiler independent. A thread runs completely independent of the other threads when its priority bit is set and when only a less or equal number of C threads have the priority bit set.

# 4    Hardware Related Aspects

When discussing the **area** aspect of SHP-ed designs, it needs to be distinguished between FPGAs and ASICs. SHP-ed designs only need a very limited number of CRs.

The CRs are equally distributed over a given combinatorial logic. SHP-ed designs need many but small memories. This makes FPGAs an ideal technology for SHP.

For ASIC technologies, further area related aspects should be considered. The registers, which usually hold the design state in the original design are now replaced by memory cells. A memory cell is considerably smaller than a register. The CRs can be non-scan registers and/or non-resetable registers to further reduce area consumption without compromising production test quality or test pattern size compared to the original design.

For the **power consumption** aspect, the following statements can be made. When multiple identical designs are implemented in the conventional way, it can be assumed that the number of registers multiplies accordingly, but the designs can still run at the original speed. When using SHP, registers are added to the design for each new design copy. Additionally the frequency must be multiplied by C when the same performance should be achieved. This leads to a disadvantageous rise of the power consumption of the clock tree.

When using CSR only, all threads have to be executed, whereas when using SHP instead, individual thread states can be parked in a memory location without generating switching activity anymore (stall state). When less than C threads need to be executed, an active thread can be re-executed to fill the unused time slot without generating switching activity, combined with a disabled memory write.

It can be argued, that the **critical path** of the original design (Forig) gets worse overall, even when the optimal timing driven placement is found, because additional physical elements (registers) are inserted. The inserted memories have most likely a higher setup and hold time compared to registers. The CR insertion is done on many paths of the design, therefore the design gets bigger, which also makes timing closure more difficult in general. This aspect is less critical in an SHP-ed design, because less CRs are inserted. Pre-build DSP blocks on FPGAs are usually automatically timing optimized by retiming the CR located at their outputs.

Empirical data from processors show that the **performance per area** (PpA) factor improves. Instead of having multiple individual instantiations of a design, SHP reuses the combinatorial logic to multiply the functionality of a design. Therefore PpA increases.

The impact of SHP on the **system performance** is manifold. The key improvements are for instance a) less bus traffic congestion in a multiprocessor system on chip (MPSoC), b) higher CPU usage in a multithreading system and c) shared memory access in multiprocessor systems (NoCs). These aspects cannot be discussed in-length in this SHP technology introductory paper. Instead the paper outlines techniques and results of how to improve the performance of individual threads in an SHP based processor environment.

SHP converts a register into a 1-bit 16-line wide memory when D = 16. This is efficient on Xilinx FPGAs, because the same FPGA resource (BRAM) is used for all D <= 16. It becomes costly, when register-files or caches need to be duplicated as well. In this case, it is more useful to reduce D to a more reasonable number. To reduce the memory size, it is also possible to limit the usage of caches (for example) to a certain number of threads and let other threads run without the possibility to access caches. One of the processors used in the result section is the OpenRISC 1200 (32-bit scalar RISC with Harvard micro-architecture, 5 stage integer pipeline, virtual memory support (MMU), basic DSP capabilities, TLB, instruction and data cache) taken from [17].

## 5    Improving the Performance of Individual Threads in an SHP Based Processor Environment

One way to improve the performance of a single thread in an SHP based processor environment is the thread switching. At the beginning of a function call, the program usually saves certain register values of the register-file on the stack. These values are then restored at the end of the function's execution. This data storing and data loading is time and power consuming. To avoid stack handling in an SHP environment, a thread can also be stored and the function call is then executed by an unused design copy (thread). Once the thread has finished the execution of the function, the thread is killed and the calling thread continues.

This technique was been tested on a 3-stage Cortex M3 Thumb2 execution engine as it is used in [19]. The PUSH/POP instructions are now handled by the thread controller (TC). It holds the current thread and starts a new thread in case of a PUSH instruction. In case of a POP instruction the active thread is killed and the calling thread continues. The scenario is shown in Figure 3d. The average runtime improvement is around 8% and like deep pipelining very application specific.

## 6    Results

The numbers in this result section are based on the OpenRISC1200 (with TLB, MMU and caches disabled) taken from [17], a 3-stage implementation of a RISCV32IM [18] core and a 3-stage Cortex M3 Thumb2 execution engine as it is used in [19].

**Table 1.** Results for SHP-ed OpenRISC1200, RISCV32IM and Cortex M3 cores

| C/D | Reg. | Mem. | FPGA Occ. Slices | | | Perform. [Mhz] | | | PpA | Power [mW] | | |
|---|---|---|---|---|---|---|---|---|---|---|---|---|
| OpenRISC1200 | | | | | | | | | | | | |
| 1 | 1280 | 2048 | 994 | Orig. | Alt. | 71 | Orig. | Alt. | 72 | 42 | Orig. | Alt. |
| 2/16 | 362 | 53248 | 1089 | 110% | 55% | 99 | 139% | 70% | 127% | 99 | 233% | 116% |
| 3/16 | 534 | 53248 | 1089 | 110% | 37% | 120 | 168% | 56% | 153% | 120 | 284% | 95% |
| 4/16 | 974 | 53248 | 1143 | 115% | 29% | 133 | 187% | 47% | 162% | 146 | 345% | 86% |
| 5/16 | 1104 | 53248 | 1177 | 118% | 24% | 147 | 206% | 41% | 174% | 162 | 382% | 76% |
| RISCV32IM | | | | | | | | | | | | |
| 1 | 189 | 2048 | 273 | Orig. | Alt. | 112 | Orig. | Alt. | 410 | 18 | Orig. | Alt. |
| 2/16 | 69 | 35792 | 293 | 107% | 54% | 175 | 156% | 78% | 146% | 47 | 261% | 131% |
| 3/16 | 111 | 35792 | 321 | 118% | 39% | 206 | 184% | 61% | 156% | 55 | 306% | 102% |
| 4/16 | 175 | 35792 | 321 | 118% | 29% | 221 | 197% | 49% | 168% | 63 | 350% | 88% |
| 5/16 | 245 | 35792 | 343 | 126% | 25% | 279 | 249% | 50% | 198% | 73 | 406% | 81% |
| Cortex M3 | | | | | | | | | | | | |
| 1 | 428 | 1024 | 1305 | Orig. | Alt. | 57 | Orig. | Alt. | 44 | 21 | Orig. | Alt. |
| 2/16 | 171 | 23232 | 1405 | 108% | 54% | 101 | 177% | 88% | 164% | 52 | 248% | 124% |
| 3/16 | 352 | 23232 | 1453 | 111% | 37% | 149 | 261% | 87% | 234% | 71 | 338% | 113% |
| 4/16 | 438 | 23232 | 1486 | 114% | 28% | 182 | 319% | 80% | 280% | 80 | 381% | 95% |
| 5/16 | 490 | 23232 | 1486 | 114% | 23% | 200 | 350% | 70% | 308% | 94 | 448% | 90% |

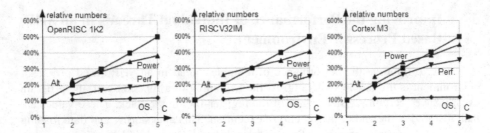

**Fig. 5.** Relative numbers of occupied slices, performance and power consumption over increasing number of design copies (C) and constant D = 16

A tool called "CoreMultiplier" is used to automatically apply SHP on the given design within seconds. The algorithm shown by Strauch in [13] is enhanced to support the SHP technology, which includes the merging of resulting shift registers with the new memories. The designs are implemented on a Xilinx Virtex-6 (xc6vlx75-3ff484). The FPGA tool's synthesis, place and route options are set to medium.

## 6.1    Occupied Slices on FPGAs

Table 1 shows the results of SHP-ed OpenRISC1200, RISCV32IM and Cortex M3 cores with increasing C [2..5] and D set to 16. Figure 5 shows the relative numbers of Table 1 graphically. The column "Reg." shows the number of registers. The original registers are now replaced by memories. The number of memory bits for D=16 (including register-file of the processor) is listed in the "Mem." column.

The number of "FPGA Occ. Slices" (occupied slices on the FPGA, (OS)) remains relatively stable. The column "Orig." shows the OS relative to a single core implementation and the column "Alt." the OS relative to the alternative implementation (called "Alt" in the remainder of this section) of instantiating C individual cores. The SHP-ed design is already smaller for C=2 compared to "Alt" and the advantage increases with C>2. The SHP-ed versions can already perform 16 independent threads (D=16).

## 6.2    Performance

The system performance increases as well for C<=5, but not as fast as the one of the alternative solution Alt. Tables 1 shows the performance per area factor PpA (in kHz per occupied slice) for each core when applying SHP. It can be seen in the PpA column, that this factor increases by up to 174% (198%, 308%) for C = 5. In other words, when SHP can be used, more performance can be realized on a given FPGA size. Nevertheless, increasing C becomes less efficient for higher C in terms of performance.

The following aspects must be considered when discussing the performance results from the system level architectural view. 1) The individual thread performance does not necessarily have to be the timing critical limitation of the system. Power and heat related aspects are most likely the upper bounds for CPU speeds. 2) When a thread is stalled (due to a cache miss for instance), alternative threads can be executed (T<=D) to increase the system performance. There are additional system relevant performance aspects which are outside the scope of this paper.

### 6.3   Power Consumption

Table 1 shows the power consumption of the SHP-ed cores with increasing C. SHP consumes slightly more power per thread. Again various additional aspects must be considered when discussing the performance results from the system level architecture view. For example, buffers can be physically shared in SHP based systems, which makes data transfer between buffers obsolete in some cases. This can improve the overall system power consumption.

## 7   Conclusion

This paper showed how C-Slow Retiming (CSR) and parallel programming can be combined to a new method called System Hyper Pipelining (SHP). SHP benefits from the higher performance per area (PpA) factor, which can be achieved when using CSR. Additionally, SHP offers also flexible thread stalling, bypassing and reordering features which are used by multithreading methods to improve the system performance.

Figure 3 shows, how the increased system performance can be distributed among multiple design copies by using a thread controller. Individual threads can run at different speeds and can even be completely stalled without consuming relevant power anymore. Design copies can be shared by any given number of threads on a cycle-by-cycle base. Most notoriously though, the fact that multiple CPUs can share the same memory through the same number of ports as in a single core implementation is very intriguing.

SHP is a formal process, that lets you convert any digital design (e.g. a CPU) into a system with identical design copies, where each running application (or program, thread etc.) can be stalled, bypassed or reordered individually. This stringent transformation process can be automatically accomplished within seconds. When the modifications are done on RTL (as shown by Strauch in [13]) the resulting system can further be verified and manually optimize. The paper gives an overview of a series of applications and design architectures which benefit from SHP.

The method is very well suited for FPGAs with their high number of registers and their flexible memory usage. SHP offers great possibilities to get more out of an FPGA by improving the system architecture and by enabling software to benefit from it at the same time.

# References

[1] Abdelfattah, M.S., Betz, V.: The power of communication: Energy- efficient NoCs for FPGAs. In: Intern. Conf. on FPL, pp. 1–8. Porto, Portugal September 2-4, 2013

[2] Matthews, E., Shannon, L., Dedorova, A.: Polyblaze: from one to many. Bringing the microblaze into the multicore era with linux SMP support. In: 22nd Intern. Conf. On FPL, pp. 224–230. Oslo, Norway August 29-31, 2012

[3] Vallina, F.M., Jachimiec, N., Saniie, J.: Multiprocessor and operating system design for signal processing on an FPGA. In: IEEE Intl. Conf. on Electro/ Information Technology, pp. 378–383. Chicago, IL, USA May 17-20, 2007

[4] Klimm, A., Braun, L., Becker, J.: An adaptive and scalable multiprocessor system for xilinx FPGAs using minimal sized processor cores. In: IEEE Inter. Symposium on Parallel and Ditributed Processing, pp. 1–7. Miami, Fl, USA April 14-18, 2008

[5] Wallentowitz, S., Lankes, A., Zaib, A., Wild, T., Herkersdorf, A.: A framework for open tiled manycore system-on-chip. In: 22nd Intern. Conf. on FPL, pp.535–538. Oslo, Norway August 29-31, 2012

[6] Henrey, M., Edmond, S., Shannon, L., Menon, C.: Bio-inspired walking: A FPGA multicore system for a legged robot. In: 22nd Inter. Conf. on FPL, pp. 105–111. Oslo, Norway August 29-31, 2012

[7] Lu, Y., Sezer, S., McCanny, J.: Advanced multithreading architecture with hardware based thread scheduling. In: Inter. Conf. on FPL, pp. 95–100. Milano, Italy 31 August –2 September 2010

[8] Tatas, K., Kyriacou, C.: Implementation of a threaded dataflow multiprocessor using FPGA. In: 6th Intern. Conf. on DTIS, pp. 1–6. Athens, Greece April 6-8, 2011

[9] Labrecque, M., Steffan, J.G.: Improving pipelined soft processors with multitherading. In: Intern. Conf. on FPL, pp. 210–215. Amsterdam August 27-29, 2007

[10] Labrecque, M., Steffan, J.G.: Fast critical sections via thread scheduling for FPGA-based multithreaded processors. In: Intern. Conf. on FPL, pp. 18–25. Prague, Czech Republic 31 August –2 September 2009

[11] Leiserson, C., Saxe, J.: Retiming Synchronous Circuitry. Algorithmica **6**(1), 5–35 (1991)

[12] Weaver, N., Wawrzynek, J.: The effects of datapath placement and C- slow retiming on three computational benchmarks. In: Proc. FCCM 2002, pp. 303–304. Napa, CA, USA April 24, 2002

[13] Strauch, T.: Timing driven C-slow retiming on RTL for multicores on FPGAs. In: ParaFPGA 2013. Munich, Germany September 10-13, 2013. www.edaptix.com/ParCo2013_Strauch_CSR_RTL.pdf

[14] Su, M., Zhou, L., Shi, C.: Maximizing the throughput-area efficiency of fully-parallel low-density parity-check decoding with c-slow retiming and asynchronous deep pipelining. In: ICCD 2007, pp. 636–643. Lake Tahoe, CA, USA October 7-10, 2007

[15] Afram, M., Khan, A., Sarfaraz, M.: C-slow technique vs. multiprocessor in designing low area customized set processor for embedded applications. In: Intern. Journal of Computer Applications **6**(7) (2001)

[16] Cadenas, J., Sherratt, S., Huerta, P., Kao, W.-C., Megson, G.M.: C-slow retimed parallel histogram archi-tectures for consumer imaging devices. Transactions on Consumer Electronics **59**(2), pp. 291–295

[17] Opencores, Stockholm, Sweden, 2007. www.opencores.org/projects

[18] The RISCV Instruction Set Architecture (riscv.org)

[19] Atmel: AT91SAM ARM based Flashed MCU. http://www.atmel.com/Images/doc11057.pdf

# Extended Abstracts (Posters)

# A Timing Driven Cycle-Accurate Simulation for Coarse-Grained Reconfigurable Architectures

Anupam Chattopadhyay[1]($\boxtimes$) and Xiaolin Chen[2]

[1] School of Computer Engineering, Nanyang Technological University,
Nanyang, Singapore
anupam@ntu.edu.sg
[2] Institute of Communication Technologies and Embedded Systems,
RWTH Aachen University, Aachen, Germany

**Abstract.** Coarse-Grained Reconfigurable Architectures (CGRAs), which provide good trade-offs between performance, hardware/ energy efficiency and flexibility, as well as offer high degree of parallelism, are fast emerging as a competing platform for the high-performance and embedded applications [3]. In this paper, we propose a timing driven approach for generating cycle-accurate high level simulator for CGRA. The simulator is generated from a high-level language describing the CGRA. Experimental results on different architectures and application kernels show that the proposed simulator is 1.5× to 4× faster than state-of-the-art RTL simulators.

## 1 Introduction

Design of a CGRA often starts from a high level abstraction of the architecture features [8][10][11], which includes, e.g. functionality and storage capacity of the basic functional units (FUs), topology and dimension of the FUs organized in the CGRA, and the interconnection resources between the FUs. Based on the supported architecture features, on one hand, a compilation tool can be built up, which integrates mapping, placement and routing to generate the configuration bitstream for applications mapped on the CGRA. On the other hand, RTL model of the CGRA can be generated and used for implementation. In a CGRA, the reconfigurable interconnects between FUs allow to build different datapaths with the FUs during the run-time. Therefore, event-driven simulators using the generated HDL [11] or SystemC models [8] are usually applied for generic simulation of applications mapped on CGRAs.

In [11] and [8], SystemC/RTL simulation is used for functional verification, thereby utilizing an event-driven simulation flow. Event-driven simulators are fairly slow in simulation speed, since the simulator needs to consider all the events generated by the changing signals inside the architecture. There are some works in literature which apply high-level simulation techniques for CGRAs [9,10,14]. Such simulators are either developed manually or are generated from specific CGRA templates, thereby limiting the design space significantly. In [10], the cycle-accurate simulator can be generated by the DRESC framework for the

© Springer International Publishing Switzerland 2015
K. Sano et al. (Eds.): ARC 2015, LNCS 9040, pp. 293–300, 2015.
DOI: 10.1007/978-3-319-16214-0_24

ADRES architecture, which uses the architecture specification and the applica-tion C code as inputs. The application is first compiled to get the configuration bitstream, which specifies the datapath configuration inside the CGRA. This datapath information is then used for generating the simulator. The disadvan-tage of this scheme is that, the simulator needs to be re-generated whenever application is changed.

High-level simulation technique has been successfully applied in designing processor architectures [1,7]. In contrast, for CGRAs, simulation techniques at levels higher than RTL abstraction is not well studied. For cycle-accurate pro-cessor simulation, the partitioning of storage and combinational logic is derived directly from the high-level specification using ADLs. In contrast, the CGRA presents a significant challenge due to its repeated reconfiguration. During static/ dynamic reconfiguration, a particular storage may or may not be active - result-ing into very different pipeline structures. In a nutshell, despite significant per-formance and debugging advantages of abstract cycle-accurate simulators, this problem is not addressed for generic CGRA design frameworks so far. This forms the motivation of this work.

## 2    Timing-Constrained Datapath

In a CGRA structure, the basic resources for constructing a datapath include the registers, the functional units, and the reconfigurable interconnects. Functional units are connected using reconfigurable interconnects, while registers are used as the relay of intermediate results between the reconfigurable datapaths. For a cycle-accurate simulation, since the registers can fully represent the computation state on the CGRA, they are considered as the focus when synthesizing the sim-ulator from the architecture model. For processors and ASICs, the architecture can usually be clearly divided into a pipelined structure, which makes it straight-forward to synthesize the cycle-accurate simulator. While in CGRAs, before the configuration bitstream is loaded, the CGRA may not always be clearly divided into pipelined structures. This creates a challenge to generate generic cycle-accurate simulators for CGRAs without the knowledge of the applications.

To solve this problem, in this paper, we apply a register-centric synthesis technique, which is different from the previous module-centric[13] and edge-centric[12] approaches. This is done by introducing a so-called *timing-constrained datapath*, which focuses on the registers and the datapath to update the reg-isters. In this section, the concept of the timing-constrained datapath is first introduced. Following the concept, a strategy to compile applications using the timing-constrained datapath is briefly described.

### 2.1    Definition

Given a CGRA intermediate representation (IR) $G_{Res} = (F, R, I)$, which is a graph of the architecture resources i.e. FUs (F), registers (R) and interconnects (I) available on the CGRA. Based on this resource graph, a timing-constrained

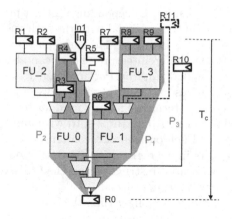

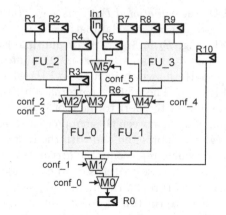

**Fig. 1.** Example of Timing-Constrained Datapath

**Fig. 2.** Generation of Register/Port Update Function

datapath for a register $R$ in the architecture is defined as a datapath $DP_{R,T}$ within a given timing constraint $T$ and rooted at the register $R$. For all registers in the CGRA, these datapaths constitute a set of direct acyclic graphs segmented from the resource graph $G_{Res}$ which can be represented as

$$S_{TCD} = \{DP_{R_0,T}, DP_{R_1,T}, ..., DP_{R_n,T}\} \tag{1}$$

Figure 1 depicts an example of the timing-constrained datapath for register $R0$. The datapath is rooted at $R0$. A backtracking is performed from $R0$ to find out all possible datapaths for updating the value of $R0$ within the timing constraint $T_c$. The end points for the backtracking are either register outputs or input ports of the CGRA. Paths which exceed the constraint $T_c$ are ignored, e.g. the dotted wire and register $R11$ in Figure 1. In practice, the timing constraint can be selected large enough, to include a reasonable number of updating paths for the register.

## 2.2 Compilation with Timing-Constrained Datapath

Based on the previous definition, a CGRA is partitioned into segments of timing-constrained datapaths. As it is shown later, the cycle-accurate simulator can be generated based on these datapaths. To ensure that the application will not use a path which is not covered by the datapaths, the compilation of the application also needs to use these extracted datapaths. To this end, we further partition each datapath into a set of patterns.

$$DP_{R_0,T_c} = \{P_{0,T_0}, P_{1,T_1}, ..., P_{n,T_n}\} \tag{2}$$

The patterns can be segments of a timing-constrained datapath, which include one or multiple FUs covered by the datapath. We call the patterns which include

FUs the *Functional Patterns*, e.g. $P_1$ and $P_2$ in Figure 1. Depending on the timing constraint, the datapath can be partitioned into functional patterns with one FU (e.g. $P_2$ in Figure 1) or multiple FUs (e.g. $P_1$ in Figure 1). These patterns are used to map application DFG into FUs on the architecture. There can also be patterns which include no FUs which are called *Routing Patterns*, e.g. $P_3$ in Figure 1. The routing patterns contain only wires and multiplexers between an input register/port to the root register. These patterns are mainly used for routing of nets between the mapped functional patterns. All patterns start with input registers/ports and end with the root register. Each pattern also contains a time unit, which represents the arrival time from its input registers/ports to the root register. These patterns can be considered as spatial instructions on the CGRA and used through the mapping, placement and routing process.

Due to the timing constraint, datapaths which are longer than the constraint are not covered. However, our experimental studies demonstrate that, by setting the timing constraint sufficiently long, the compilation result is not degraded. On the other hand, with large timing constraint, simulation speed degrades.

In this paper, we apply a traditional CGRA compilation flow with these extracted patterns. During the compilation process, a mapping method based on dynamic programming [4] is applied to convert the application data flow graph into a pattern graph of FUs. For placement and routing, a simulated-annealing based algorithm [16] or a force-directed algorithm [2,19] can be selected for placement of the patterns and routing of the nets between patterns. There is a significant body of research in CGRA mapping, including some recent works [3,5,15]. However, these are orthogonal to the scope of the current paper. Diverse mapping, placement and routing algorithms can be easily plugged into our proposed simulation framework.

## 3     Generation of High-Level Simulator

By introducing the timing-constrained datapath, the proposed high-level simulation becomes a signal flow graph simulation. Therefore, the basic functionality of the cycle-accurate simulator can be realized through a routine which performs value updating for all registers and output ports. In this section, the generation of the high-level simulator is described in detail.

### 3.1     Register/Port Update Function

Since the updating datapath is already specified by the timing-constrained datapath, the updating function for each register or output port of the CGRA can be directly generated. As shown in Figure 2, the timing-constrained datapath has a tree structure. The update function is generated assign a level-order tree traversal. For the example in Figure 2, the traversal starts from the root register $R0$. When a multiplexer is encountered, the configuration bit of the multiplexer is evaluated to decide on the branch for continuing the traversal. For FUs, separate function calls are used which come from the definition of the ELEMENTs in the high-level description. The traversal ends until all the searching paths arrive at input registers/ports.

There are two advantages for this tree-traversal scheme. *First*, the simulator can perform only the necessary operations for the given configuration bits included in the datapath. For the example given in Figure 2, when *conf_0* is set to "0" which means the routing pattern is selected, the simulator will only perform a value assignment from $R10$ to $R0$, and the execution of the complex datapath including the FUs are avoided. *Second*, the worst case time taken to execute the update function is proportional to the number of configuration bits on the longest branch of the timing-constrained datapath. This avoids an exponential increase of the simulation time with the timing constraint.

## 3.2 Simulation Routine

The main simulation routine implements three basic function blocks, which are *Input Read, Register/Port Update*, and *State Update. Input Read* reads the inputs for the current execution cycle, which include values at the input ports and configuration bits at the configuration port of the CGRA. Then, the register/port update functions are executed for the registers/ports which need to be updated, because of changing of values in input registers/ports and configuration bits. The registers are updated with the newly computed values and prepare for the next execution cycle.

## 4  Experimental Results

Three different sets of experiments are performed to evaluate the proposed approach. Two different CGRA structures are modeled using the high-level modeling language, which are CGRA-1 (modeled similar to the ADRES architecture [10]) and CGRA-2 (modeled according to the one proposed in [6]). Six different application kernels are mapped onto the two CGRAs. For CGRA-1, three application kernels are selected from the multimedia application domain, which are inverse discrete cosine transform (IDCT) from MPEG2 decoder, sum of absolute differences (SAD) from H.263 and H.264 encoder, and sum of 4x4 Hadamard transformed differences (SHTD) from H.264 encoder. For CGRA-2, the selected application kernels are matrix-matrix multiplication, matrix-vector multiplication and matrix inversion, all with the matrix dimension of $4 \times 4$.

## 4.1  Effect of Timing Constraint on Mapping Efficiency

In this case study, we apply different timing constraints for both CGRAs to extract patterns used by the compilation. Because the CGRAs have different datapath complexity in their FUs, the constraints are selected in a way that a single FU, 2 sequential FUs and 3 sequential FUs can be accommodated into the corresponding timing constraint. The relative execution time of each kernel compared to the result without timing constraint is shown in Figure 3.

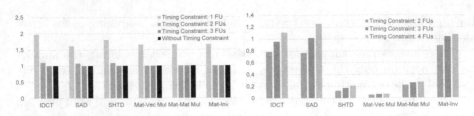

**Fig. 3.** Mapping Efficiency                    **Fig. 4.** Simulation Time

For all cases performed on both CGRAs, when the timing constraint is set to allow one FU in the datapath, the execution time of different application kernels are worse than the one without timing constraint. This is because, for the short timing constraint, the capability of the architecture is not fully explored by the pattern library. For example, the routing resources are limited to the ones extracted by the short timing constraint, and some long routing paths are not directly available in the pattern library. When the timing constraint is relaxed, e.g., to allow until two sequential FUs, the routing resources are mostly available in the timing constraint. The simulated annealing algorithm can work with almost all routing resources on the CGRA. This results in a matching performance compared to the one without timing constraint.

### 4.2   Effect of Timing Constraint on Simulation Speed

In this case study, we keep the timing constraints with 2 and 3 sequential FUs, which give compilation results close to the one without timing constraint. And we further extend the timing constraint to allow 4 sequential FUs for both CGRAs. In Figure 4, simulation time in seconds are shown for different cases. The simulation times are measured by running these kernels on a system with an AMD Phenom(TM) II X4 955 quad-core CPU and local memory of 8 GB.

From the results shown in Figure 4, the simulation time increases more or less linearly with the timing constraint in the multimedia cases on CGRA-1. This, we believe, is because in the update functions for registers/ports, the operations performed for the simulation is dependent on the number of configuration bits on the specific branch. And the number of configuration bits on the branch is approximately linearly changed according to the timing constraint.

For the cases performed on CGRA-2, the simulation time does not increase so much, especially from 3 to 4 FUs. This is because CGRA-2 is a well-pipelined architecture and does not have a very complex interconnection network as in CGRA-1. By changing the timing constraint from 3 to 4 FUs, the complexity of the timing-constrained datapath is not dramatically changed.

### 4.3   Comparison with RTL Simulators

Using the generated VHDL/Verilog HDL models of the CGRA from the implementation flow, the proposed high-level simulator is compared against two

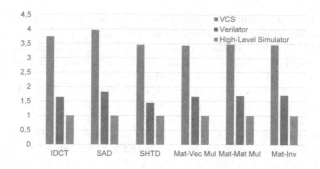

**Fig. 5.** Comparison with State-of-the-art RTL simulators

state-of-the-art HDL simulators, namely the Synopsys VCS-MX [17] (version VCS-MX 2011.03) and Verilator [18] (version 3.853) from VeriPool, an open source Verilog HDL compiler which compiles synthesizable Verilog HDL models into C++ or SystemC. Several optimizations are performed by Verilator to improve the simulation speed, which includes netlist optimization, module/function inlining, constant propagation and code levelization. For the high-level simulator, we take the one generated from the timing constraint set to 3 FUs, because the performance of the kernels are the same as the one without timing constraint. Both the generated high-level simulator and Verilator were compiled using GCC 4.4.7. The simulation time of Verilator and VCS are normalized with the simulation time of the high-level simulator and are shown in Figure 5.

The proposed simulator is about 3.5× to 4× faster than Synopsys VCS and about 1.5× to 1.8× faster than Verilator, for the selected benchmarks. The main reason is that, the proposed high-level simulator performs a signal flow graph simulation which only considers register values after each execution cycle. In contrast, the RTL simulators are event-driven simulators which also considers the updating of intermediate signals.

# References

1. Chattopadhyay, A., Meyr, H., Leupers, R.: LISA: A Uniform ADL for Embedded Processor Modelling, Implementation and Software Toolsuite Generation, chapter 5, pp. 95–130. Morgan Kaufmann (June 2008)
2. Fell, A., Rákossy, Z., Chattopadhyay, A.: Force-directed scheduling for data flow graph mapping on coarse-grained reconfigurable architectures. In: Proc. of the Intl. Conf. on ReConFigurable Computing and FPGAs (ReConFig). IEEE (December 2014)
3. Chattopadhyay, A.: Ingredients of adaptability: A survey of reconfigurable processors. VLSI Des., 10:10–10:10 (January 2013)
4. Chattopadhyay, A., Chen, X., Ishebabi, H., Leupers, R., Ascheid, G., Meyr, H.: High-level modelling and exploration of coarse-grained re-configurable architectures. In: Proc. of the Conf. on Design, Automation & Test in Europe (DATE) (2008)

5. Chen, L., Mitra, T.: Graph minor approach for application mapping on CGRAs. ACM Trans. Reconfigurable Technol. Syst. **7**(3) (2014)
6. Chen, X., Minwegen, A., Hassan, Y., Kammler, D., Li, S., Kempf, T., Chattopadhyay, A., Ascheid, G.: Flexdet: Flexible, efficient multi-mode mimo detection using reconfigurable asip. In: IEEE FCCM (2012)
7. Gao, L., Karuri, K., Kraemer, S., Leupers, R., Ascheid, G., Meyr, H.: Multiprocessor performance estimation using hybrid simulation. In: Proc. of the ACM/IEEE Design Automation Conference (DAC) (2008)
8. Filho, T.S.W.R.J., Masekowsky, S.: CGADL: an architecture description language for coarse-grained reconfigurable arrays. In: IEEE Trans. on VLSI Systems (2009)
9. Khawam, S., Nousias, I., Milward, M., Yi, Y., Muir, M., Arslan, T.: The reconfigurable instruction cell array. IEEE Trans. on VLSI Systems **16**(1) (2008)
10. Mei, B., Lambrechts, A., Mignolet, J.-Y., Verkest, D., Lauwereins: Architecture exploration for a reconfigurable architecture template. IEEE Design and Test **22**(2), 99–101 (2005)
11. Menta. http://www.menta.fr/home.html
12. Park, H., Fan, K., Mahlke, S.: Edge-centric modulo scheduling for coarse-grained reconfigurable architectures. In: Proc. of the 17th Intl. Con. on Parallel Architectures and Compilation Techniques (2008)
13. Park, Y., Park, H., Mahlke, S.: CGRA express: Accelerating execution using dynamic operation fusion. In: Proc. of the Intl. Conf. on Compilers, Architecture, and Synthesis for Embedded Systems, pp. 271–280 (2009)
14. Patel, K., McGettrick, S., Bleakley, C.: Rapid functional modelling and simulation of coarse-grained reconfigurable array architectures. Elsevier Journal of Systems Architecture **57**(2), 383–391 (2011)
15. Peyret, T., Corre, G., Thevenin, M., Martin, K., Coussy, P.: An automated design approach to map applications on cgras. In: Proc. of the 24th Edition of the Great Lakes Symposium on VLSI, GLSVLSI 2014, pp. 229–230 (2014)
16. Sharma, A., Ebeling, C., Hauck, S.: Architecture adaptive routability-driven placement for fpgas. In: ACM/SIGDA Symp. on FPGA (2005)
17. VCS-MX.    http://www.synopsys.com/tools/verification/functionalverification/pages/vcs.aspx
18. Verilator. http://www.veripool.org/wiki/verilator
19. Chen, X., Li, S., Schleifer, J., Coenen, T., Chattopadhyay, A., Ascheid, G., Noll, T.: High-level modeling and synthesis for embedded fpgas. In: Proc. of the Conf. on Design, Automation & Test in Europe (DATE), pp. 1565–1570 March 2013

# Scalable and Efficient Linear Algebra Kernel Mapping for Low Energy Consumption on the *Layers* CGRA

Zoltán Endre Rákossy[1]([✉]), Dominik Stengele[2], Axel Acosta-Aponte[1], Saumitra Chafekar[1], Paolo Bientinesi[2], and Anupam Chattopadhyay[3]

[1] Institute for Communication Technologies and Embedded Systems (ICE), Aachen, Germany
rakossy@ice.rwth-aachen.de
[2] Algorithmically-Driven Code Generation for High-Performance, Computing Architectures, AICES, RWTH Aachen University, Aachen, Germany
[3] School of Computer Engineering, Nanyang Technological University, Nanyang, Singapore

**Abstract.** A scalable mapping is proposed for 3 important kernels from the Numerical Linear Algebra domain, to exploit architectural features to reach asymptotically optimal efficiency and a low energy consumption. Performance and power evaluations were done with input data set matrix sizes ranging from 64×64 to 16384×16384. 12 architectural variants with up to 10×10 processing elements were used to explore scalability of the mapping and the architecture, achieving $< 10\%$ energy increase for architectures up to 8×8 PEs coupled with performance speed-ups of more than an order of magnitude. This enables a clean area-performance trade-off on the *Layers* architecture while keeping energy constant over the variants.

## 1 Introduction

Accelerating applications using coarse-grained reconfigurable architectures (CGRA) promises great benefits [2,3], but without an efficient compiler, designers are forced to go over tedious manual application mapping processes to find and leverage maximum performance with minimum energy. These must be repeated if architectural or application parameters are changed, therefore mapping *scalability* is an important factor.

In this paper, we propose scalable and highly efficient mapping solutions for 3 Numerical Linear Algebra kernels and apply them on a CGRA designed for scalability, called *Layers* [9]. Computationally demanding and highly parallel, NLA kernels represent the perfect application domain to fully tap the advantages of CGRA parallel execution and flexibility. However, high parallelism also requires high storage access pressure in various patterns, which is one of the limiting factors when seeking efficient execution on CGRAs. Many times, optimal execution is limited by storage bandwidth, or the hardware processing resources do not fit

© Springer International Publishing Switzerland 2015
K. Sano et al. (Eds.): ARC 2015, LNCS 9040, pp. 301–310, 2015.
DOI: 10.1007/978-3-319-16214-0_25

the optimal algorithmic execution window. We discuss how the complex interplay between application mapping, scaling and architectural features influence energy efficiency.

## 2  The *Layers* Architecture

The Layers architecture is a new multi-layered scalable and parameterizable CGRA[9], developed initially as a $4 \times 4$ fixed architecture[10], using a high-level design methodology proposed in [8]. The core philosophy aligns with the functional separation into layers of control (Q), computation (L0), communication (L1) and memory access (L2) with dedicated hardware structures for each of task class, maximizing parallelism and computational efficiency to achieve low energy. The architecture is organized in a 3D pipeline structure (Fig. 1), where data flows from the memory banks via the memory and communication layers to the computation layer in a vertical pipeline, while control flow is processed in the horizontal pipeline. Conceptually, the architecture represents for each of the task classes, a set of elementary hardware structures, which can be grouped into higher order functions by means of reconfiguration. The application data/control path is thus reconstructed out of small pieces, allowing to be arranged differently when the application changes. Rearranging the existing elementary structures is done via functional calls from assembly, in a data-independent way, for describing the application kernel. Each layer can work at a ratio $r = 2^n$ vs. the main pipeline, balancing task class bottle-necks. For each kernel, the set of function calls (i.e. configuration contexts) is stored in the program memory, as a self-contained black-box procedure derived from the mapping. An interested reader is invited to read further architectural details in the references mentioned above. For understanding the proposed mapping solutions in this paper, however, it is sufficient to keep the following key consideration in mind, when targeting *energy efficiency*: all floating-point PEs in the computation layer (L0) must be busy doing meaningful work at all times to exploit maximum parallelism. Furthermore, this consideration must be true, even if the number of processing elements and other architectural parameters change, hence he mapping must be *scalable*.

## 3  Mapping the Algorithms

### 3.1  Preliminaries

In this paper we focus on three kernels: dot product (DOT), matrix-vector (GEMV) and matrix-matrix multiplication (GEMM). The derivation of the mapping took into consideration several architectural and algorithmic parameters, while trying to keep it as generic as possible. Column-based memory loads have been avoided due to creating single-cycle access conflicts on modulo-$P$ based memory bank distributions, common for CGRAs. Efficiency evaluation is performed by taking the ratio between the theoretically required number of execution cycles $c_{kmin}$ and the number of actual cycles executed by the architecture

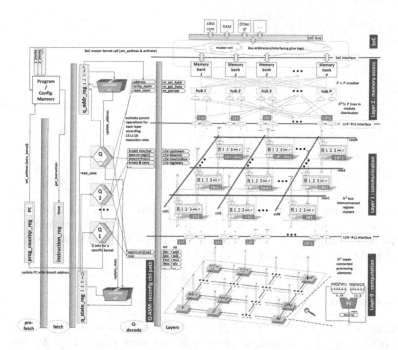

**Fig. 1.** The *Layers* architecture: scalable and modular layers dedicated for memory access, communication and computation are managed by a reconfigurable control flow stage.

$c_k$, for each problem size $N$, yielding $\eta_k(\{\cdot\}, N) := \dfrac{c_{k\,min}(\{\cdot\}, N)}{c_k(\{\cdot\}, N)}$. Theoretical values are derived from all arithmetic operations for a kernel, taking into account hardware parameters, e.g. FP division takes 4 cycles, while all other operations take 1 cycle. This allows evaluating mapping performance directly. Although architectural parameters specific to *Layers* are used here, please note that the mapping is valid for any mesh-connected architecture of processing elements, as long as the necessary data can be provided for the elements at the required time.

Generally, when mapping in a *scalable* way on a scalable architecture, the execution window size has to match the size of the array for efficiency and respect available memory bandwidth. An efficient block-based scheduling and mapping solution is discussed in earlier work[10], where *Layers* had fixed $4 \times 4$ PEs and 8 ports, yielding a fixed mapping, while automation of this is attempted in [4]. Here we show that a manual mapping can be derived for scalability yielding great performance and energy values when scaling. Further complexity arises when the array size modulo matrix size does not cleanly match at the end of the data. *Layers* uses `override` signals, set by the control layer (Q), to disable the extra execution units when required.

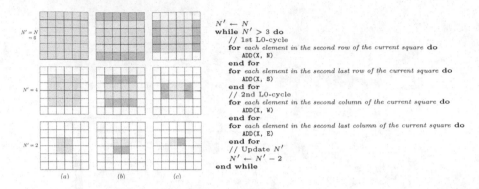

```
N' ← N
while N' > 3 do
    // 1st L0-cycle
    for each element in the second row of the current square do
        ADD(X, N)
    end for
    for each element in the second last row of the current square do
        ADD(X, S)
    end for
    // 2nd L0-cycle
    for each element in the second column of the current square do
        ADD(X, W)
    end for
    for each element in the second last column of the current square do
        ADD(X, E)
    end for
    // Update N'
    N' ← N' − 2
end while
```

**Fig. 2.** DOT algorithm with the accumulation procedure (folding). (a) initial state, (b) and (c) show the iteration transition, which reduces to the same problem of smaller size. Repeating such iterations will reduce to a $2 \times 2$ or $3 \times 3$ special case, which finally yield the final result in one element.

### 3.2 Accumulation Folding Procedure

**Mapping:** Although not a kernel *per se*, most kernels make use of this procedure, especially in the epilogue portion of hot-spot loops. Fig. 2 shows how partial sums can be folded into the final value for a $6 \times 6$ architecture, following a generic algorithm valid for any square array size. To preserve simplicity and scalability, the algorithm starts from the edge of the array, horizontally or vertically, creating two addition fronts. The procedure is repeated until the folding front reaches a $2 \times 2$ or a $3 \times 3$ data square. $N' = 2$ and $N' = 3$ have to be treated differently, because it is not possible anymore to reduce the square from top/bottom or left/right simultaneously. For these cases, only ADD(self, south) and ADD(self, east) are inserted, reducing $N' = 2$ to a single element, or, if $N$ is odd, $N' = 3$ to $N' = 2$ and to a single element afterwards.

**Complexity:** $op_{acc}(N) = N^2 - 1$ because always $i - 1$ additions are required to add up $i$ values, only depending on the architecture size $N$. When $N$ is even, the square will be reduced to a single element in $N/2$ iterations of the accumulation procedure. Every iteration consists of 2 *L0-cycles*, hence it will take $8N$ *cycles*, for $r_{L0:L1:L2} = 1 : 8 : 8$. When $N$ is odd, we cannot reduce a square with $N' = 3$ to a single element in just one iteration. Hence, we need $(N + 1)/2$ iterations, which results in $8(N + 1)$ *cycles*.

### 3.3 Dot Product (DOT): $c = \sum\limits_{i=1}^{n} a_i \cdot b_i$

**Mapping:** When mapping in a scalable way, the execution window size has to match the size of the array. Fig. 3 shows how each element of a $N^2 = 4$ element array is assigned an operation within the execution window, which partitions the two vertical data columns. If $N^2$ changes, the execution window scales accordingly. After an initial multiplication on all elements, the execution window

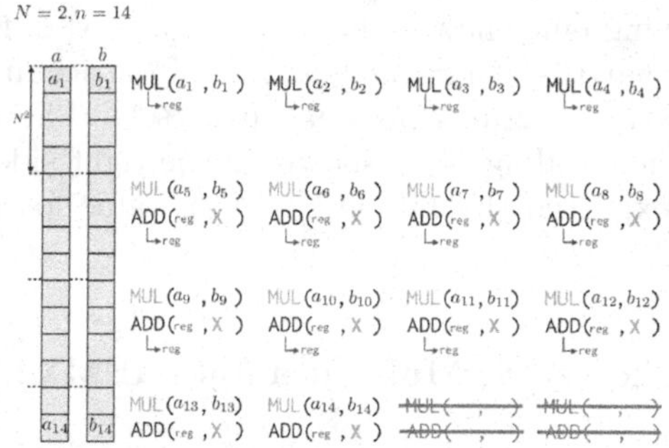

$N = 2, n = 14$

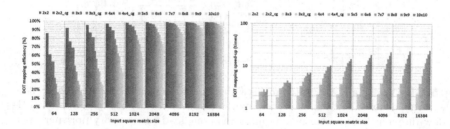

Fig. 3. DOT mapping with N=2, yielding an execution window of 4 elements, which slides downwards on the two data columns $a, b$, executing multiply and accumulate instructions alternately, until end of data is reached. If data size does not match $N^2$, overrides deactivate extra instructions. X denotes taking previous output (self).

slides downwards through the data, multiplying and accumulating the results for each processing element. Partial accumulation results are sent to L1 registers for the duration of one L0-cycle and used again in subsequent accumulation cycles, avoiding storing back to memory. When the $N^2 \% n$ does not cleanly match the array at the end of the data, overrides are set by the control core, disabling the extra execution units which have no data. This is a source of efficiency loss, however for very large matrices, the amount of full execution windows is dominating. After moving the execution window in $N^2$ steps, every element holds one partial result and the final result $c$ is the sum of all of those, hence by calling the accumulation folding procedure the kernel is completed.

Fig. 4. DOT mapping efficiency and mapping-based speed-up for various architectures (N=2..8) and data sizes (64..16384). Due to the accumulation procedure, efficiency receives a heavy penalty, especially for large arrays with small input data sizes. When enough data is used, the penalty is much smaller. Worst penalty for large data sets on large arrays is < 4%. This has the worst efficiency of the 3 kernels.

**Complexity:** For vectors of length $n$, $n$ multiplications and $n - 1$ additions are required, hence the operation complexity is $op_{dot}(\{n\}) = 2n - 1$. Hence, $c_{\text{dot}min}(\{n\}, N) = \frac{8}{N^2}(2n - 1)$.

**Efficiency:** Mapping efficiency is shown in Fig. 4 for different architecture sizes and input vector lengths, where inefficiencies of the accumulation procedure are dominating large architectures on small data sets. The expected speedup from this mapping when scaling $N$, is shown on the right side of Fig. 4, closing within $< 4\%$ to the expected theoretical speed-up value for large data sets on large arrays.

## 3.4    General Matrix-Vector Multiplication (GEMV) $c_i = \sum_{j=1}^{m} a_{ij} \cdot b_j$

**Mapping:** It is immediately visible from the formula that every multiplication can be done in parallel, but in the end every product has to be added together for every row $i$. This breaks the symmetry of the algorithmic progress through the data. It would be beneficial if the computation of $c_1, c_2, \ldots, c_{N^2}$ can be assigned to L0-elements $e_0, e_1, \ldots, e_{N^2-1}$. This would yield $N^2$ elements of $c$ after $m$ multiplications and $m-1$ additions. However, while any L0-element $e_{i-1}$ would operate exclusively on row $i$ of $A$, the input data $a_{ij}$ in every step would make loading values of a column of $A$ necessary, breaking scalability and efficiency for large $N$.

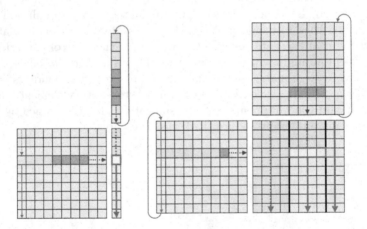

**Fig. 5.** GEMV(left) and GEMM(right) scalable execution window progress (here, $N^2 = 4$ elements), denoted in dark blue, yielding the result in yellow. The progression of this window through the data ensures no more than one load per memory port per cycle.

To operate on rows only, at any given point in time, a less optimal but scalable scheduling was implemented shown in Fig. 5(left), thus $N^2$ L0-elements can work in parallel to calculate every $c_i$. The execution window moves in $N^2$ steps horizontally in the matrix and vertically on the vector, but forces an accumulation procedure at the row boundary of each row.

**Complexity:** Operation complexity of GEMV, with input size $n$ and $m$, is equivalent to $n$ times $DOT$ for input size $m$, hence $op_{gemv}(\{n, m\}) = n \cdot op_{dot}(\{m\}) = n(2m - 1)$. Therefore, expected minimum on *Layers* is $c_{\text{gemv}\,min}(\{n, m\}, N) = \frac{8}{N^2} n(2m - 1)$.

**Efficiency:** Mapping efficiency is similar to, but better than the DOT product efficiency shown in Fig. 4, due to the extra accumulation procedures for every row. For large arrays and large data sets is $< 3\%$ close to the expected theoretical maximum.

## 3.5   General Matrix Multiplication (GEMM) $c_{ij} = \sum\limits_{l=1}^{k} a_{il} \cdot b_{lj}$.

**Mapping:** Respecting the same constraint of not loading data on the column (keeping one access per memory port), for *GEMM* the data dependencies turn out to be problematic. Most obvious mapping solutions would require to load a column of values from either $A$ or $B$ and multiply it with a row from the other. Rectangular or square windows with a height of more than 1 were not possible either since this would require to work on columns in either matrix. Block-based approaches are not scalable when modifying $N$ or memory port amount $P$ and produce complex addressing problems for a manual mapping. To bypass this, the following mapping is proposed, allowing a scalable execution window without column loads, as shown in Fig. 5(right): 1) Load $a_{11}$ 2) Multiply $a_{11}$ with $b_{11}, \ldots, b_{1N^2}$ 3) Continue with $a_{12}$ and $b_{21}, \ldots, b_{2N^2}$ and accumulate the partial results 4) When finishing with the last row, store the resulting $c_{11}, \ldots, c_{1N^2}$ and continue with the next window. This implies more loads due to reiterating through the data several times, but scales perfectly since a window of height 1 and width $N^2$ can be used, without causing memory port conflict or exceeding available bandwidth. The window iterates matrix $B$ and $C$ column-wise and only in the last column of windows there may be overrides necessary, making the override logic efficient.

**Complexity:** *GEMM*, with input size $n$, $m$ and $k$, is equivalent to $m$ times *GEMV* for input size $n$ and $k$, hence $op_{\text{gemm}}(\{n, m, k\}) = m \cdot op_{\text{gemv}}(\{n, k\}) = mn(2k - 1)$. Hence, $c_{\text{gemm}_{min}}(\{n, m, k\}, N) = \frac{8}{N^2} mn(2k - 1)$.

**Efficiency:** Even with the constraints considered, the implementation of *GEMM* is very efficient because the actual core of the implementation consists of 2 *L0-cycles* only, in which all processing elements are always occupied. For scaling by $x$ amount of elements a speedup of close to $x$ is achieved. Efficiency reaches optimality when the data set is a multiple of $N^2$ for large arrays.

# 4   Evaluation and Results

## 4.1   General Considerations

*Layers* has been coded completely in the LISA ADL of Synopsys Processor Designer, completely parametrized for easy scalability. Simulations have been conducted for random square input matrices of size 64..16384, for different combinations of $P = 2..32$ and $N = 2..10$. The assembly programs for each algorithm have been manually coded in a scalable way (auto-generation via embedded Ruby code), 5 L0-cycles for GEMM, 13 L0-cycles for GEMV, 11 L0-cycles for DOT including addition folding. Values are for single-precision floating point (32-bit).

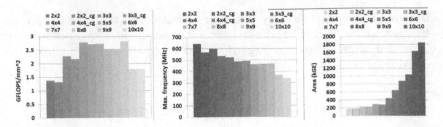

**Fig. 6.** Area, frequency and performance density for the Layers architecture

For these configurations RTL code has been generated and synthesized with DC I-2013 for Faraday $65nm$ technology library, using PowerCompiler and backward switching activity files for power estimation.

### 4.2    Time and Energy

Very interesting results are provided in Fig. 7 for GEMM kernel, where the overall time and energy values are depicted for each configuration and input matrix size. Similar results are available for DOT and GEMV. Execution time spreads over several orders of magnitude with varying input data size, while an order of magnitude speed-up can be maintained between the smallest and largest array for large input data sizes. Except for the largest architectures, where the critical path of the L1 structures severely affected frequency and thus energy, the architecture and mapping scale with almost constant energy (<10% variance), translating into a clean trade-off between area and speed, without affecting energy. Clock-gating optimizations improved results for smaller designs by roughly 20-40%. Power values range between 13.71 mW for the 2×2 clock-gated variant to 418 mW for the 10×10 array. The 3×3 clock-gated variant reaches highest average efficiency with 23.48 GFLOPs/W, while the 10×10 variant reaches lowest at 10.17 GFLOPs/W. Reducing the interconnect length in L1 would cancel out the frequency penalty for the 2 largest designs, and thus the extra energy compared to the other designs.

### 4.3    Comparisons with Related Work

Fig. 6 provides some area, frequency and performance density data. The frequency of each architecture is limited by the control flow complexity in the q-decode stage for small $N$, and by L1 critical path for larger $N$ at $r = 1 : 8 : 8$.

Unfortunately we found no works in the literature which map these kernels on a CGRA and provide detailed energy results, allowing only coarse comparisons in terms of overall power efficiency or power density [9]. Only aggregate results could be found also for GPGPU solutions[11] and a DSP[1]. In [5], authors presented a novel FPGA-based fine-grained reconfigurable architecture to map several numerical linear algebra kernels and compared with Intel Xeon Woodcrest processor to report 10-150× speed-up/energy-efficiency improvement. However, no absolute results in time or energy for any particular technology node is reported making it extremely difficult to compare with our proposed approach. A more detailed implementation for our target kernels are reported in [6], where the total performance results include the communication bandwidth with a PC. Considering the overall performance, our implementation is clearly superior by several orders of magnitude, though, the comparison is not accu-

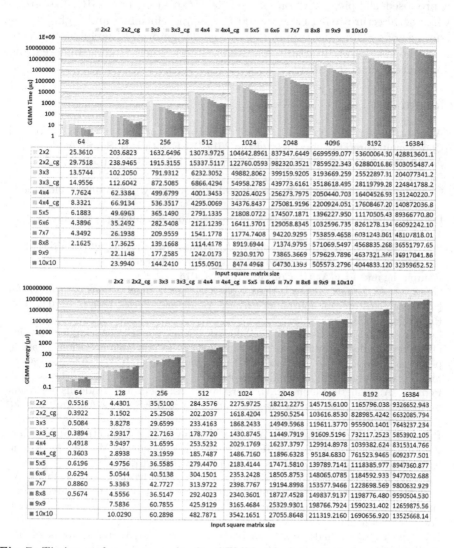

| | 64 | 128 | 256 | 512 | 1024 | 2048 | 4096 | 8192 | 16384 |
|---|---|---|---|---|---|---|---|---|---|
| 2x2 | 25.3610 | 203.6823 | 1632.6496 | 13073.9725 | 104642.8961 | 837347.6449 | 6699599.077 | 53600064.30 | 428813601.1 |
| 2x2_cg | 29.7518 | 238.9465 | 1915.3155 | 15337.5117 | 122760.0593 | 982320.3521 | 7859522.343 | 62880016.86 | 503055487.4 |
| 3x3 | 13.5744 | 102.2050 | 791.9312 | 6232.3052 | 49882.8062 | 399159.9205 | 3193669.259 | 25522897.31 | 204077341.2 |
| 3x3_cg | 14.9556 | 112.6042 | 872.5085 | 6866.4294 | 54958.2785 | 439773.6161 | 3518618.495 | 28119799.28 | 224841788.2 |
| 4x4 | 7.7624 | 62.3384 | 499.6799 | 4001.3453 | 32026.4025 | 256273.7975 | 2050440.703 | 16404526.93 | 131240220.7 |
| 4x4_cg | 8.3321 | 66.9134 | 536.3517 | 4295.0069 | 34376.8437 | 275081.9196 | 2200924.051 | 17608467.20 | 140872036.8 |
| 5x5 | 6.1883 | 49.6963 | 365.1490 | 2791.1335 | 21808.0722 | 174507.1871 | 1396227.950 | 11170505.43 | 89366770.80 |
| 6x6 | 4.3896 | 35.2492 | 282.5408 | 2121.1239 | 16411.3701 | 129058.8345 | 1032596.735 | 8261278.134 | 66092242.10 |
| 7x7 | 4.3492 | 26.1938 | 209.9559 | 1541.1778 | 11774.7408 | 94220.9295 | 753859.4658 | 6031243.861 | 4810/818.01 |
| 8x8 | 2.1625 | 17.3625 | 139.1668 | 1114.4178 | 8919.6944 | 71374.9795 | 571069.5497 | 4568835.268 | 36551797.65 |
| 9x9 | | 22.1148 | 177.2585 | 1242.0173 | 9230.9170 | 73865.3669 | 579629.7896 | 4637321.366 | 36917041.86 |
| 10x10 | | 23.9940 | 144.2410 | 1155.0501 | 8474.4968 | 64730.1393 | 505573.2796 | 4044833.120 | 32359652.52 |

Input square matrix size

| | 64 | 128 | 256 | 512 | 1024 | 2048 | 4096 | 8192 | 16384 |
|---|---|---|---|---|---|---|---|---|---|
| 2x2 | 0.5516 | 4.4301 | 35.5100 | 284.3576 | 2275.9725 | 18212.2275 | 145715.6100 | 1165796.038 | 9326652.943 |
| 2x2_cg | 0.3922 | 3.1502 | 25.2508 | 202.2037 | 1618.4204 | 12950.5254 | 103616.8530 | 828085.4242 | 6632085.794 |
| 3x3 | 0.5084 | 3.8278 | 29.6599 | 233.4163 | 1868.2433 | 14949.5968 | 119611.3770 | 955900.1401 | 7643237.234 |
| 3x3_cg | 0.3894 | 2.9317 | 22.7163 | 178.7720 | 1430.8745 | 11449.7919 | 91609.5196 | 732117.2523 | 5853902.105 |
| 4x4 | 0.4918 | 3.9497 | 31.6595 | 253.5232 | 2029.1769 | 16237.3797 | 129914.8978 | 1039382.624 | 8315314.766 |
| 4x4_cg | 0.3603 | 2.8938 | 23.1959 | 185.7487 | 1486.7160 | 11896.6328 | 95184.6830 | 761523.9465 | 6092377.501 |
| 5x5 | 0.6196 | 4.9756 | 36.5585 | 279.4470 | 2183.4144 | 17471.5810 | 139789.7141 | 1118385.977 | 8947360.877 |
| 6x6 | 0.6294 | 5.0544 | 40.5138 | 304.1501 | 2353.2428 | 18505.8753 | 148065.0785 | 1184592.933 | 9477032.688 |
| 7x7 | 0.8860 | 5.3363 | 42.7727 | 313.9722 | 2398.7767 | 19194.8998 | 153577.9466 | 1228698.569 | 9800632.929 |
| 8x8 | 0.5674 | 4.5556 | 36.5147 | 292.4023 | 2340.3601 | 18727.4528 | 149837.9137 | 1198776.480 | 9590504.530 |
| 9x9 | | 7.5836 | 60.7855 | 425.9129 | 3165.4684 | 25329.9301 | 198766.7924 | 1590231.402 | 12659875.56 |
| 10x10 | | 10.0290 | 60.2898 | 482.7871 | 3542.1661 | 27055.8648 | 211319.2160 | 1690656.920 | 13525668.14 |

Input square matrix size

**Fig. 7.** Timing and energy results for GEMM. Clock-gated designs (*_cg) perform better. GEMV and DOT show similar trends. Constant energy is required for the same problem size across architectures, giving a clean performance:area trade-off.

rate as we measured the performance of a stand-alone core without considering complete system integration and communication latency with a host CPU. No clear way of separating the performance contributors could be extracted from LAC CGRA[7] either, which shows impressive aggregate results extracted from estimations without actual post-synthesis energy consumption data.

## 5  Conclusions

The proposed mapping solutions for efficient execution on CGRA-like architectures architecture reach close to 100% mapping efficiency and highlight the advantages of scalable algorithm-hardware co-design over 12 architectural variants of the *Layers* architecture. Constant energy when trading off area and performance is made possible.

## References

1. Ali, M., Stotzer, E., Igual, F.D., van de Geijn, R.A.: Level-3 BLAS on the TI C6678 multi-core DSP. In: Proc. of the 2012 IEEE 24th Intl. Simp. on Computer Architecture and High Performance Computing (SBAC-PAD), pp. 179–186. IEEE (2012)
2. Chattopadhyay, A.: Ingredients of adaptability: a survey of reconfigurable processors. VLSI Design **2013**, 10 (2013)
3. DeHon, A.: The density advantage of configurable computing. Computer **33**(4), 41–49 (2000)
4. Fell, A., Rákossy, Z.E., Chattopadhyay, A.: Force-directed scheduling for data-flow graph mapping on coarse-grained reconfigurable architectures. In: Reconfigurable Computing and FPGAs (ReConFig), IEEE (2014)
5. Gonzalez, J., Núñez, R.C.: LAPACKrc: Fast linear algebra kernels/solvers for FPGA accelerators. In: Journal of Physics: Conference Series **180**, p. 012042. IOP Publishing (2009)
6. Lei, Y., Dou, Y., Dong, Y., Zhou, J., Xia, F.: FPGA implementation of an exact dot product and its application in variable-precision floating-point arithmetic. The Journal of Supercomputing **64**(2), 580–605 (2013). http://dx.doi.org/10.1007/s11227-012-0860-0
7. Pedram, A., van de Geijn, R.A., Gerstlauer, A.: Codesign tradeoffs for high-performance, low-power linear algebra architectures. IEEE Trans. Comput. **61**(12), 1724–1736 (2012)
8. Rákossy, Z.E., Acosta Aponte, A., Chattopadhyay, A.: Exploiting architecture description language for diverse IP synthesis in heterogeneous MPSoC. In: Reconfigurable Computing and FPGAs (ReConFig). IEEE (2013)
9. Rákossy, Z.E., Merchant, F., Acosta Aponte, A., Nandy, S., Chattopadhyay, A.: Scalable and energy-efficient reconfigurable accelerator for column-wise givens rotation. In: 22nd International Conference on Very Large Scale Integration (VLSI-SoC). IEEE (2014)
10. Rákossy, Z.E., Naphade, T., Chattopadhyay, A.: Design and analysis of layered coarse-grained reconfigurable architecture. In: Reconfigurable Computing and FPGAs (ReConFig), pp. 1–6 (2012)
11. Volkov, V., Demmel, J.W.: Benchmarking gpus to tune dense linear algebra. In: Proc. of the 2008 ACM/IEEE Conf. on Supercomputing, p. 31. IEEE Press (2008)

# A Novel Concept for Adaptive Signal Processing on Reconfigurable Hardware

Peter Figuli[1]([✉]), Carsten Tradowsky[1], Jose Martinez[1],
Harry Sidiropoulos[2], Kostas Siozios[2],
Holger Stenschke[3], Dimitrios Soudris[2], and Jürgen Becker[1]

[1] Institute for Information Processing Technologies,
Karlsruhe Institute of Technology, Karlsruhe, Germany
{figuli,tradowsky,becker}@kit.edu, jalm1204@gmail.com
[2] School of Electrical and Computer Engineering,
National Technical University of Athens, Athens, Greece
{harry,ksiop,dsoudris}@microlab.ntua.gr
[3] School of Music, University of Applied Sciences and Arts
Northwestern Switzerland, Basel, Switzerland
holger.stenschke@fhnw.ch

**Abstract.** Today, digital signal processing systems for applications like audio or video production are restricted as they do not exhaust the possibilities given by modern hardware. Reconfigurable hardware exploits a huge degree of parallelism and provides flexibility at an affordable energy budget, thus becoming a competitive alternative for high performance Digital Signal Processing (DSP) applications, previously dominated by general purpose processing cores and Application-Specific Integrated Circuits (ASICs). This paper describes the design and evaluation of a novel concept for adaptive signal processing on reconfigurable hardware by using an adaptive reverberation algorithm targeting real time streams. Novel solutions were adopted in several critical parts of the signal processing chain in order to achieve a high level of accuracy under real time constraints. Experimental results show the efficiency of the introduced implementation on a Virtex-7 FPGA, as we can provide reality accurate reverberation with ultra low latency of $\sim 20.8\,\mu s$.

**Keywords:** Adaptive signal processing · Reconfigurable hardware · Dynamic reconfiguration

## 1 Introduction

Signal processing, e.g., for audio or video, is a computational intensive task, which usually imposes requirements for expensive and high-performance computing machines. The need for processing power becomes more severe if we have to process sound streams under real-time constraints. Existing approaches to this problem involve the usage of advanced processing machines with numerous general purpose processors and dedicated Digital Signal Processor (DSP) cores.

K. Sano et al. (Eds.): ARC 2015, LNCS 9040, pp. 311–320, 2015.
DOI: 10.1007/978-3-319-16214-0_26

An initiative for developing a next generation stand-alone signal processing computer is the Open Signal Processing Workstation (OSPW). It is conceived as an open development and production platform for software researchers and programmers as well as audio/visual-designers and engineers in the field of media technology [11]. Based on state-of-the-art hardware and software co-design, *OSPW* will provide unusually high performance and flexibility, while retaining usability through high-level, intuitive user interfaces. Depending on the implemented algorithms, *OSPW* can serve as a large-scale audio matrix, an $n$-channel reverberation unit, a real-time video processing engine or a wave field synthesizer. Additionally, high bandwidth *OSPW*-interconnects will allow users to create computing clusters consisting of multiple *OSPW* units in order to scale appropriately the performance efficiency. In [13] we presented an approach using multicore DSPs. The approach targeting reconfigurable hardware will be introduced in this paper.

A typical application of sound processing is to add reverberation to the original recorded audio, emulating natural music listening spaces, like concert halls, large churches or other closed places. Key elements of natural reverberation are the unique diffusion patterns of surfaces in a closed space that cannot be simulated with filter based models as proposed by Moorer [8]. Thus the only apparent alternative to get a realistic sound is to perform a convolution with the recorded impulse response (*IR*) of the desired space.

Software programs, like Audio Ease Altiverb [2], offer this feature using impulse response libraries of different environments. Furthermore, existing approaches are adding the reverberation effect by signal processing in frequency domain using Fast Fourrier Transform (FFT). Although with modern CPUs and GPUs these processing steps are trivial, the introduced latency is at least twice the length of the impulse response of the simulated space, due to the required buffering for FFT. This translates to latency of couple of seconds for realistic reverberation, which is impractical for live applications. A reduction of latency of FFT could be achieved through partitioned overlap and save techniques. In [1] this was applied on a DSP, where the latency could be reduced to 170ms with partitioned blocks of 8192 samples. Further improvements can be achieved with sections of different lengths, as shown in [9]. But as they use manual partitioning, the implementation is subject to low scalability.

The most significant difference between our concept and existing solutions is that we implement the sound processing steps not in the frequency, but in the time domain. This imposes a significant increase of processing power requirements, especially under real-time constraints, but rewards with the lowest possible latency in the clock cycle range. In the past, this method was not feasible as the traditional digital sound processing platforms did not provide the required performance. Thus existing solutions operate on the frequency domain, compromising on latency. However, modern reconfigurable hardware offers the capabilities needed for the convolution with large impulse responses in the time domain, promising the lowest possible latency. An immediate application could be in adding the reverberation effect of a big concert hall, like La Scala, Milan's opera house, on live music played in a small concert room.

In our heterogeneous approach, a small low-power embedded processor manages the data and handles control and usability related functions of the system, while the computation intensive tasks are outsourced on highly parallel hardware accelerators, built of logic cells and high-performance DSP slices of an underlying FPGA platform. The secondary goal of our proposed implementation of natural reverberation is adaptivity by taking advantage of partial reconfiguration and allowing to:

- trade off the number of channels versus *IR* length.
- give emphasis in low latency by minimizing the number of channels and *IR* length, in case one wants to add more filters in the signal processing chain.
- integrate extra filters with the reverberation by convolution of impulse responses, for minimizing the total latency of the system.
- change the audio interface controller, depending on the periphery.

The rest of the paper is organized as follows: Section 2 presents the background of this work. Whereas in Section 3 we explain our adaptive audio signal processing architecture. Section 4 presents evaluation results on a *Virtex7 FPGA* platform. Finally, conclusions are summarized in Section 5.

## 2   Fundamentals and Constraints

This section introduces the fundamentals and the constraints imposed by the nature of the application, in our case, audio signal processing.

### 2.1   Convolution

The time-discrete convolution of two discrete signals is defined as

$$x \times h = \sum_{i=0}^{N} h[i] \times x[k - i] \qquad (1)$$

In the frequency domain this definition corresponds to element-wise multiplication of the Fourier transformed signals, as shown in [5]. Convolving a signal with the impulse response of a system, analytically results in the same effect as the signal would be transformed when passing from the input to the output of the system. We make use of this method to emulate the acoustic room effects of a building, in absence of the actual room, by convolving a live audio stream with the pre-recorded impulse response of the room.

### 2.2   Reverberation Time

Since a sound in the closed field is composed of the direct sound and reflections from the boundaries [12], a critical parameter is the reverberation time, which provides a good estimate about how long a record of the impulse response needs to be. The reverberation time is usually measured from the end of the direct sound until the sound of the reflections has a $60\,dB$ decay in the sound energy decay process [12]. A factor that influences this reverberation time is the absorption that takes place in the closed field. The equation for the reverberation time was deduced in [12] as follows:

$$T_R = \frac{0.161\,V}{-\ln(1 - \alpha)\,S}[S] \tag{2}$$

$$\alpha = \frac{\sum_i \alpha_i S_i}{S} \tag{3}$$

$V$ is the volume of the closed space and $\alpha$ denotes the average absorption coefficients of the space. $\alpha_i$ is the absorption coefficient of the $i^{th}$ portion of the surface whose area is $S_i[m^2]$ and the total area is $S[m^2]$.

### 2.3    Constraints

To realistically simulate the natural reverberation of a room, we need to take into account the capabilities of human hearing and derive system constraints.

**Latency.** In live scenarios of audio applications latency plays a major role. A perceptive latency not only degrades the audio-visual experience to the audience, but also has a negative impact on the musician's ability to perform when it occurs in the monitoring equipment. In [7], experimental tests have proven that the acceptable amount of latency in live sound monitoring can range from $42ms$ to less than $1.4ms$, depending on the instrument played and the monitoring type (wedge monitor or in-ear monitor). Thus our target is overall system latency of $< 1ms$.

**Frequency Range.** The human ear range is considered as $20Hz$ to $20,000Hz$, though there are variations between individuals, especially at high frequencies [10]. Thus for demonstration purposes we chose a sampling rate of $48KHz$, complying with the Nyquist-Shannon sampling theorem and leaving a margin for the filter transition band.

**Dynamic Range.** The human ear at its best has a dynamic range greater than $130dB$ [10]. This could be covered by a quantisation in $22bit$. Practical aspects, e. g., limitations and noise of the analog components as well as environmental noise, however make a lower quantisation acceptable and $16bit$ are standard for the most audio sources, giving a dynamic range of $96dB$. For demonstration purposes we chose $16bit$ as this is the word size of our source files and the impulse response is anyway cut after a decay of $60dB$.

## 3    Design of the Adaptive Signal Processing

Initially, the convolution definition provided in Section 2.1 is analyzed and implemented utilizing the $DSP48E1$ slices in the Xilinx Virtex-7 devices [14]. $x$ and $h$ represent the input signal and the mask to which we refer as the impulse response ($IR$), respectively. Both signals are stored internally in Block RAMs ($BRAMs$).

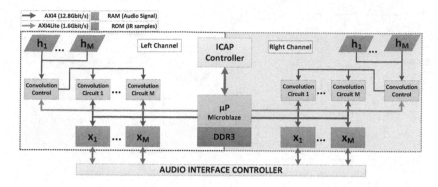

**Fig. 1.** Architecture of the introduced adaptive digital audio signal processing

To avoid excessive data movement for shifting of input data, the memory is orgranised as a ring buffer with circular addressing, incrementing the read and write address pointers, rather than moving the data.

At a sampling rate of $48\,kHz$ the time period available for all processing steps, including data read and computing of the dot product, is $\tau_p \approx 20.8\mu s$. Hence, an impulse response of $2s$ length for instance requires to multiply and accumulate two vectors of length $96,000$ element by element within this time period. In order to meet the timing requirements, the task of convolution needs to be partitioned in several parts and allocated to several concurrent convolution hardware accelerators. Also, due to the size and the accessibility limitations, the memory space needs to be partitioned into distributed $BRAMs$. Fast control units are required to manage the data access and control the processing. An efficient approach to further enhance the performance, is to tap the data bus and multiply samples as they appear on the bus while reading.

## 3.1   System Architecture

Based on the above named considerations we derive a scalable system architecture as depicted in Figure 1, where we show a two-channel example system. An extension to more channels is possible in a modular way, as they are handled independently from each other.

The audio interface controller handles input and output streams of digital audio signals and is reconfigurable in order to adapt to various interfaces and protocols of external devices, e. g., to AES/EBU [4], MADI [3] or directly to converters with $I^2S$, PCM or parallel interfaces. This unit writes the incoming audio stream sample by sample to the ring buffer memory of distributed $RAMs$ ($x_1...x_M$). Furthermore it manages the output stream as the result of the convolution.

The vector of impulse response is partitioned and stored in the $ROMs$ ($h_1...h_M$). Both, the $RAMs$ and the $ROMs$, are realized by dual ported $BRAMs$. In case of the impulse response, the decision to configure the $BRAMs$ as $ROMs$

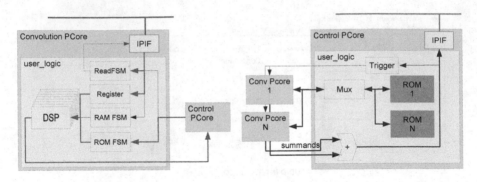

**Fig. 2.** Block diagrams of the convolution *PCore* (left) and control *PCore* (right)

leads to significant savings of memory resources. However, the impulse response can be changed only through reconfiguration.

The distributed memories are read by the *Convolution Circuits* 1..*M* through 128 *bit* wide *AXI4* Busses in burst mode. The structure of these units is depicted in Figure 2 (left). Each *Convolution Circuit* contains eight *DSP48E1* slices and is able to process eight samples in parallel. This level of parallelism per *Convolution Circuit* is derived from the maximum data width (128 *bit*) of the *PCore* interface, as wrapper of the circuits, divided by the sample data width 16 *bit*. Each circuit is programmed to read 2,048 x 128 *bit* long words every 20.8 *μs* from a *RAM* simultaneously. There are parallel processes responsible for access of *RAM* and *ROM* data (*RAM FSM* and *ROM FSM* respectively), as well as for handling of read requests from the *PCore* interface (*ReadFSM*). The *Convolution Circuits* read concurrently $\frac{2N}{M}$ data values in the sampling period $\tau_P$, $\frac{N}{M}$ from the *ROM* and $\frac{N}{M}$ from the *RAM*. Here, *M* refers to the number of convolution cores and *N* to the length of *IR*. Parallel to this process, *MAC* units, realized by *DSP48E1* slices, tap in the data busses and without detour multiply the available audio streaming data with the *IR* data and accumulate it in a register.

The *PCore* with the *Convolution Control* unit as shown in Figure 2 (right) provides to the convolution *PCore* the triggering signal and the *RAM* data signal. Also it collects the signals from each convolution *PCore*. The control *PCore* has processes to compute the summation of the results coming from the convolution *PCores* and to control the multiplexing of the *ROMs*, which is described in Subsection 3.2.

Based on the architectural requirements, the introduced solution must fulfil the upcoming challenges for computing the convolution:

– Send the trigger signal of the *ROM* read process to the *AMBA* interface.
– Read the *IR* from the $ROM(h_1, h_2, ..., h_M)$.
– Synchronize the reading of both the *IR* from the *ROM* and the streaming data from the *RAM* in order to guarantee that their multiplication is performed in the correct order.

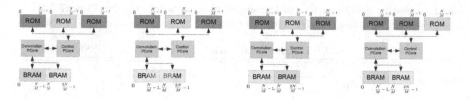

**Fig. 3.** Convolution after 0 samples (left), $\frac{N}{2M}$ samples (2nd left), $\frac{N}{M}$ samples (2nd right), and $\frac{N}{M} + 1$ samples (right)

- Simultaneously to the previous mentioned read, multiply the data and accumulate it to the previous result, until a whole read out of the $IR$ and incoming data is completed.
- Shift the data to include new samples every time a $MAC$ operation is computed.

Other control tasks, that are not critical part of the convolution mechanisms, are managed by a Microblaze processor core. This includes amongst others the initialization of the system, the communication with a higher level master system (e. g., $OSPW$) and the partial and dynamic reconfiguration of the convolution system. For the latter task, an $ICAP$ Controller module ($HWICAP$) is connected to the Microblaze. This enables to change the impulse response in the $ROMs$ $h_1...h_M$ during run time, following the partial reconfiguration method proposed in [15]. The instruction code as well as the library of impulse responses and the bit streams for partial reconfiguration are stored in an external $DDR3$ memory.

### 3.2 Memory Access Sequence

The data shifting and ROM multiplexing sequences are shown in Figure 3 for every $PCore$. The amount of *Convolution Control* modules may be one per channel, but it also depends on the number of *Convolution Circuits* that are being implemented per bus. Certainly there will be one control unit multiplexing the $ROMs$ for several *Convolution Circuits*. The *Convolution Control* needs signals from the *Convolution Circuits* in order to execute the tasks at the correct timing.

When a memory read is complete, the convolution should immediately change to the content of the $ROM$ that is being accessed for every $PCore$. Fortunately, the $ROMs$ have two ports due to the $BRAM$ implementation. In case one $PCore$ finishes a read out from memory before the other $PCore$, the $ROM$ can be accessed by the other $BRAM$ port. Thus, we avoid to collide with the

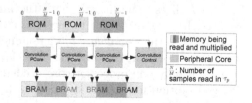

**Fig. 4.** Convolution with three $PCores$ after $\frac{N}{2M}$ samples

**Table 1.** Resource utilization of the implemented components on the *Virtex7 VC707* evaluation board targeting $48\,kHz$ with $0.5\,s$ impulse response according to Figure 1

| | Slice $LUTs$ | BRAM 36 | BRAM 18 | SliceRegisters | $DSP$ 48 Slices |
|---|---|---|---|---|---|
| *Microblaze* | 96,267 | 16 | 0 | 50,873 | 0 |
| *HWICAP* | 232 | 0 | 0 | 503 | 0 |
| Convolution *PCore* | 1,741 | 0 | 0 | 1,152 | 15 |
| Control Circuit | 1,273 | 0 | 0 | 411 | 0 |
| IR *ROM* | 0 | 0 | 1 | 0 | 0 |
| Audio *RAM* | 780 | 8 | 0 | 741 | 0 |

*PCore* that has not finished reading that memory yet. After the two memories, connected to a *PCore*, were read and multiplied, the *ROM* is changed in order to repeat the process with next portion of IR data. This procedure allows us to multiply all of the samples available in the *ROMs* with all the data saved in the *RAMs*.

After having explained the memory access sequence for one *PCore*, the equivalent case for the complete system, i.e., the same number of *PCores* as *ROMs*, is shown in the Figure 4. The memory reading process is the same as illustrated in Figure 3, but with the remaining *PCores* accessing the other *ROMs* and *RAMs*. The configurable parameters, such as the memory addresses to start and to finish, are set by the microprocessor through control registers.

# 4   Results

In this section, we present the results obtained with our adaptive signal processing on reconfigurable hardware. We present the resource utilization of the FPGA target implementation, the scalability and the applicability of the adaptive signal processing. The resource utilization is reported for the *Virtex7 VC707* board and summarized in Table 1. Each convolution *PCore* can process $\approx 0.17\,s$ of audio signal. The resources used for different quantities of *PCores*, resulting in different impulse response (*IR*) lengths, are shown in the Figure 5 (left). We investigated several scaling factors up to a size of 32 *PCores*, which results in $5.44\,s$ *IR* length. The resource utilization on the *Virtex7 VC707* board is then $72\%$ *LUTs*, $21\%$ registers, $28\%$ *BRAMs* and $17\%$ *DSP48E1* slices. While the *DSP48E1* slices scale linearly with the number of convolution units, all other resources have an offset due to the *Microblaze* component. Especially for smaller configurations the *Microblaze* has a dominant relative share on the total resource utilization. However, this becomes less the more convolution units are deployed as there is only one processor core needed, independent from the count of parallel convolution units. The decision on how many convolution units to deploy depends on the expected maximum length of the room impulse response.

With 32 convolution units we can process realistic reverberation of rooms with impulse responses of up to $5.44\,s$ in real-time. This translates to a computing performance of $\sim 25.1\,GigaMAC/s$ and internal memory accesses at a data

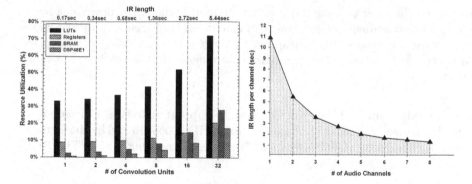

**Fig. 5.** Resource utilization of implemented components on the *Virtex7 VC707* evaluation board targeting $48\,kHz$ for different convolution units (left chart) and various impulse response lengths vs. available audio channels (right chart)

rate of $\sim 806.6\,Gbit/s$. The latency is as low as one sampling clock cycle, i.e. $\sim 20.8\,\mu s$, thus not audible.

There are different trade-offs possible regarding the presented numbers for the application of audio engineering. Of course, you can process the same *IR* to each channel to add room acoustics to your mix. However, in a studio setup it might be interesting to use different *IR*s for different mix buses, i.e., a chamber ($\approx 1.95\,s$) for the drums, a small room ($\approx 0.64\,s$) for the piano and bass and a medium plate ($\approx 2.4\,s$) for the vocals. Figure 5 (right) shows the trade-off between *IR* length and the number of audio channels. It becomes clear that there is also the possibility to use more channels like in a surround setup for video post production. All of the above mentioned adaptations are possible during run-time by using partial dynamic reconfiguration through the *ICAP* controller to, e.g., load different *IR*s from *DDR* to *ROM* or reroute to available resources to realize more/less channels.

## 5 Conclusion and Future Work

In this paper we presented a novel concept to realize adaptive audio signal processing on reconfigurable hardware. Our approach provides flexibility and very high performance and throughput and is thus capable of solving the challenges that lie ahead for the audio industry. A real-world FPGA implementation was accomplished that is able to process high resolution audio data in the time domain with very low latency at a speed that was never possible before. We have shown on a Xilinx Virtex-7 VC707 board that, based on the $48\,kHz$ sample rate, $261,120$ calculations per sample of $\sim 20.8\,\mu s$ can be executed for each stereo audio channel, resulting in a total performance of $\sim 25.1\,GigaMAC/s$ and in memory accesses at $\sim 806.6\,Gbit/s$ in a stereo setup. For future work, it would be beneficial to integrate this flexible approach into the Open Signal Processing

Workbench, in order to make this high-throughput audio signal processing available to a broad audience of developers, engineers and musicians. Additionally we want to use the generic VLIW-inspired Slot Architecture (ViSA) [6] to replace the control logic or even the Microblaze component, thus increasing the overall efficiency.

**Acknowledgments.** This work was partly supported by the German Academic Exchange Service (DAAD) under Project-ID 57055815 and by the German Research Foundation (DFG) as part of "Invasive Computing" (SFB/TR 89).

# References

1. Armelloni, E. Giottoli, C., Farina, A.: Implementation of real-time partitioned convolution on a DSP board. In: Applications of Signal Processing to Audio and Acoustics (2003)
2. Audio Ease. Audio ease altiverb - impulse responses - the altiverb library of acoustics. https://www.audioease.com/Pages/Altiverb/irs.php
3. Audio Engineering Society. AES10-2008 (r2014): AES Recommended Practice for Digital Audio Engineering - Serial Multichannel Audio Digital Interface (MADI). http://www.aes.org/publications/standards/search.cfm?docID=17
4. Audio Engineering Society. AES3-2009: AES standard for digital audio engineering - Serial transmission format for two-channel linearly represented digital audio data. http://www.aes.org/publications/standards/search.cfm?docID=13
5. Damelin, S.B., Miller Jr., W.: The mathematics of signal processing. Cambridge University Press (2011)
6. Figuli, P., Tradowsky, C., Gaertner, N., Becker, J.: ViSA: A highly efficient slot architecture enabling multi-objective ASIP cores. In International Symposium on System-on-Chip (2013)
7. Lester, M., Boley, J.: The effects of latency on live sound monitoring. In Audio Engineering Society Convention, vol. 123 (2007)
8. Moorer, J. A.: About this reverberation business. Computer Music Journal (1979)
9. Primavera, A., Cecchi, S., Romoli, L., Piazza, F., Moschetti, M.: An efficient dsp-based implementation of a fast convolution approach with non-uniform partitioning. In 5th European DSP Education and Research Conference (EDERC) (2012)
10. Self, D., Nathan, J., Duncan, B., Miller, C., Sinclair, I.: Audio Engineering: Know It All, vol. 1. Newnes, Newton (2008)
11. Stenschke, H.: Open Signal Processing Workstation (2014). http://ospw.avcreatives.com
12. Tohyama, M., Koike, T.: Fundamentals of acoustic signal processing. Academic Pr. (1998)
13. Tradowsky, C., Figuli, P., Seidenspinner, E., Held, F., Becker, J.: A new approach to model-based development for audio signal processing. In: Audio Engineering Society Convention, vol. 134 (2013)
14. Xilinx. 7 Series DSP48E1 Slice. http://www.xilinx.com/support/documentation/user_guides/ug479_7Series_DSP48E1.eps
15. Xilinx. UG744, April 2012. http://www.xilinx.com/support/documentation/sw_manuals/xilinx14_1/PlanAhead_Tutorial_Reconfigurable_Processor.eps

# Evaluation of High-Level Synthesis Techniques for Memory and Datapath Tradeoffs in FPGA Based SoC Architectures

Efstathios Sotiriou-Xanthopoulos, Dionysios Diamantopoulos,
and George Economakos[✉]

School of ECE, National Technical University of Athens, Heroon Polytechniou 9,
15780 Zografou, Athens, Greece
{stasot,diamantd,geconom}@microlab.ntua.gr

**Abstract.** While *High-Level Synthesis* (HLS) has been a research topic
for more than 30 years, modern HLS tools have made possible the development of production ready circuits, taking advantage of improvements
in areas like *Field Programmable Gate Arrays* (FPGAs) and multicore
*System-on-Chip* (SoC) architectures. The efficient use of these improvements however require technology aware coding and constraint specification, through specific tool directives. In this paper, a modern HLS
environment is used to investigate different architecture alternatives,
for the design of hardware accelerators, taking into account tradeoffs
between memory and datapath component utilization, in modern, SoC
aware FPGA devices. Experimental results show that correct architectural option selections can lead to an almost 120X speedup and better
scaling performance while the input size is increasing, with practical negligible resource utilization overheads in medium and large scale devices.

## 1 Introduction

Modern embedded systems need to comply to different requirements in order
to make a high and fast market impact. From the designer's point of view,
all requirements can be summarized into two key factors: improve quality (in
terms of performance, resource usage, power dissipation, etc.) and reduce time-
to-market. To face these goals, modern design techniques like *High-Level Synthesis* (HLS) [3] can be adopted, that involves the automatic translation of untimed
C/C++ algorithmic descriptions into *Register-Transfer Level* (RTL) architectural descriptions, ready for implementation.

HLS started as a research topic more than 30 years ago, and can be divided
into three generations [6]. The first generation, roughly covered the years between

This work was partially supported by "TEAChER: TEach AdvanCEd Reconfigurable architectures and tools" project funded by DAAD (2014) and CIDCIP and
MENELAOS projects funded by the Ministry of Development under the National
Strategic Reference Framework NSRF 2007-2013, action "Creation of innovation
clusters" "A GREEK PRODUCT, A SINGLE MARKET: THE PLANET".

© Springer International Publishing Switzerland 2015
K. Sano et al. (Eds.): ARC 2015, LNCS 9040, pp. 321–330, 2015.
DOI: 10.1007/978-3-319-16214-0_27

1980 and 1990. Its main contribution was to lay down the mathematical foundation that could solve the diversity of problems found in the automated algorithm-to-architecture transformation. The second generation, covering the years 1990 to 2000, was a very promising generation, introducing the first commercial tools. However, this generation failed to stand up to its promises, mainly because it was overestimated, offering poor quality of results. The third generation, starting in 2000 and lasting up to now, is more mature, starts from system level languages, offers a different design paradigm separated from RTL and quality of results is highly improved.

Recently, the technological advances in *Field Programmable Gate Array* (FPGA) devices, offering hundreds of GFLOPs with maximum power efficiency, has established a fast prototyping advanced implementation platform. FPGAs consist of specially designed hardware modules (*Look-Up Table* (LUT) function generators, *D-type Flip-Flops* (DFF), *Block RAM* (BRAM) and special purpose DSP blocks), offering hardware-like performance, that can be dynamically reconfigured and change functionality, based on efficient circuit switching interconnections, in a software-like manner. FPGA programming is based on *Hardware Description Languages* (HDLs), which can keep non-expert designers away, having a negative impact on productivity. This has started to change with the adoption of HLS for FPGA design. However, this adoption needs specific coding styles and tool directives for the efficient use of each hardware component found within an FPGA device, and especially those that can implement either memory or datapath primitives, or both. Building efficient FPGA memory hierarchies is a future challenge for HLS tool vendors [2].

This paper presents an HLS based methodology and the corresponding tool flow for the design of hardware accelerators installed into a programmable SoC architecture. The novelty introduced is a number of accelerator architectures, that combine datapath and memory optimizations available in modern FPGA devices. They have been designed so as to investigate tradeoffs between efficient memory hierarchies and datapath chains. Also, they are presented in a more systematic way than previous approaches [5,7], along with the required language constructs and tool directives to build them, starting from pure untimed C/C++ algorithmic descriptions. Evaluation of the accelerator architectures proposed is done through experimentation with a biomedical filtering application. Obtained results show that correct architectural option selections can lead to an almost 120X speedup, with improvements in scaling as the data set is enlarged or the number of available hardware accelerator cores is increased. As resource utilization is concerned, little overheads are found (practical negligible in medium to large scale FPGA devices). These two types of behavior make the proposed methodology a strong player in the field of improved designer productivity, which has always been the ultimate goal in all HLS related research efforts.

## 2    Motivation

Memory elements in FPGA devices can be implemented in two different ways. As distributed memories, which utilize fine grained programmable FPGA primitives like DFFs and LUTs, or as block memories, which utilize special purpose BRAM primitives. Historically, block memories are newer than distributed memories. The first FPGA devices had nothing more than DFFs and LUTs. BRAMs appeared as a way to implement embedded large memory blocks. While DFFs and LUTs can implement either memory of logic, BRAMs can implement only memory. Each BRAM block has a dedicated memory controller, with up to 2 read/write ports and impose very little overhead to the rest of the FPGA resources. On the other hand, distributed memories and their corresponding controllers (which are generally more complicated than BRAM memory controllers) are build using DFFs and LUTs and can have multiple read/write ports.

As a motivational example, we have synthesized a 1024 and a 1024x1024 memory with 16 bit values, using distributed (DRAM) and BRAM primitives and a large scale FPGA device, the Xilinx Virtex-7 VC7VX485 (303600 LUTs, 607200 DFFs, 2060 8 bit BRAMs). Table 1 shows delays and resource usage for different configurations. As it can be seen, for the 1024 memory, DRAM is faster than BRAM and the resources used leave plenty more to implement datapath chains within the same device. When this result is combined with a multiport DRAM architecture, the advantages of DRAM over BRAM is greatly magnified. However, for the 1024x1024 memory, DRAM is slower than BRAM (due to the required complicated controller) and takes almost all device resources. In that case, the selection of a BRAM is a one-way decision. While the results of table 1 are preliminary (synthesis and not implementation results), they show that DRAM can offer advantages in smaller memories that can have a great impact on application performance. So, mixed style memory hierarchies, with small DRAM memories and large BRAM memories can be designed, offering different advantages in different cases. Highly parallelizable code can gain very high speed improvements with multiport DRAM memories, while serial code can be combined with large BRAM memories, for resource usage savings. Such hierarchies will be presented as architectural templates in section 4.

**Table 1.** Delay and resource utilization for different types of memories

| Memory size/type | Delay (ns) | DFFs | LUTs | BRAM |
|---|---|---|---|---|
| 1024/DRAM | 2.523 | 16 (0%) | 292 (0%) | 0 (0%) |
| 1024/BRAM | 3.021 | 0 (0%) | 0 (0%) | 1 (0%) |
| 1024x1024/DRAM | 5.349 | 16 (0%) | 288575 (95%) | 0 (0%) |
| 1024x1024/BRAM | 2.685 | 4 (0%) | 80 (0%) | 512 (49%) |

# 3  Proposed Methodology

The design methodology proposed in this paper consists of two steps. First, the generation of a high performance hardware accelerator and second, the integration of the generated accelerator together with a reference SoC architecture. In both steps, the underlying technologies aim at improving designer productivity, while maintaining quality of results.

The proposed tool flow (without loss of generality and due to maturity) is based on Xilinx *Embedded Development Kit* (EDK), which supports SoC architectures of a single or dual core embedded processor (ARM, PowerPC, MicroBlaze), playing the role of the AXI bus [1] master. Two EDK tools are involved for hardware and software specification and design, *Xilinx Platform Studio* (XPS) and Xilinx *Software Development Kit* (SDK). XPS is a GUI enriched hardware specification tool, with links to low level implementation tools for full, top-down hardware design, and SDK is an Eclipse based software development environment. For the proposed methodology, that is the design of high performance hardware accelerators, another tool is involved, Xilinx Vivado HLS. This tool is used for the design of an AXI slave, which implements the functionality of the accelerator and is connected to the SoC architecture through simple or streaming AXI interfaces (depending on throughput and latency requirements). Vivado HLS accepts untimed C/C++ algorithmic descriptions and based on the dependencies described with the used language constructs (assignments, loops, conditionals) and user specified constraints and preferences (through appropriate directives), generates optimum technology aware RTL descriptions. The novel approach of this flow is that it accepts only C/C++ input and produces optimized final implementation bitfiles.

## 4    Proposed Architectures

This section presents four different SoC architectures, along with the language constructs and required tool directives. In this way, a clear link between specification and implementation in the Vivado HLS environment is given. The four architectures, given in figures 1a-2b, present different datapath optimizations, memory hierarchies and interconnection opportunities.

This first SoC architecture is given in figure 1a. An embedded processor is connected to on chip and off chip memories and the generated hardware accelerator, through the processor bus (for the reference tool flow, the AXI bus). For an FPGA device, the most widely used on chip memory is *Block RAM* (BRAM), which is implemented by the FPGA vendors as specific components installed within the FPGA fabric. The most widely used off chip memory is dynamic or DDR memory, connected to processor bus though an appropriate IP of a DDR controller. DDR is slow but can be very large in size and contain large data sets while BRAM is fast but limited in size. Also, parallel access to both memory types is limited by the number of controller inputs, which is most off the times two (dual port memories). Execution in the architecture of figure 1a starts with input data read from an external device (a data file in a connected filing system) and stored in DDR. Next, all or parts of the input data are moved to BRAM, to speed up execution. Then, the embedded processor reads data from BRAM and sends them through the bus to the hardware accelerator, using a set of memory mapped registers. The accelerator performs datapath operations (all the required algorithmic operations) and returns results through the same route, that is the processor bus. This architecture does not require any specific language constructs, provided the initial C/C++ algorithmic description contains legal code for the HLS tool. It needs however a set of directives, to generate appropriate hardware and software descriptions of the bus ports and their access methods, like the following, where x and y are the input and output of top level function foo.

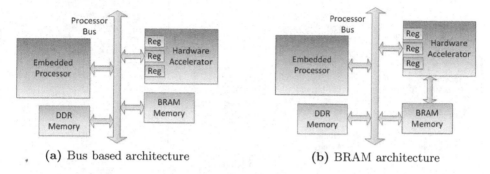

(a) Bus based architecture                          (b) BRAM architecture

**Fig. 1.** Implementation architectures

```
set_directive_interface −mode ap_ctrl_hs "foo", ap_none "foo" x, ap_vld "foo" y
set_directive_resource −core AXI4LiteS "foo" return, x, y
```

The architecture of figure 1a is limited in performance due to its close dependence with the processor bus. To overcome this, in the second SoC architecture of figure 1b, the hardware accelerator communicates directly with BRAM memory. Execution this time starts with the embedded processor initializing BRAM and then, sending just an initialization signal to the accelerator through the bus. This is their only communication and the accelerator can work at full speed, without time consuming bus transactions. Again, no specific algorithmic constructs are required, only the following directives for the memory connected port (together with the previous bus connection directives).

```
set_directive_interface −mode ap_memory "foo" mem
```

The third SoC architecture is given in figure 2a. In this architecture, the hardware accelerator is equipped with a local memory, which is implemented as a register file using LUT function generators (DRAM), found in large amounts in FPGA devices. The advantage of DRAM memory is that each component can be accessed independent of the others, so a multiport memory architecture is generated. This architecture has a more complex controller than dual port BRAM memory, but fast and parallel access times. Execution starts with the embedded processor initializing BRAM and then, the accelerator copies BRAM contents into the local DRAM memory (a local variable). After that any access command to BRAM memory is changed to the appropriate DRAM memory access command and the accelerator can work at very high speed, limited only by the dependencies found within the datapath. Both bus and BRAM bottlenecks are avoided. The disadvantage of this third architecture is that both memory and datapath are implemented with LUTs, which may be a limited resource in small and medium range FPGA devices.

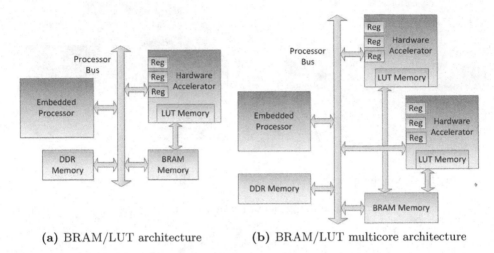

(a) BRAM/LUT architecture          (b) BRAM/LUT multicore architecture

**Fig. 2.** Implementation architectures

Regarding directives, a number of preferences can be imposed in order to exploit the full potential of this architecture. First, a directive for the BRAM memory connected port is required. Also, a directive called ARRAY_PARTITION in Vivado HLS is used to map the local memory (lut variable) into LUT and not BRAM resources. After that, all loops that access LUT/DRAM memory can be fully unrolled. This way all code that access local memory can be executed in parallel, limited only by data dependencies of the datapath. Also, the DRAM memory initialization loop can be unrolled two times, because this is the maximum parallelization that can be achieved with a dual port BRAM memory. Finally, function calls within the datapath can be either inlined or pipelined. Inlining increases the code fragments that can be accessed in parallel, with more complicated control hardware however. Pipelining improves execution time by overlapping consecutive function calls. For each algorithmic description, either inlining or pipelining may give better results so, a trial and error approach is required. In brief, a representative example of the directives of the third architecture are given below, where bram is the BRAM and lut is the LUT memory variable, and initialization and computation are labels of a LUT initialization and a heavy computational loop respectively.

```
set_directive_interface -mode ap_memory "foo" bram
set_directive_array_partition -type complete "foo" lut
set_directive_unroll -factor 2 "foo/initialization", "foo/computation"
```

Finally, the fourth SoC architecture is given in figure 2b. The accelerator is the same as the one found in the third architecture however, more than one accelerators are used. This way, provided the algorithmic description contains computations that can be executed in parallel using the local LUT based memory copy, maximum parallelism can be achieved and performance can satisfy demanding, high throughput applications. For this architecture no extra algorithmic constructs are required or tool directives. The only difference with the third architecture is that LUT/DRAM memory size in each accelerator is less than the size of the BRAM memory, determined by the number of accelerators.

## 5   Experimental Results

The four different architectures presented in section 4 have been used for experimentation. Performance, in terms of execution time, and resource usage measurements, in terms of LUTs, DFFs, BRAMs and DSPs, were taken using the tool flow presented in section 3. The SoC architecture was built based on the MicroBlaze soft processor. This selection was based on the maturity of the selected tool flow with this processor (simulation, synthesis, verification and implementation) and their illustrative user interfaces, and is by no means restricting the ideas presented in this paper. All experiments were performed using the Xilinx VC707 evaluation board with a Virtex-7 VC7VX485 device (303600 LUTs, 607200 DFFs, 2060 BRAMs, 2800 DSPs) and a clock speed of 100 MHz. The same clock was used for the MicroBlaze processor, which was connected with 1 GB DDR and 64 MB BRAM memories. All software written for the MicroBlaze was ran out of BRAM, for speed reasons.

**Table 2.** Performance for a 1024 sample size

| Experiment | Execution time (sec) |
|---|---|
| SW | 3.2198 |
| HW_BUS | 2.4059 |
| HW_BRAM | 0.0717 |
| HW_BRAM_LUT | 0.0511 |
| HW_BRAM_LUT_MULTI | 0.0274 |

The selected application to be implemented with a hardware accelerator was a biomedical filter solution, found in PhysioNet (http://www.physionet.org), for the recognition of the QRS wave of the *Electrocardiogram* (ECG) signal. The initial algorithmic description originated from a quite old but reference publication [4], and contains a 10 tap FIR filter and some classification based on the filter output, the frequency and the sampling rate of the ECG signal. Overall, five experiment sets were selected. The first was a pure software solution, where the application code was ran on MicroBlaze. The rest were the architectures of section 4, where synchronization software was ran on MicroBlaze and all application code on the hardware accelerator(s). For all five sets, an input buffer was read from a USB file and then transferred to DDR and BRAM. Finally, the fourth architecture of section 4 included 4, 8 or 16 parallel hardware accelerators.

**Table 3.** Performance for different sample sizes

| Experiment | Size | Execution time (sec) | Size | Execution time (sec) | Size | Execution time (sec) |
|---|---|---|---|---|---|---|
| HW_BUS | 1024 | 2.4059 | 2048 | 4.8021 | 4096 | 9.5944 |
| HW_BRAM | 1024 | 0.0717 | 2048 | 0.1332 | 4096 | 0.2560 |
| HW_BRAM_LUT | 1024 | 0.0511 | 2048 | 0.1256 | 4096 | 0.2408 |
| HW_BRAM_LUT_MULTI | 1024 | 0.0274 | 2048 | 0.0420 | 4096 | 0.0697 |

Performance measurements for all five experiments for an input size of 1024 are shown in table 2, where the great improvement from software to hardware solutions is made very clear. Next, since the software experiment (SW) was proved too slow, the performance measurements for the fastest four experiments (HW_BUS, HW_BRAM, HW_BRAM_LUT and HW_BRAM_LUT_MULTI) for input sizes of 1024, 2048 and 4096 samples are shown in table 3. The increase in computation time with increasing sample sizes (1024, 2048, 4096) for the fastest three hardware experiments, that utilize BRAM and LUT/DRAM local memories, is shown in figure 3 (the BUS architecture had much larger timing requirements, to fit in the same diagram). Also, performance measurements for the HW_BRAM_LUT_MULTI experiment with 4, 8 and 16 parallel accelerator cores are given in figure 4 (all figures present execution times in psec on the vertical axis). Finally, average resource usage measurements for all experiments are given in table 4, as absolute values and percentages of the total available.

For performance, tables 2 and 3 and figure 3, show that the software solution is the slowest while hardware accelerator architectures with directly connected accelerator and BRAM memory offer great improvements. Specifically, the quad accelerator HW_BRAM_LUT_MULTI architecture offers an almost 120X speedup, the HW_BRAM_LUT architecture a 65X speedup, the HW_BRAM a 45X speedup and finally, the HW_BUS a 1.5X speedup. Of the three architectures that utilize direct connection between the accelerators and BRAM memory (HW_BRAM, HW_BRAM_LUT and HW_BRAM_LUT_MULTI), again the multi accelerator architecture not only offers top performance, but also behaves much better than the others when the computational load is increased, as shown from its slope (bottom line in figure 3), which is the lowest. The speedup offered by the quad core HW_BRAM_LUT_MULTI architecture compared to the HW_BRAM_LUT is 2X while HW_BRAM_LUT compared to HW_BRAM is 1.5X faster. Also, doubling the number of parallel cores used in architecture HW_BRAM_LUT_MULTI, as shown in figure 4, offers performance advantages (0.0697 sec for 4096 inputs using 4 cores, 0.0570 sec using 8 cores and 0.0515 sec using 16 cores) but with a lower slope as expected, since large numbers of cores require even more overhead time for initializations.

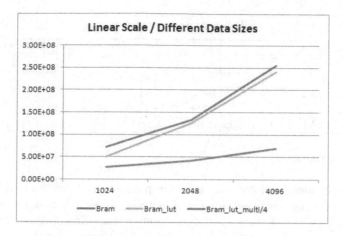

**Fig. 3.** Performance for best solutions, different sample sizes

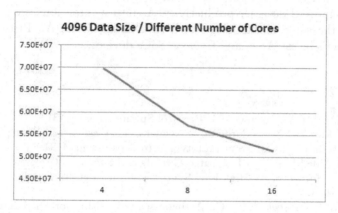

**Fig. 4.** Performance for different number of cores, 4096 sample size

For resource usage, all architectures use very few components (compared to the total number of VC7VX485 components), and particularly less than 5% for each type. This shows the potential of the proposed methodology, to realize complicated architectures with very practical resource utilization, taking advantage however of the selection of a high end FPGA device. In more detail, all architectures share a common amount of resources, (the MicroBlaze processor and its BRAM) while the hardware accelerators take a small overhead on top of this. The most demanding architecture, the quad accelerator HW_BRAM_LUT_MULTI requires almost 50% more DFFs than the software (SW) solution. This is the total highest overhead but still practically negligible compared to the number of available DFFs, and is due to the complex controller required to support parallel accesses to LUT memory. Overall, the performance improvements in each architecture more than justify the resulting area overheads.

**Table 4.** Resource usage

| Experiment | LUTs | DFFs | BRAMs | DSPs |
|---|---|---|---|---|
| SW | 9289 (3%) | 7833 (1%) | 22 (2%) | 3 (1%) |
| HW_BUS | 9520 (3%) | 8209 (1%) | 22 (2%) | 3 (1%) |
| HW_BRAM | 9879 (3%) | 8157 (1%) | 22 (2%) | 3 (1%) |
| HW_BRAM_LUT | 9949 (3%) | 8409 (1%) | 33 (3%) | 3 (1%) |
| HW_BRAM_LUT_MULTI | 12968 (4%) | 11985 (1%) | 38 (3%) | 3 (1%) |

## 6   Conclusions

In this paper a methodology and the corresponding tool flow to build efficient architectures for hardware accelerators has been presented, based on HLS and reconfigurable FPGA devices. Through extensive experimentation, it has been found that correct selection of architectural styles, through language constructs and tool directives, can lead to more than 100X speedup, with small area overheads and improved designer productivity. As future extensions, we are considering using the same methodology with the Xilinx's Zynq All Programmable SoC or Altera's latest Arria and Cyclone SoCs devices.

## References

1. ARM Ltd.: AMBA AXI and ACE Protocol Specification (2013)
2. Cong, J., Liu, B., Neuendorffer, S., Noguera, J., Vissers, K., Zhang, Z.: High-level synthesis for fpgas: From prototyping to deployment. IEEE Transactions on Computer-Aided Design of Integrated Circuits and Systems 30(4), 473–491 (2011)
3. Coussy, P., Morawiec, A.: High-level Synthesis: From Algorithm to Digital Circuit. Springer (2008)
4. Engelse, W.A.H., Zeelenberg, C.: A single scan algorithm for QRS-detection and feature extraction. In: Computers in Cardiology, pp. 37–42. IEEE (1979)
5. Hiraiwa, J., Amano, H.: An FPGA implementation of reconfigurable real-time vision architecture. In: 27th International Conference on Advanced Information Networking and Applications Workshops, pp. 150–155. IEEE (2013)
6. Martin, G., Smith, G.: High-level synthesis: Past, present, and future. IEEE Design and Test of Computers 26(4), 18–25 (2009)
7. Monson, J., Wirthlin, M., Hutchings, B.L.: Optimization techniques for a high level synthesis implementation of the sobel filter. In: International Conference on Reconfigurable Computing and FPGAs. IEEE (2013)

# Measuring Failure Probability of Coarse and Fine Grain TMR Schemes in SRAM-based FPGAs Under Neutron-Induced Effects

Lucas A. Tambara[1]([✉]), Felipe Almeida[1], Paolo Rech[1],
Fernanda L. Kastensmidt[1], Giovanni Bruni[2], and Christopher Frost[3]

[1] Instituto de Informática, PGMICRO, Universidade Federal do Rio Grande do Sul,
Porto Alegre, Brazil
{latambara,afalmeida,prech}@ifsc.usp.br, fglima@inf.ufrgs.br
[2] Dipartimento di Ingegneria dell'Informazione, Universitá di Padova, Padova, Italy
dipartimento.dei@dei.unipd.it
[3] Rutherford Appleton Laboratory, ISIS, Didcot, UK
c.d.frost@rl.ac.uk

**Abstract.** TMR is the most widely used technique to increase the reliability of SRAM-based FPGAs used in safety-critical applications. In this paper we evaluate experimentally the realistic effectiveness of several TMR schemes implemented with different levels of granularity. We measure and compare the dynamic cross-section of the TMRd circuits as well as number of accumulated bit-flips that cause a functional error. Additionally, we analyze and evaluate the effectiveness of both partial and full reconfiguration in both coarse and fine grained TMR schemes. As experimental results demonstrate, coarse-grained TMR efficiency and efficacy may be higher than a fine-grained TMR when partial reconfiguration is available.

**Keywords:** FPGA · TMR · Fault tolerance · Reliability · Radiation effects

## 1 Introduction

Systems designed to operate in safety-critical applications, such as particles accelerators, satellites, and aircrafts require high reliability. However, lately many Commercial Off-The-Shelf (COTS) products have been employed in these critical areas. Adopting COTS brings benefit to the project as they include low cost hardware and software and they are widely available in the commercial market. Nevertheless, COTS are usually very sensitive to radiation effects and efficient mitigation techniques must be employed to reduce the failure probability. In this context, reconfigurable architectures such as SRAM-based Field Programmable Gate Arrays (FPGA) have gained more and more attention over the past years.

State-of-the-art SRAM-based FPGAs present a set of features that are attractive even for systems operating in high reliability applications, such as flexibility,

K. Sano et al. (Eds.): ARC 2015, LNCS 9040, pp. 331–338, 2015.
DOI: 10.1007/978-3-319-16214-0_28

high performance and fast time-to-market. Nevertheless, as said, COTS FPGA error rate must be qualified to evaluate if the device meets the project reliability requirements. As fabricated with the latest semiconductor manufacturing processes, modern FPGAs are high density chips that integrate an up-rising number of functionalities with reduced voltage threshold and higher frequencies operation. Such advances have the drawback of significantly reducing the COTS SRAM-based FPGAs reliability by making them more susceptible to faults caused by radiation.

One of the major reliability concerns for FPGA are Soft Errors, which are transient faults provoked by the interaction of ionizing particles with the device PN junction. This upset temporally charges or discharges circuit nodes, generating transient voltage pulses that can be interpreted as internal signals, thus provoking an erroneous result [1]. When a fault changes the state of a SRAM cell, this event is referred as Single Event Upsets (SEU). Once SRAM-based FPGAs are composed of millions of SRAM cells to store their configuration, they are very susceptible to SEU and Multiple Bits Upsets (MBU) [2]. SEUs and MBUs in configuration memory bits have a persistent effect and can only be corrected by reconfiguring the FPGA.

The integration of COTS FPGAs in critical systems may then require hardening techniques able to mitigate SEU effects, especially if the device is employed in radiation harsh environments. To ensure the correct functionally of the design implemented into an FPGA it is mandatory to mask and eventually correct radiation-induced SEUs and MBUs. Triple Modular Redundancy (TMR) combined with FPGA reconfiguration is the most widely used hardening technique for masking radiation-induced errors. When engineering a TMR scheme it is fundamental to evaluate the precisely number of voters needed and the reconfiguration rate that must be used to cope with MBUs and errors accumulation. Such evaluation allows optimizing the hardening approach, avoiding the introduction of useless overhead in terms of area, performances, and power consumption.

In this work, we evaluate the robustness of several TMR schemes with different levels of granularity. Additionally, we consider both full and partial reconfiguration schemes of SRAM-based FPGAs. We analyze how the insertion of majority voters and different reconfiguration schemes can affect the fault tolerance of a system. Moreover, we evaluate the number of accumulated upsets each TMR can support before losing hardening capabilities. A preliminary analysis on TMR effectiveness in the presence of errors accumulation is presented in [3]. In this paper we extend that analysis to a 65 nm FPGA and generalize results taking a realistic application into account. Additionally, we investigate the TMR efficacy when partial and full reconfigurations are available.

## 2    TMR-FFT Circuit with Different Granularities

When an SEU occurs in a configuration memory bit of an SRAM-based FPGA, it can provoke a bitflip. This bitflip can change the configuration of a routing connection or the configuration of a LUT or flip-flop in the CLB. This can have severe repercussions in the designed circuit, since an SEU may change its functionality. An SEU in the configuration memory bits of an SRAM-based FPGA has a persistent effect and it can only be corrected with the load the correct bitstream. In the combinational logic, an SEU cause a persistent fault in one or more configuration bits of a LUT, changing its truth table. SEU in the routing architecture can connect or disconnect a wire in the matrix modifying the mapped circuit. A high number of clock cycles may be required to have the persistent error detected and initiate recovery actions such as the load of a fault-free bitstream. During this latency, the error can propagate to the rest of the system. Bitflips can also occur in the flip-flop of the CLB used to implement the user's sequential logic. In this case, the bitflip has a transient effect and a load of the flip-flop will correct it.

Triple Modular Redundancy (TMR) is usually used to cope with the persistent effect of the faults in the configuration memory bits of the FPGA. TMR consists in the triplication of the original module of the circuit whose outputs are voted by Majority Voters (MV). As to a majority voter selects the correct output, at least 2-out-of-3 modules must to be fault-free. If an error affects just one of the copies, the remaining two will continue to operate properly and the output of the majority voter will correctly mask the output of the faulty module. This traditional implementation is named Coarse Grain TMR (CGTMR). However, CGTMR is effective to cope only with single erroneous module. In order to improve the capability of masking multiple upsets in the redundant designs, researches started to apply fault tolerance techniques to a more localized and fine level. In the TMR case, this approach is usually called of Fine Grain TMR (FGTMR). FGTMR in FPGA designs consists in dividing a circuit in small TMR protected blocks. By playing with different granularities it is possible to find a trade-off in masking capability, area, performance and soft error rate. As soon as just a single failure affect each small block the overall system will not be disturbed. Moreover, the probability of having multiple failures affecting two redundant modules of the same TMR system in a FGTMR scheme is lower than in a CGTMR [4]. Thus, an FGTMR scheme is expected to present a more tolerant scheme in the presence of a massive number of SEUs. FGTMR and a similar approach called Portioned TMR were studied in [4][5][6]. XTMR [7] proposed by Xilinx is probably the most known FGTMR approach. In the XTMR, all the logic is triplicated and majority voters are used in feedback of the flip-flops to repair the SEUs. XTMR groups the data structures in a design into four different types and applies FGTMR depending on the type of the structure.

However, TMR itself can only mask the fault effect, as in SRAM-based FPGA, once one configuration memory bit is flipped by an SEU, the fault persists until the rewrite of its correct value is performed. The upset bits remain and eventually accumulate into the configuration memory, which increases the probability of failure in the system. In order to correct the accumulated faults, it is necessary to rewrite the correct configuration bits into the configuration memory of the FPGA. This process can be done without the need of stopping the design operation and it is called *Dynamic Reconfiguration*. In Xilinxs FPGAs, reconfiguration can be performed internally by using the Internal Configuration Access Port (ICAP) [8]. Dynamic reconfiguration can be implemented in different ways by reprogramming fully or partially the bitstream.

Full reconfiguration it is the easiest mode of implementation but it requires to write the full configuration memory bits despite that fact that only a small portion of bits are upset. Due to the size of the bitstream in modern FPGAs the correction time and the energy consumption involved in it is far from being negligible. In this work, we use as a synonymous full reconfiguration or scrubbing, which is when the entire design is reconfigured.

Partial reconfiguration in the other hand is the most attractive solution in terms of correction time and power because it programs only the set of frames of the bitstream that are upset. It is also called *Dynamic Partial Reconfiguration* (DPR). In the DPR, the challenge is to detect the fault position or positions to perform the repair. When used together with a TMR scheme, the majority voter outputs can inform the erroneous redundant modules in case of coarse grain TMR, or the frame ECC from the FPGA can be used to inform the erroneous frame to reconfigure. However, there is an important tradeoff between the grain used in the TMR and the ability and feasibility of performing partial reconfiguration in the chosen grain TMR topology. Although in [9] it was demonstrated that the effectiveness of TMR technique is higher when is used with scrubbing, there are not many related works that investigate different granularities of the TMR combined with different approaches of reconfiguration (full and partial).

The case-study circuit in this work is a processing core that implements a FFT with a Radix-4 algorithm, 64-point inputs and 24-bit data [10]. In order to evaluate the neutron-induced effects in TMR schemes with different levels of granularities, four different TMR-FFT schemes were designed. The first one, called of FFT_V1, uses three instances of a standard FFT block with MVs placed at the output of the circuit as CGTMR. For the FGTMR versions, FFT_V2 breaks the FFTs logic into small TMR logic blocks with MVs at the inputs and outputs of each TMR logic blocks defining the fine grain TMR as illustrated in Fig. 1. From this second design, two slightly different designs were then generated: FFT_V3 and FFT_V4. FFT_V3 removes MVs surrounding the arithmetic blocks (_r2, _r3, _r6, _r7, _r10), while FFT_V4 maintains only the MVs that surround the arithmetic blocks (_r1, _r4, _r5, _r8, _r9, _r11, _r12).

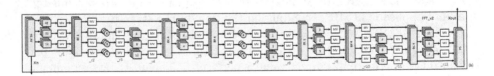

**Fig. 1.** FFT circuit protected by TMR scheme with fine grain TMR (FFT_V2)

The case-study circuits were prototyped in a Xilinx Virtex-5 XUPV5-LX110T SRAM-based FPGA [11] with an input frequency of 100 MHz and without any special placement. FFT_V1 has a total of 17,943 LUTs (3.56 times larger than the non-protected version), while FFT_V2 has a total of 29,405 LUTs (5.84 times larger than the non-protected version). In terms of performance, the FFT_V1 presents a reduction of 7.29% in speed, while FFT_V2 presents a reduction of 26.04%. As it is possible to observe, the addition of MVs has a dramatic impact in terms of area and performance of the design.

## 3   Experimental Results

The case-study circuits were exposed to a neutron flux of approximately $3.08x10^4$ $n/(cm^2.s)$ in ISIS, with neutron energies above 10 MeV. As mentioned in [12], this facility provides a white neutron source that emulates the energy spectrum of the atmospheric neutron flux. Readback of the bitstream is continuously performed in order to establish the SEU accumulation limit, which means that, until the moment in which the TMR under test presents an expected answer, the FPGA will not be reprogrammed. With regard to the reconfiguration process, it was used the reconfiguration manager presented in [13]. In a full reconfiguration scenario, when a functional failure is observed in the output of the final majority voter, readback and dynamic full reconfiguration are performed. In a partial reconfiguration scenario, when a functional failure is observed in one of the TMR modules, readback and dynamic partial reconfiguration are performed in the faulty module. The time spent performing readback and reprogramming is considered negligible.

From the exposure we calculate the dynamic cross-section ($\sigma$) that is defined as the ratio between the number of SEUs producing a wrong system output and the fluence of hitting particles. This way, we calculate the Soft Error Rate (SER) that is commonly expressed in Failure in Time (FIT). FIT defines the expected number of errors in $10^9$ hours at a certain environment. In our case, we are considering the neutron flux at New York (NY) as reference ($13n/(cm^2.h)$). The obtained dynamic cross section and FIT for the designs are: FFT_V1 has $\sigma$ = $2.10x10^{-9}cm^2$ and FIT = 28.47, FFT_V2 has $\sigma$ = $9.45x10^{-10}cm^2$ and FIT = 12.29, FFT_V3 has $\sigma$ = $1.48x10^{-9}cm^2$ and FIT = 19.24 and FFT_V4 has $\sigma$ = $1.09x10^{-9}cm^2$ and FIT = 14.17. Results show that a FGTMR (_V2) can reduce from 56% the FIT of a system when compared to a CGTMR approach.

From Xilinx Reliability Report [14], on average 20 upsets in the configuration memory bits are necessary to provoke an error in a design. This number varies according to the functionally and architecture of each design. For our TMR designs, the objective is to analyze how many upsets can be accumulated in the bitstream before a functional error. In this case, it is important to mention that we are considering the total number of upsets in the configuration memory in our analysis. FFT_V1 can tolerate 95, FFT_V2 207.25, FFT_V3 138.67 and FFT_V4 184.67 accumulated upsets in average. Results show that a FGTMR (_V2) can tolerate in average 2.18 more upsets than FFT_V1. However, through the comparison between FFT_V3 and FFT_V4, it is possible to observe that even a design with less MVs can be more reliable if such MVs are placed in critical parts of the design. In this case, most of the MVs of FFT_V4 are placed around its arithmetic blocks, which represent a large area of the FFT design in the FPGA.

We define failure when a TMR scheme has one of its three modules in an error state, so any extra upset may lead to a new module in an error state and consequently the majority voters may not be able to mask the correct output. Thus, we measured the failure probability of the designs in the presence of multiple SEUs in their configuration memory bits. The obtained results are shown in Fig. 2(a) and Table 1. The analysis of the graphs shows that, in a similar manner and as explained in the dynamic cross-section subsection, FFT_V4 presents a smaller failure probability when compared with FFT_V3. The obtained results are similar to ones presented in [3], even using a more recent device. However, authors in [3] considered only a fault accumulation scenario without using dynamic reconfiguration.

Fig. 2(b) and Table 1 show the behavior of the FFT TMR designs when the failure probability is limited for a maximum value of 10%. In this case, a design is always fully reprogrammed after it achieves a failure probability of 10%. Note that the time between two full reconfigurations can increase up to 8 times through the use of CGTMR or FGTMR as the case of the FFT_V2 version. The correction time spent during full reconfiguration is the same for all the TMR granularities and it is proportional to the FPGA size.

Fig. 3 and Table 1 show the behavior of the FFT TMR designs (coarse and fine grains) when the failure probability is limited for a maximum value of 10% and partial reconfiguration is used. For the presented partial reconfiguration results, the corrupted bitstram was readback to find out the number of accumulated upsets in the system, which in our case, leads to the failure probability. When the design achieves 10% of failure probability, the module with the higher number of accumulated SEUs is reprogrammed. Note that the time between two partial reconfigurations can increase up to 6 times through the use of CGTMR or FGTMR as the case of the FFT_V2. The correction time spent during partial reconfiguration is proportional to the part of the TMR that must be reconfigured, so the time is reduced with when FGTMR is used compared to CGTMR.

When comparing partial to full reconfiguration, the time between partial reconfigurations is slightly smaller than the time need between full reconfigurations. So, one can say that in terms of time between reconfigurations, the use of full reconfiguration is better. On other hand, full reconfiguration uses more power compared to partial reconfiguration. Consequently, considering in time, partial reconfiguration may save more energy to the system if readback is not applied, and the TMR design is able to diagnose itself the erroneous modules. Lastly, no errors in the reconfiguration manager were observed during the experiments.

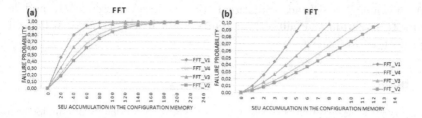

**Fig. 2.** Failure probability of the FFT TMR designs considering the obtained results from the neutron experiment (a) and considering a maximum probability of 10% (b)

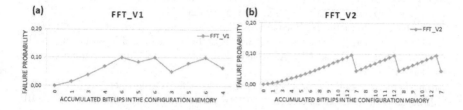

**Fig. 3.** Failure probability of FFT_V1 (c) and FFT_v2 (b) TMR designs with partial reconfiguration and considering a maximum probability of 10%

**Table 1.** Results for the designs considering full and partial reconfiguration scenarios to maintain the failure probability less than 10%

|  | Time between full reconfigurations (hours) | Correction time (ms) | Time between partial reconfigurations (hours) | Correction time (ms) |
|---|---|---|---|---|
| FFT_V1 | $2.11x10^8$ | 15.1 | $1.76x10^{08}$ | 0.0110 |
| FFT_V2 | $8.47x10^8$ | 15.1 | $6.51x10^{08}$ | 0.0026 - 0.0034 |
| FFT_V3 | $4.68x10^8$ | 15.1 | $6.35x10^{08}$ | 0.0026 - 0.0062 |
| FFT_V4 | $1.14x10^8$ | 15.1 | $4.16x10^{08}$ | 0.0027 - 0.0053 |

## 4    Conclusions

Results have shown that increasing the number of majority voters leads to a reduced dynamic cross-section and FIT. However, results also show that in intermediate grain levels there are important tradeoffs among TMR granularity, area, performance and consequently fault tolerance. For certain levels of SEU accumulation, sometimes a finer grain TMR presents a smaller fault tolerance than a similar TMR with larger granularity because of the location of the MVs in the design. The adoption of partial reconfiguration can drastically decrease the upset correction time. However, in terms of reconfiguration rate and SEU accumulation, results show that there are not so many advantages in using partial reconfiguration in a TMR scheme when the aim is to limit the failure probability

to a certain value. The SEU accumulation in the non-reconfigured TMR modules
contribute to maintain the failure probability high. In this context, a periodic
scrubbing can be more effective.

# References

1. Dodd, P.E., Massengill, L.W.: Basic Mechanism and Modeling of Single-Event
   Upset in Digital Microelectronics. IEEE Transactions on Nuclear Science **50**(3),
   583–602 (2003)
2. Quinn, H., Morgan, K., Graham, P., Krone, J., Caffrey, M.: Static proton and
   heavy ion testing of the xilinx virtex-5 device. In: 2007 IEEE Radiation Effects
   Data Workshop, pp. 177–184. IEEE, New York (2007)
3. Manuzzato, A., Gerardin, S., Paccagnella, A., Sterpone, L., Violante, M.: Effectiveness of TMR-Based Techniques to Mitigate Alpha-Induced SEU Accumulation in
   Commercial SRAM-Based FPGAs. IEEE Transactions on Nuclear Science **55**(4),
   1968–1973 (2008)
4. Niknahad, M., Sander, O., Becker, J.: Fine grain fault tolerance - a key to high
   reliability for FPGAs in space. In: 2012 IEEE Aerospace Conference, pp. 1–10.
   IEEE, New York (2012)
5. Kastensmidt, F.L., Sterpone, L., Carro, L., Reorda, M.S.: On the optimal design
   of triple modular redundancy logic for SRAM-based FPGAs. In: 2005 Design,
   Automation and Test in Europe, pp. 1290–1295. IEEE, New York (2005)
6. Wang, X.: Partitioning triple modular redundancy for single event upset mitigation in FPGA. In: 2010 International Conference on E-Product E-Service and
   E-Entertainment, pp. 1–4. IEEE, New York (2010)
7. Single-Event Upset Mitigation Selection Guide. http://www.xilinx.com/
8. Berg, M., Poivey, C., Petrick, D., Espinosa, D., Lesea, A., LaBel, K.A., Friendlich,
   M., Kim, H., Phan, A.: Effectiveness of Internal Versus External SEU Scrubbing
   Mitigation Strategies in a Xilinx FPGA: Design, Test, and Analysis. IEEE Transactions on Nuclear Science **55**(4), 2259–2266 (2008)
9. Ostler, P.S., Caffrey, M.P., Gibelyou, D.S., Graham, P.S., Morgan, K.S., Pratt,
   B.H., Quinn, H.M., Wirthlin, M.J.: SRAM FPGA Reliability Analysis for Harsh
   Radiation Environments. IEEE Transactions on Nuclear Science **56**(6), 3519–3526
   (2009)
10. Swartzlander, E.E., Young, W.W., Gibelyou, D.S., Joseph, S.J.: A Radix 4 Delay
    Commutator for Fast Fourier Transform Processor Implementation. IEEE Journal
    of Solid-state Circuits **SC–19**(5), 702–709 (1984)
11. Virtex-5 Family Overview. http://www.xilinx.com/
12. Violante, M., Sterpone, L., Manuzzato, A., Gerardin, S., Rech, P., Bagatin,
    M., Paccagnella, A., Andreani, C., Gorini, G., Pietropaolo, A., Cardarilli, G.,
    Pontarelli, S., Frost, C.: A New Hardware/Software Platform and a New 1/E Neu-
    tron Source for Soft Error Studies: Testing FPGAs at the ISIS Facility. IEEE
    Transactions on Nuclear Science **54**(4), 1184–1189 (2007)
13. Tarrillo, J., Escobar, F.A., Kastensmidt, F.L., Valderrama, C.: Dynamic partial
    reconfiguration manager. In: 5th IEEE Latin American Symposium on Circuits
    and Systems, pp. 1–4. IEEE, New York (2014)
14. Device Reliability Report First Quarter 2014. http://www.xilinx.com/

# Modular Acquisition and Stimulation System for Timestamp-Driven Neuroscience Experiments

Paulo Matias[✉], Rafael T. Guariento, Lirio O.B. de Almeida, and Jan F.W. Slaets

São Carlos Institute of Physics, University of São Paulo, São Carlos, SP, Brazil
{matias,guariento,lirio,jan}@ifsc.usp.br

**Abstract.** Dedicated systems are fundamental for neuroscience experimental protocols that require timing determinism and synchronous stimuli generation. We developed a data acquisition and stimuli generator system for neuroscience research, optimized for recording timestamps from up to 6 spiking neurons and entirely specified in a high-level Hardware Description Language (HDL). Despite the logic complexity penalty of synthesizing from such a language, it was possible to implement our design in a low-cost small reconfigurable device. Under a modular framework, we explored two different memory arbitration schemes for our system, evaluating both their logic element usage and resilience to input activity bursts. One of them was designed with a decoupled and latency insensitive approach, allowing for easier code reuse, while the other adopted a centralized scheme, constructed specifically for our application. The usage of a high-level HDL allowed straightforward and stepwise code modifications to transform one architecture into the other. The achieved modularity is very useful for rapidly prototyping novel electronic instrumentation systems tailored to scientific research.

**Keywords:** Spiking neurons · Data acquisition · Precise timing · Resource arbitration · Latency insensitive · Modular design

## 1 Introduction

Neurons usually behave by emitting stereotyped pulses of electric depolarization through their membranes, creating temporally localized spikes. It is a common belief that spiking neurons follow an all-or-none principle, similar to the processing of digital signals, by encoding information only through spike timing [1]. Although each individual cell always produces the same waveform, the most widespread experimental approach employs Analog to Digital Converters (ADCs) integrated on commercial acquisition systems to capture complete waveforms. This procedure is required when the researcher desires to analyze a large population of neurons recording only from a few electrodes, applying then a neuron classification technique known as spike sorting to discriminate individual

© Springer International Publishing Switzerland 2015
K. Sano et al. (Eds.): ARC 2015, LNCS 9040, pp. 339–348, 2015.
DOI: 10.1007/978-3-319-16214-0_29

waveforms [2]. However, because of the lack of readily available specialized acquisition hardware, many works adopt the same recording technique even though
they only need to identify the occurrence of spikes from one neuron per elec-
trode [3–6]. The resulting data files are large and spikes need to be detected by
software, demanding a considerable amount of time.

In this paper we present the design of a low-cost alternative hardware solution based on a dedicated Complex Programmable Logic Device (CPLD). We
have chosen CPLDs instead of Field Programmable Gate Arrays (FPGAs) to
demonstrate the flexibility of our approach, as CPLDs are usually limited to a
small number of logic gates, and lack common FPGA features such as Block
RAMs and Phase Locked Loops (PLLs). We implemented the logic circuits on
the CPLD adopting a modular design, which aims to facilitate future refinement
and customization for specific applications. The complete source code implemented in the Bluespec SystemVerilog (BSV) [7] language is available at [8].

BSV designs targeted at small reconfigurable devices, such as ours, are rare in
literature, since many works show that BSV usually produces a higher logic element (LE) count than Register-Transfer Level (RTL) languages [9–11]. However,
some research [12] argues that microarchitectural choices have greater impact on
the LE usage than the specification's abstraction level, although there is a lack of
studies in glue logic sized architectures with significant modularity and complexity. This paper showcases such a system, and also explores the impact of latency
insensitive module decoupling, by comparing two distinct implementations of a
resource arbitration scheme.

The acquisition input is provided to our digital logic by an analog front-
end system which generates an asynchronous TTL-compatible signal pulse at
the occurrence of each valid spike. Our entire circuit was designed to be compatible and easily inserted into a previous experimental setup [13] devised for
studying neural codification in *Chrysomya megacephala*'s visual system, but it is
sufficiently generic to be suitable for a wide range of neuroscience experiments.

**Main Contributions of this Work:**
  - Develops a portable, low-cost and precise data acquisition system for neuro-
    science and neuroethology experiments.
  - Applies the seldom used concept of recording digital events (instead of ADC-
    converted data) to increase the precision of neural spike timing.
  - Employs the BSV language in a small and resource constrained system.
  - Showcases architecture refactoring from a decoupled to a centralized scheme.

## 2    Overall System Architecture

Our system offers 6 TTL-level pulse timestamp acquisition inputs, 4 analog
16-bit resolution outputs for stimuli generation and a Join Test Action Group
(JTAG) host computer interface. It is composed by a MAX II Micro Kit (EPM-
2210F324C3 CPLD), a 74HC4050 buffer for input overvoltage protection, a

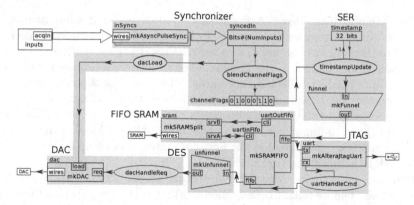

**Fig. 1.** Block diagram of the BSV modules and rules. The gray shaded areas represent internal logic, while white structures depict I/O interfaces. Modules are portrayed as quadrilaterals. Small rectangles on their side are interfaces. Ellipses designate rules.

MAX5134 Digital-to-Analog Converter (DAC) and a IDT71256 20ns 32K×8-bit SRAM. We have divided the project in following functional subunits:

**Synchronizer**: Receives asynchronous input pulses and registers 32-bit timestamps from a hardware counter, each one paired to a flag indicating which input channels fired since last counted. In most neural systems, 1 $\mu s$ is believed to be enough resolution for studying fine details of information coding [14].

**FIFO SRAM**: Provides an interface for using the external SRAM memory as a pair of First-In First-Out (FIFO) queues of 16 KiB each. One of them buffers data acquired from inputs, and the other buffers stimuli received from a computer. Our FIFO modules are compatible with the BSV standard library.

**JTAG interface**: Provides communication with a host computer. We have wrapped Altera JTAG-UART libraries into a ready-to-use BSV module. By using this protocol, the same communication module is portable to any CPLD or FPGA manufactured by the same vendor. As programmable devices are configured via JTAG, the bus is readily available through USB adapters embedded in almost every evaluation board. However, this approach introduces a significant protocol overhead by encapsulating UART emulation inside JTAG-USB, limiting the data rate to about 1 Mbit/s. Also, the interface is not interrupt nor event driven. Nevertheless, these limitations do not impair this particular application.

## 3   Design of the Modules

Figure 1 illustrates our main module. The fundamental difference between arbitration approaches resides on `SRAMFIFO` internals and on how communication with the SRAM occurs. In the dynamic approach this is done by a client-server interface mediated by FIFOs, whereas in the static one an extra central module exists which assigns a specific operation to the `SRAMFIFO`s on each cycle.

**Acquisition data flow**: Asynchronous pulses arriving from acquisition inputs are synchronized to the system clock by the AsyncPulseSync modules, resulting in the syncedIn signal. The blendChannelFlags rule accumulates one bit for each input channel in the channelFlags register, if a pulse occurred on syncedIn since the last collected timestamp. The timestampUpdate rule atomically increments the timestamp register, sends the channelFlags value and the current timestamp to the funnel, and resets channelFlags to zero. The funnel emits one byte of its input per cycle to the uartOutFifo. Finally, data coming from dataOutFifo can be read in the host computer after being collected by the JTAG-UART transmitting (tx) interface.

**Stimulus generation data flow**: Begins at the JTAG-UART receiving (rx) interface. The uartHandleCmd rule identifies if the byte received from the computer represents a start command or a DAC conversion request. A start command sets a boolean register (omitted from the figure) which unblocks the predicate of dacLoad, timestampUpdate and blendChannelFlags rules. A DAC conversion request sends the current byte and the next two bytes to uartInFifo. After coming out of the FIFO, the bytes feed the unfunnel block, merging three bytes together. The dacHandleReq controls the request flow to the DAC module. The dacLoad rule fires when the first input channel receives a pulse, unblocking the dacHandleReq rule and causing a synchronous update on all DAC outputs. This input channel is used to synchronize analog outputs to the desired stimuli clock, e.g. the display controller in a visual stimulation system.

BSV has an implicit condition mechanism which eases the specification of a provably correct system. We only needed to add error handling to four places of our design. The first one is related to tx path FIFO overflow and is put in the timestampUpdate rule, ensuring that the timestamp is always incremented at each update period. The second check is accomplished in the dacLoad rule, certifying that the DAC is ready to receive a new command and that all DAC registers were filled since the last load. The third one checks if bytes received from JTAG-UART correspond to valid commands. The last one verifies if DAC requests are still valid after leaving uartInFifo. When any of these error condition occurs, we alert the user by blinking LEDs until the system is reset.

Next, we describe characteristics of the common system sub-modules.

**SER/DES**: Serializer and deserializer modules are implemented using shift registers. Our design is generic and type parametrized, increasing its reusability.

**DAC**: In order to rapidly prototype the control of a Serial Peripheral Interface (SPI) and DAC linearity calibration procedures, we employed a standard BSV library called StmtFSM, which consists of a Domain Specific Language (DSL) for specifying Finite State Machines (FSMs). The FSMs could be easily composed and exposed in the form of a simple external module interface.

**SRAMFIFO**: This module is also type parametrized. It exposes a fifo subinterface mimicking BSV standard library's mkLFIFO, and a cli subinterface which can be connected to a SRAM or SRAMSplit server interface. Usage of Ephemeral History Registers (EHRs) [15] greatly simplified the design in order to achieve the same scheduling specifications as mkLFIFO. EHRs provide a

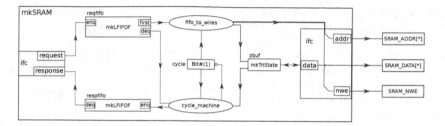

**Fig. 2.** In the dynamic arbiter based design, the SRAM controller is decoupled from the SRAMSplit module. Its state over the two cycles of operation is determined by an internal cycle register, handled by the cycle_machine rule. The fifo_to_wires rule controls the tri-state buffer and drives the outputs.

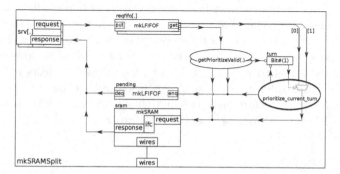

**Fig. 3.** SRAMSplit provides two SRAM server interfaces and arbitrates their access to a single SRAM controller. A set of three mutually exclusive rules arbitrate the access based on not-empty FIFO flags and on a turn register. A pending FIFO preserves the requester identification, allowing responses to be served back in the right order.

register-like interface on which same-cycle accesses can be ordered according to the logical execution order of rules or methods. Head and tail position pointers to locations inside the SRAM are held in EHRs. The SRAMFIFO stores one unit of data (in the case of this design, one byte) in a local cache FIFO implemented using flip-flop registers, whose output is connected directly to SRAMFIFO's one.

## 3.1  Dynamic Arbiter

In this design, the SRAM controller (Figure 2) is decoupled from the SRAMSplit module (Figure 3). The first dispatches requests in the order as they are received in reqfifo, using an internal cycle register to keep track of its state during a single request. The latter arbitrates the access of two other modules to a single SRAM controller. Requests received from both modules are placed into a pair of FIFOs. A set of mutually exclusive rules then controls the priority of each request. Two of them are generated by the getPrioritizeValid function, one of which is fired when a single request FIFO is not empty. However when both

**Fig. 4.** Timing diagram of SRAMFIFO transactions governed by the static arbiter. Arrows identify in which cycles the memory requests and responses occur. White rectangles represent actions on uartInFifo, while black rectangles depict operations on uartOutFifo.

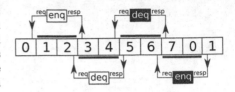

FIFOs contain data, the prioritize_current_turn rule is fired, prioritizing the Least Recently Used (LRU) FIFO.

Arbitration also needs to take place in the SRAMFIFO module, because methods for enqueuing and dequeuing data are designed not to conflict, in order to simplify module reuse. When both methods are called during the same cycle, we check if the queue's head and tail pointers are equal to each other. This means that the dequeue method has requested to read the same address which the enqueue method asked to write. In this case, we enforce requests to be sent to SRAM in the same order as the logical execution order chosen when designing the methods (dequeue before enqueue, and thus read before write). Otherwise, we follow a LRU type of memory operation approach.

## 3.2   Static Arbiter

Starting from the code of the dynamic version, we incrementally added new conditions to method predicates, testing the system after the changes. As implicit conditions which control the data flow of FIFOs are still present in the logic at this development stage, designer errors tend to prevent rules from firing, stopping data flow and making the system hang instead of producing incorrect results.

We added these predicate conditions based on a manually devised arbitration schedule, shown in Figure 4. This schedule allows for the execution of an enqueue and a dequeue operation on both uartInFifo and uartOutFifo during the course of 8 clock cycles. A central arbiter, which consists of a counter reset every 8 cycles, was implemented just below the top level module. Boolean values derived from this counter, signaling if each operation could occur during each cycle, were routed from the top level module to the inner SRAM controller, SRAMSplit and SRAMFIFOs. After the predicates were changed, some FIFOs could be removed, reducing the number of LEs needed to implement the design.

**SRAM controller**: The cycle register (compare with Figure 2) was removed and replaced by the least significant bit of the central arbiter counter. Memory requests became allowed only when this bit is zero, which happens in cycles numbered 0, 2, 4 and 6 (Figure 4).

**SRAMSplit**: Requests to one of the arbitrated servers became allowed only during the correct cycle, as defined by the timing diagram — requests coming from uartInFifo at cycles numbered 0 and 2, and those from uartOutFifo at cycles 4 and 6. Both reqfifos could then be removed from the design without

**Table 1.** Synthesis results for both arbiter designs (Altera Quartus II 14.0)

| | EPM2210F324C3 | | EPM1270F256C3 | |
|---|---|---|---|---|
| Design Arbiter | Logic elements | Maximum clock frequency | Logic elements | Maximum clock frequency |
| Static | 1017 (46%) | 54.57 MHz | 970(76%) | 54.36 MHz |
| Dynamic | 1217 (55%) | 54.07 MHz | 1168 (92%) | 53.49 MHz |

affecting its behavior. The order of responses could also be inferred from the diagram (cycles 3, 5, 7 and 1), allowing us to remove the `pending` FIFO. After all changes, the module became just an abstraction which synthesizes purely to wires (compare with Figure 3).

**SRAMFIFO**: Dequeues and enqueues became allowed only during the designated cycles (2 and 4 for dequeues, 0 and 6 for enqueues). This allowed to remove memory request output FIFOs, which were replaced by wires.

## 4 Results

### 4.1 Synthesis

Synthesis results are shown in Table 1. On the device actually adopted in our project (EPM2210F324C3), the dynamic arbitrated circuit occupies 200 more LEs than the static arbiter design. This corresponds to 9% of the LEs available in the CPLD. Almost a half of the hardware resources are still free and could be exploited to implement new features. We have also synthesized both architectures on a smaller device (EPM1270F256C3) in order to demonstrate the design can meet the requirements even when reaching the limits of the CPLD substrate.

### 4.2 Experimental Validation

Workbench validation consisted in connecting independent square-wave periodic signal generators into each input of the system for 8 hours and then analyzing the acquired data to look for spurious or missing detections. We used three periodic pulse sources (1-channel Hewlett-Packard 33120A and 2-channel Sony-Tektronix AFG320) and three free-running astable oscillators (NE555 timers).

The first input channel was programmed to synchronize DAC conversions, thus we have fed it with 500 Hz (frame rate frequency adopted by the VSImG [13] visual stimulation system). The second and third channels were supplied with close but incommensurable frequencies (6.2 kHz and 6.1 kHz). The remaining channels were fed by similar frequencies, produced by three identical NE555 circuits, differing only within component nominal tolerances.

In both architectures, no missing pulses were detected in these 8 hours, and the maximum deviation from the adjusted periods was within the acceptable generator's thermal drift. We emphasize that input frequencies employed during this test were well above those attainable by a typical spiking neuron (1 kHz at maximum, limited by its refractory period).

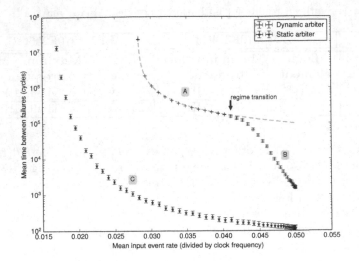

**Fig. 5.** Mean time between failures (MTBF) obtained by simulation, with designs configured for an increased timestamp resolution of $1/20$ of the system clock, and subject to large mean input event rates. The dynamic arbiter is consistently more resilient, and presented two operating regimes: in regime **A**, failures are caused by overflow of `uartOutFifo`, while in regime **B**, memory write requests occur at a high rate and eventually cannot be scheduled on time, overflowing `funnel`. As the static arbiter schedules enqueuing operations at a fixed rate of 1 byte per 8 cycles (slower than the simulated UART transmission rate), regime **C** is only due to `funnel` overflow.

## 4.3   Arbiter Resilience Evaluation

Any update rate below $1/40$ of the clock frequency (50 MHz) can always be correctly scheduled, as it leaves room for at least 5 rounds of 4 memory operations, each one taking 2 cycles (see Figure 4), sufficient to carry the 5-byte (`channelFlags`, `timestamp`) tuple in and out of the FIFOs. Thus, to be able to observe failures related to differences in SRAM arbitration schemes, we increased the timestamp counter update rate from $1/50$ to $1/20$ of the clock frequency.

In order to keep control over parameters such as UART transmission rate, we simulated the system instead of evaluating it with workbench instruments. Inputs were fed with trains of pulses generated according to a Poisson process, a stochastic model that occasionally produces activity bursts, although it possesses a parameterized mean rate. The first channel, however, was modeled as an oscillation whose frequency varies according to a narrow Gaussian distribution, which better reproduces the behavior of the stimuli reference clock.

We limited UART transmission to 1 byte per 6 cycles, aiming to observe the system in a regime in which it would eventually acquire more data than it could transmit. UART reception was constrained to 1 byte per 10 cycles, allowing 3-byte chunks of stimuli data to be provided to the system at double the speed required by the first-channel reference clock, whose mean frequency was chosen at $1/60$ of the system clock.

Varying the rate parameter of the Poisson processes, we measured the total mean input event rate to which the system was exposed, relating it to the mean time between failures (MTBF) in number of cycles. Failures were detected if any of the four error conditions discussed in Section 3 were triggered. In this experiment they happened only due to overflows in the `tx` path.

Figure 5 shows these results and demonstrates that besides supporting a mean firing rate greater than the static arbiter without missing events, the dynamic arbiter takes longer to fail when the frequency approaches its limits. At an input rate of $1/20$, the maximum meaningful frequency at the adopted timestamp resolution, the dynamic arbiter fails after circa $10^3$ cycles, whereas the static arbiter withstands for only $10^2$ cycles.

Under the simulation parameters, the static arbiter is not able to fill `uart-OutFifo`'s SRAM-contained ring with more than 1 byte. This happens because the FIFO enqueuing rate is limited to a maximum of 1 byte per 8 cycles by the central arbiter schedule (see Figure 4), while the simulated UART can reach a transmission rate of 1 byte per 6 cycles, sufficient to keep the FIFO almost empty. The observed failures were due to overflow of the `funnel`: the `uartOutFifo` never even came close to a full state. Therefore, the failure process may be viewed as nearly stationary at a time scale greater than $10^2$ cycles. Indeed, the measured data set (Figure 5–C) does not change significantly if we reset the circuit state a couple of times during the course of simulation.

On the other hand, the dynamic arbiter is able to surpass an operating regime (Figure 5–B) where failures occur because of `funnel` overflow, reaching another regime at lower frequencies (Figure 5–A) where the system does not abort until `uartOutFifo` is full. The dashed curve is proportional to $(f - f_{\lim})^{-1}$, where $f$ is the mean input frequency (abscissa) and $f_{\lim}$ is a limit frequency (in this experiment, $f_{\lim} \approx 0.0282$) such that $5f_{\lim}$ is less than the effective UART transmission rate, implying the circuit is not expected to ever fail for $f \leq f_{\lim}$.

# 5   Conclusions

The system described in this paper (source code at [8]) can be applied to neuroscience research both on *in vivo* or *in vitro* experiments requiring deterministic timing and synchronous stimuli generation, such as the study of neural coding on the visual system of flies. The employed digital pulse timestamping technique allows to achieve a measurement precision in the order of 1 $\mu$s, much higher than most ADC-based acquisition systems.

We have also shown that Bluespec SystemVerilog (BSV) can be effectively used even in projects involving small devices, and have presented an approach to refactor a decoupled and latency insensitive logic into a statically arbitrated one, which could be useful when a designer needs to quickly lower a system's LE usage — however, keeping dynamic arbitration can compensate the LE cost if the system needs to be resilient to activity bursts. The designed code is modular and reusable to implement similar systems, e.g. we have a working prototype for closed-loop experiments implemented on an EP4CGX150DF31C7 FPGA, which occupies 5728 LEs (4% of the device) and interfaces with a real-time operating system (RTOS) through PCI Express.

**Acknowledgments.** Authors were supported by grants from CAPES and FAPESP. Maxim Integrated provided free analog IC samples. Altera Corp and Bluespec Inc supplied free software licenses through their university programs.

# References

1. Dayan, P., Abbott, L.F.: Theoretical neuroscience: computational and mathematical modeling of neural systems. The MIT Press (2005)
2. Lewicki, M.S.: A review of methods for spike sorting: the detection and classification of neural action potentials. Network-Comp. Neural **9**(4), R53–R78 (1998)
3. Brochini, L., Carelli, P.V., Pinto, R.D.: Single synapse information coding in intraburst spike patterns of central pattern generator motor neurons. J. Neurosci. **31**(34), 12297–12306 (2011)
4. Spavieri Jr., D.L., Eichner, H., Borst, A.: Coding efficiency of fly motion processing is set by firing rate, not firing precision. PLoS Comput. Biol. **6**(7), e1000860 (2010)
5. Bolzon, D.M., Nordström, K., O'Carroll, D.C.: Local and large-range inhibition in feature detection. J. Neurosci. **29**(45), 14143–14150 (2009)
6. Rokem, A., Watzl, S., Gollisch, T., Stemmler, M., Herz, A.V.M., Samengo, I.: Spike-timing precision underlies the coding efficiency of auditory receptor neurons. J. Neurophysiol. **95**(4), 2541–2552 (2006)
7. Nikhil, R.: Bluespec system verilog: efficient, correct RTL from high level specifications. In: MEMOCODE 2004, pp. 69–70, June 2004
8. Matias, P.: Low-cost modular acquisition and stimulation system for neuroscience, July 2014. http://dx.doi.org/10.5281/zenodo.11034
9. Gruian, F., Westmijze, M.: BluEJAMM: a Bluespec embedded Java architecture with memory management. In: SYNASC 2007, pp. 459–466, September 2007
10. Meeus, W., Van Beeck, K., Goedemé, T., Meel, J., Stroobandt, D.: An overview of today's high-level synthesis tools. Des. Autom. Embed. Syst. **16**(3), 31–51 (2012)
11. Malik, J.S., Palazzari, P., Hemani, A.: Effort, resources, and abstraction vs performance in high-level synthesis: finding new answers to an old question. SIGARCH Comput. Archit. News **40**(5), 64–69 (2012)
12. Arvind, Nikhil, R.S., Rosenband, D.L., Dave, N.: High-level synthesis: an essential ingredient for designing complex ASICs. In: ICCAD 2004, pp. 775–782. IEEE Computer Society, Washington, DC (2004)
13. de Almeida, L.O.B., Slaets, J.F.W., Köberle, R.: VSImG: a high frame rate bitmap based display system for neuroscience research. Neurocomputing **74**(10), 1762–1768 (2011)
14. Nemenman, I., Lewen, G.D., Bialek, W., de Ruyter van Steveninck, R.R.: Neural coding of natural stimuli: information at sub-millisecond resolution. PLoS Comput. Biol. **4**(3), e1000025 (2008)
15. Rosenband, D.L.: The ephemeral history register: flexible scheduling for rule-based designs. In: MEMOCODE 2004, pp. 189–198, June 2004

# DRAM Row Activation Energy Optimization for Stride Memory Access on FPGA-Based Systems

Ren Chen[✉] and Viktor K. Prasanna

Ming Hsieh Department of Electrical Engineering, University of Southern California, Los Angeles 90089, USA
{renchen,prasanna}@usc.edu

**Abstract.** FPGA-based systems consisting external memory have been extensively employed in data intensive applications such as signal, image, and network processing. Memory energy is a dominating factor in the overall system energy dissipation. In particular, when performing non-sequential memory access patterns, significant amount of energy is dissipated due to frequent memory row activations. In this paper, we consider the classic stride memory access pattern and evaluate the energy consumption in DRAM. Lower bounds on DRAM energy consumption are derived for this widely used memory access pattern which introduces row-wise writing and column-wise reading memory operations. To achieve the lower bounds of the DRAM energy consumption, we remap data onto DRAM for both row-wise and column-wise memory operations. This significantly reduces the latency brought by frequent DRAM row activations due to column-wise memory operations. We validate experimentally our analysis using 2-D FFT as a benchmark application on FPGA-based system. The experimental results demonstrate that our proposed optimizations result in 74.8 %~77.7 % reduction in energy consumption of the overall system compared with the baseline for 1024× 1024, 4096× 4096, and 8192× 8192 points 2-D FFTs, respectively.

## 1  Introduction

Increasing density and integration of various hardware components, such as low power DSP IP cores and memory blocks, have made FPGAs an attractive option for implementation of various applications [7,8]. Compared with general purpose processors, the state-of-the-art FPGAs have advantages in much lower power with high performance, especially for data intensive applications. FPGA-based systems usually employ DRAM as the external memory to store large data sets. Such systems have been widely used in various image and digital signal processing applications [6,7]. In these applications, maximizing performance under energy dissipation constraints is a critical issue.

This work was supported by the DARPA under grant HR0011-12-2-0023, and the U.S. National Science Foundation under grants CCF-1320211 and ACI-1339756. Equipment grant from Xilinx, Inc. is gratefully acknowledged.

© Springer International Publishing Switzerland 2015
K. Sano et al. (Eds.): ARC 2015, LNCS 9040, pp. 349–356, 2015.
DOI: 10.1007/978-3-319-16214-0_30

Stride memory access patterns are widely used in data intensive applications such as 2-D FFT, matrix multiplication and convolution. When DRAM is accessed with stride memory addresses, it usually results in a large number of row activations. This increases both the data access latency as well as the power consumption. Most previous optimizations concentrate on reducing the latency due to DRAM row activations so that the DRAM bandwidth can be fully utilized. Mapping data on DRAM using a block or tiling data layout has been investigated by some researchers [5,10]. However, energy efficiency is not considered in their works. In this paper, we analyze the energy performance of DRAM when accessed with stride memory addresses. We identify the key factors which impact the energy consumption introduced by DRAM row activations. Based on our analysis, we remap data onto DRAM through on-chip stride permutation. As a result, the latency between successive row activations on the same DRAM bank are overlapped. This leads to improved memory bandwidth utilization. Compared with using block data layout, our proposed data remapping approach reduces the DRAM row activation energy with minimal extra latency overhead. Furthermore, as each DRAM row activation introduces a much higher power consumption, we also develop a data prefetch approach to minimize the number of DRAM row activations.

The proposed optimizations largely reduce the energy dissipation for accessing DRAM using strided memory addresses. The contributions in this paper are:

1. We analyze the energy performance of DRAM for stride memory access patterns. Lower bounds on the DRAM energy consumption are derived.
2. We propose a data remapping approach to reduce the latency introduced by DRAM row activation, thus improving the memory bandwidth utilization significantly.
3. We demonstrate significant energy efficiency improvement for the benchmark application. Up to 77.7% performance improvement is achieved compared with the baseline.

## 2    Background and Related Work

FPGA has abundant hardware resources including logic cells, interconnect and on-chip memory. DRAM is usually employed to store large data sets. DRAM bandwidth and capacity have been improving continuously during the last decades. Accordingly, memory energy consumption becomes a major contributor to the overall system power profile. When processing a DRAM access request, one of the DRAM banks needs to be activated so that a row in this bank could be opened to be accessed [2]. This activation process is called as the DRAM row activation. The latency between consecutive row activations to the same DRAM bank is normally 10x the DRAM clock period. This latency could be hidden by pipelining successive memory access requests using multiple DRAM banks. However, this approach is only efficient for sequential memory access pattern, where the memory address is incremented after every memory access. For *stride*

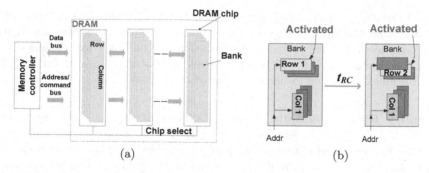

**Fig. 1.** DRAM access delay: a) Overview of DRAM organization, b) Successive accesses to the same bank and different rows

*memory access* pattern, where the stride is the distance of successively accessed memory locations, this approach becomes infeasible when the same DRAM bank has to be accessed successively. In this case, a substantial latency is introduced by DRAM row activations.

Previous work are mainly focused on optimizing the latency and throughput rather than the energy dissipation of the external memory when considering stride memory access patterns. To reduce the considerable delay caused by stride memory access in DRAM, a tile data layout was employed to improve the external memory bandwidth utilization for 2-D FFT application in [5] . Their approach maximizes the DRAM bandwidth utilization while at the expense of an extra latency of $O(N^2)$ for $N \times N$ 2-D FFT. There are also other prior research works on effectively utilizing the DRAM bandwidth [11,13], however, energy was not considered. To the best of our knowledge, all previous works do not consider energy efficiency for stride memory access. Some of them develop DRAM energy optimizations using algorithmic or architectural techniques for general purpose computing. Algorithmic techniques for reducing memory energy have been introduced in [12]. In [9], the authors proposed a conservative row activation scheme that reduces the memory power with negligible performance impact by allowing a memory rank to stay at the low-power mode longer. However, no specific memory access patterns are discussed.

# 3   Memory Energy Model

## 3.1   External Memory

We employ a high level model for external memory energy analysis and discuss lower bounds on the memory energy dissipation of algorithms [1]. The power model of the external memory (such as DRAM) is defined as:

**Memory Organization.** An external memory is composed of several ranks, each including several chips. A DRAM chip is organized into banks. Each bank consists of a two dimensional matrix of locations. At each addressable location ([Bank, Row, Column]), a fixed number of data bits (usually 8 bits) are located. The data word denotes the memory data width. The burst length denotes the minimum granularity at which external memory accesses are performed. The column index is used to locate a data word in one row.

**Memory Row Activation.** A row of a bank needs to be activated before accessed. A read/write operation on an active row is defined as page-hit access. Page hit rate represents the percentage of page-hit access to the external memory. Once the row is activated, multiple accesses on that row can be performed with low latency. When a particular row is active, and a request is for a different row in the same bank, the active row must be closed and the new row must be opened. This incurs a latency penalty due to the time it takes to close the row and activate a new row.

**Memory Energy.** External memory energy is determined by its access latency and memory power. Power components of a memory bank consist of $P_{acc}$ and $P_{non\_acc}$. $P_{acc}$ denotes the power consumed dynamically by memory read or write operations. $P_{non\_acc}$ is composed of memory activate power and background power, which are independent on memory access activities. $P_{non\_acc}$ is determined by the memory power mode. For example, DRAM has multiple power modes including active, refresh, and power down modes. $P_{non\_acc}$ in active, refresh, or power down mode is denoted as $P_{act}$, $P_{ref}$, and $P_{pdn}$ respectively.

Besides, several time constraints are involved when accessing DRAM; time constraints used in this work are described here (latency values for the time constraints mentioned here are for 2Gb DDR3 SDRAM [1])

| | |
|---|---|
| $t_{RP}$ | precharge the long wires before switching to the next row ($\approx 15$ ns) |
| $t_{RAS}$ | minimum time between issuing an activation and issuing a precharge ($\approx 25$ ns) |
| $t_{RC}$ | minimum time between issuing two successive activate commands in a single bank ($= t_{RP} + t_{RAS} \approx 40$ ns) |
| $t_{RRD}$ | minimum time between successive activate commands to different banks ($\approx 8$ ns) |

We use $E_{row}$ to denote the energy consumption of read and write operations to a row within a memory bank. $E_{row}$ can be computed as $E_{row} = (P_{non\_acc} + P_{acc}) \times t_{RC}$. Fig. 1b shows the process when executing successive accesses to different rows in the same bank. A minimum time of $t_{RC}$ is required between issuing two successive activate commands in a single bank. We define effective energy $E_{eff\_row}$ as $E_{row} \times r$, where $r$ denotes the data utilization rate within the bank row. $r$ decreases significantly when executing non-consecutive memory access patterns, such as stride memory access pattern where the memory address increases with a stride $m$ after every memory access cycle. If assuming the number of data words in a bank row is $w$, $r$ can be calculated as $\lceil w/m \rceil$ when $m < w$, and $r$ would be constantly $1/w$ when $m \geq w$.

# 4   Energy Optimizations

## 4.1   Throughput Balanced Design

A complete FPGA design usually consists of a computation kernel and an external memory. The external memory is composed of several DRAM chips, each of which has a fixed output data width (usually 16 bits). The number of DRAM chips to be in active state is determined by the memory bandwidth required by the computation kernel on FPGA. For example, if given a computation kernel running at 100 MHz requires a memory bandwidth of 3.2 GB/s, a DRAM chip with 16 data pins running at 800 MHz can be employed to meet the bandwidth requirement [1]. Note that more memory bandwidth can be obtained by using multiple DRAM chips in parallel, however, more memory energy will be consumed correspondingly. At run-time, unused DRAM chips should be set to precharge power-down mode to save energy. In Section 3.1, we derived energy consumption equations for accessing $n$ data words on $b$ memory banks. Similarly, the maximum throughput achieved in DRAM can be obtained as the ratio of $n$ to the total amount time required for accessing the $n$ data words. We can vary the data parallelism $p$ of the on-chip computation kernel with operating frequency of $f$ to balance the throughput between the DRAM and the computation kernel.

## 4.2   Data Remapping and Data Prefetching

When data are written sequentially and then read using strided addresses, successive DRAM row activations to the same DRAM bank is needed. Strided addresses are a sequence of addresses incremented with a stride. When performing such a DRAM access pattern, a 2-D data array is first created by the computation kernel and then written onto the DRAM with row-wise memory write operations. The computation time and the DRAM access time are usually overlapped through pipelining. After that, the computation kernel needs to fetch the data array with column-wise read operations. Therefore, the memory address is increased with a stride equals to the width of the data array after every memory access cycle. As a result, DRAM row activations may require to be executed frequently, thus introducing a significant delay especially for large size data arrays.

To overlap this latency, a state-of-the-art approach remaps data in blocks by on-chip permutation. Their approach minimizes the number of row activations, however, at the expense of $O(N^2)$ latency for $N \times N$ 2-D data array. Our DRAM energy model introduced in Section 3 indicates that the energy consumption of column-wise read operations can be reduced to the lower bound. In the state-of-the-art approach, $m$ is reduced to 0 unnecessarily [5]. Instead, we reduce $m$ to be lower than $wb\frac{t_{RRD}}{t_{RC}}$ through on-chip data permutation. As a result, the extra latency is reduced from $O(N^2)$ to $O(N)$. After data remapping, both the row-wise write and column-wise read operations are executed using stride memory access patterns. Therefore, for row-wise read operations, the generated 2-D data array is written with a stride $m$, which is $\left\lceil wb\frac{t_{RRD}}{t_{RC}} \right\rceil$. After that, the column-wise write operations also need to be executed with the stride $m$. As a result, the latency of both row-wise and column-wise memory operations are minimized. Using this data remapping scheme, we are able to overlap the latency between successive memory accesses on the same DRAM bank. As a result, the utilization rate per DRAM row activation is improved significantly at the expense of extra memory resource.

## 5    Experimental Results and Analysis

We use the classic 2-D FFT as the benchmark application for experimental evaluation. The 1-D FFT kernel proposed in [6] is employed in our implementation. Using this kernel, we first build a baseline 2-D FFT architecture based on the row-column 2-D FFT algorithm [7]. Then we optimized the baseline architecture through the proposed data remapping and prefetching schemes. We compare the energy efficiency of the optimized 2-D FFT architecture and the baseline architecture. Both designs achieve a sustained throughput of at least 3.2 GB/s for $1024 \times 1024$, $4096 \times 4096$ and $8192 \times 8192$ points 2-D FFT.

### 5.1    Experimental Setup

The experiments were conducted on a state-of-the-art FPGA-based MPSoC platform Zynq-7000 with 512 MB DDR3 memory [4]. The FPGA device on Zynq-7000 is Xilinx Artix 7. The experiments were performed using Xilinx Vivado 2014.2 development tools including the Vivado Power Analysis tool used for determining the power dissipation [3]. The designs were verified by post place-and-route simulation. The input matrices for the simulation were randomly generated and had an average switching activity of 50%, which is a pessimistic estimation. All of the reported results are post place-and-route simulation results. We used the VCD (Value Change Dump Format) file as input to the Xilinx Vivado Power Analyzer to produce accurate power dissipation estimation.

### 5.2    Performance Comparison

We compare performance using two metrics. The first is energy per point, which refers to power dissipated per unit throughput (points per second) in performing 2-D FFT. Another performance metric is energy efficiency (or power efficiency) which is defined as the number of complex operations performed divided by the total energy consumption (GFLOPS/W). In order to give a complete view of the energy efficiency of the entire 2-D FFT architecture, we evaluate the static power dissipation of the architecture and calculate the energy efficiency including the static power dissipation. According to our power simulation results, the static power of the Artix-7 is 0.085W for the optimized and baseline architectures, regardless of how much resources are used and the operating frequency.

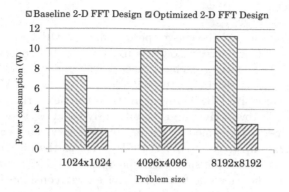

**Fig. 2.** Power performance comparison

**Table 1.** Energy performance of the optimized 2-D FFT architecture and the baseline

|  | Baseline architecture | | Optimized architecture | | |
|---|---|---|---|---|---|
| FFT size | Energy per point (nJoule) | Energy efficiency (GFLOPS/W) | Energy per point (nJoule) | Energy efficiency (GFLOPS/W) | Energy efficiency improvement |
| 1024 × 1024 | 18.2 | 2.09 | 4.6 | 8.31 | 3.9x |
| 4096 × 4096 | 24.5 | 1.89 | 5.8 | 8.01 | 4.2x |
| 8192 × 8192 | 28.2 | 1.79 | 6.3 | 8.06 | 4.5x |

By considering the energy consumed by both the DRAM and the 1-D FFT kernel, we compare the performance of the two target 2-D FFT architectures using the two metrics. Fig. 2 shows the power performance of the both architectures. By reducing the DRAM power consumption for stride memory access patterns, the power performance of the optimized 2-D FFT architecture is improved significantly. Table 1 shows the energy performance comparison between the baseline 2-D FFT architecture and the optimized 2-D FFT architecture. It shows that the entire optimized 2-D FFT architecture achieves 8.31, 8.01 and 8.06 GFLOPS/W in energy efficiency for 1024 × 1024, 4096 × 4096 and 8192 × 8192 points 2-D FFT when considering both dynamic power and static power. The energy consumption per point is reduced by 74.8%, 76.4.7%, 77.7% for 1024 × 1024, 4096 × 4096 and 8192 × 8192 points 2-D FFT, respectively. Comparing the results of the energy consumption per point in the 1-D FFT kernel and the entire 2-D FFT architecture, we observe that the optimization for DRAM access makes a major contribution to the improvement of energy performance.

# 6  Conclusion

In this paper, we evaluated the energy performance of DRAM on FPGA-based system for stride memory access. Lower bounds on DRAM energy performance were derived for these specific memory access patterns. We developed a data remapping technique to rearrange the data layout on the DRAM so that the latency between successive DRAM row activations can be overlapped. The access delay due to DRAM row activation is significantly reduced, thus saving significant amount of energy consumed by the entire FPGA system. To illustrate our proposed optimization, we selected 2-D FFT kernel as the benchmark application. The experimental results show that the optimized design outperforms the baseline in energy efficiency due to much lower energy consumption in DRAM. In the future, we plan to build a design framework targeted at energy efficient signal processing kernels, to enable automatic energy optimizations addressing memory and communication energy.

# References

1. DDR3 SDRAM System-Power Calculator. http://www.micron.com/-/media/Documents/Products/Power%20Calculator/DDR3_Power_Calc.XLSM
2. Micron DRAM. http://www.micron.com/products/dram/
3. Vivado design suite user guide: design flows overview. http://www.xilinx.com/support/documentation/
4. Xilinx. Zynq board. http://www.xilinx.com/products/silicon-devices/soc/zynq-7000.html
5. Akin, B., Milder, P., Franchetti, F., Hoe, J.: Memory bandwidth efficient two-dimensional fast fourier transform algorithm and implementation for large problem sizes. In: Proc. of IEEE FCCM 2012, pp. 188–191, April 2012
6. Chen, R., Le, H., Prasanna, V.K.: Energy efficient parameterized FFT architecture (2013)
7. Chen, R., Park, N., Prasanna, V.K.: High throughput energy efficient parallel FFT architecture on FPGAs. In: Proc. of IEEE Intl. Con. on HPEC (2013)
8. Chen, R., Prasanna, V.: Energy and memory efficient mapping of bitonic sorting on fpga. In: Proc. of ACM/SIGDA International Symposium on FPGA (2015)
9. Fang, K., Zhu, Z.: Conservative row activation to improve memory power efficiency. In: Proc. of ACM ICS 2013, pp. 81–90. ACM, New York (2013)
10. Park, N., Hong, B., Prasanna, V.: Tiling, block data layout, and memory hierarchy performance. IEEE Transactions on Parallel and Distributed Systems 14(7), 640–654 (2003)
11. Rixner, S., Dally, W.J., Kapasi, U.J., Mattson, P., Owens, J.D.: Memory Access Scheduling. SIGARCH Comput. Archit. News 28(2), 128–138 (2000)
12. Singh, M., Prasanna, V.K.: Algorithmic techniques for memory energy reduction. In: Jansen, K., Margraf, M., Mastrolli, M., Rolim, J.D.P. (eds.) WEA 2003. LNCS, vol. 2647, pp. 237–252. Springer, Heidelberg (2003)
13. Son, Y.H., Seongil, O., Ro, Y., Lee, J.W., Ahn, J.H.: Reducing memory access latency with asymmetric dram bank organizations. In: Proc. of ISCA 2013, pp. 380–391. ACM, New York (2013)

# Acceleration of Data Streaming Classification Using Reconfigurable Technology

Pavlos Giakoumakis[✉], Grigorios Chrysos,
Apostolos Dollas, and Ioannis Papaefstathiou

Microprocessor and Hardware Laboratory Department of Electronic and
Computer Engineering, Technical University of Crete, Chania, Greece
{pgiakoumakis,gregory.chrysos}@gmail.com,
{dollas,ygp}@ece.tuc.gr

**Abstract.** The challenging task for streaming data is to store, analyze and visualize massive volumes of data using systems with memory and run-time constraints. This paper presents a novel FPGA-based system to accelerate the classifier building process over data streams. The proposed system maps efficiently the well-known Very Fast Decision Tree (VFDT) streaming algorithm on a single custom processor in a high-end Convey HC-2ex FPGA platform. The experimental results show that the proposed system outperforms by two orders of magnitude the software-based solutions for streaming data processing, whereas the available resources of the platform allow for substantial further scaling.

**Keywords:** Data Stream Mining · Machine Learning · Decision Trees · VFDT · Hardware accelerator · FPGA

## 1 Introduction

Machine Learning (ML) is a research area of computer science that focuses on the extraction of useful information from raw data. The ML algorithms process data either in streaming mode or batch mode. The batch mode processing, which is driven largely by platforms like Apache Hadoop, provides mechanisms for running analytics across massive volumes. On the other hand, the streaming processing platforms need to cover two main assumptions: the reduced access to the data, which can be "seen" only once, and the time and memory restrictions during the processing stage. There are several widely used stream processing engines, like Storm and S4.

This work presents a novel FPGA-based architecture for streaming data processing. The implemented architecture maps a well-known classification streaming algorithm, i.e. the Very Fast Decision Tree (VFDT) [1] algorithm, on a reconfigurable platform with very promising performance results. The contributions of this work are:

- This is the first, to the best of our knowledge, hardware-based architecture to build the VFDT data streaming classifier on a high-end FPGA platform.
- Our proposed architecture takes advantage of the fine-grained and the coarse-grained parallelism that reconfigurable hardware can offer vs. the software coarse grained parallelism.

© Springer International Publishing Switzerland 2015
K. Sano et al. (Eds.): ARC 2015, LNCS 9040, pp. 357–364, 2015.
DOI: 10.1007/978-3-319-16214-0_31

- The single-FPGA-based single processor execution unit, which was implemented, achieves at least two orders of magnitude higher processing data rates vs. the execution of the VFDT algorithm on a single-thread platform.

The rest of this paper is organized as follows: Section 2 presents prior software and hardware-based works for data stream processing. Section 3 describes the streaming classification problem and analyzes the VFDT algorithm. Section 4 presents the architecture of the implemented system. Section 5 evaluates the performance of the proposed system. Finally, Section 6 draws the conclusions of this work.

## 2    Parallel Data Classification

Data classification is a well-studied problem and many software and hardware solutions have been proposed.

### 2.1    Software-Based Data Classification Platforms

There are many software-based platforms that focus on acceleration of the data classification workload. The Planet project [2] and the OpenPlanet project [3] used a cluster of processors to achieve linear reduction in the training execution time of the classification workload. Moreover, He *et al.* in [4] presented parallel implementations of various classification algorithms based on Hadoop's MapReduce process to achieve linear speedup vs. the size of the input dataset. Lastly, Tyree *et al.* [5] presented a parallel implementation of the gradient boosted regression tree algorithm using the MapReduce framework to achieve one order of magnitude performance speedup vs. single thread solution.

On the other hand, the most widely used software-based framework for data stream mining is the Massive On-line Analysis (MOA) framework [6]. Another important stream processing tool is the Scalable Advanced Massive Online Analysis (SAMOA) [7] framework by the Yahoo Labs.

### 2.2    Hardware-Based Data Classification Systems

This section presents some previous reconfigurable computing-based works that focused on data classification. Luo *et al.* [8] presented an FPGA-based architecture implementing a fast Decision Tree Searching for IP Traffic Classification. Papadonikolakis *et al.* [9] proposed an FPGA-based architecture for Support Vector Machine (SVM) classification and their system achieved 2–3 orders of magnitude as compared to the corresponding CPU implementation. Narayanan *et al.* [10] proposed an FPGA-based architecture that implements the most compute-intensive kernel of most DTC algorithms. Their implementation offers a 5.5x performance speedup vs. the software implementation. Chrysos *et al.* [11] presented the HC-CART system, which is an FPGA-based system that implements the Classification and Regression Tree algorithm on a multi-FPGA platform, achieving performance speedup up to two orders of magnitude vs. single threaded solutions, together with exceptional power efficiency.

Lastly, the issues involved in Big Data processing on present-day FPGA supercomputing platforms are presented by Dollas in [12].

This paper is the first work to map the widely used VFDT algorithm on hardware and the first hardware-based work on real-time machine learning streaming problems.

# 3 Classification

Classification is the process of assigning unseen instances to categories, based upon an existing model. The classification process is divided into two phases: model building and model testing.

## 3.1 VFDT Algorithm

The decision tree classification uses a decision tree as a predictive model for addressing the classification problem. The VFDT algorithm's trained model is a decision tree structure with a dynamic incremental nature. It begins with a single node, i.e. the root, and each time a new data instance arrives it calculates some functions, like the Information Gain or the Gini index, and it updates node statistics. Next, it finds the splitting rules that lead to the two best split decisions. Lastly, it uses the Hoeffding bound to decide if it is beneficial to apply the best split suggestion or not. The process continues recursively each time a new data instance arrives. The process is presented in Fig. 1.

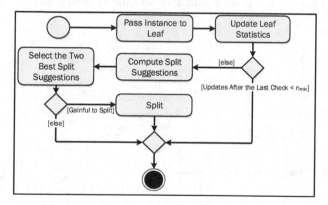

**Fig. 1.** Building of streaming classification model

## 3.2 VFDT Algorithm Analysis

This section presents some important issues as far as the nature of the VFDT algorithm. The algorithm analysis showed that:

- The training process is a much more computationally intensive process than the classification one.

- The most time consuming part of the algorithm is the computation of the split suggestions at the leaves. Thus, we focused on accelerating the leaf operations by mapping these operations on reconfigurable technology.
- The available parallelism of the problem lies into three directions.
  - Parallel traversing of the tree. Each new instance traverses the model-tree independently from the previous or the next data instance.
  - Parallel leaf processing. The operations at the model's leaves can take place in parallel.
  - Parallel attribute processing. Operations at the model's leaves such as updating the leaf statistics or the computation of split suggestions could be split into smaller parts that can take place in parallel for different attributes.

## 4     Architecture

This section presents the proposed architecture for mapping such compute intensive and streaming workloads on a reconfigurable platform, such as the Convey HC-2ex.

### 4.1     Attribute Processing Module

The Attribute Processing Module is the core unit of the proposed architecture, which is presented in Fig. 2. The proposed unit is used to update the attribute statistics and to compute the best attribute splitting rules. The Attribute Processing Module consists of two basic subunits: the Update Cache unit and the Compute Best Split Suggestion unit.

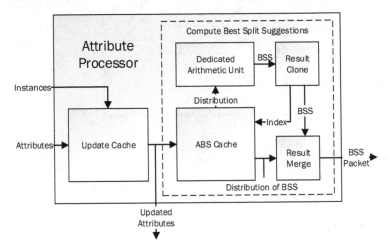

**Fig. 2.** Attribute Processing Module

The Update Cache module updates the statistics of a single tree node depending on the data instances that arrive. As shown in Fig. 2, it takes the instances that arrive to a leaf node and the statistics that are kept in these nodes. Then it updates the data and sends them back to the memory for storage and to the next module to compute the best split rule.

The Compute Best Split Suggestion unit takes as input the updated statistics and calculates the best splitting rule for the processed leaf node. The ABS Cache module and the Dedicated Arithmetic Unit implement the main workload for calculating the best attribute split rule.

## 4.2    Extended Attribute Processing Array

The Extended Attribute Processing Array is the basic unit of our proposed architecture. Our proposed solution communicates via a fast I/O data link with the corresponding software host part, as shown in Fig. 3. The proposed module consists of two basic subunits: the Attribute Processing Array (APA) and the Memory Controller Management Unit (MCMU).

The Attribute Processing Array, i.e. APA, consists of a series of parallel Attribute Processing Modules. The DMA modules residing in MCMU feed APA with attributes and instances while the dispensers deliver the data to the Attribute Processors. Each Attribute Processor outputs the updated statistics of a leaf node and the best split suggestion for each one of the attributes, which are sent back to the memory via the Updated Attribute and the Best Split Suggestion (BSS) Multiplexers. Lastly, the Selection Unit compares all the output best splitting rules and keeps the best splitting rule from all the input attributes.

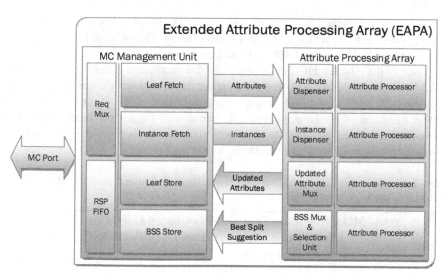

**Fig. 3.** Extended Attribute Processing Array (EAPA)

The Memory Controller Management Unit is responsible for data I/O from the shared memory. The memory requests are multiplexed by the Request Multiplexer. All four memory-based engines, i.e. Leaf fetch, Instance Fetch, Leaf store and BSS store modules, are designed to use 8-byte bursts. Furthermore, the MCMU is designed to take full advantage of the 64-bit memory controller port that runs at the same frequency with it.

The EAPA module is designed to be a firm basis for a larger architecture, where parallel EAPA modules can be employed to take advantage of more of the parallelism between attributes.

## 5     System Evaluation

This section presents the evaluation of the implemented system as far as the resources that were used and the performance results that were achieved.

### 5.1     Resources

An instance of our proposed architecture was implemented on a Convey HC-2ex server. Our system uses only about 5% of the available resources of a Virtex 6 LX760 FPGA device (out of four in the platform). Thus, our system can be easily parallelized in the future with many EAPAs on a single FPGA device, and then with multiple FPGAs in the system – as long as the memory controller can provide data. Our implemented system runs at 150 MHz, i.e. the clock rate for the memory data I/O ports.

### 5.2     Performance

This section presents the performance achieved by our proposed system vs. the single-thread Java-based implementation of the Hoeffding Tree Classification algorithm from MOA tool version 2014.4[6]. The software experiments took place on the host processor of the Convey HC-2ex platform, which includes a 4-core Intel Xeon CPU @ 2.13 GHz with 24GB RAM. We used various input datasets for our system evaluation. We built random datasets varying the parameters of the input dataset, i.e. the number of attributes per input instance, the number of classes per input instance and the number of values per attribute. The performance results from our three different groups of experiments are presented in the following Tables.

**Table 1.** Experiment with variable number of attributes (1 instance per leaf, 1024 leaves, 8 classes, 256 values per attribute)

| No. of attributes | MOA Hoeffding Tree Classification Execution Time (sec) | FPGA-based Hoeffding Tree Classification Execution Time (sec) | Speedup |
|---|---|---|---|
| 32 | 73.84 | 0.51 | 145x |
| 64 | 147.89 | 0.96 | 154x |
| 128 | 295.54 | 1.85 | 160x |
| 256 | 590.95 | 3.63 | 163x |
| 512 | 1182.55 | 7.19 | 164x |
| 1024 | 2363.11 | 14.31 | 165x |

**Table 2.** Experiment with variable number of classes (1 instance per leaf, 1024 leaves, 1024 attributes, 256 values per attribute)

| No. of classes | MOA Hoeffding Tree Classification Execution Time (sec) | FPGA-based Hoeffding Tree Classification Execution Time (sec) | Speedup |
|---|---|---|---|
| 2 | 638.11 | 3.61 | 177x |
| 4 | 1211.46 | 7.18 | 169x |
| 6 | 1785.15 | 10.75 | 166x |
| 8 | 2361.91 | 14.31 | 165x |

**Table 3.** Experiment with variable number of attributes (1 instance per leaf, 1024 leaves, 8 classes, 1024 attributes)

| No. of values per attribute | MOA Hoeffding Tree Classification Execution Time (sec) | FPGA-based Hoeffding Tree Classification Execution Time (sec) | Speedup |
|---|---|---|---|
| 32 | 79.02 | 1.83 | 43x |
| 64 | 219.62 | 3.61 | 61x |
| 128 | 673.73 | 7.17 | 94x |
| 256 | 2361.44 | 14.31 | 165x |

The above results show that our proposed architecture offers up to two order of magnitude performance speedup vs. a software solution that is implemented in a widely used tool, the MOA tool. Despite the streaming nature of the problem we showed different ways to parallelize the problem using hardware techniques like pipelining and fine-grained parallelization. In addition to this, we showed that the nature of the input datasets does not influence the performance of our proposed design. Lastly, the most important issue is that our system offers multiple distinct parallelization levels on data processing, which cannot be leveraged by processors in software.

# 6    Conclusions

This work presented an FPGA–based architecture that implements a widely used classification data streaming algorithm, the VFDT algorithm. Our proposed architecture combines fine-grained and coarse-grained parallelization level, which can be efficiently mapped on reconfigurable hardware. Also, we showed that the ensemble of modules that cooperate in a pipelined way to process a continuous stream of data seems to be a good architecture for such data streaming problems. Our proposed architecture was mapped and fully implemented on a Convey HC-2ex platform, which seems to be a good solution for data streaming problems, due to its high I/O data transmission rate and its memory organization. The proposed FPGA-based system offers substantial performance advantages vs. widely used software solutions. Future work will focus on massive parallelism on all four Convey HC-2ex FPGAs and full exploitation of the memory-FPGA bandwidth.

**Acknowledgment.** This work was funded by the General Secretariat of Research and Technology of Greece (GSRT) under the project "AFORMI- Allowing for Reconfigurable Hardware to Efficiently Implement Algorithms of Multidisciplinary Importance", funded in the call "ARISTEIA" of the framework "Education and Lifelong Learning" (code 2427).

# References

1. Domingos, P., Hulten, G.: Mining high-speed data streams. In: Proceedings of the Sixth ACM SIGKDD International Conference on Knowledge Discovery and Data Mining, pp. 71–80. ACM, August 2000
2. Panda, B., Herbach, J.S., Basu, S., Bayardo, R.J.: Planet: massively parallel learning of tree ensembles with mapreduce. Proceedings of the VLDB Endowment **2**(2), 1426–1437 (2009)
3. Yin, W., Simmhan, Y., Prasanna, V. K.: Scalable regression tree learning on Hadoop using OpenPlanet. In: Proceedings of Third International Workshop on MapReduce and its Applications Date, pp. 57–64. ACM, June 2012
4. He, Q., Tan, Q., Ma, X., Shi, Z.: The High-Activity Parallel Implementation of Data Preprocessing Based on MapReduce. In: Yu, J., Greco, S., Lingras, P., Wang, G., Skowron, A. (eds.) RSKT 2010. LNCS, vol. 6401, pp. 646–654. Springer, Heidelberg (2010)
5. Tyree, S., Weinberger, K. Q., Agrawal, K., Paykin, J.: Parallel boosted regression trees for web search ranking. In: Proceedings of the 20th International Conference on World Wide Web, pp. 387–396. ACM, March 2011
6. Bifet, A., Holmes, G., Pfahringer, B., Read, J., Kranen, P., Kremer, H., Jansen, T., Seidl, T.: MOA: A Real-Time Analytics Open Source Framework. In: Gunopulos, D., Hofmann, T., Malerba, D., Vazirgiannis, M. (eds.) ECML PKDD 2011, Part III. LNCS, vol. 6913, pp. 617–620. Springer, Heidelberg (2011)
7. De Francisci Morales, G.: SAMOA: A platform for mining big data streams. In: Proceedings of the 22nd International Conference on World Wide Web Companion, pp. 777–778. International World Wide Web Conferences Steering Committee, May 2013
8. Luo, Y., Xiang, K., Li, S.: Acceleration of decision tree searching for IP traffic classification. In: Proceedings of the 4th ACM/IEEE Symposium on Architectures for Networking and Communications Systems, pp. 40–49. ACM, November 2008
9. Papadonikolakis, M., Bouganis, C. S., Constantinides, G.: Performance comparison of GPU and FPGA architectures for the SVM training problem. In: International Conference on Field-Programmable Technology, FPT 2009, pp. 388–391. IEEE, December 2009
10. Narayanan, R., Honbo, D., Memik, G., Choudhary, A., Zambreno, J.: An FPGA implementation of decision tree classification. In: Design, Automation & Test in Europe Conference & Exhibition, DATE 2007, pp. 1–6. IEEE, April 2007
11. Chrysos, G., Dagritzikos, P., Papaefstathiou, I., Dollas, A.: HC-CART: A parallel system implementation of data mining classification and regression tree (CART) algorithm on a multi-FPGA system. ACM Transactions on Architecture and Code Optimization (TACO) **9**(4), 47 (2013)
12. Dollas, A.: Big Data Processing with FPGA Supercomputers: Opportunities and Challenges. In: Proceedings of the IEEE Computer Society Annual Symposium on VLSI. ISVLSI, pp. 474–479. IEEE, July 2014

# On-The-Fly Verification of Reconfigurable Image Processing Modules Based on a Proof-Carrying Hardware Approach

Tobias Wiersema$^{(\boxtimes)}$, Sen Wu, and Marco Platzner

University of Paderborn, Paderborn, Germany
{tobias.wiersema,platzner}@upb.de, senwu@mail.upb.de

**Abstract.** Proof-carrying hardware is an approach that has recently been proposed for the efficient verification of reconfigurable modules. We present an application of proof-carrying hardware to guarantee the correct functionality of dynamically reconfigured image processing modules. Our prototype comprises a reconfigurable-system-on-chip with an embedded virtual FPGA fabric. This setup allows us to leverage open source FPGA synthesis and backend tools to produce FPGA configuration bitstreams with an open format and, thus, to demonstrate and experimentally evaluate proof-carrying hardware at the bitstream level.

## 1 Introduction

Hardware reconfigurability holds promise for greatly reducing the deployment time for new hardware functionality and shortening time-to-market. System designers increasingly rely on IP cores from third parties, but downloading and integrating a reconfigurable module into a reconfigurable system-on-chip poses a serious security threat. Especially for systems able to adapt their functionality through dynamic hardware reconfiguration, there will be no time for rigorous testing or some other time-consuming form of validation.

Proof-carrying hardware (PCH) [4] addresses this problem by proposing a technique for a light-weight but mathematically rigorous verification on-the-fly. Using PCH, trust into the third party IP core can be established just in time, i.e., right before reconfiguration. Being a rather new concept, PCH has mainly been evaluated by simulations but not yet sufficiently demonstrated by actual prototypes. Unfortunately, the implementation of PCH at the bitstream level is hindered by the closed nature of bitstream formats for today's commercial FPGAs. In this paper, we present a PCH prototype based on a virtual FPGA fabric embedded into a reconfigurable system-on-chip. This setup allows us to leverage open source FPGA synthesis and backend tools to produce FPGA configuration bitstreams with an open format.

This work was partially supported by the German Research Foundation (DFG) within the Collaborative Research Centre "On-The-Fly Computing" (SFB 901).

K. Sano et al. (Eds.): ARC 2015, LNCS 9040, pp. 365–372, 2015.
DOI: 10.1007/978-3-319-16214-0_32

While the general approach of using a virtual FPGA fabric to gain access to bitstream details for demonstrating the PCH concept has recently been proposed [9,10], the novel contribution of this paper is the complete prototype implementation for on-the-fly verification of reconfigurable image processing modules. The prototype allows us to demonstrate and experimentally evaluate PCH at the bitstream level. Choosing image processing functions as example domain is suitable since the filters have simple interfaces and consume moderate hardware resources. Moreover, the on-the-fly replacement of image filter has a visible effect on the system and the process of reprogramming the system from specification of filters in Verilog to the visual effect is a matter of minutes.

The paper is structured as follows: Section 2 reviews related work in proof-carrying hardware. In Section 3 we present our reconfigurable system-on-chip prototype employing an FPGA overlay for running image processing functions, and in Section 4 we explain the application of the proof-carrying hardware approach to achieve on-the-fly verification. Section 5 shows experimental results and Section 6 concludes the paper.

## 2   Related Work in Proof-Carrying Hardware

The concept of proof-carrying hardware (PCH) was proposed by Drzevitzky et al. [4] as reconfigurable hardware equivalent of proof-carrying code by Necula and Lee [8]. The main idea of PCH and PCC is the fast runtime verification of certain a-priori agreed upon security properties, by having the producer of the software or hardware module create a proof in advance, at design time, so that the consumer just has to retrace or check the proof instead of generating it itself. Often, this process is light-weight compared to the producer's effort since for many properties computing a proof is exponentially more difficult than checking it afterwards. The resulting trust in the received module is equivalent to traditional verification methods on the consumer side, but the cost for this trust is now payed by the producer if the retracing is computationally less expensive than actually proving the property.

Together with the introduction of PCH as a general concept, Drzevitzky et al. [4] presented a prototype tool flow targeting an abstract FPGA architecture using the open source hardware synthesis tool flow VTR [7]. They realized the tool flow for both the consumer and producer, starting with a "golden" reference behavioral hardware description and the goal to produce a functionally equivalent implementation. While this work demonstrated the feasibility of the PCH approach, the proof-carrying bitstream was for an abstract FPGA architecture and thus could not be reconfigured onto a physical device.

Later on, Love et al. [5] shifted the focus of the PCH analysis from the post-synthesis bitstream-level up to the pre-synthesis register-transfer-level by modeling a subset of Verilog commands in the Coq theorem-proving language. Such an approach requires a Coq interpreter on the consumer side to validate the resulting proof. Moreover, the consumer has also to run synthesis and FPGA backend tools.

To achieve the transfer from abstract to real FPGAs, Wiersema et al. [9] proposed to rely on the overlay ZUMA [3], an FPGA on an FPGA with open bitstream format. They created a prototype reconfigurable system-on-chip running Linux and the ReconOS operating system [2]. Recently, in [10], the authors presented a ZUMA overlay embedded into the memory arbiter of the Linux-based reconfigurable system to guarantee memory security.

We also use such an embedding of an FPGA overlay into a Linux-based reconfigurable system-on-chip as starting point for our work, and present a complete prototype implementation for on-the-fly verification of reconfigurable image processing modules.

## 3  Reconfigurable System-On-Chip with Embedded FPGA Overlay for Image Processing

Figure 1 depicts the setup of our image processing prototype. A webcam attached to a host PC continuously captures images which are sent to the reconfigurable system-on-chip via Ethernet. The reconfigurable system runs at least a network thread in software on a MicroBlaze soft core and one or more subsequent filter threads in hardware. We use a buffering scheme that reserves an image buffer in memory for the incoming source image and for each output of a filter stage. The software thread is signaling the availability of a new source image to the first filter thread. A filter thread waits for this signal, processes the image and signals the next filter thread or the network thread, respectively. The network thread sends the processed images back via Ethernet to the host PC, where it gets displayed.

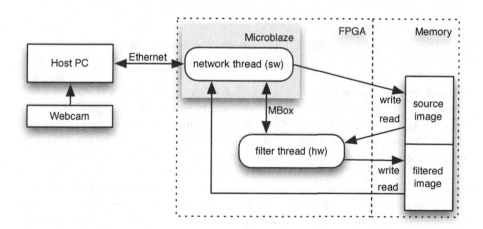

**Fig. 1.** Prototype image processing application with one hardware filter thread

We have based the implementation of our reconfigurable system-on-chip on the open source operating system ReconOS [1]. ReconOS is an architecture and execution environment for hybrid hardware/software systems featuring a multi-threaded programming model which allows for regular software threads as well as hardware threads [2,6]. Hardware threads are basically circuits that can interact with other threads and operating system services, such as semaphores, through a FIFO-based operating system interface (OSIF). Additionally, each hardware thread can access the ReconOS memory subsystem through a FIFO-based memory interface (MEMIF).

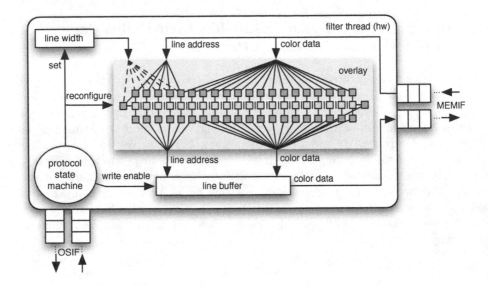

**Fig. 2.** Overlay embedding into a hardware thread for image processing

Similar to [9], we integrate a ZUMA [3] FPGA overlay into a ReconOS hardware thread. Figure 2 shows this embedding in detail. The original ReconOS hardware thread comprises a protocol state machine, an image line buffer and a line width register. The protocol state machine is connected to the OSIF for communicating with other filter threads or the network thread on the MicroBlaze and to the MEMIF for reading and writing image data from and to memory. An image line is read from memory and stored in the incoming FIFO of the MEMIF word by word, where each word contains information for one pixel, i.e., three 8-bit color and an alpha channel. The protocol state machine writes the color data for a pixel and its line address to the filter module. Thus, an image line corresponds to a row and the line index to a column of the image. For realizing image filters, the filter module can also read the line width. The output of the filter module is modified color data and a line address, i.e., the column in the line buffer where the color data is written to. Once a complete image line has been processed, the protocol state machine writes the line buffer back to memory. Additionally, the protocol state machine handles the thread-internal reconfiguration process for the FPGA overlay.

The structure of the hardware thread apparently poses constraints on the type of image filters that can be implemented. We can either implement point filters that operate independently on each pixel or filters working on one-dimensional stencils. Furthermore, since the filter can access the line width parameter, operations such as mirroring in horizontal direction can be implemented. The image processing filters are specified in Verilog.

We decided to implement moderately complex filters for our PCH prototype to keep the required area for the FPGA overlay reasonably small. Since we filter a whole line of the image in one step, our overlay is input/output-bound rather than LUT-bound or ZUMA cluster-bound, respectively. This consideration led us to a flat architecture of ZUMA clusters, as shown in Figure 2.

## 4    On-The-Fly Verification with PCH

We now apply the proof-carrying hardware (PCH) concept to our image processing prototype. As a first step, we need to discuss the different roles or parties involved. The PCH concept knows the consumer, who defines the functionality and the security specification of the hardware module, and the producer, who manufactures a module according to the specification, and then proves the conformity to the security specification. In our prototype scenario, we consider both the PC and the reconfigurable system-on-chip as the consumer, and the PC as the producer. For simplicity, the PC serves both parties without loss of generality. Furthermore, we assign not only the reconfigurable system-on-chip but also a PC to the consumer to run tools such as ABC and tracecheck; an investigation on the feasibility of running such tools on embedded CPU cores is part of future work.

Figure 3 outlines the steps performed in our PCH scenario which is similar to the steps described in [4]. The consumer specifies the functionality of the image processing filter by providing Verilog source code, as well as the security specification which in our case is demanding full functional equivalence between the (golden) Verilog source and the circuit represented by the final bitstream. The producer synthesizes the filter for the target platform, which is our instantiation of the ZUMA FPGA overlay. This step results in a virtual bitstream. The producer then extracts the logic function from the virtual bitstream to combine it with the original specification into a miter function in CNF form. This CNF formula is proven to be unsatisfiable by a SAT solver, which proves functional equivalence between specification and implementation. This works for combinational and time-bound sequential ciruits. The resulting proof trace together with the virtual bitstream is sent to the consumer, who also forms the miter with the extracted logic function in order to compare this miter CNF with the one that is the basis of the proof trace. Only if the miters match, the consumer knows

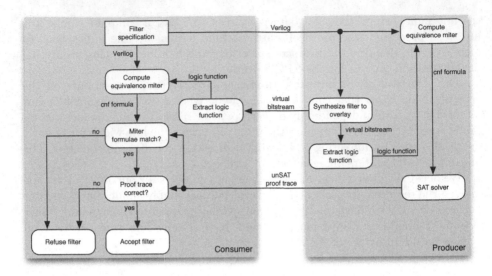

**Fig. 3.** Proof-carrying hardware flow for the image processing filters

that the provided proof trace is actually about the specified image processing function. As a next step, the consumer verifies the proof using the proof trace. If this step is successful as well, the consumer configures the FPGA overlay with the virtual bitstream. If any of the two checks fail, the consumer indicates the failure through its user interface on the PC.

## 5    Experimental Results

In this section we present experimental results measured on our prototype running a ReconOS system on a Microblaze soft-core @ 100 MHz on a Xilinx Virtex-6 FPGA ML605 board attached to a host PC with an Intel(R) Core(TM) i7-3720QM CPU @ 2.60GHz processor and 4 GiB RAM. We have configured the ZUMA overlay for the image processing filters as an $20 \times 1$ array of clusters with 4 LUTs each and 30 tracks wide routing channels.

In the first experiment, we have determined the area, timing, and synthesis and reconfiguration times for a reconfigurable system-on-chip without (original version) and with the PCH-enabling overlay (overlay version). Table 1 lists the results and overheads. Rows one and two show the required area for the complete design for both versions, i.e., including the Microblaze, I/O controllers, and ReconOS. Additionally, the resources necessary for the overlay only are shown. The use of the FPGA overlay for filtering thus increases the total area only by a factor of 1.34. The third row of Table 1 presents $f_{max}$ for the original and overlay versions, which is dramatically lower for the overlay version than for the original one. This frequency is the worst case timing estimate calculated by Xilinx tools for the overlay, and not a specific overlay configuration. Hence, this overly pessimistic estimate leads to rather slow clock rate for the hardware thread itself. However, in our experiments we have found that clock rates of up to 100MHz still produce good results, a thorough timing estimation for the FPGA overlay is part of future work. The synthesis times are displayed in the fourth row of Table 1 and show that while synthesizing the complete reconfigurable system-on-chip with or without the overlay amounts to roughly 50 minutes, the synthesis process for a single overlay configuration considerably less than a minute (actually, less than one second). Finally, row five shows the times it takes to reprogram the hardware with a new bitstream. For both versions reconfiguration from the host PC takes about one minute. Just exchanging the filter module on the overlay can be done in less than 0.2 seconds. Overall, using an FPGA overlay to enable the application of a PCH flow for on-the-fly verification increases the area only by a moderate amount, while allowing for significantly faster filter synthesis and reconfiguration.

**Table 1.** Area and timing of our prototype. Numbers given in % express the fraction of resources available on the Xilinx Virtex-6 of the ML605.

| Measure | | Original version | Overlay version | Overlay |
|---|---|---|---|---|
| area | [LUTs] | 17,888 (11%) | 23,945 (15%) | 5,512 (3%) |
| area | [LUTRAMs] | 2,038 (3%) | 7,456 (12%) | 5,418 (9%) |
| max frequency | [MHz] | 100.756 | 0.929 | – |
| synthesis time | [min] | $\approx 50$ | $\approx 50$ | $\ll 1$ |
| reconfiguration time [s] | | 60 | 60 | 0.16 |

As second experiment, we have evaluated the execution of the PCH tool flow as shown in Figure 3, starting with a filter's Verilog source and ending with either accepting or rejecting the implemented filter. Table 2 shows the times required for generating and validating the proof. for three filter types. We note that the absolute times for creating and checking proofs are rather small which can be attributed to the relatively small filter circuits being used, as the running times on both sides were largely dominated by formulating the miter function from specification and implementation of the circuit. The expected PCH workload distribution between producer and consumer is still evident, albeit barely. Applying the PCH approach to image processing filters proved to be successful, yielding easily verifiable proofs for the consumer.

**Table 2.** Proof properties for a selection of filters

| Filter | Proof generation [s] | Proof validation [s] |
|---|---|---|
| Gray filter | 0.111 | 0.105 |
| Mirror filter | 0.129 | 0.121 |
| Combined filter | 0.129 | 0.121 |

# 6    Conclusion

In this paper we have presented a complete prototype for on-the-fly verification of image processing modules for a reconfigurable system-on-chip. The prototype leverages ReconOS and ZUMA with corresponding commercial and open source tool flows. On-the-fly verification is established by a proof-carrying hardware approach that enables the reconfigurable system-on-chip to guarantee that a downloaded bitstream implements a partially reconfigurable module which is actually functionally equivalent to its specification.

Future work includes developing an accurate timing analysis for the FPGA overlay and more complex image processing functions.

# References

1. ReconOS - operating system for reconfigurable computing (2014). http://www.reconos.de/
2. Agne, A., Happe, M., Keller, A., Lübbers, E., Plattner, B., Platzner, M., Plessl, C.: ReconOS: An operating system approach for reconfigurable computing. IEEE Micro **34**(1), 60–71 (2013)
3. Brant, A., Lemieux, G.G.: ZUMA: An open FPGA overlay architecture. In: International Symposium on Field-Programmable Custom Computing Machines (FCCM), pp. 93–96. IEEE Computer Society (2012)
4. Drzevitzky, S., Kastens, U., Platzner, M.: Proof-carrying hardware: Concept and prototype tool flow for online verification. International Journal of Reconfigurable Computing **2010**, 11 (2010)
5. Love, E., Jin, Y., Makris, Y.: Proof-carrying hardware intellectual property: A pathway to trusted module acquisition. IEEE Transactions on Information Forensics and Security **7**(1), 25–40 (2012)
6. Lübbers, E., Platzner, M.: ReconOS: Multithreaded programming for reconfigurable computers. ACM Transactions on Embedded Computing Systems (TECS) **9**, 8:1–8:33 (2009)
7. Luu, J., Goeders, J., Wainberg, M., Somerville, A., Yu, T., Nasartschuk, M.N., Wang, S., Liu, T., Ahmed, N., Kent, K.B., Anderson, J., Rose, J., Betz, V.: VTR 7.0: Next generation architecture and CAD system for FPGAs. ACM Transactions on Reconfigurable Technology and Systems (TRETS) **7**(2), 6:1–6:30 (2014)
8. Necula, G., Lee, P.: Proof-carrying code. Tech. Rep. CMU-CS-96-165, School of Computer Science. Carnegie Mellon University, Pittsburgh, PA 15213, November 1996
9. Wiersema, T., Bockhorn, A., Platzner, M.: Embedding FPGA overlays into configurable systems-on-chip: ReconOS meets ZUMA. In: International Conference on ReConFigurable Computing and FPGAs (ReConFig). IEEE Computer Society, December 2014 (to appear)
10. Wiersema, T., Drzevitzky, S., Platzner, M.: Memory security in reconfigurable computers: Combining formal verification with monitoring. In: International Conference on Field-Programmable Technology (FPT), pp. 167–174. IEEE Computer Society, December 2014 (to appear)

# Partial Reconfiguration for Dynamic Mapping of Task Graphs onto 2D Mesh Platform

Mansureh S. Moghaddam$^{(\boxtimes)}$, M. Balakrishnan, and Kolin Paul

Department of Computer Science & Engineering, IIT, Delhi, India
{mansureh,mbala,kolin}@cse.iitd.ac.in

**Abstract.** This paper addresses an **optimal** mapping approach which also exploits the partial reconfiguration property of modern CGRAs. Hence this approach is not only suitable for applications which can be accommodated on the available grains but also for larger applications (or a set of applications) that need more grains than what is provided by the CGRA platform. This is achieved by mapping partitions of the application dynamically (during the life time of the application) onto the platform. The proposed mapping flow integrates *scheduling*, *binding* and *place & route* steps into one *mapping* step using a (Mixed) Integer Linear Problem formulation. The algorithm is implemented using TOM-LAB/CPLEX toolbox and we assess its efficacy on a set of 40 synthetic task graphs as well as some real life multimedia applications.

**Keywords:** Optimization · Partial Runtime Reconfiguration · CGRA · MPSoC

## 1 Introduction

The world of multimedia processing and telecommunication stacks is characterized by increasing speed and performance needs. The raw compute power necessary is fed by the ever increasing transistor densities enabled by innovations in the VLSI domain. However, this growth has to take into account increased defect densities, shorter time to market as well as high NRE costs. These two conflicting developments have made Coarse-Grained Reconfigurable Architectures (CGRAs) a popular implementation platform. The granularity of reconfiguration in CGRAs is higher than FPGAs and hence these architectures require less configuration memory for programming. This makes them achieve a significant reduction in area and energy consumed per computation as compared to FPGAs. A typical implementation of a function on CGRA vis-as-vis FPGA is tasks (higher performance) as it contains fewer switches for interconnects due to its higher granularity.

Embedded and multimedia applications can be described as task graphs. Mapping of such task graphs onto a 2D mesh of dynamically reconfigurable tiles requires temporal "partitioning" of the task graph in cases where the number of tiles is less than the number of tasks in the graph. We introduce a mapping

© Springer International Publishing Switzerland 2015
K. Sano et al. (Eds.): ARC 2015, LNCS 9040, pp. 373–382, 2015.
DOI: 10.1007/978-3-319-16214-0_33

approach to optimally map an application, given its task graph, onto a partially
and runtime reconfigurable CGRA, while minimizing total reconfiguration or
execution time of the application.

To motivate this, we use a sample CGRA to map a task graph (Fig. 1(a)).
Let us name tile in $i_{th}$ row and $j_{th}$ column of the CGRA as $\Gamma_{(i,j)}$. In Fig. 1(c),

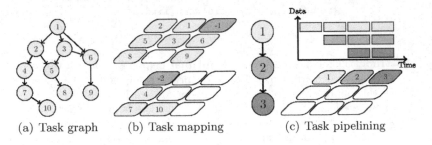

(a) Task graph      (b) Task mapping      (c) Task pipelining

**Fig. 1.** Task graph mapping onto a $3 \times 3$ platform

a simple task graph with only three tasks in sequence, is mapped onto a CGRA
of size $3 \times 3$. Whenever task 1 in tile $\Gamma_{(1,1)}$, has processed a data block, it will
send it to task 2 in tile $\Gamma_{(1,2)}$, then task 1 can immediately start processing
the next data block. The same happens between tasks 2 and 3. Therefore all
three tiles will be busy processing incoming frames in a pipeline. The capability
of CGRA in supporting such pipelined implementation, helps in decreasing the
total execution time of the application by overlapping task execution times.

Figure 1(b), illustrates mapping of the task graph onto a $3 \times 3$ CGRA. There
are only nine tiles in the CGRA, where there are 11 tasks in the task graph. One
single configuration of the CGRA when a partition of a task graph is mapped
onto it is called a "snapshot". In the present case, it is not possible to map the
entire task graph in one snapshot and hence the task graph has to be partitioned
into a number of snapshots. The main contributions of this paper are:

- An (M)ILP formulation for minimizing the reconfiguration cost as well as
  execution time of the application task graph mapped onto a partially reconfigurable CGRAs has been proposed.
- The effectiveness of the mapping algorithm has been demonstrated using
  synthetic TGFF [2] task graphs and some real applications.

The paper is organized as follows. In Section 2, we present a brief review of
the work related to mapping algorithms for CGRAs and MPSoCs. In section 3,
we formally define the problem while in section 4 an ILP formulation for the
proposed mapping flow targeting minimum context switch overhead is detailed.
This is later enhanced to an MILP to minimize the total execution time of the
application. Finally experimental results are presented in Section 5.

## 2    Related Work

The mapping techniques reported for MPSoC are on task level and even application level. The mapping techniques for MPSoCs can be categorized as static and dynamic mappings [3]. Most of the static mapping studies target minimum energy consumption, where some try to minimize total execution (computation + communication) time of the application [4], or communication cost [5], or inter-tile contention or traffic. But one key common assumption in all these works is that they target applications that can be mapped to the platform in one snapshot, implying that they do not exploit reconfiguration capabilities of the platform. Either number of tiles is more than the number of tasks of the application task graph or more than one task is mapped onto each tile.

There are only few dynamic mapping techniques that exploit reconfiguration to support mapping larger applications or a set of applications. In these techniques either tasks or links are changed during reconfiguration to make it possible for the platform to map a larger set of tasks. In [6] there is a large global memory (task memory) and whenever a tile has finished executing its allotted task, new task can be loaded from this global memory onto the tile during context-switch. In [7] there is no global memory but enough space to load new tasks to the local memory of each tile. So context-switch effort is minimized to controlling which task among these pre-loaded ones should be executed in each snapshot. In both mentioned cases there is no reconfiguration of links. Each tile has a router which is connected to its four nearest neighbouring tiles. Therefore, data from one tile can be routed to any other tile using packet switching. While dynamic mapping allows mapping of new incoming tasks/applications during runtime, no optimized solution has been proposed till date.

To the best of our knowledge, this is the first paper to present an optimal task-level static mapping technique which exploits the reconfiguration capability of the platform.

## 3    Problem Definition

The goal of our algorithm is to map a data streaming application represented as a "task graph" onto a 2D array of tiles. Tese tiles or processing elements (PEs) can be simple RISC processor [1]. The algorithm addresses the following cases; Map a large application with more PEs requirements than that available on the fabric as well as map more than one application onto the fabric simultaneously, when the area provided by the fabric is inadequate. The objective is to minimize either the total reconfiguration time or the total execution time. We make the following assumptions regarding each task; the number of incoming edges for a task of the task graph, cannot be more than the maximum possible number of neighbours in a platform (e.g. 4 in 4NN). The code size as well as data size of each task can be accommodated in the instruction and data memory respectively of each PE, otherwise the task has to be decomposed. Computation time of each task is fixed or we should be able to estimate an average execution time of each task.

The minimum number of snapshots($M$) for the application is decided based on $M \geq \left\lceil \frac{n}{K \times L} \right\rceil$, such that $n$ is the number of tasks, and $K$ and $L$ are number of rows and columns in the CGRA. Therefore for our mapping ILP, we start with minimum possible value for $M$ and if it turns out to be infeasible then we increment $M$, and repeat the mapping process.

The **Input** to the algorithm is a **Task graph** G=$< V, E >$ representing the application. $V$ is the set of tasks $V = \{v_i | i = 1, 2, ..., n\}$, and $E$ is the set of directed dependency edges representing data channels between tasks, $E = \{e_j | e_j =< i_1, i_2 >, j = 1, 2, ..., \varepsilon\}$. Two different costs are associated with each task and edge: *computation cost* and *reconfiguration cost*. Computing cost is the runtime of the task $c_i$, or time to transfer data through the edge $c_j$. Reconfiguration cost is the time to set up the task for computing $r_i$, or set up the channel for data routing $r_j$.

The **Hardware Platform** is a set of homogeneous tiles set up in K rows and L columns, $\{(k, l) | k = 1, ..., K \text{ and } l = 1, ..., L\}$, in which any tile can be used either for computing or routing purposes. The interconnection is mesh-like: each tile is connected to its four nearest neighbours (4NNs), except the boundary tiles. Data and instruction memories of all tiles are of the same size.

The **Output** is the set of $M$ snapshots $S = \{S_m | m = 1, ..., M\}$ such that $S_m = \{X_m, Ym\}$, $X_m$ is the set of computing tiles, and $Y_m$ is the set of routing tiles in snapshot $m$. It must be mentioned that while only one computing tile is assigned to each task, zero, one or multiple routing tiles could be allotted to an edge.

The **Mapping function** $f : G- > S$ partitions the application task graph into labelled partitions $p_1, p_2, ..., p_M$ such that each partition is mapped onto the same fabric at different instances of time (snapshot), respecting the data dependency constraints. In this case, computation time in each snapshot will be evaluated based on the critical path latency of that snapshot, $\delta_m$. Reconfiguration time of a snapshot is the summation of reconfiguration time of all computing and routing tasks allotted to each of the snapshots, $\gamma_m$.

The target applications in the proposed mapping flow are multimedia applications which go through a set of tasks to process a sequence of frames. Assuming, $I$ is the number of frames to be processed, then there will be $I$ iterations for the outer loop of the application. There are two possibilities: either the execution goes through all the snapshots for each incoming frame, or the execution of the application goes through an inner loop of size $J$ to process $J$ frames before switching to the next snapshot. $\tau_1$ (Eqn. 1) is for the former case and $\tau_2$ (Eqn. 2) is for the later case.

$$\tau_1 = I \times \sum_{m=1}^{M} (\delta_m + \gamma_m) \quad (1) \qquad \tau_2 = \frac{I}{J} \times \sum_{m=1}^{M} (\delta_m + (J - 1) \times h_m + \gamma_m) \quad (2)$$

The mapping process consists of mapping both tasks and edges. In the next section, we develop an Integer Linear Problem formulation (ILP) to solve this mapping problem.

# 4    Problem Formulation

In this section we will first develop an optimal mapping algorithm targeting minimum reconfiguration cost, and minimum execution time for the application. As there are likely to be both forward and backward data transfer edges in some of the task graphs, the algorithm is subsequently modified to cover edges.

## 4.1    Objective: Minimizing Total Reconfiguration Time ($ilp_r$)

Total execution time is the sum of total computation time and total reconfiguration time. We first propose an ILP formulation for minimizing total reconfiguration time. To build up the constraints set, two binary variables are introduced; $x_{iklm}$ and $y_{jklm}$.

$$x_{iklm} = \begin{cases} 1 & \text{if task } i \text{ is mapped to tile } (k, l) \text{ in snapshot } m. \\ 0 & \text{Otherwise.} \end{cases} \tag{3}$$

$$y_{jklm} = \begin{cases} 1 & \text{if edge } j \text{ is mapped to tile } (k, l) \text{ in snapshot } m \\ 0 & \text{Otherwise.} \end{cases} \tag{4}$$

Each task has to be mapped onto one and only one tile in one and only one snapshot; (Eqn. 5).

$$\forall i, \sum_k \sum_l \sum_m x_{iklm} = 1 \tag{5}$$

Each tile can be assigned to at most one task or to any number of edge segments originating from the same source task (Eqn. 6, Eqn. 7). $\varepsilon$ represents the number of edges in the task graph. Equation 6 represents that any tile $(k, l)$ in any snapshot $m$, can be occupied by either one task or at most $\varepsilon$ edges, originating from the same source node.

$$\forall k, l, m, (\varepsilon \times \sum_i x_{iklm}) + \sum_j y_{jklm} \leq \varepsilon \tag{6}$$

Equation 7 binds the edges routed through a tile to the edges that originates from the same source node.

$$\forall k, l, m, j_1, j_2 \text{ associated with } j, \text{ i.e. } < i_1, i_2 >, \; y_{j_1 klm} + y_{j_2 klm} \leq 1 \tag{7}$$

The Eqn. 8 defines "edge segment forward dependencies"; dependencies of an edge or edge segment to its destination task in the same snapshot, or to another edge segment in the same or next snapshot. Similarly we need "edge segment backward dependencies" equation, to represent dependencies of an edge segment to its source task in the same or previous snapshot as well as its dependency to another edge segment in the same or previous snapshot. Similar equations are required to represent tasks dependencies in forward or backward direction. We need to use both forward and backward constraints. These equations take care of dependencies between snapshots, otherwise the connectivity from source task to destination task of an edge maybe lost in between. But due to space limitation we have not given them here.

$$\forall k, l, m, j, \text{ in which } j =< i_1, i_2 > y_{jklm} \leq x_{i_2(k-1)lm} + x_{i_2(k+1)lm} +$$
$$x_{i_2k(l-1)m} + x_{i_2k(l+1)m} + y_{j(k-1)lm} + y_{j(k+1)lm} + y_{jk(l-1)m} + y_{jk(l+1)m} +$$
$$y_{jkl(m+1)} \quad (8)$$

We now consider the possibility of extra edge segments mapped to the last snapshot while they are not connected to anything else except themselves. The next two equations are written to avoid such cases. Equation 9 makes sure that no edge segment of an edge appears in a previous snapshot of its source task snapshot, and Eq. 10 makes sure that no edge segment of an edge is allotted in a snapshot which comes after the snapshot containing its destination task.

$$\forall j, m \sum_k \sum_l y_{jklm} \leq \sum_k \sum_l \sum_{p=1}^{m} x_{i_1klp} \quad (9)$$

$$\forall j, m \sum_k \sum_l y_{jklm} \leq \sum_k \sum_l \sum_{p=m}^{M} x_{i_2klp} \quad (10)$$

Equation 11 represents total reconfiguration cost which consists of reconfiguration cost for both tasks and edges.

$$\gamma_m = \sum_k \sum_l \{ \sum_i (x_{iklm} \times r_i) + \sum_j (y_{jklm} \times r_j) \} \quad (11)$$

The first term in Eq. 11 is fixed as each task has to be mapped onto a computing tile. Consequently the objective function reduces to minimizing the second term which is the total reconfiguration cost for edges. Minimizing the total reconfiguration cost results in minimum number of routing tiles and consequently minimum corresponds also to the number of snapshots. Equation 12 is used as objective for the ILP based on the constraint set defined in Eqs 3 to 10. The overall objective is to minimize the total cost over all frames as given by $\tau 3$ below:

$$\tau_3 = \frac{I}{J} \times \sum_m \gamma_m \quad (12)$$

## 4.2   Objective: Minimizing Total Execution Time $(ilp_x)$

In the new ILP formulation, we can use the same set of constraints described in Eqs. 3 to 10. We need to change the objective from $\tau_3$ given in Eq. 12 to $\tau_1$ or $\tau_2$ in Eqs. 1 and 2. We target the latter. While different values of $J$ will converge to the same solution using $ilp_r$ but as seen in Fig. 2, $Ilp_x$ may converge to different solutions. Different values of $J$ may cause choosing different paths

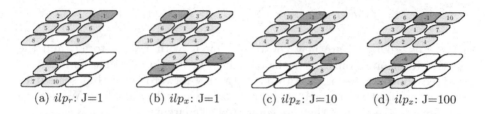

(a) $ilp_r$: J=1          (b) $ilp_x$: J=1          (c) $ilp_x$: J=10          (d) $ilp_x$: J=100

**Fig. 2.** $ilp_r$ vs. $ilp_x$ for the task graph given in Fig. 1 (I=1000)

as critical path in snapshot $m$. Accounting for reconfiguration cost ($\gamma_m$) for each snapshot was done by adding reconfiguration cost of each task and edge segment in that snapshot. However, for computation cost we need to find critical path latency $\delta_m$ and the maximum task latency $h_m$ in each snapshot as stated in $\tau_2$ (Eqn. 2). Finding critical path latency and maximum task latency in each snapshot while maintaining linearity of the optimization problem is resolved by definition of a new function called "Path Lister". The Path Lister function receives a task graph as input and gives two matrices as output. In both matrices the number of rows is equal to number of paths in the task graph. In the first matrix, $p_t$, each row states which tasks exist in the corresponding path while in the other matrix $p_e$ each row states which edges exist on the corresponding path (e.g. Fig. 3). Output of function "Path Lister" is formulated in Eqs. 13 and 14. Following equations are

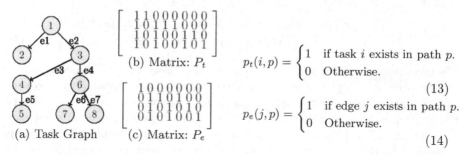

(b) Matrix: $P_t$

$$p_t(i,p) = \begin{cases} 1 & \text{if task } i \text{ exists in path } p. \\ 0 & \text{Otherwise.} \end{cases}$$

(13)

(c) Matrix: $P_e$

$$p_e(j,p) = \begin{cases} 1 & \text{if edge } j \text{ exists in path } p. \\ 0 & \text{Otherwise.} \end{cases}$$

(a) Task Graph

(14)

**Fig. 3.** Task and Edge path ($P_t$, $P_e$) matrices

new constraints besides Eqs. 3 to 10 for our new ILP problem. $\delta_{pm}$ is the latency of path $p$ in snapshot $m$, and $h_{pm}$ is the maximum latency task in path $p$ in snapshot $m$.

$$\forall m, p \in \{1..P\}, \delta_m \geq \delta_{pm} \tag{15}$$

$$\delta_{pm} = \sum_k \sum_l \{\sum_i \{x_{iklm} \times C_i \times p_t(i,p)\} + \sum_j \{y_{jklm} \times C_j \times p_e(j,p)\}\} + (J-1) \times h_{pm} \tag{16}$$

$$\forall i, m, p, \quad h_{pm} \geq \sum_k \sum_l \{x_{iklm} \times C_i \times p_t(i,p)\} \tag{17}$$

So far, Eqs. 16 to 17 are new constraints along with Eqs. 3 to 11, and the objective function of our ILP is the one given in $\tau_2$ (Eqn. 2). The formulation presented above works for task graphs with only forward edges, but some data streaming applications (e.g. H.264 codec) also have backward edges. We need to treat snapshots as though they are connected as a circular list. If data generated by a task in snapshot 2 is going to be used in snapshot 1, the same tile assigned to the task in snapshot 2 must do data buffering in snapshots 3, 4 and 1. Based

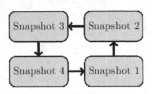

**Fig. 4.** Circular perspective of snapshots

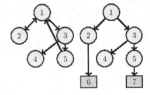

**Fig. 5.** PreProcessing Step

on this simple view, we replace Eq. 8 with the following equation, to cover both forward and backward edges.

$$\forall k, l, m, j, \text{ in which } j = <i_1, i_2>; \; y_{jklm} \leq x_{i_2(k-1)lm} + x_{i_2(k+1)lm} +$$
$$x_{i_2k(l-1)m} + x_{i_2k(l+1)m} + y_{j(k-1)lm} + y_{j(k+1)lm} + y_{jk(l-1)m} + y_{jk(l+1)m} +$$
$$(m! = M)y_{jkl(m+1)} + ((m == M)\&(i_2 < i_1))y_{jkl1} \tag{18}$$

We also change "Path Lister" appropriately so by inserting "PreProcessing" and "Postprocessing" steps to the default "Path Lister" algorithm which help convert the circular buffer view into the task graph with only forward edges. The (M)ILP formulation runs in a reasonable time if number of tasks and edges is not more than 20. In the next section, we present the experimental results of running the proposed algorithm on some synthetic and real application task graphs.

## 5   Experiments

In order to evaluate the accuracy of the (M)ILP formulation, we use two set of task graphs; forty synthetic task graphs generated using TGFF package as well as some real streaming applications. TOMLAB/CPLEX optimization toolbox is used in Matlab to implement our (M)ILP approach, using cut-and-branch solver. The Platform is a 2D mesh array of tiles of size $2 \times 2$, $3 \times 3$, and $4 \times 4$. For the 40 synthetic task graphs some random values are assigned as execution as well as reconfiguration time. The chosen range for random values is between (1000, 100) for a task and (100, 10) for an edge. Experiments are performed on

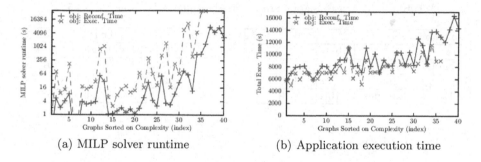

(a) MILP solver runtime                    (b) Application execution time

**Fig. 6.** Application execution time and Solver runtime for both $ilp_r$ and $ilp_x$

a Intel core 2 duo CPU (1.60GHz with 6GB memory). Based on the illustrated results while $ilp_x$ improves the total execution time of the target application by only 13.97 percent but it takes $31X$ more time than $ilp_r$ approach. $ilp_x$ also occupies $2.3X$ more space in RAM during execution than $ilp_r$. The graphs are sorted based on their complexity; number of tasks and edges. But we noticed that (M)ILP solver for two task graphs with the same number of tasks and edges takes different time to converge to a solution. The reason is a third factor; length of edges. The proposed (M)ILP solver requires more time to converge to optimal solution for the task graphs with a higher variety in their edges length compared to the task graphs with almost equal length of edges. Note we could not map the last four graphs using $ilp_x$ approach due to the RAM size limitation. We also mapped other applications like JPEG Encoder, Sobel Low-Pass Filter, Huffman Coding and JPEG2000 Decoder to assess the accuracy and efficacy of the (M)ILP formulation. In Fig. 7 task graph of the JPEG Encoder along with its implementation on a 3 × 3 array of reMORPH is given. Runtime and reconfiguration cost of the tasks and edges is measured after implementation on reMORPH; as given in Table 1. We implemented these applications on an array of MicroBlazes using XUP-V5 FPGA board and summary results are shown in Table 2.

**Table 1.** Task Costs

| Task | runtime #cycles | reconf. cost #cycles |
|------|------|------|
| S | 720 | 11 |
| D | 133324 | 62 |
| QZ | 2296 | 47 |
| H1 | 7934 | 71 |
| H2 | 1587 | 56 |
| H3 | 1651 | 151 |
| H4 | 2300 | 180 |
| H5 | 6823 | 109 |

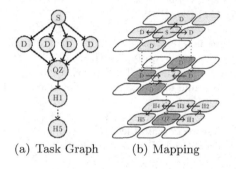

(a) Task Graph       (b) Mapping

**Fig. 7.** Mapping Jpeg Encoder to 3 × 3 grid

**Table 2.** Testcases mapped to 2D mesh of microblazes in XUP-V5

| Textcases | | | | 2*2 Platform | | | Larger Platforms | | |
|---|---|---|---|---|---|---|---|---|---|
| Name | #byte | n | ε | M | #routing | exec. (#clk) | M | #routing | exec(#clk) |
| Soble LowPass Filter | 64 | 5 | 5 | 2 | 1 | 36195 | 1 | 0 | 26708 |
| Huffman Coding | 512 | 7 | 6 | 2 | 1 | 5270626 | 1 | 0 | 5121010 |
| JPEG2000 Encoder | 16K | 8 | 7 | 3 | 2 | 55650087 | 1 | 0 | 53406896 |

## 6  Conclusion

This paper presents an optimal mapping technique for reconfigurable CGRA fabrics. The results of mapping synthetic examples derived from TGFF as well as real multimedia test cases show that the algorithm is able to achieve the minimum execution time or minimum reconfiguration time. The algorithm is scalable for mapping large task graphs as well as multiple task graphs that cannot be accommodated in the given silicon area. In the future, we would like to explore overlapping of execution of some of the grains while updating of other grains with the next snapshot. We also intend to generalize the approach for 3D fabrics as well as other interconnect topologies.

## References

1. Kolin, P., Chinmaya, D., Mansureh, S.M.: reMORPH - a runtime reconfigurable architecture. In: 15th Euromicro Conference on Digital System Design, September 5–8, Cesme, Izmir, Turkey (2012)
2. Dick, R.P., Rhodes, D.L., Wolf, W.: TGFF: Task graphs for free. In: Proc. Int. Workshop Hardware/Software Codesign, pp. 97–101 (1998)
3. Sahu, P.K., Chattopadhyay, S.: A survey on application mapping strategies for Network-on-Chip design (2013)
4. Bender, A.: MILP based task mapping for heterogeneous multiprocessor systems. In: Proceedings of the Conference on European Design Automation, pp. 190–197. IEEE Computer Society Press, Geneva (1996)
5. Soumya, J., Sharma, A., Chattopadhyay, S.: Multi-Application Network-on-Chip Design Using Global Mapping and Local Reconfiguration. J. Reconfigurable Techol. Syst. **7**, 1–24 (2014)
6. Carvalho, E., Calazans, N., Moraes, F.: Heuristics for dynamic task mapping in NoC-based heterogeneous MPSoCs. In: 18th IEEE/IFIP International Workshop on Rapid System Prototyping (RSP 2007) (2007)
7. Singh, A.K., Srikanthan, T., Kumar, A., Jigang, W.: Communication-aware heuristics for run-time task mapping on NoC-based MPSoC platforms. J. Sys. Arch. **56**, 242–255 (2010)
8. Singh, A.K., Kumar, A., Srikanthan, T., Ha, Y.: Mapping real-life applications on run-time reconfigurable NoC-based MPSoC on FPGA. In: 2010 International Conference on Field-Programmable Technology (FPT), pp. 365–368 (2010)

# A Challenge of Portable and High-Speed FPGA Accelerator

Takuma Usui[✉], Ryohei Kobayashi, and Kenji Kise

Tokyo Institute of Technology, 2-12-1, Ookayama, Meguro-ward, Tokyo, Japan
{usui,kobayashi}@arch.cs.titech.ac.jp, kise@cs.titech.ac.jp
http://www.arch.cs.titech.ac.jp/index-e.html

**Abstract.** FPGA accelerators can achieve higher computation performance and better power efficiency than CPUs and GPUs, because designers can implement circuits that realize application-specific pipelined hardware and data supply system. In this paper, we propose a portable and high-speed FPGA accelerator employing USB3.0 which is a data transfer interface with high versatility and high speed. We choose sorting as a practical application for the FPGA accelerator, and then design and implement the FPGA accelerator that executes sorting at high speed. To demonstrate the high portability, we evaluate the FPGA accelerator with several desktop PCs and laptop PCs. The evaluation result shows the sorting speed of the proposed FPGA accelerator is 1.26x and 2.60x higher than Intel Core i7-3770K operating at 3.5GHz and Intel Core i3-4010U operating at 1.83GHz, respectively. From this evaluation, we also show that the proposed FPGA accelerator has high portability.

**Keywords:** FPGA · Accelerator · Portable · High-speed · Sorting

## 1 Introduction

In order to achieve high computation performance and good power efficiency, it is promising to accelerate poor tasks for CPUs by GPUs or FPGAs. In particular, FPGA accelerators can achieve higher computation performance and better power efficiency than CPUs and GPUs, because designers can implement circuits that realize application-specific pipelined hardware and data supply system[4,10].

In this paper, we choose integer sorting as a practical application accelerated with FPGA, because it is an extremely important computation kernel that has been tried to be accelerated in a lot of fields, such as database, image processing, data compression [6,7,9].

There are a lot of sorting algorithms. In particular, quick sort and merge sort are known to be more practical algorithms than the others. Table 1 shows the measured execution time of quick sort and merge sort. We used two input-data sequences consisting of 32M and 64M elements, respectively. The data type of the elements is 4-byte integer. Each input-data sequence has three types; random

© Springer International Publishing Switzerland 2015
K. Sano et al. (Eds.): ARC 2015, LNCS 9040, pp. 383–392, 2015.
DOI: 10.1007/978-3-319-16214-0_34

**Table 1.** Execution Time of Quick Sort and Merge Sort

| # of Elements | 32M | | | 64M | | |
|---|---|---|---|---|---|---|
| Data Sequence | Random | Sorted | Reverse | Random | Sorted | Reverse |
| QuickSort | 2.754sec | >2hours | >2hours | 5.817sec | Unmeasured | Unmeasured |
| MergeSort | **4.121**sec | 1.562sec | 1.494sec | 8.512sec | 3.253sec | 3.125sec |

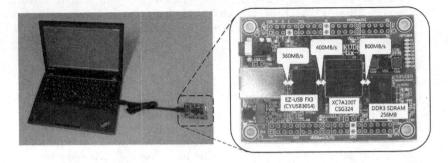

**Fig. 1.** The Evaluation Environment (a Host PC and The FPGA board supporting USB3.0)

data sequence ("Random"), sorted data sequence ("Sorted"), and reverse sorted data sequence ("Reverse"). We implement quick sort and merge sort in C, compile them with Microsoft Visual C++ Compiler 2013 (/Ox optimization), and measure the execution time of them. Quick sort and merge sort are executed as single thread of Intel Corei7-3770K operating at 3.5GHz. The execution time is the processing time of only sorting, and does not include the time of initializing data and displaying sorted data.

As shown in Table 1, although "Random" of quick sort is faster than merge sort, "Sorted" and "Reverse" of merge sort are much faster than quick sort. This is because the computational complexity of quick sort in the worst-case, where data is already sorted, is $O(n^2)$, while the worst-case computational complexity of merge sort is $O(n \log n)$. In general, quick sort is known as the fastest sorting algorithm. However, quick sort depends on the input-data sequence type. For this result, we figure out merge sort is a more practical sorting algorithm than quick sort because merge sort is insulated from the influence of the input-data sequence type. Then, we aim to accelerate sorting by FPGA accelerators, compared with merge sort.

In the case of developing FPGA accelerators, a data transfer interface between the host PC and the FPGA accelerators has to be considered. There are several interfaces, such as UART, eSATA, Ethernet, PCI Express, and USB. Among them, USB3.0 has the following advantages.

- High data transfer speed (up to 5Gbps).
- Hot swapping.

– With the 900mA bus power supplies, low power devices can be operated by just connecting a single USB cable.
– It is supported by most of modern computers.

Because these advantages are very desirable as a data transfer interface between a PC and an FPGA accelerator, we propose an FPGA accelerator supporting the USB3.0 connection. Fig.1 shows the proposed FPGA accelerator connected with a Laptop PC. The FPGA accelerator receives the unsorted data from the host PC, executes sorting, and sends back the fully sorted data. In this paper, we evaluate the sorting performance of the FPGA accelerator employing USB3.0. To demonstrate its high portability, we compare the sorting performance of the FPGA accelerator with several desktop PCs and laptop PCs.

The paper is organized as follows. We present related works in Section 2. In Section3, the design and implementation of the proposed FPGA accelerator are explained. Section 4 shows the evaluation of the sorting performance. Finally, we conclude this paper in Section 5.

## 2   Related Works

There are a lot of sorting algorithms that can be implemented on FPGAs. The merge sorter tree [5] can achieve highly effective performance and efficient hardware resource usage. The merge sorter tree is a datapath that executes merge sort. Each sorter cell compares two input-values and output one of them depending on the comparison result.

Koch et.al [5] proposed an FPGA-based sorting method, which combines an FIFO-based merge sort with the merge sorter tree. In this method, first the FIFO-based merge sort is used. Then, the sorting is executed by using the merge sorter tree several times. We employ this method to design our sorting logic.

In [7], sorting networks on FPGAs are discussed in detail. Sorting networks can realize even-odd merge sort, bitonic sort, bubble sort, insertion sort and so on, by changing the connection of the comparators. However, the input-dataset width for this method depends on the implementation. If the input-dataset width is wider, it is necessary to execute merge sort on a CPU. This means that the sorting cannot be finished within FPGAs.

Recent works show that many applications are more highly accelerated by FPGAs than CPUs and GPUs [4,10]. In [10], an FPGA accelerator for stencil computation is proposed. Stencil computation is used in lots of field, such as fluid calculation and weather calculation. This FPGA accelerator is implemented by using multiple DE3 FPGA boards, each of which has an ALTERA Stratix II I FPGA. Compared with Intel Core i7-3930K with six cores operating at 3.2 GHz, this FPGA accelerator achieves up to 13.7x higher computation performance. [4] also proposes an FPGA accelerator for stencil computation. Unlike [10], this accelerator is implemented by using multiple small FPGAs. This performance/Watt value is about 3.8x better than NVIDIA GTX280 graphic card.

Recently, some companies use FPGAs to accelerate several specific applications [1,8]. [1] develops FPGA accelerators with hundreds of pipeline stages and

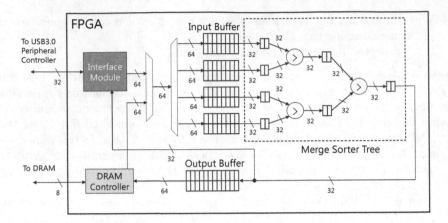

**Fig. 2.** Datapath of Sorting Logic Implemented on an FPGA

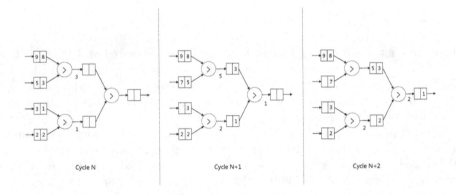

**Fig. 3.** Sorting Process in Merge Sorter Tree

sells them to companies, especially finance and oil exploration companies. In [8], FPGAs are employed to accelerate data center tasks. This technology improves PageRank throughput of Bing at twice.

# 3   Design and Implementation

## 3.1   Sorting Logic

Fig.2 shows the datapath of the sorting logic implemented on an FPGA.

The dotted line region in Fig.2 is the merge sorter tree, which executes the main part of sorting. Squares and circles in the merge sorter tree represent FIFOs and sorter cells respectively. The sorter cell is a combinational circuit that compares two input-values, and then outputs one of them depending on the comparison result.

Interface Module in Fig.2 receives the unsorted data from a host PC and sends back the fully sorted data. Interface Module sorts two elements each (this parameter depends on the size of merge sorter tree and the number of elements to be sorted) of this input-data sequence, and then stores them to Input Buffers. Each Input Buffer is an asymmetry FIFO whose input-data width is 64bits (two elements) and output-data width is 32bits (one element). A data sequence, which is partially sorted in the merge sorter tree, is temporarily stored to an Output Buffer. After that, the partially sorted data sequence is stored into DRAM. The Output Buffer is an also asymmetry FIFO whose input-data width is 32bits (one element) and output-data width is 64bits (two elements). Note that the DRAM controller's data width is 64bits.

Fig.3 shows how sorting is executed in the merge sorter tree. In this paper, each leaf of the merge sorter tree is referred as a **way**. Next, we explain the sorting process in the 4-way merge sorter tree shown in Fig.3.

First, at Cycle N, four numbers (8, 3, 1, 2) are read, each from a way. Then, "8" and "3", as well as "1" and "2" are compared. Note that the sorted data sequences are stored in the leftmost FIFOs. The sorter cells output smaller elements, unless their output FIFOs are full.

At Cycle N+1, "3" and "1", "8" and "5", "3" and "2" are compared by three sorter cells. Every sorter cell outputs the smaller element of two input elements, because all of the FIFOs are not full.

At Cycle N+2, every sorter cell compares two input elements. The sorter cell that compares "8" and "7" does not output "7" because its output FIFO is full. If this FIFO is not full, "7" is emitted. Finally, the whole sorted data sequence is obtained from the root of the merge sorter tree.

4-way merge sorter tree can merge four sorted data sequences into one sorted data sequence. If the number of sequences is more than four, the merge process has to be repeated. For executing this process, the partially sorted data sequence emitted from the merge sorter tree is temporarily stored in Output Buffer. This buffer is used to mitigate the DRAM access overhead. After that, the data sequence is stored in DRAM. We explain these processes in Section 3.2.

## 3.2    Entire Sorting Process

Fig.4 shows how the unsorted data (128 elements) sent from a host PC is sorted as time goes on.

We define "Unit" as a portion of partially sorted data sequences, which is in the input-data sequence of the merge sorter tree. A step that Units are merged is defined as a "Phase", and the number of executed Phases is defined as $P$. When Phase is never executed ($P = 0$), $U_0$ is the number of Units and $E_0$ is the number of elements in each Unit. In the same way, when Phase has been executed one time ($P = 1$), $U_1$ is the number of Units and $E_1$ is the number of elements in each Unit.

Fig.5 shows the entire sorting process. In Process A, Interface Module sorts two elements each of the unsorted data, and then stores them into Input Buffers.

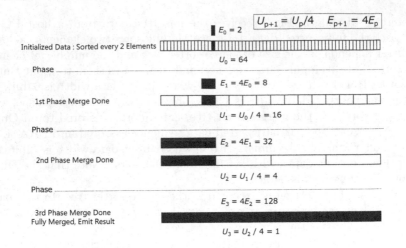

**Fig. 4.** Sorting Method in The Merge Sorter Tree

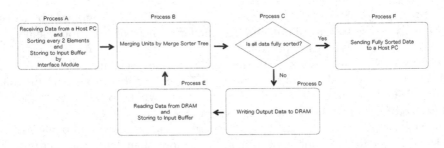

**Fig. 5.** Entire Sorting Process

"Initialized Data" in Fig.4 means a set of data sequences including the sorted two elements. Here, $U_0$ is 64 and $E_0$ is 2 because Phase is never executed.

In Process B, these Units are merged in the merge sorter tree.

After Process B, Process C determines whether the input-data is fully sorted. If sorting is finished, the fully sorted data sequence is sent to a host PC (Process F). If sorting is not finished, the data sequence emitted from the merge sorter tree is stored into DRAM (Process D). For example, 4-way merge sorter tree can merge four Units into one Unit within one Phase. Consequently, in the case of Fig.4, the data sequence ($U_1 = 16$, $E_1 = 8$) is emitted from the merge sorter tree. As shown in Fig.4, the input-data sequence sent from a host PC is not fully sorted. Therefore, the data sequence ($U_1 = 16$, $E_1 = 8$) is stored into DRAM (Process D).

In Process E, in order to sort the data sequence stored in DRAM, the data sequence is read from DRAM and is stored in Input Buffers.

By repeating Process B-E, the input-data is fully sorted ($U_3 = 1$, $E_3 = 128$). In the implementation of the proposed FPGA accelerator, Process B-E

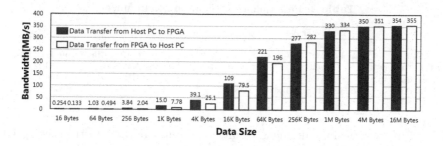

**Fig. 6.** Data Transfer Speed of USB3.0

are overlapped in order to improve performance. Finally, the fully sorted data sequence is sent back to a host PC via Interface Module.

In the data sequence $(U_P, E_P)$ with $K$-way merge sorter tree, the following equations are obtained.

$$U_{P+1} = \frac{U_P}{K} \qquad E_{P+1} = E_P K \tag{1}$$

where $U_0 > K$. In order to sort the input-data sequence sent from a host PC, the number of required Phases is $log_K U_0$.

### 3.3   Implementation Environment

In order to implement the proposed accelerator, we use TKDN_ART7_BRD-2[3] shown in the right side of Fig.1. This FPGA evaluation board contains a Xilinx Artix-7 FPGA and a DDR3 SDRAM (256MB) by Micron Technology. The maximum data-transfer speed is 800MB/s between the FPGA and the DRAM. To transfer data via USB3.0, EZ-USB (FX3CYUSB3014) by Cypress Semiconductor is used as the USB3.0 peripheral controller. The maximum data-transfer speed is 360MB/s between a host PC and EZ-USB, and is 400MB/s between EZ-USB and the FPGA.

We implemented the sorting logic (shown in Fig.2) in Verilog HDL. To implement Interface Module, we use an IP core provided by Tokushudenshikairo Inc[3], and use an IP core provided by Xilinx for DRAM Controller implementation[2]. All of the modules implemented on the FPGA operate at 100MHz, and DRAM operates at 400MHz. This implemented accelerator occupies 20% of Block RAMs and 18% of slices.

## 4   Evaluation

### 4.1   Efficient Data Transfer via USB3.0

We measured the data transfer speeds from a host PC to the FPGA board and vice versa. To measure them, we prepared 11 different data sizes from 16 bytes to 16M bytes.

**Table 2.** Performance Evaluation Environment

| Host PC | Computer A | Computer B | Computer C | Computer D |
|---|---|---|---|---|
| Type | Tower | Laptop | Slim Desktop | Laptop |
| CPU | Intel Core i7 3770K | Intel Core i3 4010U | Intel Core i7 870 | Intel Core Duo T2400 |
| CPU Frequency | 3.5 GHz | 1.70 GHz | 2.93 GHz | 1.83 GHz |
| Memory Capacity | 16 GB | 4.0 GB | 4.0 GB | 1.0 GB |
| USB Ports | USB3.0 × 4 USB2.0 × 6 | USB3.0 × 2 | USB2.0 × 8 | USB2.0 × 2 |

Fig.6 shows the measurement results. Although both data-transfer speeds are low when small data size is used, these data-transfer speeds get close to 360MB/s (the maximum data-transfer speed between a host PC and EZ-USB), as data size becomes bigger.

This result shows that high data-transfer speed between a host PC and the FPGA accelerator cannot be achieved unless data size is big. In the case of our sorting, data transfer speed close to the maximum value when the size of our targeting data set is 128M bytes.

As mentioned in 3.2, Interface Module sorts two elements each of the unsorted data sequence, and stores it in Input Buffers. Therefore, the FPGA accelerator can perform sorting while receiving unsorted data sequence from the host PC. Similarly, in the last Phase, the FPGA accelerator can perform sorting while sending fully sorted data sequence to the host PC. Thus, by sending and receiving data more efficiently, we enhance the sorting performance of the FPGA accelerator.

### 4.2    Performance Evaluation of The Proposed FPGA Accelerator

To demonstrate high portability of the proposed FPGA accelerator, we prepared four host PC shown in Table 2, as the evaluation environment. Because the library provided by Tokushudenshikairo Inc [3] to transfer data between a host PC and the FPGA board is designed for Windows, we installed Windows7 on all of them. We connect the FPGA accelerator via USB3.0 to Computer A and Computer B, and connect it via USB2.0 to Computer C and Computer D. We compared the execution time of the FPGA accelerator with that of merge sort in the host PCs. All host PCs run merge sort by single thread. Note that merge sort are implemented in C, and compiled it with Microsoft Visual C++ Compiler 2013 (/Ox optimization).

Fig.7 shows the elapsed time of sorting on four computers. Note that the result shown in Table 1 was measured with Computer A. The sorting performance of the FPGA accelerator is lower than that of Computer C and Computer D, but higher than that of Computer A and Computer B. Especially, in Computer B, the FPGA accelerator achieves 2.60x higher sorting performance.

### 4.3    Discussion

In this section, we discuss the reason why the sorting performance of the FPGA accelerator is higher than that of Computer A and Computer B. As shown in

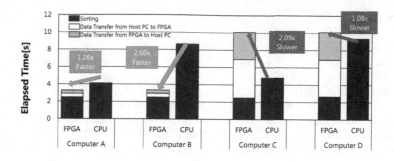

**Fig. 7.** Sorting Time (32bit × 32M Elements)

Fig.7, the elapsed time for sorting is the same in all of the evaluation environments, but the data transmission time for sending and receiving is substantially reduced. This fact shows that the FPGA accelerator benefits significantly from the high communication speed of USB3.0.

In Computer C and Computer D connected to the FPGA accelerator via USB2.0, the sorting performance of the FPGA accelerator is lower. Especially, in Computer C, the sorting performance decreases 2.09x. Thus, when connecting the FPGA accelerator with host PCs via USB2.0, sorting performance decreases due to the much lower data transfer speed.

In contrast, in Computer A and Computer B connected to the FPGA accelerator via USB3.0, the sorting performance of the FPGA accelerator is improved to 1.26x and 2.60x, respectively, because of the much faster data transfer speed. Therefore, it can be said that if the host PCs support USB3.0 connection, the FPGA accelerator can achieve higher sorting performance.

## 5   Conclusion

In this paper, we proposed a portable and high-speed FPGA accelerator employing USB3.0. We described its design and implementation, and evaluate its sorting performance. If we connect the FPGA accelerator with host PCs via USB2.0, the sorting performance decreased due to the low data transfer speed. However, if USB3.0 is used, the sorting performance is improved up to 2.60x.

In future work, we will increase the number of ways of the merge sorter tree and evaluate its performance. Besides, we will port the library for data transfer via USB3.0 [3] to other operating systems in order to enhance the portability of the proposed FPGA accelerator, and try to speed up other computational kernels using the FPGA accelerator.

# References

1. Maxeler Technologies. https://www.maxeler.com/
2. Memory Interface Generator (MIG). http://www.xilinx.com/products/intellectual-property/MIG.htm
3. Tokushudenshikairo Inc. http://www.tokudenkairo.co.jp/art7/index.html
4. Kobayashi, R., Kise, K.: Scalable stencil-computation accelerator by employing multiple small fpgas. IPSJ Transactions on Advanced Computing Systems **6**(4), 1–13 (2013). http://ci.nii.ac.jp/naid/110009616689/
5. Koch, D., Torresen, J.: Fpgasort: A high performance sorting architecture exploiting run-time reconfiguration on fpgas for large problem sorting. In: Proceedings of the 19th ACM/SIGDA International Symposium on Field Programmable Gate Arrays, FPGA 2011, pp. 45–54. ACM, New York (2011). http://doi.acm.org/10.1145/1950413.1950427
6. Martinez, J., Cumplido, R., Feregrino, C.: An fpga-based parallel sorting architecture for the burrows wheeler transform. In: International Conference on Reconfigurable Computing and FPGAs, ReConFig 2005, p. 7 (September 2005)
7. Mueller, R., Teubner, J., Alonso, G.: Sorting networks on fpgas. The VLDB Journal **21**(1), 1–23 (2012). http://dx.doi.org/10.1007/s00778-011-0232-z
8. Putnam, A., Caulfield, A., Chung, E., Chiou, D., Constantinides, K., Demme, J., Esmaeilzadeh, H., Fowers, J., Gopal, G., Gray, J., Haselman, M., Hauck, S., Heil, S., Hormati, A., Kim, J.Y., Lanka, S., Larus, J., Peterson, E., Pope, S., Smith, A., Thong, J., Xiao, P., Burger, D.: A reconfigurable fabric for accelerating large-scale datacenter services. In: 2014 ACM/IEEE 41st International Symposium on Computer Architecture (ISCA), pp. 13–24 (June 2014)
9. Ratnayake, K., Amer, A.: An fpga architecture of stable-sorting on a large data volume: application to video signals. In: 41st Annual Conference on Information Sciences and Systems, CISS 2007, pp. 431–436 (March 2007)
10. Sano, K., Hatsuda, Y., Yamamoto, S.: Multi-fpga accelerator forscalablestencil computation with constant memory bandwidth. IEEE Transactions on Parallel and Distributed Systems **25**(3), 695–705 (2014)

# Total Ionizing Dose Effects of Optical Components on an Optically Reconfigurable Gate Array

Retsu Moriwaki[1], Hiroyuki Ito[1], Kouta Akagi[1], Minoru Watanabe[1]($\boxtimes$),
and Akifumi Ogiwara[2]

[1] Electrical and Electronic Engineering, Shizuoka University,
3-5-1 Johoku, Hamamatsu, Shizuoka 432-8561, Japan
tmwatan@ipc.shizuoka.ac.jp
[2] Kobe City College of Technology, Kobe, Japan

**Abstract.** Recently, optically reconfigurable gate arrays (ORGAs) have been developed as radiation-hardened field programmable gate arrays (FPGAs) to realize a 10 Mrad total ionizing dose-tolerance. Specifically, ORGAs offer important benefits of high-speed reconfiguration, numerous reconfiguration contexts, and robust configuration. These three factors are important to remove the soft-error of a configuration circuit on a programmable gate array and to increase the total ionizing dose tolerance. Although the robust configuration capability has been confirmed using radiation emulation, no actual radiation experiment has been reported to date in the relevant literature. This paper therefore presents experiments demonstrating the enhanced radiation tolerance of an optically reconfigurable gate array using a cobalt-60 gamma radiation source.

## 1 Introduction

Embedded devices of spacecraft, satellites, and space stations are damaged constantly by the total dose effect of radiation [1]–[3]. For that reason, radiation-hardened SRAM-based field programmable gate arrays (FPGAs) have been developed [4]–[7]. Such radiation-hardened FPGAs have been used for some space missions already.

In a space system, weight is a crucially important concern since launch costs are extremely high. According to JAXA's newsletter, for a H2A rocket, the launch cost is 8,862 USD/kg [8]. Therefore, radiation-hardened devices should be used for space systems to decrease radiation-shielding weight. Currently, Xilinx Corp. is providing the space-grade Virtex-5QV FPGA, which has a 700 krad total ionizing dose (TID) tolerance. However, since the FPGA's TID is insufficient for shieldless systems, shielding must be used to decrease the TID effect. That shielding could be removed if the TID tolerance of FPGA were increased.

Therefore, recently, optically reconfigurable gate arrays (ORGAs) have been developed as radiation-hardened FPGAs to realize a 10 Mrad total ionizing dose tolerance [9]–[14]. A shield-less programmable embedded system would be

K. Sano et al. (Eds.): ARC 2015, LNCS 9040, pp. 393–400, 2015.
DOI: 10.1007/978-3-319-16214-0_35

realized if the 10 Mrad total ionizing dose tolerance could be achieved on ORGA architecture.

An ORGA consists of a holographic memory, an optically reconfigurable gate array VLSI [11], and a laser array [9][12]. Many configuration contexts can be stored on a holographic memory. To date, ORGAs with 256 configuration contexts have been demonstrated [14]. The configuration contexts can be addressed by the laser array. By turning one laser on, one corresponding configuration context can be read out from a holographic memory and can be programmed onto an ORGA-VLSI. An ORGA-VLSI has a fine-grained programmable gate array, as does an FPGA, and a photodiode array to receive an optically applied configuration context from a holographic memory. In an ORGA, a configuration procedure can be executed perfectly in parallel. Therefore, an ORGA can achieve nanosecond-order high-speed reconfiguration. A 10 ns optical reconfiguration has been demonstrated [10].

## 1.1    Total Ionizing Dose-Tolerance of ORGA

*Current radiation-hardened FPGA:* Currently, radiation-hardened FPGAs are available [4]–[6]. Xilinx Corp. has produced a space-grade FPGA (Virtex-5QV) with a 700 krad total ionizing dose (TID) tolerance. A radiation-hardened EEP-ROM is also available [15]. For comparison, one might consider a radiation-hardened nonvolatile 1Mbit (128K  8) EEPROM (W28C0108; Northrop Grumman Corp.) has 300 krad TID tolerance. Each time 100 krad radiation is absorbed on the EEPROM, a rewrite operation must be executed on the EEPROM. However, as long as one performs that rewrite operation, the data on EEPROM can be maintained up to 300 krad radiation. A configuration SRAM on an FPGA is extremely sensitive to radiation: the configuration context on the configuration SRAM is therefore constantly damaged by radiation. However, even if a configuration context on a configuration SRAM is damaged, then the damaged configuration context can be repaired by conducting a partial reconfiguration or full reconfiguration. Currently, a 300–700 krad TID tolerance FPGA system can be realized easily using such a radiation-hardened FPGA and a radiation-hardened EEPROM.

However, currently, we are aiming at 10 Mrad TID tolerance for an FPGA, thereby enabling the removal of shielding material from embedded systems intended for use in space. In this case, a non-faulty condition cannot be expected on an FPGA. Many parts of an FPGA can be damaged by radiation.

However, current FPGAs cannot allow such use because their configuration circuits are invariably damaged first, before a gate array part is damaged. The reason is simple. In an FPGA, many circuits serve to support the configuration procedure. Therefore, the circuit area related to the configuration procedure or a cross-section area for radiation is extremely large so that the configuration circuit becomes extremely sensitive to radiation. Moreover, such circuits are connected serially to each other. Therefore, the probability of failure of a configuration circuit is much higher than the failure probability of each logic gate. As a result, in FPGAs, a configuration circuit is the first to fail: its configuration becomes impossible. Therefore, its use in a faulty area is impossible on FPGAs.

*Total ionizing dose tolerance of ORGA:* However, an ORGA's configuration is a parallel configuration. Even if a part of the configuration circuit is damaged, the other area can be reconfigured correctly. Therefore, even if only one look-up-table (LUT) is functioning on a programmable gate array, the rest of the LUTs can be reconfigured and be used on an ORGA. The ORGA's parallel configuration enables use of a partly faulty gate array. If optical components, holographic memory and a laser array can withstand 10 Mrad TID so that the optical configuration can be executed under 10 Mrad TID, then 10 Mrad TID tolerance ORGA can be realized.

This paper therefore experimentally clarifies the 10 Mrad enhanced radiation tolerance of optical components on ORGA using a cobalt 60 gamma radiation source.

## 2   Experiment of an FPGA's Radiation Tolerance

To demonstrate that a configuration circuit is first damaged in an FPGA, a gamma radiation experiment was done for Cyclone II FPGA (EP2C70F) using a cobalt 60 gamma radiation source. The FPGA board was exposed to a 0-35 krad total ionizing dose in 5 krad increments. Results show that the JTAG configuration circuit on the Cyclone II was first damaged at a 35 krad total ionizing dose. However, a counter circuit on its programmable gate array was able to function correctly at 30 krad immediately before the JTAG was damaged. Therefore, this demonstration showed that the fault probability of configuration circuit of an FPGA is much higher than that of the other components because of the serial connection. In actuality, FPGAs cannot support a partly fault gate array since the configuration itself is impossible.

## 3   ORGA Experiments

### 3.1   Polymer-Dispersed Liquid Crystal Holographic Memory Material

Here, a polymer-dispersed liquid crystal holographic memory including the pre-polymer composed of dipentaerythritol hydroxyl penta-acrylate (Wako Pure Chemical Industries Ltd.) with liquid crystal materials was used. The mixture ratio of the prepolymer was 60 wt%. A liquid crystal material (DIC RDP98487) was added to the previously described prepolymer mixture at 40 wt % in the fraction of all ingredients. N-phenylglycine and xanthene dye (dibromofluores-cein) were introduced, respectively, as a co-initiator and a photo-initiator. Then, the mixture of the liquid crystal material and prepolymers was injected and poured into the 10 $\mu$m air gap separating two glass plates. The glass plate cell

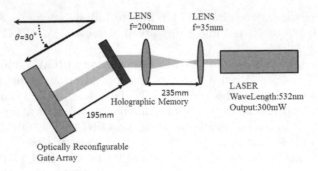

**Fig. 1.** Block diagram of the reconfiguration system in which a light source was placed at +30°. The configuration is executed with a +30° incident angle for a holographic memory.

was fabricated by two glass plates with dimensions of 25 mm × 20 mm × 1 mm. A photograph is presented in Fig. 3(a).

The multi-context information is written to the isolated regions in the photo area of $25 \times 20$ mm$^2$ in the angle-multiplexed holographic memory. The angle-multiplexing recording of multi-context is described as follows. After the position of movable pinhole for the laser exposure is fixed at the specific region on the liquid crystal composites by driving the X–Y stage, the configuration context in the photomask is selected by shifting the photo area using the motorized X-stage. Then, the laser light is illuminated for 2 min by opening of an optical shutter. After the first exposure of laser interference at a slanted angle of 30°, the second exposure is implemented in the same photo area at the symmetric angle of -30° by controlling the location of half mirror using the motorized rotating stage. The formation of the holographic memory by angle-multiplexing recording of a multi-context is fabricated by repeating the previously described process successively.

## 3.2   ORGA Reconfiguration System

The constructed optical system is presented in Fig. 1. The photograph is portrayed in Fig. 2. A laser of the same wavelength as that of the recording system, a 532 nm – 300 mW laser (torus 532; Laser Quantum), was used. The ORGA reconfiguration system was constructed simply using a laser, a polymer-dispersed liquid crystal holographic memory, and an ORGA-VLSI including a fine-grained programmable gate array [9]–[12]. The laser beam was collimated and was then incident to a polymer-dispersed liquid crystal holographic memory, as depicted in Fig. 3. The ORGA-VLSI was placed 195 mm distant from the polymer-dispersed liquid crystal holographic memory. The ORGA-VLSI was fabricated using a 0.35 $\mu$m three-metal $4.9 \times 4.9$ mm$^2$ CMOS process chip. In this fabrication, the distance between photodiodes was designed as 90 $\mu$m. Each of the 340 photodiodes is $25.5 \times 25.5 \ \mu$m$^2$ to ease the optical alignment. The configuration context

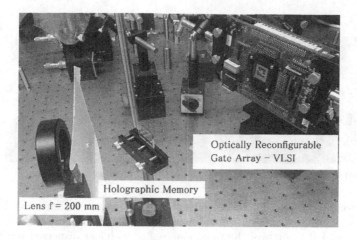

**Fig. 2.** Photograph of an experimental system in which a light source was placed at +30°. The configuration is executed with a +30° incident angle for a holographic memory.

size is 20 × 17 bits. The gate array's gate count is 68. Results of preliminary experiments confirmed that the ORGA-VLSI itself can be reconfigured in 10 ns.

### 3.3    Experimental Results

Here, a simple NAND circuit among 18 recorded configuration contexts on an original polymer-dispersed liquid crystal holographic memory was selected and implemented onto the ORGA-VLSI. First, an original polymer-dispersed liquid crystal holographic memory was implemented onto the ORGA system shown in Figs. 1 and 2. A photograph of the original polymer-dispersed liquid crystal holographic memory is shown in Fig. 3(a). The configuration context generated from the original polymer-dispersed liquid crystal holographic memory is also shown in Fig. 4(a). Finally, it was confirmed that the configuration context was programmed correctly onto the ORGA-VLSI.

Next, the radiation tolerances of optical components, or a holographic memory and a laser were confirmed. First, the original polymer-dispersed liquid crystal holographic memory described above was exposed to a cobalt 60 gamma radiation source. A photograph of the polymer-dispersed liquid crystal holographic memory after 29 Mrad radiation was applied is shown in Fig. 3(b). Its appearance has been changed from a transparent condition to a brown color. Nevertheless, a configuration procedure using the 29 Mrad total ionizing dose holographic memory was executed successfully. The CCD captured configuration context pattern is shown in Fig. 4(b).

In addition, the radiation tolerance of lasers was examined. In an ORGA, a laser-array is used to address configuration contexts inside a holographic memory. Therefore, an optical configuration procedure must be executed using a

(a) Original holographic memory    (b) 29 Mrad total ionizing dose holographic memory

**Fig. 3.** Polymer-dispersed liquid crystal holographic memory. Panel (a) depicts an original polymer-dispersed liquid crystal holographic memory before gamma radiation is applied. Panel (b) portrays the radiation-applied polymer-dispersed liquid crystal holographic memory after 29 Mrad was applied using a cobalt 60 gamma radiation source.

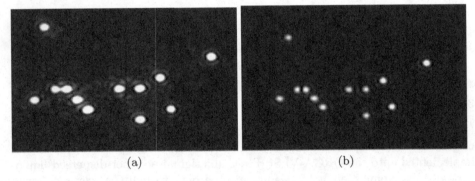

(a)                                (b)

**Fig. 4.** CCD-captured configuration context images of an NAND circuit generated from (a) original holographic memory and (b) 29 Mrad total ionizing dose holographic memory, shown respectively in Figs. 3(a) and 3(b)

laser-array in addition to a holographic memory. As presented above, holographic memories are extremely robust against radiation. However, to demonstrate an optical configuration's robust ability, the radiation tolerance of a laser must be measured. Therefore, here, the radiation tolerance of laser was also measured as shown in Fig. 5. The laser is a vertical cavity surface emitting laser (VCSEL, AS-0001-K; Fuji Xerox Co. Ltd.). The wavelength is 850 nm. The VCSEL was exposed up to 10 Mrad cobalt 60 gamma radiation. Even when the VCSEL was exposed to 10 Mrad radiation, the VCSEL worked correctly. No degradation of the voltage current relation and light power was found.

Therefore, an optical configuration mechanism along with a holographic memory and a laser-array is strong for radiation compared with the robust configuration ability of 300–700 krad of currently available radiation-hardened FPGA

**Fig. 5.** Gamma radiation experiment of a laser (VCSEL-AS-0001-K: Fuji Xerox Co. Ltd.). The wavelength is 850 nm. The VCSEL was exposed up to 10 Mrad cobalt 60 gamma radiation. Even after a VCSEL was exposed to 10 Mrad radiation, the VCSEL functioned correctly. No degradation of the voltage current relation and light power was found.

and radiation-hardened EEPROM. Even if optical devices are exposed 10 Mrad radiation, the correct configuration procedure can be executed on an ORGA.

## 4 Conclusion

Recently, optically reconfigurable gate arrays (ORGAs) have been developed as radiation-hardened field programmable gate arrays (FPGAs). ORGAs offer important benefits of high-speed reconfiguration, numerous reconfiguration contexts, and robust configuration. These three benefits are extremely important to mitigate or prevent soft-errors on a programmable gate array and to increase the total ionizing dose tolerance. To date, although the robust configuration capability has been confirmed through radiation emulation, no actual radiation experiments have been reported in the relevant literature. This paper therefore has presented experimental results showing that optical components of an optically reconfigurable gate array can withstand up 10 Mrad radiation from a cobalt 60 gamma radiation source. Future work will demonstrate that the ORGA's gate array part can also withstand up 10 Mrad radiation, although many parts might be damaged.

**Acknowledgments.** This research was partly supported by Nuclear Safety Research & Development Center of the Chubu Electric Power Corporation. Also, this research was partly supported by the Ministry of Education, Science, Sports and Culture, Grant-in-Aid for Scientific Research (B), No. 24300017. The VLSI chip in this study was fabricated in the chip fabrication program of VLSI Design and Education Center (VDEC), the University of Tokyo in collaboration with Rohm Co. Ltd. and Toppan Printing Co. Ltd.

# References

1. Yunlong, L., Xinyu, L., Chaohe, H., Haifeng, S., Zhengsheng, H., Qian, H.: Total dose radiation experiments in CMOS/SOI 4 Kb SRAM. In: Intl. Con. on Solid-State and Integrated-Circuit Technology, pp. 676–678 (2001)
2. Hass, K.J., Treece, R.K., Giddings, A.E.: A radiation-hardened 16/32-bit micro-processor. IEEE Transactions on Nuclear Science 36(6), 2252–2257 (1989)
3. Bertazzoni, S., Di Giovenale, D., Salmeri, M., Mencattini, A., Salsano, A., Florean, M.: Monitoring methodology for TID damaging of SDRAM devices based on retention time analysis. In: IEEE Intl. Symp on Defect and Fault Tolerance in VLSI Systems, pp. 106–110 (2004)
4. Rockett, L., Patel, D., Danziger, S., Cronquist, B., Wang, J.J.: Radiation hardened FPGA technology for space applications. In: IEEE Aerospace Conference, pp. 1–7 (2007)
5. Martin-Ortega, A., Alvarez, M., Esteve, S., Rodriguez, S., Lopez-Buedo, S.: Radiation hardening of FPGA-based SoCs through self-reconfiguration and xtmr techniques. In: Southern Conference on Programmable Logic, pp. 261–264 (2008)
6. Ramaswamy, S., Rockett, L., Patel, D., Danziger, S., Manohar, R., Kelly, C.W., Holt, J.L., Ekanayake, V., Elftmann, D.: A radiation hardened reconfigurable FPGA. In: IEEE Aerospace Conference, pp. 1–10 (2009)
7. XILINX corp., Space-grade Virtex-5QV FPGA. http://www.xilinx.com/products/silicon-devices/fpga/virtex-5qv.html
8. JAXA. http://global.jaxa.jp/
9. Kubota, S., Watanabe, M.: A four-context programmable optically reconfigurable gate array with a reflective silver-halide holographic memory. IEEE Photonics Journal 3(4), 665–675 (2011)
10. Nakajima, M., Watanabe, M.: Fast optical reconfiguration of a nine-context DORGA using a speed adjustment control. ACM Transaction on Reconfigurable Technology and Systems 4(2) (2011)
11. Seto, D., Nakajima, M., Watanabe, M.: Dynamic optically reconfigurable gate array very large-scale integration with partial reconfiguration capability. Applied Optics 49(36), 6986–6994 (2010)
12. Morita, H., Watanabe, M.: Microelectromechanical Configuration of an Optically Reconfigurable Gate Array. IEEE Journal of Quantum Electronics 46(9), 1288–1294 (2010)
13. Nakajima, M., Watanabe, M.: Optical buffering technique under space radiation environment. Optics Letters 34(23), 3719–3721 (2009)
14. Yamaji, Y., Watanabe, M.: A 256-configuration-context MEMS optically reconfigurable gate array. In: International Conference on Solid State Devices and Materials, pp. 232–233 (2012)
15. Northrop Grumman Corp., Radiation Hardened 128K x 8 CMOS EEPROM. http://www.northropgrumman.com/Capabilities/RadiationHardenedEEPROMS/Documents/1mbiteeprom.pdf

# Exploring Dynamic Reconfigurable CORDIC Co-Processors Tightly Coupled with a VLIW-SIMD Soft-Processor Architecture

Stephan Nolting, Guillermo Payá-Vayá$^{(\boxtimes)}$, Florian Giesemann,
and Holger Blume

Institute of Microelectronic Systems, Leibniz Universität Hannover,
Appelstr. 4, 30167 Hannover, Germany
{nolting,guipava,giesemann,blume}@ims.uni-hannover.de

**Abstract.** Most of embedded signal processing applications require the computation of complex arithmetic operations. Tightly coupled with a host processor, the CORDIC algorithm is one possible solution to establish a processing base, which is capable of performing a wide spectrum of operations with high precision. A software implementation as well as fully programmable and dedicated hardware implementations of the CORDIC algorithm are compared with each other in this paper. Especially, the use of non-programmable, area-efficient modules with a pre-determined functionality is particularly suited for use in dynamical partial reconfiguration (DPR) systems. This paper discusses the different aspects and design issues of different implementation strategies and shows that the initial reconfiguration overhead introduced by DPR systems is negligible in contrast to the speedup gained by the reconfiguration of the hardware accelerator when computing the same function more than 51 times consecutively (depending on the arithmetic function to be computed).

**Keywords:** CORDIC · Soft-core processor · FPGA · Dynamic partial reconfiguration

## 1 Introduction

Modern multimedia applications, for example in the field of robotics or computer vision systems, are becoming increasingly complex, requiring higher processing performance while also demanding high computational precision. One possibility to meet these demands is to implement application-specific instruction-set processors (ASIPs), where a baseline processor is specialized for the efficient execution of a specific application or a set of applications. This specialization is usually performed by extending a baseline processor with new application-specific instructions or co-processors.

The TUKUTURI project [3] at the Institute of Microelectronic Systems studies the possibility of using reconfigurable devices to increase the capability of specialization of an ASIP by taking advantage of dynamic partial reconfiguration

© Springer International Publishing Switzerland 2015
K. Sano et al. (Eds.): ARC 2015, LNCS 9040, pp. 401–410, 2015.
DOI: 10.1007/978-3-319-16214-0_36

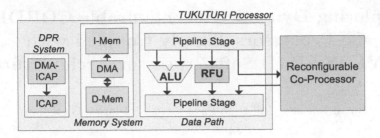

**Fig. 1.** Simplified architecture block diagram of the TUKUTURI VLIW-SIMD soft-core processor [3]. Reconfigurable parts are highlighted in blue. The processor contains a DMA-ICAP for transferring the bitstreams into the Xilinx ICAP module.

(DPR). DPR is provided by commercial Xilinx FPGA devices and can be used to reconfigure parts of the ASIP architecture while simultaneously executing a target application on the ASIP. For example, the TUKUTURI processor [3], depicted in Fig. 1, makes use of a DMA-ICAP controller to dynamically self-reconfigure the data-path. However, there is a drawback: *the time required to reconfigure a specific region of a Xilinx FPGA directly depends on the size of the region and highly influences the achievable processing performance.* For example, in video-based processing algorithms, depending on the required reconfiguration time, DPR can be used during inter- and/or intra-frame processing. It is mandatory, therefore, to explore the design space before implementing either large static application-specific hardware units or small reconfigurable ones.

*Elementary arithmetic functions*, like sine, cosine, square root or exponential functions, are commonly used in most embedded media applications. In applications, where the use of this kind of operations is spare, a software-based computation might be sufficient, but for higher usage frequencies, a hardware-based implementation by means of a co-processor architecture is more suitable. Furthermore, since the actually necessary operations might change during the processing of the application, a flexible processing kernel is needed. This paper explores the design space of using small reconfigurable co-processor units against large ones or simple software solutions for computing such elementary arithmetic functions on a soft-core ASIP, i.e., TUKUTURI processor. For that, a parametrized CORDIC hardware module as well as dedicated software kernels have been implemented. Both schemes comply with the requirements of embedded media applications. Due to the utilization of dynamic partial reconfiguration and the high configuration degree of the CORDIC module, a certain specialization can be performed to reduce the reconfiguration time. This requires the analysis of the target application in order to plan the use of the DPR mechanisms. The methodology to find an optimal implementation scheme (i.e, based on a programmable CORDIC co-processor, a function-specific reconfigurable CORDIC co-processor, or a software approach) as well as the proposed parametrized CORDIC co-processor architecture, hereafter called *rCORDIC*, is the main topic of this paper. For that, four elementary arithmetic functions are used as a case study. These are sine and cosine ($SINCOS$), square root ($SQRT$), exponential function ($EXP$) and division ($DIV$). In this paper, all exemplary functions use fixed-point arithmetic.

This paper is organized as follows: Section 2 presents previous work, where CORDIC architectures have been implemented on FPGAs. In Section 3, the proposed rCORDIC architecture is presented in detail. Besides the architecture, this section also explains the implementation parameters, the coupling with the TUKUTURI processor, the hardware implementation as well as additional design considerations. Then, Section 4 evaluates the results of using the proposed reconfigurable function-specific rCORDIC against a programmable rCORDIC and a software approach for the given functions. Finally, the conclusion of this work is given in Section 5.

## 2 Related Work

The classical radix-2 CORDIC algorithm [1] is a good choice to implement a basic kernel, which is capable of computing the required functions while providing a high precision. The desired functionality is determined by the content of the internal look-up-tables and the operation mode. Moreover, each specific functionality (e.g., square root) requires a dedicated pre-processing to eventually map the input argument(s) into the convergence area of the CORDIC algorithm. Furthermore, a post-processing step is required to undo the convergence mapping from the initial pre-processing stage and to multiply the processing result with a fixed final scale factor. Both steps can be implemented in hardware, resulting in high hardware costs, or in software, slowing down the processing throughput. Due to the iterative shift-and-add nature of the CORDIC algorithm itself, it can be easily implemented in hardware. Therefore, the low implementation complexity of the CORDIC kernel makes it profitable for hardware implementation.

Even though the original CORDIC algorithm is older than 50 years, it is still very popular and has been continually researched and improved. Lakshmi et al. [4] present a survey explaining different types of CORDIC algorithms, including signed-digit and carry-save arithmetic, various scale factor computation schemes, pipelined and serial architectures as well as different high-radix versions. In addition, we have previously presented in [2] a programmable radix-4 CORDIC co-processor for the use as arithmetic accelerator of a soft-core processor system. In [5], Valls et al. examine the use of redundant arithmetic for FPGA implementation to reduce the critical path. The impact on the hardware costs caused by the specialized arithmetic is also analyzed. Mencer et al. [6] researched for an automatic CORDIC design methodology for FPGAs to allow generation of optimal application-specific CORDIC implementations. Wang et al. [7] incorporated the partial dynamic reconfiguration feature to connect several CORDIC modules via a configurable fabric, so they can be boarded to perform complex operations like FFT algorithms.

This work uses the dynamic partial reconfiguration mechanism to reconfigure programmable or optimized CORDIC-based accelerators if a software implementation is not sufficient for a given application.

# 3   The rCORDIC Co-Processor

In order to meet the requirements of changing processing demands, a flexible computation scheme is necessary. The proposed rCORDIC co-processor architecture implements a fully *programmable rCORDIC co-processor* module, which can be configured by the TUKUTURI processor for performing a specific elementary arithmetic function. However, the required programmation overhead (performed by the TUKUTURI processor) can be avoided by directly implementing a specific configuration of the proposed rCORDIC. By making use of the dynamical partial reconfiguration feature of Xilinx FPGAs, *function-specific rCORDIC co-processor* modules can be "inserted" into the TUKUTURI processor during run-time.

## 3.1   Architecture

The rCORDIC co-processor architecture implements three basic pipeline stages, illustrated in Fig. 2: Whenever a new processing task is started, the *pre-processing stage* configures the CORDIC kernel to compute the corresponding operations, pre-processes the input argument(s) (e.g., in case of the sine computation, a quadrant-mapping is performed to achieve convergence) and starts the actual CORDIC computation. In the *CORDIC stage*, the number of kernel iterations of the CORDIC algorithm per clock cycle can be set during implementation. The last stage performs the *post-processing*. Here, final modifications are applied to the kernel's output data (i.e., quadrant remapping, operand re-sorting into the output register).

Amongst the internal hardware-implemented pre- and post-processing, an additional, software-based pre- and post-processing has to be performed before and after each CORDIC module computation. The software part of the pre-processing transforms the input operands into the convergence area of the algorithm. In many cases (e.g., *DIV*, *SQRT*) this is done by obtaining the number of leading zeroes of the arguments and performing shifts to adapt the fixed-point format. For this purpose, the TUKUTURI processor implements a custom count-leading-zeroes instruction. The additional post-processing software step undoes the initial argument remapping and performs the multiplication with the fixed final scaling factor using the multiplier functional unit of the TUKU-TURI processor. The additional software-based pre- and post-processing steps have been chosen to reduce complexity, timing, hardware resources and, therefore, the reconfiguration time of the rCORDIC co-processor.

An initialization of the module's internal configuration memories (i.e., micro-rotation look-up-table, arithmetic constants, function ID) is necessary once before the module is used for the first time. Besides the configuration for the desired function, the number representation of the look-up-table content also determines the used fixed-point format. This step is only required, if a full or partly programmable rCORDIC is used. Otherwise, when using a function-specific rCORDIC, the configurable parameters have to be set during implementation.

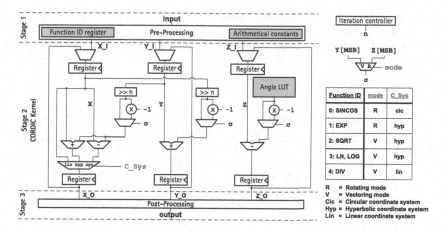

**Fig. 2.** Block diagram of the rCORDIC co-processor architecture. Configurable register are highlighted in gray.

## 3.2  Parameters

The rCORDIC co-processor architecture offers different configuration parameters, which can be used to specialize the hardware to a specific requirement of a target application (see Fig. 2). These parameters can be programmed by the TUKUTURI processor during run-time or configured during implementation, limiting the functionality and flexibility of the resulting implemented rCORDIC co-processor. The resulting limitation of functionality has a direct impact on the required FPGA hardware resources and, therefore, on the reconfiguration time (in case of using DPR). Moreover, for many applications, a subset of the maximum flexibility is sufficient. This section presents the available configuration parameters, summarized in Table 1, and their effects.

The programming of the rCORDIC co-processor for a specific function (e.g., sine) is performed by initializing the micro-rotation angle LUT, the arithmetic constants, and the function ID register, which determines the actual computed function. By setting the function ID during implementation, the rCORDIC co-processor is limited to a specific function, but the required hardware resources are dramatically reduced (due to the elimination of all these logic shifters or multiplexers which are not required anymore). The function ID register is used to select the operating mode (*rotating, vectoring*) and the coordinate systems (*circular, linear, hyperbolic*) required by the desired arithmetic operation.

Implementing all these configuration possibilities as RAM/registers (*programmable mode, "prog"*) in a FPGA gives the maximal flexibility but certainly leads to higher hardware resource utilization and reconfiguration times. By using a programmable angle LUT and registers for storing parameters, the actual fixed-point format of the computation is still programmable and can be altered during operation. If no adaptable fixed-point format is required, this RAM/registers can also be implemented as ROM/constants (*fixed mode, "fixed"*) initialized at

**Table 1.** Available configuration parameters in rCORDIC co-processor. These parameters can be programed during run-time (when using a programmable rCORDIC co-processor) or set during implementation, implementing static, function-specific rCORDIC co-processors.

| Parameter | Description |
|---|---|
| config. mode | The rCORDIC module can either be **full** *programmable* to compute any function, *function-specific* **programmable** to reconfigure only the fixed-point format of a specific function or *function-specific with a **fixed** function*. |
| function ID | The function ID determines the actual computed function of the module. All functions (SINCOS, EXP, SQRT, DIV, ...) get specific indetifying numbers, which are fed to an LUT to obtain the operation mode and the used coordinate system of the CORDIC kernel (see table in Fig. 2). |
| SIMD mode | When this implementation option is enabled, the **single**-issue rCORDIC module is equipped with an additional processing path (***double**-issue*). |
| CORDIC iterations | The parameter $M$ determines the number of implemented CORDIC iterations, which are processed in every clock cycle. |

implementation time. This fully specialized rCORDIC modules provide the lowest implementation costs but since no programmability is left, a change of the function or the fixed-point format during run-time is only possible by completely replacing the module via partial reconfiguration of the FPGA.

The hardware kernel normally processes only one computation at a time (*single-issue*). By using the SIMD mode, a second processing path is added allowing it to compute two task, e.g., two square roots, at once (*double-issue*). Due to the shared internal resources, like iteration control, angle look-up-table, etc., the two issues have to compute the same arithmetical function (e.g., division), but the hardware costs are less than using two single-issued rCORDIC modules.

The parameter "$M$" determines the actual number of processed CORDIC iterations per clock cycle (e.g., $M=1 \rightarrow 1$ CORDIC iteration per issue-slot and clock cycle). With increasing $M$, additional CORDIC kernels are added to the module's processing pipeline stage. Using a high $M$ allows the desired precision to be reached in less clock cycles but increases the hardware cost as well as the critical path. For instance, $M$ can be set to a maximum value, where the longest path of the rCORDIC module is still shorter than that of the remaining system.

### 3.3   Coupling and Scheduling

The rCORDIC co-processor is accessed by the TUKUTURI by performing memory transfers. This allows high transfer rates and provides a mechanism to control the precision of the CORDIC results by scheduling the load/store instructions. This mechanism is also used for programming the angle table, the arithmetic constants, and the function ID of a programmable rCORDIC co-processor.

The rCORDIC co-processor starts whenever new operands (amount depends on the actual processed function) are written to the specific input registers.

After computing the pre-processing stage in the first cycle, the CORDIC kernel stage will start processing M iterations every cycle (where M is the number of consecutive implemented iterations in the CORDIC kernel stage). When the maximum number of iterations (which depends on the number of entries in the angle LUT) is reached, the computation stops. For each kernel result, the post-processing stage also generates a valid output one cycle later. Therefore, a valid result can only be obtained after at least three cycles (i.e., the CORDIC kernel has been processed only for one cycle, since the pre- and post-processing stages also require a single cycle each), due to the three pipeline stages. The precision of the final result depends on the number of executed kernel iterations. Because of this, the rCORDIC access operations (load and stores) can be exactly scheduled in the application program to meet the target accuracy by setting the number of cycles between starting the rCORDIC computation and reading the result [2].

## 3.4   FPGA Hardware Implementation

The kernel stage, illustrated in Fig. 2, is the crucial element of the rCORDIC module. Here, the core of the algorithm is processed, presenting the dominant part of the required hardware resources, determining the overall critical path of the co-processor. Appending additional kernel stages (increasing parameter $M$) leads to more CORDIC iterations being processed in each clock cycle. This improves throughput on the one hand, but also adversely affects the maximum operation frequency and hardware costs on the other hand. Some function-specific kernels, like $DIV$, do not incorporate as much logic for each kernel as others like $SQRT$. Therefore, a dedicated $DIV$ rCORDIC module might be synthesized with a higher parameter $M$ without having a major impact on the critical path and the amount of required hardware resources.

Different configurations of the proposed CORDIC co-processor were synthesized and mapped on a Xilinx Virtex-6 FPGA. Fig. 3 shows that doubling the kernel stages does not imply a double amount of hardware resources. In some cases, different iteration stages can be merged together to reduce overall implementation costs. Additionally, some operations (like $DIV$) use partly-hardwired shifters in adjacent stages due to their linear sequence of shifts, which again reduces hardware claims. Due to the synchronous coupling with the TUKU-TURI, which operates at 100 MHz, the same frequency is desired. Therefore, only the rCORDIC configuration with M=1 and M=2 are considered hereafter.

Another interesting effect is related to the minimum number of reconfiguration blocks required by each configuration. The minimal reconfiguration partition in a Virtex-6 is a 40 CLB height by 1 CLB width block. As it is shown in Fig. 3, this number is related to the amount of LUTs and FFs required per configuration, however this relation is not linear. During the implementation of the "static" part of the design, i.e., the TUKUTURI processor and I/O system, the connection inputs and outputs (called virtual pins) of the reconfiguration block are fixed to LUTs located in the border of the reconfiguration partition. The location of these LUTs influences the implementation results greatly during the place-and-route process.

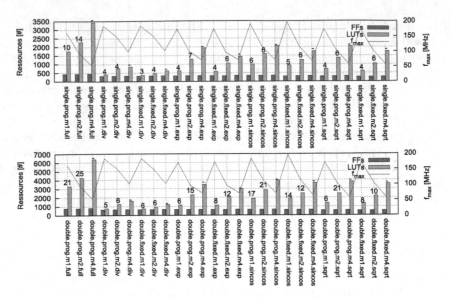

**Fig. 3.** Synthesis results for different implementations of the rCORDICs co-processor on a Virtex-6 XC6VLX240T-1 FPGA. For each rCORDIC configuration, the number of reconfiguration frames required for its implementation together with a TUKUTURI processor is also given (only for configurations that implement 1 and 2 iterations).

## 4    Evaluation

In order to analyze the speedup gained by using the function-specific rCORDIC co-processors, four processing kernels (*DIV, EXP, SINCOS, SQRT*) have also been implemented in software, optimized for the TUKUTURI processor and for the same precision. Table 2 shows the number of required processing cycles for each kernel implementation to compute a function. Obviously, the pure software implementations represent the kernels with the highest run-time. Since no hardware reconfiguration at all is necessary for the software kernels to operate, this implementation scheme might be very well suited for applications, that require only a few computations. However, when using the same function over and over again, the impact of the initial partial reconfiguration and the programming (in case of a programmable module) moves to the background and the actual processing cycles dominate.

Fig. 4 shows the number of total clock cycles over the number of computed *SINCOS* and *EXP* functions, respectively. In case of the *SINCOS* kernel, a dynamical reconfiguration using an accelerator is better suited when computing *SINCOS* more than 70 times. The dedicated (fixed) single-issue implementation with $M=1$ is the best option (*hw.single.fixed.m1*), since it computes the most tasks within a minimum of cycles. For computing more than 495 times the *SINCOS* function, the programmable or the fixed-function modules with $M=2$ present optimal cycle usage (*hw.single.{fixed,prog}.m2*). In case of *EXP*,

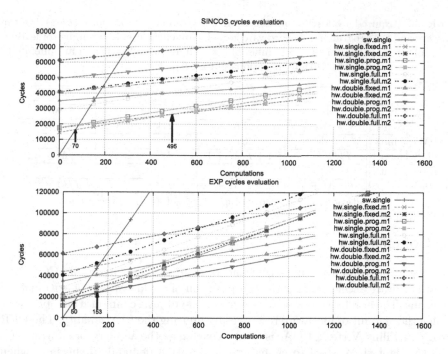

**Fig. 4.** Number of cycles required to compute the *SINCOS* (top) and *EXP* (bottom) function for random inputs. All the rCORDIC modules are initially reconfigured by using DPR before using them (for 0 computations the number of cycles correspond to the required reconfiguration time).

an accelerator is more efficient when processing more than 50 functions. While computing less than 153 computations, the fixed-function and the programmable single-issue versions (*hm.single.{fixed,prog}.m1*) both present an optimal cycle usage, since the initialization cycles for the programmable module are negligible. If more computations in a row are required by the application, the programmable SIMD (double) module features an optimal throughput per cycle.

For a high number of computations, the initial cycles for reconfiguration and programming become irrelevant. Only the cycles needed for a single computation have an impact on the actual cycles required. Therefore, the SIMD (double-issue) CORDIC kernels with a maximum of CORDIC iterations per issue and clock cycle (here $M=2$) are ideally suited implementations when focusing only on the overall execution cycles. These modules, of course, offer the highest throughput, but also bear the highest hardware costs.

410    S. Nolting et al.

**Table 2.** Required cycles for initialization (*init*) and computation (*comp*) for the software and the programmable hardware kernel. Nomenclature: N = number of leading zeroes of the input argument, I = number of kernel iterations, A = {input argument}/ln 2, and M = number of CORDIC iterations per clock cycle.

| | | DIV | EXP | SINCOS | SQRT |
|---|---|---|---|---|---|
| SW | init | 48 | 48 | 48 | 48 |
| | comp[1] | $5N + 16I + 16$ | $5A + 20I + 22$ | $[10..21] + 16I + 25$ | $5N + 19I + 26$ |
| HW single | init | 51 | 51 | 51 | 51 |
| | comp[1] | $I/M + 33$ | $5A + I/M + 18$ | $I/M + 22$ | $I/M + 34$ |
| HW double | init | 51 | 51 | 51 | 51 |
| | comp[1] | $IT/M + 57$ | $5A + I/M + 18$ | $I/M + 15$ | $I/M + 34$ |

[1]Computations = (pre-processing +) kernel + post-processing

## 5  Conclusions

This paper presents a parametrized and dynamically reconfigurable CORDIC-based hardware accelerator for the computation of a wide variety of arithmetical functions. The accelerator provides several pre-synthesis configuration options to reduce the amount of hardware resources by limiting the functionality. The DPR feature of Xilinx Virtex FPGAs is used to exchange the accelerators during run-time to adapt the system to changing computation demands. Especially when computing the same function several times in a row, the DPR mechanism can be successfully. The evaluation shows, that the reconfiguration overhead is negligible in contrast to the speedup gained by the rCORDIC hardware accelerator when computing the same function more than 50 times consecutively (depending on the arithmetic function to be computed).

## References

1. Walther, S.J.: A Unified Algorithm for Elementary Functions. In: 38th Spring Joint Computer Conference, p. 379, Atlantic City (1971)
2. Nolting, S., Payá-Vayá, G., Schmädecke, I., Blume. H.: Evaluation of a Generic Radix-4 CORDIC Coprocessor Tightly Coupled with a Generic VLIW-SIMD ASIP Architecture. ICT Open 2012 (2012)
3. Payá-Vayá, G., Burg, R., Blume, H.: Dynamic data-path self-reconfiguration of a VLIW-SIMD soft-processor architecture. In: Workshop on Self-Awareness in Reconfigurable Computing Systems, SRCS 2012 (2012)
4. Lakshmi, B., Dhar, A.S.: CORDIC Architectures: A Survey. Hindawi Publishing Corporation, VLSI Design (2010)
5. Valls, J., Kuhlmann, M., Parhi, K.K.: Evaluation of CORDIC algorithms for FPGA Design. Journal of VLSI Signal Processing **32**, 207-222 (2002)
6. Mencer, O., Séméria, L., Morf, M., Delosme, J.-M.: Application of Reconfigurable CORDIC Architectures. Journal of VLSI Signal Processing Systems for Signal, Image and Video Technology **24**(2–3), 211–221 (2000)
7. Wang, H., Leray, P., Palicot, J.: A CORDIC-based dynamically reconfigurable FPGA architecture for signal processing algorithms. In: The XXIX General Assembly of the International Union of Radio Science, URSI 2008 (2008)

# Mesh of Clusters FPGA Architectures: Exploration Methodology and Interconnect Optimization

Sonda Chtourou[1]([✉]), Zied Marrakchi[2,3], Vinod Pangracious[2],
Emna Amouri[2], Habib Mehrez[2], and Mohamed Abid[1]

[1] CES Research Laboratory, National School of Engineers of Sfax,
University of Sfax, Sfax, Tunisia
`sonda.chtourou@ceslab.org`
[2] LIP6 Research Laboratory, University of Pierre et Marie Curie, Paris, France
[3] Flexras Technologies, Paris, France

**Abstract.** In this paper, we present an improved Mesh of Clusters (MoC) architecture with new hierarchical Switch Box (SB) topology and depopulated intra-cluster interconnect with flexible Rent's parameter. The aim of this paper is to explore the effect of different architecture parameters like architecture Rent's, design Rent's and channel width. Then, we analyze how these factors interact and the way to tune them to satisfy various specific application constraints and quality metrics like power consumption and area. The proposed exploration methodology unifies two procedures which are analytical method based on Rent's rule modeling and experimental method based on benchmarks circuits implementation. A comparison with VPR mesh architecture shows gains in terms power and area equal respectively to 30% and 32%.

## 1 Introduction

Modern Mesh FPGA architectures are based on a clustered architecture where several Look-Up-Tables (LUTs) are grouped together to act as a Cluster Logic Block (CLB). Experiments show that using these architectures allows exploiting signal sharing among LUTs locally and then improving overall performance of the FPGA [1]. The best characterization to date which empirically estimates interconnect requirements is Rent's Rule [2]. Rent's rule could be applied as follows to MoC-based cluster architecture: $IO = c * k^p$ where k is the cluster arity, $c$ is the number of inputs/outputs of a Logic Block (LB), $IO$ is the number of inputs/outputs of the cluster and $p$ is the Rent's parameter. Intuitively, $p$ quantifies the locality of interconnect requirements. This parameter is used to qualify and control both architecture clusters bandwidth (architecture Rent's parameter) and design clustering characteristics (design Rent's parameter). We can distinguish in previous works two families of MoC-based FPGAs:

– A VPR-style interconnect [3] which has a sparsely populated connection block and a fully populated intra-cluster crossbar with low Rent's parameter (small inputs bandwidth). The fully populated intra-cluster crossbar

© Springer International Publishing Switzerland 2015
K. Sano et al. (Eds.): ARC 2015, LNCS 9040, pp. 411–418, 2015.
DOI: 10.1007/978-3-319-16214-0_37

is simple and ensures a complete local routability, but it takes no advantage of the logical equivalency of LUT inputs and induces a significant area overhead.
- An improved VPR-style interconnect which was proposed by Feng [4]. He investigates joint optimization of Configurable Blocks (CBs) and intra-cluster crossbars depopulation while using a high Rent's parameter ($p = 1$). He achieves an area saving of 28%. However, he optimized only connection of external signals to LB inputs and keeps the use of a full crossbar to connect feedbacks (LB outputs) to LB inputs, which can be very penalizing.

In this paper, we propose an improved MoC-based architecture with new hierarchical SB and depopulated intra-cluster interconnect based on the Butterfly-Fat-Tree (BFT) topology with flexible Rent's parameter. The goal of our work is to explore the effect of architecture parameters on performance. Then, we analyze how they interact in order to balance different trade-offs and satisfy application constraints. In order to compare and evaluate various architectures, we rely on two different procedures which are analytical method based on Rent's rule modeling and experimental method based on benchmarks circuits implementation.

The remaining of this paper is organized as follows. Section 2 presents the proposed MoC-based FPGA architecture. Section 3 presents the used exploration methodologies. Section 4 details the experimentation platform and used metric models. Experimental results are discussed in Section 5.

## 2      Proposed MoC-based FPGA Architecture Overview

Inspired by the Tree topology [5], we propose an improved MoC-based architecture with new hierarchical SBs, depopulated intra-cluster interconnect and unidirectional routing network. This architecture is a matrix of clusters placed into regular 2D grid.

### 2.1   Cluster Architecture

Each cluster contains local LBs connected with a depopulated local switch block. Each LB consists of a 4-input LUT and a Flip-Flop (FF). Figure 1 illustrates an example of cluster with 8 LBs. The depopulated local switch block is divided into Mini Switch Blocks (MSBs). The local interconnect is composed of a downward network and an upward network. The downward network is based on the BFT topology, which connects Downward MSBs (DMSBs) outputs to LBs inputs. Each DMSB connects each LB in only one input. The upward network connects LB outputs to an Upward MSB (UMSB) and allows all LBs outputs to reach all DMSBs and cluster outputs.

$$Nb\_DMSB = LB\_inputs$$
$$DMSB\_inputs = \frac{Cluster\_inputs}{Nb\_DMSB} \text{ and } DMSB\_outputs = Cluster\_size$$
$$UMSB\_inputs = UMSB\_outputs = Cluster\_size$$

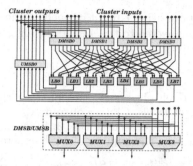

Fig. 1. Cluster Interconnect with 8 LBs and architecture of the interconnect crossbar

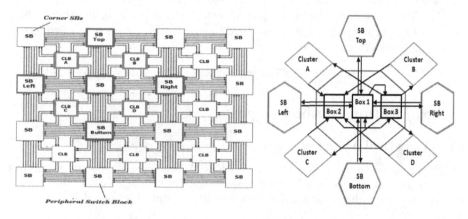

Fig. 2. MoC-based FPGA Architecture:
Unidirectional interconnect

Fig. 3. Multilevel SB Interconnect

## 2.2 Mesh Routing Interconnect

In the proposed mesh routing interconnect, a new multi-levels interconnect of
the SB is proposed to assure connection between horizontal and vertical adjacent
routing channels and also between clusters inputs/outputs and adjacent routing
channels. Figure 3 shows a detailed view of the interconnect of a SB and a
global view of the 4 adjacent SBs (Top, Bottom, Right, Left) and the 4 adjacent
clusters (A, B, C, D) highlighted in Figure 2. Similarly to cluster, the SB has a
multilevel topology including 3 main Boxes organized as follows:

1. SB to SB: Each SB is connected to the 4 adjacent SBs using short wires
   through Box 1. Box 1 is composed of MSB each one drives only one track in
   the 4 neighboring channels. This topology is similar to VPR disjoint SB [3].
   Thus, the number of MSB in Box 1 is given by:

$$Nb\_MSB\_1 = \frac{Channel\_width}{2} \text{ and } MSB\_1\_inputs = Nb\_short\_adj\_SBs = 4$$

2. SB to Cluster: Each SB is connected to the 4 neighboring clusters through
   2 interconnect levels. Outputs of MSB located at Box 1 drive MSB located

at Box 3 whose outputs drive 1 input of each of the 4 neighboring clusters. Since the cluster is connected to the 4 neighboring SBs, the number of MSB located at Box 3 is given by:

$$Nb\_MSB\_3 = \frac{Cluster\_inputs}{4} \text{ and } MSB\_1\_outputs = 1 + Nb\_short\_adj\_SBs = 5$$

3. Cluster to Cluster: Each cluster is connected to the neighboring clusters through 2 interconnect levels. Cluster outputs drive MSB located at Box 2 whose outputs drive MSB located at Box 3. Since each cluster is connected to the 4 neighboring SBs, the number of MSB located at Box 2 is given by:

$$Nb\_MSB\_2 = \frac{Cluster\_outputs}{4} \text{ and } MSB\_3\_inputs = \frac{Nb\_MSB\_1}{Nb\_MSB\_3} = \frac{2*Channel\_width}{Cluster\_inputs}$$

4. Cluster to SB: Outputs of MSB located at Box 2 drive MSB located at Box 1 whose outputs drive 1 input of each of the 4 neighboring SBs. Therefore, Cluster outputs which drive Box 2 are connected to 4 neighboring SBs through 2 interconnect levels:

$$MSB\_2\_inputs = Nb\_adj\_Clusters \text{ and } MSB\_2\_outputs = \frac{2*Channel\_width}{Cluster\_outputs}$$

# 3 Exploration Methodologies

## 3.1 Analytical Model

As we parameterize proposed MoC-based FPGA, we can now evaluate switches requirement. We consider a MoC arranged in a NxN array with k cluster size and W channel width. The total switch number in the MoC-based FPGA:

$$Nb_{switch} = Nb_{switch}(SB) * (N + 1)^2 + Nb_{switch}(CLB) * N^2$$

$$Nb_{switch}(SB) = Nb_{switch}(Box\_1) + Nb_{switch}(Box\_2) + Nb_{switch}(Box\_3)$$

Since MSBs are full crossbar, we have:

$$Nb_{switch}(Box\_1) = Nb\_MSB\_1 * MSB\_1\_inputs * MSB\_1\_outputs$$

$$Nb_{switch}(Box\_1) = 10 * W$$

Similarly, we have: $Nb_{switch}(Box\_2) = 2 * W$ and $Nb_{switch}(Box\_3) = 2 * W$. Thus, the number of switch per SB: $Nb_{switch}(SB) = 14 * W$

$$Nb_{switch}(CLB) = Nb_{switch}(DMSBs) + Nb_{switch}(UMSB)$$

Since DMSBs and UMSB are full crossbar, we have: $Nb_{switch}(UMSB) = k^2$ and $Nb_{switch}(DMSBs) = Cluster\_inputs * k$. Thus, the number of switch per CLB:

$$Nb_{switch}(CLB) = Cluster\_inputs * k + k^2$$

So, the total number of switch in the FPGA:

$$Nb_{switch} = 14 * W * (N + 1)^2 + (Cluster\_inputs * k + k^2) * N^2$$

Based on Rent's rule, we have:

$$Cluster\_inputs + Cluster\_outputs = c * k^p$$

where c is the number of inputs/outputs of a LB and p is the Rent's parameter. As $Cluster\_outputs = k$, we get: $Cluster\_inputs = c * k^p - k$. Finally, the total number of switch in the FPGA can be modeled with the following equation:

$$Nb_{switch} = 14 * W * (N + 1)^2 + (c * k^{p+1}) * N^2 \qquad (1)$$

As illustrated in the equation 1, the interconnect flexibility of proposed MoC-based FPGA is controlled by these architecture parameters: Rent's parameter, cluster size, channel width and LB inputs/outputs. Rent's parameter and cluster size control local clusters interconnect whereas channel width controls external clusters interconnect.

## 3.2   Experimental Comparison

Rent's rule provides an empirical estimation of switching requirements. Nevertheless, this is not sufficient since it does not give accurate information about interconnect routability. To explore the interconnect flexibility of proposed MoC-based FPGA, we aim at varying, on one hand, architecture parameters described in equation 1 and, on the second hand, resulting design clusters communication locality. We can distinguish two Rent's parameters:

- Architecture Rent's: It depends on the inputs/outputs number of architecture cluster.
- Design Rent's: It depends on the inputs/outputs number of a design cluster. This inputs number constraint is taken into account by the T-VPACK clustering tool[6].

## 4   Exploration Platform and Metrics Models

To explore our architecture, we investigate the configuration flow illustrated in figure 4. In this configuration flow, we use the T-VPack tool [6] to achieve the packing and clustering phase of the Netlist. We use simulated annealing algorithm [3] to place the CLBs/IOs and Pathfinder routing algorithm [7] to route the circuit. A description of the used FPGA architecture is provided to the MoC-based FGPA CAD tool in the form of an architecture file containing information such as cluster size, LUT size, segment length and process parameters.

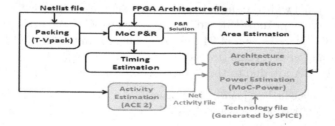

**Fig. 4.** Proposed MoC configuration flow

ACE2 and MoC-Power modules, integrated in proposed MoC configuration flow, are used to estimate power consumption. The first module is the activity estimator (ACE2 [8]) which employs a transition density model to determine the switching density of all nets. The second module is the MoC-Power which incorporates two components: Architecture generator and Low-Level Power Estimation. The architecture generator uses the routing resource graph to decompose the entire MoC-based FGPA circuit into low-level components which are inverters, multiplexers and wires. Then, the Low-Level power estimates the dynamic and static powers of each component as defined in VersaPower model [9].

Used area model is based on transistor-counting function to compute components area. We use routing graph resource to parse all FPGA components (MSBs, LBs and buffers) to accurately compute the total number of transistor in the FPGA. The area is expressed as function of $\lambda$ which is equal to the half of the minimum distance between source and drain of transistor.

Timing analysis allows evaluating performances of a circuit implemented on a FPGA in term of functional speed. The length of local wires is determined by approximating the size of entities through transistor-counting functions. Then, wire and switch (crossbar, multiplexer) delays are extracted from the SPICE circuit simulator using ST Micros 130nm Technology node.

# 5   Exploration Results

## 5.1   VPR MoC-based vs. Proposed MoC-based FPGA Architectures

In this section, we perform detailed exploration comparison between VPR and proposed MoC-based FPGA architectures in term of power, area, delay, total buffer number in the FPGA and minimal channel width. Comparison results using biggest MCNC[1] and IWLS[2] benchmarks are illustrated in table 1. In this experimentation, we use VPR7.0 [10] and proposed MoC configuration CAD tools while using same packing options and same place and route algorithms. For both architectures, we consider clusters arity 8 and LUT size 4, a unidirectional routing network with single length segments and a disjoint switch block. VPR cluster architecture contains 18 inputs and 8 outputs. For proposed MoC-based FPGA, the design Rent's parameter is fixed to 0.89 (Design cluster inputs = 24) and the architecture Rent's parameter is fixed to 1(cluster inputs = 32). Table 1 shows that proposed MoC-based architecture can implement all circuits with lower channel width. In fact, the maximal channel width used is equal to 85 and 56 respectively in the VPR and the proposed MoC-based architecture. This induces an average reduction of 24% in total buffer number in the FPGA. Most of the power and area savings (respectively 30% and 32%) obtained in proposed MoC-based FPGA are due to the reduction in total buffer number.

---

[1] http://er.cs.ucla.edu/benchmarks/ibm-place.

[2] http://iwls.org/iwls2005/benchmarks.html

**Table 1.** Comparison Results : VPR and Proposed MoC-based FPGA

| Bench | Primitives | VPR MoC | | | | | | Proposed MoC | | | | | | Gain | | |
|---|---|---|---|---|---|---|---|---|---|---|---|---|---|---|---|---|
| | | Power mW | Area $10^6\lambda^2$ | Delay ns | Total Buff | Min CHW | FPGA size | Power mW | Area $10^6\lambda^2$ | Delay ns | Total Buffer | Min CHW | FPGA size | Power % | Area % | Buff % |
| clma | 8416 | 264 | 2560 | 31.5 | 175032 | 78 | 33x33 | 170.39 | 1593 | 45.53 | 116688 | 52 | 33x33 | 37 | 38 | 33 |
| elliptic | 4726 | 100.8 | 970 | 24.93 | 52624 | 60 | 22x22 | 71.2 | 650 | 32.18 | 44528 | 44 | 22x22 | 29 | 33 | 15 |
| ex1010 | 4898 | 142.2 | 1368 | 26.94 | 75400 | 70 | 25x25 | 86.95 | 810 | 29.84 | 57600 | 48 | 24x24 | 39 | 41 | 24 |
| ex5p | 1064 | 36.1 | 272 | 13.54 | 16224 | 54 | 12x12 | 26.39 | 211 | 15.45 | 15600 | 50 | 12x12 | 27 | 22 | 4 |
| frisk | 3556 | 110.4 | 1204 | 24.24 | 62744 | 68 | 22x22 | 72 | 666 | 31.86 | 46552 | 46 | 22x22 | 35 | 45 | 26 |
| misex3 | 1397 | 46.2 | 352 | 13.74 | 18480 | 50 | 14x14 | 31 | 246 | 15.72 | 15960 | 38 | 14x14 | 33 | 30 | 14 |
| pdc | 4575 | 170.1 | 1601 | 30.29 | 96200 | 86 | 25x25 | 96 | 886 | 38.62 | 67200 | 56 | 24x24 | 44 | 45 | 30 |
| s298 | 1930 | 38.3 | 345 | 28.62 | 19584 | 34 | 16x16 | 32.41 | 295 | 28.64 | 17408 | 32 | 16x16 | 15 | 14 | 11 |
| s38417 | 6406 | 168.7 | 1501 | 22.8 | 83520 | 52 | 29x29 | 109.8 | 986 | 26.34 | 59160 | 34 | 29x29 | 35 | 34 | 29 |
| s38584 | 6447 | 188.9 | 1479 | 17.3 | 87000 | 50 | 29x29 | 126.43 | 1266 | 19.56 | 59160 | 34 | 29x29 | 33 | 14 | 32 |
| USB_Funct | 6537 | 127.5 | 1344 | 41.5 | 88400 | 68 | 25x25 | 102.02 | 905 | 20.67 | 65000 | 50 | 25x25 | 20 | 32 | 26 |
| B22_C | 5293 | 429 | 4632 | 41.5 | 291648 | 62 | 48x48 | 376.35 | 3179 | 48.91 | 206976 | 44 | 48x48 | 12 | 31 | 29 |
| AVA2 | 10437 | 227.9 | 2406 | 41.5 | 160512 | 76 | 32x32 | 158.96 | 1507 | 42.33 | 109824 | 50 | 32x32 | 30 | 37 | 32 |
| AES_Core | 9378 | 243 | 2293 | 41.5 | 142800 | 60 | 34x34 | 177.49 | 1592 | 49.46 | 104720 | 44 | 34x34 | 27 | 31 | 27 |
| Average | | | | | | | | | | | | | | 30 | 32 | 24 |

## 5.2 Architecture Optimization

**Rent's exploration** The objective consists in exploring and analyzing how design Rent's and the architecture Rent's parameters interact and the way to tune them to satisfy various specific application constraints. The architecture used here contains clusters with 8 LBs. Results correspond to interconnect area and the average power of MCNC benchmarks using the biggest array and channel width that implement all circuits. Figures 5, 6 and 7 show the variation of respectively the total power, area and channel width with architecture Rent's for different design Rent's. Each curve corresponds to a design Rent's parameters. Figure 8 illustrates the variation of FPGA size with design Rent's. In figures 5 and 6, we remark that for each design Rent's parameter, there is a reduction in interconnect power and area until we reach a certain architecture Rent's parameter (the break point) from which the increase of architecture Rent's induces an increase in power and area. In fact, at this point, the reduction of the channel width with the increase of architecture Rent's becomes insufficient to route circuits (see figure 7).

Results shows that the area and power consumption increase with low design Rent's parameter. In fact, when design rent's is equal to 0.56, we depopulate cluster interconnect and we reduce the congestion and then we can reduce the channel width(see figure 7). Nevertheless, the total number of clusters in the FPGA increases (45x45) as illustrated in figure 8. Based on results of transistor-count area model, the most optimized MoC-based architecture in term of power and area corresponds to design Rent's parameter equal to 0.89 and architecture Rent's parameter equal to 1.05. However, if we opt for the use of architecture rent's of 1 or higher, meaning full connectivity, there might be a lot of congestion in the routing lines and then the development of 2D physical design becomes complex [11] because the wires might have a lot of vias to cross each other. This would affect the wire capacitance and power. Thus, we can relax wire complexity by choosing lower architecture rent's (equal to 0.98) with low wires at the cost of increasing active area by 7%.

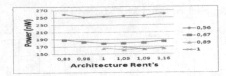

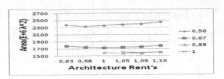

**Fig. 5.** Variation of Power with the Architecture Rent's for different Design Rent's

**Fig. 6.** Variation of Area with the Architecture Rent's for different Design Rent's

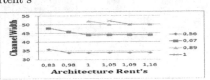

**Fig. 7.** Variation of Channel width with the Architecture Rent's for different Design Rent's

**Fig. 8.** Variation of FPGA size with the Design Rent's

# 6    Conclusion

In this paper, we present and explore a new MoC-based FPGA architecture. As a future work, we plan to develop the layout of the proposed architecture and explore the impact of wiring complexity on performances.

# References

1. Ahmed, E., et al.: The effect of LUT and cluster size on deep-submicron FPGA performance and density. Very Large Scale Integration (VLSI) Systems (2004)
2. Landman, B., et al.: On Pin Versus Block Relationship for Partition of Logic Circuits. IEEE Transactions on Computers **20**, 1469–1479 (1971)
3. Betz, V., et al.: Architecture and CAD for Deep-Submicron FPGAs. In: ACL Symposium on Parallel Algorithms and Architectures Series (2000)
4. Feng, W., et al.: Designing efficient input interconnect blocks for LUT clusters using counting and entropy. In: Proc. of FPGA 2007, Monterey, Calif, USA, p. 2332 (2007)
5. Marrakchi, Z., et al.: FPGA Interconnect Topologies Exploration. Int. J. Reconfig, Comp. (2009)
6. Marquart, A., et al.: Using cluster-based logic block and timing-driven packing to improve FPGA speed and density, FPGA, Monterey, p. 3746 (1999)
7. McMurchie, L., et al.: Pathfinder: A Negotiation-Based Performance-Driven Router for FPGAs. In: Proc. FPGA 1995 (1995)
8. Lamoureux, J., et al.: Activity Estimation for FieldProgrammable Gate Arrays. In: FPL (2006)
9. Goeders, J., et al.: VersaPower: Power Estimation for Diverse FPGA Architectures. In: International Conference on Field-Programmable Technology (FPT) (2012)
10. Rose, J., et al.: The VTR Project: Architecture and CAD for FPGAs from Verilog to Routing. In: FPGA, pp. 77–86 (2012)
11. DeHon, A., et al.: Compact. Multilayer Layout for Butterfly Fat-Tree. IEEE Trans. VLSI **12**(10), 1051–1065 (2004)

# DyAFNoC: Dynamically Reconfigurable NoC Characterization Using a Simple Adaptive Deadlock-Free Routing Algorithm with a Low Implementation Cost

Ernesto Castillo[1]([✉]), Gabriele Miorandi[2],
Davide Bertozzi[2], and Wang Jiang Chau[1]

[1] Departamento de Sistemas Eletrônicos, Universidade de São Paulo,
Escola Politécnica da Universidade de São Paulo (EPUSP), São Paulo, Brazil
{cristovc,jcwang}@lme.usp.br
[2] Dipartimento di Ingegneria, Universitá degli Studi di Ferrara, Ferrara, Italy
mrngrl@unife.it, dbertozzi@ing.unife.it

**Abstract.** NoC-Based Dynamic Reconfigurable Systems (DRSs) implemented over FPGA devices change their configuration during operation time by positioning or replacing new processing modules over the network structure, being known as Dynamically Reconfigurable NoCs (DRNoCs). In the literature, there are different proposals of DRNoCs implementing adaptive routing algorithms in order to handle the network structure alteration. Nevertheless, their implementation cost is high in terms of chip area, and in the time required to reconfigure the routing algorithm, which result in non-well-scalable solutions for DRSs. In this work, we propose an alternative DRNoC, based on a traditional 2-D mesh, using a logic-based implementation of the Flexible Direction Order Routing (FDOR) algorithm, characterized by its simplicity, low complexity and deadlock-freeness. Simulation examples were made in order to test the feasibility of the FDOR algorithm for a DRNoC, accompanied by performance and synthesis results.

**Keywords:** DRNoCs · FPGA · Routing algorithm · Deadlock · Dynamic reconfiguration

## 1   Introduction

Dynamically Reconfigurable Systems (DRS) are characterized by their high level of modularity and flexibility, which allows to implement a higher number of processing modules over a smaller chip area than the traditional System on-Chip (SoC), altering their functioning according to the computation needs by reconfiguring themselves during operation time. One particular case of DRSs, is known as Dynamically Reconfigurable Network on-Chip (DRNoC), which is an extension of the Networks on-Chip (NoC), capable of changing their communication structure during the allocation and placement of processing modules over the network structure during dynamic reconfiguration.

© Springer International Publishing Switzerland 2015
K. Sano et al. (Eds.): ARC 2015, LNCS 9040, pp. 419–426, 2015.
DOI: 10.1007/978-3-319-16214-0_38

The same properties of traditional NoCs are presented in DRNoCs, as topology, routing algorithm, arbitration policy, etc. The routing algorithm is directly related to the network topology, because it adapts itself to the new irregular topologies obtained by the positioning of new processing modules after the dynamic reconfiguration processes. The routing algorithm plays an important role in DRNoCs, since they must guarantee safe communications for all the contexts, even with the presence of obstacles generated by the processing modules placement. Ensuring this condition is not so simple because the transition between two routing algorithms induces extra dependencies that may lead to deadlock and/or livelock.

Some related works about DRNoCs have been proposed presenting different implementations of routing algorithms. Some examples, as DyNoC [1] and CuNoC [2] based on a 2-D mesh structure composed of routers, use a modified Dimension-Order-Routing or DOR algorithm (e.g. XY and YX algorithms) known as Surrounding XY (S-XY), which requires a high implementation cost. Other works can accomplish a safer deadlock-free communication, as QNoC [3] and CoNoChi [7], that use a Table-Based Routing (TBR) algorithm as an alternative, these solutions require a pretty long time to update all the routing tables during the dynamic reconfiguration process, thus turning out as non-scalable solutions.

Other routing algorithms have been proposed for the implementation of fault-tolerant NoCs [9,11]. A 2 Virtual Channel (VC) switching approach is adopted to avoid deadlock conditions, but the algorithms require significant extra resources for their implementation. In [11], the algorithm is based on an extra communication link in the network for backtracking in order to perform an adaptive routing, while [9] implements a Logic-Based Distributed Routing (LBDR) changing 26 configuration bits per router in order to reconfigure the network.

In this work, we present the Dynamic AFDOR-based NoC (DyAFNoC), a DRNoC adopting the Flexible Dimension Order Routing (FDOR) algorithm [8], which is a deadlock-free routing solution with a significantly lower complexity in comparison with the LBDR and TBR implementations, turning out to be an interesting alternative for DRNoCs than the related works. It is based in a single Virtual Channel switching approach and guarantees full connectivity in irregular shaped topologies obtained from the distribution of processing modules over the network [8]. It is based on the 2-D mesh DyNoC structure [1], due to its simplicity and the use of conventional 5-port routers. The DyAFNoC architecture was described in VHDL and simulated by using the Dynamic Circuit Switching (DCS) Technique [4] to test the partial dynamic reconfiguration process. A performance analysis was also made in order to characterize the traffic in different FDOR topologies that can help the designer to choose the adequate module positioning for obtaining the best traffic performance in the different contexts that conform a DRS. The remainder of this paper is organized as follows: Section 2 presents the DyAFNoC architecture, Section 3 presents the Experimental Results and finally Section 3 presents the Conclusions and Future Works of this work.

## 2   DyAFNoC Architecture

The DyAFNoC architecture is composed of its 2-D Mesh structure, and the control blocks responsible for the 2-D Mesh routing algorithm reconfiguration and the dynamic reconfiguration processes, named as Mesh Reconfiguration Control System (MRCS) and Partial Dynamic Reconfiguration Control System (PDRCS) respectively.

### 2.1   The Mesh Structure - Topologies and Reconfigurability

The DyAFNoC's 2-D Mesh i composed of NxN routers, whose architecture was developed taking as base the HERMES network architecture [5]. The routers have five bidirectional ports with two registers for storing incoming flits of a packet. The register size is defined for a flit in order to be used for the Wormhole Switching mode. In a basic regular topology, each router is connected to a Processing Element (PE) by the local port. Application's Processing Modules (PMs), which can be the PEs size or its multiple, will be allocated and positioned over the network forming different reconfigurable contexts during the run time of DyAFNoC, as it is required by the system application needs. Figure 1a shows an example of a 5x5 mesh structure formed by routers and PEs, while Figures 1b and 1c are examples of different large modules are placed over the network structure. The resulting router network becomes irregular corresponding to particular topologies.

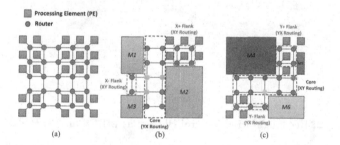

**Fig. 1.** (a) 5x5 Mesh structure, Module positioning forming a 's' topology (b) along the Y direction, (c) along X direction

It can be observed in Figure 1b that if M3 sends a packet to any one of the blue PEs, the XY routing algorithm will fail because M2 will blocks any packet directed to the right. The FDOR [8] circumvents this problem, besides avoiding deadlock, by defining two types of regions: the flanks, with the XY (or YX) routing, and the core, with an YX (or XY) routing, as shown in the examples in Figure 1. The flank(s)-core relative positions determine the types of topology. For instance, Figures 1b and c presents 's' and 'inverted s' topologies. Due to the flank and core opposite routing algorithms, FDOR can only work in non-concave topologies.

## 2.2   Reconfiguration Control

The reconfiguration control process is performed in the DyAFNoC through two main blocks: MRCS (Figure 2a) is in charge of automatically adapting the routing algorithm of each router to network topology variations when placing new PMs over its structure. Each router has a control signal from the MRCS to determine which DOR algorithm will be used (XY or YX). Each router will have a different routing configuration depending on the region (core or flanks) where it belongs, explained in the FDOR theory in [8]. More details about this controller are presented in [10]. The second control block is the PDRCS (Figure 2b), responsible for the partial dynamic reconfiguration process of the network. It receives signals from all the PMs and PEs, indicating that their respective processing tasks are finished and their logic resources are able to be reconfigured for implementing new PMs. It is also in charge of sending the configuration maps to the MRCS when the network structure will be affected. More details are explained in [10].

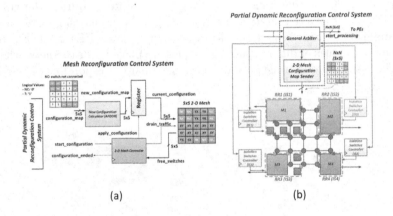

(a)                                   (b)

**Fig. 2.** Reconfiguration Control Blocks: a) MRCS and b) PDRCS

## 3   Experimental Results

### 3.1   DyAFNoC Validation

Figure 3 shows an example of the DyAFNoC operation in a time-line composed of different reconfigurable contexts forming different irregular topologies which are considered as valid by the FDOR algorithm. It can be observed that the system starts with its basic structure composed of basic PEs, then when some of them have finished their respective tasks (red curved arrow), their hardware resources are used to implement bigger PMs applying partial dynamic reconfiguration.

This application example in Figure 3 was generated by DRSimGen, a tool based on MATLAB scripts developed in order to generate a VHDL code of the DyAFNoC architecture for DCS simulation and its testbenches. It was simulated

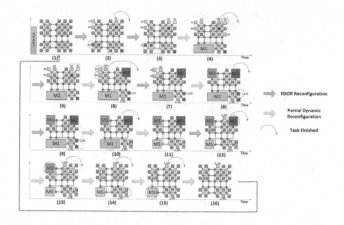

**Fig. 3.** Time Diagram of the different scenarios in the DyAFNoC processing

and validated using the ISim tool from Xilinx. The results showed that just one clock cycle is necessary to calculate and apply a new routing scheme using the FDOR algorithm, then the reconfiguration overhead will depends on the packets draining time, which also depends on the traffic presented on the network when the reconfiguration starts. However, the partial reconfiguration process does not introduce an overhead because packets can be transmitted immediately after the new FDOR configuration was applied. While the partial ares is being reconfigures, the PMs continue their respective tasks and packets can be transmitted over the network.

### 3.2 Mesh Traffic Analysis

The FDOR algorithm was implemented over a high level system simulator, Noxim [6], in order to evaluate the traffic performance for some common irregular valid topology in a 8x8 mesh indicating the FDOR sub-regions (core or flanks) with their respective DOR algorithm (XY ou YX), as shown in Figure 4. To have a fair comparison, all topologies presented similar number of active PEs, in this case 48. The performance is evaluated based on two main parameters: Average Latency and Average Throughput.

The Average Latency results are shown in Figure 5, in function of the packet injection rate (PIR) for the range of $[0; 0.4]$ $flits/cycles/Switch$. Results and discussions for Maximum Latency are similar, therefore will not be presented. It can be observed that topology 'd' has the highest average latency results. It is due to the intense traffic at the bounding line that separates the core and X-flank regions. The topologies with lower average latency values are the 'inv s' topology and its symmetric shape 'inv s 2', because the number of active PEs are most in the core region, which is centralized with respect to the mesh. It is also considered the arbitration policy that gives priority to the ports in the Y direction (North to South) and then to the X direction (West to East), this makes

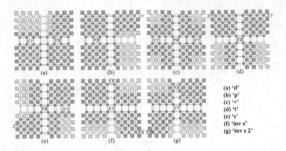

Fig. 4. Irregular FDOR topologies for an 8x8 mesh

that the 'inv s' and 'inv s 2' topologies have a lower average latency value in comparison with the 's' topology. The 't' topology presents the same properties as 's' topology, obtaining similar results of average latency, however, the flanks are in the same height with respect to the mesh, which reduces the average distance between routers. For the 'p' topology case, it has an inverted shape of the 'd' topology with a higher number of PEs in the core region, reducing the number of transitions from the flank to the core. This makes that packets do not clog the vertical line that separates the two regions as in the case of 'd' topology, therefore the average latency is lower. Finally, the results obtained for the '+' topology show that the average latency is lower than the 'd' topology case, but higher than the rest of them, although its shape is similar to the 't' topology.

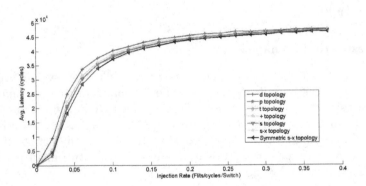

Fig. 5. Average Latency vs. Injection Rate

The Average Throughput results in Figure 6, show that 'd' topology obtained the lowest value, because a high number of PEs in the X-flank transfer packets within the core region, clogging the vertical line of the core region adjacent to the X-flank. All these packets pass this vertical line of routers obligatory, so the average throughput value is reduced. The highest value of the average throughput is for the 'p' topology case, because no clogging lines are generated,

**Table 1.** Synthesis Results for Virtex-6

|  | Router | PDRCS | MRCS(5x5) | MRCS(8x8) | MRCS(12x12) |
|---|---|---|---|---|---|
| *Slice FFs* | 302 | 21 | 81 | 201 | 438 |
| LUTs | 304 | 48 | 140 | 367 | 817 |
| *Slices* | 360 | 31 | 121 | 284 | 542 |

although it has the same shape as 'd' topology, it has a higher number of PEs in the core region. As most of the traffic is presented in this region, routing the packets is similarly as a NoC with a DOR algorithm. The '+' and 't' topology cases have the highest average throughput results after the 'p' topology. Their similar structures composed of two flanks horizontally aligned and separated by a centralized core region, are where most of the traffic occurs, obtaining similar average throughput values. These results are higher than the 's', 'inv s' and 'inv s 2', due to the average distance increment between routers and the clogged lines adjacent to the flanks in the core regions.

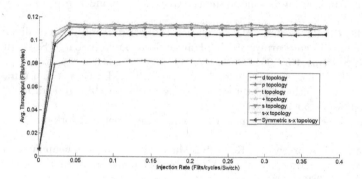

**Fig. 6.** Average Throughput vs. Injection Rate

## 3.3 Synthesis Results

The Synthesis Results of the DyAFNoC architecture were obtained for three different mesh sizes (5x5, 8x8 and 12x12) and targeting Xilinx Virtex-6 XC6VLX75T FPGA. The hardware resources cost of DyAFNoC blocks responsible for dynamic reconfiguration is comparable to a simple 5-port router, as shown in Table 1.

## 4   Conclusion

The DyAFNoC has been proposed with the main target to be a platform to implement a DRS that requires large number irregular topologies while ensuring a deadlock-free communication. Using the FDOR algorithm, these was be obtained with a low hardware implementation cost. The simulation results demonstrate the desired functionality of the DyAFNoC architecture for the dynamic reconfiguration processes, whose required time just depends on the packets draining time. The performance analyses demonstrated the limitations of each FDOR irregular topology, whose results of Average Latency and Throughput would help the designer to choose the best modules placement over the mesh for obtaining the best performance in each context of the DRS.

# References

1. Bobda, C., Ahmadinia, A.: Dynamic interconnection of reconfigurable modules on reconfigurable devices. IEEE Design Test of Computers **22**(5), 443–451 (2005)
2. Jovanovic, S., Tanougast, C., Bobda, C., Weber, S.: Cunoc: A dynamic scalable communication structure for dynamically reconfigurable FPGAs. Microprocessors and Microsystems **33**(1), 24–36 (2009). Selected Papers from ReCoSoC 2007 (Reconfigurable Communication-centric Systems-on-Chip)
3. Jovanovic, S., Tanougast, C., Weber, S.: A new high-performance scalable dynamic interconnection for fpga-based reconfigurable systems. In: International Conference on Application-Specific Systems, Architectures and Processors, ASAP 2008, pp. 61–66, July 2008
4. Lysaght, P., Stockwood, J.: A simulation tool for dynamically reconfigurable field programmable gate arrays. IEEE Transactions on Very Large Scale Integration (VLSI) Systems **4**(3), 381–390 (1996)
5. Moraes, F., Calazans, N., Mello, A., Mller, L., Ost, L.: Hermes: an infrastructure for low area overhead packet-switching networks on chip. Integration, the VLSI Journal **38**(1), 69–93 (2004)
6. Palesi, M., Patti, D., Fazzino, F.: Noxim - an open network-on-chip simulator (2007)
7. Pionteck, T., Albrecht, C., Koch, R., Maehle, E.: Adaptive communication architectures for runtime reconfigurable system-on-chips. Parallel Processing Letters **18**(02), 275–289 (2008)
8. Skeie, T., Sem-Jacobsen, F., Rodrigo, S., Flich, J., Bertozzi, D., Medardoni, S.: Flexible dor routing for virtualization of multicore chips. In: International Symposium on System-on-Chip, SOC 2009, pp. 073–076, October 2009
9. Strano, A., Bertozzi, D., Trivino, F., Sanchez, J., Alfaro, F., Flich, J.: Osrlite: Fast and deadlock-free noc reconfiguration framework. In: 2012 International Conference on Embedded Computer Systems (SAMOS), pp. 86–95, July 2012
10. Villegas, E., Miorandi, G., Chau, W.J.: Dyafnoc: Characterization and analysis of a dynamically reconfigurable noc using a dor-based deadlock-free routing algorithm. In: Proceedings of the 8th IEEE/ACM International Symposium on Networks-on-Chip, September 2014
11. Wachter, E., Moraes, F.: Mazenoc: Novel approach for fault-tolerant noc routing. In: 2012 IEEE International SOC Conference (SOCC), pp. 364–369, September 2012

# A Flexible Multilayer Perceptron Co-processor for FPGAs

Zeyad Aklah$^{(\boxtimes)}$ and David Andrews

Computer Science and Computer Engineering, University of Arkansas, Fayetteville, AR 72701, USA
{zaklah,dandrews}@uark.edu
http://www.hthreads.uark.edu

**Abstract.** Implementing a custom Artificial Neural Network (ANN) in hardware lacks the scalability and the flexibility of changing from one topology to another at run time. This paper presents a Multilayer Perceptron Co-processor (MLPCP) targeting FPGAs that is configurable during design time and programmable during run time. The MLPCP can be reprogrammed at run time to rapidly change network topologies and use different activation functions. This allows application developers to change parameters of a given network without the need to resynthesize. This also allows the MLPCP to be used for different applications during run time. Run time results show the MLPCP can deliver performance levels close to those of a custom ANN, and can execute network topologies that cannot fit into FPGAs with limited resources. Performance comparisons against software versions show up to 70x speedup compared to a MicroBlaze running at 100 MHz, and 4x compared to a Zynq running at 667 MHz.

## 1 Introduction

Researchers have been exploring the performance benefits of implementing custom Artificial Neural Networks (ANNs) within FPGAs [1][10][9][8][3][7]. Although FPGA densities are growing their finite set of resources will limit the size and accuracy of the ANN. Investigations have occurred to reduce the resource footprint required to implement a custom ANN [9],[1],[6].

However constructing a custom ANN requires that the topology of layers, as well as the types of arithmetic and activation functions used in the neural network be defined before synthesis. This prevents run time changes to the topology of the network as well as key parameters that effect accuracy such as arithmetic precision and types of activation functions implemented in the neural network[11]. Clearly it would be desirable to synthesize once, and then reuse the neural network under different configurations for different applications.

Esmaeilzadeh et al. [4] addressed this lack of flexibility by proposing a programmable neural network co-processor targeted for implementation as an Application Specific Integrated Circuit (ASIC). The co-processor is first optimized through design space exploration prior to fabrication. Once a design is selected

© Springer International Publishing Switzerland 2015
K. Sano et al. (Eds.): ARC 2015, LNCS 9040, pp. 427–434, 2015.
DOI: 10.1007/978-3-319-16214-0_39

and fabricated it can then sequence the execution of multiple topologies at run time.

This paper presents a configurable and programmable Multilayer Perceptron Co-Processor ( MLPCP) for implementation on FPGAs that extends the configurability of the design reported in [4]. During the design phase the number of PEs, data representation (floating point or fixed point), Activation Function (AF) implementation approach (BRAM lookup tables or synthesized using Vivado HLS) can be configured by setting parameters. Once configured the MLPCP co-processor design automatically scales the register set and interconnect to support the number of PEs specified. Once synthesized the MLPCP is then programmable at run time to implement any topology (up to a set maximum) and use mixes of different types of activation functions. This provides the flexibility to change the precision and accuracy of results, or reuse the co-processor to support the needs of multiple application domains without having to resynthesize hardware.

The results in section(4) show the benefits as well as performance costs of this flexibility. Performance results show the flexibility and reprogrammability of the MLPCP do come at a modest decrease in peak performance compared to fully custom implementations of small to modest sized neural networks. Results then show the same MLPCP can continue to compute larger neural networks that exceed the resource limitations of the FPGA for a custom implementation.

## 2    MLPCP Architecture

Figure 1 shows the generic structure of an MLPCP core. The MLPCP architecture consists of a linear array of Processing Elements (PEs), a scheduler, controller, configuration registers, local memory and three external interface connections. Both input data and weights are transferred through the same input channel. The MLPCP

is automatically generated based on a set of configuration parameters provided by the user. The main parameters are the number of PE's, type of activation functions, and arithmetic precision. Designers can vary these parameters to explore area and performance tradeoffs for a particular FPGA. Once the parameters have been set, the core scales itself and can then be synthesized. Regardless of how the parameters are set, all configurations are still run time programmable and will support different topologies, number of neurons, and activation functions (up to a set maximum). Thus designers can perform cost performance tradeoffs to arrive at an MLPCP tailored for their FPGA and set of system requirements.

**Processing Elements** Figure 1.b shows a block diagram of the neuron PEs.

Each PE contains support for three types of AFs: a step function, log sigmoid, and tangent sigmoid. During the design phase, designers can choose to implement the AFs as either computed functions (synthesized hardware) or using

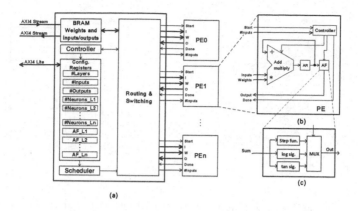

**Fig. 1.** MLPCP Architecture; (a). MLPCP structure; (b). a PE structure (AR: Accumulation Registers); (c). AF unit.

LUTs. Each layer can utilize different AFs programmed through the configuration registers at run time. This provides the flexibility to implement different networks at run time.

**Scheduler** The scheduler divides each layer into group(s) of neurons equal in size to the available number of PEs.

Thus for some topologies, the number of neurons in a layer is not divisible evenly by the number of PEs. In these cases, the remaining neuron(s) will be assigned to the first PE(s) during the next cycle. For example, with 8 PEs and 20 neurons in a layer, the scheduler will sequence two groups of eight neurons and one group of four. All neurons in a group are processed concurrently, with different groups processed sequentially. Based on the scheduler assignment, the controller aligns weights and inputs for each neuron in each PE's FIFO. Figure 2 illustrates how the scheduler computes neurons in an MLPCP with four PEs. The network is divided into 7 groups (G1 to G7). The scheduler then assigns each group sequentially onto the PEs. The outputs of each group within a layer are saved in the Layer Buffer, and assigned as inputs to the next layer.

**Controller** The controller is responsible for organizing weights and inputs for the neurons. During setup time, if AFs are not built in HW (synthesized), the controller reads the AFs values throughout the streaming input channel and stores them in PEs' local memory. Also, it calculates the number of weights that will be streamed to the MLPCP based on the configured registers. The controller divides the weight matrix into groups equal to the number of PEs and aligns them into each PE's FIFO. The controller also aligns the outputs of each layer with the appropriate weights to be used in the next layer. At the output layer, the controller streams the results out of the programmable MLPCP and generates "last" signal.

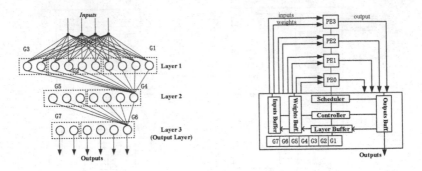

**Fig. 2.** Scheduling neurons in MLPCP with four PEs

**Configuration Registers** The following programmable registers are provided:

- #Layers: number of layers in the network.
- #Inputs: number of inputs.
- #Outputs: number of outputs.
- #Neurons_L1: number of neurons in first layer.
- #Neurons_L2: number of neurons in second layer.
- #Neurons_Ln: number of neurons in $n^{th}$ layer.
- #AF_L1: the type of activation function in first layer.
- #AF_L2: the type of activation function in second layer.
- #AF_Ln: the type of activation function in $n^{th}$ layer.

The number of registers scales based on the maximum network settings such as: Maximum Number of Layers (MNL), Maximum Number of Neurons (MNN), Maximum Number of Neurons in Largest Layer (MNNLL), Maximum Number of Inputs (MNI), and Maximum Number of Outputs (MNO).

## 3   Evaluation and Results

The MLPCP was written in C++ and generated using Xilinx's Vivado-hls 14.2 tools. We configured, synthesized and ran four versions of the MLPCP and compared their performance against software implementations for three applications. Comparisons were performed against a 660 MHz diffused ARM processor on the Zedboard(xc7z020clg484-1) and a 100 MHz soft IP MicroBlaze processor.

Performance results for these tests are presented in Section 3. We then implemented two custom neural network versions of three different test applications on the Zedboard for size comparisons. These results are presented in Section 3.1.

**MLPCP Configurations:** The following four versions of the MLPCP were used in our evaluations:

1. MLPCP-1: Four PEs, arithmetic floating point, AFs: synthesized (Vivado-Hls).

**Table 1.** Execution times for software (MicroBlaze, ARM) and MLPCP-x

| Func. | Network | | SW($\mu$s) | | MLPCP-1 | MLPCP-2 | MLPCP-3 | MLPCP-4 |
|-------|---------|---|-----------|-----|---------|---------|---------|---------|
| | Order | Topology | Microbl. | ARM | run time($\mu$s) | run time($\mu$s) | run time($\mu$s) | run time($\mu$s) |
| Sched. | 1 | 9,2,6 | 52.36 | 2.52 | 5.91 | 5.24 | 5.04 | 4.6 |
| | 2 | 9,4,6 | 78.43 | 4.82 | 6.5 | 5.7 | 5.42 | 4.9 |
| | 3 | 9,16,8,6 | 296.49 | 17.84 | 17.63 | 11.22 | 12.22 | 8.7 |
| | 4 | 9,40,6 | 449.83 | 30.40 | 29.8 | 17.96 | 19.54 | 13.72 |
| | 5 | 9,12,27,6 | 510.91 | 31.54 | 29.8 | 17.96 | 20.22 | 15.93 |
| JPEG | 6 | 64,16,64 | 1319.48 | 94.86 | 83.66 | 50.31 | 58.45 | 39.36 |
| | 7 | 64,32,16,64 | 2848.89 | 158.9 | 137.93 | 81.58 | 93.19 | 60.74 |
| | 8 | 64,32,16,32,64 | 4021.37 | 279.62 | 190.2 | 112.67 | 125.91 | 80.15 |
| | 9 | 64,32,16,48,40,16,64 | 6682.37 | 411.32 | 213.41 | 133.84 | 143.32 | 95.52 |

2. MLPCP-2: Eight PEs, arithmetic floating point, AFs: synthesized (Vivado-Hls).
3. MLPCP-3: Four PEs, arithmetic fixed point, AFs: lookup table in BRAM (100 samples with 8-bit resolution).
4. MLPCP-4: Eight PEs, arithmetic fixed point, AFs: lookup table in BRAM (100 samples with 8-bit resolution).

Both MLPCP-3 and MLPCP-4 used (sign=1,word size=8,fraction=4) inputs, (1,17,8) weights, (1,29,16) weighted sum, and (1,8,4) outputs in fixed point data representation. The configuration parameters were set to the following values to bound the maximum network size that each MLPCP would run: MNL=6, MNN=348, MNNLL=64, MNI=64, MNO=64.

**Test Applications** Three applications were used in our evaluations. The first is inversek2j an inverse kinematics application for a 2-joint arm[4].

The second is an adaptive smart-scheduler reported in [2]. The third is a standard JPEG encoder. Each application was first trained offline on a desktop PC in MATLAB. Different topologies were evaluated during the training phase. The topologies used in this study are not guaranteed to provide the best efficiency and accuracy.

**Performance Evaluation** The four versions of the MLPCP were evaluated against software implementations on both a MicroBlaze and ARM .The software source code could be found in [5]. It was modified and optimized to run on embedded processors. Data and instruction caches were turned on for both processors. Input data sets were transfered using DMA into local BRAMs for all test cases (processors and MLPCPs). The reported time in Table 1 included transfer and execution time.

Table 1 lists execution times for the smart scheduler and JPEG encoder applications trained using nine different topologies. Each of the four MLPCP systems were programmed at run time to implement each of the topologies. For a given topology, the first number represents the number of inputs. The

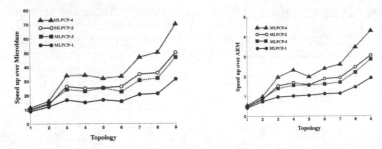

**Fig. 3.** Speed up over software on MicroBlaze (left) and ARM (right) processors

cardinality of the $n-1$ remaining integers represent the number of layers, with each integer representing the number of neurons in that particular layer.

The execution times from Table 1 are replotted in Figure 3 to show the speed up over software implementations run on the MicroBlaze and ARM processors respectively.

The MicroBlaze was running at 100 MHz, the same clock frequency as the co-processor. The ARM however, was running at 667 MHz, 6.6x faster than the 100 MHz MLPCP. Even with the 6.6x advantage, the MLPCP begins outperforming the ARM at topology (3); a relatively small and simple neural network with three layers and 30 neurons. In both cases, speedups generally increase as the size and complexity of the topology increases.

## 3.1 Resource Comparisons

Generalization typically comes with performance and resource efficiency costs compared to customization. This analysis shows the performance and resource efficiency costs associated with the programmable MLPCP. We quantified these costs by building and then comparing the following two custom designs with our four MLPCP systems.

**Custom hardware Designs:** The following two custom hardware design approaches are from [1],[10] and [6]:

1. CNN1: A fully parallel network (the number of PEs equal to the number of neurons in the network) with pipelining between layers.
2. CNN2: A network with the number of PEs equal to the number of neurons in the largest layer. Each layer was then multiplexed on the array of PE's.

Table 2 shows the resource usage for our four MLPCP systems on the Zedboard.

**Comparisons Between MLPCP-4 and CNNx** : For comparisons we implemented the two custom networks on the Zedboard. One specific topology was used for each application and then implemented using the CNN1 and CNN2

**Table 2.** Resource Utilizations on Zedboard

| Version | PEs | AF | BRAM_18k | DSP48E | FF | LUTs |
|---|---|---|---|---|---|---|
| MLPCP-1 | 4 | Synth | 8.9% | 37% | 6.59% | 16.21% |
| MLPCP-2 | 8 | Synth | 13.2% | 74.09% | 12.13% | 31.15% |
| MLPCP-3 | 4 | LUTs | 4% | 4% | 0.2% | 3.2% |
| MLPCP-4 | 8 | LUTs | 8.2% | 7.7% | 2.9% | 4.9% |

**Table 3.** Resources Comparisons for MLPCP-4 and CNNs on Zedboard

| Function | Design | PEs | BRAM_18k | DSP48E | FF | LUTs | Performance ($\mu s$) |
|---|---|---|---|---|---|---|---|
| Inversek2j (2,4,2) | CNN1 | 6 | 0 | 2.2% | 1.1% | 6% | 2.29 |
| | CNN2 | 4 | 0 | 1.3% | 0.9% | 4.9% | 2.49 |
| | MLPCP-4 | 8 | 7.5% | 7.2% | 2.9% | 4.9% | 3.86 |
| Scheduler (9,10,6) | CNN1 | 16 | 0.3% | 13.6% | 4.2% | 16.32% | 3.8 |
| | CNN2 | 10 | 0.3% | 9.0% | 3.4% | 12.6% | 4.4 |
| | MLPCP-4 | 8 | 7.5% | 7.2% | 2.9% | 4.9% | 5.9 |
| JPEG (64,8,64) | CNN1 | 72 | 25.7% | 37.7% | 15.4% | 122% | - |
| | CNN2 | 64 | 22% | 30% | 11% | 100% | - |
| | MLPCP-4 | 8 | 7.5% | 7.2% | 2.9% | 4.9% | 25.67 |

approaches. Inversek2j was first trained and then implemented using fixed point arithmetic and lookup tables for the AFs. The MLPCP-4 system was chosen for comparison.

Several interesting results can be drawn from the comparisons in Table 3. The inversek2j application represents a very small custom neural network with fewer than the eight PEs contained within MLPCP-4. Thus the MLPCP-4 includes two PEs and additional control and sequencing logic not used. For this case the CNNs were more resource efficient. The smart scheduler and JPEG applications show the MLPCP-4 becoming more resource efficient as the size of the neural network exceeds its 8 PEs. Both custom designs showed how the resource requirements grow with size of the network topology compared to the MLPCP-4. It can be seen in Table 3 that the custom implementations for the JPEG application exceeded the LUT resources available on the Zynq and could not be synthesized.

Table 3 shows the performance cost of programmability. As would be expected a fully custom, pipelined implementation (CNN1) outperformed the custom design that limited PEs to the largest layer (CNN2) as well as a very general and programmable co-processor (MLPCP-4).

## 4    Conclusion

This paper presented a new Multilayer Perceptron Co-Processor (MLPCP) designed for implementation on FPGAs. The MLPCP provides the advantages of reuse and scalability over custom designed ANNs. Once synthesized for a particular FPGA, the MLPCP can be configured through a programmable set of registers at run time to assume different topologies and achieve different accuracy of results. This allows the MLPCP to be used for different sets of requirements and across different applications.

# References

1. Canas, A., Ortigosa, E., Ros, E., Ortigosa, P.: FPGA implementation of a fully and partially connected MLP. In: Omondi, A., Rajapakse, J. (eds.) FPGA Implementations of Neural Networks, pp. 271–296. Springer, US (2006). http://dx.doi.org/10.1007/0-387-28487-7_10
2. Cartwright, E., Sadeghian, A., Ma, S., Andrews, D.: Achieving portability and efficiency over chip heterogeneous multiprocessor systems. In: Proc. of the 24th Intl. Conf. on Field Programmable Logic and Applications (FPL), pp. 1–4 (2014)
3. Cheung, K., Schultz, S., Luk, W.: A large-scale spiking neural network accelerator for FPGA systems. In: Villa, A., Duch, W., Érdi, P., Masulli, F., Palm, G. (eds.) ICANN 2012, Part I. LNCS, vol. 7552, pp. 113–120. Springer, Heidelberg (2012). http://dx.doi.org/10.1007/978-3-642-33269-2_15
4. Esmaeilzadeh, H., Sampson, A., Ceze, L., Burger, D.: Neural acceleration for general-purpose approximate programs. In: 2012 45th Annual IEEE/ACM International Symposium on Microarchitecture (MICRO), pp. 449–460, December 2012
5. Gure, A.: Multilayer perceptron neural network in c. https://github.com/sanjeevk001/workingfiles/tree/master/mlp-bp-fxp-5
6. Himavathi, S., Anitha, D., Muthuramalingam, A.: Feedforward neural network implementation in FPGA using layer multiplexing for effective resource utilization. IEEE Trans. on Neural Networks 18(3), 880–888 (2007)
7. Jung, S., Kim, S.S.: Hardware implementation of a real-time neural network controller with a DSP and an FPGA for nonlinear systems. IEEE Transactions on Industrial Electronics 54(1), 265–271 (2007)
8. Krips, M., Lammert, T., Kummert, A.: FPGA implementation of a neural network for a real-time hand tracking system. In: Proc. of the 1st Intl. Workshop on Electronic Design, Test and Applications, pp. 313–317 (2002)
9. Misra, J., Saha, I.: Artificial neural networks in hardware: A survey of two decades of progress. Neurocomputing 74(13), 239–255 (2010). Artificial Brains http://www.sciencedirect.com/science/article/pii/S092523121000216X
10. Moussa, M., Areibi, S., Nichols, K.: On the arithmetic precision for implementing back-propagation networks on FPGA: a case study. In: Omondi, A., Rajapakse, J. (eds.) FPGA Implementations of Neural Networks, pp. 37–61. Springer, US (2006). http://dx.doi.org/10.1007/0-387-28487-7_2
11. Ortega-Zamorano, F., Jerez, J., Franco, L.: FPGA implementation of the c-mantec neural network constructive algorithm. IEEE Trans. on Industrial Informatics 10(2), 1154–1161 (2014)

# Reconfigurable Hardware Assist for Linux Process Scheduling in Heterogeneous Multicore SoCs

Maikon Bueno[1(✉)], Carlos R.P. Almeida Jr.[2], José A.M. de Holanda[2], and Eduardo Marques[2]

[1] ICEN - Institute of Exact and Natural Science,
UFMT - Federal University of Mato Grosso, Cuiabá, Brazil
`maikon@usp.br`
[2] ICMC - Institute of Mathematics and Computer Science,
USP - University of São Paulo, São Paulo, Brazil
{`carlos,arnaldo`}`@usp.br`, `emarques@icmc.usp.br`

**Abstract.** This paper presents a model of an FPGA-based scheduler which identifies the processes' demands and indicates to the Linux operating system running over SPARC Leon the most suited set of processes to each core type. In this regard, performance monitors were implemented within the processors, which in real-time identifies the demands of processes. The demand for each process is projected for the other processors in the architecture, and then it is executed a balancing to maximize the total system performance by distributing processes among processors. The scheduler has been validated through the parallel execution of several benchmarks, resulting in decreased execution times compared to the scheduler without the heterogeneity support.

**Keywords:** Heterogeneus multiprocessing · Load balancer · Multicore

## 1 Introduction

Heterogeneous multicore can achieve higher performance and reduce energy consumption from processes by matching them to appropriated cores. The performance is dependent on an efficient scheduling mechanism, able to identify in real-time the demands of processes. However, the process and processor matching procedure can be a challenge for designers since it should take into account the performance of both, processor and process, to choose the most suited assignment.

The model presented by this paper seeks to improve the system performance by assigning the process to a processor that will offer the best estimated performance for the overall system. The decisions are dynamic, and they are based on online process monitoring by using performance counters without requiring sampling performance in all cores[1]. The results of monitoring are the amount of stalls generated by a process in a processor at a given instant. These stalls

© Springer International Publishing Switzerland 2015
K. Sano et al. (Eds.): ARC 2015, LNCS 9040, pp. 435–442, 2015.
DOI: 10.1007/978-3-319-16214-0_40

are used to estimate the performance projection for all processors, using weights assigned to each resource type that may influence the architecture stalls. Based on these projections, the scheduler uses a combinatorial optimization algorithm implemented in hardware which aims to maximize the system's performance by operating an optimal assignment of processes to processors, based on their resource's needs and weights. The results reached by running benchmarks on processors with minimal micro architectural differences show that the use of the proposed scheduler assisted by hardware can increase the effective use of each processor in the architecture.

This paper is organized as it follows. Section 2 and 3 introduce the heuristic proposed by this paper and its architecture. Section 4 discusses the experimental setup and results and, Section 5 presents our conclusion.

## 2    Scheduler Model

Several approaches have been used to measure the performance of a process in different types of processors. The results of this measurement are useful for guiding the scheduler on making a real time decision about which processor should be chosen for a given process. Many of these approaches use simulations or statistical data provided by the processor itself, implementing the scheduler entirely in software. However, the processor may not have sufficient statistical information about the resource's needs of the running processes to perform a more precise schedule. Thus, using the hardware itself to assist in scheduling, the results generated by the scheduler are more specific and may be essential in architectures that use a set of processors with different capabilities [5].

The approach used by the scheduler's heuristic is focused on the architectural features of embedded processors that cause an effect of heterogeneity on multiprocessors. Features like cache size, FPU (Float Point Unit) type, TLB (Translation Lookaside Buffer) size and branch prediction, are usually part of trade-offs in embedded processor designs, with regard to logical space, performance and power. Some studies indicate that the use of distinct types of processors, each one containing different features, can result in an architecture with less power consumption, less logical space and greater performance when guided by an efficient scheduling [4].The CPI stack is the metric discussed by this work and it is the decomposition of the number of cycles spent on executing instructions in components of a stall [2]. These components show where the CPU is spending more time executing a process.

The components of stall chosen to decompose the CPI are directly related to the architecture. The most common examples of components that can cause stalls in processes are: number of cycles spent on executing floating-point instructions; latency of multiplication operations; latency of division operations; delay related to direct dependencies found in the pipeline in load and store instructions; delay related to the cancelling and to the loading of instructions in the pipeline due to the occurrence of jumps; instruction and data cache-related delays; and cycles of latency in case of absence of references in instruction or data TLB.

The components mentioned above are the basis for calculating the performance of the processes in each processor architecture. Thereby, there must be a method to extract the CPI decomposition from running processes. This task can be carried out by a component named performance monitor. As one of the goals of the proposed scheduler is to achieve real-time monitoring, it is considered that the performance monitor must be located within the processor. Therefore, it can receive information about the execution of the current process, such as control data from cache and TLB. This data can be decomposed to produce more accurate results on the amount of cycles spent in each of the aforementioned components. The decomposition of process stalls into components is called the performance histogram in the remainder of this article and it generates the time percentage of each component for the current execution of a process.

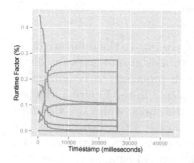 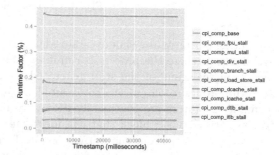

**Fig. 1.** Fbench running over $CPU_0$     **Fig. 2.** Fbench running over $CPU_1$

The same metric of decomposing the CPI into components is also used to qualify the performance of one processor in relation to the other processors in the architecture. It can be achieved by weights assignments for each resource type, which can affect the performance of a CPI component. Therefore, each processor has a set of weights, called performance vector. The weight of a component is the percentage of its performance in relation with the performance of the same component in the others' processors.

When a process executes on processors with different architectures, the distribution of stalls can also change, as can be seen in Figure 1 and  2. Both processors were used to run the FBench benchmark. The $CPU_1$ has a architecture that benefits the execution of float point instruction, while $CPU_0$ has both data and instruction caches with larger sizes. Although the benchmark FBench has its focus on float point algorithms, the smaller caches' sizes provided by $CPU_1$ were the bottleneck during the FBench execution, obtaining a greater delay in completion of the execution.

The number of cycles spent in each component on a particular processor necessarily depends on its own features. For example, if more resources are offered for a component in a processor (like a bigger cache), fewer cycles tend to be spent on running instructions on this feature. Hence, this dependence implies that data from the performance histogram of a given process before being considered in

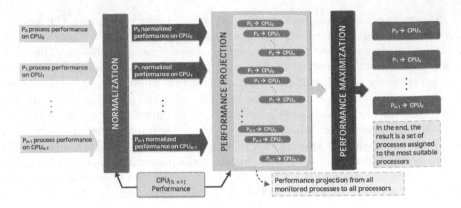

**Fig. 3.** Heuristic flow

projecting performance, should be standardized according to the influence of the architecture where the process is running. The normalization makes the distribution in real time of the stall generated by each processor to be minimized according to its resources set. For example, as depicted in the Figure 3, the performance monitors are continually decomposing the stalls, which are the input to the normalization block that considers the resources set, called here as performance vectors. From the normalized performance histogram, the next step consists of calculating the performance projections of all running processes for all processors in the architecture. The projections indicate the gains or losses that would be achieved if a process was executed on other processors. The method of performance projection is executed with the normalized performance values, also taking into account the performance weights of the processors.

The result of the projection is a matrix of fixed-point values that represents the performance percentage gain of each pair composed by a process and a processor. The columns represent the processors and the rows represent the performance's projections of a process for each processor. The maximization method returns the set of assignments that maximizes all projections. The choice of projections that maximize performance is considered a classic problem in the field of linear programming, also named the assignment problem. In this work, we adopted the Hungarian algorithm because it uses only integer operations of addition and subtraction, which facilitates its implementation in hardware [3].

## 3   Implementation

Inside each processor there is a performance monitor that communicates directly with the performance projection block, which measures how much a process would gain or lose in performance when running on another processor. From the performance projections, the Hungarian algorithm carries out performance maximization, where processes are uniformly assigned to processors. Figure 4 illustrates the communication between components.

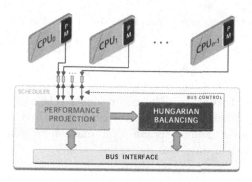

**Fig. 4.** Communication among components (PM represents the Performance Monitor)

The proposed hardware was developed using an FPGA (Field Programmable Gate Array), due to its great flexibility, which allows to prototype complete systems, from small logic circuits to complex architectures involving multiple processors, buses, and many other devices. We also use the framework GRLIB to implement the architecture. This framework was developed by Gaisler[1] and contains a VHDL implementation of the 32-bit SPARC V8 Leon3 processor, available under GPL (General Public License).

The main scheduler component has an interface for connecting to the AMBA bus, through which the processor can communicate with its hardware. A processor may access any desired hardware block because each component has a physical address range in the bus.

### 3.1   Software

The Buildroot tool was used in this project to generate the file system and the kernel image to load Linux on the FPGA. We employed the version 2.6.32, mainly because it already uses scheduler CFS (Completely Fair Schedule) and for its widespread use, it is easier to find solutions for any problem. This scheduler seeks a fair execution across all system processes.

In the algorithm view, the ideal processor would be the one that could perform all tasks in parallel with equal speeds. Thus, virtually, the algorithm attempts to approximate this ideal execution, making the processor's time equally divided among all processes. For this, we use the concept of virtual execution time, which is simply the processor time given to each process. The processes with smaller virtual execution times are the next to make use of the processor.

The Linux scheduler was modified to enable process monitoring and to perform migrations among processors according to the results generated by the hardware load balance. The scheduler module in hardware has several registers mapped into the memory address space used by the Linux kernel to control the

---

[1] Aeroflex Gaisler: http://www.gaisler.com

start and the end of process execution, as also to make available for the scheduler results.

## 3.2   Hardware

**Inter-components Interface** The components related to performance projection, and load balancing communicate using the AMBA AXI4-Stream protocol.The AXI protocol defines signals that make it as generic as possible to support a wide variety of data-transfer types.

**Performance Counter** The performance counter is the component responsible for observing each instruction executed by the processor and for measuring the number of cycles spent by it. This measure is used to decompose the CPI and is automatically computed by the component. The basic operation of the performance counter consists of decoding the received instruction, so that it knows to which group such instruction belongs, i.e., whether it is a branch, a load/store or a floating-point instruction, for example. From the decoding, the time delay for this instruction to be affected is measured. The operating system scheduler controls the beginning and the end of the monitoring. The performance counter has an input signal coming from the bus interface that indicates to the running process and the beginning and theend of monitoring activity.

**Normalization and performance projection** Continuous data from the decomposition of the processes generated by performance counters are the inputs to the block that performs the normalization and performance projection. This block has the role of arbitrating between the decomposition entries, sampling and sending them serially through the AXI interface. For each process, the percentage from its performance histogram over the total spent cycles is calculated. The next step is to perform the data normalization according to the weights of the current processor. Once these results are calculated, they are used along the weights of the processor to be projected to performs the direct data correlation, generating information corresponding to the projection of the current process on another processor. These projections are sent to the balancing block and later they will be read by the operating system.

**Balancing** The idea of the Hungarian algorithm is to receive a matrix and perform arithmetic operations in all elements between rows and between columns, so the number of zeros in the matrix increases until it is possible to choose a set of $n$ elements (*null*), where each element is unique in its row and column. This set of $n$ elements is the result of the optimal assignment which maximizes (the algorithm can maximize as much as minimize) the performance distribution between processes and processors. The matrix must be filled with the results of the performance projections from all processes for all processors.

**Table 1.** Architecture configurations

| Arch. | CPUs(0/1) / Resources | | | | | | | | | | | | | | |
|---|---|---|---|---|---|---|---|---|---|---|---|---|---|---|---|
| | Branch Pred. | Multip. (cycles) | D/Cache sets/way KB | | D/CACHE Rplcmt. | | I/Cache sets/way KB | | I/CACHE Rplcmt. | | D/TLB entries | | I/TLB entries | | FPU |
| 1 | Yes No 2 | 5 | 4/1 | 1/1 | LRU | No | 4/1 | 1/1 | LRU | No | 8 | 8 | 8 | 8 | LITE | FULL |
| 2 | Yes No 2 | 5 | 4/1 | 4/1 | LRU | Random | 4/1 | 1/1 | LRU | No | 8 | 32 | 32 | 8 | LITE | FULL |
| 3 | Yes No 2 | 5 | 4/1 | 2/1 | LRU | LRR | 4/1 | 4/1 | LRU | LRR | 32 | 16 | 16 | 32 | LITE | FULL |
| 4 | No No 2 | 5 | 4/1 | 4/1 | LRU | LRU | 4/1 | 4/1 | LRU | LRU | 8 | 8 | 8 | 8 | LITE | FULL |

# 4 Results

The embedded platform used in this project offers fewer resources compared to a modern personal computer. However, many benchmarks currently available in the market are designed to run in an environment with more resources. Thus, due to resource limitations in the embedded platform and also the low operation frequency of the processor and the other devices, the benchmarks were selected from different sources, so that they were in accordance with the embedded environment used. In this context, the following benchmarks were selected: *bzip2*, *libquantum*, *dhrystone*, *stanford*, *fbench*, *inverse*, *sphinx* and *whetstone*.

In the experiments, we used time effective time concept which stands for the amount of CPU time used by a process to execute. The effective CPU time is used to evaluate separately the performance projections made by the scheduler, without take into account the load balancing among the processors. Four different architectures were used for experimental evaluation, each containing two processors. The processor architectures are described in Table 1.

## 4.1 Performance Projection Results

Experiments were conducted by running four copies of the same benchmark simultaneously. This scenario is repeated ten times using the Linux scheduler and ten times using the heterogeneous scheduler on the processes. This procedure is repeated for the four architectures presented previously. Apart from the simultaneous execution of copies of the same benchmarks, three groups of different benchmarks were used. Benchmarks for each group are: Group 0: *dhry*, *fbench*, *stanford* and *inverse*; Group 1: *libquantum*, *whetstone*, *bzip2* and *fbench*; Group 2: *dhry*, *stanford*, *bzip2* and *sphinx*.

Before migrating a process, the standard Linux scheduler verifies if the processor already has a cache-hot. If so, the scheduler does not perform the migration. This approach may bring a disadvantage for heterogeneous multiprocessor systems. Sometimes the scheduler may prevent a process from running on a higher-performance processor, despite having a cache-cold for the process. In many cases, process migration should occur regardless of cache issues, mainly when the new processor offers a set of desirable features. Therefore, new experiments were made following the previous method, but without cache-hot verification at migration time. Importantly, the use of this procedure may cause some performance loss due to the lack of cache verification. Figure 5 and 6 illustrate the

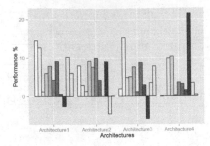

**Fig. 5.** With cache-hot          **Fig. 6.** Without cache-hot

results for all architectures with and without cache-hot checking, respectively. The results for the heterogeneous scheduler are compared to the results for the Linux native scheduler. As a consequence, it is realized a significant increase in performance achieved by the scheduler without the cache-hot checking.

## 5   Conclusion

This paper has presented a scheduler model implemented in hardware to determine in real time the performance projections of any running process to all processors of the architecture. The model was validated through its implementation in FPGA, using SPARC V8 Leon processor and Linux operating system. Through the performance projection provided by the scheduler module in hardware, the processes are migrated to the processors that have the most suitable resources, reducing effective execution times for these processes. We showed through the parallel execution of several benchmarks that the proposed scheduler improved the effective time up to more than 40%.

## References

1. Bueno, M., Holanda, J., Pereira, E., Marques, E.: Operating system support to an online hardware-software co-design scheduler for heterogeneous multicore architectures. In: Proceedings of the 2014 IEEE International Conference on Embedded and Real-Time Computing Systems and Applications, RTCSA 2014. IEEE Computer Society (2014)
2. Eyerman, S., Eeckhout, L., Karkhanis, T., Smith, J.E.: A top-down approach to architecting cpi component performance counters. IEEE Micro **27**(1), 84–93 (2007)
3. Kuhn, H.W., Yaw, B.: The hungarian method for the assignment problem. Naval Res. Logist. Quart, 83–97 (1955)
4. Kumar, R., Tullsen, D.M., Ranganathan, P., Jouppi, N.P., Farkas, K.I.: Single-isa heterogeneous multi-core architectures for multithreaded workload performance. SIGARCH Comput. Archit. News **32**(2), 64 (2004)
5. Srinivasan, S., Zhao, L., Illikkal, R., Iyer, R.: Efficient interaction between os and architecture in heterogeneous platforms. SIGOPS Oper. Syst. Rev. **45**(1), 62–72 (2011)

# Towards Performance Modeling of 3D Memory Integrated FPGA Architectures

Shreyas G. Singapura$^{(\boxtimes)}$, Anand Panangadan, and Viktor K. Prasanna

University of Southern California, Los Angeles, CA 90089, USA
{singapur,anandvp,prasanna}@usc.edu

**Abstract.** Recent advances in three dimensional integrated circuits have enabled large amounts of memory to be stacked in layers and accessed by a logic unit using high bandwidth vertical interconnects. Several 3D architectures have been proposed with different organizations of memory and logic layers. In particular, 3D stacks of memory dies can be interfaced with a reconfigurable logic layer such as FPGA to enable highly optimized implementation of memory-intensive applications. We refer to these as 3D Memory Integrated FPGAs. Mapping algorithms to such architectures is a challenging task due to the complex interaction between memory and logic and the relation between energy consumption and memory access. Performance modeling of these architectures can enable the design space to be systematically explored while mapping a specific algorithm. In this paper, we analyze the current landscape of 3D Memory Integrated FPGAs and identify the key parameters that have a significant impact on bandwidth and energy. We specify an "abstract architecture" that captures the features of such architectures and provide a parameterization of the design space with the eventual goal of developing a performance model for optimizing algorithm implementation.

**Keywords:** 3DIC · Vertical interconnect · Hybrid memory cube

## 1 Introduction

VLSI technologies are reaching their limits on their ability to pack more transistors on 2-dimensional areas of silicon. Three dimensional integrated circuits (3DIC) technology is one of the most promising ways to increase device densities in accordance with Moore's law. 3DICs add a dimension to the planar IC by stacking layers vertically. These layers communicate with each other using vertical interconnects such as high bandwidth Through Silicon Vias (TSVs). 3DIC technology is most advanced in the design of memory chips. For instance, in 3D Stacked DRAMs [9], layers of DRAM memory banks are stacked on top of each other with TSVs used for vertical interconnects. A further advance is

This material is based in part upon work supported by the National Science Foundation under Grant Number ACI-1339756.

© Springer International Publishing Switzerland 2015
K. Sano et al. (Eds.): ARC 2015, LNCS 9040, pp. 443–450, 2015.
DOI: 10.1007/978-3-319-16214-0_41

the stacking of layers of logic and memory vertically and connecting these layers with high-bandwidth vertical interconnects. These 3D Memory Integrated Architectures can enable processing near memory with high bandwidth access to memory [3–5,10–13]. The large number of interconnects between memory and logic coupled with frequent accesses to memory results in significant energy consumption. The goal of performance model-based optimization is to enable algorithms that can exploit the resources of 3D memory integrated architectures in an energy-efficient manner.

In this paper, we focus on 3D Memory Integrated Architectures with FPGA as the logic layer and consider the issues in developing performance models of 3D Memory Integrated FPGA. A challenge for developing an efficient implementation of an algorithm on a 3D Memory Integrated Architecture is the large number of architecture features that need to be optimized. These include parameters such as number of memory banks, vaults, layers and interconnects. The complex interactions between logic and memory require more control parameters such as access cost for a row, bank, vault in terms of both time and energy. A *design* refers to the mapping of an application onto an architecture. The *design space* is the set of all possible designs that are obtained by instantiating all possible values of the different parameters. The design space of 3D Memory Integrated FPGAs is large but must be explored within a reasonable amount of computation time. It is infeasible to perform a detailed evaluation of every possible design in the design space using simulation tools since the size of the design space grows exponentially with the number of parameters. Hence, it is important to identify the specific parameters which have a significant impact on performance and develop a high-level performance model based only on these parameters. We study the current 3D Memory Integrated FPGA landscape, identify these parameters, and propose an abstract architecture consisting of the parameters that significantly affect bandwidth and energy-efficiency.

The contributions of this paper are:

- a study of the current landscape of 3D Memory Integrated FPGAs
- an "abstract architecture" that captures the features of such architectures as the basis of a high-level performance model
- identification of a set of design space parameters for the abstract architecture

The rest of the paper is organized as follows. Section 2 presents the overview of 3D Memory Integrated FPGAs. In Section 3, we identify the critical parameters required to explore the design space of 3D Memory Integrated FPGAs and we conclude in Section 4.

## 2    3D Memory Integrated FPGA (3D MI-FPGA)

3DIC technology is being applied to develop the next generation of FPGAs [1,2, 6,7]. These include 3D FPGAs (stacking multiple layers of FPGA to benefit from the high bandwidth interconnections in 3DICs) and 3D MI-FPGAs (stacking memory and FPGA). In this paper, we focus on 3D MI-FPGAs and provide an overview of the different 3D MI-FPGAs. We then use these architectures to identify the potential parameters for a performance model.

The 3D architecture in [6], "Reconfigurable System-in-Stack" stacks memory layers on top of FPGA layers. The architecture is made up of multiple memory layers and the logic layer is split into two FPGA layers, with one layer acting as Datapath unit (accelerator) and the other as Control unit. The datapath unit layer of FPGA is made up of application specific logic and BRAMs with interconnections to the DRAM and the control unit layer. The control unit layer implements a finite state machine to manage the datapath unit.

Recently, a 3D demonstration board developed by Altera and Micron [2] features one 3D memory device from Micron connected to four Altera Stratix V FPGAs. The 3D memory is a vertical stack of DRAM memory dies connected using TSVs [8]. Although, this board does not have the memory stacked vertically on an FPGA, it enables designers to test 3D memory models and its communication with multiple FPGAs.

### 2.1  Features and Performance

**Reconfigurable System-in-Stack [6]:** In this architecture, each memory layer has 8 ports with 256 Mb per bank. TSVs connect the memory and FPGA layers. The maximum operating frequency of 3D memory is 2 GHz and this can sustain a bandwidth of 512 GB/s with a latency of 9 ns. The interconnects between FPGA layers use 3D interconnects. The maximum frequency of the FPGA is approximately 200 MHz.

**Altera + Micron Demonstration Board [2]:** The number of memory layers in the 3D memory is 8 and the number of logic layers in the demonstration board is 4. There are 512 interconnects between layers of the 3D memory. Banks stacked vertically one above the other form a *rank* or *vault*. Each layer of 3D memory is made of 16 vaults and 1 bank per layer per vault. The 3D memory interface is made of four links with each link connected to one FPGA. The total bandwidth from the 3D memory is approximately 130 GB/s and approximately 32 GB/s between one FPGA and the 3D memory.

## 3  Parameterization of 3D MI-FPGA

One of the promising characteristics of 3D architectures is that they address the memory wall problem and hence we focus on parameters which affect the bandwidth of 3D MI-FPGAs. On the other hand, 3D architectures can be energy intensive due to heavy utilization of the memory layers. Therefore, we also specify parameters affecting power or energy consumption of 3D MI-FPGAs. We present an *abstract architecture* comprising of layers of memory and layers of logic interacting through an interconnect layer. This is illustrated in Figure 1. The design space for this abstract architecture consists of parameters defining the Memory, FPGA Logic, and Logic-Memory Interconnect (LMI) layers. These parameters are described next.

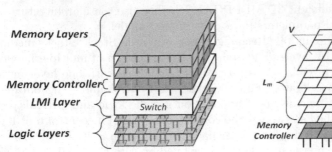

**Fig. 1.** 3D MI-FPGA Architecture

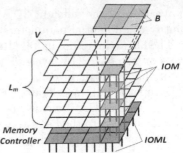

**Fig. 2.** 3D Memory

### 3.1 Memory Layer

**Bandwidth Parameters:** The bandwidth of memory is a function of parameters including its operating frequency ($f_{mem}$), size ($M$), and the number of memory layers ($L_m$). In the case of 3D memory, other parameters also affect bandwidth. In addition to the above, we define the following fine-grained parameters:

- Banks per vault per layer ($B$)
- Number of interconnections ($N_{iom}$)
- Number of vaults ($V$)
- Activation overhead ($t_{row}$)
- Interconnect latency ($t_{iom}$)

The organization of each layer has a significant impact on the bandwidth. A representation of the 3D memory is shown in Figure 2. Each layer of memory is partitioned into banks. Group of banks on each layer share a set of interconnections to other layers. We denote this set of interconnects as *IOM*. This *group of banks* which are stacked vertically one above the other in different layers form a *vault*. All the banks belonging to the same vault share the IOM with other layers. The number of these connections, $N_{iom}$ define the bandwidth available between the layers. In Figure 2, the memory layer can be visualized as being made of $V$ vaults of memory sharing a group of interconnections and each vault made of $B$ banks in each of the $L_m$ layers. The latency of accessing memory depends on the time needed to activate a bank in a vault and on the data transfer time on the IOM. Let $t_{row}$ denote the time to access a row in one bank of one layer and $t_{iom}$, the transfer time on IOM. $t_{row}$ consists of the activation time of the bank and the data movement from the bank to IOM. The latency of accessing two rows in the same bank is higher than accessing two rows in different banks because the activation time of banks can be reduced by overlapping the activation. This pipelining of activation of banks can be extended to different layers. But, the vaults do not share the IOM and hence, all the vaults can be active at the same time.

**Energy Parameters:** Energy consumption of memory is affected by latency parameters (defined above) and the power parameters. In a memory, accessing two rows consumes more power than accessing one row. We denote by $P_{row}$ the power to activate one row in a bank. In addition, the banks in memory can be set to standby mode or power-down mode. In each of these modes, there are two states: *active* and *precharge*. Keeping the bank in precharge power-down state $(P_{down})$ consumes the lowest power whereas active standby state $(P_{act})$ consumes the highest. Thus, data layout and number of row activations in a bank significantly affect the total power consumption in memory. The power consumption due to the IOM is defined by the parameter $P_{iom}$, the power consumed per interconnect per unit data transferred. Other parameters include read power $(P_{read})$ and write power $(P_{write})$ which are dependent on the amount of data accessed and refresh power $(P_{refresh})$, a constant.

## 3.2   Logic Layer

**Bandwidth Parameters:** An FPGA-based logic layer in our architecture consists of logic blocks, DSP blocks, memory blocks, and memory controllers (Figure 3). A functional unit can be replicated in multiple layers or a logic unit can be divided across multiple layers. We denote the set of vertical interconnects between these logic blocks by $IOL$. In addition, memory controllers on different layers share a separate set of vertical interconnects which are used to communicate with each other and the memory layers through the Logic-Memory Interconnect Layer (denoted $IOLM$ and described in Section 3.3). Parameters such as the number of LUTs and slices occupied by the application determine if the logic fits on the FPGA. Similarly, the maximum frequency of operation is dependent on the application and specific implementation. The FPGA parameters that significantly impact the memory bandwidth are:

- Frequency of operation $(f_{logic})$ and number of layers $(L_l)$
- number of interconnects between logic layers $(N_{iol})$
- interconnect latency $(t_{iol})$
- configuration of on-chip memory $(N_{bram}, S_{bram})$
- number of memory controllers $(N_{mcl})$

The frequency of operation of FPGA logic determines the amount of data that can be processed by the logic layer and hence the bandwidth between logic and memory increases with $f_{logic}$. The number of layers of logic $(L_l)$, size of IOL $(N_{iol})$, and delay from routing through IOL $(t_{iol})$ determine the number of parallel functional units that can run together. The IOL reduces the routing and improves the pipeline with output of logic block on one layer acting as input to logic block on another layer. The structure of on-chip memory affects the performance of FPGAs significantly. BRAMs are dedicated memory blocks with the mode of operation (read/write), the size of each block and width of each data location as configuration parameters. In each of the $N_{bram}$ BRAMs of size $S_{bram}$, there are two separate read and write ports per block. The BRAMs are

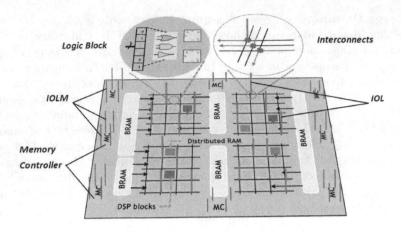

**Fig. 3.** FPGA-based logic layer

connected to the memory layer through $N_{mcl}$ memory controllers. Note that we do not consider Distributed RAMs (Dist. RAMs) in this work as they are dependent on the implementation and are not dedicated memory blocks.

**Energy Parameters:** In an FPGA, memory is one of the major consumers of energy. We define the parameter $P_{bram}$ as the power consumed by one block of BRAM. The total power consumption in BRAMs can be reduced by implementing a memory activation schedule that switches off blocks that are not in use. Dist. RAMs can be used as a local buffer so that the BRAM can be switched off to save energy. The power consumption of Dist. RAM, $P_{dist}$, is lower than $P_{bram}$ because of its smaller size. The power consumption due to routing through IOL is determined by $P_{iol}$. Other components that consume power in an FPGA are slice logic, functional units, and signals. Such blocks have their own power consumption parameters, for example, Multiply and Accumulate block ($P_{mac}$), adder ($P_{add}$), slice logic ($P_{slice}$) and signals ($P_{sig}$).

### 3.3   Logic-Memory Interconnect (LMI) Layer

The interconnect topology shown in Figure 4 acts as the communication link between logic and memory layers carrying the address of data in the memory and the data itself. The organization of these interconnects affect the bandwidth. The parameters of the interconnect layer specify the number of interconnects, latency, and the topology of the interconnect. The aggregate bandwidth from all the vaults in the memory should be made available to the logic layers. This is determined by the topology, latency ($t_{lmi}$) and number of interconnects *between* the memory controller layer in memory and memory controllers in the logic layer. Denote by $N_{ioml}$ the number of links from one vault in the memory layer to be connected to the logic layers through LMI. Then the total number of links from the memory layer ($IOML$) is $V \times N_{ioml}$.

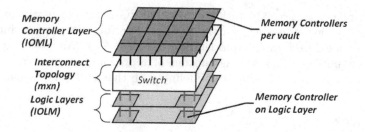

**Fig. 4.** Logic-Memory Interconnect

**Table 1.** Memory Layer Parameters [2,6]

| Parameter | $L_m$ | $M$ | $V$ | $B$ | $N_{iom}$ |
|---|---|---|---|---|---|
| Reconfigurable System-in-Stack | 2 | 2 GB | 8 | 1 | $\sim 310$ |
| Altera + Micron | 8 | 2-4 GB | 16 | 1 | 512 |

Similarly, denote by $N_{iolm}$ the number of links from each memory controller on a logic layer to be connected to the memory layers through LMI. Then, the total number of links from the logic layers ($IOLM$) are $N_{mcl} \times N_{iolm}$. For example, a crossbar switch of size $m \times n$, can be used to form the interconnection topology, where $m = V \times N_{ioml}$ and $n = N_{mcl} \times N_{iolm}$. In addition, we denote by $t_{lmi}$ to include both the setup time to configure the LMI and the data transfer time between memory controllers on memory and logic layers. $P_{lmi}$ denotes the power consumption due to the LMI layer per connection made between the memory and logic layers.

### 3.4  Examples of the Abstract Architecture

The parameters defined in this section can be used to describe the architectures in Section 2. The memory layer parameters for both the architectures are tabulated in Table 1. In Altera + Micron Demonstration Board, the FPGA is not connected to the memory via 3D interconnects and hence, the parameters of the logic and the LMI layer is limited to Reconfigurable System-in-Stack architecture in Table 2.

**Table 2.** Logic and LMI Layer Parameters [6]

| Parameter | $L_l$ | $S_{bram}$ | $N_{bram}$ per logic unit | $N_{iol}$ | $N_{iolm}$ | $N_{ioml}$ |
|---|---|---|---|---|---|---|
| Reconfigurable System-in-Stack | 2 | 4 KB | 5 | 880 | $\sim 310$ | $\sim 310$ |

## 4  Conclusion

We summarized the current state of development of 3D MI-FPGAs and identified architectural features which are critical for performance modeling. These features were used in the design of an abstract architecture whose parameters can form the basis for design space exploration of 3D MI-FPGAs with memory bandwidth and energy efficiency as the primary metrics. For future work, we intend to develop a detailed performance model for a 3D MI-FPGA. We will compare the data throughput and energy consumption of representative memory-intensive applications based on performance modeling with that of detailed simulations.

# References

1. Ababei, C., Maidee, P., Bazargan, K.: Exploring potential benefits of 3D FPGA integration. In: Becker, J., Platzner, M., Vernalde, S. (eds.) FPL 2004. LNCS, vol. 3203, pp. 874–880. Springer, Heidelberg (2004)
2. Altera, Micron: Hybrid Memory Cube Demonstration Platform. http://www.altera.com/technology/memory/serial-memory/hybrid-mem-cubes/mem-cubes.html
3. Black, B., Annavaram, M., Brekelbaum, N., DeVale, J., Jiang, L., Loh, G.H., McCauley, D., Morrow, P., Nelson, D.W., Pantuso, D., et al.: Die stacking (3D) microarchitecture. In: 39th Annual IEEE/ACM International Symposium on MICRO-39, pp. 469–479. IEEE (2006)
4. Das, S., Fan, A., Chen, K.N., Tan, C.S., Checka, N., Reif, R.: Technology, performance, and computer-aided design of three-dimensional integrated circuits. In: Proc. of the 2004 Intl. Simp. on Physical design, pp. 108–115. ACM (2004)
5. Davis, W.R., Wilson, J., Mick, S., Xu, J., Hua, H., Mineo, C., Sule, A.M., Steer, M., Franzon, P.D.: Demystifying 3D ICs: The Pros and Cons of Going Vertical. IEEE Design & Test of Computers 22(6), 498–510 (2005)
6. Gadfort, P., Dasu, A., Akoglu, A., Leow, Y.K., Fritze, M.: A power efficient reconfigurable system-in-stack: 3D integration of accelerators, FPGAs, and DRAM. In: 2014 27th IEEE International System-on-Chip Conference (SOCC), pp. 11–16. IEEE (2014)
7. Gayasen, A., Narayanan, V., Kandemir, M., Rahman, A.: Designing a 3-D FPGA: Switch Box Architecture and Thermal Issues. IEEE Transactions on Very Large Scale Integration (VLSI) Systems 16(7), 882–893 (2008)
8. Hybrid Memory Cube Consortium: Hybrid Memory Cube Specification. http://hybridmemorycube.org/files/SiteDownloads/HMC_Specification%201_0.pdf
9. Loh, G.H.: 3D-stacked memory architectures for multi-core processors. In: ACM SIGARCH Computer Architecture News, vol. 36, pp. 453–464. IEEE Computer Society (2008)
10. Loh, G.H., Xie, Y., Black, B.: Processor Design in 3D Die-Stacking Technologies. IEEE Micro 27(3), 31–48 (2007)
11. Papanikolaou, A., Soudris, D., Radojcic, R.: Introduction to three-dimensional integration. In: Three Dimensional System Integration, pp. 1–12. Springer (2011)
12. Patti, R.: Homogeneous 3d integration. In: Three Dimensional System Integration, pp. 51–71. Springer (2011)
13. Topol, A.W., La Tulipe, D., Shi, L., Frank, D.J., Bernstein, K., Steen, S.E., Kumar, A., Singco, G.U., Young, A.M., Guarini, K.W., et al.: Three-Dimensional Integrated Circuit. IBM Journal of Research and Development 50(4.5), 491–506 (2006)

# Pyverilog: A Python-Based Hardware Design Processing Toolkit for Verilog HDL

Shinya Takamaeda-Yamazaki[✉]

Nara Institute of Science and Technology,
8916-5, Takayama-cho, Ikoma-shi, Nara, Japan
shinya@is.naist.jp
http://arch.naist.jp

**Abstract.** Verilog HDL is the most-used hardware design language for
FPGAs. In this paper, we introduce *Pyverilog*, an open-source toolkit for
RTL design analysis and code generation of Verilog HDL. Pyverilog offers
efficient functionality to implement a CAD tool that treats Verilog HDL
with small amount of effort. Pyverilog consists of four key libraries: (1)
parser, (2) dataflow analyzer, (3) control-flow analyzer, and (4) Verilog
code generator. We show a case study that uses Pyverilog as the fundamental back-end library. We have developed flipSyrup, a framework
for efficient rapid prototyping by virtually enlarging FPGA resources.
By using Pyverilog, the framework is implemented with small amount of
additional codes; it is implemented in about 2700 lines of code in Python.

**Keywords:** Verilog HDL · Parser · Analyzer · Toolkit · FPGA

## 1 Introduction

Verilog HDL is the most-used design language to express the fabric of a hardware
structure in the register transfer level (RTL) for both ASIC implementation
and FPGA-based implementation. Since Verilog HDL has been used for many
years, a lot of useful information and common design patterns are available in
the literature and on the web. Additionally, constructing an effective hardware
structure for high performance and low power requires cycle-by-cycle scheduling
definitions for computations and data movements. In cases that the high-level
design languages do not fit with the application characteristics, designers would
prefer to use a conventional register transfer level HDL. Verilog HDL is certainly
useful for such fine-grain hardware definitions in any cases, because Verilog HDL
has enough capability to express cycle-level circuit behaviors. Thus, Verilog HDL
will be important as both a cycle-by-cycle modeling language for highly tuned
hardware structures.

Unfortunately, Verilog HDL lacks sufficient abstractions for higher productivity of hardware design. In the standard hardware development flow using
Verilog HDL, low-level descriptions of the hardware structure are required to
arrange inherent fine-grain components. It is hard to re-use hardware designs in

© Springer International Publishing Switzerland 2015
K. Sano et al. (Eds.): ARC 2015, LNCS 9040, pp. 451–460, 2015.
DOI: 10.1007/978-3-319-16214-0_42

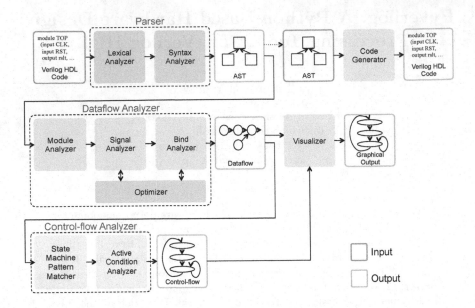

Fig. 1. Pyverilog overview

other environments. To overcome this drawback, some emerging alternatives of hardware design languages, such as Chisel[1], and high-level synthesis tools have been proposed. While these have powerful capabilities of component abstraction to support microarchitectural explorations for a better hardware configuration, most CAD tools do not directly support them as the input of the tools in standard. Therefore the software tools of those high-level languages generally generate RTL codes in Verilog HDL (or VHDL) for such standard CAD tools. Verilog HDL will be important as the intermediate representation of hardware, like assembly languages of general software environments.

In this paper, we introduce *Pyverilog*, an open-source toolkit for design analysis and code generation of RTL designs written in Verilog HDL. Pyverilog offers (1) code parser, (2) dataflow analyzer, (3) control-flow analyzer, (4) visualizer, and (5) code generator for Verilog HDL. The objective of Pyverilog is to make it easy for researchers and engineers to implement a novel CAD tool for Verilog HDL design.

## 2   Pyverilog

In point of modern high-level synthesis and new generation HDL researches, Verilog HDL and VHDL are commonly used as an intermediate representation for vender CAD tools. In order to implement such tools and languages, a code generator of traditional HDL is essential. Additionally, some approaches provide virtualization capability of FPGA resources that abstract away on-chip and off-chip fabrics, such as CoRAM[2,3] and LEAP[4]. These frameworks build their abstraction layers on existing HDLs. To realize such abstraction functions as actual hardware, a code parser, a static analyzer, and a code translator are required. In point of software engineering, RTL designs can be treated just as source codes described in parallel computing paradigm. To improve quality of RTL designs, some software engineering approaches are proposed, such as refactoring[5] and code coverage analysis[6]. In order to implement such approaches, a code parser, a static analyzer, and a code translator are required, as well.

There are some popular open-source Verilog simulators that support hardware development[7–9]. These simulators surely have a parser and a static analysis function that translate input Verilog codes into an internal representation used in the simulators. Unfortunately, since these simulators are originally designed just for practical Verilog simulations, reusing design analysis result by other software tools is not considered. Additionally, to the best of our knowledge, there are no available open-source products that support both code analysis and code generation of Verilog HDL. Therefore a comprehensive toolkit for Verilog HDL is needed.

In order to assist development of new CAD tools for efficient FPGA computing, we developed Pyverilog. Pyverilog is an open-source software toolkit for processing hardware designs of Verilog HDL. As its name suggests, Pyverilog has been completely implemented in Python, a major scripting language. Figure 1 shows the overview of Pyverilog toolkit. Pyverilog offers four key libraries: (1) parser, (2) dataflow analyzer, (3) control-flow analyzer, and (4) Verilog code generator. For ease of understanding a hardware structure, Pyverilog offers a visualizer of the dataflow graph and control-flow graph. The objective of Pyverilog is to make it easy for researchers and engineers to implement a novel CAD tool for Verilog HDL design. Pyverilog is a quite small toolkit; it consists of 12,359 lines of code in Python and 167 lines of template text.

## 2.1  Parser

Figure 2 illustrates an example design of a stopwatch in Verilog HDL. This hardware has three user inputs: *start*, *stop*, and *init*, and it has two outputs: *busy* and *timecount*. The hardware measures the time period from the start signal is asserted until the stop signal is asserted. If the init signal asserted, the value of timecount will be reset. The hardware includes a finite state machine (FSM) of *state* to handle three states: *IDLE*, *COUNTING*, and *WAITINIT*.

The parser of Pyverilog is a fundamental tool to analyze a source code written in Verilog HDL. The parser generates an abstract syntax tree (AST) from the code of Verilog HDL for later analysis and external tools. Pyverilog calls Icarus Verilog[7] with -*E* option as the preprocessor. After the preprocessing, all macros, such as *#define* and *#ifdef*, are extracted, and the fabricated source code in the form of text are available. Then the parser of Pyverilog reads the source code and builds up an AST in the form of nested class objects in Python. Finally the generated AST is ready for the next analysis step. Figure 3 shows a part of a text output of an AST generated from the example source code illustrated in

```
1   module stopwatch
2     (
3     input CLK,
4     input RST,
5     input start,
6     input stop,
7     input init,
8     output reg busy,
9     output reg [31:0] timecount
10    );
11    localparam IDLE = 0;
12    localparam COUNTING = 1;
13    localparam WAITINIT = 2;
14    reg [3:0] state;
15    always @(posedge CLK) begin
16      if(RST) begin
17        state <= 0;
18        timecount <= 0;
19      end else begin
20        if(state == IDLE) begin
21          if(start) begin
22            state <= COUNTING;
23            timecount <= 0;
24            busy <= 1;
25          end
26        end else if(state == COUNTING) begin
27          timecount <= timecount + 1;
28          if(stop) begin
29            state <= WAITINIT;
30            busy <= 0;
31          end
32        end else if(state == WAITINIT) begin
33          if(init) begin
34            timecount <= 0;
35            state <= IDLE;
36          end else if(start) begin
37            timecount <= 0;
38            state <= COUNTING;
39          end
40        end
41      end
42    end
43  endmodule
```

```
Source:
  Description:
    ModuleDef: stopwatch
      Paramlist:
      Portlist:
        Ioport:
          Input: CLK, False
            Width:
              IntConst: 0
              IntConst: 0
        Ioport:
          Input: RST, False
            Width:
              IntConst: 0
              IntConst: 0
        Ioport:
          Input: start, False
            Width:
              IntConst: 0
              IntConst: 0
        Ioport:
          Input: stop, False
            Width:
              IntConst: 0
              IntConst: 0
        Ioport:
          Input: init, False
            Width:
              IntConst: 0
              IntConst: 0
        Ioport:
          Output: busy, False
            Width:
              IntConst: 0
              IntConst: 0
            Reg: busy, False
              Width:
                IntConst: 0
                IntConst: 0
        Ioport:
          Output: timecount, False
            Width:
              IntConst: 31
              IntConst: 0
            Reg: timecount, False
              Width:
                IntConst: 31
                IntConst: 0
```

**Fig. 2.** Verilog HDL code example (stopwatch)

**Fig. 3.** Generated AST (I/O declaration section)

Figure 2, which represents that the example source code is correctly analyzed and converted into an appropriate AST representation.

To build the parser, PLY (Python Lex-Yacc)[10] is used as the parser generator (compiler-compiler), which is a lightweight implementation of a lexical analyzer and an LR-parser. Since PLY is entirely implemented Python, portability of the parser is naturally satisfied. The parser consists of 2,903 lines of code in Python.

## 2.2   Dataflow Analyzer

The dataflow analyzer of Pyverilog is for constructing a dataflow graph that represents relationships among signals. The generated dataflow graph will be used as an intermediate representation in a next step for control-flow analysis. The dataflow analyzer has 3 subsystems to make clear the entire structure of the hardware: (1) *module analyzer*, (2) *signal analyzer*, and (3) *bind analyzer*. All the subsystems are implemented using a standard visitor pattern that a specific function for each visited AST node is called by its class name recursively.

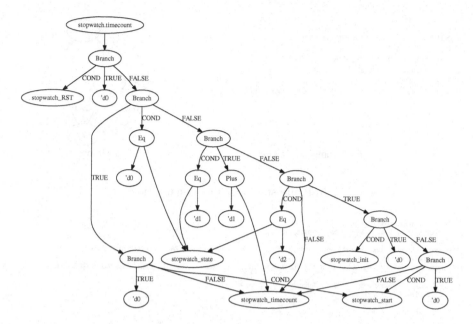

**Fig. 4.** Generated dataflow graph

The module analyzer first traverses an input AST to build a list of entire modules. In this step, a signal list of input, output, and parameters is created for each module definition, but any assignments of specific values are not analyzed. After that, the list is used to clarify signal connectivities across module hierarchy.

Then the signal analyzer then traverses the same AST again in order to collect signal definitions. In this step, all signal declarations are analyzed, and scope of effect for each signal is recorded. At the same time, the optimizer resolves the constant value definitions, such as a parameter and a localparam. Parameters in a module definition can be overwritten by its parent module. Therefore the actual hardware structure depending on such parameters will be fixed after those parameters are fixed. By utilising the analysis results of the optimizer, actual parameters in each module instance and the entire module hierarchy are determined.

Finally the bind analyzer generates a dataflow graph for each signal. Since the analysis and optimization of constant values and module hierarchy are already completed until this step, a dataflow definition is absolutely determined. Pyverilog offers a visualizer of the dataflow graph and control-flow graph. Figure 4 shows a dataflow graph picture of the variable *timecount* in Figure 2. The graphical representation of dataflow graphs makes us easy to find out the definition of a value by intuition. A dataflow graph in Pyverilog is provided in a tree of value definitions. The tree consists of several (1) arithmetical or logical operators, (2) assignment conditions represented as *Branch* in the figure, and (3) assigned values or signals. The bind analyzer constructs a tree incrementally from the head

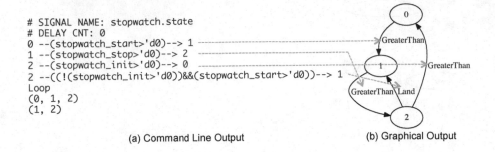

```
# SIGNAL NAME: stopwatch.state
# DELAY CNT: 0
0 --(stopwatch_start>'d0)--> 1
1 --(stopwatch_stop>'d0)--> 2
2 --(stopwatch_init>'d0)--> 0
2 --((!(stopwatch_init>'d0))&&(stopwatch_start>'d0))--> 1
Loop
(0, 1, 2)
(1, 2)
```

(a) Command Line Output                    (b) Graphical Output

**Fig. 5.** Finite state machine visualization

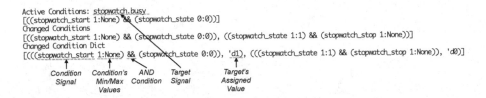

**Fig. 6.** Analysis result output of activated conditions

of an AST. The tree is usually rearranged so that assignment conditions are located in the root side of the tree and assigned values or signals are located on the leaf side of the tree. Then assigned values (or signals) and their conditions are obviously separated, which helps to easily construct a control-flow graph in the next step.

The visualizer uses Graphviz[11] with its Python binding. The principal operations of the visualizer are to convert a graph of a dataflow or a finite state machine (control-flow) into a graphic representation of the Graphviz format. The dataflow analyzer consists of 6,461 lines of code in Python.

## 2.3    Control-flow Analyzer

The control-flow analyzer of Pyverilog is for generating a graph representation of finite state machines (FSMs) in the hardware. In this work, we call such FSM as control-flow graph. The control-flow analyzer uses an analysis result of the dataflow analysis to utilize a list of signals and assignments among those signals. The control-flow analyzer has 2 subsystems: (1) state machine pattern matcher and (2) active condition analyzer.

The state machine pattern matcher explores appropriate signals constructing FSMs from the dataflow graph. By using pattern matching schemes that search signals with a predictable name, such as *state*, the analyzer selects candidate signals for the next analysis step. Then the active condition analyzer analyzes conditions that the value of a candidate signal for FSMs is modified. The

```
 1   import pyverilog.vparser.ast as vast
 2   from pyverilog.ast_code_generator.codegen import ASTCodeGenerator
 3
 4   params = vast.Paramlist(())
 5   clk = vast.Ioport( vast.Input('CLK') )
 6   rst = vast.Ioport( vast.Input('RST') )
 7   width = vast.Width( vast.IntConst('7'), vast.IntConst('0') )
 8   led = vast.Ioport( vast.Output('led', width=width) )
 9   ports = vast.Portlist( (clk, rst, led) )
10   items = ( vast.Assign( vast.Identifier('led'), vast.IntConst('8') ) ,)
11   ast = vast.ModuleDef("top", params, ports, items)
12
13   codegen = ASTCodeGenerator()
14   rslt = codegen.visit(ast)
15   print(rslt)
```

```
1   module top
2   (
3     input [0:0] CLK,
4     input [0:0] RST,
5     output [7:0] led
6   );
7     assign led = 8;
8   endmodule
```

**Fig. 7.** Code generation

**Fig. 8.** Generated Verilog HDL code

dataflow analyzer provides assignment definitions of each signal. They contain the assigned value and its assignment condition. The control-flow analyzer infers the values of candidate conditions from these assignment conditions. Results of active condition analyses are presented as a number of pairs of a cause signal name and its actual values for each state transition.

Figure 5(a) shows the analysis result of an FSM in Figure 2 in the form of text. At the same time, the control-flow analyzer generates a graphic file of the FSM. Figure 5(b) illustrates a corresponding FSM of variable *state* as a graph. The graph represents that the FSM consists of a cyclic transition pattern. The graphical representation of such control-flow graphs also makes us easy to figure out the control structure of the hardware.

The control-flow analyzer has a function to identify the conditions that a signal is asserted or de-asserted, so that it can identify the conditions of state transitions. Figure 6 shows the analysis result of conditions that value of the variable *busy* in Figure 2 is updated. According to the example code, the variable *busy* is updated when *state* is 0 (IDLE) and *start* is asserted, or *state* is 1 (COUNTING) and *stop* is asserted. The analyzer reports the correct analysis result of update conditions. The report result includes (1) conditional signal names, (2) pairs of maximum and minimum values that the condition is satisfied, and (3) values assigned when the condition is satisfied. This feature can be used to identify the asserted conditions of non-FSM signals. It helps to automatically synthesize an additional circuit that works only when some conditions are satisfied. The control-flow analyzer consists of 1,596 lines of code in Python.

## 2.4   Code Generator

The code generator of Pyverilog is for generating a source code written in Verilog HDL from the intermediate representation of an AST. Figure 7 shows an example code to generate a Verilog source code from an intermediate representation of AST. In the example, the structure of Verilog source code is directly defined by making an AST object. In line 13 of Figure 7, an object of *ASTCodeGenerator* is created. Then the object generates a corresponding source code in the form of text from the AST object. Figure 8 illustrates the generated source code by the Python script in Figure 7.

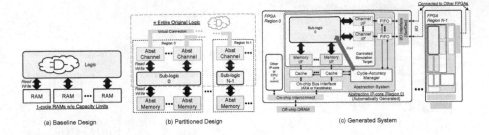

**Fig. 9.** Hardware design steps with the framework support

Common source code generators in any languages contain a set of template texts of output codes in their internal source codes. Therefore, the amount of the source codes is usually larger than the other parts. In order to separate the implementation of the entire code generator into the code write parts using template texts and the control parts, we used a template engine. In this implementation, we chose Jinja2[12], a major template engine used in various web applications with Python. By utilising the template engine, all template texts of Verilog HDL codes are removed from the source code in Python. It simplifies the software structure of the tool. As well as the dataflow analyzer, the code generator uses the standard visitor pattern that calls an appropriate function of the visited AST node recursively. The code generator consists of 988 lines of code in Python and 167 lines of template text.

## 3   Case Study: Development of a Rapid Prototyping Framework

We show a case study that uses Pyverilog as the fundamental back-end library. We have developed flipSyrup[13,14], a framework for rapid prototyping. Flip-Syrup enables to implement an FPGA-based prototyping system without any concerns of on-chip memory capacity limits and inter-FPGA communication property by the resource abstraction.

The framework provides two key abstractions of FPGA resources as instantiation templates in HDL level: (1) *abstract memory* for memory systems and (2) *abstract channel* for inter-FPGA communications. By utilizing these abstractions, designers can build prototyping target hardware with little concern of available on-chip memory capacity and interfaces among multiple FPGAs. Figure 9(a) illustrates a baseline design of target hardware. Figure 9(b) illustrates a partitioned design made from the baseline design. If multiple FPGAs are utilized in order to expand the logic capacity, designers should partition the the original design into multiple parts and define an instance of an abstract channel (represented as *Abst channel* in Figure 9(b)) in each partitioned design.

Figure 9(c) shows the complete prototype system using generated IP-core packages. Each separate FPGA includes one IP-core corresponding to each

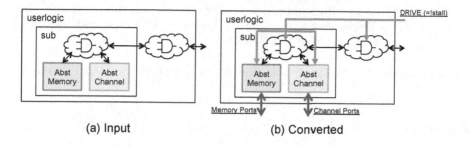

(a) Input                              (b) Converted

**Fig. 10.** RTL design conversion

partition of the target hardware. The framework creates (1) a memory system (*cache* in Figure 9(c)) corresponding to each abstract memory interface (Abst memory) and (2) a synchronization FIFO buffer (*FIFO* in Figure 9(c)) corresponding to each abstract interface among partitioned hardware (abstract channel). The framework then synthesizes a management hardware (*cycle-accuracy manager* in Figure 9(c)) that throttles the target hardware for cycle-accurate emulation under utilizing the given abstractions.

When any miss events happen, the cycle-accuracy manager (in Figure 9(c)) stops the entire modeled hardware for the cycle-level accuracy of target hardware behavior. To this end, the framework automatically translates the pure RTL designs of the target hardware into controllable RTL designs by the controller. The RTL design conversion takes two steps: (1) inserting control ports for abstract objects, and (2) inserting a throttling port for the cycle-accuracy manager. Figure 10(a) illustrates a structure of an input RTL design before the RTL conversion. Figure 10(b) illustrates a structure of the converted RTL design after the RTL conversion. The designers are not required to prepare any signal ports that control abstract objects from outside of the user-level RTL.

The tool-chain of flipSyrup is implemented by utilizing Pyverilog. The RTL analyzer and translator are implemented with very small amount of source code by using the parser and the dataflow analyzer provided by Pyverilog: The amount of additional source code of these tools is **1055 lines** in Python. At the final step of the IP-core synthesis, translated RTL designs are converted to Verilog source code with some control hardware. The code generator of flipSyrup is implemented with just two lines of source code by using the code generator of Pyverilog. Totally flipSyrup is implemented in about **2700 lines** of code in Python by using Pyverilog.

## 4    Conclusion

We introduced *Pyverilog*, an open-source toolkit for design analysis and code generation of RTL designs written in Verilog HDL. We showed a case study that uses Pyverilog as the fundamental back-end library. We have developed a framework for rapid prototyping by using Pyverilog. The framework is implemented with small amount of additional codes. We believe that utilizing Pyverilog effectively simplifies development of modern CAD tools. Pyverilog and its related frameworks are available from PyPI[15–17].

**Acknowledgments.** We thank Kenji Kise for his useful comments and support on this research.

# References

1. Bachrach, J., Vo, H., Richards, B., Lee, Y., Waterman, A., Avižienis, R., Wawrzynek, J., Asanović. K.: Chisel: constructing hardware in a scala embedded language. In: Proceedings of the 49th Annual Design Automation Conference, DAC 2012, pp. 1216- 1225. ACM, New York (2012)
2. Chung, E.S., Hoe, J.C., Mai, K.: Coram: an in-fabric memory architecture for fpga-based computing. In: Proceedings of the 19th ACM/SIGDA International Symposium on Field Programmable Gate Arrays, FPGA 2011, pp. 97–106. ACM, New York (2011)
3. Takamaeda-Yamazaki, S., Kise, K., Hoe, J.C.: PyCoRAM: yet another implementation of CoRAM memory architecture for modern FPGA-based computing. In: Intersections of Computer Architecture and Reconfigurable Logic (CARL 2013) (2013)
4. Adler, M., Fleming, K.E., Parashar, A., Pellauer, M., Emer, J.: Leap scratchpads: automatic memory and cache management for reconfigurable logic. In: Proceedings of the 19th ACM/SIGDA International Symposium on Field Programmable Gate Arrays (2011)
5. Duley, A., Spandikow, C., Kim, M.: A program differencing algorithm for verilog hdl. In: Proceedings of the IEEE/ACM International Conference on Automated Software Engineering, ASE 2010, pp. 477–486. ACM, New York (2010)
6. Athavale, V., Ma, S., Hertz, S., Vasudevan, S.: Code coverage of assertions using rtl source code analysis. In: 2014 51st ACM/EDAC/IEEE Design Automation Conference (DAC), pp. 1–6, June 2014
7. Icarus verilog. http://iverilog.icarus.com/
8. Gplcver. http://gplcver.sourceforge.net/
9. Verilator. http://www.veripool.org/wiki/verilator
10. Ply (python lex-yacc). http://www.dabeaz.com/ply/
11. Graphviz - graph visualization software. http://www.graphviz.org/
12. Jinja. http://jinja.pocoo.org/
13. Takamaeda-Yamazaki, S., Kise, K.: flipSyrup: cycle-accurate hardware simulation framework on abstract FPGA platforms. In: Proceedings of 24th International Conference on Field Programmable Logic and Applications (FPL 2014) (2014)
14. Takamaeda-Yamazaki, S., Kise, K.: A framework for efficient rapid prototyping by virtually enlarging FPGA resources. In: Proceedings of 2014 International Conference on ReConFigurable Computing and FPGAs (ReConFig 2014) (2014)
15. pyverilog: Python package index. https://pypi.python.org/pypi/pyverilog
16. pycoram: Python package index. https://pypi.python.org/pypi/pycoram
17. flipsyrup: Python package index. https://pypi.python.org/pypi/flipsyrup

# Special Session 1: Funded R&D Running and Completed Projects (Invited Papers)

# Towards Unification of Accelerated Computing and Interconnection For Extreme-Scale Computing

Toshihiro Hanawa[1]($\boxtimes$), Yuetsu Kodama[2], Taisuke Boku[2], Hideharu Amano[3], Hitoshi Murai[4], Masayuki Umemura[2], and Mitsuhisa Sato[2]

[1] Information Technology Center, The University of Tokyo, Kashiwa, Japan
hanawa@cc.u-tokyo.ac.jp
[2] Center for Computational Sciences, University of Tsukuba, Tsukuba, Japan
{kodama,taisuke,msato}@cc.tsukuba.ac.jp, umemura@ccs.tsukuba.ac.jp
[3] Department of Information and Computer Science, Keio University,
Yokohama, Japan
hunga@am.ics.keio.ac.jp
[4] RIKEN Advanced Institute for Computational Science, Kobe, Japan
hmurai@riken.jp

**Abstract.** Heterogeneous clusters using accelerators are widely used for high-performance computing system. In such systems, the inter-node communication among accelerators becomes bottleneck due to the data transfer between the accelerator and the host.

To eliminate this overhead, we have been developing a novel communication system realizing direct communication among accelerators over computation nodes under the HA-PACS (Highly Accelerated Parallel Advanced system for Computational Sciences) project. Also we are investigating high-level parallel programming language, and several practical application programs on our concept, as well as studying the enhancement of TCA and developing system software stack in the CREST project.

**Keywords:** Accelerator computing · Interconnection network · PCI express · Remote DMA · GPU direct

## 1 Introduction

Accelerators, as represented by Graphics Processing Units (GPUs), are widely used in high performance computing due to their high performance/price ratios and high performance/power ratios. In the Top500 List, the number of high performance computing systems that include accelerators has increased yearly, and several dozen systems use accelerators in the current list (Nov. 2014) [9].

However, all the accelerators are connected to the CPU by PCI Express (PCIe), which is commonly used as IO bus. Thus, while the accelerators provide high computing performance, the total performance of the application using

© Springer International Publishing Switzerland 2015
K. Sano et al. (Eds.): ARC 2015, LNCS 9040, pp. 463–474, 2015.
DOI: 10.1007/978-3-319-16214-0_43

accelerators degrades heavily due to PCIe performance bottleneck. Especially in the cluster using accelerators, inter-node communications among multiple accelerators require extra latencies. Since accelerator memory is separately located behind the CPU, several memory copies via the CPU memory are required. Furthermore, accelerator itself cannot communicate to the other accelerators over the interconnect. The latency caused by multiple memory copies severely degrades the performance, especially in the case of a short message.

In order to address this problem, we have proposed and have been developing the direct communication system among accelerators over the compute node, referred to as Tightly Coupled Accelerators (TCA) architecture. Since TCA provides the inter-node communication by PCI Express directly with fast packet switching mechanism, it could achieve ultra-low latency without the protocol overhead such as InfiniBand and MPI as well as the memory copy overhead.

In this paper, the research and development of TCA architecture, its programming environment, and applications based on TCA communication are presented under the HA-PACS project in Center for Computational Sciences, University of Tsukuba (CCS). Also, we introduce the CREST project entitled "Research and Development on Unified Environment of Accelerated Computing and Interconnection for Post-Petascale Era," in cooperation with a couple of organizations around CCS.

## 2    Overview of HA-PACS and TCA Architecture

The Highly Accelerated Parallel Advanced system for Computational Sciences (HA-PACS system) is the eighth generation of the PACS/PAX series supercomputer at CCS. This project was performed under the approach based on "Interdisciplinary Computational Science" with collaboration of computational scientists using high performance computing system and computer scientists. It was funded by Ministry of Education, Culture, Sports, Science and Technology (MEXT), Japan since Apr. 2011 for three years.

In developing the HA-PACS system, target applications, including particle physics, astrophysics, and life sciences applications, are pre-defined. In order to achieve maximum performance within limited power supply and a limited installation area, a large-scale cluster using accelerators is introduced to perform these applications effectively.

We promoted the project with organizing two project offices of Exascale Computational Sciences and Exascale Computing System Development in CCS, for application development toward accelerated computing and actual system development, respectively.

The HA-PACS system was designed not only just as the large-scale commodity GPU cluster but also as the testbed for development and demonstration of element technology towards the next-generation HPC. In practice, we focused on the following goals:

- Development of TCA (Tightly Coupled Accelerators) architecture to allow to enhance the communication performance, and
- acceleration of computational science applications based on TCA.

## 2.1  Base Cluster

For the development and product run of advanced scientific computations toward next-generation accelerated computing, the HA-PACS base cluster is equipped with the latest GPUs at the time of installation.

Each computation node of HA-PACS uses two sockets of an Intel Xeon E5 2600 (Sandy Bridge-EP) CPU and four NVIDIA M2090 GPUs. As an interconnection network, InfiniBand QDR with a dual-rail configuration is used, which is suitable for PCIe Gen3 x8 with approximately 8 GB/sec bandwidth. A total of 268 computation nodes is connected by the fat-tree configuration with full bisection bandwidth.

The system began operating in February 2012 with a peak performance of 802 TFlops and was ranked at 41st on the Top500 list issued June 2012.

## 2.2  Tightly Coupled Accelerators Architecture

As mentioned above, for the accelerator technology of the next-generation HPC, improvement of the latency and bandwidth in the communication among accelerators is the most important issue. In order to address this problem, we proposed a novel interconnect dedicated to direct communication among accelerators beyond nodes. This technology is referred to as the TCA architecture[14],[13].

The TCA architecture is based on the concept of using the PCIe link [22] not only as intra-node IO bus but also as the communication network link between communication nodes and accelerators. Therefore, in the TCA architecture, the accelerators can communicate directly via the PCIe protocol to the other accelerators on the remote node. As a result, the TCA architecture can eliminate extra memory copy via the host memory in the conventional cluster with accelerators and can also avoid protocol overhead such as that associated with InfiniBand and MPI.

## 2.3  PEACH2: An Implementation Based on TCA Architecture

In order to build up the cluster using TCA architecture, the interface board for TCA, referred to as the PCI Express Adaptive Communication Hub version 2 (PEACH2) board, which uses an FPGA chip referred to as the PEACH2 chip, has been developed.

PCIe is the standard serial interface for attaching the device to a host[22]. Originally, PCIe performs primarily memory read/write operations between the Root Complex (RC) on the host side (master) and the Endpoint (EP) on the device side (slave). However, the actual behavior is simply point-to-point bidirectional packet communication. Therefore, we adapted fast serial packet communication on the PCIe link to inter-node communication.

In the PEACH2 chip, four PCIe Gen2 ports are allocated, each of which has eight lanes, i.e., each port can transfer data at up to 4 Gbytes/sec as same as a port of InfiniBand QDR 4x. We implement the PEACH2 chip using a field programmable gate array (FPGA) for flexible control and prototyping. Altera's

Stratix IV GX FPGA, which can provide four PCIe Gen2 x8 modules as the hard IP, was introduced [5]. The DMA controller is equipped for operating the fast communication with the complicated communication pattern as described later. As the packet buffer, the embedded memory in the FPGA and DDR3 SDRAM are available. DDR3 SDRAM is also used for the main memory of the controller, which is described in the following. The PEACH2 chip also includes Altera's Nios II processor as a microcontroller. The controller that is small and low-power works only to monitor and configure TCA function.

In order to possibly reduce the routing overhead, the routing function in the PEACH2 chip is designed without table search and address conversion. Although PCIe uses a 64-bit address space, the host and the devices attached to the host use only limited areas of the address space, and there are many unused bit fields in 64-bits. In the PEACH2, the upper vacant bit fields in 64-bit address is used for specifying the destination node ID, and the destination port can simply be determined by comparing address range with the bit mask.

Due to the difficulty of the reasonable implementation for Memory Read Request, only Memory Write Request is available for the communication to the remote node in the PEACH2 by hardwired logic. Instead of Memory Read, the "proxy write" mechanism can realize the same effect with the driver support.

The PEACH2 provides two types of communication: PIO and DMA. PIO communication is useful for short message transfers, and the CPU can only perform the store operation to remote nodes.

A DMA controller with four channels is embedded in the PEACH2 chip. The DMA controller provides a chaining DMA function in order to transfer multiple data segments. In this function, multiple DMA requests by multiple DMA descriptors can be chained by a pointer on the host memory in advance. Once the top of the DMA descriptors is activated, DMA transactions are continued automatically according to the chain of the DMA descriptors by hardwired logic. Moreover, in order to eliminate the overhead for the transfer of the DMA descriptors, a small amount of DMA requests can be referred to as "register mode". In this mode, up to 16 of DMA requests can be registered to the DMA control register space on the PEACH2 in advance for a faster invocation. The DMA controller also permits a block-stride transfer which can be specified with a single descriptor.

For more detailed implementation of PEACH2 chip, please refer [13],[15].

Fig. 1 shows the PEACH2 board. The PEACH2 board is compatible with the PCIe board specification [21] and includes an edge connector with Gen2 x8 to be connected to the host CPU and three PCIe external cable ports at its edge to be connected to other nodes.

Most of the PEACH2 chip operates at a clock frequency of 250 MHz, which is the operating clock frequency of the PCIe Gen2 x8 logic block.

**Fig. 1.** Photograph of PEACH2 Production Board (Side View(Left), Top View(Right))

**Table 1.** Specifications of The HA-PACS/TCA

| Compute Node | |
|---|---|
| Motherboard | SuperMicro X9DRG-QF |
| CPU | Intel Xeon-E5 2680v2 2.8 GHz × 2 sockets |
| | (IvyBridge 10 cores + 25 M cache) / socket |
| Memory | DDR3 1866 MHz × 4 ch, 128 Gbytes |
| Peak performance | 448.0 GFlops |
| GPU | NVIDIA Tesla K20X 732 MHz × 4 |
| Memory | GDDR5 2.6 GHz, 6 Gbytes / GPU |
| Peak Performance | 5.24 TFlops |
| Interconnect | InfiniBand: Mellanox Connect-X3 Dual-port QDR |
| | TCA: PEACH2 Board |
| | (Altera Stratix-IV GX FPGA, PCIe Gen2 x8 / port) |
| System Speficiations | |
| Number of Nodes | 64 |
| Interconnect | InfiniBand QDR 108 ports switch × 2 ch |
| Peak Performance | 364 TFlops |
| Number of Racks | 10 |
| Maximum Power Consumption | 99.3 kW |

## 2.4  HA-PACS/TCA Cluster

HA-PACS/TCA system is built as an extension of HA-PACS base cluster as shown in Fig. 2, and it consists of five racks by two rows on the near side of this photograph.

Table 1 presents the specifications of the HA-PACS/TCA cluster. A total of 64 computation nodes is connected by two groups of IB QDR in the fat-tree configuration with full bisection bandwidth. Furthermore, each node is also connected by TCA.

The system achieves a peak performance of 364 TFlops. The system exhibited a good performance/power efficiency of 3.52 GFlops/W as the peak, and the system was ranked third on the Green500 list issued on November 2013 [10].[1]

---

[1] This record is made before the system is entirely equipped with PEACH2 board installation, and it is done only by IB interconnection.

**Fig. 2.** Photograph of the Entire HA-PACS System (HA-PACS/TCA: 5 racks ×2 rows, HA-PACS base cluster: other racks)

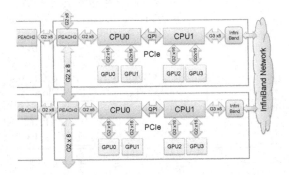

**Fig. 3.** Block Diagram of the Computation Node in HA-PACS/TCA

**Configuration of the TCA Compute Node.** As shown in Table 1, each compute node employs two sockets of an Intel Xeon E5-2680v2 (IvyBridge-EP) CPU and four NVIDIA K20X GPUs as the accelerator device.

Fig. 3 shows a block diagram of the data transfer in the compute node of HA-PACS/TCA. In this figure, each compute node is illustrated as a red-framed box. Each GPU is directly attached to the PCIe x16 slots from a CPU socket. Apparently, the PEACH2 board is inserted into another PCIe x8 slot independently from the GPUs. In this case, all of the devices, including GPUs, InfiniBand HCA and the PEACH2 board, also share a single PCIe address space logically, and the PEACH2 board can directly communicate with GPUs via the PCIe switch embedded in the Intel Xeon E5 CPU socket.

This configuration is similar to that of commodity GPU cluster, such as the HA-PACS base cluster, with the exception of the PEACH2 board. It means that an accurate comparison can be performed to investigate the advantages of TCA with the ordinary GPU cluster. Two of three external ports on the PEACH2 board are used to configure the ring topology (vertical arrows in the figure). A remaining port is used to combine two rings by connecting to the other PEACH2 board on the neighboring nodes (horizontal arrow).

Accessing the GPU memory from the other devices is normally prohibited, and a technology called GPUDirect Support for RDMA (GDR) provided by NVIDIA allows direct memory access through the PCIe address space under a CUDA 5.0 or above environment with a Kepler-architecture and Tesla-class GPU [19]. Once this feature enables the GPU memory at page granularity to be mapped to the PCIe address space, the devices on the same PCIe bus can access the memory directly. In practice, since we observed that the direct access over QPI between sockets degrades the performance significantly, we assume that PEACH2 only accesses GPU0 and GPU1 in Fig. 3. Recently, Mellanox also releases GDR solution named PeerDirect for InfiniBand OFED (Open Fabrics Enterprise Distribution) [16] collaborated with NVIDIA, and the same situation happens. In this configuration, the InfiniBand HCA can achieve good performance only by the use of GPU2 and GPU3 without the use of QPI.

## 2.5  Performance Results

We evaluated the basic performance of TCA communication using HA-PACS/ TCA. We develop two device drivers: the PEACH2 driver for controlling the PEACH2 board and the P2P driver for enabling GPUDirect Support for RDMA. We also evaluate the performance using a CUDA-aware MPI, MVAPICH2-GDR 2.0b for comparison. The detailed environment is summarized in the poster draft, and we use up to 16 nodes as a TCA sub-cluster for this evaluation.

Fig. 4(a) shows the ping-pong latency in the case of CPU-CPU and GPU-GPU using DMA, under small data size conditions. Using TCA, the minimum latency in the case of CPU-CPU is 1.9 $\mu$sec, and that in the case of GPU-GPU is 2.3 $\mu$sec. The overhead of GPU communication is 0.4 $\mu$sec, and it is caused by read operation from GPU memory. On the other hand, the minimum latency in the case of MVAPICH2 is 17 $\mu$sec. TCA result is 7.4 times better than MVAPICH2 in terms of the minimum latency on GPU-to-GPU communication. MVAPICH2-GDR is an improved version for latency using GPUDirect for RDMA on GPU-to-GPU communication. However, the latency is 6 $\mu$sec, and TCA performance is still 2.6 times better than MVAPICH2-GDR.

Fig. 4(b) shows the performance of the halo exchange pattern in the stencil computation. When the size of cubic array is $N \times N \times N$ with a contiguous memory for $k$ direction, the memory transfer on each halo plane can be described as follows:

- $jk$-plane: a block transfer with $N \times N$ of block size
- $ik$-plane: $N$ times of block-stride transfers with $N$ of block size and $N \times N$ of stride size
- $ij$-plane: $N \times N$ times of stride transfers with a single data block and $N$ of stride size

MPI are measured using `MPI_Type_vector` on the $ik$- and $ij$-plane. The maximum bandwidth is 2.7 Gbyte/sec at $N = 192$, and we could obtain better performance than MVAPICH2-GDR at message lengths up to $N = 320$

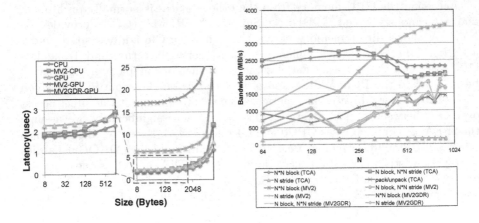

**Fig. 4.** Performance Comparison among PEACH2 and MPI+InfiniBand; (a) Ping-pong Latency (left), (b) Bandwidth on Halo exchange of $N^3$ cube (right) [CPU: CPU-to-CPU neighbor comm., GPU: GPU-to-GPU neighbor comm., MV2: MVAPICH2, MV2GDR: MVAPICH2-GDR 2.0a]

with 800 Kbytes. The effect of DMA chaining function shows a great performance gain in the case of block stride with $N$ block and $N$ stride ($jk$-plane) where the performance of TCA is 3x to 6x better than both MVAPICH2 and MVAPICH2-GDR.

## 3   Research and Development of Unified Environment of Accelerated Computing and Interconnection

Our project entitled "Research and Development on Unified Environment of Accelerated Computing and Interconnection for Post-Petascale Era" was adopted as the CREST program in the research area of "Development of System Software Technologies for post-Peta Scale High Performance Computing" by Japan Science and Technology Agency (JST) at Oct. 2012 and scheduled to continue for six years.

In this research, we will investigate the unified environment of accelerators and interconnection network for HPC system in post-petascale era. One of the serious performance bottlenecks of next generation of accelerated computing is the communication latency among accelerators especially for strong scaling, and we will provide the total solution for this problem from the hardware to application layer toward massively parallel accelerated computing systems in exascale era.

In practice, our research team studies the enhancement of PEACH2 and the development for the next generation of PEACH2, system software stack, high-level parallel programming language, and several application programs based on this concept.

## 3.1    Enhancement and Next Generation of PEACH2

Currently, we are implementing the hardware support such as the function offloading in the PEACH2 FPGA according to the characteristic of the application. In the current PEACH2 chip, the logic utilization is only 22%, and memory usage is 14% whereas the GXB (Gigabit Transceiver Block) resources are fully used for PCIe ports. Thus, we can utilize such free logic for the additional functions.

On the other hand, the current PEACH2 consists of Altera's Stratix IV GX and provides four PCIe Gen2 ports for connecting a host CPU and three neighbors to form a double ring network. Considering the next generation of PEACH2, we have discussed the design and implementation of a switching hub architecture with PCIe Gen3 using a common FPGA. We are developing the PEACH3 using Altera's Stratix V GX FPGA, and demonstrated the first empirical evaluation results with a PCIe Gen3 off-the cabinet network.

As the result, the data transfer between two PCs using PEACH3 with PCIe Gen3 ports was successful and 6.9 GB/sec bandwidth, and the evaluation results show its feasibility to achieve almost twice the bandwidth of PEACH2 [6].

## 3.2    XcalableACC: a Directive-based Language Extension for Accelerated Parallel Computing

To develop an application on accelerator clusters, programmers must use hybrid programming models in order to transfer data among nodes and to offload computations to accelerators. In general, a combination of MPI and one of the available accelerator programming models, such as CUDA, or OpenACC [1].

With the aim of replacing MPI, we have been engaged in the design and development of XcalableMP (XMP) [4],[17], which is a directive-based language extension based on the Partitioned Global Address Space (PGAS) [2] model.

Based on studies of XMP and OpenACC, we propose a new programming model called XcalableACC (XACC), which is an XMP extension that uses OpenACC for accelerator clusters. In XACC, programmers can use both XMP and OpenACC directives seamlessly. Therefore, XACC allows programmers to develop applications on accelerator clusters easily. In addition, the Omni XACC compiler provides functions that can transfer a halo region on accelerator memory via TCA for transferring data directly among accelerators efficiently.

We evaluate the productivity and the performance of XACC through implementations of the Himeno Benchmark. The results show that XACC requires less than half the source lines of code compared to a combination of MPI and OpenACC [18].

## 3.3    Applications Using TCA

Currently, we have been applying the TCA communication to several field of applications, including the numerical libraries, graph traversal problems, particle physics, astrophysics, and life sciences.

Here, we introduce an example applying TCA communication to QUDA, which is a Lattice QCD library for GPU. QUDA is an open-source Lattice Quantum Chromo-Dynamics (LQCD) framework library developed by Mike Clark et al. that supports NVIDIA GPU accelerators [8],[3]. Roughly speaking, there are two kinds of computations in QUDA: stencil computations in the Dirac operator and computations to solve linear equations using Krylov solvers.

The communication of QUDA is described by the abstraction layer, and mostly the MPI is used for the actual communication API. We have added TCA support to QUDA as an extension of the MPI [11].

The original QUDA uses send-receive semantics, i.e., a point-to-point protocol. On the other hand, since TCA supports Remote Memory Access (RMA) model, we need to change the communication structure of QUDA from its original point-to-point protocol. First, we rewrote QUDA's communication protocol using MPI-3 Remote Memory Access (RMA), and then, replaced the MPI-3 RMA APIs with the TCA communication APIs.

The results show that our solution significantly reduces communication latency compared with MPI. The execution time for Conjugate Gradient (CG) iteration in QUDA shows that the TCA implementation is 2.14x faster than peer-to-peer MPI implementation and 1.96x faster than MPI remote-memory access (RMA) implementation [11].

## 4  Related Work

The non-transparent bridge (NTB), which is embedded in the PCI-E switch, allows inter-node communication by means of a special function[12]. Several products based on NTB capability are released. However, the NTB is not defined in the standard of PCI-E and is incompatible with the chip vendors of PCI-E switches. The BIOS detection for NTB at the boot time causes many issues. On the other hand, PEACH2 only behaves ordinary device, and the link state can be determined independently.

APEnet+ is the original 3-D Torus network using FPGA[7],[23]. APEnet+ enables GPU direct copy over the nodes using Fermi-architecture GPUs. However, APEnet+ introduced different protocol from GDR, and our approach achieves better performance for the latency and bandwidth.

As mentioned in section 2.4, CUDA 5 and above programming environment for NVIDIA GPU provides GDR function with Kepler-class GPU[20]. This function enables the zero-copy communication between the InfiniBand Host Adaptor and GPUs referred to as PeerDirect for InfiniBand OFED [16]. PEACH2 also uses the same function and obtains the better performance regarding latency and bandwidth.

Recently, NVIDIA has announced NVLink as a proprietary IO interface. However, it is restricted to the wiring on a print circuit board, and we expect to continue the PCIe based architecture as a standard interface, such as PCIe Gen4.

# 5   Conclusion

In the present paper, we described a novel interconnect for direct communication among accelerators over nodes, referred to as the TCA architecture, and PEACH2 as an implementation of TCA architecture was presented. Also, the HA-PACS project and the CREST project were introduced, which supported our work.

Our future plan includes applying TCA architecture to Xeon Phi cluster and development of optimal hybrid communication framework between TCA and InfiniBand.

**Acknowledgments.** The authors would like to thank the members of the project offices of Exascale Computational Sciences and Exascale Computing System Development in the Center for Computational Sciences, University of Tsukuba. The authors would also like to thank Dr. Davide Rossetti, Dr. Dale Southard, and other members of NVIDIA and NVIDIA Japan for their helpful discussions and assistance. The present study was supported in part by MEXT special fund program for Univeristy of Tsukuba entitled "Research and Education on Interdisciplinary Computational Science Based on Exascale Computing Technology Development," and in part by the JST/CREST program entitled "Research and Development on Unified Environment of Accelerated Computing and Interconnection for Post-Petascale Era" in the research area of "Development of System Software Technologies for post-Peta Scale High Performance Computing."

# References

1. OpenACC. http://www.openacc-standard.org
2. PGAS - Partitioned Global Address Space Languages. http://www.pgas.org
3. QUDA - A Library for QCD on GPUs. http://lattice.github.io/quda/
4. XcalableMP Specification Version 1.2, November 2012. http://www.xcalablemp. org/spec/xmp-spec-1.2.pdf
5. Altera Corp.: Stratix IV Device Handbook. http://www.altera.co.jp/literature/ lit-stratix-iv.jsp
6. Amano, H., Kuhara, T., Kaneda, T., Hanawa, T., Kodama, Y., Boku, T.: A preliminarily evaluation of PEACH3: a switching hub for tightly coupled accelerators. In: Proc. of 2nd International Workshop on Computer Systems and Architectures (CSA 2014), in Conjunction with the 2nd International Symposium on Computing and Networking (CANDAR 2014), December 2014
7. Ammendola, R., et al.: APEnet+: high bandwidth 3D torus direct network for petaflops scale commodity clusters. Journal of Physics **331**(Part 5) (2011)
8. Clark, M.A., Babich, R., Barros, K., Brower, R.C., Rebbi, C.: Solving lattice QCD systems of equations using mixed precision solvers on GPUs. Comput. Phys. Commun. **181**, 1517–1528 (2010)
9. Dongarra, J., Meuer, H., Stromaier, E., Simon, H.: Top500 list. http://www. top500.org
10. Feng, W.C., Cameron, K.W.: Green500 list. http://www.green500.org

11. Fujita, N., Fujii, H., Hanawa, T., Kodama, Y., Boku, T., Kuramashi, Y., Clark, M.: QCD library for GPU cluster with proprietary interconnect for GPU direct communication. In: Lopes, L., et al. (eds.) Euro-Par 2014, Part I. LNCS, vol. 8805, pp. 251–262. Springer, Heidelberg (2014)
12. Gudmundson, J.: Enabling multi-host system designs with PCI Express technology, May 2004. http://www.plxtech.com/products/expresslane/techinfo
13. Hanawa, T., Kodama, Y., Boku, T., Sato, M.: Interconnect for tightly coupled accelerators architecture. In: Proc. of IEEE 21st Annual Sympsium on High-Performance Interconnects (HOT Interconnects 21), pp. 79–82, August 2013
14. Hanawa, T., Kodama, Y., Boku, T., Sato, M.: Tightly coupled accelerators architecture for minimizing communication latency among accelerators. In: The Third International Workshop on Accelerators and Hybrid Exascale Systems (AsHES2013) in Conjunction with IPDPS, pp. 1030–1039, May 2013
15. Kodama, Y., Hanawa, T., Boku, T., Sato, M.: PEACH2: FPGA based PCIe network device for tightly coupled accelerators. ACM SIGARCH Computer Architecture News **42**(4), 3–8 (2014)
16. Mellanox Technologies: Mellanox OFED GPUDirect. http://www.mellanox.com/content/pages.php?pg=products_dyn&product_family=116&menu_section=34
17. Nakao, M., Lee, J., Boku, T., Sato, M.: Productivity and performance of global-view programming with XcalableMP PGAS language. In: The 2012 12th IEEE/ACM International Symposium on Cluster, Cloud and Grid Computing (CCGrid 2012), pp. 402–409, May 2012
18. Nakao, M., Murai, H., Shimosaka, T., Tabuchi, A., Hanawa, T., Kodama, Y., Boku, T., Sato, M.: XcalableACC: extension of XcalableMP PGAS language using OpenACC for accelerator clusters. In: Proc. of Workshop on a Accelerator Programming Using Directives (WACCPD 2014), in Conjunction with SC14, pp. 27–36, November 2014
19. NVIDIA Corp.: Developing A Linux Kernel Module Using RDMA For GPUDirect. http://developer.download.nvidia.com/compute/cuda/5_0/rc/docs/GPUDirect_RDMA.pdf
20. NVIDIA Corp.: NVIDIA GPUDirect. http://developer.nvidia.com/gpudirect
21. PCI-SIG: PCI Express Card Electromechanical (CEM) Specification, Rev. 2.0, April 2007
22. PCI-SIG: PCI Express Base Specification, Rev. 3.0, November 2010
23. Rossetti, D., et al.: Leveraging NVIDIA GPUDirect on APEnet+ 3D torus cluster interconnect, May 2012. http://developer.download.nvidia.com/GTC/PDF/GTC2012/PresentationPDF/S0282-GTC2012-GPU-Torus-Cluster.pdf

# SPARTAN/SEXTANT/COMPASS: Advancing Space Rover Vision via Reconfigurable Platforms

George Lentaris[1]([✉]), Ioannis Stamoulias[1], Dionysios Diamantopoulos[1],
Konstantinos Maragos[1], Kostas Siozios[1], Dimitrios Soudris[1],
Marcos Aviles Rodrigalvarez[2], Manolis Lourakis[3], Xenophon Zabulis[3],
Ioannis Kostavelis[4], Lazaros Nalpantidis[4], Evangelos Boukas[4],
and Antonios Gasteratos[4]

[1] School of Electrical and Computer Engineering, NTUA, Athens, Greece
{glentaris,dsoudris}@microlab.ntua.gr
[2] Advanced Space Systems and Technologies, GMV, Tres Cantos, Spain
maaviles@gmv.com
[3] Institute of Computer Science, FORTH, Heraklion, Greece
{lourakis,zabulis}@ics.forth.gr
[4] Department of Production and Management Engineering, DUTH, Xanthi, Greece
{gkostave,agaster}@pme.duth.gr

**Abstract.** Targeting enhanced navigational speed and autonomy for
the space exploration rovers, researchers are gradually turning to reconfigurable computing and FPGAs. High-density space-grade FPGAs will
enable the acceleration of high-complexity computer vision algorithms
for improving the localization and mapping functions of the future Mars
rovers. In the projects SPARTAN/SEXTANT/COMPASS of the European Space Agency, we study the potential use of FPGAs for implementing a variety of stereo correspondence, feature extraction, and visual
odometry algorithms, all with distinct cost-performance tradeoffs. The
most efficient of the developed accelerators will assist the slow space-
grade CPU in completing the visual tasks of the rover faster, by one order
of magnitude, and thus, will allow the future missions to visit larger areas
on Mars. Our work bases on a custom HW/SW co-design methodology,
parallel architecture design, optimization techniques, tradeoff analysis,
and system tuning with Martian-like scenarios.

**Keywords:** Space rovers · Computer vision · Stereo correspondence ·
Feature extraction · Visual odometry · HW/SW co-design · FPGA acceleration

## 1 Introduction

Planetary exploration relies heavily on the navigational speed, accuracy, and
autonomy of the robotic vehicle employed in each space mission. Autonomy is

Projects funded by the European Space Agency (reference numbers
AO/1-6512/10/NL/EK, 4000103357/11/NL/EK, 4000111213/14/NL/PA).

important for overcoming the difficulty of tele-operation due to poor communication conditions. Accuracy is important for the safety of the billion-dollar cost vehicle and for performing precision scientific experiments. Speed, together with accuracy and autonomy, will enable the vehicle to explore larger areas on the planet during the lifespan of its mission and bring even more results/discoveries to the scientific community.

One major factor slowing down today's Mars rovers is their very slow on-board space-grade CPU. Due to physical constraints and the error mitigation techniques employed in radiation environments, the space-grade CPUs suffer from extremely low performance, i.e., achieving only 22 to 400 MIPS. When combined with the increased complexity of the sophisticated computer vision algorithms required for rover navigation, the space-grade CPUs become a serious bottleneck consuming several seconds for each step of the vehicle and decreasing its velocity to only 10-20m/h [1][2][3]. The most promising solution being considered today for the rovers of the future is reconfigurable computing and, more specifically, co-processing with space-grade FPGAs.

Space-grade FPGAs are already being used in several space missions, however, not for performing highly-complex Computer Vision (CV) tasks. These rad-hardened devices of Xilinx, Microsemi/Actel, and Atmel, are built on Flash, Antifuse or SRAM technology. Similar to their earthbound counterparts, they can outperform CPUs by allowing parallel computation, power-efficient architectures, and reconfiguration at run-time. The latter is of utmost importance in space missions, because it allows for multi-purpose use and repairing of hardware, which is located millions of miles away from the engineers and would otherwise be rendered useless. The benefits of remote programming and reconfiguration have already been demonstrated in practice for the Mars rovers (e.g., changing between flight/wake/dream modes, repairing high-energy particle glitches, etc). Energy efficiency is important due to the limited power supply of these rovers (e.g., power in the area of 100 Watts, during daytime). Parallel circuits are important for managing numerous sensors/controls concurrently and, in the future, for accelerating the calculation of demanding CV functions.

FPGA acceleration of CV algorithms for rover navigation on Mars is the primary objective of the projects SPARTAN (SPAring Robotics Technologies for Autonomous Navigation), SEXTANT (Spartan EXTension Activity), and COMPASS (Code Optimisation and Modification for Partitioning of Algorithms developed in SPARTAN/SEXTANT), of the European Space agency (ESA). The second objective, of equal significance with acceleration, is to improve the accuracy of the CV algorithms and assemble CV pipelines of increased reliability. The advent of high-density space-grade FPGA devices allows us to explore various HW/SW co-design possibilities for implementing and optimizing CV pipelines tailored to the needs of future Mars rovers. The options increase by considering single- or multi-FPGA approaches, on-chip softcores or off-chip CPUs, altogether with a variety of algorithms offering distinct cost-performance tradeoffs.

The algorithms considered in SPARTAN/SEXTANT/COMPASS relate to two very basic functions of the rover: *mapping* and *localization*, essentially 3D reconstruction and visual odometry, which are used to solve the more general SLAM problem. Simultaneous Localization and Mapping (SLAM, or in our case VSLAM, because we use Vision to tackle it), is the computational problem of constructing a map of an unknown environment while simultaneously keeping track of the rover's location within the environment. Typically, the rover is equipped with two stereo cameras of distinct characteristics (resolution, field of view, etc) to feed the *mapping* and *localization* functions. The 3D reconstruction part bases on stereo correspondence algorithms, which proceed by comparing the pixels recorded from the two views of the stereo camera to perform triangulation and deduce the depth of the scene. The visual odometry part proceeds by detecting and matching salient features between the images of the stereo pair, as well as between successive stereo pairs, the apparent motion of which is used to deduce the actual motion of the rover on the Martian surface. This feature-based approach to visual odometry breaks down to the sub-problems of accurate feature detection, sufficient feature description, correct feature matching, and robust egomotion estimation. The bibliography includes a plethora of computer vision algorithms for each one of the above sub-problems. The purpose of SPARTAN/SEXTANT/COMPASS is to explore a number of these algorithms and combine them in distinct visual odometry and 3D reconstruction pipelines, which we then partition into HW and SW functions, accelerate using FPGA(s), optimize, tune, and validate, for selecting the most efficient HW/SW solution for the future space rovers. In the remaining of the paper we give an overview of the work being performed in these projects, starting with the system specifications.

## 2   System Overview

### 2.1   Specifications and System Configuration

The Automation and Robotics group of the European Space Agency (ESA) determines certain specifications for the systems under development and provides valuable guidelines. In our case, the specifications include certain limits on the type and size of the HW to be used, on the execution time of the algorithms, as well as on the accuracy of the algorithmic results.

For the localization algorithms (visual odometry, VSLAM), the developed pipeline must process one stereo image per second. The images are input from a dedicated stereo camera, namely the "localization" camera. The distance between two successive stereo images during the motion of the rover will be 6cm. That is, the system must be able to sustain a rover velocity of 6cm/sec and travel 100m in 1667 rover steps. At the end of each 100m path, the output of the localization algorithm must have an error of less than 2m in position and 5 degrees in attitude. Regarding the 3D reconstruction (stereo correspondence algorithms), the developed pipeline must generate one 3D local map in 20sec. The map must cover a circular area of 120 degrees and 4m radius in front of the rover. For such an increased coverage, the "navigation" camera will acquire three high-definition stereo images in three distinct directions (left, middle, right) in front of the rover and, subsequently, we will generate and stitch three partial maps. The accuracy of the 3D maps must be better than 2cm even at 4m depth.

The arrangement of the rover cameras are depicted in fig. 1. The localization camera is placed close to the ground and is intended mainly for feeding the visual odometry pipeline. It has 1Hz sampling rate, a baseline distance of 12cm between its two monocular cameras, focal lengths of 3.8mm (pin-hole model), and image resolution of 512x384 with 8-bit pixels. Notice that, the algorithms will operate on greyscale values. The localization camera is mounted 30cm above ground level and is tilted by 31.55° with respect to the horizon. The monocular cameras are parallel to each other. Their field of view is 66° horizontally and 49.5° vertically. The navigation camera is placed higher, at 1m above ground, and has the ability to rotate left and right to acquire images at distinct directions. The two monocular cameras have a baseline distance of 20cm, focal length of 6.6mm (pin-hole model), are parallel to each other, tilted by 39° with respect to the horizon, and output images of 1120x1120 resolution with 8-bit pixels. The above stereo setups help us overcome the depth/scale ambiguity, while the given parameters help us tune the algorithms, and also, to generate synthetic image sequences for system testing.

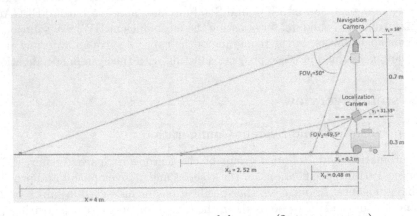

**Fig. 1.** Camera arrangement of the rover (2 stereo cameras)

The HW specifications limit the amount of processing power that can be employed by the system due to the nature of such space applications. At the same time, the HW specifications consider the potential capabilities of future HW components (these research projects refer to future space missions of 2018 and 2020+). Overall, the HW used in SPARTAN/SEXTANT/COMPASS is a hypothetical LEON-based space-grade CPU and a hypothetical space-grade FPGA of near-future technology; as a working hypothesis, based on current technology trends, the limits are set to 150 MIPS for the CPU (32-bit ISA, 512MB RAM) and to roughly 100K LUTs and 2MB on-chip RAM for the FPGA. Notice that, in the SPARTAN/SEXTANT/COMPASS projects, we avoid the increased price of actual space-grade devices by emulating them on conventional off-the-self components; to emulate the FPGA, we use a Xilinx XC6VLX240t-2 Virtex6 device, whereas to emulate the low-performance CPU, we use a Intel Core2-Duo CPU (E8400 at 3.00GHz), the time results of which are scaled by a factor of 18.4x (based on CPU benchmarking). Additionally to the single-FPGA solution, we examine multi-FPGA approaches and HW-HW partitioning on 2, 3 or 4 devices of lower performance (more conservative approach of future space-grade technology, e.g., 65nm process, 4-input LUTs, 0.8MB on-chip RAM).

Following the above specifications and recommendations of ESA, we built a proof-of-concept system consisting of a general purpose PC (scaled to 150 MIPS) and an actual Virtex6 evaluation board or a HAPS multi-FPGA board (four Virtex5 devices with predefined constraints on their resources). We develop a custom 100Mbps Ethernet communication scheme for the FPGA and the CPU to exchange data. We connect the cameras to the CPU and we also store a variety of test sequences on a hard disk drive for off-line use. We design a high-level software architecture in a three-level hierarchy. Level-0 interacts with the OS of the CPU and includes the kernel drivers (cameras, custom Ethernet) and the wrappers of the three most basic functions: imaging, mapping, and localization. Hypothetically, Level-0 also interacts with other parts/modules of the rover, e.g., the IMU sensor, the wheel encoders, navigation algorithm, etc. On top of Level-0, we build Level-1 to include all the C/C++ procedures of our vision algorithms. Finally, Level-2 includes a subset of the algorithms, i.e., the most computationally intensive, which are implemented on the FPGA.

## 2.2 Datasets

To evaluate and fine-tune the developed system, we perform several tests based on pre-recorded videos and stereo images resembling the Martian surface. ESA specifies a number of qualitative characteristics for the test images to comply with, i.e., they depict an arbitrary mixture of fine grained sand, rock outcrops and surface rocks of various sizes, with the percentage of each component ranging from 0 to 100% among frames. Visually, the images have rather diffuse lighting and low contrast, as is expected to be happening on the "red" planet.

The test sequences are recorded in natural Earth terrains of Martian appearance and in synthetic Mars-like environments. The former provide the highest degree of realism when it comes to image features, lighting conditions, content diversity, etc., which prove to be absolutely necessary for reliable system tuning and pipeline validation. The latter offer the advantage of 100% certainty when measuring errors (in a synthetic model, the position of every element in the environment is known a priori, with maximum accuracy), which proves extremely useful for detailed fine-tuning and accurate trade-off evaluations. Our tests combine both type of environments to exploit both of their advantages, and also, we use distinct sequences from each environment to exploit their diversity and examine as many situations as possible. Hence, the selected datasets:

- help us improve the developed HW/SW pipelines by exposing every potential error/problem (e.g., photometric/blurring variations between the stereo pair, intensity changes between frames, highly-varying amount of features, etc),

– they allow us to perform word length optimization and cover the dynamic range of all variables, safely, without overestimating their HW cost,
– they facilitate design space and/or algorithmic exploration to select the most efficient cost-performance pipeline by making detailed measurements
– customize the system to the visual content expected on the surface of Mars

The synthetic image test sequences are generated by 3DROV (fig. 2). 3DROV is a complete virtual simulator based on SimSat [4]. We feed the simulator with precise models of the rover (camera positions) and samples of known Martian environment. By simulating the actuation operations and data acquisition functions, we record thousands of successive stereo frames showing arbitrary 100m paths of the rover, as well as still-images of high resolution for testing our 3D reconstruction algorithms. Specifically, to test the localization algorithms (visual odometry, VSLAM), we generate three sequences of 1667 stereo frames each, with 512x384 resolution and 6cm between successive frames (fig. 3, upper row). To test the mapping algorithms (stereo correspondence, 3D reconstruction), we generate two sequences of 34 stereo frames each, with 1120x1120 resolution and depths ranging from 1 to 4m (similar content with fig. 3, upper row).

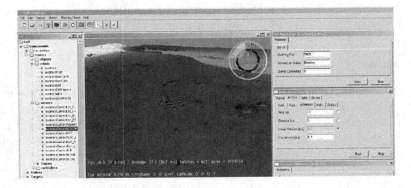

**Fig. 2.** 3DROV virtual simulator used to create synthetic Mars-like datasets

The natural image test sequences originate from three distinct places on Earth, which were carefully selected to resemble as much as possible the Martian landscape (fig. 3, bottom row). First, we use the video recorded on the Atacama desert of Chile, which was specifically designed to recreate Mars-like scenarios [5]. We use 1999 stereo images of 512x384 resolution and approx. 6cm distance between frames (the 334 are stationary). To make measurements with 100% certainty, we set the first 1000 frames to depict a forward rover motion and the remaining 999 to depict a backward rover motion (the previous frames played in reverse order), such that the rover ends up at its initial position. Second, we use the Devon island sequences [6], which are more challenging than Atacama and depict rover motion with approx. 19cm distance per frames on rough terrains with increased vibration. For Devon, we use the GPS measurements as groundtruth. Third, we use a custom video recorded in Ksanthi, DUTH, Greece, by using a stereo rig with the Bumblebee2 camera.It depicts a rocky and sandy landscape and it has been acquired under low lighting conditions with alow elevation angle of the sun. Also for DUTH, we use as groundtruth the data acquired with the Promark 500 Magellan Differential GPS.

**Fig. 3.** Sample frames from six distinct test sequences. Above: synthetic image datasets showing sand and rocks. Below: Natural image datasets form the Atacama desert in Chile (left), Devon Island in Canada (middle), Ksanthi-DUTH in Greece (right).

## 3   Related work and Overview of the Algorithms

The majority of the algorithms explored and accelerated by FPGA in SPARTAN/SEXTANT/COMPASS fall in two categories of Computer Vision: stereo correspondence and feature extraction/matching. The former algorithms are used for reconstructing the 3D scene in-front of the rover, i.e., for its *mapping* function. The latter are used to develop visual odometry pipelines and estimate the motion of the rover in a frame-by-frame basis during its path within the environment, i.e., for its *localization* function. For both categories, we perform algorithmic exploration and HW/SW implementation of multiple pipelines to evaluate their cost-performance and select the most efficient solution.

For stereo correspondence, we examine and implement two of the most widely used algorithms in the field: disparity and spacesweep [7][8]. Essentially in both cases, from an implementation point of view, the process boils down to comparing a region of left-image pixels to a region of right-image pixels (e.g., of size 13x13). The comparison will occur for all such regions within the two images in a full-search fashion, however, by taking into account the epipolar geometry of the stereo pair to decrease the search space of the correspondence problem. The details for fetching and comparing each one of the areas are determined by the algorithm. The distance of the areas matched between the two images (their disparity) determines the depth of the scene (via algorithm-specific calculations, e.g., triangulation) at all points of the image (dense stereo).

Feature detection, description, and matching are the tree algorithmic phases preceding the actual egomotion estimation of a feature-based visual odometry pipeline [9]. The egomotion estimation will input two point-clouds (set of 3D or 2D points of the environment, as captured by the camera and reconstructed by the CV algorithms) from two distinct positions/frames of the rover and will try to align them for deducing the motion of the rover (pose estimation of the translation/rotation parameters). For egomotion, we consider approaches such as the *absolute orientation* of Horn and the $SO(3)$ based solution of Lu, Hager and Mjolsness. Before employing egomotion, first, we detect salient features on each image, most often by examining its intensity gradients.We explore and implement well-known detection algorithms such as SURF [10], Harris [11], FAST [12]. Second, we describe each detected feature by processing its surrounding pixels to collect information in a succinct and resilient vector, most often a histogram based on the gradients' magnitude/orientation. We explore and implement well-known description algorithms such as SURF [10], SIFT [13], BRIEF [14]. Third, we match the descriptors between stereo images for triangulating and deducing their 3D coordinates, as well as between successive frames to feed the egomotion with the correspondences of the two point-clouds. We explore and implement distinct matching methods based on epipolar geometry and on Euclidean distance, Hamming distance, and the $\chi^2$ distance (from the $\chi^2$ test statistic).

## 4    FPGA Acceleration

The algorithms described in the previous section are used individually or in combination to form distinct pipelines for *mapping* and *localization*. For instance, we can use spacesweep to construct a dense 3D point cloud of the environment (mapping); or, we can put SURF detection/description, Euclidean matching and Horn's egomotion to estimate the visual odometry of the rover (localization). The execution time of the algorithms varies greatly with respect to their complexity and image content. In some cases, it exceeds by far the 20sec constraint of mapping (e.g., spacesweep requires approx. 1 hour on the space-grade CPU for processing 3 high-definition stereo images) or the 1sec constraint of localization (e.g., feature detection alone requires up to 2sec for one stereo pair). In other cases, it requires around 10 msec (e.g., Horn's egomotion). By analyzing their execution time, complexity, communication requirements, arithmetic precision, and the platform's characteristics, we develop a custom HW/SW co-design methodology to determine those kernels and/or sub-kernels that should be executed on CPU and those that must be accelerated by the FPGA for the pipelines to meet all time/accuracy/cost specifications of ESA.

To accelerate the most demanding kernels and at the same time avoid over-utilizing the FPGA resources, we propose HW architectures based on a number of diverse design techniques. First of all, to overcome the FPGA memory bottleneck, we perform decomposition of the input data on the CPU side and download each set to the FPGA, separately. Each set (e.g., a stripe of the image) is downloaded, processed, and then uploaded to the CPU, before the following set can be processed by re-using the same FPGA resources. Second, we perform pipelining at pixel basis, which accounts for one of the main reasons for achieving high speed-up factors. The nature of the image processing algorithms (repetitive calculations on successive pixels) allows for efficient design and increased pipeline utilization. Third, we design parallel memories allowing multiple data to be fetched at a single cycle and support the throughput of the pixel-based pipeline. Fourth, we parallelize the calculation of the mathematical formulas and support the throughput of the pipeline. Next, we explain the techniques by describing a representative example of our HW kernels: the SURF descriptor.

## 4.1   Architecture of the SURF Descriptor

The proposed architecture accelerates the Haar wavelet based processing part of SURF [10]. It utilizes both HW and SW modules (Fig. 4) to divide the area of each feature (interest point, ipts) in 16 smaller areas, which are then processed by the FPGA sequentially starting from the top and moving to the bottom of the image. Breaking down the problem of describing an interest point to describing several smaller boxes has a twofold purpose. First, we decrease the area required to be cached on the FPGA by almost $1/16^{th}$. Second, we reuse our HW resources by developing a custom sliding window: the on-chip memory of the FPGA stores only a horizontal stripe of the integral image, instead of 512x384 values, which is updated iteratively until the entire image is scanned downwards. Therefore, given that we detect ipts in 13 scales of SURF and that, in the worst case, the orientation of an interest point will be at $45^{\circ}$, the maximum height of an interest point's box is reduced to 130 rows (instead of almost the entire image height). Hence, our sliding window has a size of 512×130 integral values.

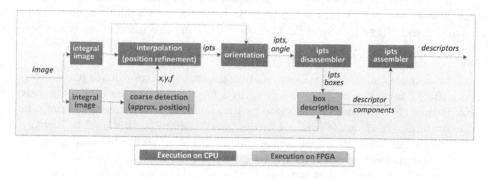

**Fig. 4.** Proposed HW/SW Partitioning of the SURF algorithm

To support the FPGA process, we perform certain SW modifications on OpenSURF. We develop the *Ipts Disassembler* component (Fig. 4) to divide each ipt to its 16 main squares, namely to its "boxes" (1 ipt = $4 \times 4$ boxes). The set of all boxes of the image (up to 1600) is sorted according to their $y$ coordinate.

This sorting allows the HW descriptor to process the boxes in order, i.e., to use a sliding window, which will always move downwards on the image unloading old data and reusing memory space. We implement a custom data structure on SW to sort and store the boxes in linear time: we use one 1-D matrix of lists containing stacks of boxes, which are grouped according to their $y$ coordinate. The data used to identify each box are transmitted to the FPGA starting from the left-most list. Upon completion of the FPGA, the *Ipts Assembler* receives the box descriptors and stores them within our custom data structure. Finally, it normalizes the HW results and forms the 64-value descriptor of each ipt.

The HW accelerator of SURF description consists of 7 components (Fig. 5): the *Boxes Memory* (BM), the *SampleX & SampleY Computation* (SSC), the *Component of Memories* (CM), the *HaarX & HaarY Calculator* (HHC), the *Gauss Computation* (GC), the *Box Descriptor Computation* (BDC) and the *Descriptors Memory* (DM). It processes the received boxes iteratively by moving its sliding window downwards on the integral image (by 1 row at each iteration) and describing all possible boxes lying on the central row of the window.

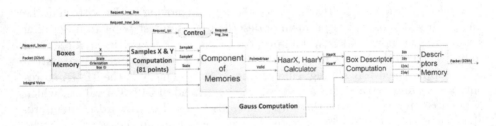

**Fig. 5.** Proposed HW architecture of SURF's Box Descriptor

The Box Memory stores all the information regarding the boxes to be described ($\{x, y, \text{scale, sin, cos, ID}\}$). Each 6-tuple is received in two 32-bit words and is unpacked and placed in a local FIFO memory. During execution, whenever a box description is completed, the CU will pop a new box from the FIFO to initiate the next box description, until the FIFO is empty.

The SampleX & SampleY Computation generates 81 coordinate pairs specifying the 81 neighboring "samples" required for the description of a single box [10]. It uses the information associated with each box (the 6-tuple) to compute $X = \text{round}(x + (-j \cdot scale \cdot sin + i \cdot scale \cdot cos))$, where $(i, j)$ is used to identify each sample and $X$ is its actual image coordinate ($Y$ is computed analogously).

The Component of Memories acts as a local cache of the integral values, i.e., it implements our sliding window on the integral image. During the description of a box, it inputs the aforementioned 81 sample coordinate pairs in a pipeline fashion and fetches 8 integral values per sample. The parallel memory will provide all 8 values with a single cycle access facilitating the high throughput computation of the HaarX-HaarY characterization of each sample (1 per cycle). The parallel memory storing the 512×130 stripe of the integral image utilizes 16 true dual port banks and is organized based on the non-linear mapping $BANK(x,y) = (x + y \times 3) \bmod 16$     and     $ADDR(x,y) = x \operatorname{div} 16 + (y \bmod 130) \times (512/16)$. The above organization allows for a single cycle access of the 8 integral values required for the computation of any Haar wavelet used by SURF (i.e., dx and dy responses), for up to 13 scales (besides scale 8), and from anywhere on the image. Note this this requirement implies random access to multiple rectangle-shaped patterns, and hence, increases the complexity of the organization.

The HaarX & HaarY Calculator inputs the 8 integrals coming from the parallel memory to calculate (add/sub) the HaarX and HaarY for each sample [10].

The Gauss Computation (GC) generates the values used to weight each one of the 81 samples. The generation bases on the distance of the sample from the center of its box. We decrease its hardware complexity by simplifying the rounding of the scale value and the coordinate pair used to calculate the exponential terms. As a result, we avoid implementing exponentiation and division circuits, we reduce the set of possible inputs for each sample to 13 or 25 numbers stored in LUTs , and we use only one multiplication for their final combination.

Finally, the Box Descriptor Computation inputs the HaarX & HaarY of the samples and weights them to produce the descriptor of the box. The box descriptor consists of 4 values, i.e. $\Sigma dx$, $\Sigma dy$, $\Sigma|dx|$, and $\Sigma|dy|$, which are computed via the summation of the 81 samples. The responses $dx$ and $dy$ are computed separately for each sample using 20 bit fixed-point multipliers. Specifically, for $dx$ (and similarly for $dy$), it computes $dx = \text{gauss\_weight} \cdot (-\text{HaarX} \cdot \sin + \text{HaarY} \cdot \cos)$.

## 4.2   Results

The accelerators are implemented on the XC6VLX240T-2 FPGA and the results show significant speed-up factors compared to the SW execution on the 150MIPS CPU. The speed-up ranges from 60x for feature detection to over 1000x for stereo correspondence. Such speed-up is necessary for meeting the time specifications of future rovers. The quality/accuracy of the FPGA output proves to be sufficient for the rover needs; by careful customization, it becomes comparable to the full floating point accuracy of the CPU, even though we tend to employ fixed-point arithmetic and do mild simplifications on the FPGA. The FPGA resource utilization per accelerator, due to our efficient architecture design with hand-written VHDL and customization/tuning, decreases to 7-21% of the FPGA slices, and to less than 1/3 of the on-chip memory. Specifically for the SURF Descriptor presented above, the processing of the boxes completes in 5ms for 200 features (ipts) by utilizing 4.3K LUTs, 5.7K registers, 13 DSPs, and 136 RAMB36.

## 5   Conclusion

The current paper presented an overview of the projects SPARTAN, SEXTANT, and COMPASS of the European Space Agency, which are part of the ongoing research to improve the autonomous planetary exploration rovers. Our work bases on single- and/or multi-FPGA acceleration and optimization of selected computer vision algorithms for advancing the localization and mapping skills of the future rovers. Ongoing results show significant speedup factors with improved algorithmic accuracy and quantify the benefits of using space-grade FPGAs for 3D reconstruction and visual odometry.

# References

1. Matthies, L., Maimone, M., Johnson, A., Cheng, Y., Willson, R., Villalpando, C., Goldberg, S., Huertas, A., Stein, A., Angelova, A.: Computer Vision on Mars. International Journal of Computer Vision **75**(1), 67–92 (2007)
2. Howard, T.M., Morfopoulos, A., Morrison, J., Kuwata, Y., Villalpando, C., Matthies, L., McHenry, M.: Enabling continuous planetary rover navigation through FPGA stereo and visual odometry. In: IEEE Aerospace Conference (2012)
3. Johnson, A., Goldberg, S., Cheng, Y., Matthies, L.: Robust and efficient stereo feature tracking for visual odometry. In: IEEE International Conference on Robotics and Automation, ICRA 2008, pp. 39–46, May 2008
4. Poulakis, P., Joudrier, L., Wailliez, S., Kapellos, K.: 3DROV: a planetary rover system design, simulation and verification tool. In: Proc. of the 10th Int'l Symposium on Artificial Intelligence, Robotics and Automation in Space (i-SAIRAS-08) (2008)
5. Woods, M., Shaw, A., Tidey, E., Pham, B.V., Artan, U., Maddison, B., Cross, G.: SEEKER-autonomous long range rover navigation for remote exploration. In: Int'l Symp. on Artificial Intelligence, Robotics and Automation in Space, Italy (2012)
6. Furgale, P., Carle, P., Enright, J., Barfoot, T.D.: The Devon Island Rover Navigation Dataset. Int'l Journal Robotics Research **31**(6), 707–713 (2012)
7. George, L., Diamantopoulos, D., Siozios, K., Soudris, D., Rodrigalvarez, M.A.: Hardware implementation of stereo correspondence algorithm for the exomars mission. In: 2012 22nd International Conference on Field Programmable Logic and Applications (FPL), pp. 667–670. IEEE (2012)
8. Szeliski, R.: Computer Vision: Algorithms and Applications. Springer (2010)
9. Scaramuzza, D., Fraundorfer, F.: Visual odometry [tutorial]. IEEE Robot. Automat. Mag. **18**(4), 80–92 (2011)
10. Bay, H., Ess, E., Tuytelaars, T., Van Gool, L.: Speeded-Up Robust Features (SURF). Comp. Vision and Image Understanding **110**(3), 346–359 (2008)
11. Harris, C., Stephens, M.: A combined corner and edge detector. In: Proceedings of the 4th Alvey Vision Conference, pp. 147–151 (1988)
12. Rosten, E., Porter, R., Drummond, T.: Faster and better: A machine learning approach to corner detection. IEEE Trans. Pattern Anal. Mach. Intell. **32**(1), 105–119 (2010)
13. Lowe, D.G.: Distinctive image features from scale-invariant keypoints. Int'l Journal of Computer Vision **60**(2), 91–110 (2004)
14. Calonder, M., Lepetit, V., Strecha, C., Fua, P.: Brief: binary robust independent elementary features. In: Daniilidis, K., Maragos, P., Paragios, N. (eds.) ECCV 2010, Part IV. LNCS, vol. 6314, pp. 778–792. Springer, Heidelberg (2010)

# Hardware Task Scheduling
# for Partially Reconfigurable FPGAs

George Charitopoulos[1,2], Iosif Koidis[1,2], Kyprianos Papadimitriou[1,2],
and Dionisios Pnevmatikatos[1,2(✉)]

[1] Institute of Computer Science,
Foundation for Research and Technology – Hellas, Heraklion, Greece
[2] School of Electronic and Computer Engineering,
Technical University of Crete, Chania, Greece
pnevmati@ics.forth.gr

**Abstract.** Partial reconfiguration (PR) of FPGAs can be used to dynamically extend and adapt the functionality of computing systems, swapping in and out HW tasks. To coordinate the on-demand task execution, we propose and implement a run time system manager for scheduling software (SW) tasks on available processor(s) and hardware (HW) tasks on any number of reconfigurable regions of a partially reconfigurable FPGA. Fed with the initial partitioning of the application into tasks, the corresponding task graph, and the available task mappings, the RTSM considers the runtime status of each task and region, e.g. busy, idle, scheduled for reconfiguration/execution etc., to execute tasks. Our RTSM supports task reuse and configuration prefetching to minimize reconfigurations, task movement among regions to efficiently manage the FPGA area, and RR reservation for future reconfiguration and execution. We validate its correctness using our RTSM to execute an image processing application on a ZedBoard platform. We also evaluate its features within a simulation framework, and find that despite the technology limitations, our approach can give promising results in terms of quality of scheduling.

## 1   Introduction

Reconfiguration can dynamically adapt the functionality of hardware systems by swapping in and out HW tasks. To select the proper resource for loading and triggering HW task reconfiguration and execution in partially reconfigurable systems with FPGAs, efficient and flexible runtime system support is needed [6]. In this paper we propose and implement a Run-Time System Manager (RTSM) incorporating efficient scheduling mechanisms that balance effectively the execution of HW and SW tasks and the use of physical resources. We aim to execute as fast as possible a given application, without exhausting the physical resources.

Our motivation during the development of RTSM was to find ways to overcome the strict technology restrictions imposed by the Xilinx PR flow [8]:

© Springer International Publishing Switzerland 2015
K. Sano et al. (Eds.): ARC 2015, LNCS 9040, pp. 487–498, 2015.
DOI: 10.1007/978-3-319-16214-0_45

- Static partitioning of the reconfigurable surface in reconfigurable regions (RR).
- Reconfigurable regions can only accommodate particular hardware core(s), called reconfigurable modules (RM). The RM-RR binding takes place at compile-time, after sizing and shaping properly the RR.
- An RR can hold one RM only at any point of time, so a second RM cannot be configured into the same RR even if there are enough free logic resources for it.

Our RTSM runs on Linux x86-based systems with a PCIe FPGA board, e.g. XUP V5, or on embedded processors (Microblaze or ARM) within the FPGA; it can be used on other processors and FPGAs. We validated the behavior of RTSM on a fully functional system on a ZedBoard platform executing an edge detection application [7]. We also created a simulation framework that incorporates current technology restrictions in order to evaluate our RTSM. The main contributions of this work are:

- an RTSM with portable functionality in its main core, capable to control HW and SW tasks in PR FPGA-based systems;
- dynamic execution of complex task graphs, with forks, joins, loops and branches;
- combination of different scheduling policies, such as relocation, reuse, configuration prefetching, reservation and Best Fit.

In the following two sections, we first discuss previous work in the field, and then we present the key concepts and provide details on the RTSM input and operation. Then, in Section 4 we offer a performance evaluation in a simulation environment and validation on a real FPGA-based system, and in Section 5 we summarize the paper.

## 2    Related Work

In one of the first works on hardware task scheduling for PR FPGAs, Steiger et al. addressed the problem for the 1D and 2D area models by proposing two heuristics; Horizon and Stuffing [1]. Marconi et al. were inspired by [1] and presented a novel 3D total contiguous surface heuristic in order to equip the scheduler with "blocking-awareness" capability [2]. Subsequently, Lu et al. created the first scheduling algorithm that considers the data dependencies and communication amongst hardware tasks, and between tasks and external devices [3].

Efficient placement and free space management algorithms are equally important. Bazargan et al. [4], offers methods and heuristics for fast and effective on-line and off-line placement of templates on reconfigurable computing systems. Compton et al., in a fundamental work in the field of task placement, proposed run-time partitioning and creation of new RRs in the FPGA [5]. However, the proposed transformations are still beyond the currently supported FPGA technology.

Burns et al., in one of the first efforts to create an operating system (OS) for partially reconfigurable devices, extracted the common requirements for three different applications, and designed a runtime system for managing the dynamic reconfiguration of FPGAs [6]. Göhringer et al. addressed the efficient reconfiguration and execution of tasks in a multiprocessing SoC, under the control of an OS [11], [12].

The managing of hardware tasks in partially reconfigurable devices by RTSMs is very interesting and active [9], and some efforts have evaluated the proposed scheduling and placement algorithms on actual FPGA systems [7], [11]. What seem to be missing are complete solutions that take into consideration all the current technology restrictions. In [11] the actual overhead of the scheduler compared to the execution time of each task is not calculated and also the reconfiguration time measured is the theoretical one, and the application execution is presented in a theoretical way. The run-time manager presented on [7] is able to map multiple applications on the underlying PR hardware and execute them concurrently and takes all restrictions in consideration; however the mechanics of the scheduling algorithm are simple and the overhead considerable.

# 3      The Run-Time System Manager

The RTSM manages physical resources employing scheduling and placement algorithms to select the appropriate HW Processing Element (PE), i.e. a Reconfigurable Region (RR), to load and execute a particular HW task, or activate a software-processing element (SW-PE) for executing the SW version of a task. HW tasks are implemented as Reconfigurable Modules, stored in a bitstream repository.

## 3.1     Key Concepts and Functionality

During initialization, the RTSM is fed with basic input, which forms the basic guidelines according to which the RTSM takes runtime decisions:

*(1) Device pre-partitioning and Task mapping:* The designer should pre-partition the reconfigurable surface at compile-time, and implement each HW task by mapping it to certain RR(s) [8]. This limitation was discussed in [6] and [7].

*(2) Task graph:* The RTSM should know the execution order of tasks and their dependencies; this is provided with a task graph. Our RTSM supports complex graphs with properties like forks and joins, branches and loops for which the number of iterations is unknown at compile-time.

*(3) Task information:* Execution time of SW and HW tasks, and reconfiguration time of HW tasks should be known to the RTSM; they can be measured at compile-time through profiling. A task's execution time might deviate from the estimated or profiled execution time so the RTSM should react adapting its scheduling decisions.
The RTSM supports the following features:

*(1) Multiple bitstreams per task:* A HW task can have multiple mappings, each implemented as a different RM. All versions would implement the same functionality, but each may target a different RR (increasing placement choices) and/or be differently optimized, e.g. in terms of performance, power, etc. A similar approach is used in [6], and accounts for the increased scheduling flexibility and quality [7].

*(2) Reservation list:* If a task cannot be served immediately due to resource unavailability, it is reserved in a queue for later configuration/execution. A HW task will wait in the queue until an RR is available, or it is assigned to the SW-PE.

*(3) Reuse policy:* Before loading a HW task into the FPGA, the RTSM checks whether it already resides in an RR and can be reused. This prevents redundant reconfigurations of the same task, reducing reconfiguration overhead. If an already configured HW task cannot be used, (e.g. it is busy processing other data, etc.), the RTSM may find it beneficial to load this task's bitstream to another RR is such a binding exists.

*(4) Configuration prefetching:* Allows the configuration of a HW task into an RR ahead of time [14]. It is activated only if the configuration port is available.

*(5) Relocation:* A HW task residing in an RR can be "moved" by loading a new bitstream implementing the same functionality to another RR, as illustrated in Figure 1. Two RMs are being scheduled for configuration into two RRs; RM1 is already configured in RR2. RM2 should also execute, so it is waiting to be configured, but its RR is not available. The proposed relocation mechanism first moves the HW task by configuring the RM1 to RR1, and then configures the RM2 to the now empty RR2. This differs from the previously proposed relocation mechanism [5]. To fully exploit the benefits of this approach context save techniques are needed [10].

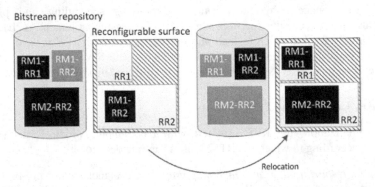

**Fig. 1.** RM2-RR1 does not exist, thus the hardware task laying in RR2 is relocated by first configuring RM1-RR1, and then RM2-RR2

*(6) Best Fit in Space (BFS):* It prevents the RTSM from injecting small HW tasks into large RRs, even if the corresponding RM-RR binding exists, as this would leave many logic resources unused. BFS minimizes the area overhead incurred by unused logic into a used RR, pointing to similar directions with studies on sizing efficiently the regions and the respective reconfigurable modules [13].

*(7) Best Fit in Time (BFT):* Before an immediate placement of a task is decided, the BFT checks if reserving it for later start time would result in a better overall execution time. This can happen due to reuse policy: when HW tasks are called more than once (e.g. in loops). For example, consider a HW task that is to be scheduled and already exists in an RR due to a previous request. Scheduling decision evaluates which action (reservation, immediate placement and relocation) will result in the earliest completion time of this task. For instance, BFT might invoke reconfiguration of a HW task into a new RR, even though this HW task (equal functionality, but different bitstream) already resides in another RR (but it is busy executing or has been already scheduled for execution).

*(8) Joint Hardware Modules (JHM):* It is possible to create a bitstream implementing at least two HW tasks, thus allowing more than one tasks to be placed onto the same RR. JHM, illustrated in Figure 2, exploits this ability by giving priority to such bitstreams, which can result in better space utilization and reduced number of reconfigurations. A similar concept was presented in [15].

The above features are incorporated in the RTSM, and have been tested within a simulation framework presented in the following Section. The combination of BFT with the Reservation list and their reaction with the Reuse policy constitute an interesting feature, leading the scheduler to hybrid decisions that potentially benefit an application. To this end, we believe it is important to study if complex techniques and features are actually required to serve efficiently different kind of applications.

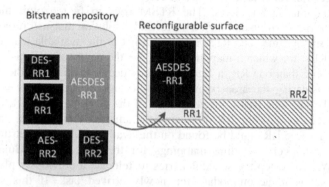

**Fig. 2.** Implementations for all crypto modules are available for and can be loaded into any RR, however a large amount of resources will be under-utilized. JHM utilizes more efficiently the RR area, given that the corresponding bitstream (the combined AESDES module) is available.

## 3.2   RTSM Input and Execution Flow

The input to the RTSM is the partitioning of the FPGA in partially reconfigurable HW-PE resources, the availability of SW-PE resources, the tasks to be scheduled, the task graph representation describing task dependencies, and the available task mappings, i.e. bitstreams for the different implementations of each hardware task, and tasks implemented in software that can be served by a SW-PE. Additionally, the RTSM needs the reconfiguration and execution times of each task, and optionally the task deadlines. This information is used to update the RTSM structures and perform the initial scheduling. We use lists to represent the reconfigurable regions (RR list); the tasks to be executed (task list); the bitstreams for each task (mappings list); and reservations for "newly arrived" tasks waiting for free space (reservation list). Since we do not consider random arrival times of tasks, we provide a definition by which a task is characterized as "arrived task": *If a task has completed its execution at time t=x, then the next in sequence dependent task as retrieved from the task graph has an arrival time $t_{arr}=x+1$.* During application execution the RTSM changes its scheduling decisions dynamically. Specifically, it reacts according to dynamic parameters such as the runtime status of each HW/SW task and region, e.g. busy executing, idle, scheduled for reconfiguration, scheduled for execution, free/reconfigured-idle/reconfigured-active region etc. Our approach is dynamic, i.e. at each point of time the RTSM reacts according to the FPGA condition and task status.

We structure the RTSM in two phases. In the first phase the RTSM continuously checks for newly arrived tasks. After the scheduling decision is made, the RTSM checks if the task can be served immediately and then whether the *Reuse Policy* can be invoked, and accordingly issues an execution or reconfiguration instruction. Then, it checks if a task has completed execution, and decides which task to schedule next according to the task graph. Finally, the RTSM checks if there are reserved tasks that should start executing.

The second phase is the main scheduling function of the RTSM. In order to reach a scheduling decision for a task, the RTSM follows a complex process, employing a variety of functions and policies. The RTSM tries to first exploit the available bitstreams in terms of space and then tries to find a solution that will provide the task with the best ending time. The RTSM creates a list of the available mappings and of the available RRs, for which a mapping exists, for the newly arrived task. If the later list contains more than one RR, a Best Fit policy decides which RR the task will be placed on, considering the area occupied by the task. Our scheduler will pick the bitstream of the task that best utilizes the area of the corresponding RR, i.e. it places the newly arrived task on the RR producing the smallest unused area, provided this RR is free. If no free RR could be found on the available RRs list, but there are free RRs that have no corresponding mappings for the task, the scheduler performs *Relocation*. With this step the scheduler tries to relocate a previously placed task to another RR so as to accommodate the newly arrived task. If this step is also unsuccessful, the scheduler will attempt to make a reservation for the newly arrived task, thus execute it at a later time.

Even if the scheduler finds a suitable RR for immediate placement, it will also perform a Best Fit in Time (BFT) in order to check if by reserving the task for later execution and reusing a previously placed core, the incoming task will finish its execution at an earlier time. It is important to note that the RTSM besides the RR and SW PEs, treats also the configuration controller as a resource that must be scheduled.

### 3.3   Tasks with Deadlines

For applications with task deadlines, the RTSM can consider them prior to taking scheduling and placement decisions. If no alternative -either via relocation, reservation or SW execution- can meet the deadline, the task is rejected. Note that the proposed relocation moves a HW task only if its deadline will be met. This feature is inactive in our current work, as we focus on applications that run in a streaming fashion.

### 3.4   Discussion

*Task reconfiguration and execution times:* These inputs can be derived through profiling, which may be done by the end user. It can also be computed using theoretical reconfiguration times and the HW bitfile size, while the execution time can be estimated by the compilation tools or can be provided by the programmer during the design phase of the application. This information is provided to the RTSM in its initialization. However, in practice, a task may execute for more than its predicted execution time, hence the RTSM should be notified when a task completes execution, so that it may revise its scheduling decisions dynamically.

*BFS:* The BFS aims to place a newly arrived task (implemented as bitstream) on the RR producing the smallest unused area. Without BFS, the size of an RM does not pose any restriction for loading it into a RR, given that such a bitstream exists. The programmer can disable this feature; however in all our experiments it is enabled.

*Size of RRs and RMs:* These parameters are defined at design-time and have fixed values. BFS reacts based on these parameters.

## 4    Experimental Simulation Framework, Testbed, and Results

We evaluated the RTSM within a simulation framework, and tested its correctness executing an edge detection application on the ZedBoard platform. To demonstrate all concepts described previously we also used the RTSM to control synthetic workloads.

Figure 3 shows the task graph that the RTSM will manage. In this Figure we express the HW/SW execution times and reconfiguration time in arbitrary time units in order to make the understanding easier. The task graph has one instance in which three tasks have more than one dependency, i.e. T3, T7 and T8, which results in join operations. Also, in T2 there are fork operations. The available resources consist of two RRs and one SW-PE, as well as the FPGA configuration port, which is also treated as a resource to be scheduled. Also, the RTSM accepts as input the width and height of each RR; these are used by the *Best Fit in Space* function.

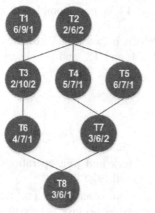

**Fig. 3.** Application task-graph annotated with HW and SW execution time and reconfiguration time for each task

**Table 1.** I RM-RR Bindings and required space

| Tasks | Mapping Characteristics | | |
|---|---|---|---|
|  | *#RR* | *Width* | *Height* |
| T1 | 1,2 | 1 | 2 |
| T2 | 2 | 1 | 3 |
| T3 | 2 | 1 | 3 |
| T4 | 1,2 | 1 | 2 |
| T5 | 1 | 2 | 2 |
| T6 | 2 | 1 | 2 |
| T7 | 1,2 | 1 | 2 |
| T8 | 1,2 | 1 | 2 |

Table 1 shows the available task mappings that drive the options of RTSM for making the best scheduling decision for a given task, e.g. T1 can be loaded either in RR1 or RR2. If a task has only one RR-RM, (e.g. T2) binding, options are limited. We assume that every task has a software implementation as well, in order to study how the RTSM reacts in exploiting both hardware and software resources, always to the advantage of the overall application execution time. It is important to note that the software implementation of a task has a longer execution time than the hardware one.

The scheduling result of the experiment presented is shown in Figure 4. In this execution most of the RTSM features were activated. Relocation is activated to accommodate task T2. Since Best Fit in Space (BFS) function has placed task T1 on RR2, in order to place task T2 on the FPGA, the RTSM first performs relocation and reconfiguration of task T1 on RR1, and then reconfigures T2 to the now empty RR2. Additionally, the decision to execute task T5 on SW-PE is due to the Best Fit in Time (BFT) function as a later reservation of task T5 on a RR gave a longer completion time.

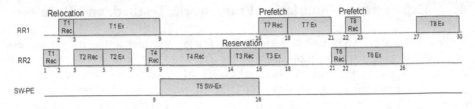

**Fig. 4.** The scheduling outcome of our example, showing features such as relocation, reservation and prefetching. The use of the SW version of task T5 completes faster the overall execution.

Also we can see the use of Reservation on the decision taken for task T3. The arrival time of task T3 is on t=10 and since the only available bitstream binds task T3 to RR2, there is no other option but to reserve task T3 for later execution on RR2. Note that the scheduler does not relocate task T4 to RR1, because T4 is near completion of its execution (otherwise it would restart its execution).

Finally, there is a high level of inner task parallelism between tasks of the same level but also from different levels, i.e. tasks T1, T2, T4, and T5, and we observe the use of configuration prefetching for tasks T7 and T8.

## 4.1   Discussion

In the example above we observe the following:

- The task graph is complex enough to demonstrate fork and join operations. We assumed multiple bitstreams per task to show the flexibility of RTSM.
- We demonstrated almost all RTSM features: relocation, reservation, prefetching, BFT and BFS. The reuse policy was not demonstrated as no task is repeated, nor does the task graph contain a loop. We also did not demonstrate the use of JHM, as we did not assume availability of such bitstreams.
- In Figure 4, we obtain that relocation takes place from the very beginning of the scheduling. This evidences that our approach is dynamic, i.e. at each point of time the RTSM reacts according to the FPGA condition and task status.
- We assumed that the SW-PE execution takes more time than the combined hardware execution and reconfiguration operation, prompting the scheduler to choose the hardware accelerator to program in the FPGA.
- Finally, we assumed that HW task execution time is 2-3 times larger than the reconfiguration time, to model fast reconfiguration times or coarser grain tasks.

## 4.2    Validating the RTSM with a Real-World Application

We validated the behavior of RTSM on a fully functional system on a ZedBoard platform executing an edge detection application [7]. Figure 5 shows the system architecture that features two ARM Cortex-A9 cores, two reconfigurable regions acting as the HW-PEs each of which is connected to a DMA engine, and a DDR3 memory. We used CPU0 for the RTSM and CPU1 as the SW-PE, executing SW tasks.

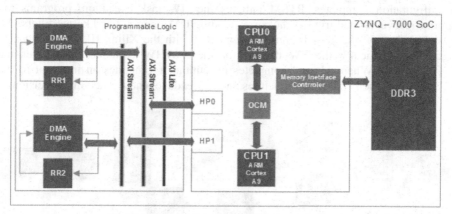

**Fig. 5.** System architecture of the Zynq platform

At system start-up, the system is initialized by the on-board flash memory; the boot loader initializes CPU0 with the RTSM code, sets-up CPU1 as the Processing Element (PE), and loads the initial bitstream in the programmable logic. Then the RTSM loads the application description (task graph, task information, task mappings, etc.) from the SD card. It also transfers the partial bitstreams from the SD to the main (DDR3) memory. During normal operation the RTSM takes scheduling decisions and issues tasks, on the SW-PE, i.e. CPU1, and the two HW-PE, i.e. RR1 and RR2.

The edge detection application consists mainly of four filter kernels executing in a sequence: Gray Scale, Gaussian Blur, Edge Detection and Threshold [7]. For these tasks, we have both a HW version as partial bitstreams, and a SW version; the RTSM will decide which version (SW or HW) is better to use based on the run-time availability of HW- and SW-PEs. The input image is loaded from the SD card, while intermediate images resulting after processing each task and the final output image are also written back to SD card. The transfer from and to the SD card is performed by SW tasks running on CPU1, which also controls partial reconfiguration of HW tasks. Figure 6 depicts the task graph of the application, showing only task dependencies but not how the application will execute over time. We also include the (implicit) SW tasks that perform the reconfiguration process.

The CPUs communicate with each other through the on-chip shared memory using two memory locations, one for each communication direction, using a simple handshake protocol (set and acknowledge/clear). One flag shows the PE status where a "-1" indicates that the PE is idle and the RTSM can issue any SW task to it; when the PE is busy, the flag indicates the task assigned, e.g. "2" for SW_imageRead, "3" for SW_imageWrite, etc. Once the PE completes the task execution, it informs the RTSM using the other flag indicating the type of the completed task.

In the system architecture of Figure 5, the two RRs are connected to the processing ARM cores through an AXI_Lite bus running at 75MHz, and through a DMA engine, each one having read and write channels on a dedicated AXI_Stream running at 150 MHz. The AXI_Stream is connected to the processor High Performance ports that provide access to DDR memory. To execute a HW task, the RTSM issues a reconfiguration command to CPU1, which in turn configures the FPGA with the corresponding bitstream through the PCAP configuration port. Once partial reconfiguration completes, RTSM initiates the HW task execution, programs the appropriate values and triggers the corresponding DMA engines and kernel filters. All HW mappings of the kernels were implemented with the Xilinx HLS tool that also creates automatically the SW drivers for the SW/HW communication over the AXI_Lite bus. When a kernel completes execution, it generates an interrupt to the RTSM, which then updates its structures and proceeds to a new scheduling decision.

**Fig. 6.** Edge Detection Application Task Graph

The RTSM operation can be broken down into different phases shown in Table 2. The Table also lists the total time spent on an ARM A9 Cortex CPU for each distinct phase, both in clock cycles and μs. The *RTSM initialization phase* is performed only once and it includes fetching from the flash memory the initialization file that describes the tasks the control flow graph and the task mappings, parsing it, and initializing the RTSM data structures. In the RTSM initialization time we do not include the overheads for loading the file from flash memory and for transferring the partial bitstreams to DDR3 memory. The *Schedule phase* refers to the time needed to execute the Schedule function in order to take a decision about the task to be executed next, i.e. when and where this task is going to be executed. The *Issue Execution phase* refers to the time required to issue either a reconfiguration or execution task instruction, depending on what the scheduling decision was. Also, depending on whether a HW core is reused, the RTSM checks if configuration prefetching can be performed. The *HW Task completion phase & SW Task completion phase* refer to updating the RTSM data structures after the completion of a HW or SW task, and to resolving the dependencies in order to set the next task in the graph as "arrived". Finally, the *Reconfiguration task completion & HW task execution issue phase* refer to the interval in which the RTSM receives a reconfiguration completion notification from the PE, issues a task execution command, and checks whether it can perform configuration prefetching of a not yet "arrived" task.

The overall execution time of the application was measured to be 129.62 ms, while the total RTSM overhead derived from Table 2 is 0.112 ms. The theoretical reconfiguration overhead, given that PCAP has a throughput of 400MB/sec, is 0.6 ms.

This is added only once, since in the rest cases of our example configuration prefetching takes place and hides the reconfiguration overhead with HW execution. However, since we use a SW task to perform reconfiguration, the throughput is considerably lower at 50MB/sec, increasing the reconfiguration cost to 5ms. Still, compared to the total execution time of application, this overhead is negligible.

**Table 2.** Time per each distinct phase of the RTSM, running on ARM A9 at 667MHz

| RTSM phases | #Clock Cycles | Elapsed time (µs) |
|---|---|---|
| RTSM Initialization | 7,707 | 23.121 |
| Schedule | 17,346 | 52.038 |
| Issue Execution | 5,995 | 17.985 |
| HW Task completion | 2,493 | 7.479 |
| Reconfiguration task completion & Hardware task execution issue | 1,224 | 3.672 |
| SW Task completion | 2,748 | 8.244 |

Finally, we compare the performance of our system with the one presented in [7]. That work used the same application running on a Xilinx Virtex-5 FPGA and reported a throughput of 18 fps for a 640x480 image. In our case, we used a 1920x1080 image, and we measured a throughput of 7 fps. By converting the two results into pixels per second throughput, our system is faster by a factor of 2.6. Since the two platforms are quite different, a direct comparison is not easy; for example in the Zynq we use the ARM hard processors while the V5 supports only soft-core MicroBlaze processors.

Regarding portability, our initial RTSM was developed on an x86 ISA desktop; porting it to the ARM architecture required only (i) cross-compiling the code, and (ii) the re-implementation of architecture specific drivers and communication protocols between the RTSM and the Processing Elements.

# 5    Conclusions

We presented a run-time system to efficiently schedule HW and SW tasks in systems with partially reconfigurable FPGAs. We plan to develop complex use-cases, e.g. task graphs with branches and loops that will allow for demonstrating and evaluating all the features of RTSM on actual FPGA platforms. One obstacle to this effort (by us and other researchers) is the lack of standard interface across different applications, and designers have to manually intervene to adjust the RTSM and the task application interfaces, according to the specifics of each platform. Our RTSM relieves the designer from the task invocation complexities; he/she only has to address the task data interface with the core part of the RTSM.

**Acknowledgment.** This work was supported by the European Commission FP7 FASTER project (#287804) and the HiPEAC Network of Excellence (#287759). We also thank Marco Santambrogio and NECST Lab from the Politecnico di Milano for providing the initial image processing (Edge Detection) application.

# References

1. Steiger, C., Walder, H., Platzne, M.: Operating Systems for Reconfigurable Embedded Platforms: Online Scheduling of RealTime Tasks. IEEE Transactions on Computers **53**(11) (2004)
2. Marconi, T., Lu, Y., Bertels, K., Gaydadjiev, G.: 3D compaction: a novel blocking-aware algorithm for online hardware task scheduling and placement on 2d partially reconfigurable devices. In: Sirisuk, P., Morgan, F., El-Ghazawi, T., Amano, H. (eds.) ARC 2010. LNCS, vol. 5992, pp. 194–206. Springer, Heidelberg (2010)
3. Lu, Y., Marconi, T., Bertels, K.L.M. Gaydadjiev, G.N.: A communication aware online task scheduling algorithm for FPGA-based partially reconfigurable systems. In: Proc. of the IEEE Symposium on Field-Programmable Custom Computing Machines (2010)
4. Bazargan, K., Kastner, R., Sarrafzadeh, M.: Fast Template Placement for Reconfigurable Computing Systems. IEEE Design and Test of Computers **17**(1), 68–83 (2000)
5. Compton, K., Li, Z., Cooley, J., Knol, S., Hauck, S.: Configuration Relocation and Defragmentation for Run-Time Reconfigurable Systems. IEEE Trans. on VLSI, **10**(3) (2002)
6. Burns, J., Donlin, A., Hogg, J., Singh, S., de Wit, M.: A dynamic reconfiguration run-time system. In: Proc. of the 5th Annual IEEE Symposium on Field-Programmable Custom Computing Machines (1997)
7. Durelli, G., Pilato, C., Cazzaniga, A., Sciuto, D., Santambrogio, M.D.: Automatic run-time manager generation for reconfigurable MPSoC architectures. In: 7th International Workshop on Reconfigurable Communication-centric Systems-onChip (ReCoSoC) (2012)
8. Lysaght, P., Blodget, B., Mason, J., Young, J., Bridgford, B.: Invited paper: enhanced architectures, design methodologies and CAD tools for dynamic reconfiguration of xilinx FPGAs. In: Proc. FPL 2006, pp. 1–6 (2006)
9. Bauer, L., Grudnitsky, A., Shafique, M., Henkel, J.: PATS: a performance aware task scheduler for runtime reconfigurable processors. In: Proc. of IEEE Symposium on Field-Programmable Custom Computing Machines (FCCM) (2012)
10. Morales-Villanueva, A., Gordon-Ross, A.: On-chip context save and restore of hardware tasks on partially reconfigurable FPGAs. In: Proc. of IEEE Symposium on Field-Programmable Custom Computing Machines (FCCM) (2013)
11. Göhringer, D., Hübner, M., Nguepi Zeutebouo, E., Becker, J.: Operating System for Runtime Reconfigurable Multiprocessor Systems. Int. J. Reconfig. Comp. **2011** (2011)
12. Göhringer, D., Werner, S., Hübner, M., Becker, J.: RAMPSoCVM: runtime support and hardware virtualization for a runtime adaptive MPSoC. In: Proc. FPL 2011, pp. 181–184 (2011)
13. Conger, C., Gordon-Ross, A., George, A.D.: Design framework for partial run-time FPGA reconfiguration. In: ERSA 2008, pp. 122–128 (2008)
14. Li, Z., Hauck, S.: Configuration prefetching techniques for partial reconfigurable coprocessor with relocation and defragmentation. In: FPGA 2002, pp. 187–195 (2002)
15. Vipin, K., Fahmy, S.A.: Architecture-aware reconfiguration-centric floorplanning for partial reconfiguration. In: Choy, O.C., Cheung, R.C., Athanas, P., Sano, K. (eds.) ARC 2012. LNCS, vol. 7199, pp. 13–25. Springer, Heidelberg (2012)

# SWAN-iCARE Project: On the Efficiency of FPGAs Emulating Wearable Medical Devices for Wound Management and Monitoring

Vasileios Tsoutsouras[1](✉), Sotirios Xydis[1], Dimitrios Soudris[1], and Leonidas Lymperopoulos[2]

[1] ECE Department, National Technical University of Athens, Athens, Greece
billtsou@microlab.ntua.gr
[2] EXUS, 73-75 Mesogeion Av and Estias Str 1, 115 26 Athens, Greece

**Abstract.** In this paper we examine the efficiency of FPGA-based reconfigurable systems for emulating complex embedded medical devices. We focus our analysis on embedded wearable medical devices targeting remote wound monitoring and management. The application scenario originates from the Swan-iCare EU funded project which aims at developing an integrated autonomous device for the monitoring and personalized management of chronic wounds, mainly diabetic foot ulcers and venous leg ulcers. Taking into account the functional requirements of such medical systems, we show that FPGA based functional emulation forms a promising solution that enables easy programming of bare-metal medical applications with micro-architectural and port connectivity/availability characteristics matching well the requirements of the specific application domain. The hardware platform and the embedded software for the supported medical application are described in detail and a set of qualitative and quantitative evaluations are provided to show the effectiveness of the approach.

## 1 Introduction

In recent years there has been an increased focus on getting patients out of the hospital and back into their own homes as soon as possible. To reach these goals, new technologies that enable and assist this transfer have to be developed. SWAN-iCare[1] project aims to achieve these goals for the case of chronic wound management, i.e. venous leg ulcers, and diabetic foot ulcers. Chronic venous insufficiency and leg ulcers affect approximately 1-2 people per 1000 of the general population, with approximately 10-20 people per 1,000 ever affected. In addition, approximately 1-4% of those with diabetes will develop a foot ulcer annually, and approximately 15% of those with diabetes will develop at least one foot ulcer during their lifetime [1], [2].

---

[1] Swan-iCare: Smart wearable and autonomous negative pressure device for wound monitoring and therapy, EU funded project, contract no FP7-ICT-20011-8. This work is funded by the aforementioned project.

© Springer International Publishing Switzerland 2015
K. Sano et al. (Eds.): ARC 2015, LNCS 9040, pp. 499–510, 2015.
DOI: 10.1007/978-3-319-16214-0_46

The Negative Pressure Wound Therapy (NPWT) is increasingly applied in hospitals to treat this kind of chronic wound and performs by removing exudate and potentially infectious material, promoting also the formation of granulation tissue thus accelerating the wound healing. At the moment, the healthcare costs of NPWT are relatively high since it necessitates hospitalization and medical acts. Although, there are many reasons for hospitalization; some patients who require NPWT are hospitalized simply because they require constant monitoring and immediate access to wound care specialists. This means that the total health care costs for the application of NPWT in this particular group of patients are relatively high despite decreasing prices of the NPTW systems themselves. Recently, portable NPWT systems have been developed and commercialized, providing several advantages for the patients such as discreteness and ease of operation. *However, these devices still only offer the single service of negative pressure on the wound and basic vacuum control.*

To enable monitoring and treatment of patients in their own home environment or long term care, the SWAN-iCare project [3] aims to develop a Smart Negative Pressure Device (SNPD). SNPD will integrate non-invasive sensors that allow objective, continuous, real-time monitoring of critical parameters with personalized therapy tailored to supporting the patients wound condition. In addition, the device will have the potential to remotely release active agents to assist in the wound healing process. SNPD will i) collect data and monitor several wound parameters via non-invasive integrated micro-sensors ii) offer the opportunity to provide innovative personalized therapy in combination with the negative pressure wound therapy, iii) allow health care providers to be remotely aware of the patient's condition and receive alerts highlighting situations that require direct actions

Such complex wearable devices require large cycles of design, analysis and validation of the employed hardware (HW) and software (SW) components. The traditional design approach that serialize hardware and software development is usually very time consuming, especially within the context of innovative research projects in which portion of time is allocated on defining the initial system design. Pure software simulation suffers from long simulation times, while at the same time it requires severe deprecation of the original code, since many components. e.g. bluetooth devices, user IF etc, are not efficiently/realistically modelled. In order to enable an early functional prototyping of the embedded medical application, in this paper we propose FPGAs to be used as preliminary emulation frameworks for medical devices. We show how the proposed emulation framework instantiated the HW and SW coefficients defined within the original prototype of the SNPD device. We evaluate the proposed approach both qualitatively regarding to the coverage of the functional requirements, as well as qualitatively regarding to the evaluation of design decisions faced during the design of the original device.

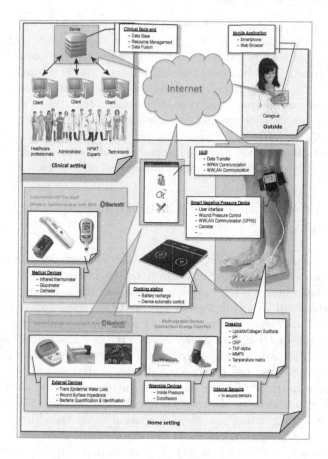

**Fig. 1.** Architecture of SWAN-iCare eco-system

## 2  SWAN-iCare System Architecture

Figure 1 shows the overall architecture of the SWAN-iCare System as well as the localization of the respective sensors for wound healing/monitoring. The infrastructure is composed of a set of subsystems namely: (i) the Clinical Back-End integrated to the hospital infrastructure which includes the back-end server where the application and database run, and one or many front-ends, where the users can interact with the system, according to their assigned roles, (ii) the Mobile Client for enabling access the Patient data on the Server, (iii) the Home Device Area Network, i.e. the Hub and one or more Stationary Medical Devices, one or more Wearable Devices and one or more External Devices, which will link to the Back-End by means of the Hub, and the (iv) Smart Negative Pressure Wearable Device that applies the negative pressure wound therapy, and provides monitoring information as well as warning and alarms to both the patient and the clinical back-end.

We further describe the Smart Negative Pressure Wearable Device (SNPWD), which is the focus of this paper. It is composed of the Smart Negative Pressure Device (SNPD), which is non-disposable and comes with a disposable part (Canister, Tubing, Dressing and Integrated Multi-Sensors). SNPD controls the pressure of a pump used to extract the excess of exudate generated by the wound and collects it in a canister or a waste bag. The device also integrates an activity sensor, and electronic interface for reading real-time values from the integrated multi-sensors, i.e. MMPs, CRP and TNF-alpha, pH and wound temperature sensors. The monitored data from the SNPD's integrated multi-sensors will be utilized for real-time evaluation of the wound inflammation and infection levels.

## 3  Requirements of a HW Emulation Platform for SNPWD

Designing embedded software for a wearable device, especially in the absence of an operating system, is directly coupled to the hardware, since there is no intermediate layer between the high level tasks and the low level software. The operating system will be substituted by a series of low level drivers implemented in order to provide means to the high level software to control the underlying software. This inherently creates dependence in the development of the high level software. To enable early development, avoid the dependence with the SNPWD hardware prototype and the unexpected delays related to hardware assembly cycle, an emulation device for the high level software has been used with hardware characteristics close to the original specifications of the SNPWD. In this way, issues regarding timing and communication could be addressed and software architectural design choices could be validated and re-evaluated in case of inability to meet specific requirements. The emulation platform should at least satisfy the two following requirements:

i  The hardware architectural features of the emulation device should match those of SNPWD.
ii  The emulation platform must provide modules and means to facilitate the highest amount of hardware related modules described in the SNPWD hardware design.

In an effort to determine the best available platform to realize the SNPWD emulator, several options were examined. The basic qualitative selection criteria are i) the ease of the platform to be programmed in the absence of an OS, ii) the similarity of the CPU of the platform compared to the specifications of the CPU of SNPWD and iii) the available I/O interfaces in order to facilitate the building blocks of the SNPWD emulator. Specifically, we compare the cases of i) pure software emulation on personal desktop computers, ii) emulation using ARM-based embedded platforms with slow and fast cores and enriched peripheral hardware components (e.g. BeagleBoard[7]) and iii) reconfigurable FPGA devices. Table 1 reports the pros (+) and cons (-) of each device solution according to the desired qualitative criteria. As shown, the fine-grained emulation efficiency of FPGA devices fulfil the necessary requirements for building

**Table 1.** Selection criteria and scoring for SNPWD emulation

| | Ease of programming w/o OS | uArch and performance close to original SNPWD | PCB port availability for high connectivity |
|---|---|---|---|
| SW emulation | + | - | - |
| Fast processors | - | - | - |
| Slow processors | + | + | - |
| FPGA | + | + | + |

up the SNPWD system emulator, making possible to incorporate or simulate almost all peripheral devices of the SNPWD and develop the high level software in environment without the presence of an operating system.

## 4    Description of the FPGA-Based Emulation Platform for SNPWD

Figure 2 shows a photograph of the HW emulation platform, annotated with the specific components used to resemble the original SNPWD hardware. The basic element of the HW emulation platform is a Xilinx Spartan-III FPGA device[4]. The Spartan-III FPGA instantiates the control microprocessor and every interface of the peripheral devices is connected to it. We synthesize the MicroBlaze, a soft-core IP processor, provided by Xilinx. It is a RISC processor with 3-stage pipeline and clock frequency up to 50 MHz. Microblaze supports architectural parameters customization thus enabling exploration of differing design configurations to be performed, in order to tailor the design to the characteristics of the application's SW components.

The FPGA comes as a subset of a rich development kit which provides many on-board modules and extension interfaces around which the components of the SNPWD will be emulated. The on-board Ethernet module of Spartan-III has been used to implement the communication of the embedded device with clinical Back-end server. The LWIp tcp/ip protocol stack[8] was used and the processing of the packets was a task which was handled by the main processor. The communication between the on-wound sensors and the SNPWD will be performed in a wireless way using Bluetooth Low Energy (BLE) protocol. In the presented prototype an external BLE transceiver from dialog-semiconductor[9] was used to simulate this type of communication. Since development time is an essential parameter, the transceiver was not fully incorporated into the FPGA since all the communication interface between these two components would have to be replicated and this is out of the scope of the emulation framework. A desktop computer was used, which executed the Bluetooth stack building the transceiver. This software was customized to forward all the incoming sensor readings to a serial port which was connected to the main processor of the SPARTAN-III FPGA. This is quite close to the real SNPWD hardware, in which the embedded Bluetooth transceiver also communicates with the main processor using a UART interface.

As far the User Interface is concerned, a set of buttons on the SPARTAN-III kit were used as input. The output was (i) the SPARTAN-III LCD display

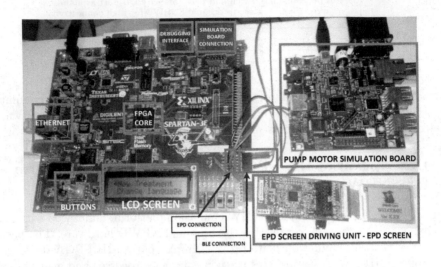

**Fig. 2.** The components of the HW emulation platform

and (ii) an external ePaper display[6], the same used in the original SNPWD platform. The integrated ePaper Display was the 1.44 EPD panel of Pervasive Displays. To reduce complexity, the processor of the FPGA communicates via UART interface with an external board which runs the EPD firmware and on which the EPD is connected. The main processor sends data and commands to this board using a protocol designated by the firmware of the latter.

Finally, the HW emulation framework integrates a software module for the pump speed controller, which forms one of the most critical components of the SNPWD functionality. To maximize flexibility and avoid burdening the emulation framework with extra hardware, the decision was made to create a model of a pump, driven by a DC motor and to program another embedded board, external to the FPGA, to simulate the behaviour of the motor in real time. The additional advantage of this choice is that it requires a simple control loop to be implemented thus simulating to a certain extend the final control mechanism of the SNPWD where the high level software will designate a certain pump reference point and it will be the task of dedicated hardware, external to the main processor, to appropriately control the speed of the dc motor in order to achieve that reference point. The communication of the pump motor simulation board and the main processor synthesized on the FPGA is also performed via a UART interface.

## 5    The Embedded SW Application

The embedded SW application of the SNPWD medical device will be responsible for the control of all the systems on the device. To further describe the

SW application, the term task will be employed, to group a number of functions related to a specific sub-system of the device. Task grouping enables the implementation of a finite state machine of the interactions and priorities of tasks. The supported main tasks are: i) start-up system check & calibration tasks, ii) User Interface tasks, iii) communication tasks, iv) reading sensor data tasks, v) sensor data fusion, vi) pump flow control tasks

The logic behind the combination and succession of all the events inside the high level software of the SNPWD is implemented by the task management engine, which eventually is the core of the embedded SW application. The overview of the task management logic is depicted Figure 3 as a Finite State Machine. The rectangles with round edges correspond to tasks and their interior is described by other FSMs. The pump control interrupt service routing is also depicted in the same format given that it is big enough to be considered a separate task. The rest of the interrupt service routines are considered a separate state due to their small size and simple internal structure.The events handled by this engine can be categorized in three basic categories:

i Periodic events which take place in predefined intervals in an interrupt driven way. The main periodic task and a most descriptive case of one is the pump control engine. The interrupt driven manner of their execution is highlighted because this feature ensures that their periodic constraints are met. This contradicts to normal task execution which is bound by a periodicity but not as strict since it is highly affected by elapsed time in the execution of asynchronous events.

ii Asynchronous events referring to interrupt driven events whose occurrence is highly unpredictable. For example, there can be an estimation about when a sensor is expected to provide new data but the exact moment is totally stochastic.

iii Main program tasks which group functions related to a specific operation required by the device i.e. the UIF management task encapsulates all the necessary functions to provide information to and control the hardware modules which compose the UIF front-end of the SNPWD. The succession of these tasks is designated both in periodic manner and as a consequence of other events.

A SW sensor data fusion engine is integrated with the SW application for evaluating and combining the data sampled by the various sensors. The fusion engine can generate either alarms, related to the detection of mechanical malfunctions, or warnings related to the detection of medical related critical situations. The architecture of the data fusion engine consists of four levels:

– **Level 1:** This level is responsible for identifying hardware malfunction problems related to sensors. Due to the criticality of a medical system, this level produces alarms to protect the patient from the possible harm of a malfunctioning medical apparatus. An example of a malfunction would be a pH sensor to indicate value greater than 14.

– **Level 2:** In this level, a warning is produced whenever the input of the sensor is extreme according to the expected range indicated by the medical experts. In other words, a pH value of 13 is correct in terms of normal sensor operation but it is not likely to be acquired in a wound tissue.

– **Level 3:** In this case, measured values are within expected range but also within the range of what the medical experts believe to indicate a deteriorating course for the status of the wound.

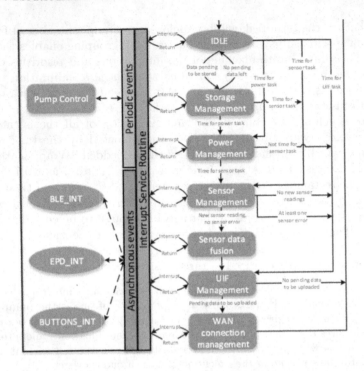

**Fig. 3.** The interrupt handling and task management engine

– **Level 4:** This final level incorporates modern data management and classification algorithms which enable the system to infer the status of the wound using complex correlations of sensor data. These correlations are probably impossible to be discovered by mere inspection of data and as a consequence the use of these analytical tools is imperative. The encoded medical conditions that suggest an alarm or warning generation can be found in [10]. These directives were used to create an artificial labelled data set which in turn was used to train machine learning algorithms and the subset of the algorithms that achieved an acceptable classification accuracy threshold, where tested to discover whether their computational needs are met by the hardware resources. Eventually, the classification algorithms used where Neural Networks (NN), Support Vector Machines (SVM) and Decision Trees (D. Trees) [5].

The controller algorithm was chosen to be a PI controller in order to ensure the stability of the control by sacrificing settling time. This choice was made on the premise that it is important to ensure that the pump will not momentarily assert great pressure on the wound which could probably damage the tissue on and around the wound. A model of the pump in the time-domain was created in Matlab [11] using nominal values from the actual DC motor. The PI controller was tuned to satisfy the control requirements mentioned earlier. The source of the system is the voltage source (V) applied to the armature of the motor and the output is the position of the shaft ($\theta$).

The rotor and the shaft are assumed to be rigid. Additionally, a viscous friction model is assumed meaning that the torque is proportional to the angular velocity of the shaft.
The model is described by the following system of equations:

$$J\theta + b\dot{\theta} = Ki \tag{1}$$

$$L\frac{di}{dt} + Ri = V - K\dot{\theta} \tag{2}$$

The units involved in the equation are described below:

- J: moment of inertia of the rotor equal to $5.02 \cdot 10^{-7} kg \cdot m^2$
- B: motor viscous friction constant equal to $14.32 \cdot 10^{-7} N \cdot m \cdot s$
- K: motor torque constant equal to $0.0165 N \cdot m/A$
- R: electric resistance equal to $3.5\Omega$
- L: electric inductance equal to $0.12 \cdot 10^{-3} H$

The rotational speed is considered the output of the system while the armature voltage is considered its input.

$$P(s) = \frac{\theta(s)}{V(s)} = \frac{K}{(Js + b)(Ls + R) + K^2}(\frac{rad}{V \cdot s}) \tag{3}$$

This open loop system is controlled using the aforementioned PI controller in series with it. The entire closed loop system has been converted to its digital equivalent using a sampling rate of 0.05 sec which equals to a sampling frequency of 20Hz which is proposed as an adequate sampling frequency for the correct control of the pump motor. Since the pump control task is the most crucial of the SNPWD high level embedded software, it is executed in an interrupt handler, the one with the highest priority. This interrupt handler is the one corresponding to the expiration of the main system timer.

# 6    Qualitative Evaluation: Functional Requirements Coverage

In order to qualitatively evaluate the effectiveness of our approach, we examined the coverage of the functional requirements using the proposed emulation framework. Four attributes are used to define the status of the requirements:

Figure 4 provides a summary of coverage of the functional requirements, originally defined in the specifications of the system and achieved by the first prototype of the embedded SW application. As shown, 48% of the SW requirements are completely covered by the proposed first prototype, while another 15% is partially covered. Thus, the overall coverage achieved is about 63%, where the remaining 37% is split among obsolete (4%), irrelevant (4%) and open requirements.

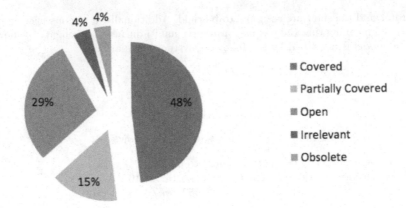

**Fig. 4.** Analysis of functional requirements coverage

# 7 Experimental Evaluation: Exploring the Impact of Design Alternatives

In this section, we utilize the proposed HW/SW framework to analyse the impact of differing architectural decisions on the timing and resource usage. We focus our timing analysis on the data fusion engine that forms the heaviest computational component of the system. Specifically, we explore architectural decisions regarding to (i) the memory architecture, i.e. instruction and data cache system configuration, and (ii) the inclusion/exclusion of the a Floating Point Unit (FPU), across embedded application instances with differing machine learning algorithms for the data fusion engine, i.e. NN, SVM and D. Trees.

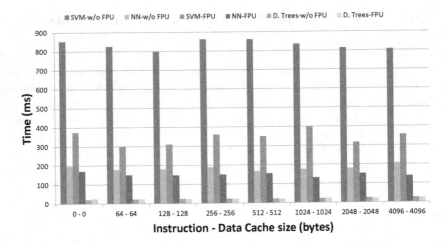

**Fig. 5.** Architectural configurations impact on performance

Figure 5 depicts the impact of cache size (instruction and data) and FPU allocation on the performance of the fusion engine. As shown the D. Trees forms the most efficient decision regarding to performance. The existence of an FPU in the microprocessor reduces the execution time of the algorithms operating on floating point data, like SVM and NN. Decision trees are not affected since their code structure is based on branch instructions, which are not requiring complex FP operations to benefit from the FPU. In contrast to the FPU, the cache memory size should be carefully chosen in order to speed-up the execution, since the data access patterns in memory can be such that the average execution is increased even compared to the design with no cache memory, e.g. 256 cache size configuration for the SVM w/o FPU.

Figure 6 depicts the regulation capabilities of the PI controller of the DC motor. The reference point is 1 rad/s and every point in time equals to 50 ms. From points 1-100 the DC motor is successfully regulated from being stopped to reaching 1 rad/sec. From points 101-200 in three points the speed of the motor is suddenly reduced to 0 rad/sec. The speed is regulated and the overshoot spans only for 4 points which is about 200ms. From points 201-300 we impose step response disturbance where output is constantly reduced by 0.5 rad/sec. In this case the speed is also regulated with slightly greater overshoot and roughly the same settling time of about 200ms. From points greater than 301 random noise of amplitude smaller or equal to 0.05 rad/sec is either added or subtracted to or from the output of the DC motor model. We can see that the controller is actually robust at regulating this disturbance and not resulting in an undesirable output.

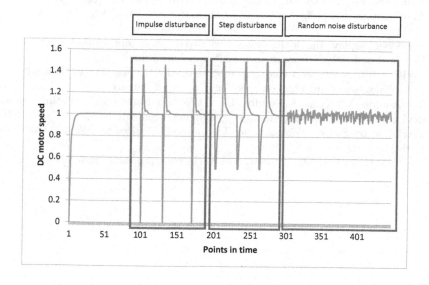

**Fig. 6.** Pump regulation

# 8  Conclusion

In this work a framework to utilize the abilities of an FPGA device to efficiently emulate a wearable embedded medical device is presented. The case study was a wound management and monitoring medical device as designed and specified as the key element of the SWAN-iCare European project. By extending the FPGA using a set of off-the-shelf hardware components, a modular HW platform was created emulating a state-of-art medical device. Using this hardware platform, we achieved the goal to develop an Embedded Application Software prototype which managed to cover the majority of the specified requirements for the software stack of the medical device.

# References

1. Bartus, C.L., Margolis, D.J.: Reducing the incidence of foot ulceration and amputation in diabetes. Current Diabetes Reports. **4**, 413–418 (2004)
2. Apelqvist, J., Larsson, J.: What is the most effective way to reduce incidence of amputation in diabetic foot. Diabetes/Metabolism Research and Reviews. **16**(Suppl. 1), 75–83 (2000)
3. Texier, I., Xydis, S., Soudris, D., Marcoux, P., Pham, P., Muller, M., Correvon, M., Dudnik, G., Voirin, G., Kristenssen, J., Laurenza, M., Raptopoulos, A., Saxby, C., Navarro, T., di Francesco, F., Salvo, P., Romanelli, M., Lymperopoulos, L.: SWAN-iCare Project: towards smart wearable and autonomous negative pressure device for wound monitoring and therapy. In: Proc. of IEEE International Workshop on Smart Wearable and Autonomous Devices for Wound Monitoring (2014)
4. Xilinx Inc. http://www.xilinx.com/products/silicon-devices/fpga/spartan-3.html
5. Abu-Mostafa, Y.S., Magdon-Ismail, M., Lin, H-T.: Learning from Data. AMLBook (2012)
6. Pervasive Displays Inc. http://www.pervasivedisplays.com/kits/adapTag
7. Beagle Board. http://beagleboard.org/beagleboard-xm
8. LWIP. http://www.xilinx.com/ise/embedded/edk91i_docs/lwip_v2_00_a.pdf
9. www.dialog-semiconductor.com/products/bluetooth-smart
10. Tsoutsouras, V., Xydis, S., Soudris, D.: A HW/SW framework emulating wearable devices for remote wound monitoring and management. In Proc. of IEEE Intl. Workshop on Smart Wearable and Autonomous Devices for Wound Monitoring (2014)
11. MathWorks Matlab. http://www.mathworks.com/products/matlab/

# Special Session 2: Horizon 2020 Funded Projects (Invited Papers)

# DynamIA: Dynamic Hardware Reconfiguration in Industrial Applications

Nele Mentens[1]([✉]), Jochen Vandorpe[1], Jo Vliegen[1], An Braeken[2],
Bruno da Silva[2], Abdellah Touhafi[2], Alois Kern[3],
Stephan Knappmann[3], Jens Rettkowski[4], Muhammed Soubhi Al Kadi[4],
Diana Göhringer[4], and Michael Hübner[4]

[1] ESAT/SCD-COSIC & iMinds and ES&S, KU Leuven, Leuven, Belgium
{nele.mentens,jochen.vandorpe,jo.vliegen}@kuleuven.be
[2] INDI and ETRO, Vrije Universiteit Brussel (VUB), Brussels, Belgium
{an.braeken,bruno.da.silva,abdellah.touhafi}@vub.ac.be
[3] Institut fuer Mikro- und Informationstechnik der Hahn-Schickard-Gesellschaft
(HSG-IMIT), Villingen-Schwenningen, Germany
{alois.kern,stephan.knappmann}@hsg-imit.de
[4] Ruhr-University Bochum (RUB), Bochum, Germany
{jens.rettkowski,muhammed.alkadi,diana.goehringer,
michael.huebner}@rub.de

**Abstract.** This paper presents the work that will be done in the research project "DynamIA: Dynamic Hardware Reconfiguration in Industrial Applications". The project focuses on transferring knowledge on partial and dynamic reconfiguration of FPGAs from the academic partners to small and medium enterprises (SMEs), because the success stories on partial and dynamic reconfiguration were mainly only realized in large companies with a substantial amount of R&D activities. The reason is that the technology is still perceived as being difficult to adopt and expensive in terms of NRE costs. Therefore, the goal of the DynamIA project is two-fold. (1) It develops a number of use cases and guidelines in different application domains, tailored to the activities of the SMEs in the user group and in the broader target group. These use cases demonstrate a number of benefits of partial and dynamic FPGA reconfiguration, namely a faster startup, a faster design cycle and a lower occupation of resources leading to a lower static power consumption. (2) It develops a low-cost, vendor-independent emulation environment for dynamic and partial reconfiguration, which is non-existing in commercial and academic EDA tools. Another benefit of this emulation environment is that it can also be used for static designs. This allows SMEs to have a low-cost emulation environment for their applications instead of developing their own emulation environment manually (which is very time-consuming) or buying big cost-intensive commercial emulators.

**Keywords:** FPGA · Dynamic reconfiguration · Partial reconfiguration · Emulation platform

© Springer International Publishing Switzerland 2015
K. Sano et al. (Eds.): ARC 2015, LNCS 9040, pp. 513–518, 2015.
DOI: 10.1007/978-3-319-16214-0_47

# 1    Introduction

Dynamic and partial reconfiguration of FPGAs was introduced in the mid '90s [3,7]. By 'dynamic' reconfiguration we mean the reconfiguration of an FPGA at run-time. When a specific part of the FPGA is static, the reconfiguration is referred to as 'partial'. Typically, in systems that are partially dynamically reconfigurable, the static part contains a component that controls the reconfiguration of the dynamic part of the FPGA.

In the last decade, dynamic and partial reconfiguration of SRAM-based FPGAs has made major scientific and application-oriented progress through faster reconfiguration time, smaller granularity of the reconfigurable partitions, a large diversity of FPGAs that supports the technology and easier access to the technology through improved EDA tools. This resulted in a number of success stories that were mainly based on faster startup, faster design cycle, lower occupation of resources and lower static power consumption.

**Faster startup.** The larger the FPGA, the longer it takes to be reconfigured and operative after power-up. Many protocols such as PCI Express or CAN bus have very strict timing requirements, which cannot be fulfilled by starting up large FPGAs. In these cases partial reconfiguration can be used to allow a fast startup of the needed functionality, e.g. by first loading the PCI Express or CAN interface using partial reconfiguration and afterwards reconfiguring the rest of the FPGA. A method to improve the startup time of Xilinx FPGA is described in [4]. The approach described in this paper enables the startup of FPGA within 10ms, independently to the size of the device. This feature allows the deployment of large FPGAs in more applications as it was possible before.

**Faster design cycle.** Processing a large design takes a lot of time. A small modification in a subsystem of the design, forces the designer to go through the synthesis and place & route process all over again. Partial reconfiguration can offer a solution to this problem through an incremental design approach in which subsystems can be processed separately. This significantly decreases the time-to-market of FPGA-based electronic systems.

**Lower occupation of resources and lower static power consumption.** Dynamic and partial reconfiguration is very beneficial for systems, which have mutual exclusive functions. These functions can then be swapped in and out depending on the run-time requirements of the application. This way, smaller FPGAs can be used to save both costs as well as power consumption. One of the first applications benefiting from dynamic and partial reconfiguration was Software Defined Radio. Another application domain is image processing. Here dynamic and partial reconfiguration is used to reconfigure the digital image filters depending on the image content. The advantage for these kinds of systems are (1) no frames will be lost, as the camera interface stays active while the digital filter is reconfigured, and (2) as only parts of the FPGA are reconfigured this can happen so fast that between two frames the digital filter can be modified.

It turned out, however, that these success stories were mainly only realized in large companies with a substantial amount of R&D activities, while a lot of SMEs could also benefit from the use of the technology. The reason is that the technology is still perceived as being difficult to adopt and expensive in terms of NRE costs. Therefore, the goal of this project is two-fold:

– It develops a number of use cases and guidelines in different application domains, tailored to the activities of the SMEs in the user group and in the broader target group. These use cases demonstrate the abovementioned benefits of partial and dynamic FPGA reconfiguration.
– It develops a low-cost, vendor-independent emulation environment for dynamic and partial reconfiguration, which is non-existing in commercial and academic EDA tools. Another benefit of this emulation environment is that it can also be used for static designs. This allows SMEs to have a low-cost emulation environment for their applications instead of either making their own emulation environment manually (which is very time-consuming) or buying big cost-intensive commercial emulators. On the other hand, the project shows that professional emulators like for example Synopsys' ChipIT are also capable to emulate dynamic and partial reconfigurable systems. A first approach was presented in [5].

This project was submitted to the CORNET call in September 2013. CORNET stands for COllective Research NETworking. It is a network for information exchange and collaboration between national and regional programmes for collective research in Europe. The objective is to promote close cooperation between the responsible national/regional ministries and agencies and to create opportunities for transnational collective research with national/regional funding. This means that CORNET partners in the participating countries/regions are working together to align programme conditions and procedures.

The CORNET coordination activities are financially supported by the German Federal Ministry of Economics and Technology (BMWi). The Belgian partners will receive funding from the Agency for Innovation by Science and Technology (IWT Flanders) and the German partners will receive funding from the German Federation of Industrial Research Associations (AiF). The project period is from January 1, 2015 to December 31, 2016. The consortium partners are the Katholieke Universiteit Leuven, the Vrije Universiteit Brussel, the Ruhr-University Bochum, the Hahn-Schickard-Gesellschaft e.V. (HSG-IMIT) and 10 SMEs in Flanders and Germany that support the project with their experience and use cases.

## 2   Economic Relevance for SMEs

### 2.1   Targeted Market Sector

The technology of dynamic and partial reconfiguration is commercially offered by Xilinx and Altera - vendors of FPGAs and tools that, together, represent almost 90% of the market share [2]. They represent an even larger market share in SRAM-based FPGAs, i.e. the only type of FPGAs with the technological capability of being dynamically reconfigured. After a company buys FPGAs and licenses, it can freely use dynamic and partial reconfiguration [1,8].

The direct target group of the project consists of SMEs that are active in the development of FPGA-based systems and sometimes also tools. In Flanders this means around 50 SMEs that have the absorption capacity to apply the project results in future products. In Germany we talk about several hundreds. The technology of dynamic and partial reconfiguration has only recently become mature enough to be beneficial in several application domains. Nevertheless, it requires a substantial effort for SMEs to adopt the technology. This project helps SMEs taking the first steps to product innovation based on dynamic and partial reconfiguration. The indirect target group are hundreds of companies and organizations that use FPGA-based end products. Through dynamic and partial reconfiguration these products become more efficient in terms of startup speed, power consumption and/or cost. The project DynamIA especially targets the development of cost effective possibilities to emulate dynamic reconfigurable systems. The current development process of dynamic and partial reconfigurable systems goes more or less over a trial and error process. A prototype is developed and the system is tested on it. In case of a re-design, a complete new prototype has to be developed. For prototyping, many solutions are on the market. E.g. Cadence and Synopsys offer systems which allow to prototype and emulate a digital system on several FPGAs. However, these systems don't support dynamic and partial reconfiguration. A recent research work however showed, that also these systems are capable to provide this feature [5]. With the introduction of this degree of freedom, also partially and dynamically reconfigurable systems can be emulated with these machines. However, the costs of such emulators are immense. Therefore DynamIA also targets to develop a cost efficient substitute for these professional emulators. For this purpose, standard off-the-shelf FPGA boards will be used to build the emulator architecture. Like in the professional emulators, the design has to be distributed over several FPGAs in case the design doesn't fit on one board. The dynamic and partial reconfiguration will be enabled with specific IP cores using the internal configuration access port of the used FPGAs. Fast interconnections between the boards are used to enable the communication of the distributed modules. A host PC is utilized as data source and sink. A tool flow, which will be developed within the project, performs the partitioning of the application and the generation of the different configuration bitstreams for the several boards and the partial bitstreams which will be loaded on demand. A scheduler on chip level performs the download of the bitstreams as described in [6]. The application scenarios come from different domains and are provided by the SMEs participating in the project as a part of the user group.

## 2.2    Economic Impact

The goal of the project is to improve the competitive position of Flemish and German SMEs by enabling them to develop products with a better performance (faster startup behavior, low power consumption, lower cost) and with a shorter design cycle (through an incremental design approach). The improved products and reduced NRE costs increase the turn-over of the companies and contribute to their growth. Furthermore, it is mandatory to enable SMEs in Belgium and

Germany the entry in an upcoming market which will definitely increase significantly in the next years. Reasons for this are the next revolution of the industry
called Industry 4.0. Here novel kinds of embedded systems need to provide a computational platform which is able to keep strict deadline requirements, reliability
and robustness. A further important requirement is the combination of domains
such as process automation, factory automation, production and logistics. This
comes into our daily lives with the "Internet of Things". If the SMEs are not
ready as soon as these new systems are required, the huge companies take over
this important market leading to another reduction of SMEs in Europe, which
is definitely a huge drawback. DynamIA wants to help to lower the barrier for
an entrance of SMEs into this beneficial and promising technology.

# 3    Research Approach and Expected Results

## 3.1    Research Approach

The innovation target consists of two aspects: (1) innovation of the SMEs' products and (2) development of an innovative emulation platform. The product
innovation consists of designing and implementing new FPGA architectures that
provide dynamic and partial reconfiguration and support run-time adaptation.
On the one hand, these architectures increase the startup speed, shorten the
design cycle, decrease the power consumption and/or reduce the resource occupation. On the other hand, the novel architectures need to have sufficient internal
and/or external memory to store the configuration data. The use cases are chosen in different application domains and contain different architectural challenges
such as intensive internal/external memory access, real-time processing requirements, computation intensive algorithms, specific interfacing requirements. The
variety in the application domain and the architecture of the use cases guarantees the applicability for the SME target group. The SMEs in the user committee
will be involved in fine-tuning the use cases in the first phase of the project. In
parallel to the development of the use cases, techniques for emulating dynamic
reconfiguration will be developed. For this purpose, a CHIPit prototyping system
which consists of 6 large FPGAs in one system will be used to demonstrate the
feature of dynamic and partial reconfiguration. CHIPit from Synopsys is originally meant for developing ASICs. However, it is possible to introduce dynamic
reconfiguration into this emulator box. For this purpose the internal configuration access port is used to update the FPGA partially at run-time. This
approach is fully new and would lead to a novel use case of this emulator. In
a further step, the technique is used with individual FPGA evaluation boards.
These boards, which can be obtained at low costs from e.g. Digilent, Avnet and
Xilinx, can also be used as emulators. For this purpose, a novel technique to bring
these boards into a network and distribute the reconfigurable system on it will
be developed. The reason why the consortium wants to target this approach
is the fact that cheaper boards are more attractive to SMEs and universities.
However, the two options are envisioned in this project to be able to make a
performance comparison between the CHIPit and the novel low-cost solution.

## 3.2 Expected Project Results

The result of DynamIA is the analysis, implementation and evaluation of applications using dynamic and partial reconfiguration. For the implementation and evaluation, tools and hardware methods will be developed in order to test the dynamicity of the system before an application-specific prototype is built. For this purpose, a design flow using the Synopsys CHIPit system will be developed which enables to perform dynamic and partial reconfiguration. In a further step, such a design flow will be developed for standard off-the-shelf FPGA boards. A free version of the flow will be provided for SMEs and academics. The implemented use cases will be described in application notes that allow reproduction.

## 4     Conclusion

DynamIA focuses on translating knowledge and expertise on dynamic and partial reconfiguration to Belgian and German SMEs. This will be done through the development of four use cases that represent different benefits of the technology. The use cases are from domains like sensor signal processing, embedded security, network of systems and image processing. This variety of applications enables a full exploration of the capability of dynamic reconfiguration and the required gain in experience to provide valuable feedback to the SMEs within the project. Low-cost emulation platforms will be developed and demonstrated through the use cases. These platforms can also be used for static designs and can be adopted by the SMEs as an alternative for expensive emulation platforms.

## References

1. Altera. Increasing design functionality with partial and dynamic reconfiguration in 28-nm FPGAs. White Paper, Altera Corporation (2010)
2. FPGA developer: Tools and tutorials for FPGA designers. List and comparison of FPGA companies (2011). http://www.fpgadeveloper.com/2011/07/list-and-comparison-of-fpga-companies.html
3. De Hon, A.: Reconfigurable architectures for general-purpose computing. AI Technical Report 1586, MIT Artificial Intelligence Laboratory (1996)
4. Huebner, M., Meyer, J., Sander, O., Braun, L., Becker, J., Noguera, J., Stewart, R.: Fast sequential FPGA startup based on partial and dynamic reconfiguration. In: Proc. of the IEEE Computer Society Annual Symp. on VLSI (ISVLSI) (2010)
5. Al Kadi, M.S., Ferger, M., Stegemann, V., Huebner, M.: Multi-FPGA reconfigurable system for accelerating MATLAB simulations. In: Proc. of the Intl. Conf. on Field Programmable Logic (FPL). IEEE (2014)
6. Schwiegelshohn, F., Huebner, M.: An application scenario for dynamically reconfigurable FPGAs. In: Reconfigurable and Communication-Centric Systems-on-Chip (ReCoSoC). IEEE (2014)
7. Trimberger, S., Carberry, D., Johnson, A., Wong, J.: A time-multiplexed FPGA. In: Proc. of the 5th Annual IEEE Symp. on FPGAs for Custom Computing Machines, vol. 4833, pp. 22–28 (1997)
8. Xilinx. Xcell journal (1988–2012). http://www.xilinx.com/publications/xcellonline

# Robots in Assisted Living Environments as an Unobtrusive, Efficient, Reliable and Modular Solution for Independent Ageing: *The RADIO Perspective*

Christos Antonopoulos[1], Georgios Keramidas[1], Nikolaos S. Voros[1(✉)],
Michael Hübner[2], Diana Göhringer[2], Maria Dagioglou[3],
Theodore Giannakopoulos[3], Stasinos Konstantopoulos[3], and Vangelis Karkaletsis[3]

[1] Technological Educational Institute of Western Greece, Patras, Greece
{cantonopoulos,gkeramidas,voros}@teimes.gr
[2] Ruhr-Universitaet Bochum, Bochum, Germany
{Michael.Huebner,Diana.Goehringer}@rub.de
[3] Institute of Informatics and Telecommunications,
NCSR "Demokritos", Athens, Greece
{mdagiogl,tyianak,constant,vangelis}@iit.demokritos.gr

**Abstract.** Demographic and epidemiologic transitions in Europe have brought a new health care paradigm where life expectancy is increasing as well as the need for long-term care. To meet the resulting challenge, European healthcare systems need to take full advantage of new opportunities offered by technical advancements in ICT. The RADIO project explores a novel approach to user acceptance and unobtrusiveness: an integrated smart home/assistant robot system where health monitoring equipment is an obvious and accepted part of the user's daily life. By using the smart home/assistant robot as sensing equipment for health monitoring, we mask the *functionality* of the sensors rather than the sensors themselves. In this manner, sensors do not need to be discrete and distant or masked and cumbersome to install; they do however need to be perceived as a natural component of the smart home/assistant robot functionalities.

## 1 Introduction

Demographic and epidemiologic transitions have brought a new health care paradigm with the presence of both growing elderly population and chronic diseases [1]. Life expectancy is increasing as well as the need for long-term care. Institutional care for the aged population faces economical struggles with low staffing ratios and consequent quality problems [2], [3].

Although the aforementioned implications of ageing impose societal challenges, at the same time technical advancements in ICT, including robotics, bring new opportunities for the ageing population of Europe, the healthcare systems, as well as the European companies providing relevant technology and services at the global scale. The full realization of this technological potential depends on:

© Springer International Publishing Switzerland 2015
K. Sano et al. (Eds.): ARC 2015, LNCS 9040, pp. 519–530, 2015.
DOI: 10.1007/978-3-319-16214-0_48

- Concrete evidence for the *benefits for all stakeholders*, including the elderly end-users and their formal and informal care givers (secondary end-users), as well as the health care system
- *Safety of and acceptability by* the end-users
- *Cost-effectiveness* in acquisition and maintenance, *reliability*, and *flexibility* in being able to meet a range of needs and societal expectations
- The provision of functionalities that can *reduce admissions and days spent in care institutions*, and prolong the *time spent living in own home.*

RADIO project will develop an **integrated smart home/assistant robot system**, pursuing **a novel approach to acceptance and unobtrusiveness**: a system where sensing equipment is not discrete but an **obvious and accepted part of the user's daily life**. By using the integrated smart home/assistant robot system as the sensing equipment for health monitoring, we mask the *functionality* of the sensors rather than the sensors themselves. In this manner, sensors do not need to be discrete and distant or masked and cumbersome to install; they do however need to be perceived as a natural component of the smart home/assistant robot functionalities. In pursuing these goals, the main objectives of RADIO are:

- To develop methods for detecting the *activities of daily life (ADL)* and *mood* conditions that are pertinent for *detecting early symptoms of cognitive impairment* and *social exclusion*, and to compare their accuracy against that of more obtrusive setups.
- To place the robot as the *central focus of interaction* for a whole range of automations offered by the smart home, besides the assistance offered by the robot itself. This enhances acceptance of the robot's *sensing equipment* as a necessary part of the robot's functionality.
- To base the design on existing *reliable, safe,* and *low-cost robotic and home automation solutions*, without requiring specialized hardware.
- To embed recognition methods in *hardware sensing and processing components*, which form a *modular system* that can be deployed in *different configurations and mixes of components* without requiring extensive effort or specialized knowledge for reconfiguration.
- To evaluate how well the RADIO-provided information can *drastically reduce precautionary admissions and days spent in care institutions* by detecting early symptoms of cognitive impairment.
- To integrate individual home deployments into a wide area network of RADIO home deployments, medical institutions, and mobile devices of informal care givers; into an *information transmission and management system* that is by design *scalable* and *secure and privacy-preserving*.

In order to achieve its ambitious objectives, the RADIO project will carry out research in several ICT fields. In the remainder of this paper we first frame this research in the context of the RADIO architecture (Section 2) and then proceed to present the envisaged smart home/robotics environment (Section 3), data analysis (Section 4), embedded system design (Section 5) and communications infrastructure (Section 6), and conclude (Section 7).

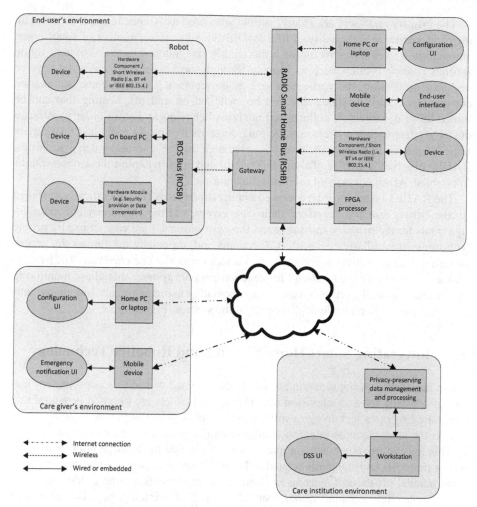

**Fig. 1.** Conceptual architecture of the RADIO system

## 2 Use Cases and System Architecture

One of the core premises that RADIO will test is that *user acceptance* can be achieved by minimizing the levels of awareness being monitored: system actions and behaviours are apparently serving the end user's convenience and no action is explicitly motivated by health monitoring. RADIO also assumes a pragmatic stance towards the technology readiness level of robotic autonomy and cognitive systems, and actually turns into its advantage the relatively low level of autonomy that robots enjoy: it lowers user expectations on its cognitive abilities and gains acceptance and familiarity by not presenting itself as an omnipotent helper but rather as a pet that depends on the user more than the user depends on it.

The primary end users are elderly people who need assistance in order to maintain their independence and quality of life. *RADIO* aims to offer a number of smart home automation conveniences including a thoroughly integrated *domestic assistant* robot. Besides running errands such as looking through the house for eyewear or keys or bringing medication, the robot also acts as the contact point for home automation conveniences, such as lights that can be switched on and off, heating that can be turned up or down, etc. It collects and analyses behavioural data in order to attract a doctor's attention when necessary, helping diagnose symptoms early and take timely remedial action. Through its direct involvement in the end-users daily activities, RADIO observes *Activities of Daily Life (ADL)* and aims to exploit these observations to establish ADL patterns and to identify deviations.

The RADIO system will be accessed via *user interfaces (UI)* specifically designed for the elderly *primary end-users*, their *care givers*, and the *clinicians*. The main design goals for the *primary end-users* and the *care givers* UI are ease of use by people with minimal familiarization with ICT systems and, especially the former, by people suffering from cognitive impairments that affect memory. The *clinicians UI*, by contrast, is a more complex front-end for *decision support systems* that allow monitoring by clinicians as well as research and experimentation using aggregate and anonymous data collected from multiple deployments of the system (Figure 1).

## 3    Integrating Smart Home Systems and Robotics Technology

Home automation is not a passing trend but is expected to become as prominent feature of our daily lives as television sets, phones and tablets are today. It is natural that integrating robotics technologies into home automation infrastructure is going to afford us the most seamless integration of the robot in its smart home environment.

This integration, however, is a major undertaking due to the large number of competing protocols and standards related to home automation. Smart home systems integrate mature, off-the-self sensing and actuation components around a *home gateway* that provides telecommunications, central control, and intelligence. However, fast development by many companies who wanted to position their products on the market led vendors to develop incompatible communication protocols for their products. Although some standardization has been achieved, there are still several standards for physically wiring devices in actual use in homes that need to be considered in the context of RADIO:

- The *Digital Addressable Lighting Interface (DALI)* is used to control light systems, means transformers, dimmers, LED lights, and other endpoints.
- The *European Installation Bus (EIB)* standard describes how sensors and actuators in a house automation system have to be connected. It also describes the communication protocol. EIB is used for alarm systems, light control, and shutter for windows.
- *Konnex-Bus (KNX)* describes the connection of sensors and actuators in house automation and integrates three bus systems: EIB, BatiBus, and EHS.

- *Local Operating Network* (LON) is a Fieldbus and US standard with was adopted also in Europe. The standard allows that devices of different vendors can communicate.
- Last but not least, the *Standard Motor Interface (SMI)* allows to control drives e.g., in shutters for windows.

The wireless communication systems are also manifold. Currently the following standards are used for wireless home automation: *EnOcean*, *ZigBee*, *Z-Wave*, *WLAN*, and *Bluetooth*. In robotics, integration is typically centred on an on-board PC that uses the *Robot Operating System (ROS)*[1] middleware to integrate sensing and actuation over the Ethernet, WiFi, and USB communication channels typically available to PCs.

The RADIO project focuses to handle the communication between the most relevant wired and wireless home automation standards and the robots. For this purpose, based on a standard the gateway functionality will be deployed. The *OSGi Framework*[2] is an open, modular and scalable *service delivery platform*. It enables as software basis platform the networking of devices from different vendors. However, the platform has to be extended and evaluated to handle also the domain of robotic. Since the standard was developed for connecting end points e.g., from Telemetry, Assisted Living, mobile phones, and PDAs, it is not dedicated for the usage in the robot domain. However, since this is an open standard which is established, the consortium decided to use this platform as the start for the integration of robots into house automation.

# 4    Data Collection and Processing

RADIO aims to detect ADL related to *basic self-care tasks*, such as dressing, eating, feeding and functional mobility, as well as *instrumental ADL* related to housework and device usage (e.g., telephone). ADL detection will be based on visual, depth, and audio signal analysis as well as their fusion. For instance, detecting eating-related events will be based on audio-visual analysis, while functional mobility will be based on recognizing motion patterns in depth and range data.

Apart from the ADL mentioned above, the project will also experiment with detecting more complex events, such as meal preparation, cleaning up, using technology and taking medications. RADIO will also face significant communication and technology integration challenges, ranging from efficient and secure data transfer, cooperative communication, data processing, sensors-actuators efficient cooperation, low power operation, and communication technologies heterogeneity. Besides ADL, the project will also integrate methods for recognizing *mood* from speech and facial characteristics. Since the robotic platform will only be able to react to simple spoken commands and not engage in any type of conversation, audio analysis will be mostly

---

[1] ROS is maintained by the *Open Source Robotics Foundation (OSRF)*. More information about ROS and OSRF can be found at http://www.ros.org and http://www.osrfoundation.org

[2] More information about OSGi can be found on the homepage of the OSGi alliance (http://www.osgi.org)

based on acoustic features rather than the content of the user's utterances. In addition, *speaker diarization* will be used to isolate utterances by the person of interest, but also to provide information about social life and other signs of social exclusion.

The relevant literature is rich, but extension and adaptation will be needed in order to meet RADIO requirements. In instance, [4] try to monitor certain dressing activity failures, using both radio frequency Identification (RFID) tracking and computer vision processing. The failures they monitored were: putting on clothes a) in the wrong order, b) backwards or other way around, c) only partially d) at an inappropriate number of layers for the current temperature and e) at a wrong part of the body. They used a Bayesian model in order to infer the dressing step using the RFID tags, which had been embedded in clothes and a clustering scheme to infer simple dressing events using rules and finally fused the results. [5] tackled also the problem of clothes change, however in that case only the result is tracked (i.e., the change of a particular clothing) based on depth and RGB information that stems from a Kinect sensor.

Various already existing efforts will be considered for the purposes of RADIO. [6] used RFIDs to detect nine ADL activities. Wireless gloves with embedded RFIDs have been successfully used, among which oral hygiene, toileting, washing and personal appearance. Fusion of RFID and visual properties have also been addressed: [7] tackles the problem of automatically learning of object models from video by using sparse and noisy RFID readings, common-sense knowledge and visual features, in a kitchen, in order to recognize activities by identifying the objects which are being used in the scene. [8] focuses on five basic ADL activities: telephone use, hand washing, meal preparation, eating and medication use, and cleaning. They used various sensors (e.g., motion, temperature, sensors that monitor water and stove burner use etc.) They applied naive Bayes classifiers and Markov models so as to recognize the aforementioned activities. [9] presents a system that uses visual features and custom logic rules in order to recognize steps in hand washing by tracking a) of hand location and b) of step-specific object locations, specifically the soap and towel. [10] successfully fused several sensors with an SVM classification scheme to recognize several ADLs (e.g., dressing, hygiene). [11] uses kinematic sensors (specifically, wearable wireless accelerometers) to detect several ADLs. [12] uses an RGB-D camera to recognize potentially dangerous activities for elderly people, along with several ADLs. They track joints on the human body, which have been provided by Microsoft Kinect API1 and extract kinematic features. For the recognition of simple activities, they use several one-vs-all SVM classifiers, while for finer activities (i.e., ADLs) they adopt a bag-of-motion-features approach and then apply SVM classifiers. [13] also used the Kinect sensor in order to monitor intake gestures in the context of spotting specific ADL's of eating and drinking in a home setting.

A critical and quite challenging area will be sound and speech processing algorithms. Sound analysis has been mainly used to detect bathroom activity, e.g., [13], in the context of recognizing bathing, toilet use, and personal hygiene ADLs. Also, acoustic information has been used (e.g., in the USEFIL project) in order to detect sounds relevant to general events: doorbell, phone ring and speech, while [14] adopts baseline audio analysis approaches to detect ADL-specific audio events (dish washing, step sounds etc.). In addition, audio information can be rather useful when recognizing emotions from speech [15]. In most cases, due to the importance of face in emotion expression and perception, most of the affect recognition studies focus on combining information from visual-based facial expression analysis [16]. It has to be noted here, that speaker diarization [17] will be used in order to discover speaker-specific information before applying the speech-based emotion recognizer. In addition, the application of a speaker diarization step will help us to extract useful information regarding the social activity of the users (dialogue detection, types of dialogues etc.).

## 5    Embedded Systems Design and Hardware Accelerators

In the RADIO project, a significant effort will be given to the design and implementation of the underlying hardware platform. Our vision is to equip the robotic system with dedicated FPGA-based processors, memory systems, and accelerators. Apart from the low power requirements, prime design objectives of the hardware substrate will be safety, availability, reliability, and fault-tolerance. We plan to strike the best balance between those partially contradictory design goals through two main directions.

First, sophisticated offloading techniques will be devised. Our target towards this direction is to formulate a synergistic environment in which specific parts of the computational workload will be forwarded to the backbone for (further) processing. Those parts of the workloads can be either computational intensive pieces of code or critical parts of the executing applications. A combination of local and remote execution taking into account the well known communication vs. computation ratio will be also examined. However, in our case, this classic "communication vs. computation" trade-off will be extended to include the concerts of reliability and fault-tolerance [35]. For example, given a set of processing (local or remote) units, which is the most reliable unit for a given algorithm or a program phase of an algorithm? In principal, bit-level processors can execute more reliable bit-level algorithms (e.g., security algorithms), but bit level processors are too slow, that in turn means, power inefficient. In addition, the data transactions between the local (robotic) system and the remote system (back office) are also a significant source of errors.

Second, at the lower level, we plan to attack the challenges posed at the hardware level thought extensive reconfiguration [36]. While reconfiguration is widely considered as a technique to improve the performance or the power of a system [37], our aim is to use the concept of reconfiguration in order to increase the reliability, the safety, and the responsiveness of the robotic system. This requires to build power vs. performance vs. reliability (as well as safety) Pareto curves and use the notion of a reconfiguration in order to traverse those curves (statically or dynamically) in order to identify the ideal point(s) that meet specific (user or system) objectives. More importantly, in order to maximize the resulting benefits, we plan to include in the design space, application-level reconfigurations [36]. The application domain of the RADIO project is amenable to reconfiguration either at the algorithmic level (e.g., more relaxed data transformations) or at the data representation level (e.g., floating point vs.

fixed points variables). In other words, the innovation in our case is that core and memory reconfigurations are going to happen in concert with application reconfiguration so as to be synergistic towards meeting specific objectives.

Memory reconfiguration entails a vast array of techniques: resizing on-chip memory to fit program needs [37], optimizing cache architectures for dynamic and static power consumption [38], optimizing shared-memory communication via custom cache coherence protocols [39], modifying the replacement policies for minimizing miss rates in caches [40], compressing data and removing data redundancies, managing caches shared by multiple applications, partitioning the on-chip memory for different functionalities (caches, scratchpads, loop buffers, etc.) and any combination of the above. While the reconfiguration space is vast in this project we will combine the mechanisms that work synergistically and provide global, application-driven policies for applying these mechanisms. Our goal is to provide a malleable core and memory system that can be efficiently adapted to the needs of an application using both static (application information) and run-time information (hardware monitoring & feedback).

## 6     Communication Infrastructure Using WSN

Concerning *Wireless Sensor Network (WSN)* technologies, the embedded sensor that will be used in the context of distributed sensor data analysis will include experimental development boards as well as off-the-shelf commercial products. In the context of the RADIO platform, communication and interfacing capabilities of WSN sensors will be enhanced through low power advanced operation as well as advanced communication approaches including cooperative communication, data fusion and multi-hop communication.

In that respect, significant progress beyond the state-of-art is anticipated in ICT areas including efficient wireless sensor networks. Targeting on one hand a system able to handle a wide range of different and diverse sensors and one the other a highly extendible and evolving platform an adequate codification approach must be followed enabling communication in a structured and open way. Such schemes will significant ease the management of enormous and diverse amount of information. Significant input to this approach will be provided by open standards such as VITAL [18] and DICOM [19] and relevant research efforts [20]. During the last few years interesting research efforts have been presented concerning home monitoring of people with a specific condition. However most of them are based on a passive approach [21], [22] whereas RADIO aims towards a more active approach which will engage the user himself in order to make him feel more active, creative, self-reliant and useful.

Additionally, most efforts assume a single, specific communication technology and/or limited types of sensor which significantly limits flexibility and extendibility. In both aspects RADIO aims to offer wide support of available options so as to maximize usefulness and practicality [22], [23], [24]. Supporting state-of-the-art communication technologies such as Bluetooth v4 and IEEE 802.15.4 and extending low power communication capabilities will comprise a critical goal of the project. At the same time enhancements will be pursued in data management areas concerning context aware data process, data fusions etc. aiming to offer a more intelligent and efficient wireless sensor network. When multiple and mobile sensors are deployed in a home environment a critical challenge that must be addressed is potential disconnections of specific nodes (e.g., a person wearing sensors transferring data using IEEE 802.15.4 and the respective receiver are more than two rooms away from each other will probably lose direct connectivity to the receiver). In such scenarios the nodes can still be connected over multi-hop communication paths. Of course multi-hop communication is not new to WSN but RADIO aims to study the possibility to furthered enhance the usefulness and practicality of such features compared to existing state-of-the-art efforts. A common characteristic of relative efforts is the goal to address a very specific case usually characterized by quite limiting assumption including the use of specific communication technology or the transferring of specific sensor data [25], [26], [27], [28]. In that respect RADIO aims to offer to enhance usefulness in terms of flexible support of various communication technologies and data types using a common and extendible codification scheme. A very interesting approach is presented in [29] where multi-hop communication is used as a way to actually enhance security. Such approaches can also be extended in RADIO through the use of efficient encryption components while identifying and taking into consideration adequate data management processes able to address soft security issues such as data mishandle, authorized access, EC security regulations compliance etc.

Another area able to offer significant performance and efficient benefits yet not receiving adequate interesting in WSNs is cooperative communication [30]. In general the term cooperative communication in RADIO is used for approaches where nodes receiving (or overhearing) data don't just convey them to the final receiver but instead they use data in order to enhance communication efficiency. Such approaches have attracted significant interest in more resource rich network technologies such as Wi-MAX [31], [32] but can also benefit RADIO network setups as well. In [33] and [34] a very interesting use of cooperative communication aiming to enhance communication security is offered, which can also be exploited in the context RADIO and extended through the use of state-of-the-art encryption components.

## 7    Conclusion

The RADIO project provides an integration of robotic equipment in the environment of house automation. The high number of solutions in terms of protocols requires the development of a platform, which unifies all these different standards to enable a common interface for the robot's data access. This platform can be seen as gateway between the robot's data access and the connection to the house automation busses. Such a platform needs to support different real-time requirements, specific bus operations (e.g., cyclic messages, spontaneous messages etc.). A setup like this has the complexity like a gateway in the automotive domain. Due to this fact, a platform with sufficient computational capacity has to be selected. We envision here an FPGA-based design which is high performant and also flexible to future bus systems, which may be developed after the projects end.

An FPGA-based platform is also envisioned to host the algorithms used on the robotics platform. Here the best trade-off between communication and computation (at the local node) has to be found. Definitely, the processing of data near the sensor node might be the preferred solution in terms of power efficiency, but the highly dynamic scenario within the context of RADIO might lead to new approaches and solutions.

**Acknowledgment.** This study is funded by the European Commission through the Horizon 2020 Programme (H2020/PHC-19-2014) under the Research and Innovation Action "RADIO - *Robots in assisted living environments: Unobtrusive, efficient, reliable and modular solutions for independent ageing".*

# References

1. Lee, R.: The Outlook for Population Growth. Science **333** (2011)
2. Kash, B.A., Hawes, C., Phillips, C.D.: Comparing staffing levels in the Online Survey Certification and Reporting (OSCAR) system with the Medicaid Cost Report data: are differences systematic?. Gerontologist (2007)
3. Weech-Maldonado, R., Meret-Hanke, L., Neff, M.C., Mor, V.: Nurse staffing patterns and quality of care in nursing homes. Health Care Manage. Rev. (2004)
4. Matic, A., Mehta, P., Rehg, J.M., Osmani, V., Mayora, O.: Monitoring dressing activity failures through RFID and video. Methods of Information in Medicine (2012)
5. Sgouropoulos, D., Giannakopoulos, T., Petridis, S., Perantonis, S.: Clothes change detection using the Kinect sensor. Submitted to International Conference on Signal Processing and Multimedia Applications (2014)
6. Philipose, M., Fishkin, K.P., Perkowitz, M., Patterson, D.J., Fox, D., Kautz, H., Hähnel, D.: Inferring activities from interactions with objects. IEEE Pervasive Computing (2004)
7. Wu, J., Osuntogun, A., Choudhury, T., Philipose, M., Reh, J.M.: A scalable approach to activity recognition based on object use. In: Proceedings of the IEEE International Conference on Computer Vision (2007)
8. Cook, D.J., Schmitter-Edgecombe, M.: Assessing the quality of activities in a smart environment. Methods of Information in Medicine (2009)
9. Mihailidis, A., Carmichael, B., Boger, J.: The use of computer vision in an intelligent environment to support aging-in-place, safety, and independence in the home. IEEE Transaction on Information Technology in Biomedicine (2004)
10. Fleury, A., Noury, N., Vacher, M.: Supervised classification of activities of daily living in health smart homes using SVM. In: Proceedings of the IEEE Annual International Conference in Engineering in Medicine and Biology Society (2009)
11. Dalton, A., Morgan, F., Olaighin, G.: A preliminary study of using wireless kinematic sensors to identify basic activities of daily living. In: Proceedings of the IEEE Annual International Conference in Engineering in Medicine and Biology Society (2008)
12. Zhang, C., Tian, Y.: RGB-D Camera-based Daily Living Activity Recognition. Journal of Computer Vision and Image Processing (2012)
13. Hondori, H.M., Khademi, M., Lopes. C.V.: Monitoring intake gestures using sensor fusion (microsoft kinect and inertial sensors) for smart home tele-rehab setting. In: Proceedings of the IEEE Healthcare Innovation Conference (2012)

14. Vacher, M., Fleury, A., Portet, F., Serignat, J.F., Noury, N.: Complete sound and speech recognition system for health smart homes: application to the recognition of activities of daily living. In: Campolo, D. (ed.) New Developments in Biomedical Engineering, Chapter 33 (2010)

15. Koolagudi, S.G., Rao, K.S.: Emotion recognition from speech: a review. International Journal of Speech Technology (2012)

16. Zeng, Z., Pantic, M., Roisman, G.I., Huang, T.S.: A survey of affect recognition methods: Audio, visual, and spontaneous expressions. IEEE Trans. on Pattern Analysis and Machine Intelligence 31(1) (2009)

17. Giannakopoulos, T., Petridis, S.: Fisher linear semi-discriminant analysis for speaker diarization. IEEE Transaction on Audio, Speech, and Language Processing (2012)

18. CEN. Health informatics – Vital signs information representation – VITAL. CEN ENV13734 (1999)

19. ACR. DICOM Supplement 30: Waveform Interchange, Revision 1.1. Document for Letter Ballot: NEMA Standard Pub. (1999)

20. Anagnostaki, A.P.: A Novel Codification Scheme Based on the VITAL and DICOM Standards for Telemedicine Applications. IEEE Transactions on Biomedical Engineering (2002)

21. Alwan, M.: Passive in-home health and wellness monitoring: overview, value and examples. In: Proceedings of IEEE Annual International Conference of the IEEE EMBS (2009)

22. Marko, H.: Wireless system for patient home monitoring. In: Proceedings of International Symposium on Wireless Pervasive Computing (2007)

23. Raj, S.: Implementation of pervasive computing based high secure smart home system. In: Proceedings of IEEE International Conference on Computational Intelligence & Computing Research (2012)

24. Maciuca, A.: Wireless sensor network based on multilevel femtocells for home monitoring. In: Proceedings of IEEE International Conference on Intelligent Data Acquisition and Advanced Computing Systems: Technology and Applications (2013)

25. Fernandez-Luque, F.J., Zapata, J., Ruiz, R.: A system for ubiquitous fall monitoring at home via a wireless sensor network. In: Proceedings of IEEE Annual International Conference in Engineering in Medicine and Biology Society (2010)

26. Xu, M.: Design and implementation of a wireless sensor network for smart homes. In: Proceedings of IEEE International Workshop on Mobile Cyber-Physical Systems (2010)

27. Rashid, R.A.: Home healthcare via wireless biomedical sensor network. In: Proceedings of IEEE International RF and Microwave Conference (2008)

28. Lai, C.C.: Deployment analysis for wireless multi-hop home healthcare networks. In: Proceedings of IEEE Region 10 Conference (2007)

29. Liang, X.: Enabling pervasive healthcare with privacy preservation in smart community. In: Proceedings of IEEE International Conference on Communications (2012)

30. Kailas, A.: Wireless communications technology in telehealth systems. In: Proceedings of International Conference on Wireless Communication, Vehicular Technology, Information Theory and Aerospace & Electronic Systems Technology (2009)

31. Yoon, J.S.: Performance analysis of mutual decode-and-forward cooperative communication for ofdma based mobile wimax system. In: Proceedings of IEEE International Symposium on Personal, Indoor and Mobile Radio Communications (2009)

32. Fakih, K.: On the cooperative and non-cooperative relaying in WiMAX communication systems. In: Proceedings of IEEE Vehicular Technology Conference (2010)

33. Lu, R.: GRS: The Green, Reliability, and Security of Emerging Machine to Machine Communications. IEEE Communications Magazine (2011)

34. Chang, J.M.: CBDS: a cooperative bait detection scheme to prevent malicious node for MANET Based on hybrid defense architecture. In: Proceedings of International Conference on Wireless Communication, Vehicular Technology, Information Theory and Aerospace & Electronic Systems Technology (2011)
35. Keramidas, G., Mavropoulos, M., Karvouniari, A., Nikolos, D.: Spatial pattern prediction based management of faulty data caches. In: Proceedings of ACM Conference on Design, Automation & Test in Europe (2014)
36. Wong, S., Carro, L., Kavvadias, S., Keramidas, G., et al.: Embedded reconfigurable architectures. In: Proceedings of IEEE Conference on Compilers, Architectures, and Synthesis for Embedded Systems (CASES) (2012)
37. Keramidas, G., Datsios, C., Kaxiras, S.: A framework for efficient cache resizing. In: Proceedings of IEEE Conference on Embedded Computer Systems (2012)
38. Keramidas, G., Spiliopoulos, V., Kaxiras, S.: Interval-based models for run-time DVFS orchestration in superscalar processors. In: Proceedings of ACM International Conference on Computing Frontiers (2010)
39. Kaxiras, S., Keramidas, G.: SARC coherence: scaling directory cache coherence in performance and power. IEEE MICRO (2010)
40. Keramidas, G., Petoumenos, P., Kaxiras, S.: Cache replacement based on reuse-distance prediction. In: Proceedings of IEEE International Conference on Computer Design (2007)

# Reconfigurable Computing for Analytics Acceleration of Big Bio-Data: The AEGLE Approach

Andreas Raptopoulos[1], Sotirios Xydis[2]($\boxtimes$), and Dimitrios Soudris[2]

[1] EXUS, 73-75 Mesogeion Av and Estias Str 1, 115 26 Athens, Greece
[2] School of Electrical and Computer Engineering,
National Technical University of Athens, Athens, Greece
sxydis@microlab.ntua.gr

**Abstract.** This paper presents the main directions of the AEGLE project, that targets to integrate cloud technologies together with heterogeneous reconfigurable computing in large scale healthcare systems for Big Bio-Data analytics. AEGLE's concept brings together the 'hot' big-data technologies with the health 'industry' eventually leading to integrated care and creating a win-win situation for both. We provide the addressed Big Data health scenarios and we describe the structural elements of the proposed solution, with emphasis given in the exploitation of high-performance reconfigurable engines for Big Data analytics acceleration integrated to the AEGLE ecosystem, enabling personalized and integrated health-care services, while also promoting related research activities.

## 1 Introduction

At the centre of health debates there are open questions on how to manipulate data and how to produce value out of it, share it and secure it [1]. Answers to these questions will create opportunities "to predict long-term health conditions and identify non-traditional intervention points, as well as to design better diagnostics tools, prevent diseases, and increase access to, and reduce the costs of healthcare". As discussed in [2], effective use of data in the US health sector could generate USD 300 billion in value per year. The implementation of big data analytics in the healthcare sector has the potential to "boost the integration of user-generated data with official medical data, leading to healthcare that is more integrated and personalised" [3].

Several European initiatives [4] have already pinpointed the importance and usefulness of healthcare big data, e.g. to predict the outbreak of an epidemic etc. However, the strategic advantage brought by Big-Data in healthcare still materializes at slow paces, as only some large-scale organizations have established few pilot or proof-of-concept projects.

Nowadays, there is an obvious gap in the area of big data analytics for Health Bio-data. Data-driven services are still needed to cater for the data versatility,

K. Sano et al. (Eds.): ARC 2015, LNCS 9040, pp. 531–541, 2015.
DOI: 10.1007/978-3-319-16214-0_49

volume and velocity within the whole data value chain of healthcare analytics. A true opportunity exists to produce value out of big data in healthcare with the goal to revolutionize integrated and personalised healthcare services, which have been recently introduced for the management of complex medical conditions e.g. various chronic disease conditions, chronic malignant and non-malignant disorders. Evidently, the implementation of data value chains for healthcare big data analytics has the potential to lead Europe gain the leading position worldwide, pioneering by leveraging Big Data analytics solutions in a domain that is of critical importance for all European countries and their citizens.

The AEGLE[1] project targets to address the aforementioned open issues by implementing a full data value chain to create new value out of rich, multi-diverse, 'big' health data. The project builds upon the synergy of heterogeneous High Performance Computing (HPC) exploiting reconfigurable architectures, Cloud and Big Data computing technologies, offering tools for a seamless use of different sorts of capacity across HPC, Cloud, Grid and Big Data computing for the benefit of all areas of Horizon 2020. AEGLE will provide a framework for Big Data analytics for healthcare that will overall enable and promote innovation activities that place 'health', at the spotlight.

## 2    AEGLE's Relevance and Positioning in Respect to Other R&D Projects

AEGLE aims to generate value from the healthcare data value chain data with the vision to improve translational medicine and facilitate personalized and integrated care services overall improving healthcare at all levels, to promote data-driven research across Europe and to serve as an enabler technology platform enabling business growth in the field of big data analytics for healthcare Currently numerous R&D projects are running, regarding health and ICT technologies. Most of them are targeting to obtain a proof of concept (having limited and controlled validation phases) on the impact of sensing and monitoring devices in the treatment and management of a disease.

Some of the projects have already examining in more depth the concept of integrated care concerning chronic diseases like WELCOME[2] or SWAN-iCare[3]. Additionally health projects have started exploiting cloud capabilities, like e-health GATEway to the Clouds[4] or BIOBANK Cloud[5] as well as perform large scale analysis like MD-Paedigree[6] and OPENPHACTS[7]. Most of these

---

[1]  AEGLE: An analytics framework for integrated and personalized healthcare services in Europe

[2]  http://www.welcome-project.eu/

[3]  http://www.swan-icare.eu

[4]  http://www.jisc.ac.uk/whatwedo/programmes/di_research/researchtools/ehealth. aspx

[5]  http://www.biobankcloud.com

[6]  http://www.md-paedigree.eu

[7]  http://www.openphacts.org

projects however aim to the storage and analysis of mainly biological data (e.g. genomics), and this is the field where commercial products can be found like CLCbio[8] platform aiming to the analysis of DNA, RNA and protein.

In addition, none of the existing Big-Data projects are completely dedicated to healthcare and the provision of corresponding healthcare services, or the management of diseases. AEGLE combines all elements of the full value chain (storage of large volumes of data, big data analytics, cloud computing and provisioning of integrated care services), targeting to cover the whole field of health big data analytics. It will also liaise with other projects (e.g OPENPHACTS etc), for taking advantage from their developments, resulting to a more advanced and extended system.

# 3   Health Scenarios for Big BioData Analytics

## 3.1   Chronic Lymphocytic Leukemia (CLL) Big BioData Management

CLL is a cancer of the blood system, more precisely a B-cell lymphoma, affecting mainly people of advanced age (median age at diagnosis of 70 years). CLL is a chronic, incurable disease, leading to great distress for patients and their families as well as huge costs for the health care system. The relevant Big Data include: (i) the growing output of multiple -omics technologies, such as proteomics and metabolomics, exome/whole-genome sequencing (genomics), RNA-sequencing and methylation sequencing; (ii) results from functional studies focusing on immune signaling; (iii) results from in vitro drug screening; and (iv) demographic and clinico-biological information from patients. With the advent of high-throughput technologies, a wealth of information has become available about CLL at an unprecedented scale in medical research.

Analysis will be performed both on local repositories provided by AEGLE partners as well as public repositories such as Gene Expression Omnibus (GEO) [5] and Sequence Read Archive (SRA) [6] that archive and freely distribute functional genomics data of multi-terabyte- scales submitted by the scientific community. In the context of CLL data management and analysis services, the AEGLE Big Data platform will operate on integrated sources that will be able to address complex clinical questions and scenarios associating phenotypic data with personal genetic profiles. Ultimately, the AEGLE conceptual and methodological platform will enable to bridge the gap from improved molecular characterization to improved and rational management of CLL.

## 3.2   Intensive Care Unit (ICU) Big Bio-signal Streams

In an Intensive Care Unit (ICU) context, patient bio-signals are continuously monitored and displayed towards recognizing alerting events. The continuous recordings of clinical, laboratory data and physiologic waveforms could be analysed

---

[8] http://www.clcbio.com

and displayed in an easy-to-understand manner by clinicians, who cannot interpret more than 3-4 variables at any given time. A basic principle for such analysis is that these signals cannot really be regarded independently, as they express systems and their interactions in stable or deteriorating states. Also in this particular situation, where the human factor steps in with inadequacy, sound critical decisions cannot simply be made without risks. AEGLE scalable data analytics will provide automated analysis of the fast changing multi-dimensional functions of variables for the detection of unusual, unstable or deteriorating states in patients.

Advanced data analytics shall be employed under the AEGLE for the critical detection and prevention of patient states to deterioration to eventually save lives and reduce the rates of mortalities in hospital ICUs. AEGLE analytics infrastructure for sepsis diagnosis and prediction in ICU shall promote the development of large data bases for variability and complexity analysis of physiological data (such as heart rate, blood pressure and temperature) captured from monitors in real time and alerting clinicians when the patients clinical status may deteriorate, particularly in the early stages of life- threatening illnesses. In this respect, early and personalized treatment will be feasible using AEGLE technology for higher survival in ICUs around European Hospitals.

### 3.3    Multi-parametric Management for Type II Diabetes

The risk of developing T2D can be increased by various factors; usually a mixture of modifiable and non-modifiable elements: i) age, ii) weight, iii) genetics and iv) ethnicity [7]. Based on the risk factors and screening measurements outlined, and their variety from biochemical data, ultrasound, to general demographic data it is necessary to develop a scalable infrastructure such as the AEGLE platform that will process streams of distributed and heterogeneous biomedical, imaging and demographic Big Data, while offering multi-parametric data analytics services. AEGLE infrastructure will cope with important computational issues generated by: a) the complex and heterogeneous, huge volumes of data and, b) the inherent complexity of the multi-parametric data analyses to provide meaningful data to multi-level of healthcare professionals, researchers to inform diabetes early diagnoses, screening and counselling. It must be noted that high-throughput data are usually provided in semi-structured or unstructured format and hence the AEGLE platform will need to provide a multi-step processing modification and analysis of data in order to be operational for the end users. The processing of all the above prognostic and complication indicators in their variety should enable the early detection, treatment and modifications of complications developing in type II diabetes, leading to a decrease in morbidity, mortality and excessive health care costs.

## 4    The AEGLE Infrastructure

Figure 1 depicts the main building blocks of AEGLE's big data analytics framework. Reflecting the requirements of different stakeholders involved in the full data value chain for healthcare analytics, the AEGLE framework consists of big data analytics services at two levels:

- **Local level:** The local level implements big data analytics services for real-time processing of large volumes, fast generated and multiple-formatted raw data originating from patient monitoring services deployed within a healthcare unit, complemented with dedicated medical databases. An example is the real-time analytics service that AEGLE will implement over an HPC substrate for the scenario of Intensive Care Unit (ICU). The goal of the analytics service is to detect unusual, unstable or deteriorating states of patients given the fast changing multi- dimensional variables conveyed within the bio-signals generated by ICU dedicated equipment. The stakeholders of the local level analytics are healthcare units/systems and of course the patients a ultimate beneficiaries that will benefit from the advanced treatment modalities enabled by adopting the analytics services. For example, in the ICU scenario, a prompt reaction to detected instabilities or abnormal behavior of the patient's status could significantly help to save the lives of patients being treated within the ICU.
- **Cloud level:** The cloud level analytics services will offer an experimental big data research platform to data scientists, workers and data professionals across Europe. The platform consists of a large pool of semantically-annotated and anonymized healthcare data, a set of libraries implementing state-of-the-art big data analytics methods including the local level big data analytics AEGLE services and APIs for federating with public and private data sets. Advanced visualisation tools will be implemented by AEGLE as an instrument for gaining new knowledge and expertise, advancing the European know-how in healthcare big data analytics, by allowing data scientists to steer the cloud level analytics mechanisms with their own insights. SMEs across Europe will be given the ability to use of the AEGLE platform (according to the business model that AEGLE will define) in order to deploy and assess the validity of their innovative data analytics solutions which aim at creating new value in the field of healthcare.

## 4.1 Exploiting Heterogeneous High Performance Reconfigurable Architectures

Over the past few years, high performance computing environments have increasingly embraced hardware heterogeneity as a means to offering improved performance and particularly, performance/Watt. Rather than a homogeneous collection of a single-type of processing element (i.e. single core CPUs), heterogeneous systems utilize multiple types of resources allowing workloads to be partitioned across those resources depending on the best match of the type of processing to the capabilities of the processing unit. A typical heterogeneous system will contain conventional multi-core processors providing a general purpose computing capability and one or more type of co-processors such as GPUs, DSPs or FPGA-based Dataflow Engines (DFEs) which are optimized for parallel workloads.

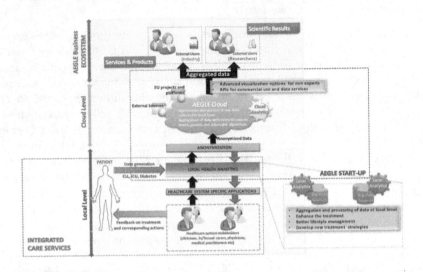

**Fig. 1.** AEGLE infrastructure

Most hardware systems consist of rackmount servers, where each server contains some number of CPUs and PCI Express attached co-processor cards such as GPUs or DFEs. This type of system is simple to deploy but can be hard to optimize since either CPUs or co-processors are often under-utilized due to the fixed ratio of resources within the chassis. An alternative deployment methodology is represented by the MAXELER MPC-X Series [8], which decouple DFEs from CPUs by having separate CPU servers and DFE systems connected via a high speed network. This method achieves somewhat lower bandwidth between the CPUs and DFEs but at the benefit of significantly increased flexibility of task assignment which can lead to much improved performance and efficiency.

MAXELER high-performance dataflow solutions are designed to integrate into production server environments, supporting standard operating systems and management tools. Mature software tools are provided by MAXELER for dataflow oriented application customization. In addition, MAXELER's dataflow computing platforms form promising infrastructures for 'big data' problems, with large on-board memories backed by high performance computation capabilities. For example, the MPC-X series dataflow nodes provide up to 384GB of DRAM and ultra-high speed connectivity to other nodes, allowing problems that might normally use disk or multiple nodes to run in memory on a single node. In addition, DFEs can incorporate lossless or lossy data compression into application data flows, directly multiplying memory capacity and bandwidth and allowing terabytes of data to be held in memory within a single node.

Despite growing adoption in narrow contexts, heterogeneous infrastructures are not widely used for the kind of Big Data analytics applications that will be tackled in AEGLE. This is due to a number of factors, including that not all analytics algorithms map well to co-processors (and particularly to GPUs, which are optimized specifically for floating point arithmetic), the increased programming difficulty in a heterogeneous environment, complexities of managing multiple resource types and the prevalence of a simplified view of the Map Reduce programming model which maps well to homogeneous processors. AEGLE will address the final steps necessary to enable heterogeneous HPC infrastructure to have a real impact on healthcare. In particular, we will utilize MAXELER DFEs which are based on reconfigurable hardware and can be optimized for specific algorithms and the project brings together both algorithm experts and computational experts to ensure that the analysis applications are efficiently implemented on the target technology. The project will develop optimized implementations of the core algorithms on the MAXELER platform, as well as developing the technology necessary to manage a large-scale infrastructure of heterogeneous systems.

## 5  Big Data Analytics Acceleration

### 5.1  State-of-Art Technological Approaches for Big Data

BigData healthcare analytics operate on collections of large and complex data sets which are difficult to process using common database management tools. Improving the performance of Big Data analytics has currently gained a lot of attention in industry and academia. Especially in healthcare systems, analytics acceleration is expected to form the main enabler for making decisions faster, analyse bigger data sizes and processing live data streams real-time.

Several techniques and tools have been emerged for Big Data acceleration to address the increased complexity of applications' requirements. Widely used for BigData processing, MapReduce is a distributed data processing framework for large clusters built of commodity servers. MapReduce frameworks are exploiting the inherent parallelism found in data driven applications, by splitting computation to set of parallel jobs (mappers) that generate intermediate results and propagate them to the reduction tasks to produce the final outcome. Google originally proposed and developed the MapReduce framework to process their proprietary Big Data [9]. Apache Hadoop [10] is open source MapReduce software that has emerged as the de facto standard of MapReduce for big data processing. Typical MapReduce frameworks target cluster based organizations of computing working nodes, thus assuming that each working nodes has its own address space. These computing fabric organizations usually impose a communication bottleneck between the maps and reduce phase. The Phoenix framework [? ] proposes a runtime environment for supporting MapReduce on shared-memory multicore processors, taking advantage of the physical proximity of the computing and memory resources.

At the data management level, in-memory databases have gained a lot of attention in the field of Big Data analytics. Modern commodity servers equipped with 1 TByte main memory are currently available for a very reasonable price.

An in-memory database [11], [12] relies on main memory storage mechanisms rather than disk storage, in order to eliminate seek time when querying the data, thus providing faster and more predictable performance. In- memory databases are faster than disk-optimized databases since the internal optimization algorithms are simpler and execute fewer CPU instructions. Recently, IBM has launched DB2 with BLU [13] acceleration database infrastructure to speed up BigData analytics using dynamic in-memory columnar technologies. Unnecessary processing is eliminated by data skipping that automatically detects and skips large sections of data that do not qualify for a query. In-memory columnar technologies provide an efficient way to scan and find relevant data. BLU acceleration utilizes instruction level parallelism through SIMD vector processing techniques to pack instructions and execute them in a single time slot, thus improving processing efficiency. In general, there is a growing interest in accelerating data management and event stream processing with devices exhibiting high capabilities on parallel resources.

## 5.2   Dataflow Reconfigurable Computing for Big Data Analytics

Within AEGLE, we target to go beyond state-of-art on Big Data services by introducing an integrated infrastructure that exploits FPGA-based dataflow acceleration across three different software levels, i.e.:

- the algorithmic level,
- the MapReduce runtime level and
- the storage and data management level.

More specifically, at the algorithmic level, customized DataFlow Engines (DFEs) will be developed in order to accelerate the computation intensive kernels found in the targeted Big Data analytics procedures. At this level, acceleration is achieved through the well-known hardware-software co-design paradigm [? ], in which the software kernels that are utilized frequently and exhibit high computation demands will be designed as hardware DFEs and mapped to MAXELERs device. Advanced compiler- and datapath-level optimization techniques [19], [20] will be adapted for spatial computing with DFEs. Along with per accelerator datapath optimization, maximization of accelerator's scalability issues given the FPGA's computational and memory organization constraints [18] will be a considered.

At the runtime level, specialized DFEs will be designed targeting to the acceleration of the underlying MapReduce programming model, i.e. the map, combine and reduce functions. MapReduce allocates several resources from the software processors, reducing the overall performance of the Big Data application. In this case, acceleration targets to the efficient implementation of internal procedures found in MapReduce runtime. Early experimental analysis considering the implementation of a MapReduce accelerated framework for FPGAs, showed speedup gains up to 32x in respect to a purely software solution [14].

In addition, customized memory management schemes tailored to the memory hierarchy and organization of MAXELER's devices will be incorporated to efficiently handle the large number of key-value pairs usually generated by MapReduce semantics, as well as platform specific task schedulers for balancing the load across the software processors and the DFEs. Previous work on customized dynamic memory management for multi-threaded workloads showed that significant performance and memory footprint gains can be achieved, when careful design of customized [15], platform dependent [16] and adaptable [17] memory management mechanisms are performed.

Finally, regarding the storage and data management level, the database management system (DBMS) would be extended to support both adaptive data layout optimizations, e.g. columnar versus row-wise storage model according to the type of queries, and query-specific hardware pipelines dataflow-based acceleration. There is a lot of calculation intensive operations that are executed by the DBMS to maintain the stored data e.g. merging the update buffer into the main storage of an in-memory column store, that can be efficiently accelerated though dataflow-based FPGA acceleration. Regarding the DBMS acceleration for data analytics, MAXELER's in-memory capabilities is expected to fulfill the needs for high demanding and fast data retrieval.

# 6    Expected Scientific and Societal Benefits

Business growth and technology advancements have resulted in growing amounts of enterprise data. To gain valuable insights and competitive advantages, there is a growing demand for performing fast and in some cases, e.g. responsive healthcare, real-time analytics on such data. The AEGLE project invests on effective acceleration of such workloads, by incorporating the latest advances in hardware, i.e. HPC computing nodes to support parallelization and heterogeneous dataflow acceleration on reconfigurable devices to perform several tasks in just one instruction. Within AEGLE it is foreseen to extent the scope and the benefits of acceleration also in domains related with big bio and health data and database management. It is expected that in this era of big data, the methodologies and tools developed within AEGLE project will transform to an extremely helpful tool-suite not only for health practitioners and researchers but also for business and IT leaders across all industries that are looking for ways to easily and cost-effectively unlock the value of enterprise data and are trying to quickly implement new solutions to gain additional insight from this data to improve outcomes across all areas of the business and science.

Additionally the outcomes of this project that would comprise the AEGLE platform shall impact the biomedical informatics domain in providing new and fast tools to the end users for performing high throughput analysis, as well as provide to the end users a solid and efficient framework for developing clinical studies (observational and/or interventional) for reliable medical decision support, and for the production of evidence based medicine incorporating information from the social media. It would impact the issue of accessing data from various inputs and the evolution of an open health data virtual space comprising of all the personalized and translational medicine related data. Thus, the impact to the ICT world is expected to be significant since health is one of the most important social and financial areas for R&D and innovation, and further, the S/W products are expected to be useable to a large extend to other big data that are related with the economy, environment, energy, behavior and psychology.

Regarding the healthcare domain AEGLE will provide more advanced mechanisms for analysis of data, while offer predictive modeling especially in critical situations. This could lead in short term evaluation of patient's condition estimation of evolution for any type of illness and at the same time facilitate doctor's role by providing significant assistance via pattern recognition of the severity and the countermeasures for patient's condition. The social benefits in terms of integrated care and the use of big-data are the following:

- Improved interaction between patients, their relatives and carers, facilitating more active participation of patients and relatives in care processes
- Improved cooperation between the providers of health, social and informal care
- Reinforced medical knowledge with respect to efficient management of comorbidities
- Increased confidence in decision support systems for disease/patient management
- Increased level of education and acceptance by patients and care givers of ICT solutions for personalised care
- Reduced admissions and days spent in care institutions, improved disease management and treatment at the point of need, actual improvements in the daily activities of patients through the effective use of ICT and the better coordination of care processes

## 7    Conclusions

In this paper, we presented the AEGLE approach for enabling high performance Big Bio-Data analytics. AEGLE aims to efficiently integrate cloud computing together with heterogeneous high performance computing technologies to enable both a publicly available global medical repository for wide adoption within the healthcare research, as well as to support fast analysis for aiding medical decisions at the local level of intervention. Here, we focused our analysis on the advanced reconfigurable technologies to be exploited throughout the AEGLE project.

## References

1. Transforming health care through big data, Institute for Health Technology Information. http://www.ihealthtran.com/big_data_in_healthcare.html
2. http://ec.europa.eu/information_society/newsroom/cf/dae/document.cfm?doc_id=3488
3. http://ec.europa.eu/digital-agenda/news/digital-agenda-eu-task-force-advise-how-promote-ehealth-help-patients-and-healthcare-systems

4. http://ec.europa.eu/digital-agenda/en/news/big-data-what-it-and-why-it-important

5. Barrett, T., Wilhite, S.E., Ledoux, P., et al.: NCBI GEO: archive for functional genomics data sets update. Nucl. Acids Res. **41**(D1), D991–D995 (2013)

6. Kodama, Y., Shumway, M., et al.: The sequence read archive: explosive growth of sequencing data. Nucl. Acids Res. **40**(D1), D54–D56 (2012)

7. National Institute for Health and Care Excellence. Preventing type 2 diabetes: risk identification and interventions for individuals at high risk. NICE public health guidance 38 (2012). http://www.guidance.nice.org.uk/ph38

8. Maxeler Technologies. http://www.maxeler.com

9. Dean, J., Ghemawat, S.: MapReduce: simplified data processing on large clusters. In: Proc. Sixth Symp. on Operating System Design and Implementation (OSDI 2004), pp. 137–150 (2004)

10. Apache Hadoop. http://hadoop.apache.org

11. Grund, M., Kruger, J., Plattner, H., Zeier, A., Cudre-Mauroux, P., Madden, S.: HYRISE - a main memory hybrid storage engine. In: VLDB (2012)

12. Stonebraker, M., et al.: The end of an architectural era (its time for a complete rewrite). In: VLDB (2007)

13. Raman, V., Attaluri, G., Barber, R., Chainani, N., Kalmuk, D., KulandaiSamy, V., Leenstra, J., Lightstone, S., Liu, S., Lohman, G.M., Malkemus, T., Mueller, R., Pandis, I., Schiefer, B., Sharpe, D., Sidle, R., Storm, A., Zhang, L.: DB2 with BLU acceleration: so much more than just a column store. Proc. VLDB Endow. **6**, 11, 1080–1091 (2013)

14. Shan, Y., Wang, B., Yan, J., Wang, Y., Xu, N., Yang, H.: FPMR: mapReduce framework on FPGA. In: Proceedings of the 18th Annual ACM/SIGDA International Symposium on Field Programmable Gate Arrays (FPGA 2010)

15. Xydis, S., Bartzas, A., Anagnostopoulos, I., Soudris, D., Pekmestzi, K.: Custom multi-threaded dynamic memory management for multiprocessor system-on-chip platforms. In: 2010 International Conference on Embedded Computer Systems (SAMOS), July 19–22, pp. 102–109 (2010)

16. Anagnostopoulos, I., Xydis, S., Bartzas, A., Zhonghai, L., Soudris, D., Jantsch, A.: Custom Microcoded Dynamic Memory Management for Distributed On-Chip Memory Organizations. IEEE Embedded Systems Letters **3**(2), 66–69 (2011)

17. Xydis, S., Stamelakos, I., Bartzas, A., Soudris, D.: Runtime tuning of dynamic memory management for mitigating footprint-fragmentation variations. In: Proc. of PARMA Workshop, pp. 27–36. VDE Verlang (2011)

18. Diamantopoulos, D., Xydis, S., Siozios, K., Soudris, D.: Dynamic memory management in vivado-hls for scalable many-accelerator architectures. In: Sano, K. (ed.) ARC 2015. LNCS, pp. XX–YY. Springer, Heidelberg (2015)

19. Xydis, S., Palermo, G., Zaccaria, V., Silvano, C.: SPIRIT: Spectral-Aware Pareto Iterative Refinement Optimization for Supervised High-Level Synthesis. IEEE Transactions on Computer-Aided Design of Integrated Circuits and Systems **34**(1), 155–159 (2015)

20. Xydis, S., Pekmestzi, K., Soudris, D., Economakos, G.: Compiler-in-the-loop exploration during datapath synthesis for higher quality delay-area trade-offs. ACM Trans. Des. Autom. Electron. Syst. **18**(1), Article 11, 35 pages (2013)

# COSSIM : A Novel, Comprehensible, Ultra-Fast, Security-Aware CPS Simulator

Ioannis Papaefstathiou[1]([✉]), Gregory Chrysos[2], and Lambros Sarakis[3]

[1] Embedded Systems Group, Synelixis Solutions Ltd, 34100 Chalkida, Greece
ygp@synelixis.com
[2] ECE Department Technical, University of Crete, 73100 Chania, Greece
chrysos@mhl.tuc.gr
[3] Electrical Engineering Dept, TEI of Sterea Ellada, 34400 Psahna, Greece
sarakis@teiste.gr

**Abstract.** This paper present a recently started multi-national project which will provide an innovative comprehensible, ultra-Fast, security-Aware CPS Simulator (called COSSIM) that will seamlessly simulate both the networking and the processing parts of the Cyber Physical Systems (CPS) significantly faster and more accurate than any existing solution. In order to achieve that COSSIM will develop a novel simulator framework based on a processing simulation subsystem (i.e. a "full-system simulator") which will be integrated with a novel network simulator. Furthermore, innovative power consumption and security measurement models will be developed and incorporated to the end framework. On top of that, COSSIM will also address another critical aspect of an accurate CPS simulation environment: the performance as measured in required simulation time. COSSIM will create a framework that is orders of magnitude faster, while also being more accurate and reporting more CPS aspects, than existing solutions, by applying hardware acceleration through the use of field programmable gate arrays (FPGAs), which have been proven extremely efficient in relevant tasks. This paper presents the high-level architecture of the end-system as well the most innovative aspects of it that will allow it to be the fastest and most accurate such simulator, while it does not cover the security aspects of this novel system.

## 1 Introduction

Cyber Physical Systems (CPS) are considered "The Next Computing Revolution" after Mainframe computing (60's - 70's), Desktop computing & Internet (80's - 90's) and Ubiquitous computing (00's). CPS are growing in capability at an extraordinary rate, promoted by the increased presence and capabilities of electronic control Units as well as of the sensors and actuators and the interconnecting networks. In order to meet the growing requirements of automated and assisted features and the inherent complexity, developers have to model and simulate those sophisticated systems at all the design stages; simulation has proven itself in the last 15 years by providing an analytical approach to solutions for complex problems.

© Springer International Publishing Switzerland 2015
K. Sano et al. (Eds.): ARC 2015, LNCS 9040, pp. 542–553, 2015.
DOI: 10.1007/978-3-319-16214-0_50

One of the main problems that CPS designers face is "the lack of simulation tools and models for system design and analysis"[1]. Even in the Wireless Sensor Network (WSN) field, which can be considered a subset CPS (e.g. a CPS can, among others, comprise of a set of WSNs), it has been reported [2] that over one third of the researchers use a testbed in the design process while more than an additional quarter of them design their own WSN simulator in order to model their system as a result of the severe limitations of all the existing solutions. This is mainly because the majority of the existing simulation tools handle efficiently only parts of the CPS (e.g. only the processing nodes or only the network) while they mainly focus on the performance of the CPS. Moreover, the existing simulators need extreme amounts of processing resources and computation time to simulate a system at a low level (e.g. when simulating the execution of the complete software stack, including the Operating System, in a target platform at a close to cycle accurate level). Faster approaches are available however they function at higher levels of abstraction and cannot provide the precision and accuracy that are necessary in order to model the exact behavior of a system under design so as to guarantee that it meets its requirements.

The COSSIM simulation framework will address all those important needs by providing a novel open-source approach which can

- seamlessly simulate, in an integrated way, both the networking and the processing parts of the CPS,
- perform the simulations one to two orders of magnitude faster,
- provide significantly more accurate results, especially in terms of power consumption, than existing solutions
- report the, critical for many applications, security levels of the simulated CPS.

COSSIM will achieve the above by incorporating a full system simulator (i.e. "a simulator that simulates an electronic system at such a level of detail that complete software stacks from real systems can run on the simulator without any modification"[2]) with a novel network simulator. Furthermore, novel power consumption and security models will be developed and integrated to the proposed framework. Additionally, COSSIM will create a framework that is significantly faster than existing solutions, by applying hardware acceleration through the use of field programmable gate arrays (FPGAs), which have been proven extremely efficient in relevant tasks. In this paper we focus on all the innovative aspects of COSSIM except of the security ones that are described in another paper that is under preparation.

## 2    Related Work

There are numerous simulators and emulators that have been developed and implemented mainly for the simulation of WSNs. Those simulators can be used as part of a CPS framework since a CPS frequently comprises of a set of WSNs. However the CPS are significantly more complex than WSNs in terms of both the processing in the nodes and the interconnecting networks so certain specific CPS toolsets are required; nevertheless, no such simulation system incorporating all the aspects of a complex

CPS exists. The aforementioned WSN simulators and emulators can be mainly placed in the following two categories: (a) those that do not support instruction level simulation of the processing units and (b) those that support simulation at the instruction level but only for specific, very simple microcontrollers.

In the first category there are TOSSIM (with the PowerTOSSIM extension [3]), OMNET++[4] based simulators like Castalia, MiXiM, NesCT, SENSIM and PAWiS [5] and NS-2 based ones like NRLSensorsim[6], and J-SIM[7] . The common characteristic of these simulators is that in order to be scalable, they run the target applications as a native executable on the simulation machine rather than directly simulate a node's CPU at the instruction level. Therefore to provide performance and power measurements, they employ either a code-transformation technique to estimate the number of CPU cycles executed by each node or a limited set of different power modes. Then, the trace of each node's activity is fed into a detailed model of hardware performance as well as energy consumption, yielding per-node timing and energy consumption data. This approach yields acceptable accuracy in terms of performance and energy consumption estimation for very simple CPUs without any memory hierarchy and/or complex peripherals.

On the other hand there are simulators or actual emulators which support specific CPUs at the instruction level and provide cycle accurate results. Those include ATEMU, Avrora, VMNet and EmSim that all support the MicaZ AVR-based CPUs; MSPsim and WSim that support the MSP430-based CPUs as well as Freemote Emulator which supports both AVR and MSP430-based nodes. Those systems report at a very high accuracy both the performance and the energy consumption of the CPUs.

The drawback of the simulators of the first category is that they cannot accurately estimate the performance as well as the energy consumption of modern complicated pipelined and multi-core CPUs that have many levels of memories and are interconnect with sophisticated peripherals. The error in such high-level estimations, if a non-cycle accurate model is present, can be up to 62% in terms of the performance as well as of the energy consumption of a complex CPU [8] making the estimation basically useless. On the other hand the simulators and emulators of the second category do support cycle accurate models of the CPUs but they provide such capabilities only for very simple microcontrollers (i.e. AVR and MSP430) that are not even pipelined, do not support memory hierarchy of any kind or are interconnected so as to form multi-cores.

At the same time, over the last few years, the availability of large FPGAs together with the newly introduced high-level synthesis tools has provided a new opportunity for CPU cycle-accurate simulations. It is now possible to perform cycle accurate simulations of realistic designs, e.g., a small number of out-of-order processors, on a single FPGA chip. These FPGA-based simulators are able to provide three orders of magnitude improvement in performance over software simulators. Chung et al[9], Pellauer et al [10], Chiou et al[11], Tan et al[12]  and Khan et al[12] have all designed and implemented such very efficient emulation frameworks. At the same time numerous researchers such as Bachman et al[13], Park et al[14] , Sunwoo et al[15], Tsao et al[16] and Krieg et al [17] proposed frameworks for accurate estimation of either one or more CPUs interconnected in a SoC which are based on implementing certain parts of the CPUs or CPU models to an FPGA; the result is an up to 500x faster simulation that the purely software approach while providing the exact same energy accuracy. Moreover, there are certain approaches such as the work from Nasreddine et al[18], Quadri et al [19], Lin et al[20] and Tan et al[21] that accelerate the network simulation by up to two orders of magnitude when implementing them on FPGAs.

As stated above there are numerous FPGA-based power estimation methodologies that have been proposed in the last few years [22],[23],[24]. Their approach is to port the hardware description of the CPU to the FPGA together with the associated power models. In all cases the emulation systems run from 50x to over 1000x faster than a SW based simulator. The drawbacks of those approaches are that (i) it is difficult and time consuming to port a complex CPU to the FPGA including its peripherals (ii) the power models integrated increase the latency of executing each emulated instruction on the FPGA while the more accurate the models the higher the execution time. More importantly all such emulation-based solutions are limited to one FPGA thus they cannot emulate complex multi-cores/SoCs. Another more promising approach is that by Ghodat et a' [25] were a hybrid model is utilized so as to execute certain tasks, which cannot be synthesized, in software and the synthesizable parts in the FPGA. The main drawback of this approach, which makes it of very little use, is that in order to be efficient the modules simulated in software should have very low intercommunication with those implemented on FPGAs; this is not the case of the complex CPS SoCs where effectively all the intra CPU and peripherals modules are connected to each other at very high speeds.

On the other hand, especially in the early 2000' there were certain regression-based power estimation systems that have been proposed[26],[27],[28],[29]. Their main drawback is that their accuracy is limited due to the fact that they do not model cycle-by-cycle power while they are only working on estimating relatively simple CPUs with simple known constituents; as a result those systems cannot easily be used for system-level evaluation while they use very complex mathematics at high precision so they cannot probably be accelerated even if implemented on FPGAs. There is also a framework proposed by Sunwoo et al [30] which generates FPGA-based power estimators consisting of linear models that are designed to be integrated into fast, accurate FPGA-based performance simulators of microprocessors and the work from Bansal et al[31] that utilizes statistical methods to generate power models of the hardware modules integrated within a complex SoC; the latter provides accurate results however, due to its nature, it cannot be mapped to an FPGA hence it cannot be accelerated. Another very important drawback of the majority of those systems (except the ones from Sunwoo, Bhattacharjee and Bansal) is that they cannot support multi-cores and SoC with CPUs, accelerators and peripherals which are expected to be the norm in tomorrow's CPS while none of the existing systems support the energy and power consumption estimation for the active network interconnection components (such as transmitters, repeaters, receivers, routers, switches) which is an extremely important feature for CPS.

The common characteristics of all those approaches is that by taking advantage of the high-processing power of the FPGA the system provide not only faster but also significantly (up to 80%[34],[35]) more accurate results mainly due to the facts that a) they utilize much more complex power models than the standard software approaches and b) they simulate orders of magnitude more testcases therefore reaching a much better estimation.

## 3    High Level Architecture

The COSSIM framework will be the first one that will support, at a cycle accurate level, the simulation in a fully integrated manner of a) CPS nodes comprising of sophisticated multi-core homogeneous or heterogeneous CPUs, including several levels of memory hierarchy, complex on-chip interconnection and peripherals and b) the internetworking between those nodes. All the existing simulation tools, as analytically described in the previous section, can either perform high-level non accurate simulations of complex CPUs and networks (the error is up to 62% in terms of energy and performance[32] making them impractical) or instruction level simulations of very simple non-pipelined, single-level memory hierarchy CPUs. Moreover, in terms of energy consumption, as also described in the last section, the approaches are quite similar: either high-level non accurate models are utilized or very accurate models of quite simple microcontrollers are offered..

So COSSIM will design and implement a CPS simulation framework that will:

1. Simulate at the Instruction Level the software execution of the CPS multi-core nodes and extract highly accurate performance and energy estimations for the software execution
2. Incorporate the network-related aspects of the CPS together with the CPU processing aspects in one single framework
3. Develop new models for more accurate estimations of the energy consumption of the final CPS including the consumption of both complex CPS nodes and interconnected networks,
4. Execute certain parts of the simulations on Reconfigurable Devices (i.e. FPGAs); FPGAs will provide the huge processing power needed so as to report all the features above in a timely and accurate manner.

Hardware acceleration on reconfigurable logic of certain parts of the framework is expected to provide orders of magnitude improvement in the performance of the overall simulation environment. This is of utter importance as unrealistic high, for any practical application, simulation times have till now been the most prohibitive factor in fully unlocking the potential of such integrated simulation tools. Through the proposed scheme it will be possible for the first time to simulate a complete complex CPS at an acceptable level of accuracy. This will include numerous complex CPS nodes and the complex network interconnecting them. Simulations will be at a low level, so as to provide highly accurate performance and energy consumption estimations, while for the first time security aspects of the system under simulation will be examined; those estimations are important so as to (1) verify that power budgets and security levels are met by the different parts of the design as well as of the entire CPS, and (2) evaluate the effect of high-level optimizations, which have greater impact on power than low-level ones [33].

To achieve those ambitious research goals, while also provide a tool familiar to CPS designers (i.e. it has a very large use-base already), COSSIM will try to build on top of existing simulation systems and augment / modify them so as to address the new requirements. Towards this end, COSSIM will investigate the existing full system, Network and Power Simulators (most of which are open-source) and identify whether some of their subsystems can be employed, after the required modifications, in the developed COSSIM framework. The use of existing cores as the basis of the development has the additional advantage that the exploitation of COSSIM will be significantly facilitated and the impact will be greater. If, for example, COSSIM adopts the interface of an existing network simulation framework (like NS3 or OMNet++), a large part of the CPS design community that is already familiar with the selected framework from their WSN simulations, will be able to embrace, without any hassle, the COSSIM framework, which will provide them with significantly more functionality (for example much better energy and performance estimations) at a much higher speed without requiring an extensive learning curve.

Regarding the inputs of the overall system, they will be as follows:

- the code that will be executed on the processing Units (including the OS)
- the characteristics of the processing units (e.g. number of CPUs, characteristics of interconnections and peripherals, caches sizes, number of external memories etc) or the name of the System on Chip(SoC), from a predefined set for the most common SoCs used in CPS
- the network architecture (e.g. active network systems, network topology, network protocol, links speed, characteristics of the links in terms of BER etc)
- all necessary data to perform security testing of the system's exposed interfaces: permissible input values, or possible input ranges for the code to be simulated (i.e., input constraints for fuzz-testing model behavior) as well as a list of vulnerabilities to test the system against

The Output of the system will be a trace file and certain overall characteristics (e.g. total execution time, energy consumed, security level supported etc). The overall block diagram of the proposed system is shown in Figure 1.

The vision of COSSIM is that of an infrastructure that combines in a seamless way heterogeneous sub-tools that evaluate the performance, energy and security of individual nodes and complete networks. This integrated infrastructure, shown in Figure 2, consists of two main components: a processing simulator and a network simulator. The processing simulator is split into a functional (addressing the sequence of tasks that have to be executed) and a timing (addressing task sequence execution latency) model allowing the implementation of the time critical component of the simulator in FPGA(s). Apart from evaluating the exact timing of the tasks' execution, COSSIM places particular focus on the efficient modeling of the CPS power consumption and its security aspects and will come up with efficient realizations of such novel models including their efficient mapping to reconfigurable hardware. The node simulator will be able to address different CPU architectures and execute unmodified application software written for the target devices including support for full OS code execution. In this way, COSSIM will address the simulation of real software execution on complex CPS interconnected with complex network and access its implications on the performance and power consumption (as well as the security) of the CPS.

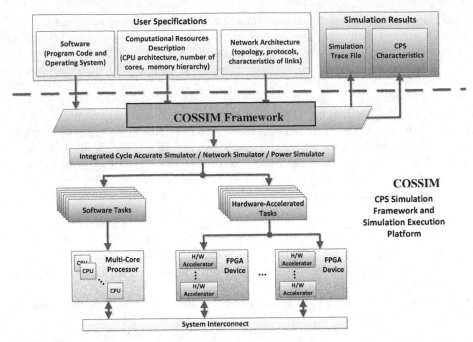

**Fig. 1.** COSSIM Framework

In the next subsection we analytically describe why the COSSIM framework will be highly innovative.

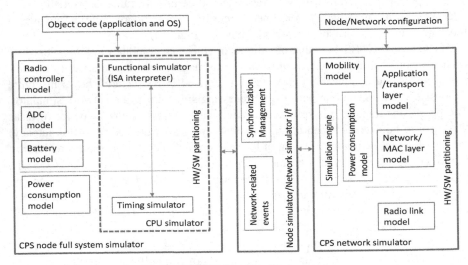

**Fig. 2.** COSSIM Combined Infrastructure

# 4    Novelty

The novelty of COSSIM is twofold: it is a novel overall system comprising of innovative sub-systems. Summarizing the current systems, as described in the Related Work Section, there are numerous systems that perform and accelerate the simulation of different aspects of CPS (i.e. CPU performance, power consumption and networking performance) but each of them is following a different approach, is working in a stand-alone mode and there is no seamless way to interconnect them. Moreover, none of them support the notion of security. On the other hand a complete CPS simulation framework should incorporate such sub-systems in a seamlessly to the developer way and this is the design need that COSSIM will fill-in with a novel offering.

Moving to the innovative aspects of the complete framework in most of current, and more importantly, future CPS the main CPS nodes will consist of multi-core complex CPUs and peripherals interconnected with NoCs, while there will be a complex network interconnecting the CPS nodes. Such a system cannot be simulated or emulated by any of the existing frameworks; one of the main reasons is that it is very slow to simulate, at a low level (e.g. the instruction level), even a single complex CPU together with the associated memory system and peripherals. *COSSIM will design and develop the first known simulation framework that will allow for the simulation of a complete CPS utilizing complex SoCs interconnected with sophisticated networks.* This will be achieved by executing certain parts of the combined processing and network simulations on FPGAs. As it has been proved in by the existing systems listed above and simulating the CPUs, such an approach can accelerate the simulation of the Processing system by one and up to two orders of magnitude. Moreover, the COSSIM system will support more accurate power estimations than the existing tools as demonstrated in the next section_

The related work section clearly demonstrates that many of the tools developed especially for WSN simulations combine CPU and network simulators by modeling the system components at different levels of abstraction determined by the performance and accuracy requirements of the tool. These CPU simulators, either built for the proposed framework (like in Avrora and ATEMU), or integrated from pre-existing components (like in DiSens, Cooja and Sunshine) limit their applicability to only specific WSN platforms. There are also complex CPU/SoC simulators that have neither any notion of networking nor of the peripherals found in a CPS. In contrast, in COSSIM we will build a simulation framework that will be capable of simulating existing complex SoC architectures while also be friendly to experimentation with design alternatives. We argue that such experimentation is a key factor to drive innovation in the field of CPS computational and power-efficient hardware platforms.

COSSIM will develop a modular and flexible processing simulator utilizing certain sub-systems of the existing CPU and SoC system simulators but tailored to the needs of CPS (e.g. supporting less CPU-features and the correct level of abstraction of the hardware components). It will also implement a networking simulator either based on, or utilizing certain modules of, one of the existing such systems which are currently under active development and have considerable support from the international research community; this will allow the exploitation of state-of-art simulation engines, possibly complemented with facilities for distributed network simulations over a computer cluster, which incorporate accurate simulation models for e.g. mobility and radio channels. For both sub-simulation engines, we will define system-agnostic interfaces and provide a reference architecture for their interconnection.

To summarize, the main innovation of COSSIM in the area of the integrated processing and network simulator will be the development of processing and network simulation engines handling the CPS-specific characteristics and interconnected with a novel scheme. We will also define the appropriate novel system-agnostic interface that will accommodate (a) different data representations that traditionally exist in processing and network simulators (data representation in bit/byte and packet levels, respectively), (b) efficient communication of events and (c) versatile time synchronization. Matching a processing simulator to a CPS simulation-capable, generic network simulation tool will pave the way to more complete and realistic simulations of CPS with computational and control execution facilities hosted in platforms (network elements) that are located beyond the boundaries of wireless sensor and actuator networks.

Moving to the novel power estimation system of COSSIM, and in comparison with the existing approaches described in the related work section, the COSSIM sub-tool will be innovative since it will also cover the power consumption of the interconnection between the CPUs as well as with the peripherals since present and, more importantly, future CPS will comprise of multi-core devices incorporated with accelerators and complex peripherals in the same SoC. Moreover, the system will handle the power/energy consumption of the active network components of the interconnection wired and/or wireless network; this includes the power consumption of the active network nodes while transmitting (and very often re-transmitting) over non-reliable networks at different power nodes. No such system that estimates the power and energy of both the processing and the interconnection network exists today.

Moreover, the COSSIM sub-system performing the evaluation of the energy consumption of the Processing units of the CPS as well as of the active network components will be more innovative than existing solutions since it will be the first known system that will utilize certain techniques for increasing the simulation efficiency namely spatial and temporal power sampling[36], power caching[37], and trace abstraction[38]. Those techniques will improve both the speed and the accuracy of the framework. In any case, based on the results triggered by the existing systems (as described in the last sub-section) the accuracy of the power estimation of our system is expected to be more than 50% higher than the existing approaches while by applying those novel technique it can be up twice as accurate as the current CPS-related software based simulation systems.

## 5    Conclusions

The COSSIM project will create the first known system that (a) Simulates at a cycle accurate level the executable(s) in the processing nodes of a CPS and the actual network interconnecting the CPS nodes, (b) Provides significantly more accurate power/energy estimations than any existing system (c) Supports and simulates certain security features of the overall CPS (d) It is one to two orders of magnitude faster than existing systems providing also more features.

So the system as a complete framework will be highly innovative since no similar systems supporting all those CPS aspects exist whereas it will also be significantly faster than the limited feature already proposed approaches. Moreover, in order to implement such a system there are certain research challenges that should be addressed and thus there are certain subparts of the overall system that will also be innovative as described in this paper; those innovative modules will include:

- The sub-system that will implement certain parts of the simulation on reconfigurable devices
- The accurate Power/energy estimation models that will be developed which would also take advantage of the cycle accurate simulations and the large processing power, for certain tasks, of the FPGAs
- The FPGA-based acceleration framework which will be capable of seamlessly supporting anything from a single middle-size FPGA to a cluster of highly interconnected very large reconfigurable devices

# References

1. Foundations for Innovation in Cyber-Physical Systems, NIST (January 2013)
2. Abuarqoub, A., et al.: Simulation issues in wireless sensor networks: A survey. In: SENSORCOMM 2012, The Sixth International Conference on Sensor Technologies and Applications (2012)
3. Shnayder, V., Hempstead, M., Rong Chen, B., Werner-Allen, G., Welsh, M.: Simulating the power consumption of large-scale sensor network applications. In: Proceedings of the Second ACM Conference on Embedded Networked Systems (SenSys) (November 2004)
4. Chen, F., Dietrich, I., German, R., Dressler, F.: An Energy Model for Simulation Studies of Wireless Sensor Networks using OMNeT++. Praxis der Informationsverarbeitung und Kommunikation (PIK) 32(2), 133–138 (2009)
5. Glaser, J., Weber, D., Madani, S.A., Mahlknecht, S.: Power aware simulation framework for wireless sensor networks and nodes. EURASIP J. Embedded Syst. 2008, Article 3 (January 2008)
6. Using Mannasim Framework (March 2014). http://www.mannasim.dcc.ufmg.br
7. Sobeih, A., et al.: J-sim: A simulation environment for wireless sensor networks. In: Proceedings of the 38th annual Symposium on Simulation. IEEE Computer Society (2005)
8. Heirman, W., Sarkar, S., Carlson, T.E., Hur, I., Eeckhout, L.: Power-aware multi-core simulation for early design stage hardware/software co-optimization. Proceedings of the 21st international conference on Parallel architectures and compilation techniques (PACT '12), pp. 3–12. ACM, New York, NY, USA (2012)
9. Chung, E.S., Papamichael, M.K., Nurvitadhi, E., Hoe, J.C., Mai, K., Falsafi, B.: ProtoFlex: Towards Scalable, Full-System Multiprocessor Simulations Using FPGAs. ACM Trans. Reconfigurable Technol. Syst. 2(2), 1–32 (2009)
10. Pellauer, M., Vijayaraghavan, M., Adler, M., Arvind, Emer, J.: Quick performance models quickly: Closely-coupled partitioned simulation on FPGAs. In: ISPASS '08: Proceedings of the International Symposium on Performance Analysis of Systems and software

11. Chiou, D., Sunwoo, D., Kim, J., Patil, N.A., Reinhart, W., Johnson, D.E., Keefe, J., Angepat, H.: FPGA-Accelerated simulation technologies (fast): Fast, full-system, cycle-accurate simulators. In: MICRO '07: Proceedings of the 40th Annual IEEE/ACM International Symposium on Microarchitecture. Washington, DC, USA

12. Khan, A., Vijayaraghavan, M., Boyd-Wickizer, S., Arvind: Fast and cycle-accurate modeling of a multicore processor. In: Proceedings of the 2012 IEEE International Symposium on Performance Analysis of Systems & Software (ISPASS 2012) (2012)

13. Bachmann, C., Genser, A., Steger, C., Weiß, R., Haid, J.: Accelerating Embedded Software Power Profiling Using Run-Time Power Emulation. In: Monteiro, J., van Leuken, R. (eds.) PATMOS 2009. LNCS, vol. 5953, pp. 186–195. Springer, Heidelberg (2010)

14. Park, Y.-H., et al.: A multi-granularity power modeling methodology for embedded processors. In: IEEE Transactions on Very Large Scale Integration (VLSI) Systems, **19.4** pp. 668–681 (2011)

15. Sunwoo, D., et al.: PrEsto: An FPGA-accelerated power estimation methodology for complex systems. In: 2010 International Conference on Field Programmable Logic and Applications (FPL), IEEE (2010)

16. Tsao, S.-L., et al.: Hardware-assisted energy consumption evaluation tool for multi-core embedded systems. In: 2nd International Workshop on Analysis Tools and Methodologies for Embedded and Real-time Systems (WATERS 2011)

17. Krieg, A., et al.: POWER-MODES: POWer-EmulatoR-and MOdel-Based DEpendability and security evaluations. In: ACM Transactions on Reconfigurable Technology and Systems (TRETS) **5.4**(19) (2012)

18. Nasreddine, N., Boizard, J.L.; Escriba, C., Fourniols, J.-Y.: Wireless sensors networks emulator implemented on a FPGA. In: 2010 International Conference on Field-Programmable Technology (FPT), vol., no., pp. 279–282. December 8-10, 2010

19. Quadri, Uzma, Rangaree, P., Asutkar, G.M.: FPGA implementation of an emulator for Wireless Sensor Node with Pt100 temperature sensor. ENCON 2013-2013 IEEE Region 10 Conference (31194). IEEE (2013)

20. Lin, H., et al.: GECO: Global Event-Driven Co-Simulation Framework for Interconnected Power System and Communication Network. IEEE Transactions on Smart Grid **3**(3), 1444–1456 (2012)

21. Tan, Z., Krste A., David, P.: Datacenter-Scale Network Research on FPGAs. In: Proc. Workshop on Exascale Evaluation and Research Techniques (2011)

22. Coburn, J., Ravi, S., Raghunathan, A.: Power emulation: a new paradigm for power estimation. DAC, pp. 700–705 (2005)

23. Atienza, D., Valle, P.D., Paci, G., Poletti, F.: A fast HW/SW FPGA-based thermal emulation framework for multi-processor system-on- chip. DAC January 2006

24. Bhattacharjee, A., Contreras, G., Martonosi, M.: Full-system chip multiprocessor power evaluations using FPGA-based emulation. In: Proceedings of ISLPED January 2008

25. Ghodrat, M., Lahiri, K., Raghunathan, A.: Accelerating System-on-Chip power analysis using hybrid power estimation. DAC, 883–886 (2007)

26. Chen, Z., Roy, K., Chou, T.: Power sensitivity-a new method to estimate power dissipation considering uncertain specifications of primary inputs. ICCAD (1997)

27. Wu, Q., Qiu, Q., Pedram, M., Ding, C.-S.: Cycle-accurate macromodels for RT-level power analysis. IEEE Transactions on VLSI Systems **6**(4), 520–528 (1998)

28. Gupta, S., Najm, F.: Power modeling for high-level power estimation. IEEE Transactions on VLSI Systems **8**(1), 18–29 (2000)

29. Bogliolo, A., Benini, L., Micheli, G.D.: Regression based RTL power modeling. ACM Trans. on Design Automation of Electronic Systems **5**(3), 337–372 (2000)

30. Sunwoo, D., Wu, G.Y., Patil, N.A., Chiou, D.: PrEsto: An fpga-accelerated power estimation methodology for complex systems. In: 2010 International Conference on Field Programmable Logic and Applications (FPL)
31. Bansal, N., Lahiri, K., Raghunathan, A.: Automatic power modeling of infrastructure IP for system-on-chip power analysis. In: Proceedings of VLSI Design, pp. 513–520 (2007)
32. Heirman, W., Sarkar, S., Carlson, T.E., Hur, I., Eeckhout, L.: Power-aware multi-core simulation for early design stage hardware/software co-optimization. Proceedings of the 21st international conference on Parallel architectures and compilation techniques (PACT '12), pp. 3–12. ACM, New York, NY, USA (2012)
33. Eisley, N., Peh, L.-S.: High-level power analysis for on-chip networks. In: Proc. CASES, pp. 104–115 (2004)
34. Wu, Q., Qiu, Q., Pedram, M., Ding, C.-S.: Cycle-accurate macromodels for RT-level power analysis. IEEE Transactions on VLSI Systems 6(4), 520–528 (1998)
35. Sunwoo, D., Wu, G.Y., Patil, N.A., Chiou, D.: PrEsto: An FPGA-accelerated power estimation methodology for complex systems. In: 2010 International Conference on Field Programmable Logic and Applications (FPL)
36. Macii, E., Pedram, M., Somenzi, F.: High-level power modeling, estimation, and optimization. In: Proc. Design Automation Conf., pp. 504–511 June 1997
37. Lajolo, M., Raghunathan, A., Dey, S., Lavagno, L.: Co-Simulation Based Power Estimation for System-on-Chip Design. IEEE Trans. VLSI Systems 10, 253–266 (2002)
38. Li, Y., Henkel, J.: A Framework for estimating and minimizing the energy dissipation of HW/SW embedded systems. In: Proc. Design Automation Conf., pp. 188– 193 June 1998

# Author Index